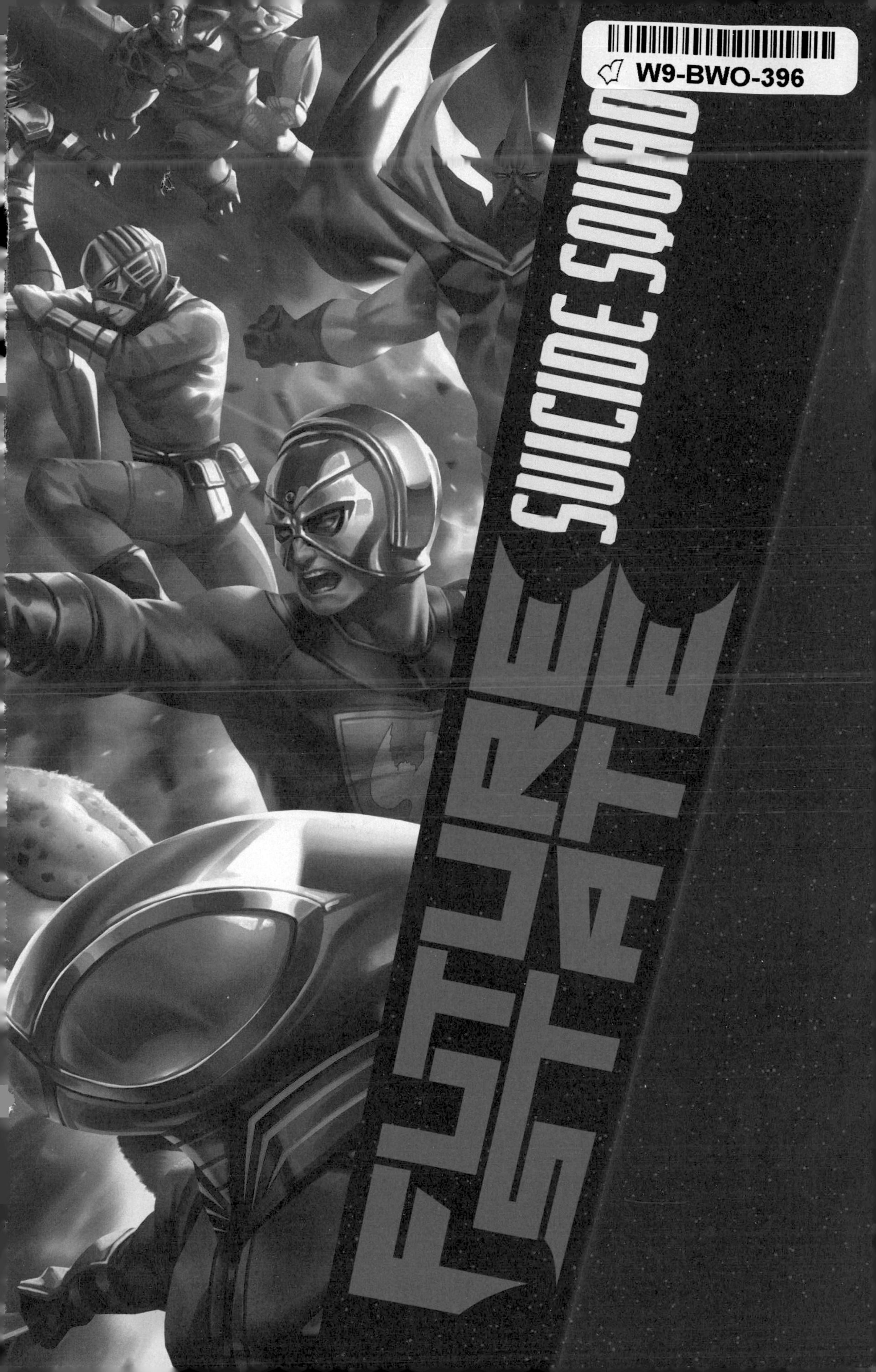
FUTURE STATE
SUICIDE SQUAD

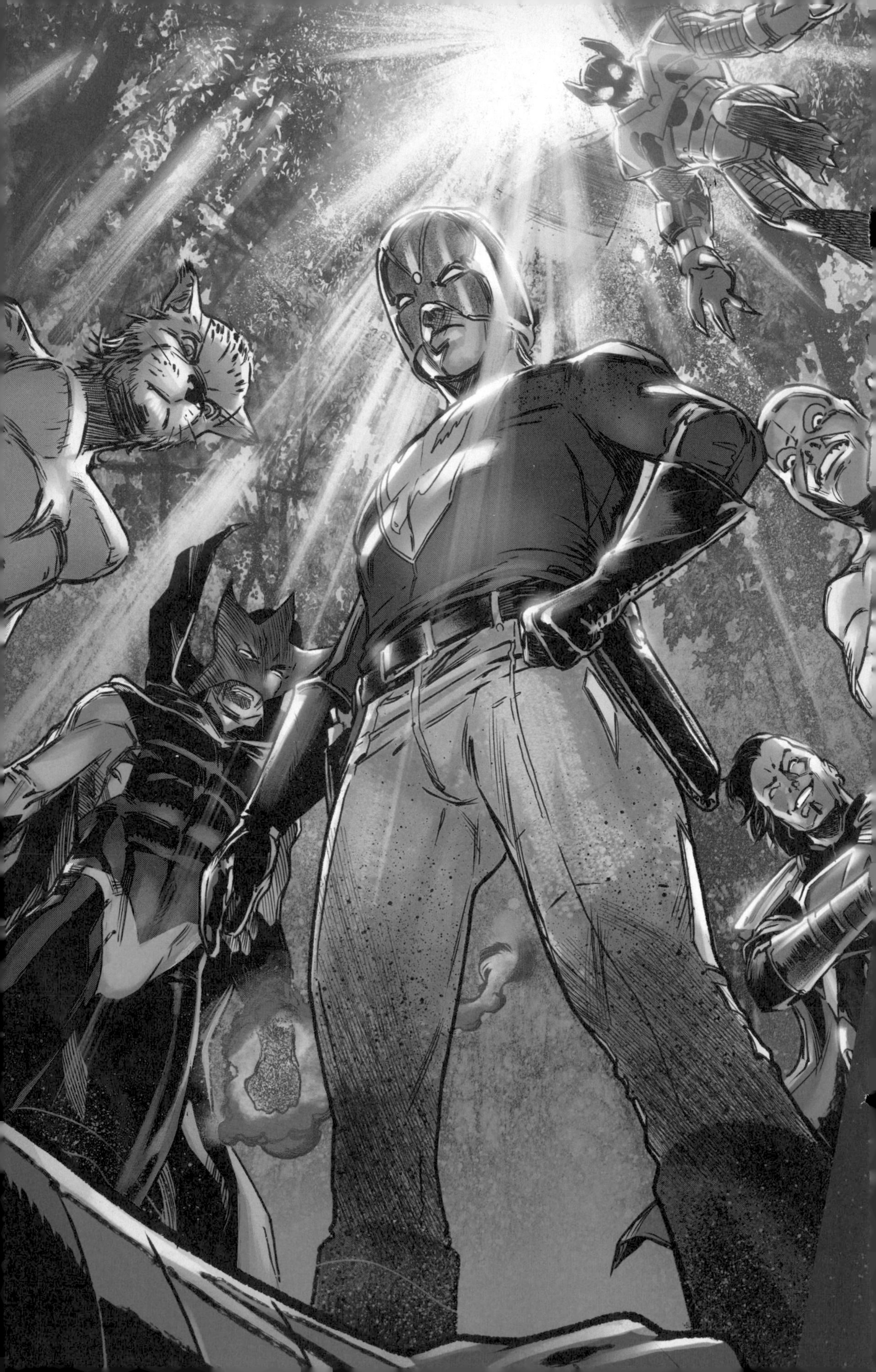

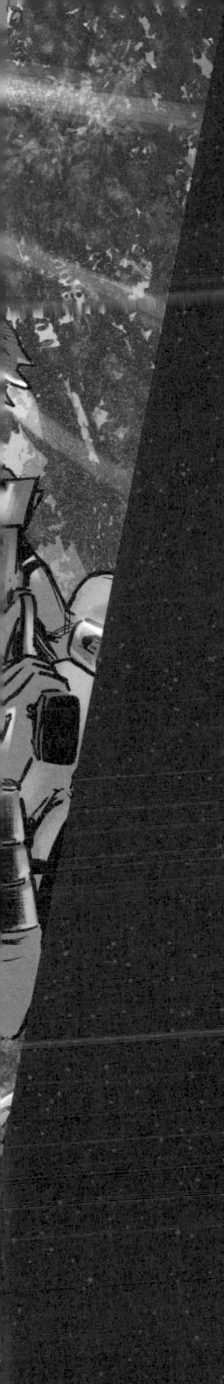

FUTURE STATE
SUICIDE SQUAD

WRITERS
ROBBIE THOMPSON
TIM SHERIDAN
JEREMY ADAMS
RAM V

PENCILLERS
JAVIER FERNANDEZ
EDUARDO PANSICA
RAFA SANDOVAL
FERNANDO PASARIN
MIKE PERKINS

INKERS
JAVIER FERNANDEZ
JULIO FERREIRA
JORDI TARRAGONA
OCLAIR ALBERT
MIKE PERKINS

COLORISTS
ALEX SINCLAIR
MARCELO MAIOLO
ALEJANDRO SANCHEZ
JEROMY COX
JUNE CHUNG

LETTERERS
WES ABBOTT
ROB LEIGH
ADITYA BIDIKAR

COLLECTION COVER ARTISTS
JAVIER FERNANDEZ
& MARCELO MAIOLO

SWAMP THING CREATED BY
LEN WEIN & BERNIE WRIGHTSON
SUPERBOY CREATED BY JERRY SIEGEL
BY SPECIAL ARRANGEMENT
WITH THE JERRY SIEGEL FAMILY

MIKE COTTON
Editor – Original Series & Collected Edition
ALEX R. CARR
Editor – Original Series
MARQUIS DRAPER
Assistant Editor – Original Series
STEVE COOK
Design Director – Books
& Publication Design
SUZANNAH ROWNTREE
Publication Production

MARIE JAVINS
Editor-in-Chief, DC Comics

DANIEL CHERRY III
Senior VP – General Manager
JIM LEE
Publisher & Chief Creative Officer
JOEN CHOE
VP – Global Brand & Creative Services
DON FALLETTI
VP – Manufacturing Operations & Workflow Management
LAWRENCE GANEM
VP – Talent Services
ALISON GILL
Senior VP – Manufacturing & Operations
NICK J. NAPOLITANO
VP – Manufacturing Administration & Design
NANCY SPEARS
VP – Revenue

FUTURE STATE: SUICIDE SQUAD

DC Comics, 2900 West Alameda Ave., Burbank, CA 91505
Printed by LSC Communications, Owensville, MO, USA.
6/4/21. First Printing.
ISBN: 978-1-77951-072-3

Library of Congress Cataloging-in-Publication Data is available.

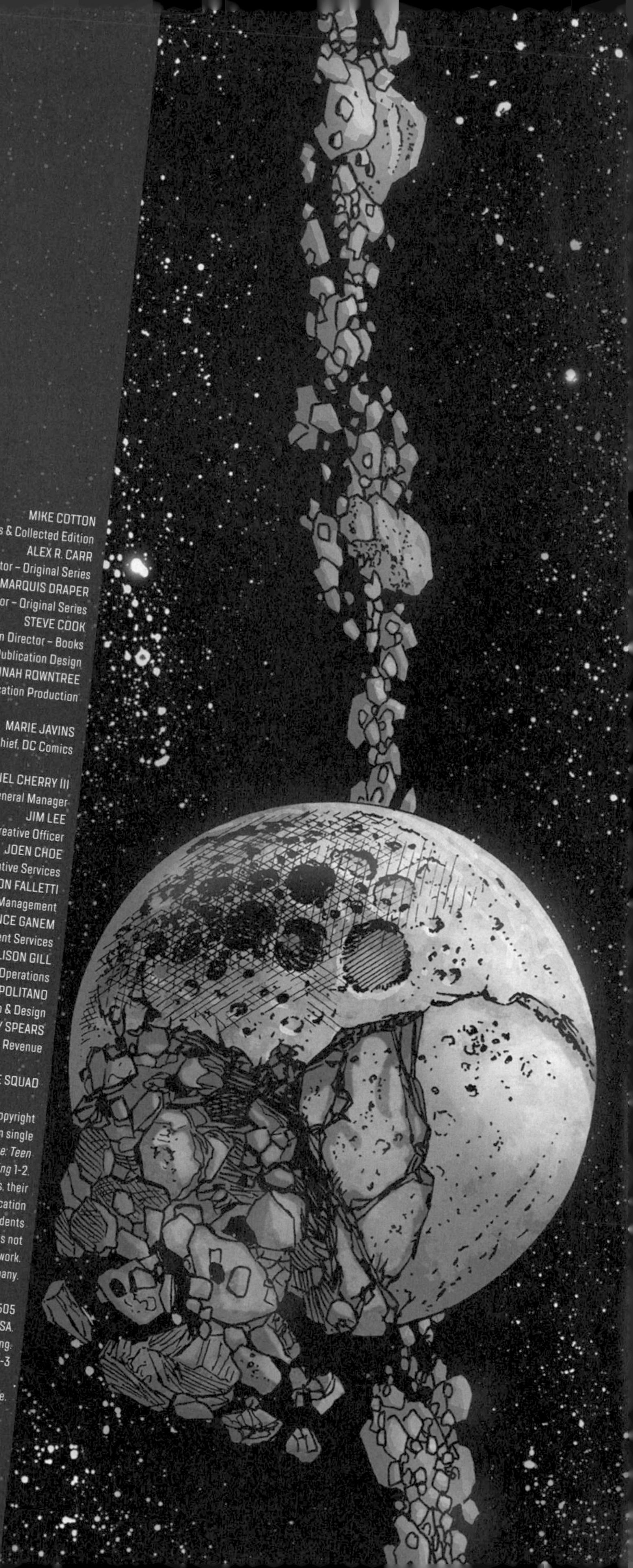

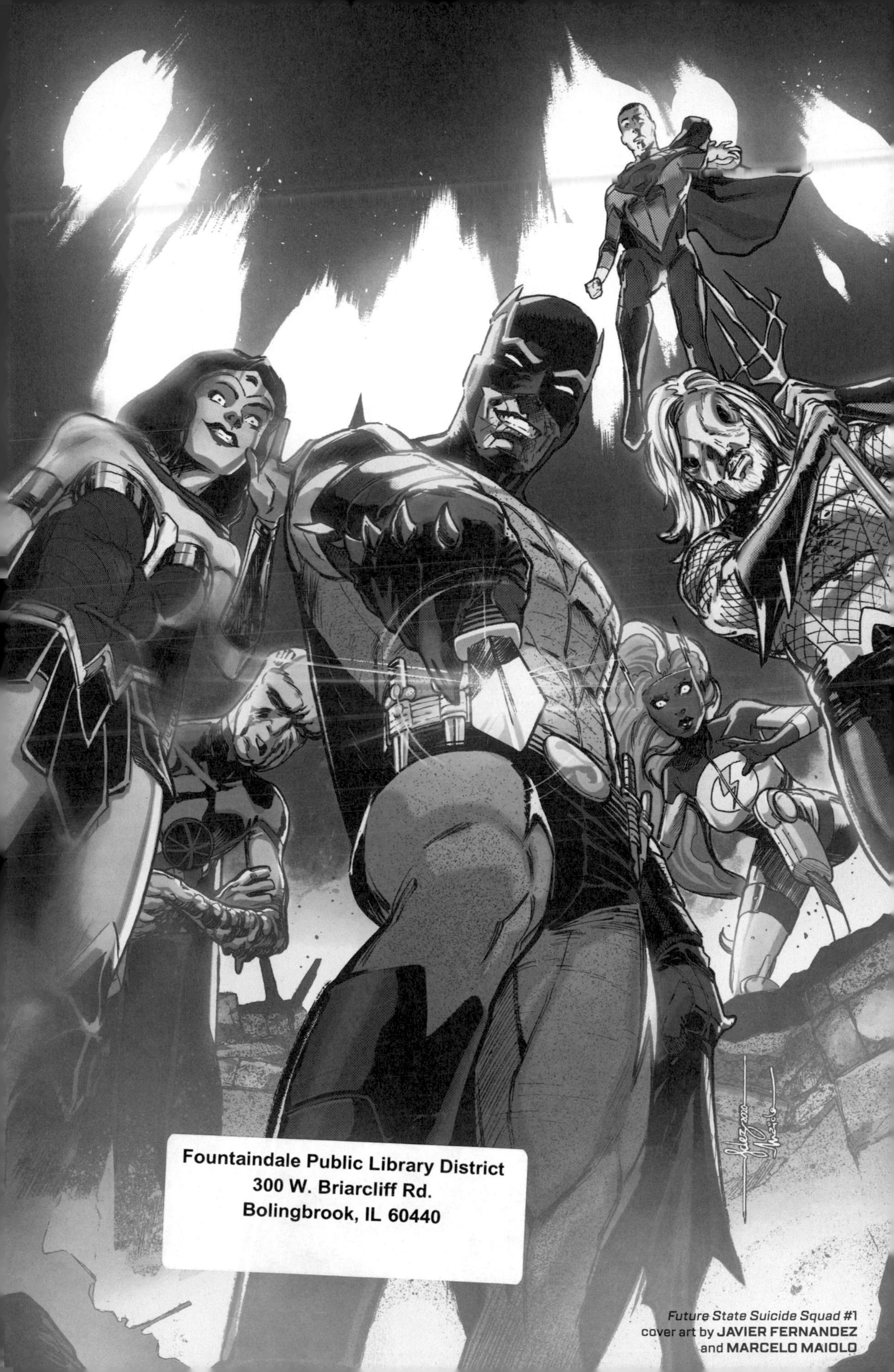

Future State Suicide Squad #1
cover art by **JAVIER FERNANDEZ**
and **MARCELO MAIOLO**

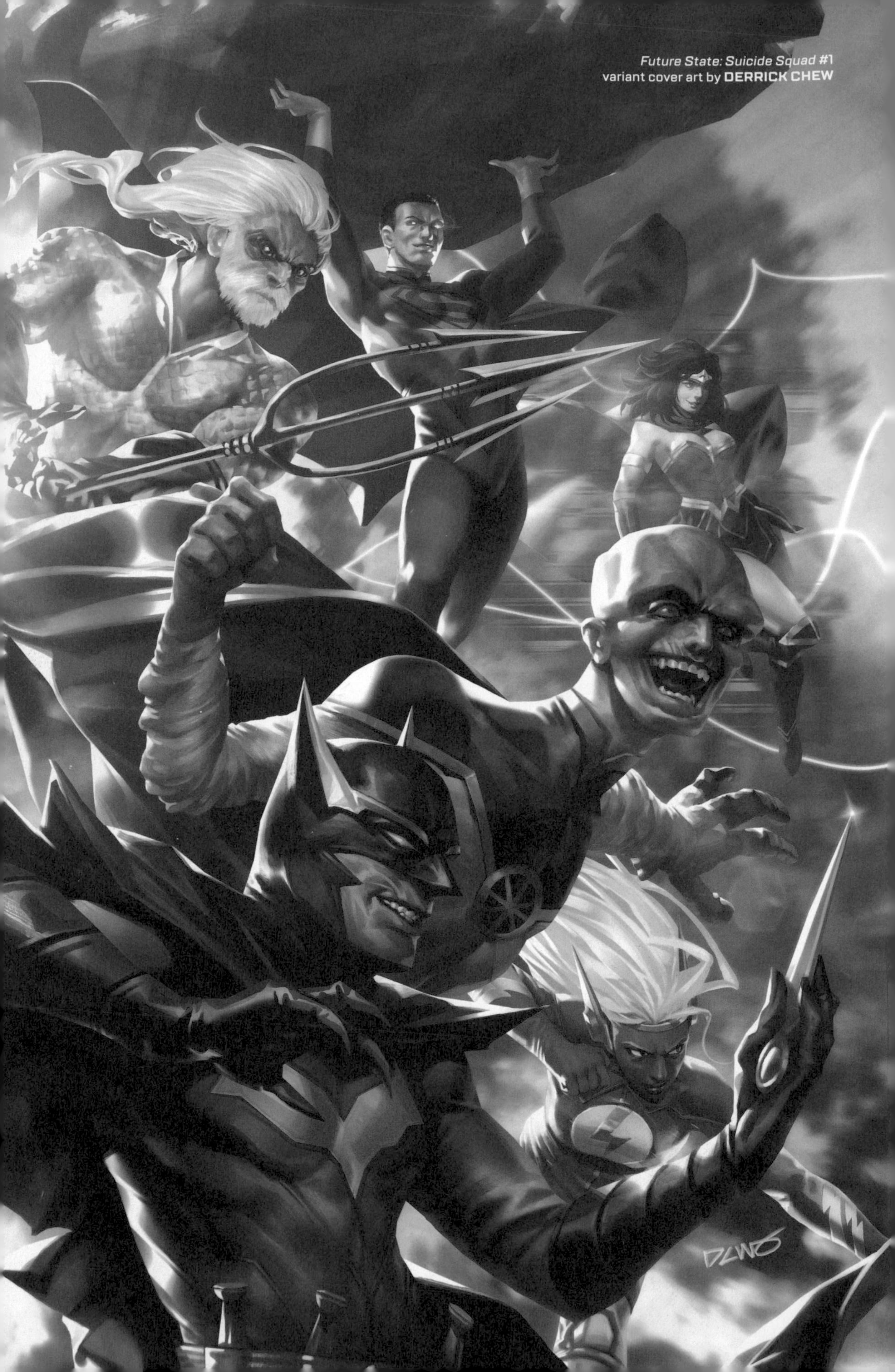

Future State: Suicide Squad #1
variant cover art by **DERRICK CHEW**

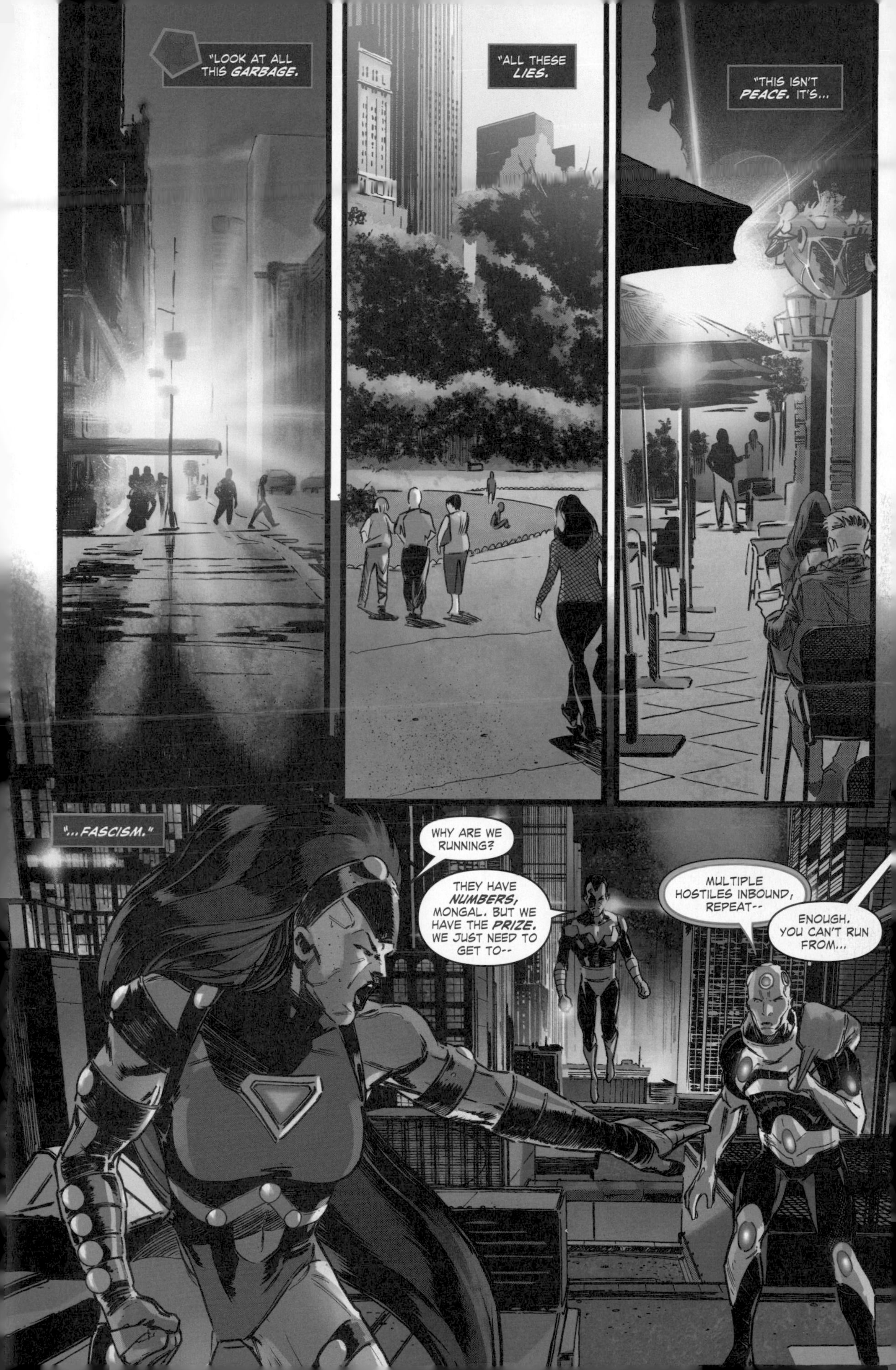
"LOOK AT ALL THIS GARBAGE.
"ALL THESE LIES.
"THIS ISN'T PEACE. IT'S...
"...FASCISM."
WHY ARE WE RUNNING?
THEY HAVE NUMBERS, MONGAL. BUT WE HAVE THE PRIZE. WE JUST NEED TO GET TO--
MULTIPLE HOSTILES INBOUND, REPEAT--
ENOUGH. YOU CAN'T RUN FROM...

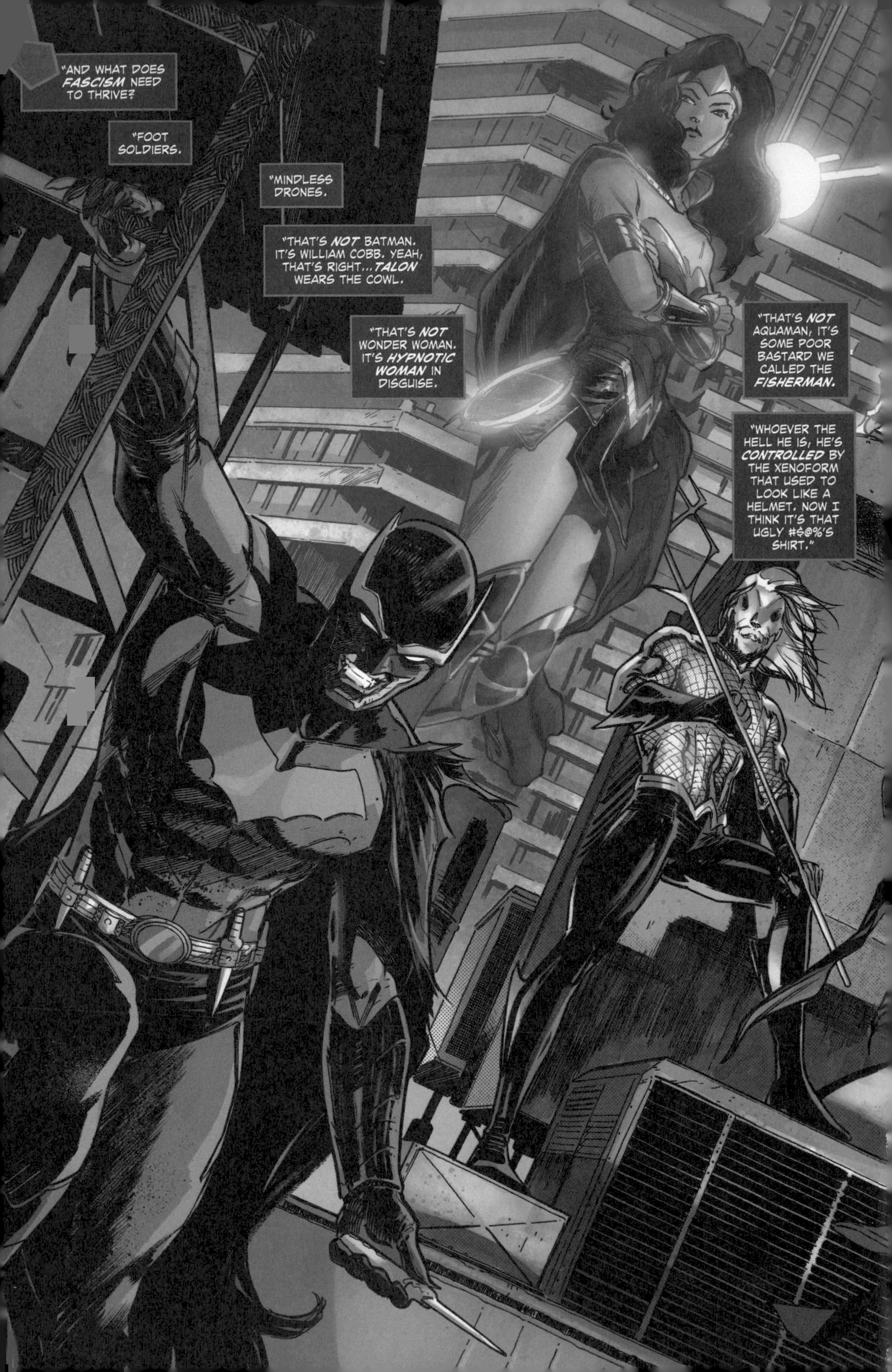
"AND WHAT DOES *FASCISM* NEED TO THRIVE?
"FOOT SOLDIERS.
"MINDLESS DRONES.
"THAT'S *NOT* BATMAN. IT'S WILLIAM COBB. YEAH, THAT'S RIGHT... *TALON* WEARS THE COWL.
"THAT'S *NOT* WONDER WOMAN. IT'S *HYPNOTIC WOMAN* IN DISGUISE.
"THAT'S *NOT* AQUAMAN, IT'S SOME POOR BASTARD WE CALLED THE *FISHERMAN.*
"WHOEVER THE HELL HE IS, HE'S *CONTROLLED* BY THE XENOFORM THAT USED TO LOOK LIKE A HELMET. NOW I THINK IT'S THAT UGLY #$@%'S SHIRT."

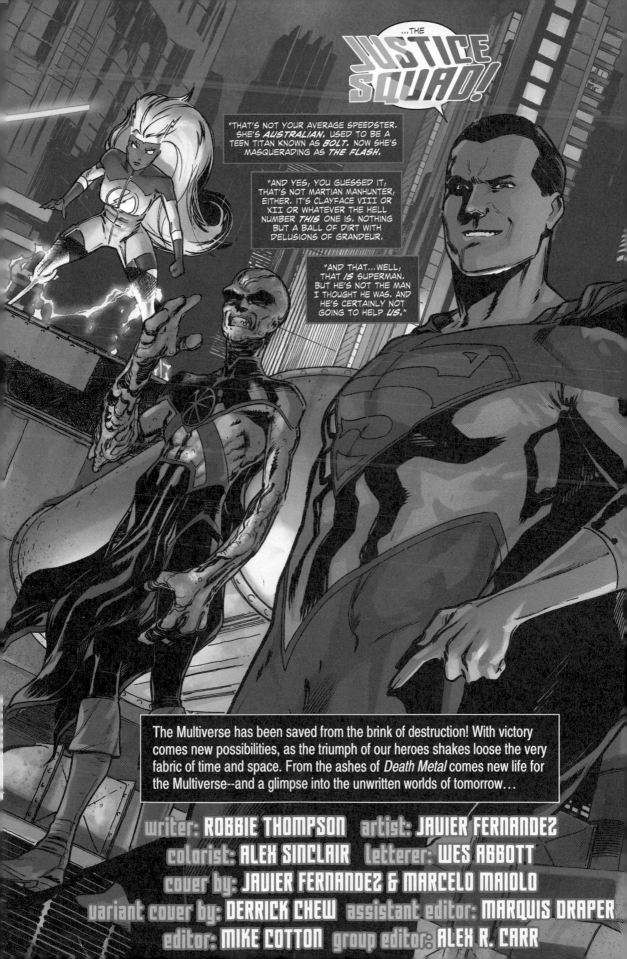

...THE **JUSTICE SQUAD!**

"THAT'S NOT YOUR AVERAGE SPEEDSTER. SHE'S *AUSTRALIAN.* USED TO BE A TEEN TITAN KNOWN AS *BOLT.* NOW SHE'S MASQUERADING AS *THE FLASH.*"

"AND YES, YOU GUESSED IT, THAT'S NOT MARTIAN MANHUNTER, EITHER. IT'S CLAYFACE VIII OR XII OR WHATEVER THE HELL NUMBER *THIS* ONE IS. NOTHING BUT A BALL OF DIRT WITH DELUSIONS OF GRANDEUR.

"AND THAT...WELL, THAT *IS* SUPERMAN. BUT HE'S NOT THE MAN I THOUGHT HE WAS. AND HE'S CERTAINLY NOT GOING TO HELP *US.*"

The Multiverse has been saved from the brink of destruction! With victory comes new possibilities, as the triumph of our heroes shakes loose the very fabric of time and space. From the ashes of *Death Metal* comes new life for the Multiverse--and a glimpse into the unwritten worlds of tomorrow...

writer: ROBBIE THOMPSON   artist: JAVIER FERNANDEZ
colorist: ALEX SINCLAIR   letterer: WES ABBOTT
cover by: JAVIER FERNANDEZ & MARCELO MAIOLO
variant cover by: DERRICK CHEW   assistant editor: MARQUIS DRAPER
editor: MIKE COTTON   group editor: ALEX R. CARR

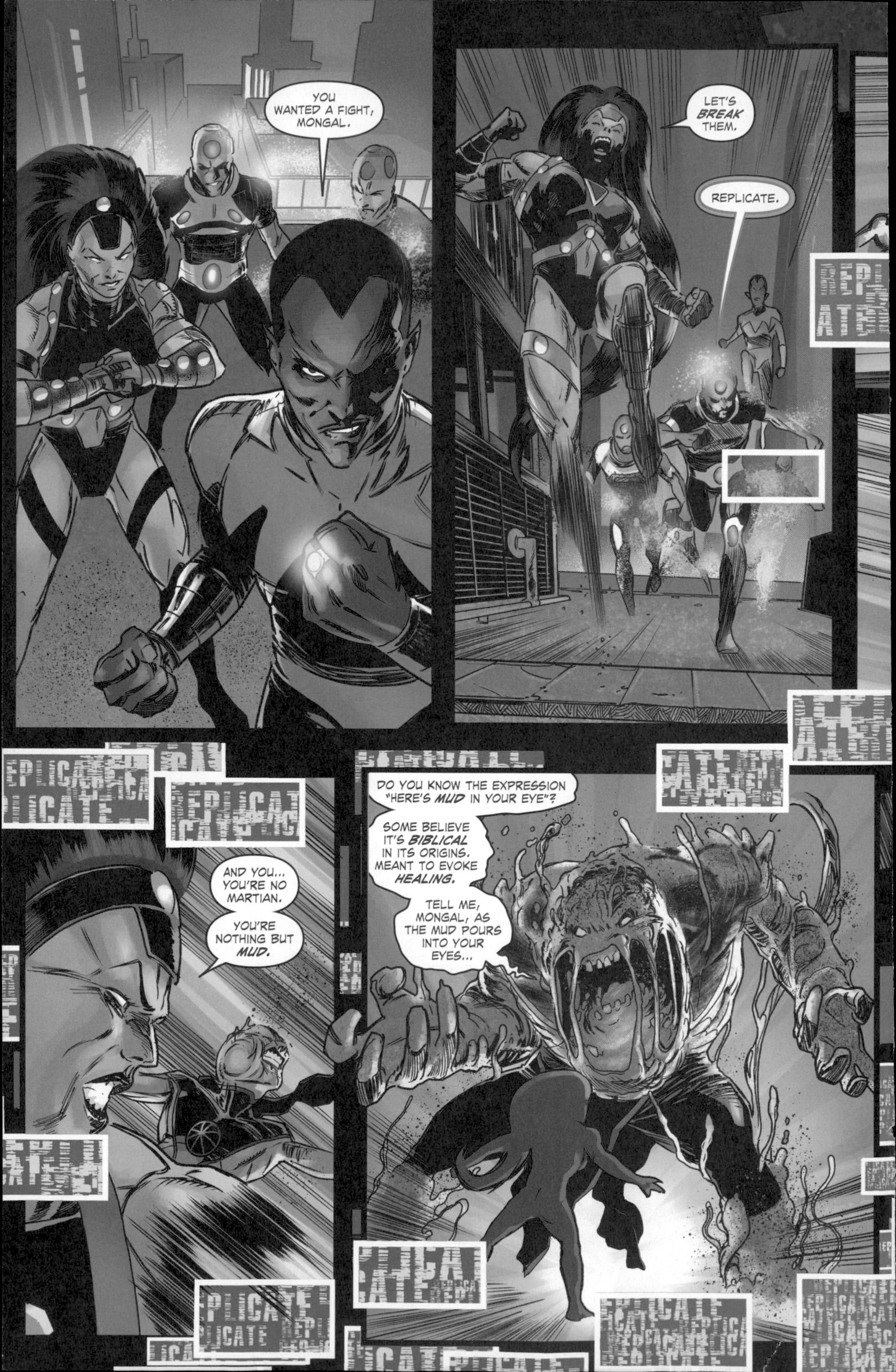
YOU WANTED A FIGHT, MONGAL.
LET'S BREAK THEM.
REPLICATE.
AND YOU... YOU'RE NO MARTIAN.
YOU'RE NOTHING BUT MUD.
DO YOU KNOW THE EXPRESSION "HERE'S MUD IN YOUR EYE"?
SOME BELIEVE IT'S BIBLICAL IN ITS ORIGINS. MEANT TO EVOKE HEALING.
TELL ME, MONGAL, AS THE MUD POURS INTO YOUR EYES...
REPLICATE

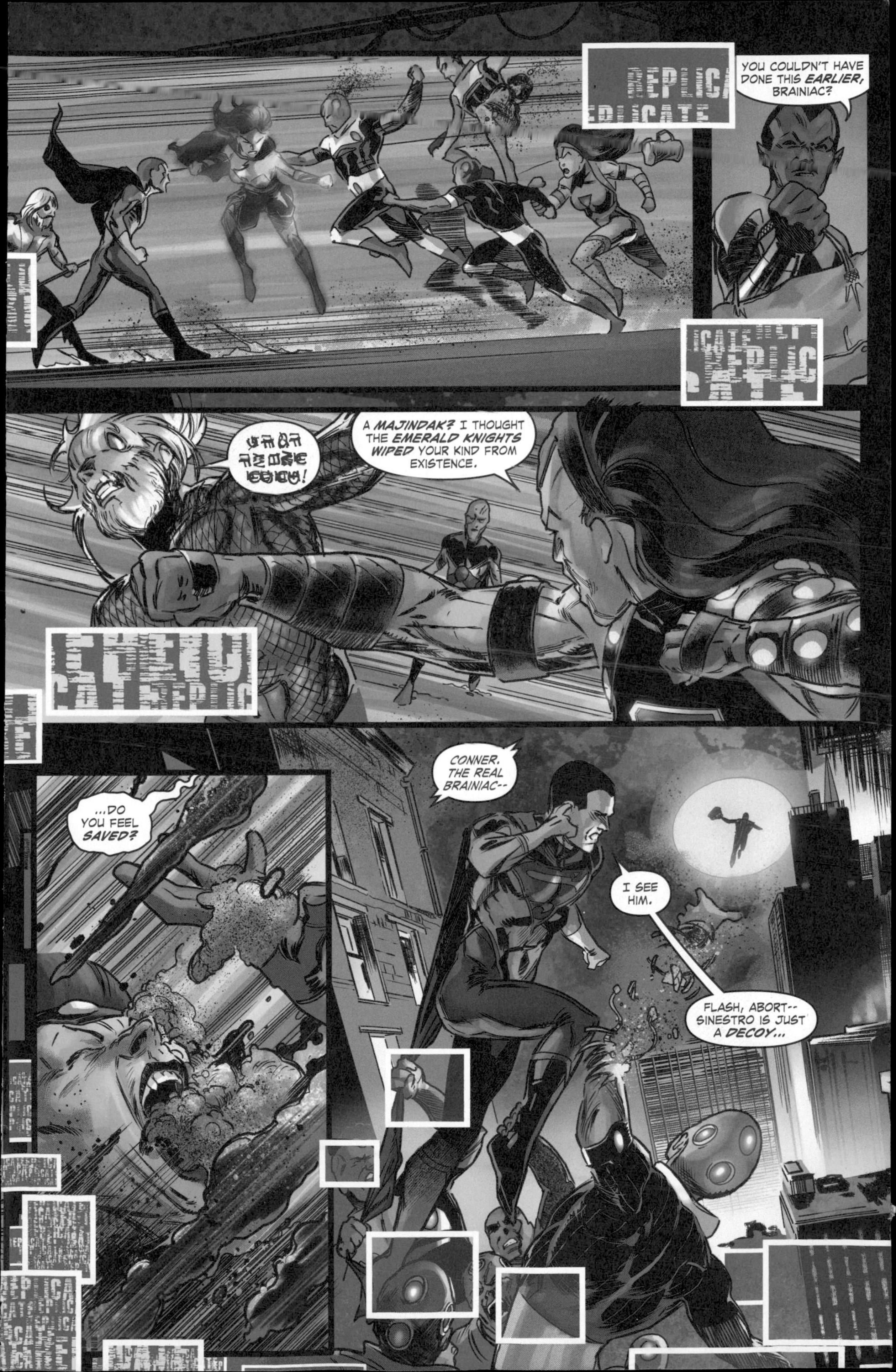
REPLICA
EDLICATE
YOU COULDN'T HAVE DONE THIS EARLIER, BRAINIAC?
A MAJINDAK? I THOUGHT THE EMERALD KNIGHTS WIPED YOUR KIND FROM EXISTENCE.
...DO YOU FEEL SAVED?
CONNER. THE REAL BRAINIAC--
I SEE HIM.
FLASH, ABORT-- SINESTRO IS JUST A DECOY...

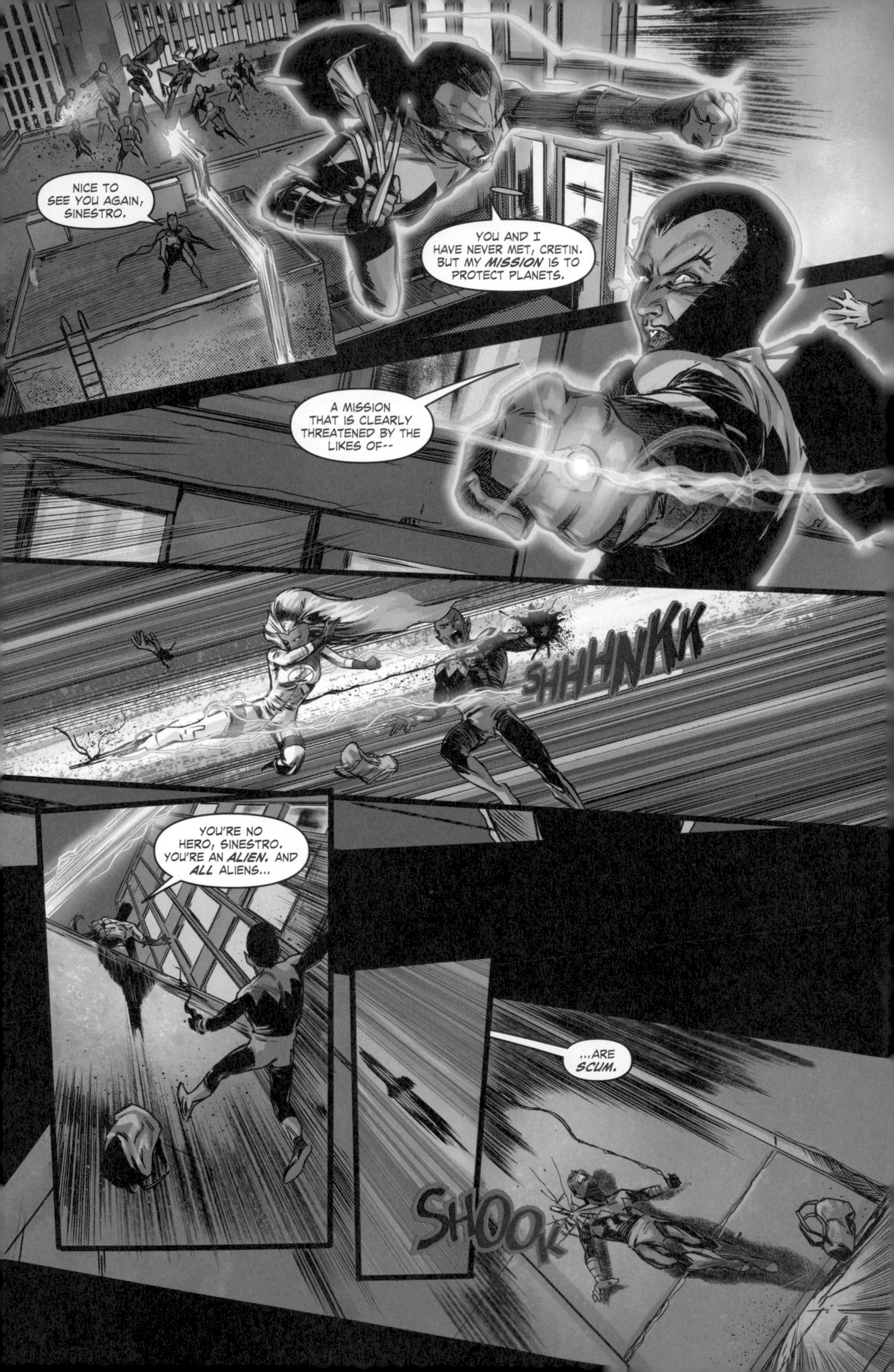
NICE TO SEE YOU AGAIN, SINESTRO.
YOU AND I HAVE NEVER MET, CRETIN. BUT MY MISSION IS TO PROTECT PLANETS.
A MISSION THAT IS CLEARLY THREATENED BY THE LIKES OF--
SHHHNKK
YOU'RE NO HERO, SINESTRO. YOU'RE AN ALIEN. AND ALL ALIENS...
...ARE SCUM.
SHOOK

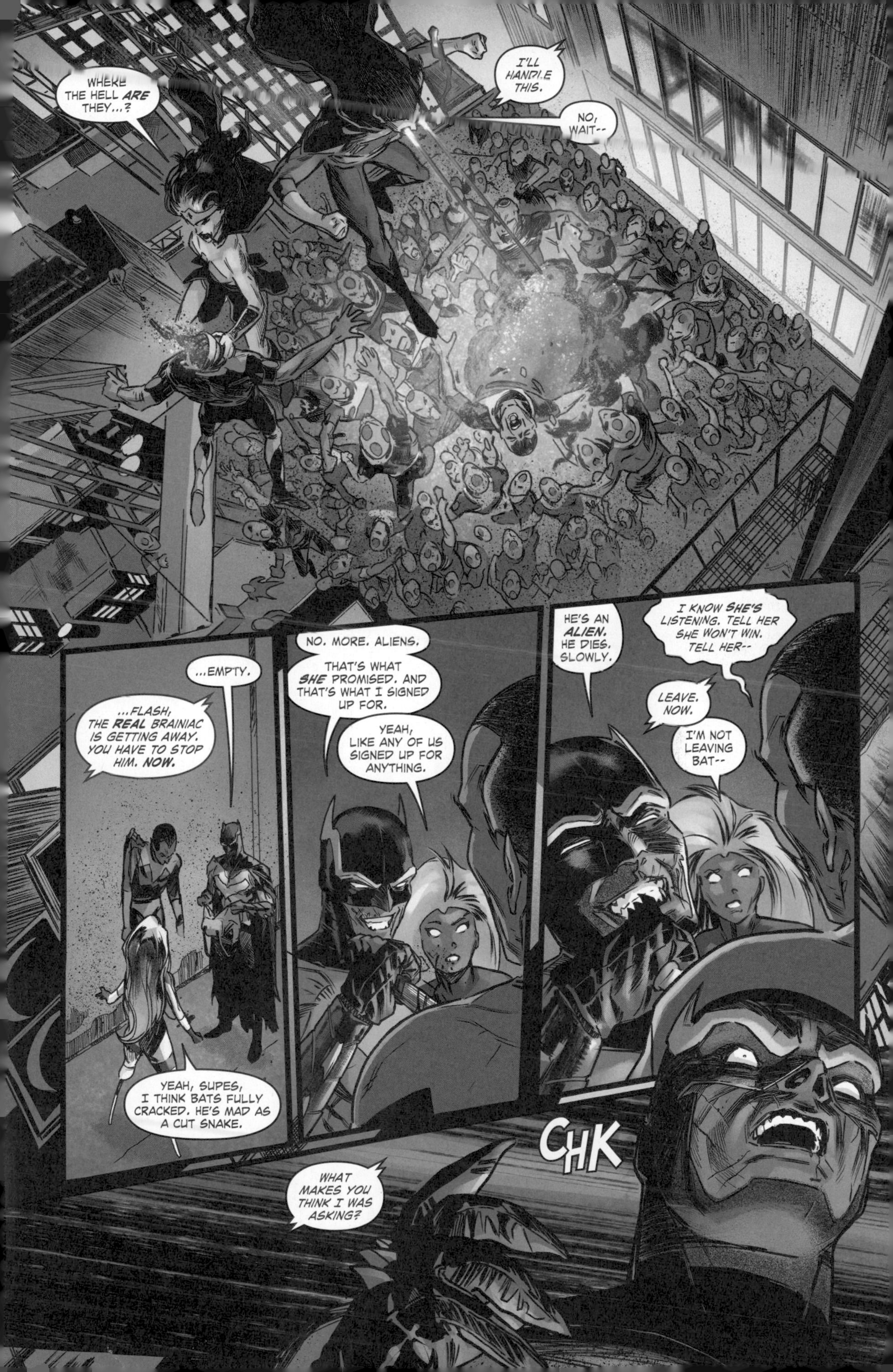
WHERE THE HELL ARE THEY...?
I'LL HANDLE THIS.
NO, WAIT--
...EMPTY.
...FLASH, THE REAL BRAINIAC IS GETTING AWAY. YOU HAVE TO STOP HIM. NOW.
YEAH, SUPES, I THINK BATS FULLY CRACKED. HE'S MAD AS A CUT SNAKE.
NO. MORE. ALIENS.
THAT'S WHAT SHE PROMISED. AND THAT'S WHAT I SIGNED UP FOR.
YEAH, LIKE ANY OF US SIGNED UP FOR ANYTHING.
HE'S AN ALIEN. HE DIES. SLOWLY.
I KNOW SHE'S LISTENING. TELL HER SHE WON'T WIN. TELL HER--
LEAVE. NOW.
I'M NOT LEAVING BAT--
CHK
WHAT MAKES YOU THINK I WAS ASKING?

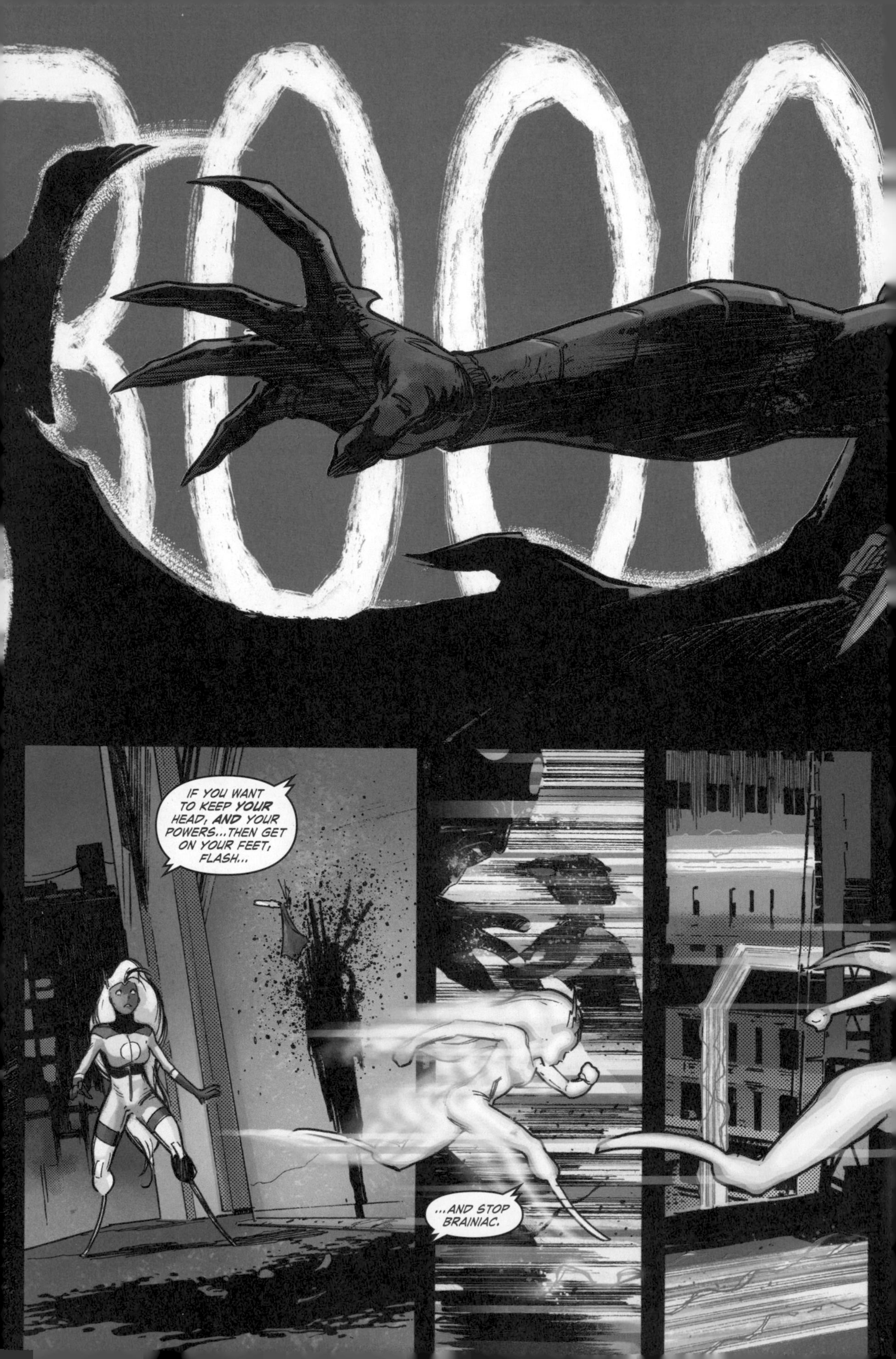
BOOOO
IF YOU WANT TO KEEP YOUR HEAD, AND YOUR POWERS...THEN GET ON YOUR FEET, FLASH...
...AND STOP BRAINIAC.

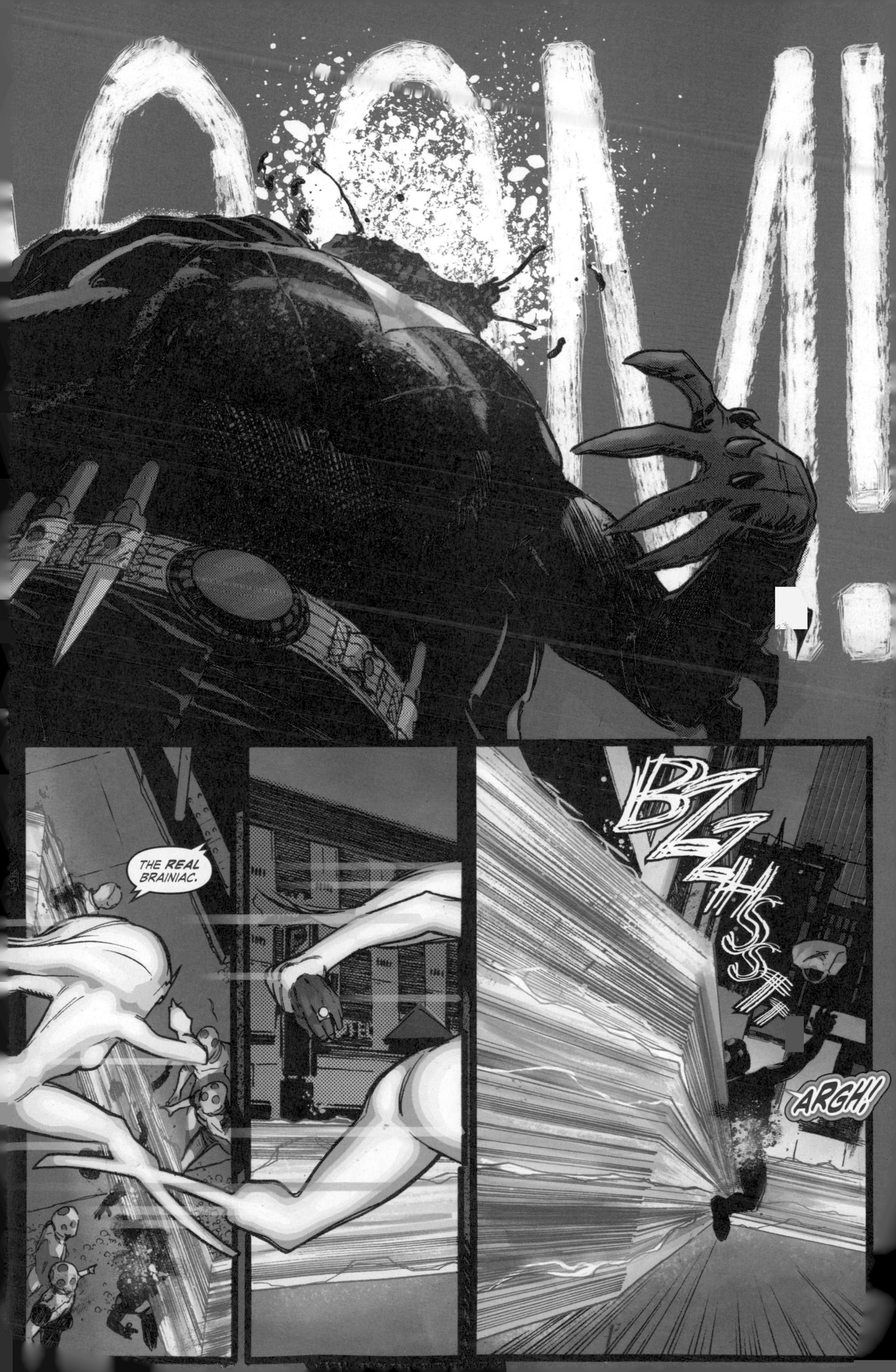
THE REAL BRAINIAC.
BZZHSST
ARGH!

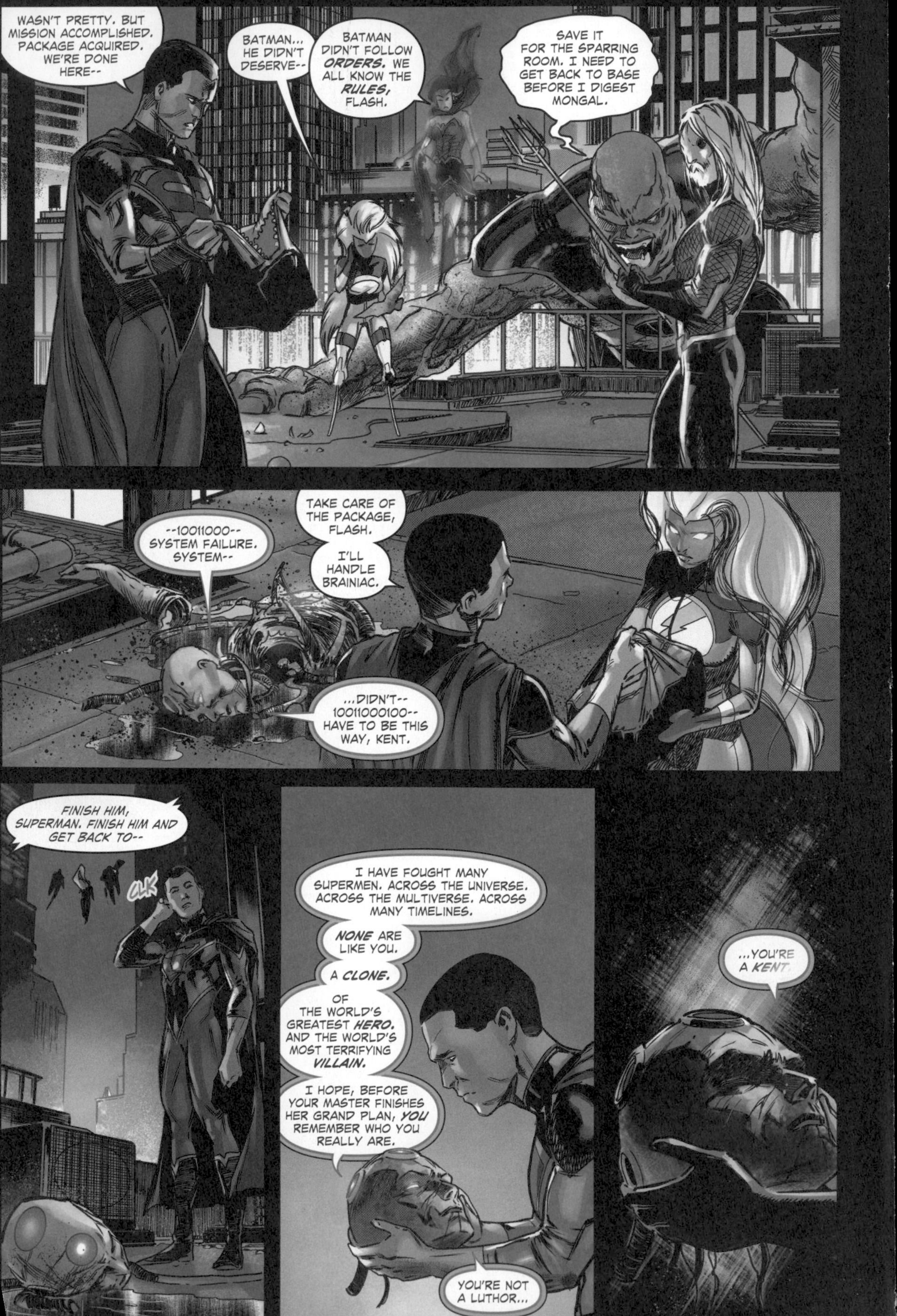
WASN'T PRETTY. BUT MISSION ACCOMPLISHED. PACKAGE ACQUIRED. WE'RE DONE HERE--
BATMAN... HE DIDN'T DESERVE--
BATMAN DIDN'T FOLLOW ORDERS. WE ALL KNOW THE RULES, FLASH.
SAVE IT FOR THE SPARRING ROOM. I NEED TO GET BACK TO BASE BEFORE I DIGEST MONGAL.
--10011000-- SYSTEM FAILURE. SYSTEM--
TAKE CARE OF THE PACKAGE, FLASH.
I'LL HANDLE BRAINIAC.
...DIDN'T-- 10011000100-- HAVE TO BE THIS WAY, KENT.
FINISH HIM, SUPERMAN. FINISH HIM AND GET BACK TO--
CLK
I HAVE FOUGHT MANY SUPERMEN. ACROSS THE UNIVERSE. ACROSS THE MULTIVERSE. ACROSS MANY TIMELINES.
NONE ARE LIKE YOU.
A CLONE.
OF THE WORLD'S GREATEST HERO. AND THE WORLD'S MOST TERRIFYING VILLAIN.
I HOPE, BEFORE YOUR MASTER FINISHES HER GRAND PLAN, YOU REMEMBER WHO YOU REALLY ARE.
YOU'RE NOT A LUTHOR...
...YOU'RE A KENT.

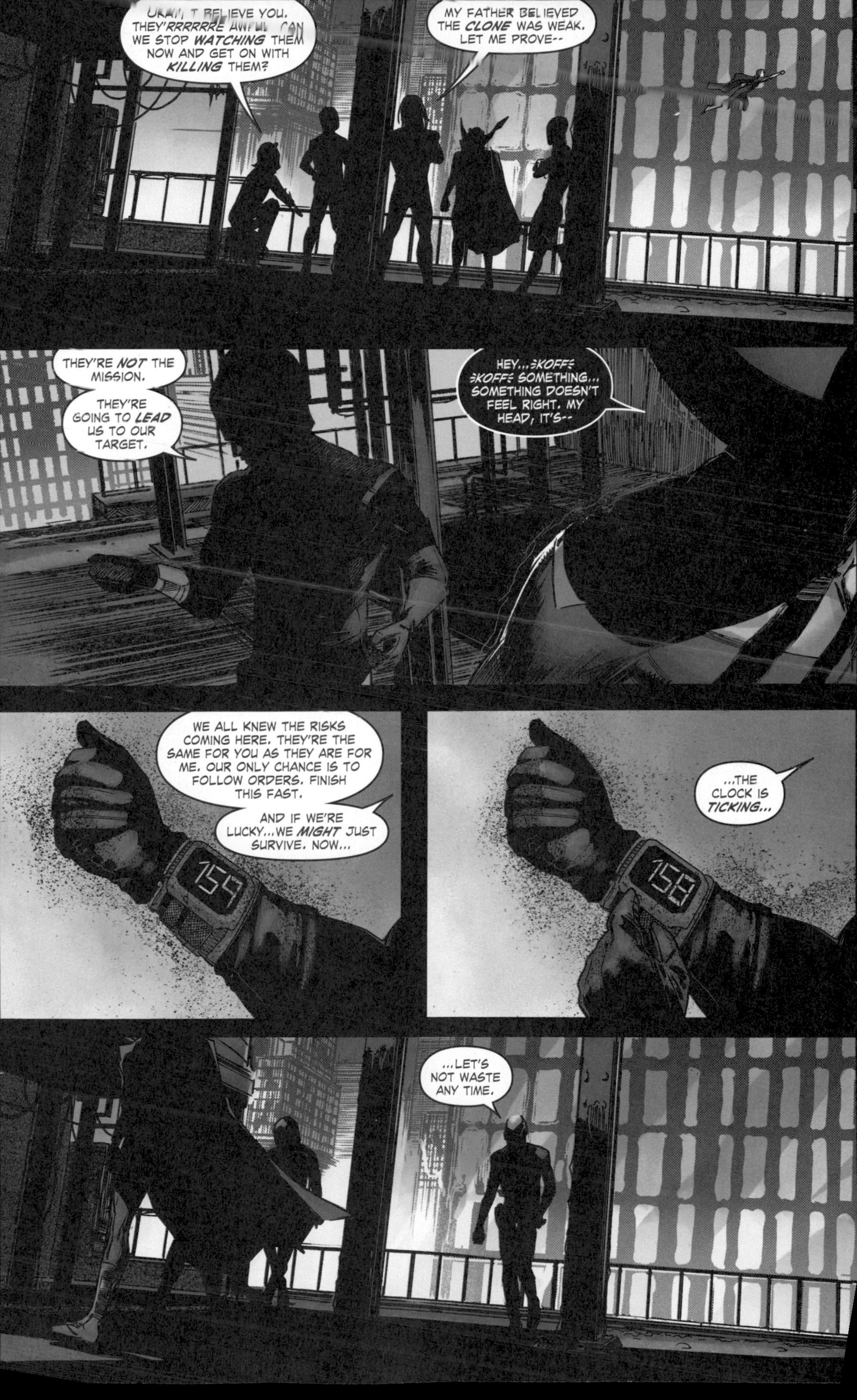
OKAY, I BELIEVE YOU. THEY'RRRRRRE AWFUL. CAN WE STOP WATCHING THEM NOW AND GET ON WITH KILLING THEM?
MY FATHER BELIEVED THE CLONE WAS WEAK. LET ME PROVE--
THEY'RE NOT THE MISSION.
THEY'RE GOING TO LEAD US TO OUR TARGET.
HEY... *KOFF* *KOFF* SOMETHING... SOMETHING DOESN'T FEEL RIGHT. MY HEAD, IT'S--
WE ALL KNEW THE RISKS COMING HERE. THEY'RE THE SAME FOR YOU AS THEY ARE FOR ME. OUR ONLY CHANCE IS TO FOLLOW ORDERS. FINISH THIS FAST.
AND IF WE'RE LUCKY... WE MIGHT JUST SURVIVE. NOW...
159
...THE CLOCK IS TICKING...
158
...LET'S NOT WASTE ANY TIME.

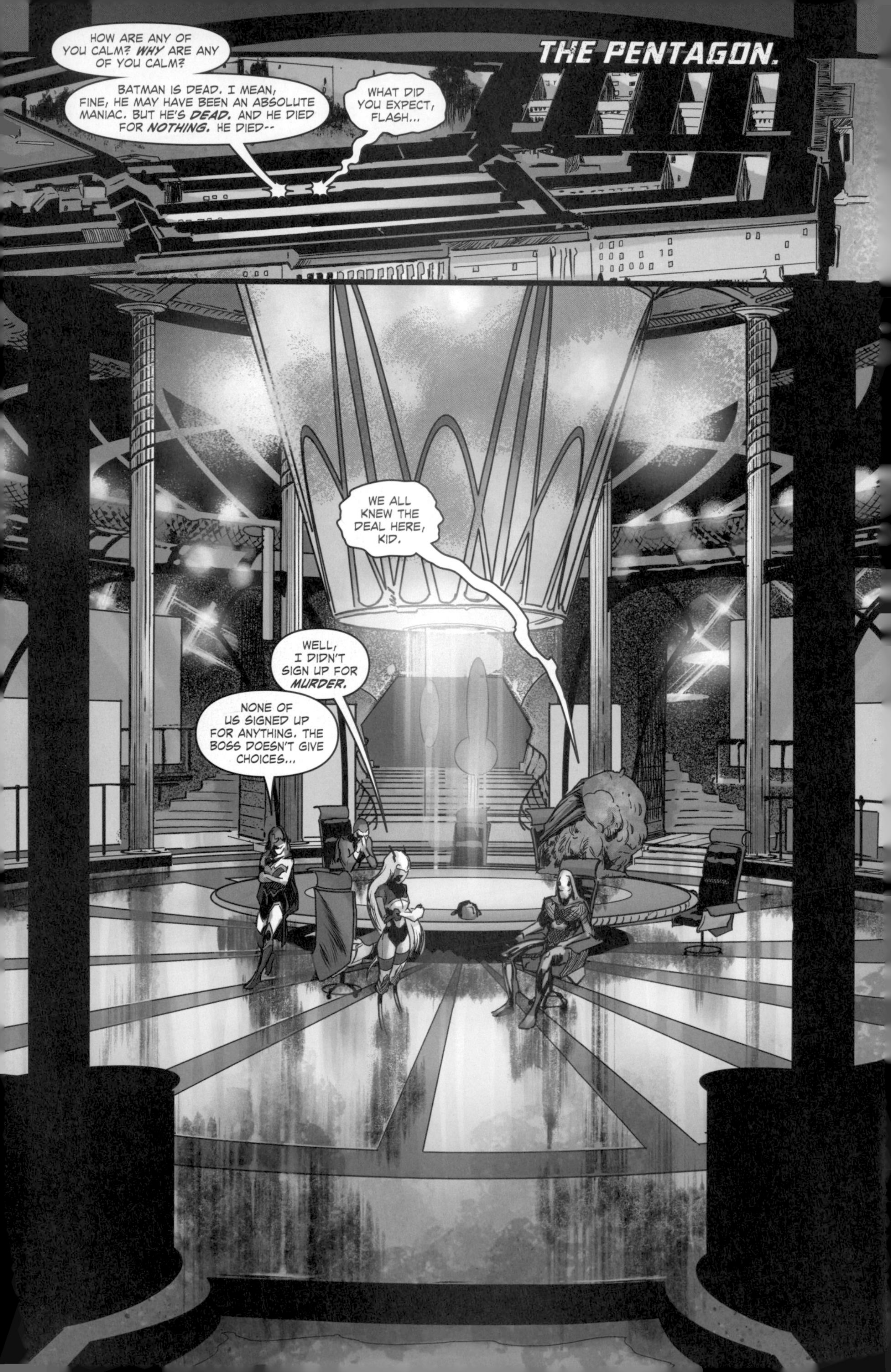
THE PENTAGON.
HOW ARE ANY OF YOU CALM? *WHY* ARE ANY OF YOU CALM?
BATMAN IS DEAD. I MEAN, FINE, HE MAY HAVE BEEN AN ABSOLUTE MANIAC. BUT HE'S *DEAD.* AND HE DIED FOR *NOTHING.* HE DIED--
WHAT DID YOU EXPECT, FLASH...
WE ALL KNEW THE DEAL HERE, KID.
WELL, I DIDN'T SIGN UP FOR *MURDER.*
NONE OF US SIGNED UP FOR ANYTHING. THE BOSS DOESN'T GIVE CHOICES...

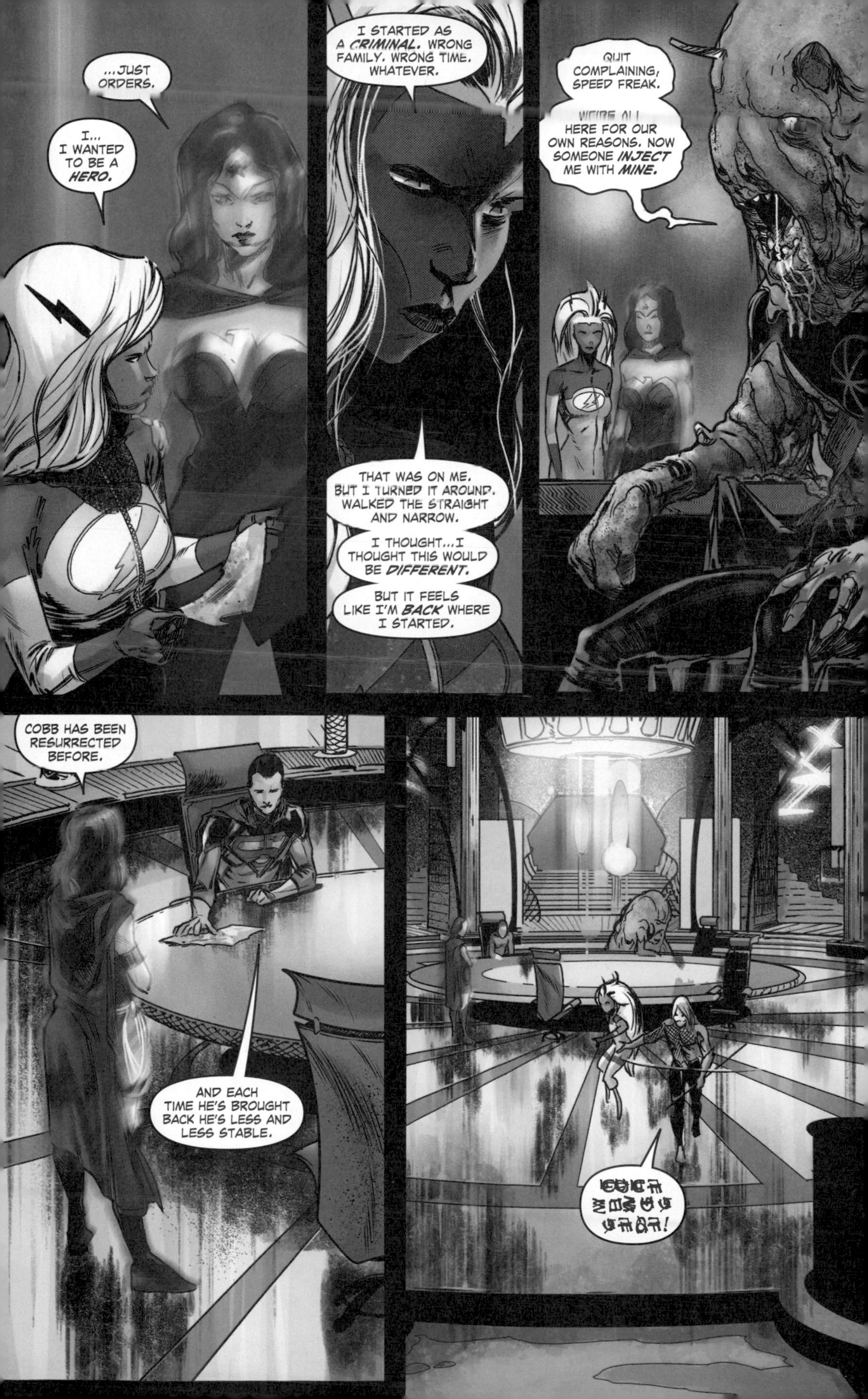
...JUST ORDERS.
I... I WANTED TO BE A *HERO.*
I STARTED AS A *CRIMINAL.* WRONG FAMILY. WRONG TIME. WHATEVER.
THAT WAS ON ME. BUT I TURNED IT AROUND. WALKED THE STRAIGHT AND NARROW.
I THOUGHT...I THOUGHT THIS WOULD BE *DIFFERENT.*
BUT IT FEELS LIKE I'M *BACK* WHERE I STARTED.
QUIT COMPLAINING, SPEED FREAK.
WE'RE ALL HERE FOR OUR OWN REASONS. NOW SOMEONE *INJECT* ME WITH *MINE.*
COBB HAS BEEN RESURRECTED BEFORE.
AND EACH TIME HE'S BROUGHT BACK HE'S LESS AND LESS STABLE.

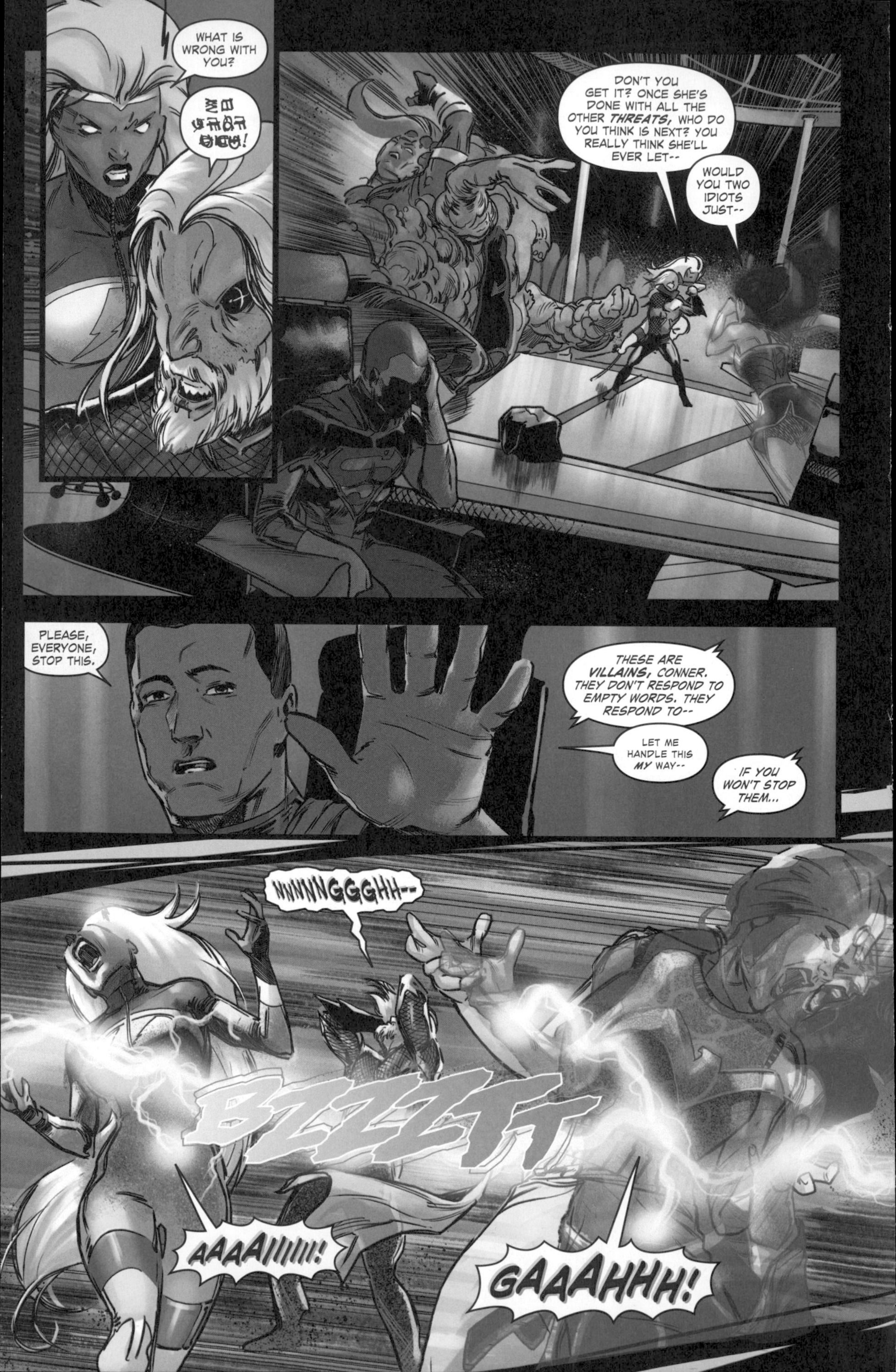
WHAT IS WRONG WITH YOU?
DON'T YOU GET IT? ONCE SHE'S DONE WITH ALL THE OTHER *THREATS,* WHO DO YOU THINK IS NEXT? YOU REALLY THINK SHE'LL EVER LET--
WOULD YOU TWO IDIOTS JUST--
PLEASE, EVERYONE, STOP THIS.
*THESE ARE **VILLAINS,** CONNER. THEY DON'T RESPOND TO EMPTY WORDS. THEY RESPOND TO--*
LET ME HANDLE THIS ***MY*** WAY--
IF YOU WON'T STOP THEM...
NNNNNGGGHH--
BZZZTT
AAAAIIIIII!
GAAAHHH!

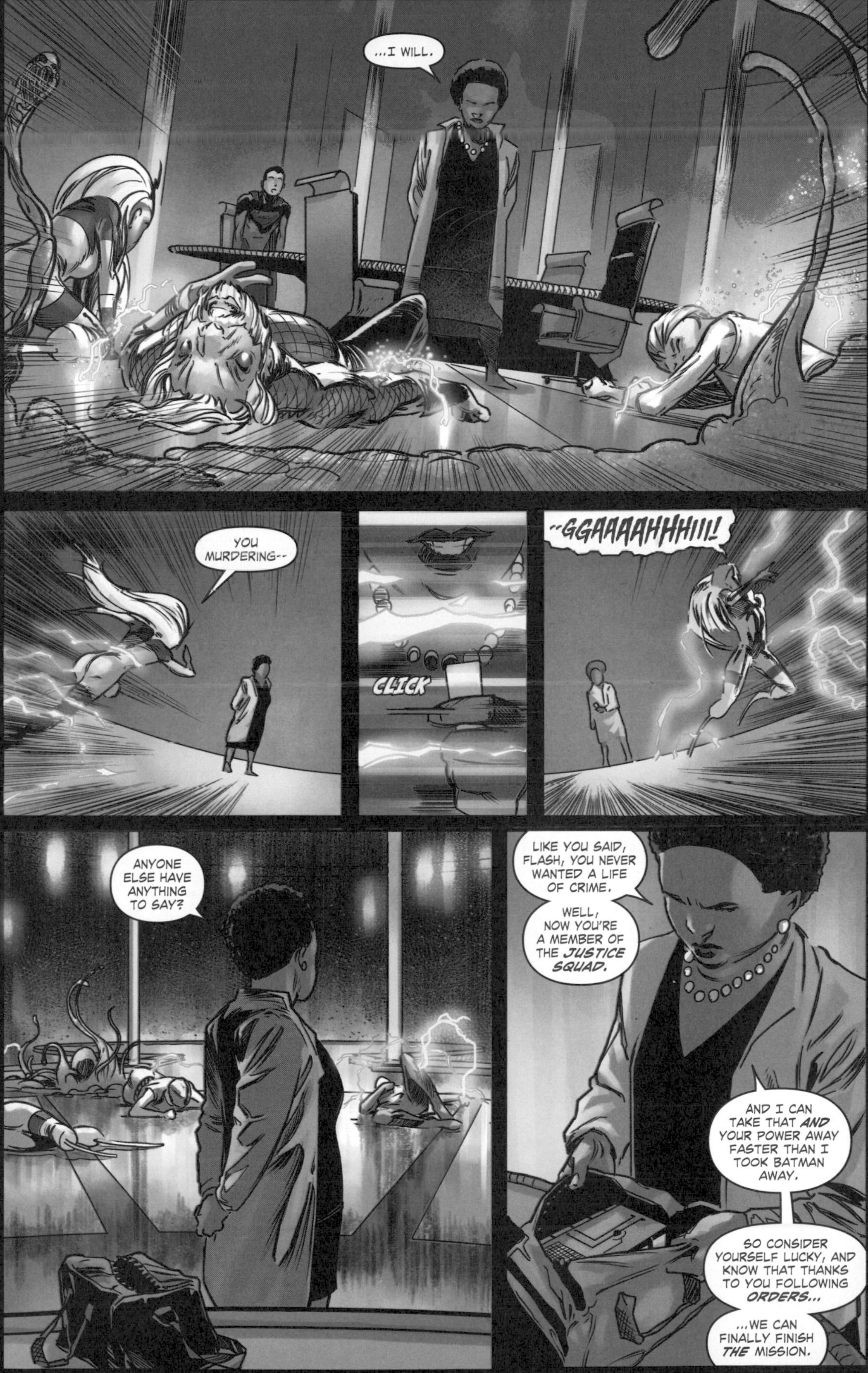
...I WILL.
YOU MURDERING--
CLICK
--GGAAAAAHHHH!!
ANYONE ELSE HAVE ANYTHING TO SAY?
LIKE YOU SAID, FLASH, YOU NEVER WANTED A LIFE OF CRIME.
WELL, NOW YOU'RE A MEMBER OF THE JUSTICE SQUAD.
AND I CAN TAKE THAT AND YOUR POWER AWAY FASTER THAN I TOOK BATMAN AWAY.
SO CONSIDER YOURSELF LUCKY, AND KNOW THAT THANKS TO YOU FOLLOWING ORDERS...
...WE CAN FINALLY FINISH THE MISSION.

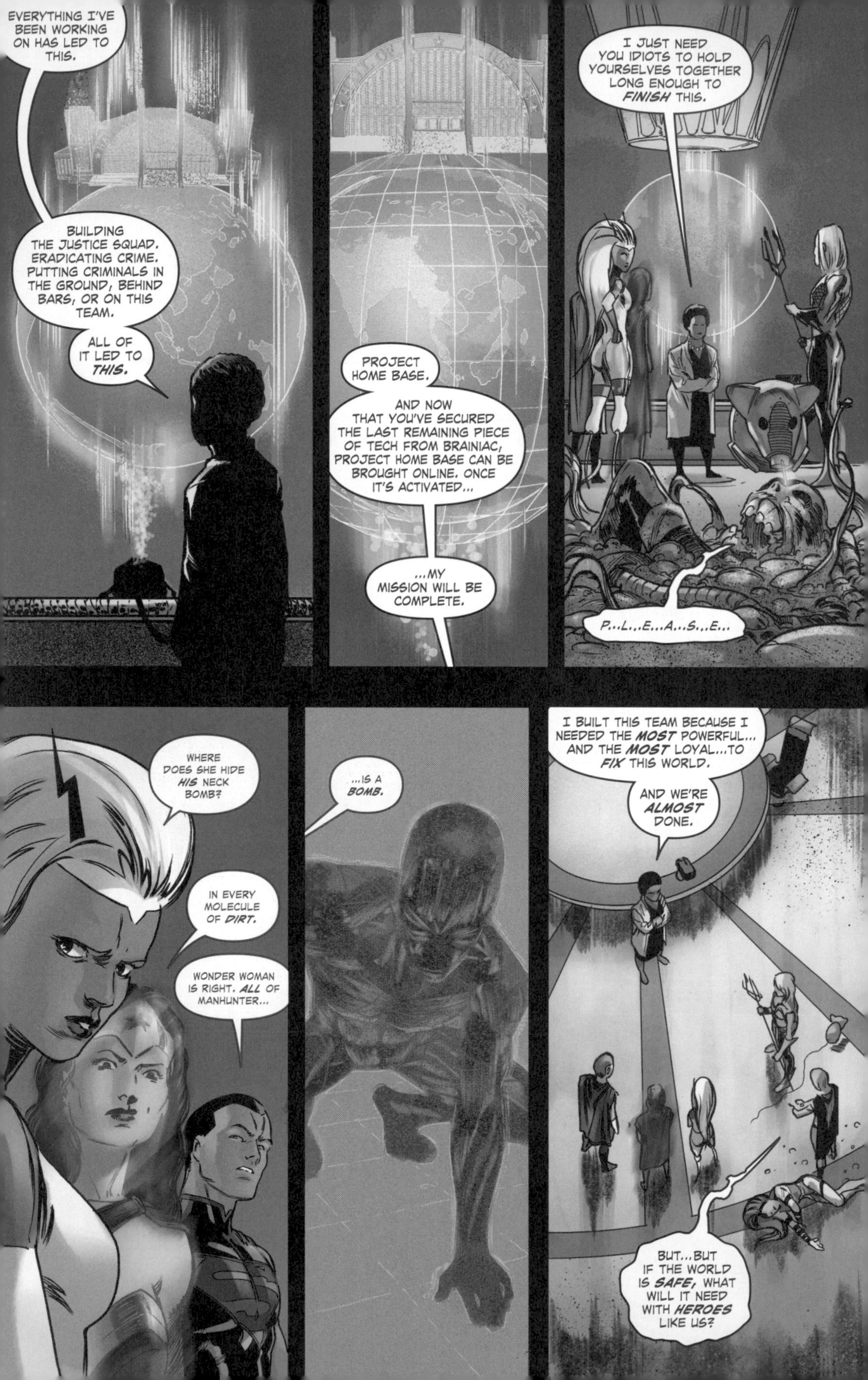
EVERYTHING I'VE BEEN WORKING ON HAS LED TO THIS.
BUILDING THE JUSTICE SQUAD. ERADICATING CRIME. PUTTING CRIMINALS IN THE GROUND, BEHIND BARS, OR ON THIS TEAM.
ALL OF IT LED TO *THIS.*
PROJECT HOME BASE.
AND NOW THAT YOU'VE SECURED THE LAST REMAINING PIECE OF TECH FROM BRAINIAC, PROJECT HOME BASE CAN BE BROUGHT ONLINE. ONCE IT'S ACTIVATED...
...MY MISSION WILL BE COMPLETE.
I JUST NEED YOU IDIOTS TO HOLD YOURSELVES TOGETHER LONG ENOUGH TO *FINISH* THIS.
P...L...E...A...S...E...
WHERE DOES SHE HIDE *HIS* NECK BOMB?
IN EVERY MOLECULE OF *DIRT.*
WONDER WOMAN IS RIGHT. *ALL* OF MANHUNTER...
...IS A *BOMB.*
I BUILT THIS TEAM BECAUSE I NEEDED THE *MOST* POWERFUL... AND THE *MOST* LOYAL...TO *FIX* THIS WORLD.
AND WE'RE *ALMOST* DONE.
BUT...BUT IF THE WORLD IS *SAFE,* WHAT WILL IT NEED WITH *HEROES* LIKE US?

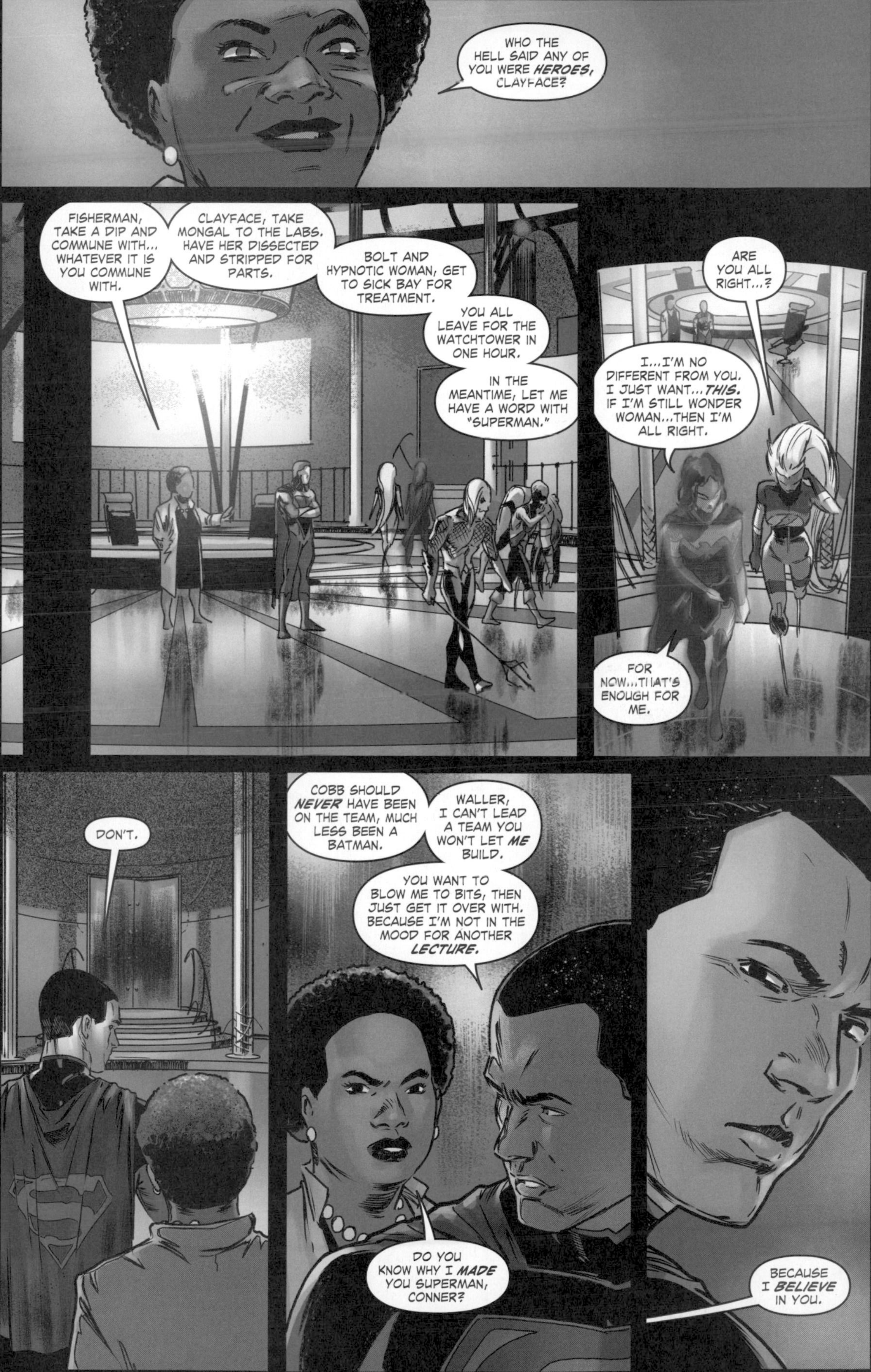
WHO THE HELL SAID ANY OF YOU WERE HEROES, CLAYFACE?
FISHERMAN, TAKE A DIP AND COMMUNE WITH... WHATEVER IT IS YOU COMMUNE WITH.
CLAYFACE, TAKE MONGAL TO THE LABS. HAVE HER DISSECTED AND STRIPPED FOR PARTS.
BOLT AND HYPNOTIC WOMAN, GET TO SICK BAY FOR TREATMENT.
YOU ALL LEAVE FOR THE WATCHTOWER IN ONE HOUR.
IN THE MEANTIME, LET ME HAVE A WORD WITH "SUPERMAN."
ARE YOU ALL RIGHT...?
I...I'M NO DIFFERENT FROM YOU. I JUST WANT...THIS. IF I'M STILL WONDER WOMAN...THEN I'M ALL RIGHT.
FOR NOW...THAT'S ENOUGH FOR ME.
DON'T.
COBB SHOULD NEVER HAVE BEEN ON THE TEAM, MUCH LESS BEEN A BATMAN.
WALLER, I CAN'T LEAD A TEAM YOU WON'T LET ME BUILD.
YOU WANT TO BLOW ME TO BITS, THEN JUST GET IT OVER WITH. BECAUSE I'M NOT IN THE MOOD FOR ANOTHER LECTURE.
DO YOU KNOW WHY I MADE YOU SUPERMAN, CONNER?
BECAUSE I BELIEVE IN YOU.

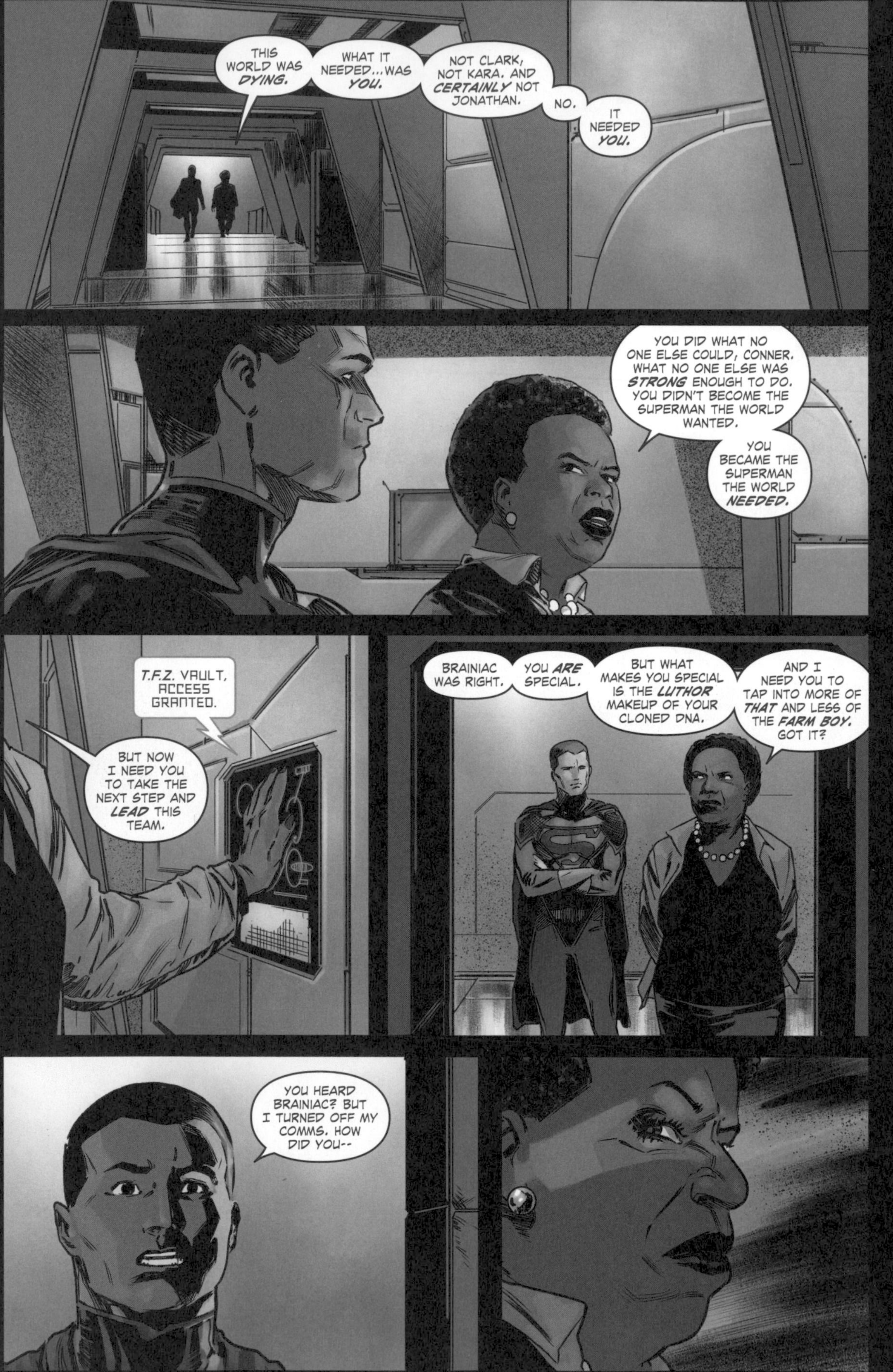
THIS WORLD WAS *DYING.*
WHAT IT NEEDED...WAS *YOU.*
NOT CLARK, NOT KARA. AND *CERTAINLY* NOT JONATHAN.
NO.
IT NEEDED *YOU.*
YOU DID WHAT NO ONE ELSE COULD, CONNER. WHAT NO ONE ELSE WAS *STRONG* ENOUGH TO DO. YOU DIDN'T BECOME THE SUPERMAN THE WORLD WANTED.
YOU BECAME THE SUPERMAN THE WORLD *NEEDED.*
T.F.Z. VAULT, ACCESS GRANTED.
BUT NOW I NEED YOU TO TAKE THE NEXT STEP AND *LEAD* THIS TEAM.
BRAINIAC WAS RIGHT.
YOU *ARE* SPECIAL.
BUT WHAT MAKES YOU SPECIAL IS THE *LUTHOR* MAKEUP OF YOUR CLONED DNA.
AND I NEED YOU TO TAP INTO MORE OF *THAT* AND LESS OF THE *FARM BOY.* GOT IT?
YOU HEARD BRAINIAC? BUT I TURNED OFF MY COMMS. HOW DID YOU--

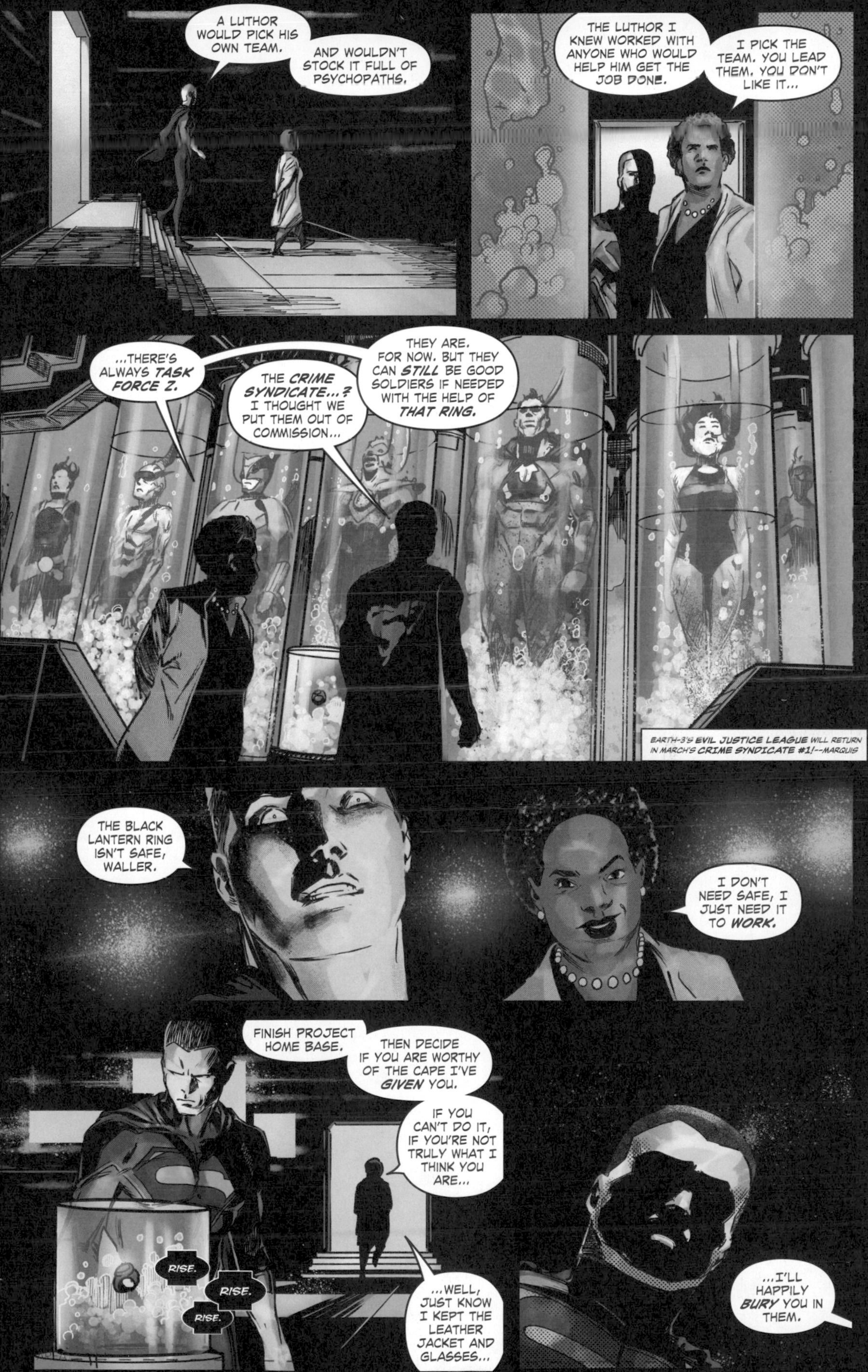
A LUTHOR WOULD PICK HIS OWN TEAM.
AND WOULDN'T STOCK IT FULL OF PSYCHOPATHS.
THE LUTHOR I KNEW WORKED WITH ANYONE WHO WOULD HELP HIM GET THE JOB DONE.
I PICK THE TEAM. YOU LEAD THEM. YOU DON'T LIKE IT...
...THERE'S ALWAYS TASK FORCE Z.
THE CRIME SYNDICATE...? I THOUGHT WE PUT THEM OUT OF COMMISSION...
THEY ARE. FOR NOW. BUT THEY CAN STILL BE GOOD SOLDIERS IF NEEDED WITH THE HELP OF THAT RING.
EARTH-3'S EVIL JUSTICE LEAGUE WILL RETURN IN MARCH'S CRIME SYNDICATE #1!--MARQUIS
THE BLACK LANTERN RING ISN'T SAFE, WALLER.
I DON'T NEED SAFE, I JUST NEED IT TO WORK.
FINISH PROJECT HOME BASE.
THEN DECIDE IF YOU ARE WORTHY OF THE CAPE I'VE GIVEN YOU.
IF YOU CAN'T DO IT, IF YOU'RE NOT TRULY WHAT I THINK YOU ARE...
...WELL, JUST KNOW I KEPT THE LEATHER JACKET AND GLASSES...
RISE.
RISE.
RISE.
...I'LL HAPPILY BURY YOU IN THEM.

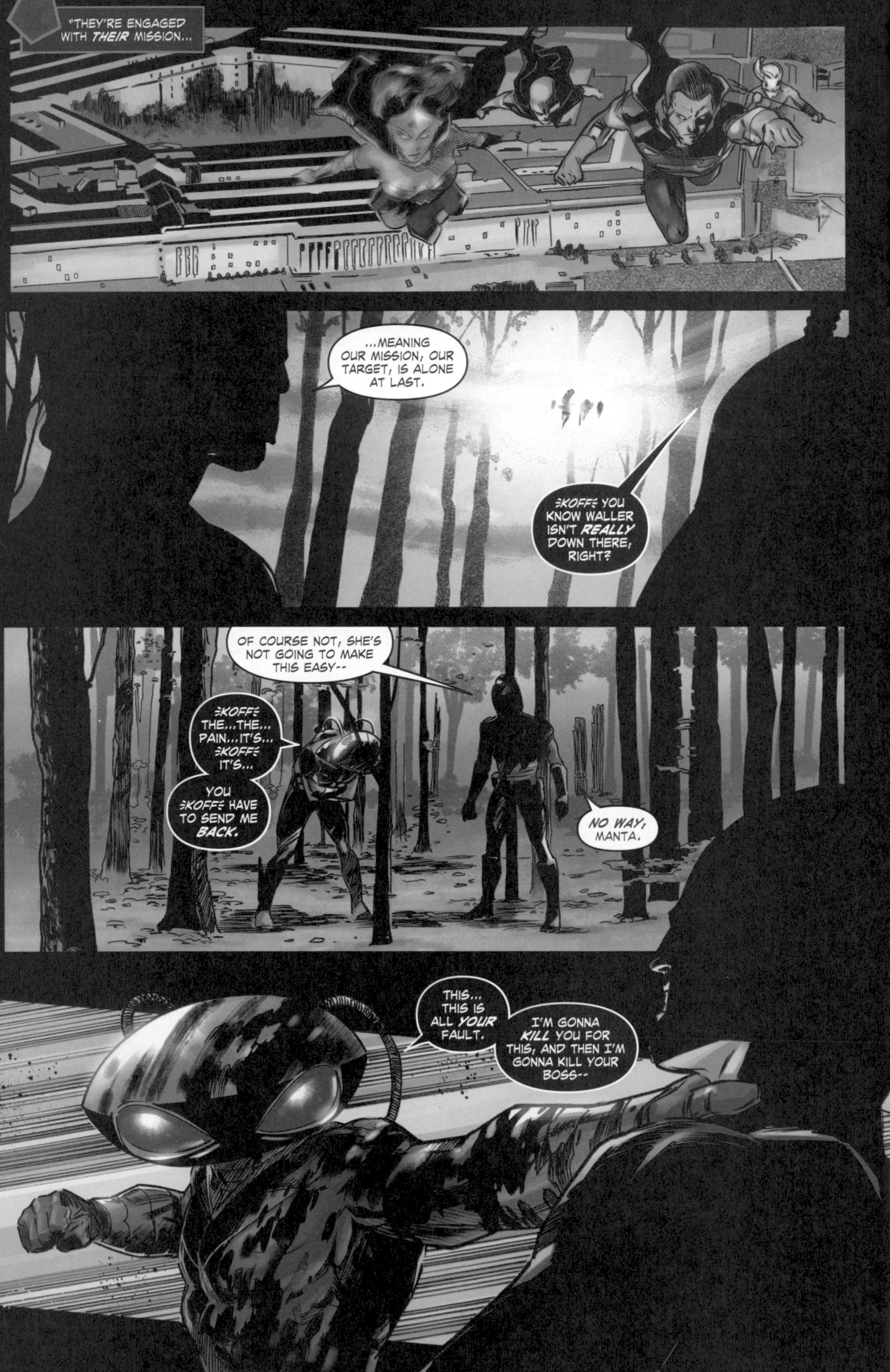
"THEY'RE ENGAGED WITH THEIR MISSION...
...MEANING OUR MISSION, OUR TARGET, IS ALONE AT LAST.
≶KOFF≶ YOU KNOW WALLER ISN'T REALLY DOWN THERE, RIGHT?
OF COURSE NOT, SHE'S NOT GOING TO MAKE THIS EASY--
≶KOFF≶ THE...THE... PAIN...IT'S... ≶KOFF≶... IT'S...
YOU ≶KOFF≶ HAVE TO SEND ME BACK.
NO WAY, MANTA.
THIS... THIS IS ALL YOUR FAULT.
I'M GONNA KILL YOU FOR THIS, AND THEN I'M GONNA KILL YOUR BOSS--

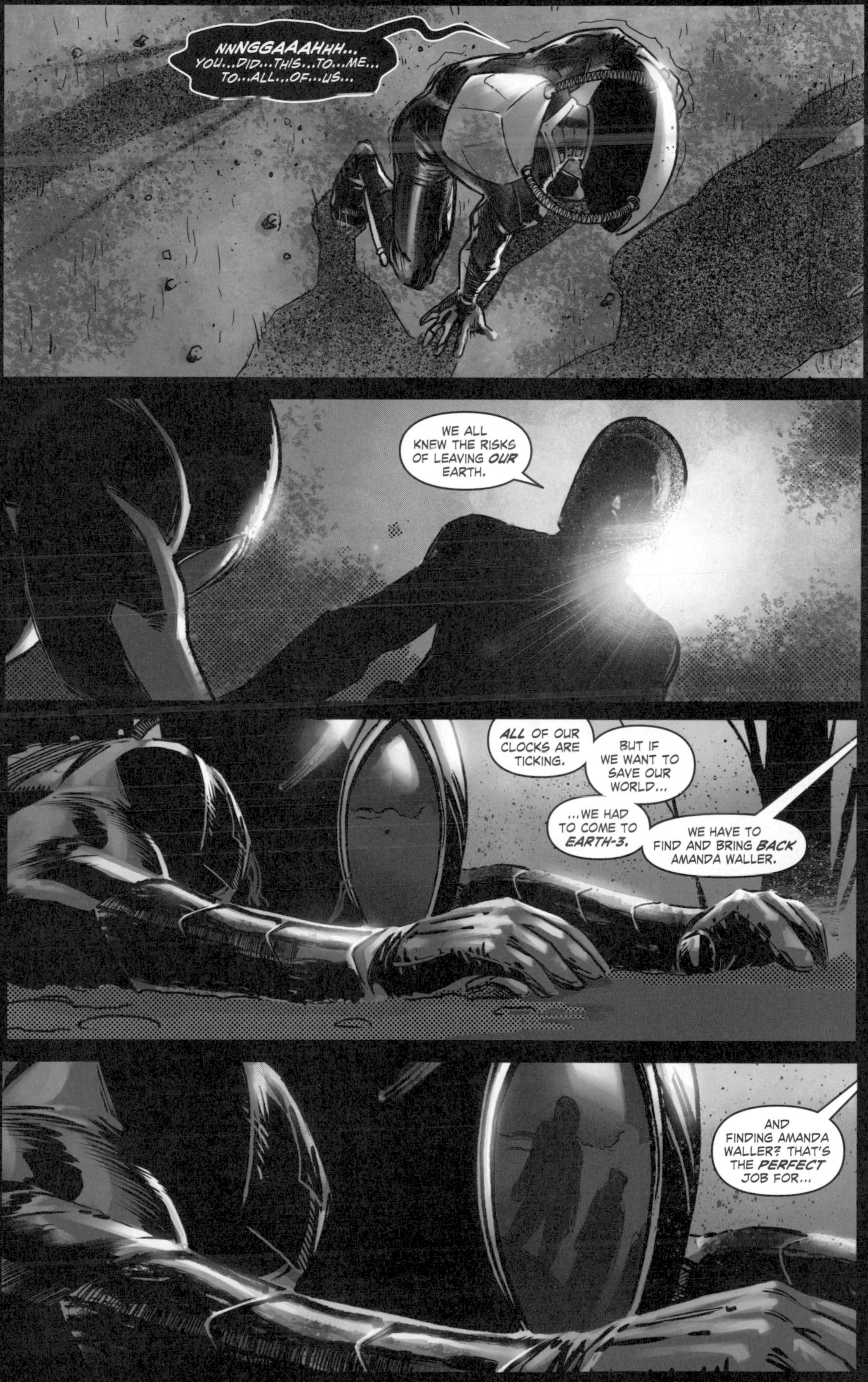
NNNGGAAAHHH... YOU...DID...THIS...TO...ME... TO...ALL...OF...US...
WE ALL KNEW THE RISKS OF LEAVING OUR EARTH.
ALL OF OUR CLOCKS ARE TICKING.
BUT IF WE WANT TO SAVE OUR WORLD...
...WE HAD TO COME TO EARTH-3.
WE HAVE TO FIND AND BRING BACK AMANDA WALLER.
AND FINDING AMANDA WALLER? THAT'S THE PERFECT JOB FOR...

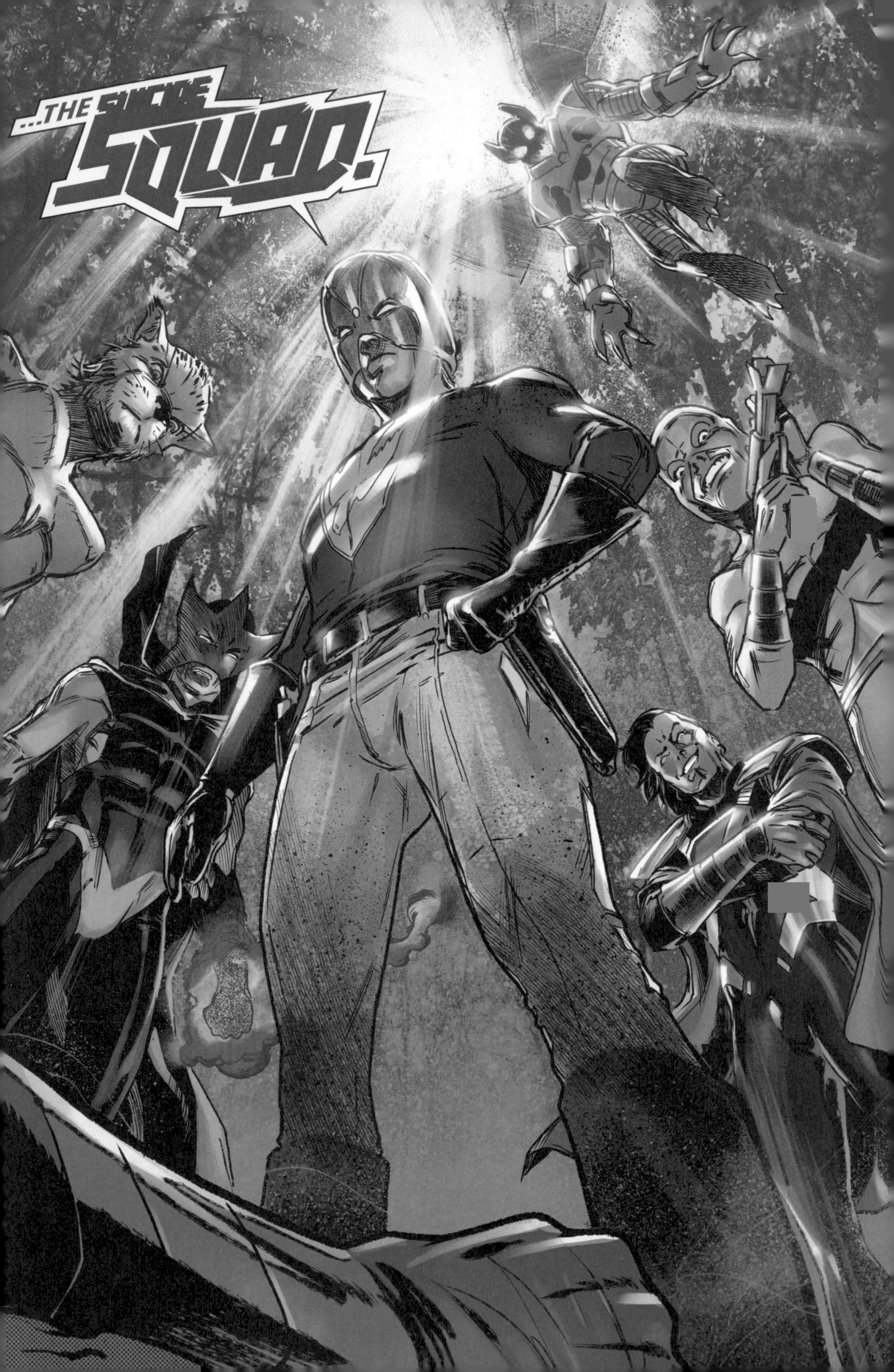
...THE SUICIDE SQUAD.

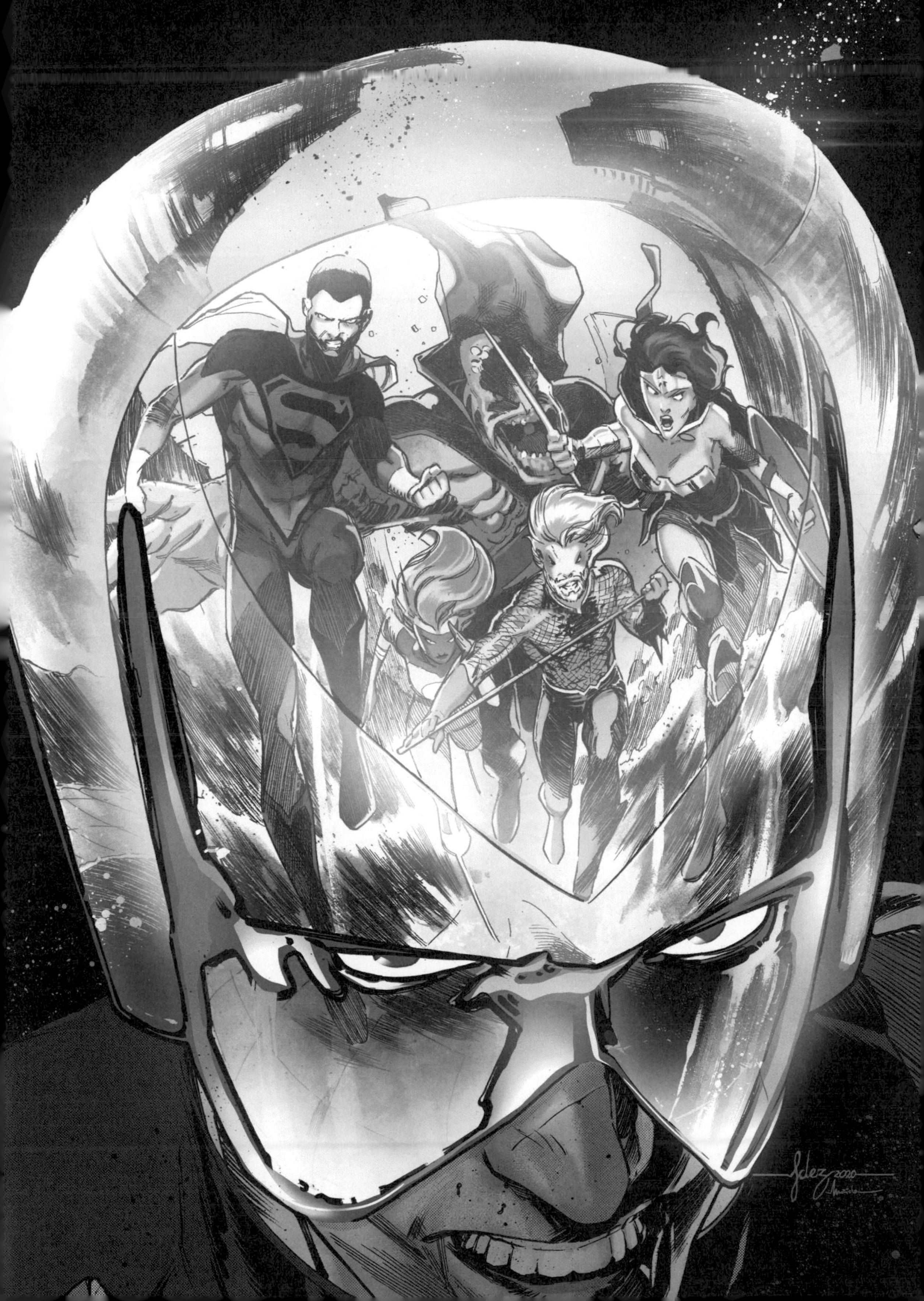

Future State: Suicide Squad #2
cover art by **JAVIER FERNANDEZ**
and **MARCELO MAIOLO**

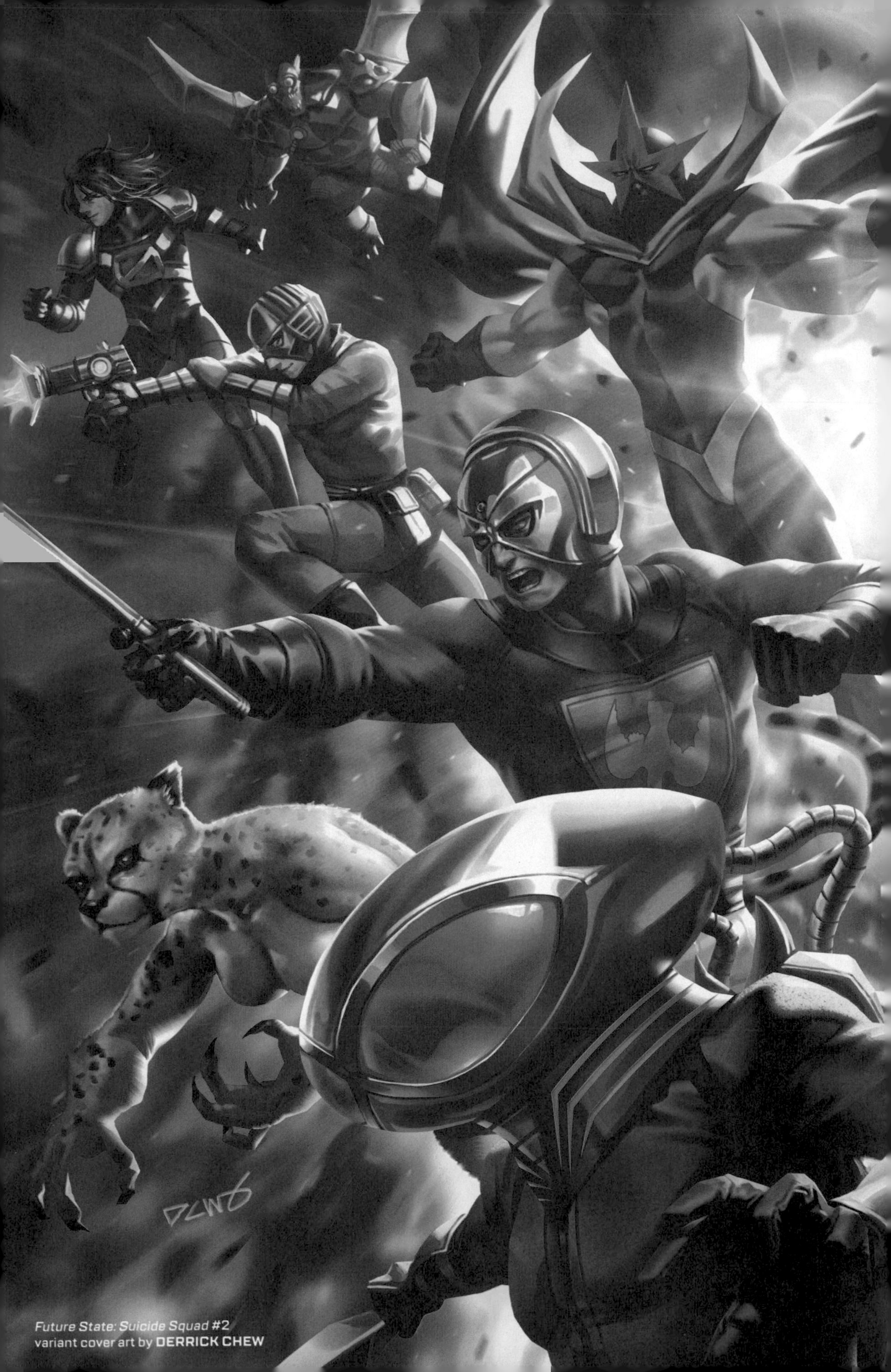

Future State: Suicide Squad #2
variant cover art by **DERRICK CHEW**

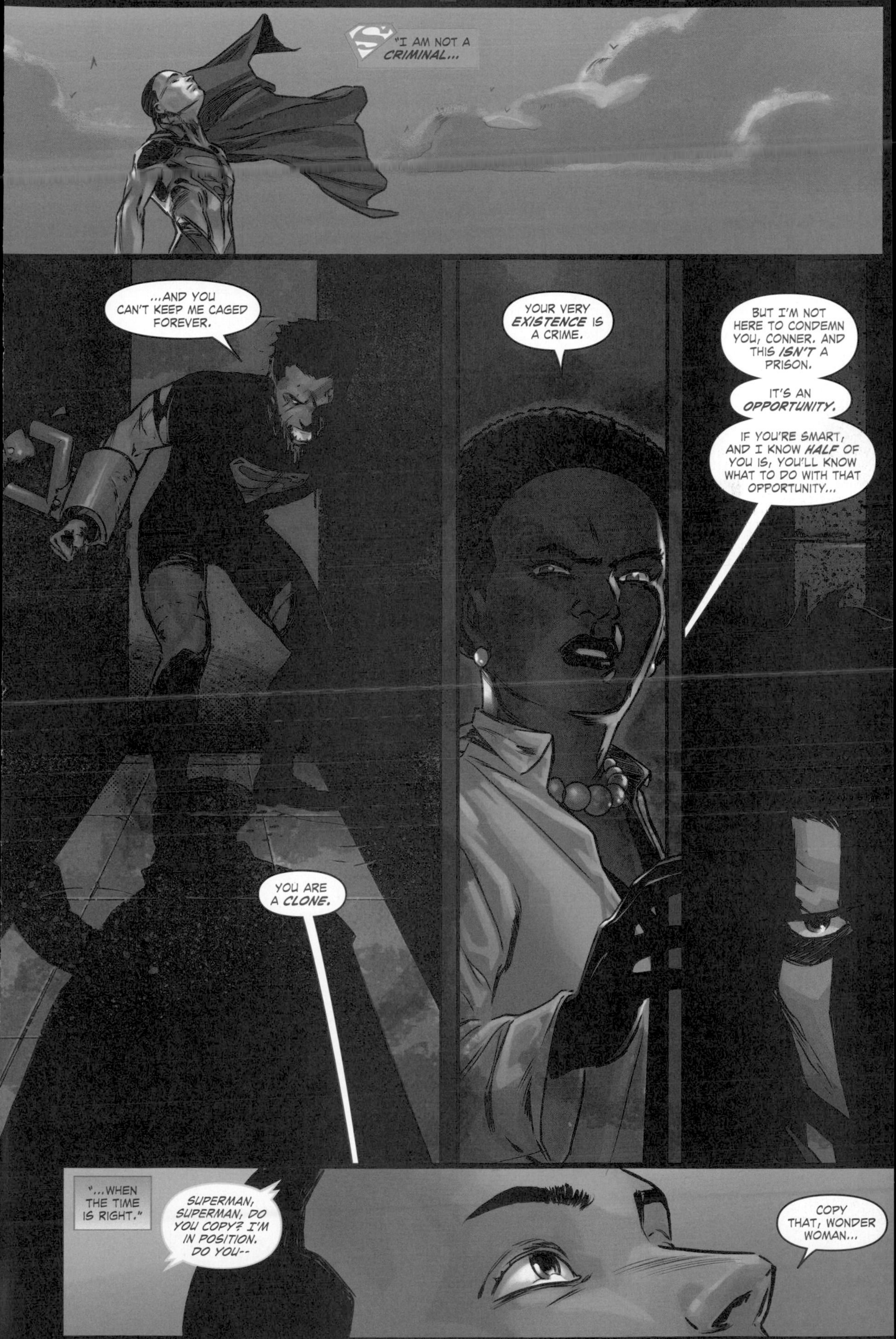
"I AM NOT A CRIMINAL...
...AND YOU CAN'T KEEP ME CAGED FOREVER.
YOUR VERY EXISTENCE IS A CRIME.
BUT I'M NOT HERE TO CONDEMN YOU, CONNER. AND THIS ISN'T A PRISON.
IT'S AN OPPORTUNITY.
IF YOU'RE SMART, AND I KNOW HALF OF YOU IS, YOU'LL KNOW WHAT TO DO WITH THAT OPPORTUNITY...
YOU ARE A CLONE.
"...WHEN THE TIME IS RIGHT."
SUPERMAN, SUPERMAN, DO YOU COPY? I'M IN POSITION. DO YOU--
COPY THAT, WONDER WOMAN...

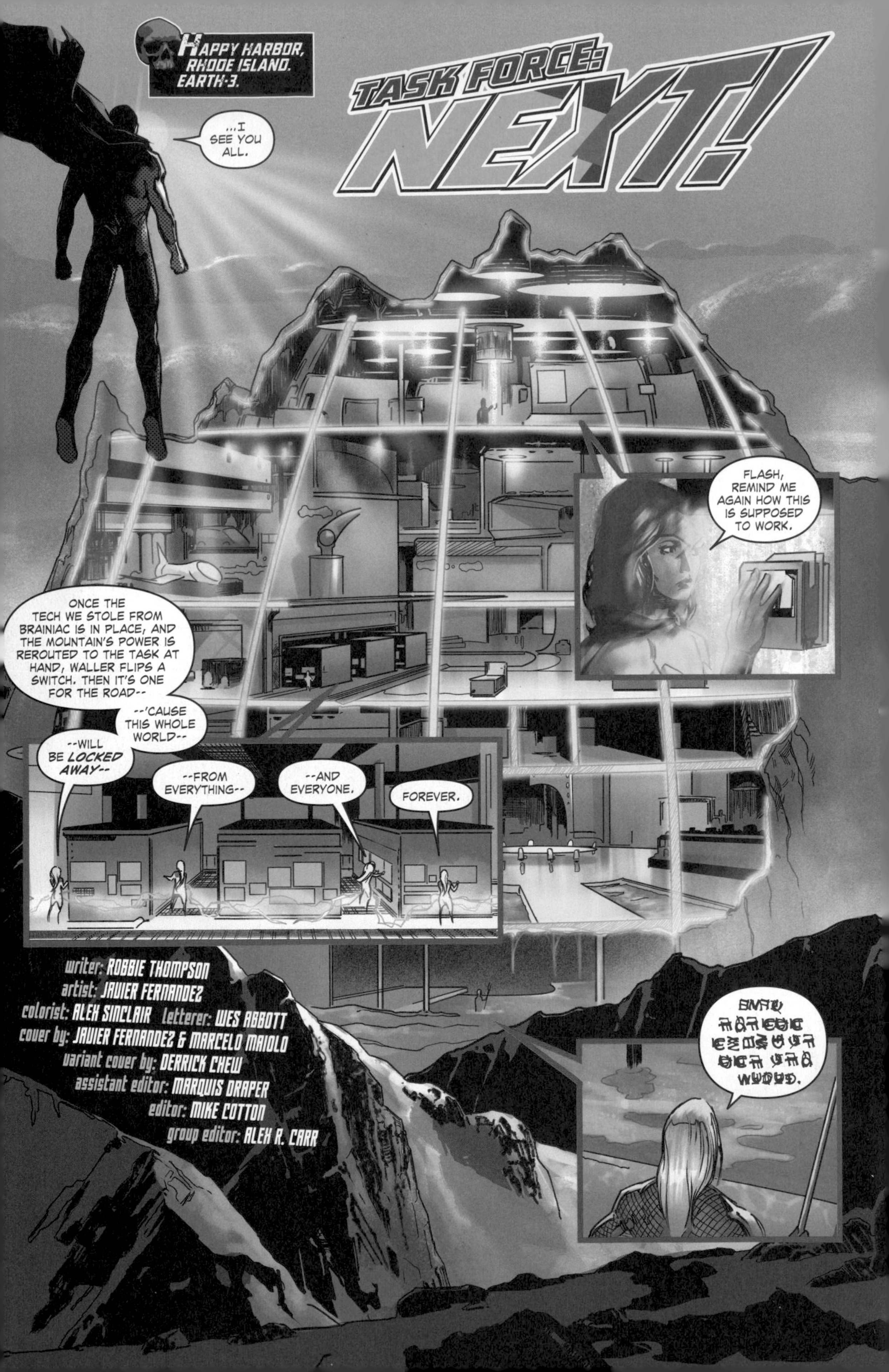
HAPPY HARBOR, RHODE ISLAND. EARTH-3.
...I SEE YOU ALL.
TASK FORCE: NEXT!
FLASH, REMIND ME AGAIN HOW THIS IS SUPPOSED TO WORK.
ONCE THE TECH WE STOLE FROM BRAINIAC IS IN PLACE, AND THE MOUNTAIN'S POWER IS REROUTED TO THE TASK AT HAND, WALLER FLIPS A SWITCH. THEN IT'S ONE FOR THE ROAD--
--'CAUSE THIS WHOLE WORLD--
--WILL BE LOCKED AWAY--
--FROM EVERYTHING--
--AND EVERYONE.
FOREVER.
writer: ROBBIE THOMPSON
artist: JAVIER FERNANDEZ
colorist: ALEX SINCLAIR letterer: WES ABBOTT
cover by: JAVIER FERNANDEZ & MARCELO MAIOLO
variant cover by: DERRICK CHEW
assistant editor: MARQUIS DRAPER
editor: MIKE COTTON
group editor: ALEX R. CARR

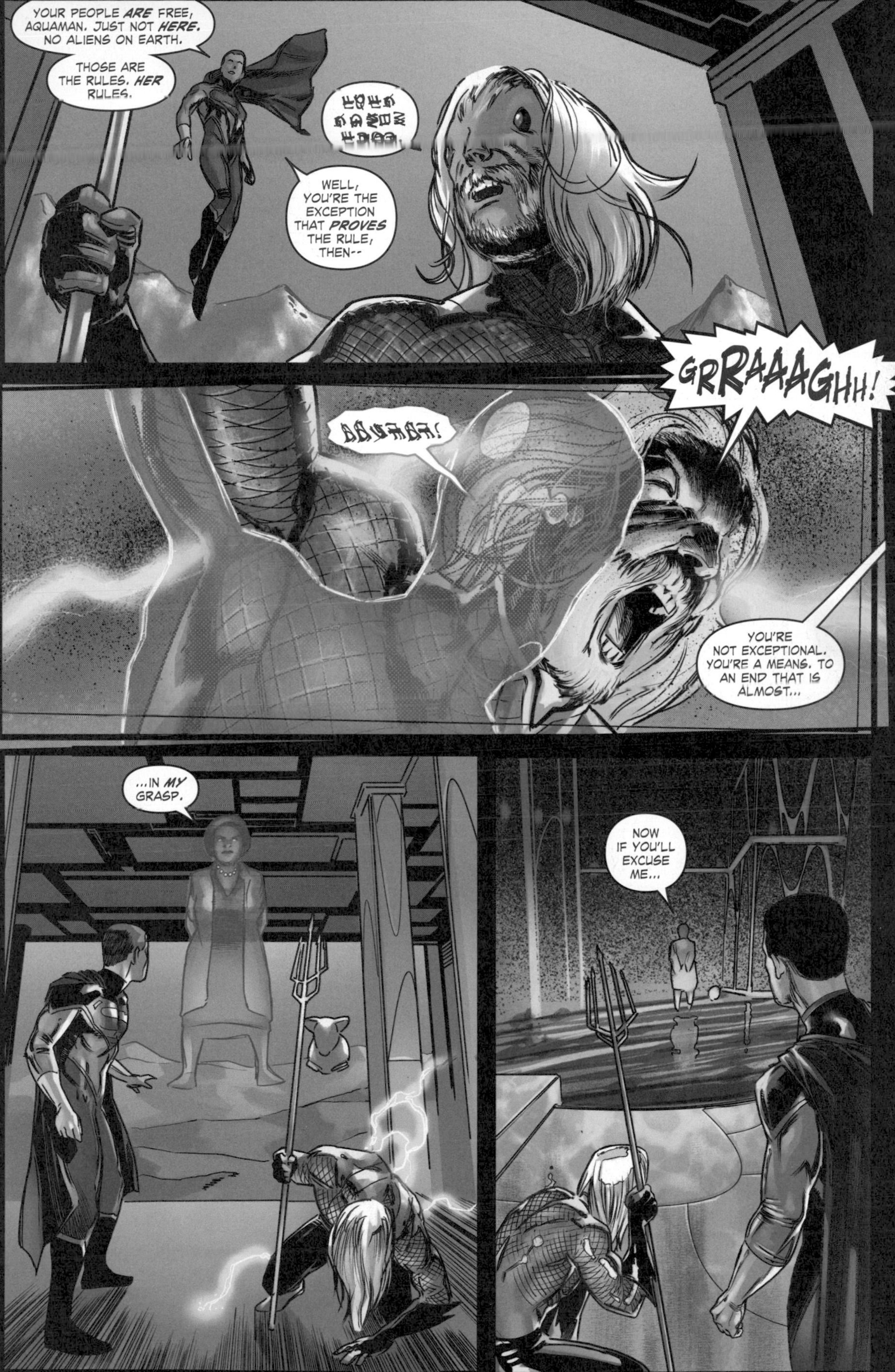
YOUR PEOPLE ARE FREE, AQUAMAN. JUST NOT HERE. NO ALIENS ON EARTH.
THOSE ARE THE RULES. HER RULES.
WELL, YOU'RE THE EXCEPTION THAT PROVES THE RULE, THEN--
GRRAAAGHH!
YOU'RE NOT EXCEPTIONAL. YOU'RE A MEANS. TO AN END THAT IS ALMOST...
...IN MY GRASP.
NOW IF YOU'LL EXCUSE ME...

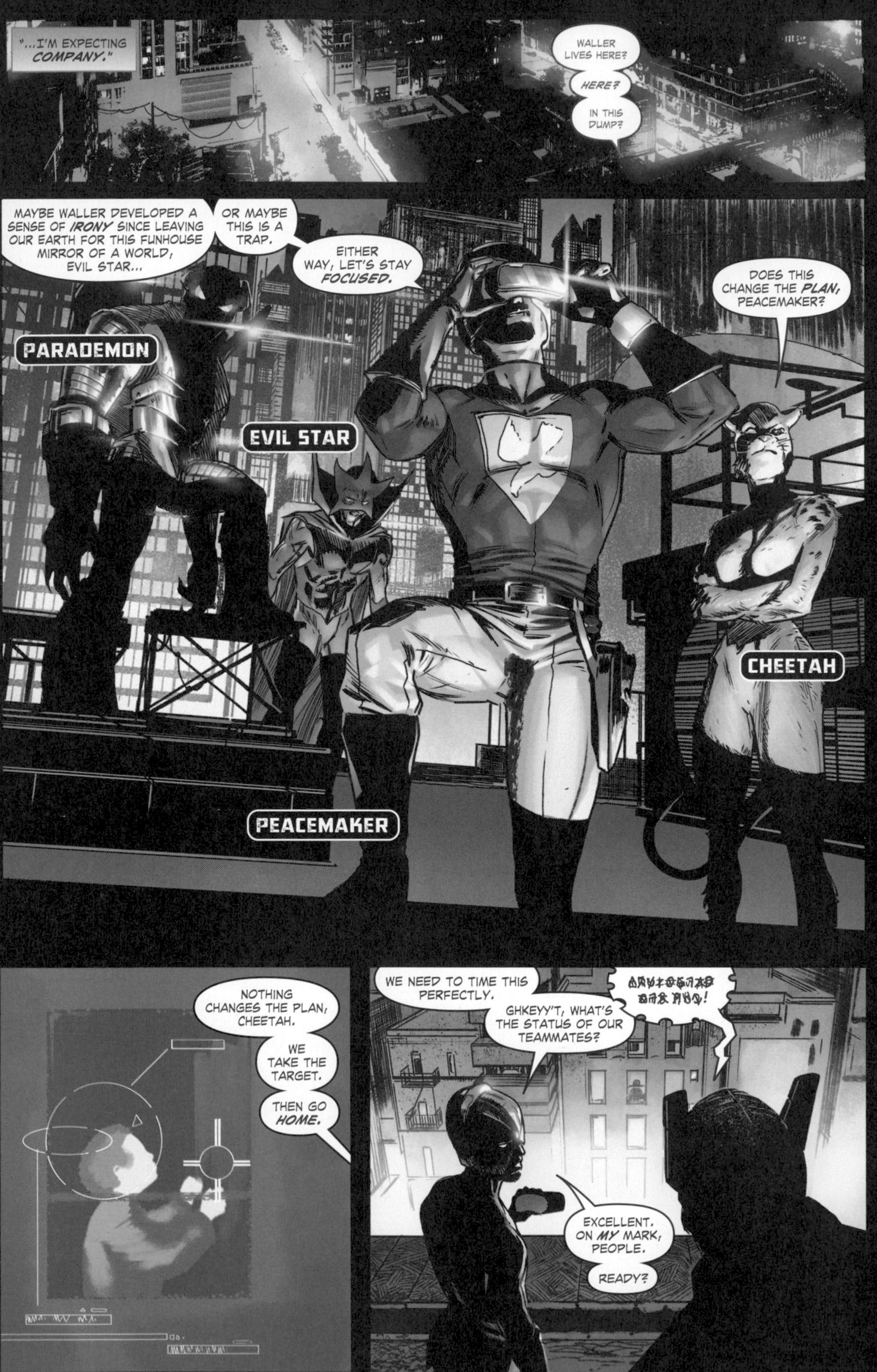
"...I'M EXPECTING COMPANY."
WALLER LIVES HERE?
HERE?
IN THIS DUMP?
MAYBE WALLER DEVELOPED A SENSE OF IRONY SINCE LEAVING OUR EARTH FOR THIS FUNHOUSE MIRROR OF A WORLD, EVIL STAR...
OR MAYBE THIS IS A TRAP.
EITHER WAY, LET'S STAY FOCUSED.
DOES THIS CHANGE THE PLAN, PEACEMAKER?
PARADEMON
EVIL STAR
PEACEMAKER
CHEETAH
NOTHING CHANGES THE PLAN, CHEETAH.
WE TAKE THE TARGET.
THEN GO HOME.
WE NEED TO TIME THIS PERFECTLY.
GHKEYY'T, WHAT'S THE STATUS OF OUR TEAMMATES?
EXCELLENT. ON MY MARK, PEOPLE.
READY?

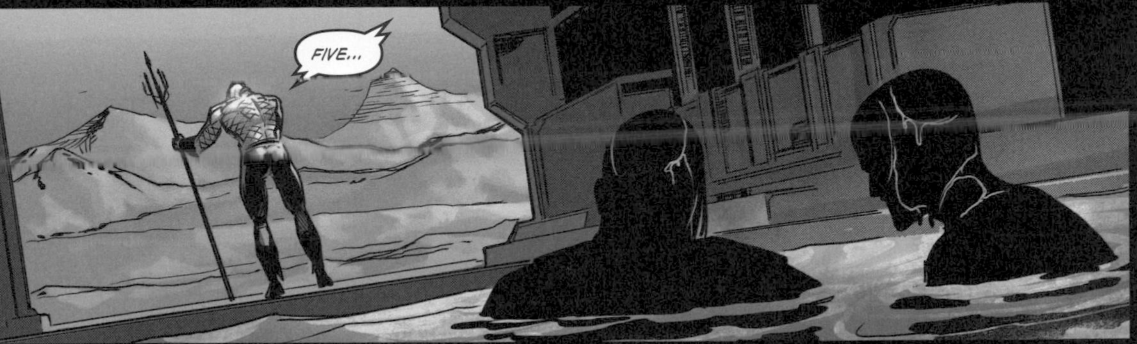
FIVE...

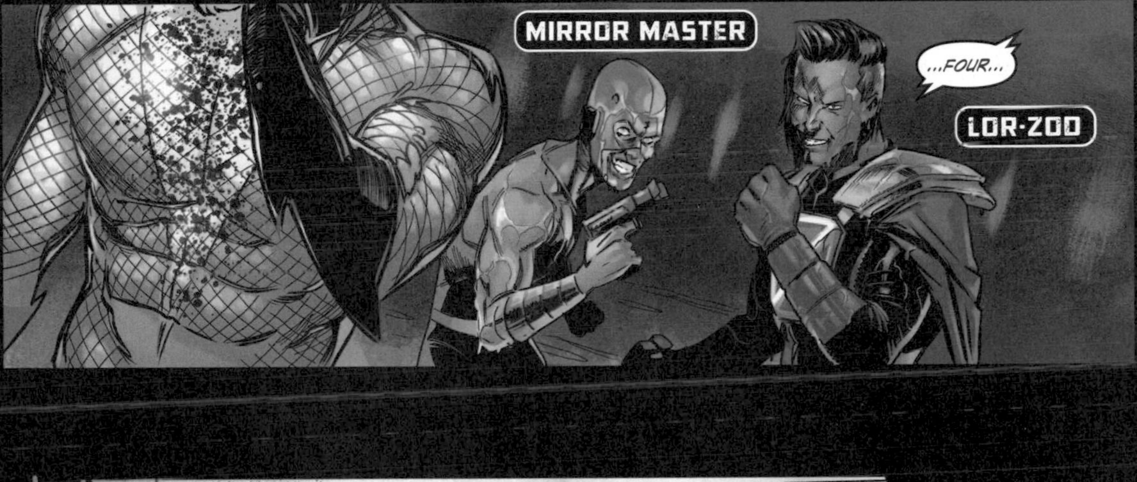
MIRROR MASTER
...FOUR...
LOR-ZOD

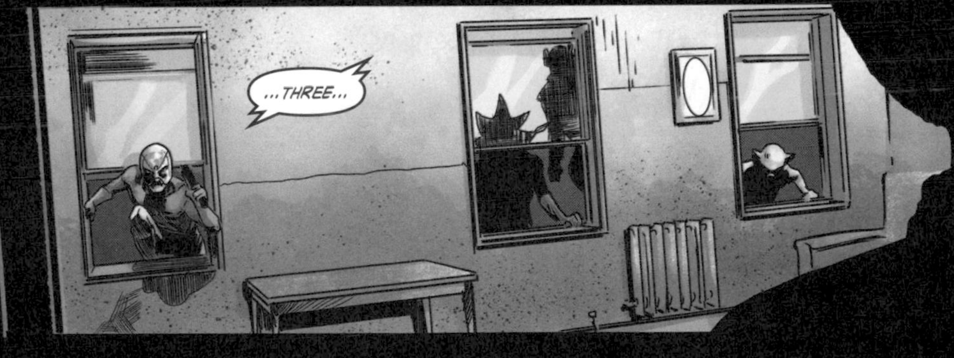
...THREE...

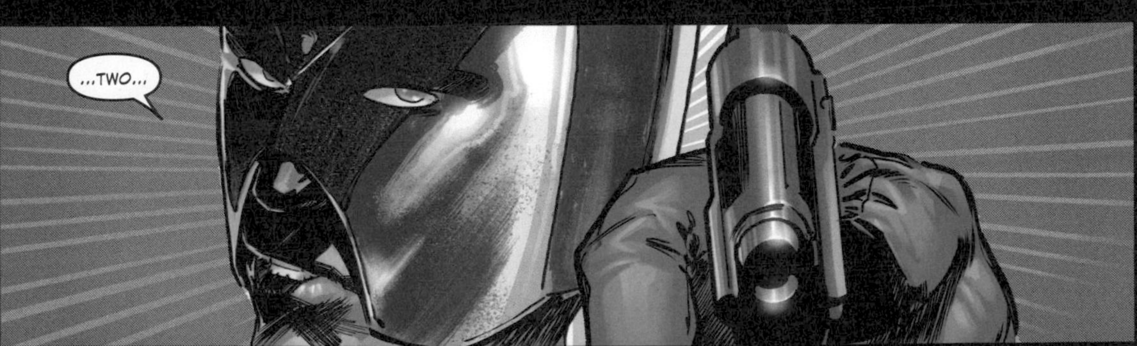
...TWO...

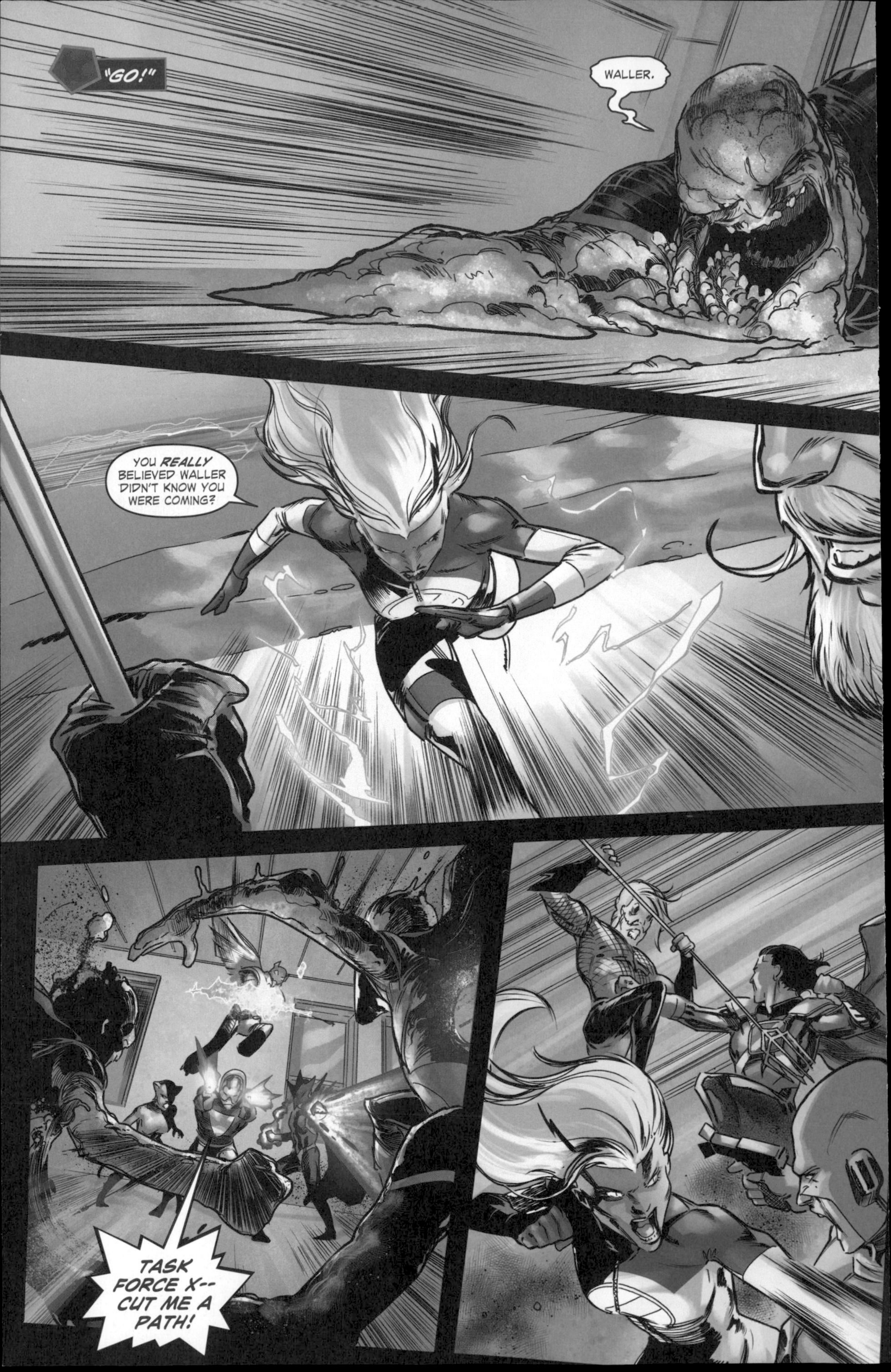

"GO!"
WALLER.
YOU REALLY BELIEVED WALLER DIDN'T KNOW YOU WERE COMING?
TASK FORCE X-- CUT ME A PATH!

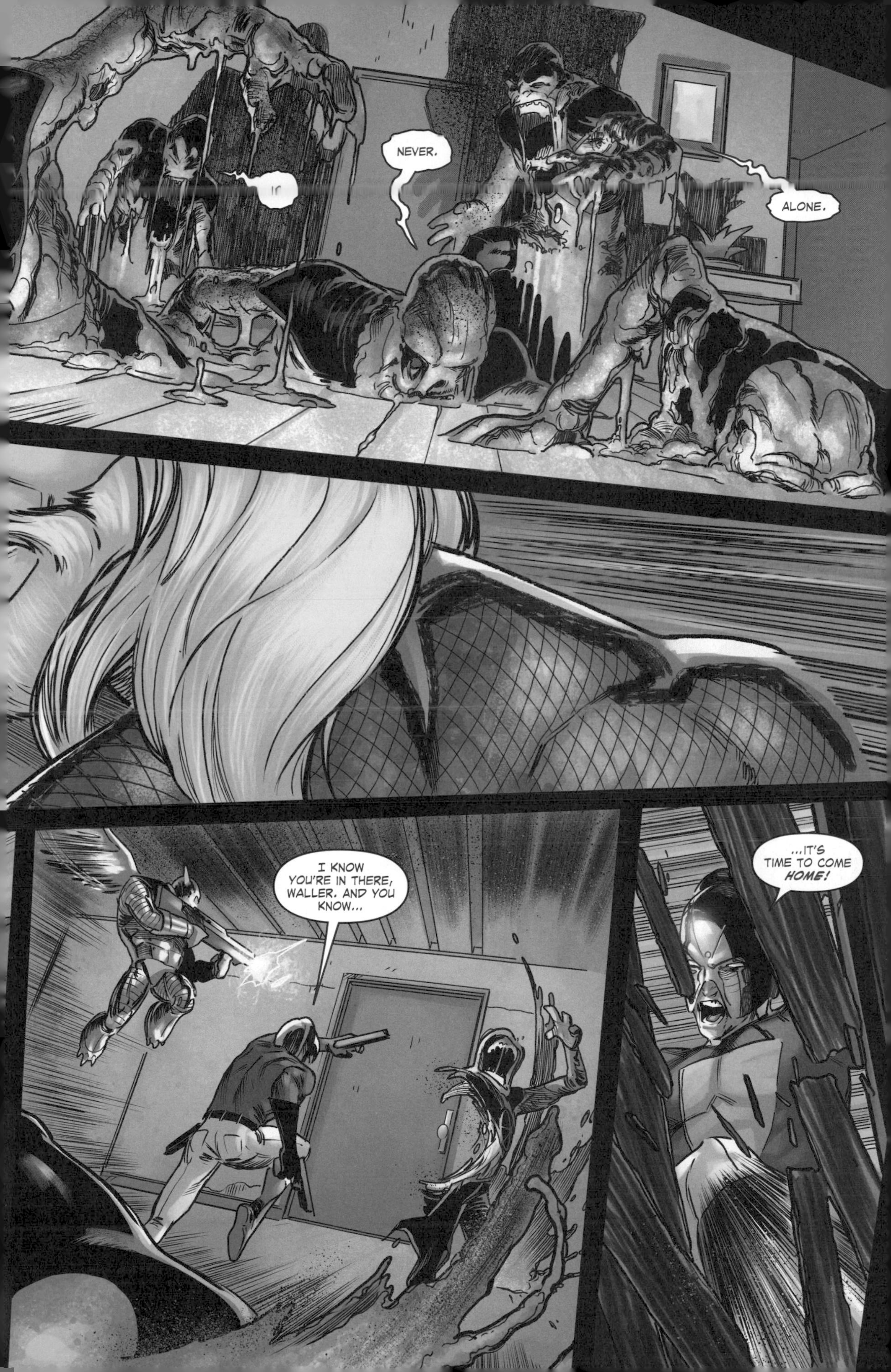
NEVER.
ALONE.
I KNOW YOU'RE IN THERE, WALLER. AND YOU KNOW...
...IT'S TIME TO COME ***HOME!***

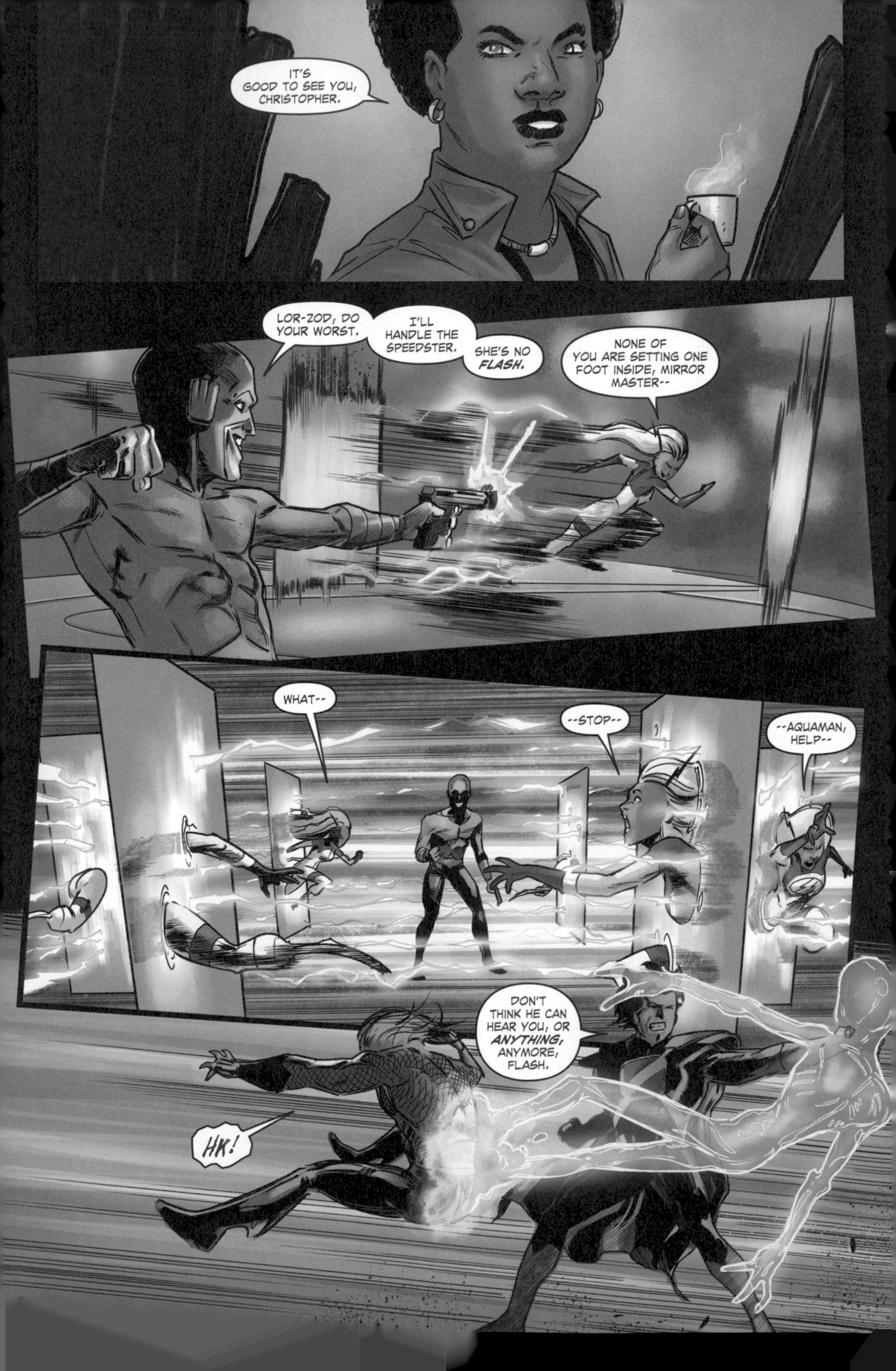
IT'S GOOD TO SEE YOU, CHRISTOPHER.
LOR-ZOD, DO YOUR WORST.
I'LL HANDLE THE SPEEDSTER.
SHE'S NO FLASH.
NONE OF YOU ARE SETTING ONE FOOT INSIDE, MIRROR MASTER--
WHAT--
--STOP--
--AQUAMAN, HELP--
DON'T THINK HE CAN HEAR YOU, OR ANYTHING, ANYMORE, FLASH.
HK!

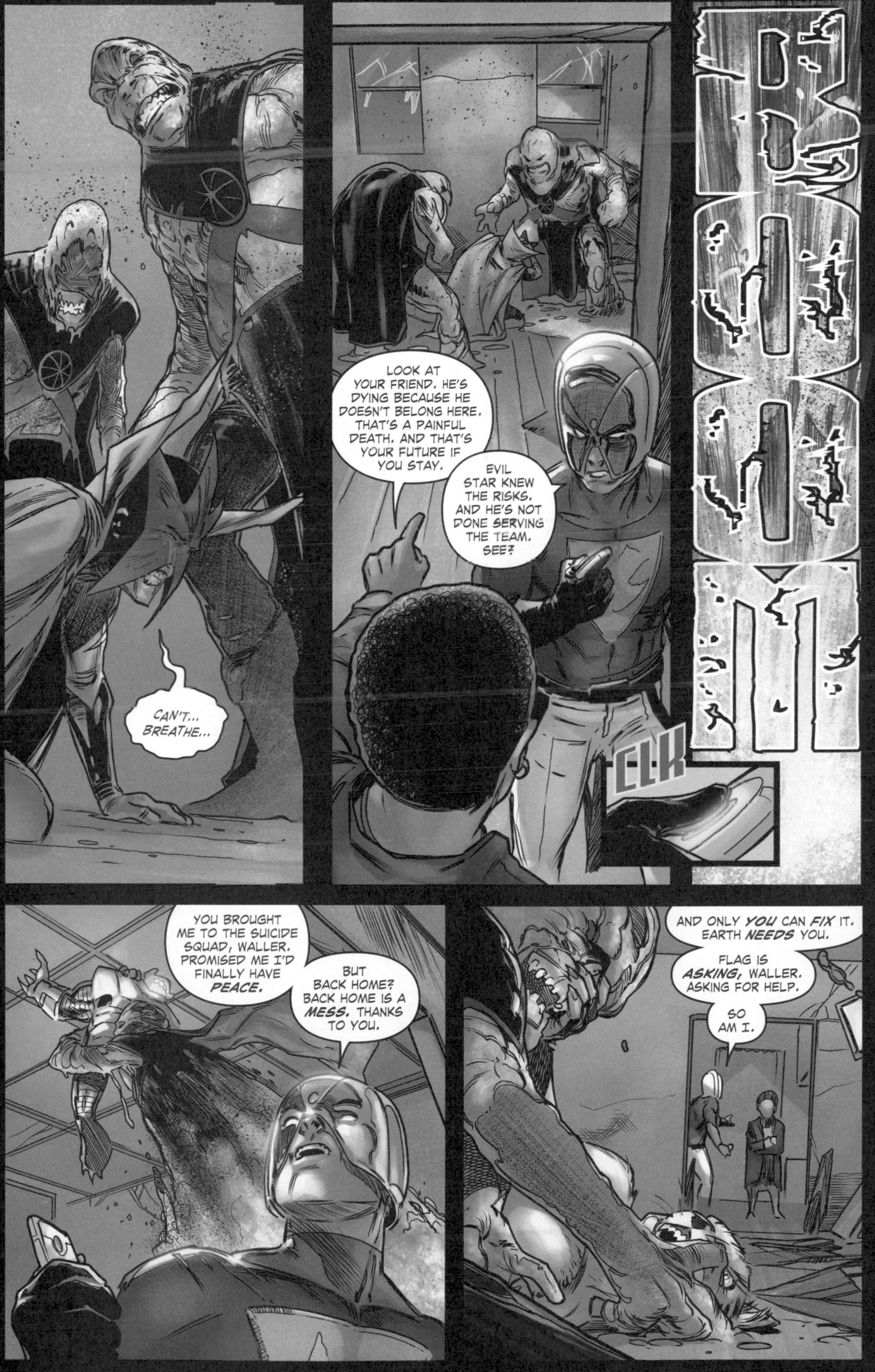

CAN'T... BREATHE...
LOOK AT YOUR FRIEND. HE'S DYING BECAUSE HE DOESN'T BELONG HERE. THAT'S A PAINFUL DEATH. AND THAT'S YOUR FUTURE IF YOU STAY.
EVIL STAR KNEW THE RISKS. AND HE'S NOT DONE SERVING THE TEAM. SEE?
CLK
YOU BROUGHT ME TO THE SUICIDE SQUAD, WALLER. PROMISED ME I'D FINALLY HAVE PEACE.
BUT BACK HOME? BACK HOME IS A MESS. THANKS TO YOU.
AND ONLY YOU CAN FIX IT. EARTH NEEDS YOU.
FLAG IS ASKING, WALLER. ASKING FOR HELP.
SO AM I.

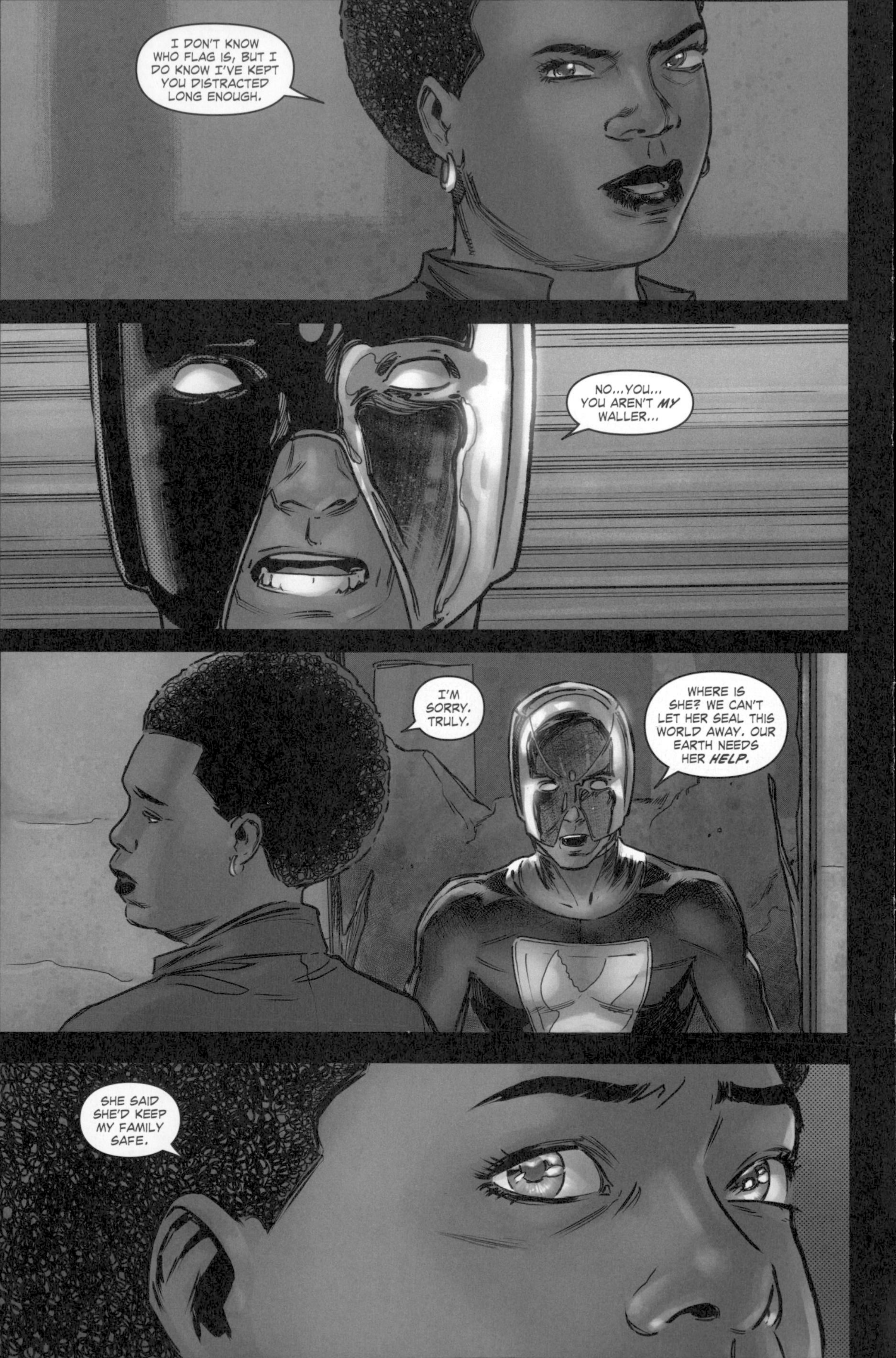
I DON'T KNOW WHO FLAG IS, BUT I DO KNOW I'VE KEPT YOU DISTRACTED LONG ENOUGH.
NO...YOU... YOU AREN'T *MY* WALLER...
I'M SORRY. TRULY.
WHERE IS SHE? WE CAN'T LET HER SEAL THIS WORLD AWAY. OUR EARTH NEEDS HER *HELP.*
SHE SAID SHE'D KEEP MY FAMILY SAFE.

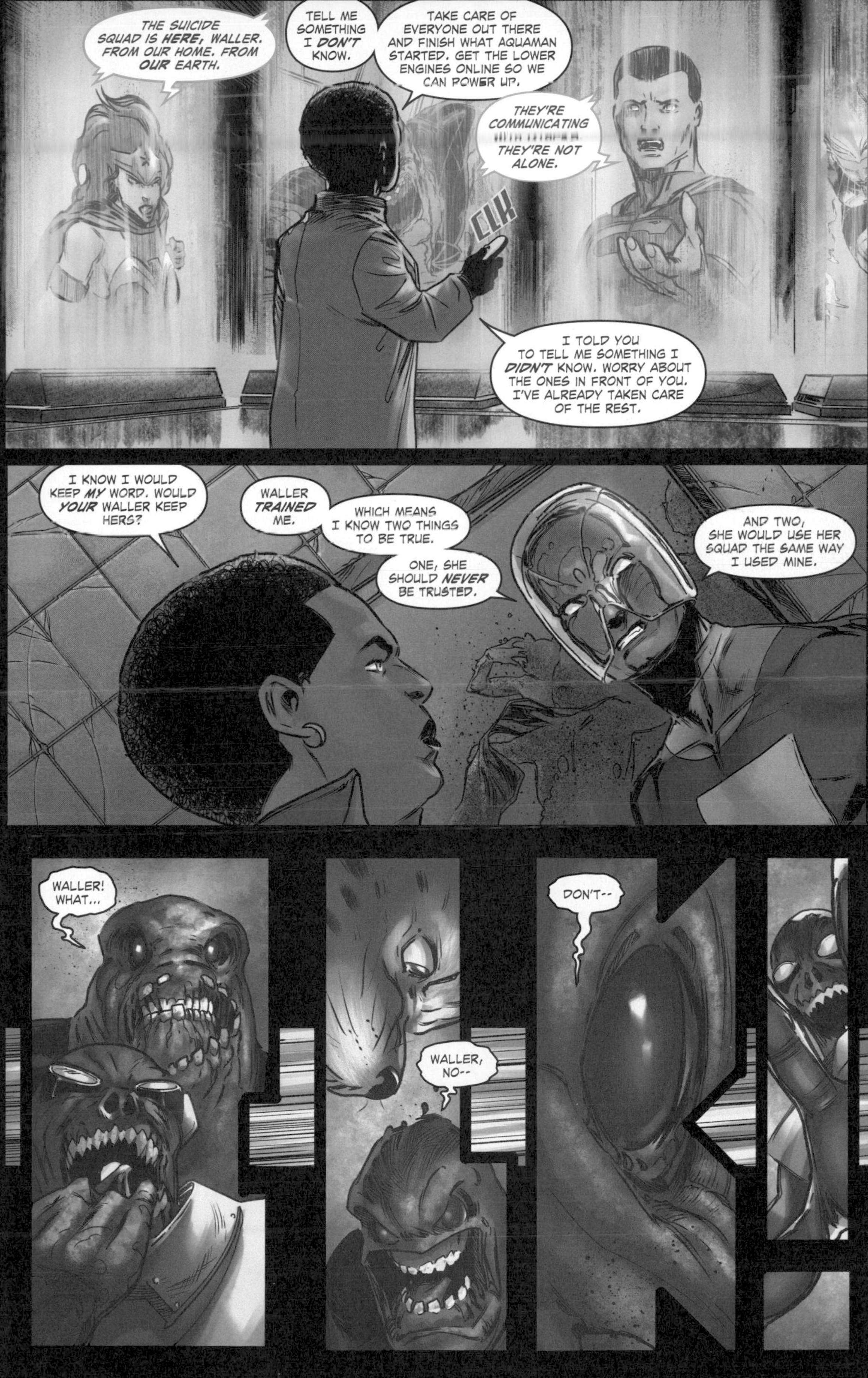

THE SUICIDE SQUAD IS HERE, WALLER. FROM OUR HOME. FROM OUR EARTH.
TELL ME SOMETHING I DON'T KNOW.
TAKE CARE OF EVERYONE OUT THERE AND FINISH WHAT AQUAMAN STARTED. GET THE LOWER ENGINES ONLINE SO WE CAN POWER UP.
THEY'RE COMMUNICATING THEY'RE NOT ALONE.
CLK
I TOLD YOU TO TELL ME SOMETHING I DIDN'T KNOW. WORRY ABOUT THE ONES IN FRONT OF YOU. I'VE ALREADY TAKEN CARE OF THE REST.
I KNOW I WOULD KEEP MY WORD. WOULD YOUR WALLER KEEP HERS?
WALLER TRAINED ME.
WHICH MEANS I KNOW TWO THINGS TO BE TRUE.
ONE, SHE SHOULD NEVER BE TRUSTED.
AND TWO, SHE WOULD USE HER SQUAD THE SAME WAY I USED MINE.
WALLER! WHAT...
WALLER, NO--
DON'T--

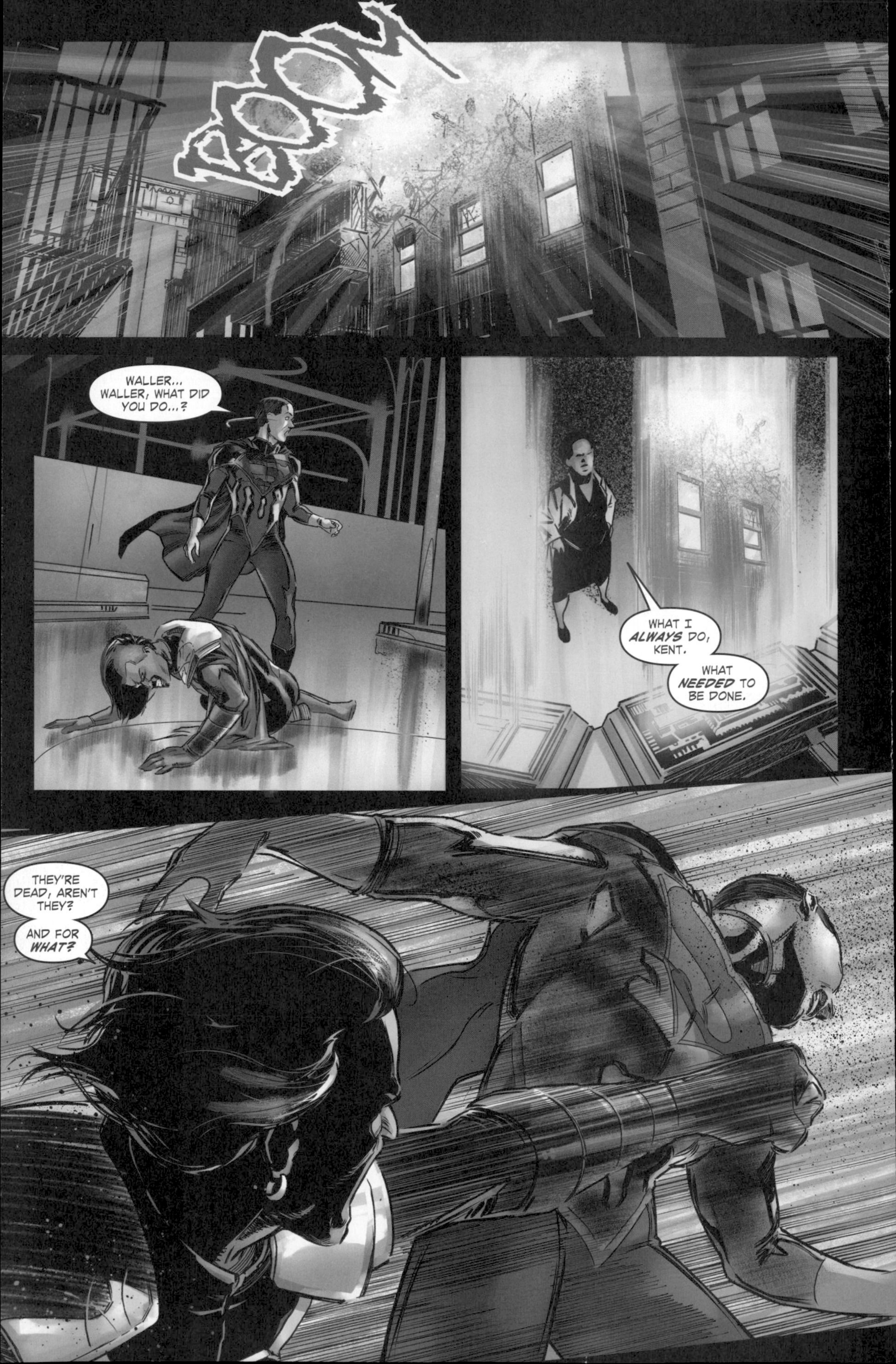
BOOOM
WALLER... WALLER, WHAT DID YOU DO...?
WHAT I ALWAYS DO, KENT.
WHAT NEEDED TO BE DONE.
THEY'RE DEAD, AREN'T THEY?
AND FOR WHAT?

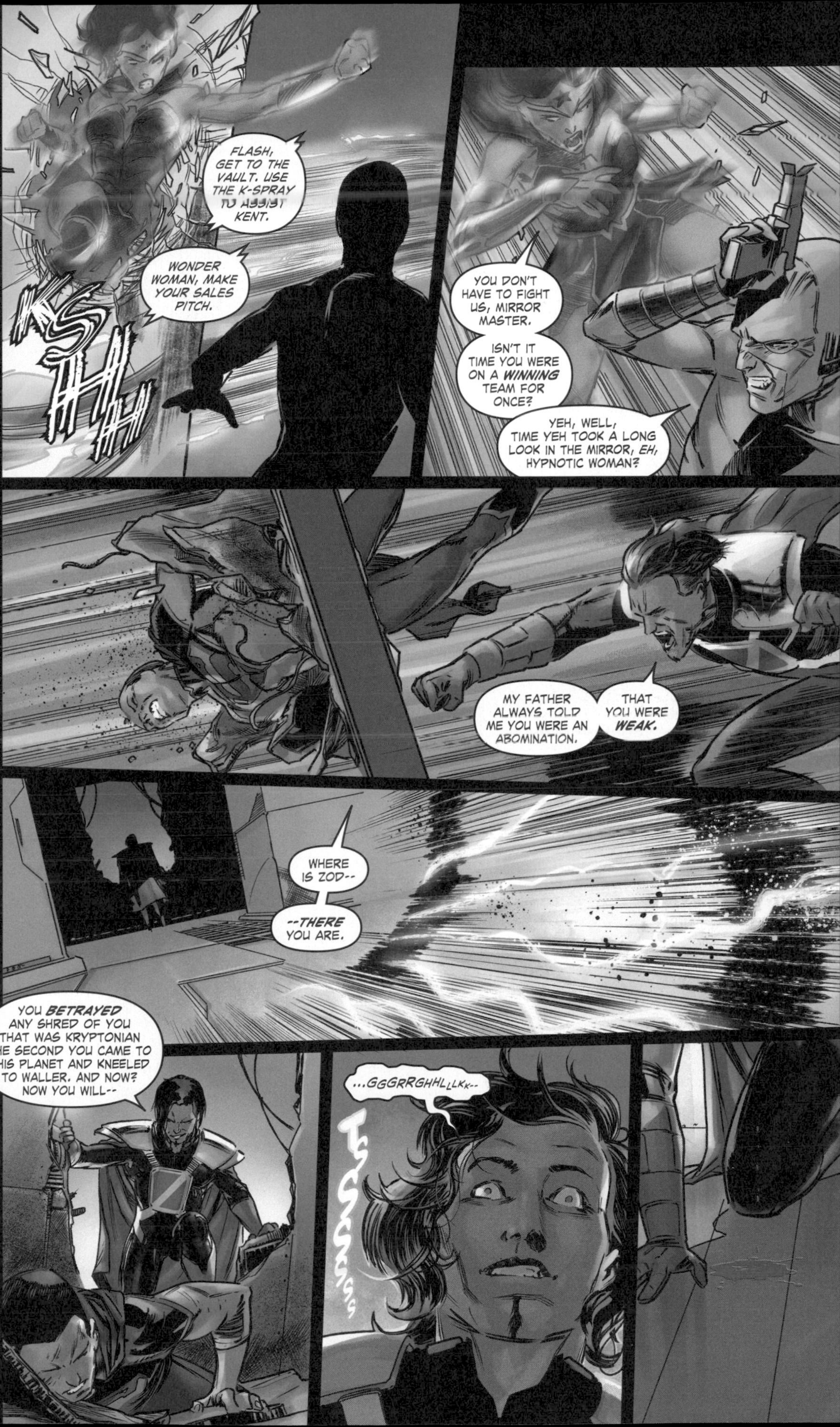
FLASH, GET TO THE VAULT. USE THE K-SPRAY TO ASSIST KENT.
WONDER WOMAN, MAKE YOUR SALES PITCH.
KSSHHH
YOU DON'T HAVE TO FIGHT US, MIRROR MASTER.
ISN'T IT TIME YOU WERE ON A WINNING TEAM FOR ONCE?
YEH, WELL, TIME YEH TOOK A LONG LOOK IN THE MIRROR, EH, HYPNOTIC WOMAN?
MY FATHER ALWAYS TOLD ME YOU WERE AN ABOMINATION.
THAT YOU WERE WEAK.
WHERE IS ZOD--
--THERE YOU ARE.
YOU BETRAYED ANY SHRED OF YOU THAT WAS KRYPTONIAN THE SECOND YOU CAME TO THIS PLANET AND KNEELED TO WALLER. AND NOW? NOW YOU WILL--
...GGGRRGHHLLLKK--

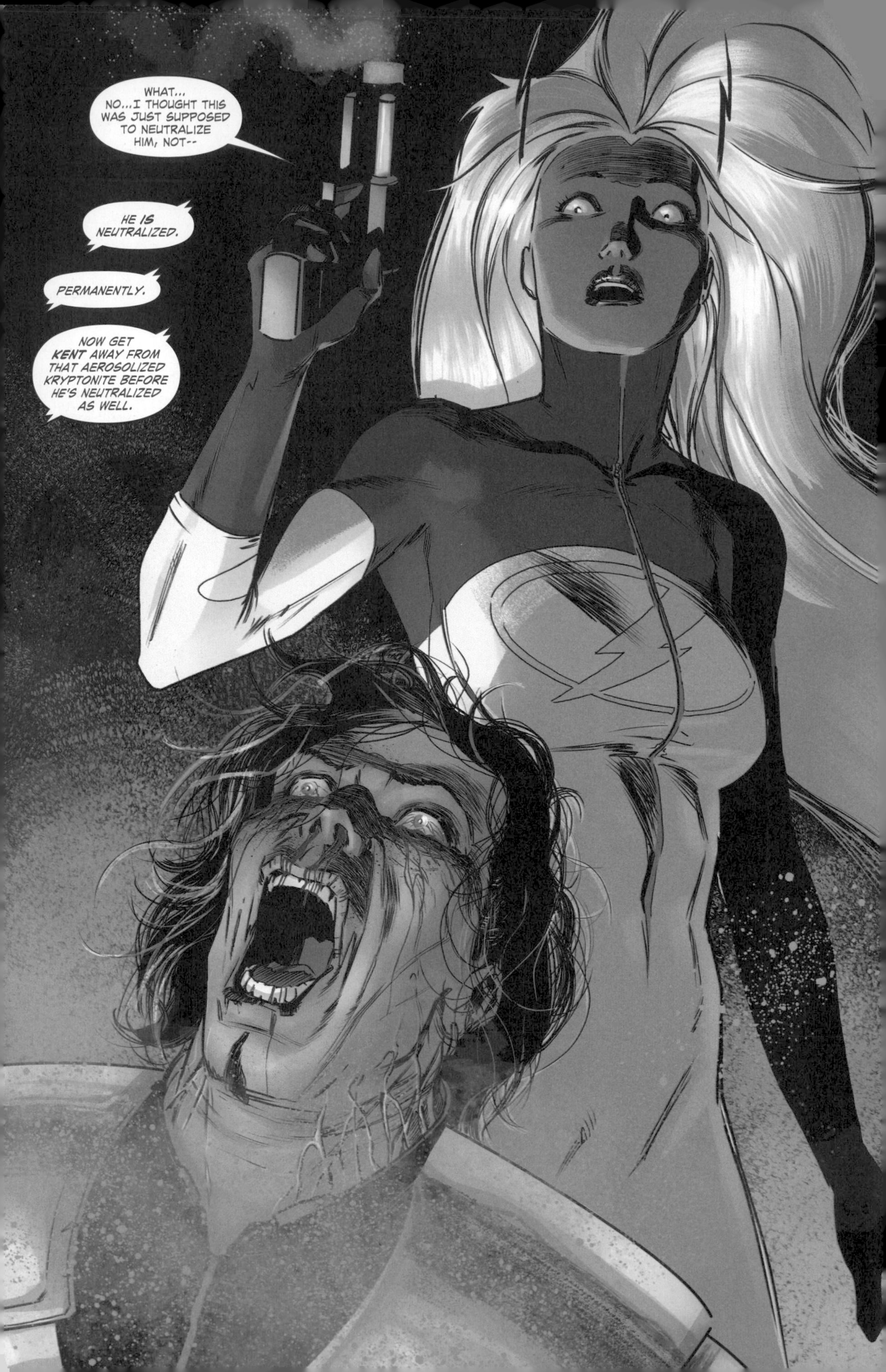
WHAT... NO...I THOUGHT THIS WAS JUST SUPPOSED TO NEUTRALIZE HIM, NOT--
HE *IS* NEUTRALIZED.
PERMANENTLY.
NOW GET **KENT** AWAY FROM THAT AEROSOLIZED KRYPTONITE BEFORE HE'S NEUTRALIZED AS WELL.

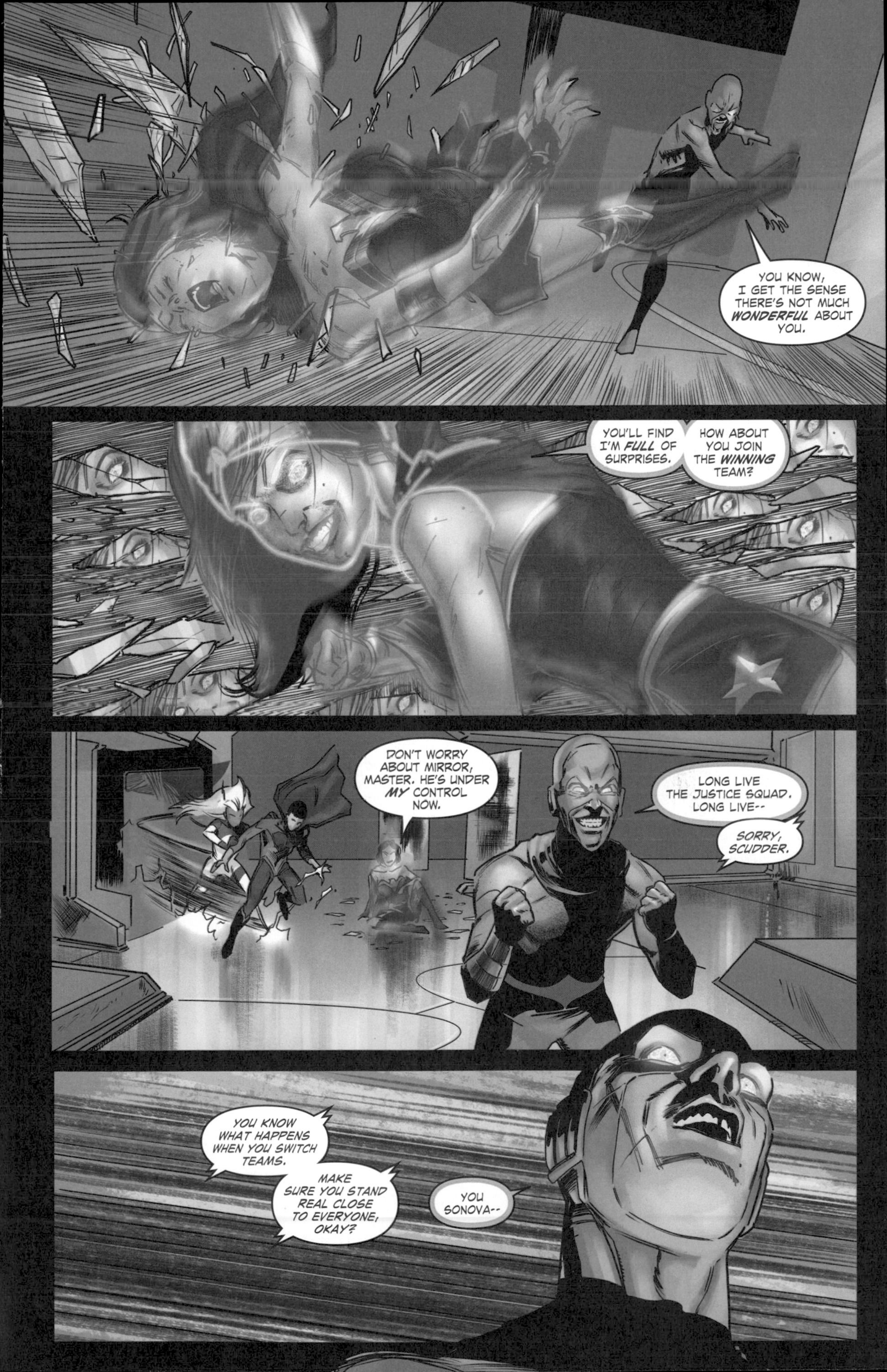
YOU KNOW, I GET THE SENSE THERE'S NOT MUCH ***WONDERFUL*** ABOUT YOU.
YOU'LL FIND I'M ***FULL*** OF SURPRISES.
HOW ABOUT YOU JOIN THE ***WINNING*** TEAM?
DON'T WORRY ABOUT MIRROR, MASTER. HE'S UNDER ***MY*** CONTROL NOW.
LONG LIVE THE JUSTICE SQUAD. LONG LIVE--
SORRY, SCUDDER.
YOU KNOW WHAT HAPPENS WHEN YOU SWITCH TEAMS.
MAKE SURE YOU STAND REAL CLOSE TO EVERYONE, OKAY?
YOU SONOVA--

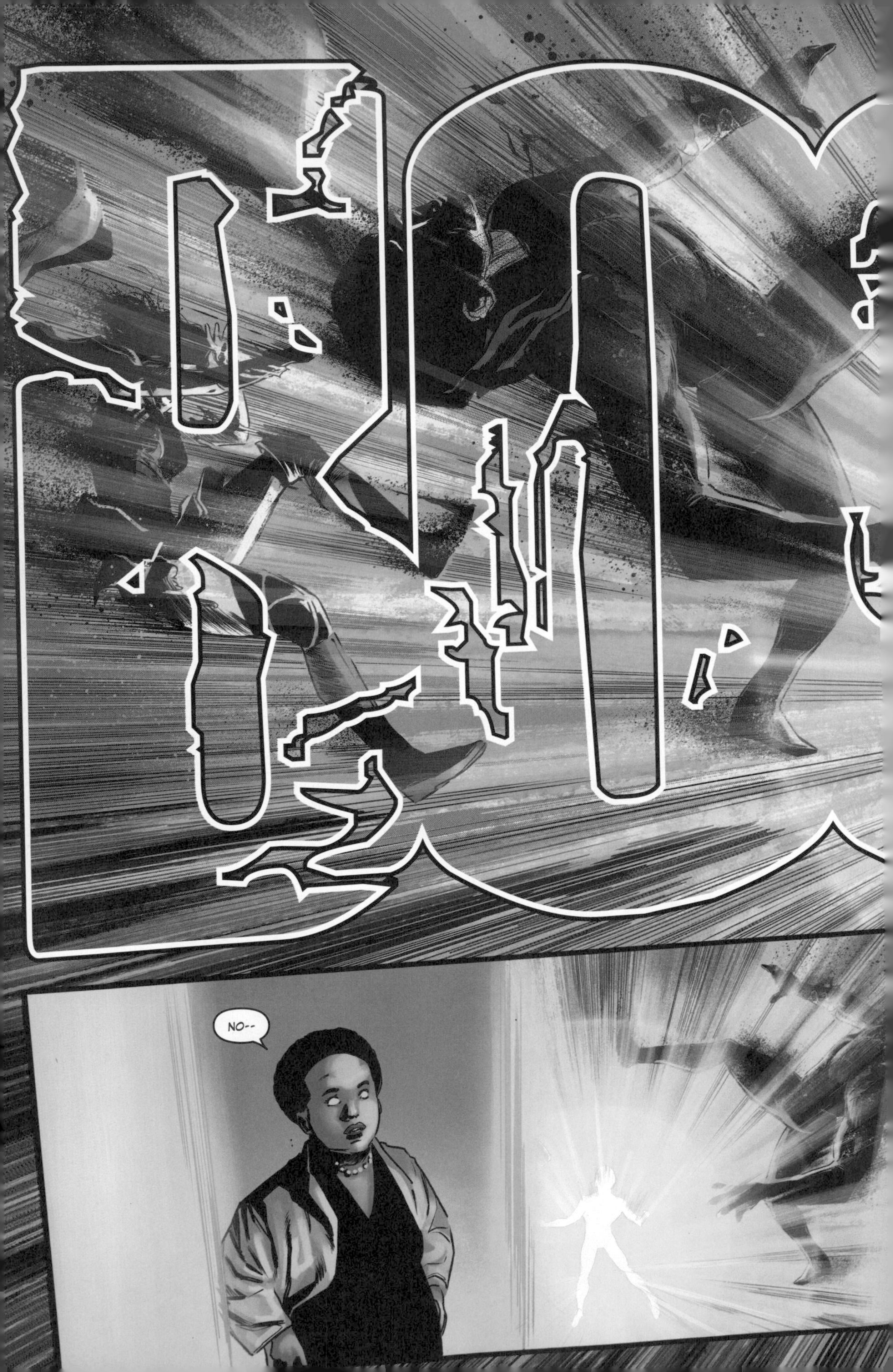
NO--

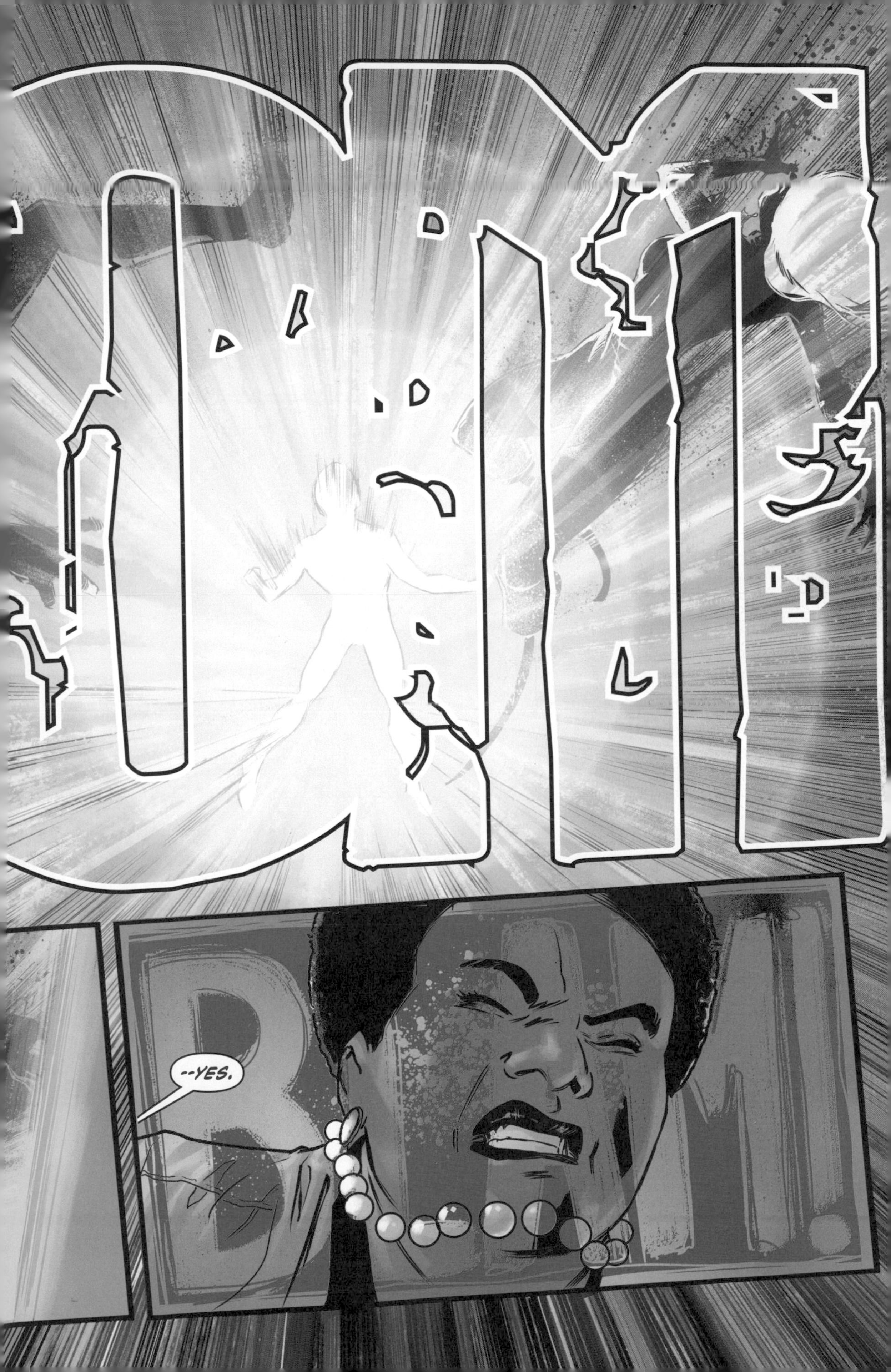
--YES.

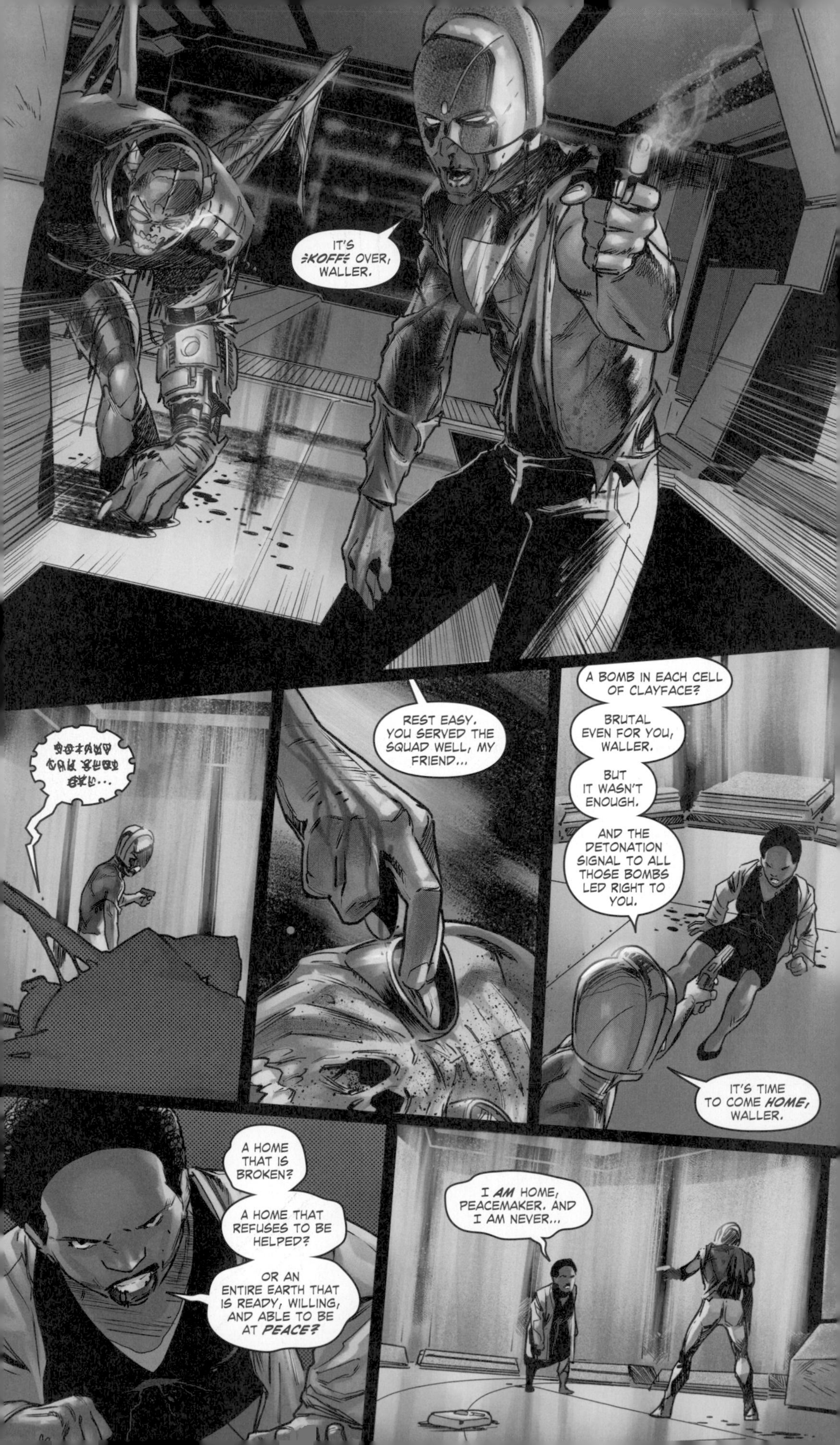
IT'S *KOFF* OVER, WALLER.
REST EASY. YOU SERVED THE SQUAD WELL, MY FRIEND...
A BOMB IN EACH CELL OF CLAYFACE?
BRUTAL EVEN FOR YOU, WALLER.
BUT IT WASN'T ENOUGH.
AND THE DETONATION SIGNAL TO ALL THOSE BOMBS LED RIGHT TO YOU.
IT'S TIME TO COME *HOME*, WALLER.
A HOME THAT IS BROKEN?
A HOME THAT REFUSES TO BE HELPED?
OR AN ENTIRE EARTH THAT IS READY, WILLING, AND ABLE TO BE AT *PEACE?*
I *AM* HOME, PEACEMAKER. AND I AM NEVER...

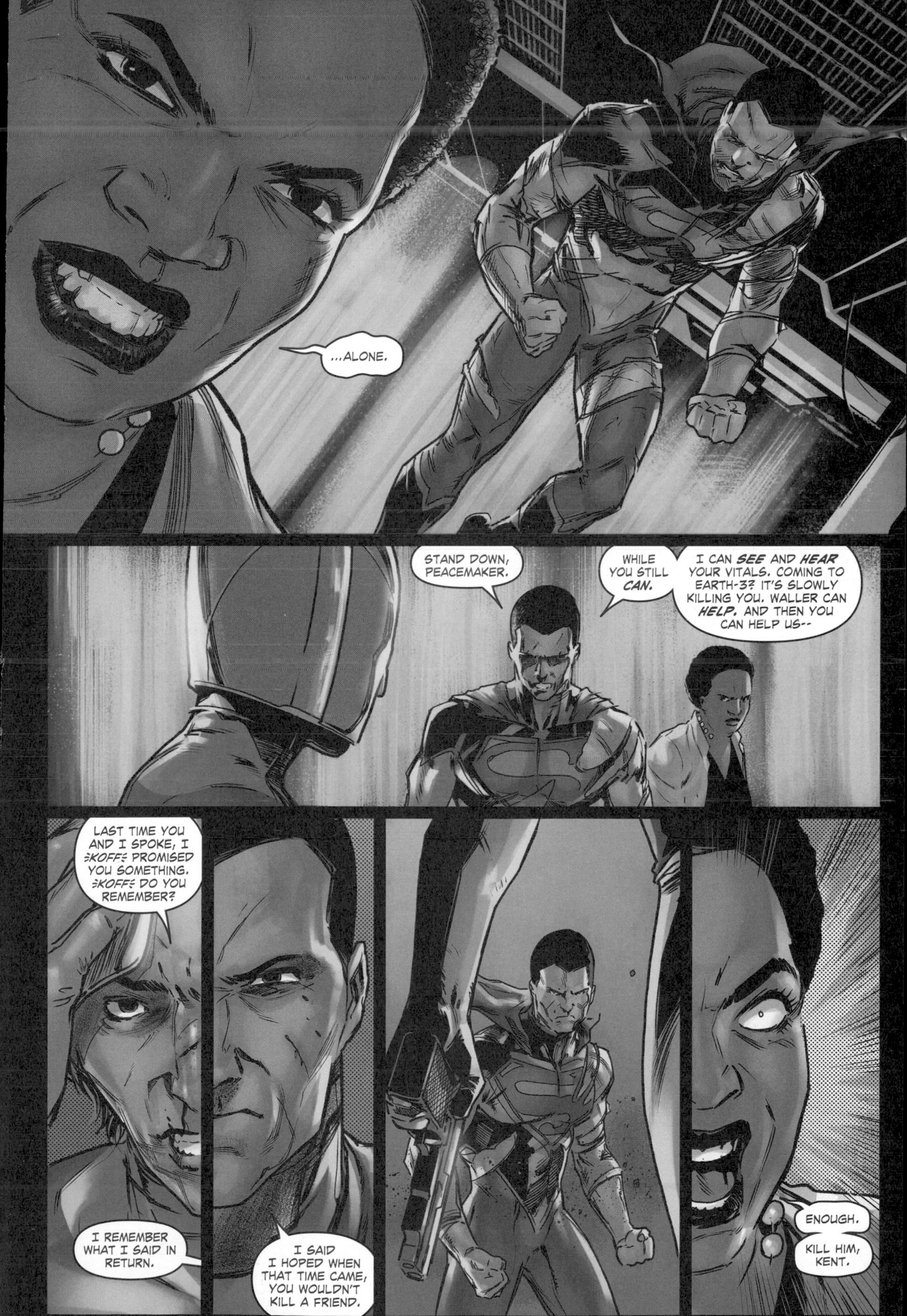
...ALONE.
STAND DOWN, PEACEMAKER.
WHILE YOU STILL CAN.
I CAN SEE AND HEAR YOUR VITALS. COMING TO EARTH-3? IT'S SLOWLY KILLING YOU. WALLER CAN HELP. AND THEN YOU CAN HELP US--
LAST TIME YOU AND I SPOKE, I *KOFF* PROMISED YOU SOMETHING. *KOFF* DO YOU REMEMBER?
I REMEMBER WHAT I SAID IN RETURN.
I SAID I HOPED WHEN THAT TIME CAME, YOU WOULDN'T KILL A FRIEND.
ENOUGH.
KILL HIM, KENT.

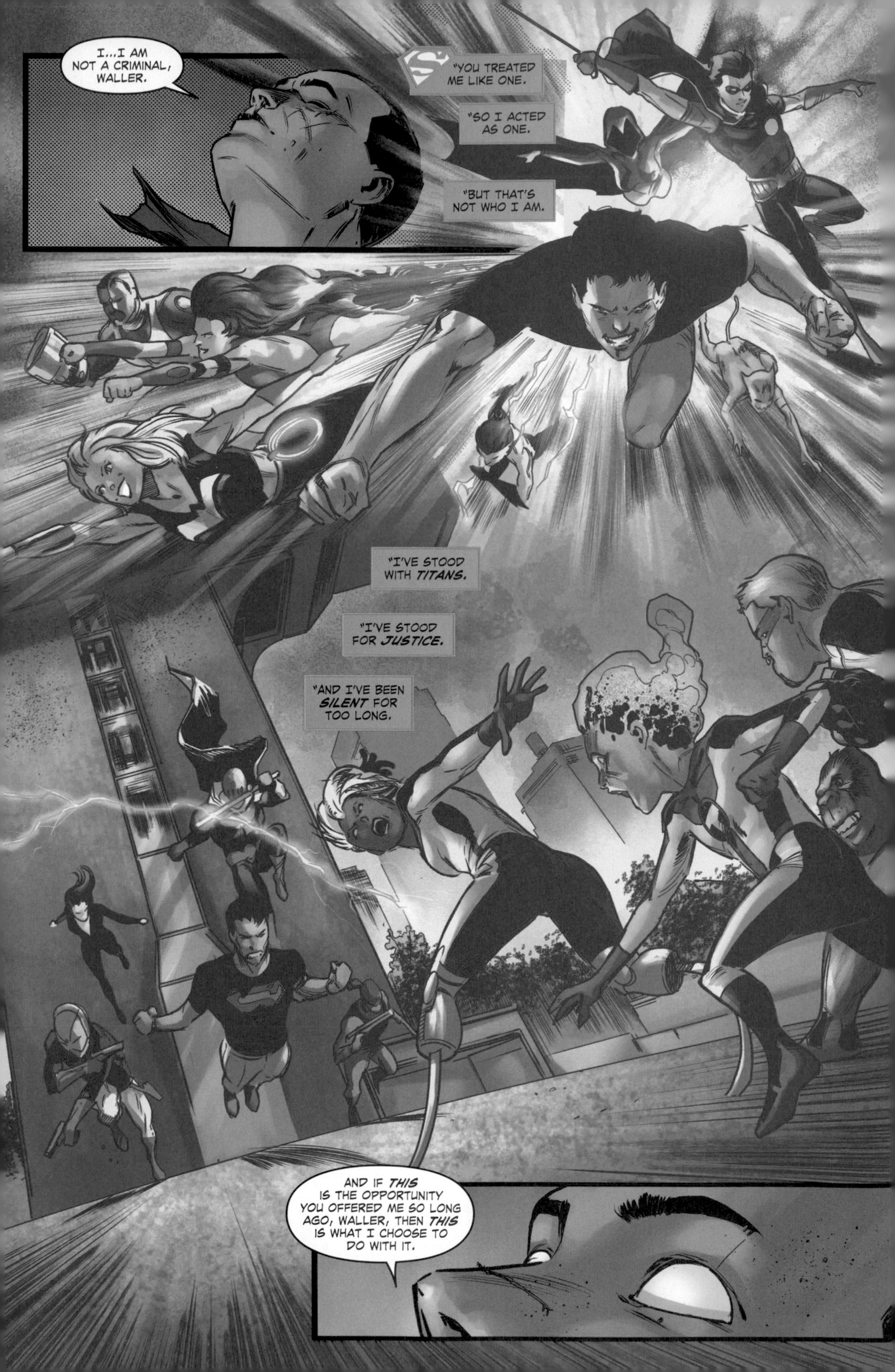
I...I AM NOT A CRIMINAL, WALLER.
"YOU TREATED ME LIKE ONE.
"SO I ACTED AS ONE.
"BUT THAT'S NOT WHO I AM.
"I'VE STOOD WITH TITANS.
"I'VE STOOD FOR JUSTICE.
"AND I'VE BEEN SILENT FOR TOO LONG.
AND IF THIS IS THE OPPORTUNITY YOU OFFERED ME SO LONG AGO, WALLER, THEN THIS IS WHAT I CHOOSE TO DO WITH IT.

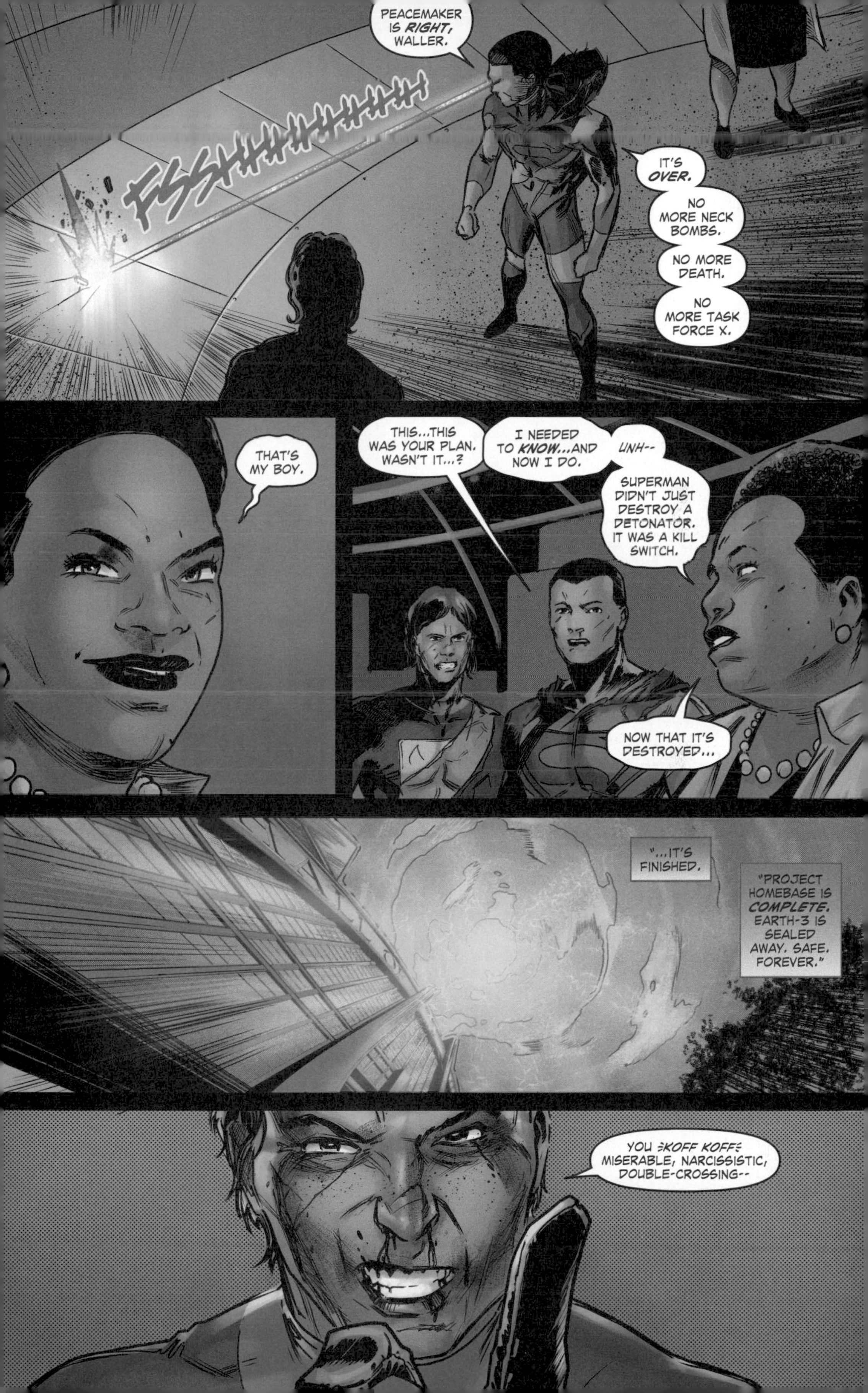
PEACEMAKER IS RIGHT, WALLER.
FSSHHHHHHHH
IT'S OVER.
NO MORE NECK BOMBS.
NO MORE DEATH.
NO MORE TASK FORCE X.
THAT'S MY BOY.
THIS...THIS WAS YOUR PLAN. WASN'T IT...?
I NEEDED TO KNOW...AND NOW I DO.
UNH--
SUPERMAN DIDN'T JUST DESTROY A DETONATOR. IT WAS A KILL SWITCH.
NOW THAT IT'S DESTROYED...
"...IT'S FINISHED.
"PROJECT HOMEBASE IS COMPLETE. EARTH-3 IS SEALED AWAY. SAFE. FOREVER."
YOU =KOFF KOFF= MISERABLE, NARCISSISTIC, DOUBLE-CROSSING--

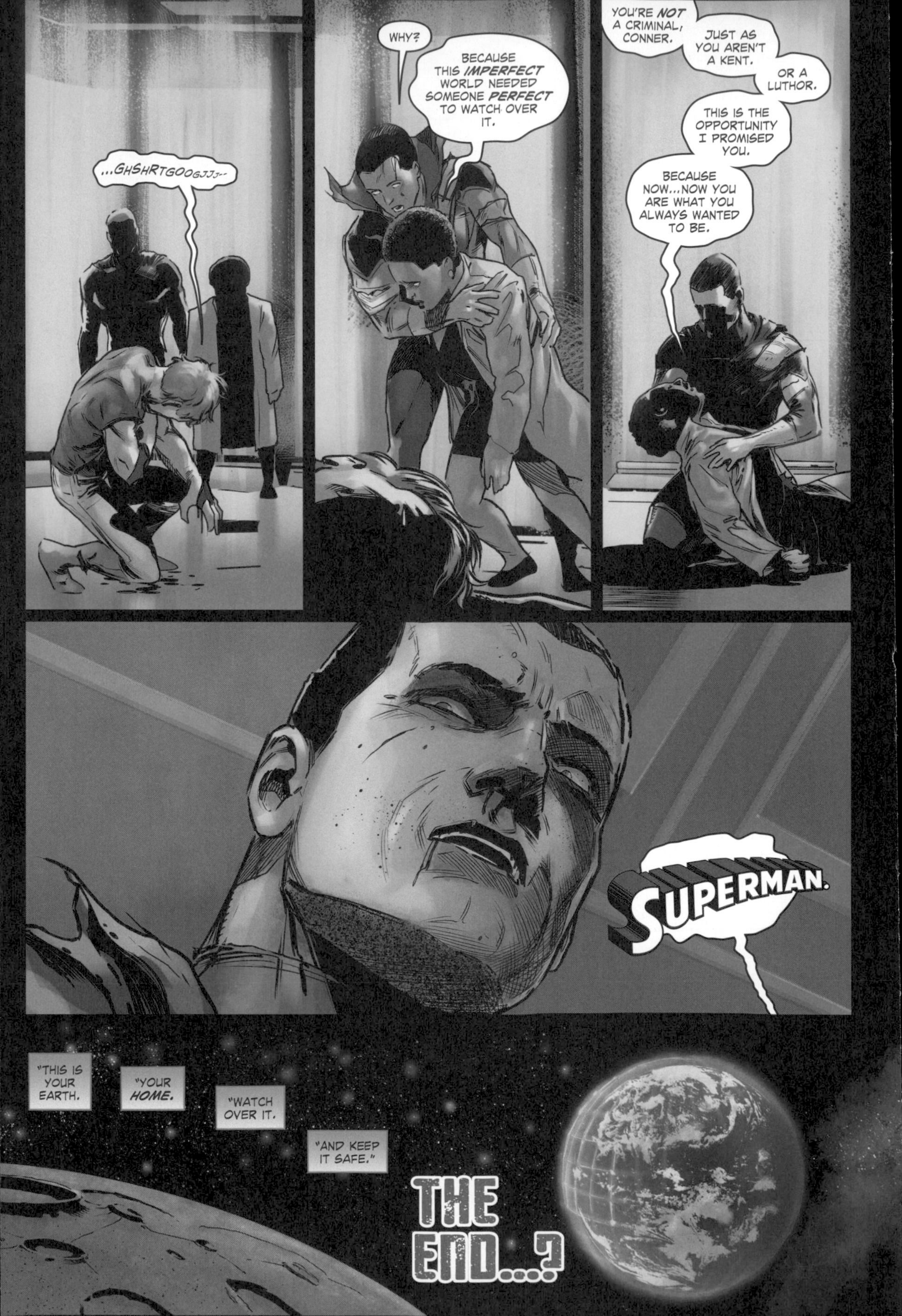
...GHSHRTGOOGJJJ--
WHY?
BECAUSE THIS *IMPERFECT* WORLD NEEDED SOMEONE *PERFECT* TO WATCH OVER IT.
YOU'RE *NOT* A CRIMINAL, CONNER.
JUST AS YOU AREN'T A KENT.
OR A LUTHOR.
THIS IS THE OPPORTUNITY I PROMISED YOU.
BECAUSE NOW...NOW YOU ARE WHAT YOU ALWAYS WANTED TO BE.
SUPERMAN.
"THIS IS YOUR EARTH.
"YOUR *HOME.*
"WATCH OVER IT.
"AND KEEP IT SAFE."
THE END...?

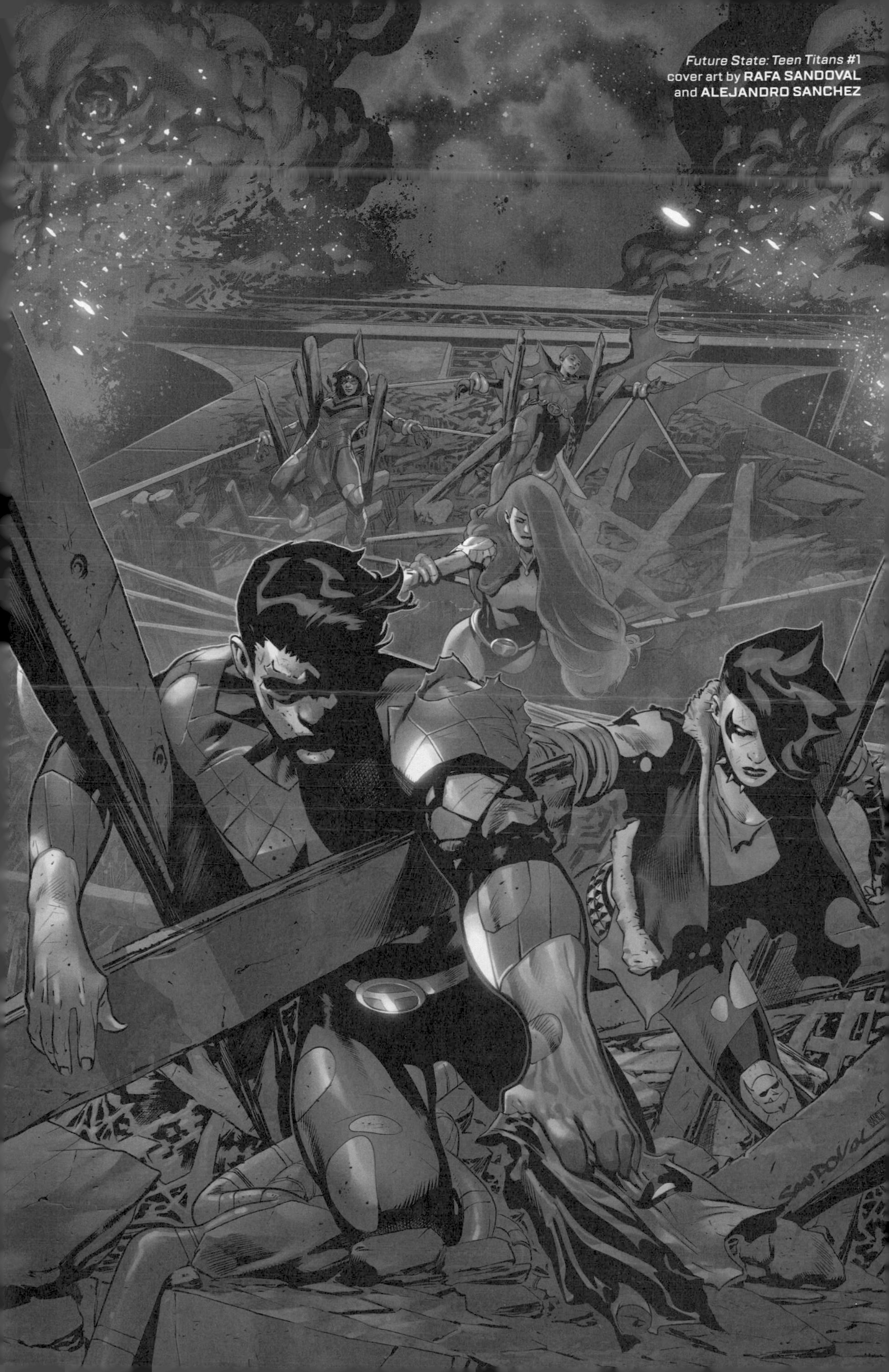

Future State: Teen Titans #1
cover art by **RAFA SANDOVAL**
and **ALEJANDRO SANCHEZ**

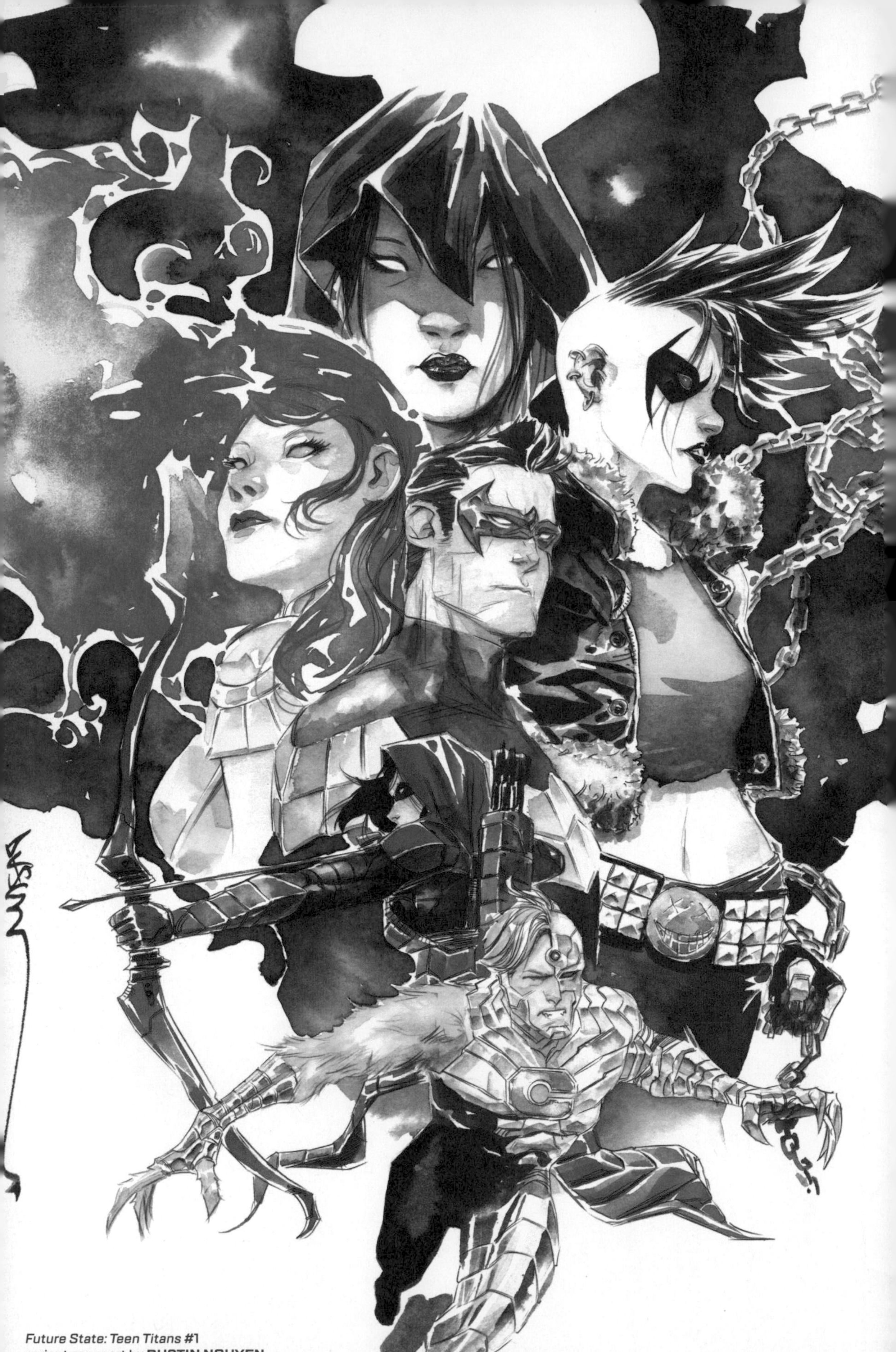

Future State: Teen Titans #1
variant cover art by **DUSTIN NGUYEN**

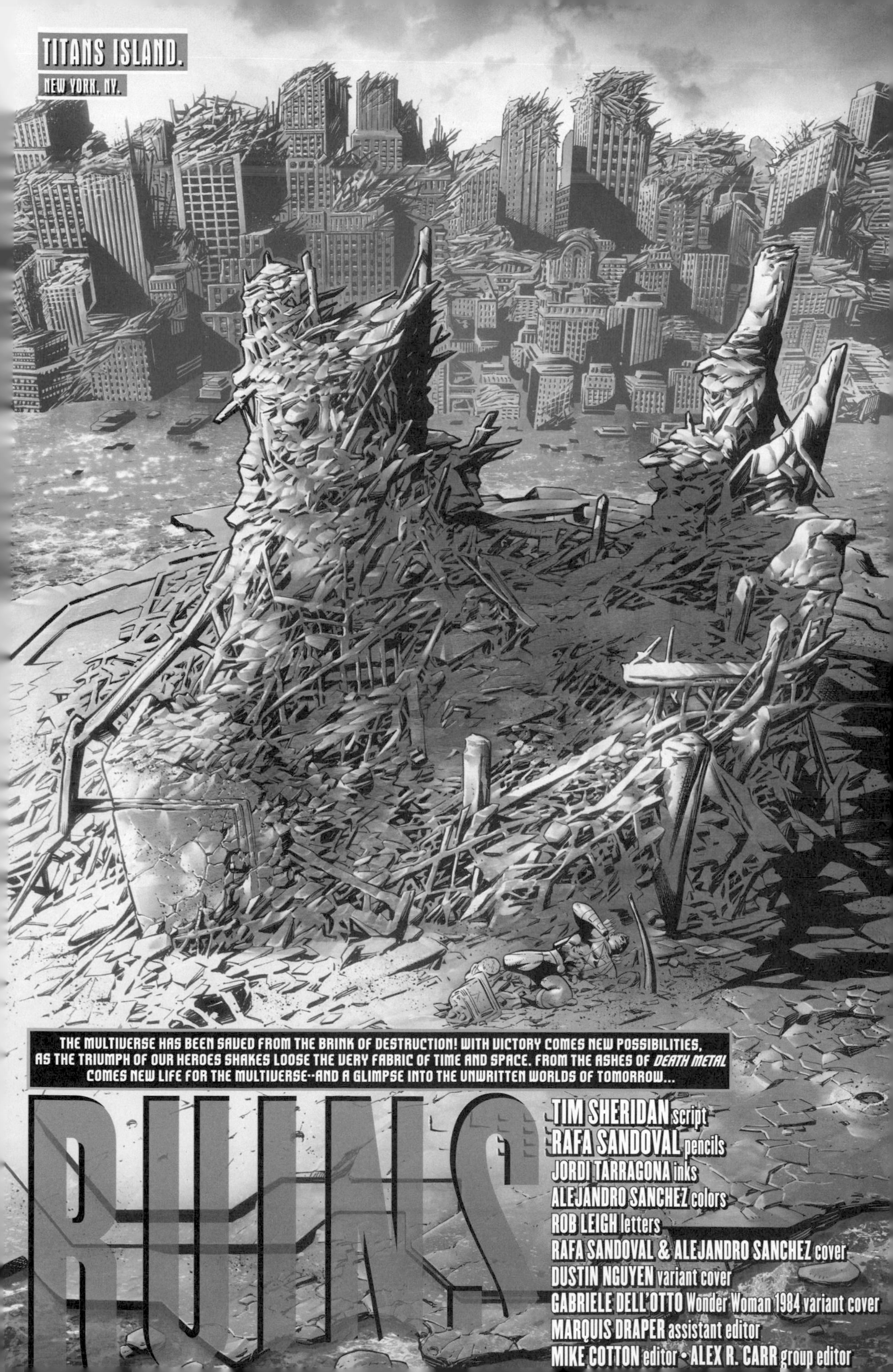
TITANS ISLAND.
NEW YORK, NY.
THE MULTIVERSE HAS BEEN SAVED FROM THE BRINK OF DESTRUCTION! WITH VICTORY COMES NEW POSSIBILITIES, AS THE TRIUMPH OF OUR HEROES SHAKES LOOSE THE VERY FABRIC OF TIME AND SPACE. FROM THE ASHES OF *DEATH METAL* COMES NEW LIFE FOR THE MULTIVERSE--AND A GLIMPSE INTO THE UNWRITTEN WORLDS OF TOMORROW...
RUINS
TIM SHERIDAN script
RAFA SANDOVAL pencils
JORDI TARRAGONA inks
ALEJANDRO SANCHEZ colors
ROB LEIGH letters
RAFA SANDOVAL & ALEJANDRO SANCHEZ cover
DUSTIN NGUYEN variant cover
GABRIELE DELL'OTTO Wonder Woman 1984 variant cover
MARQUIS DRAPER assistant editor
MIKE COTTON editor • ALEX R. CARR group editor

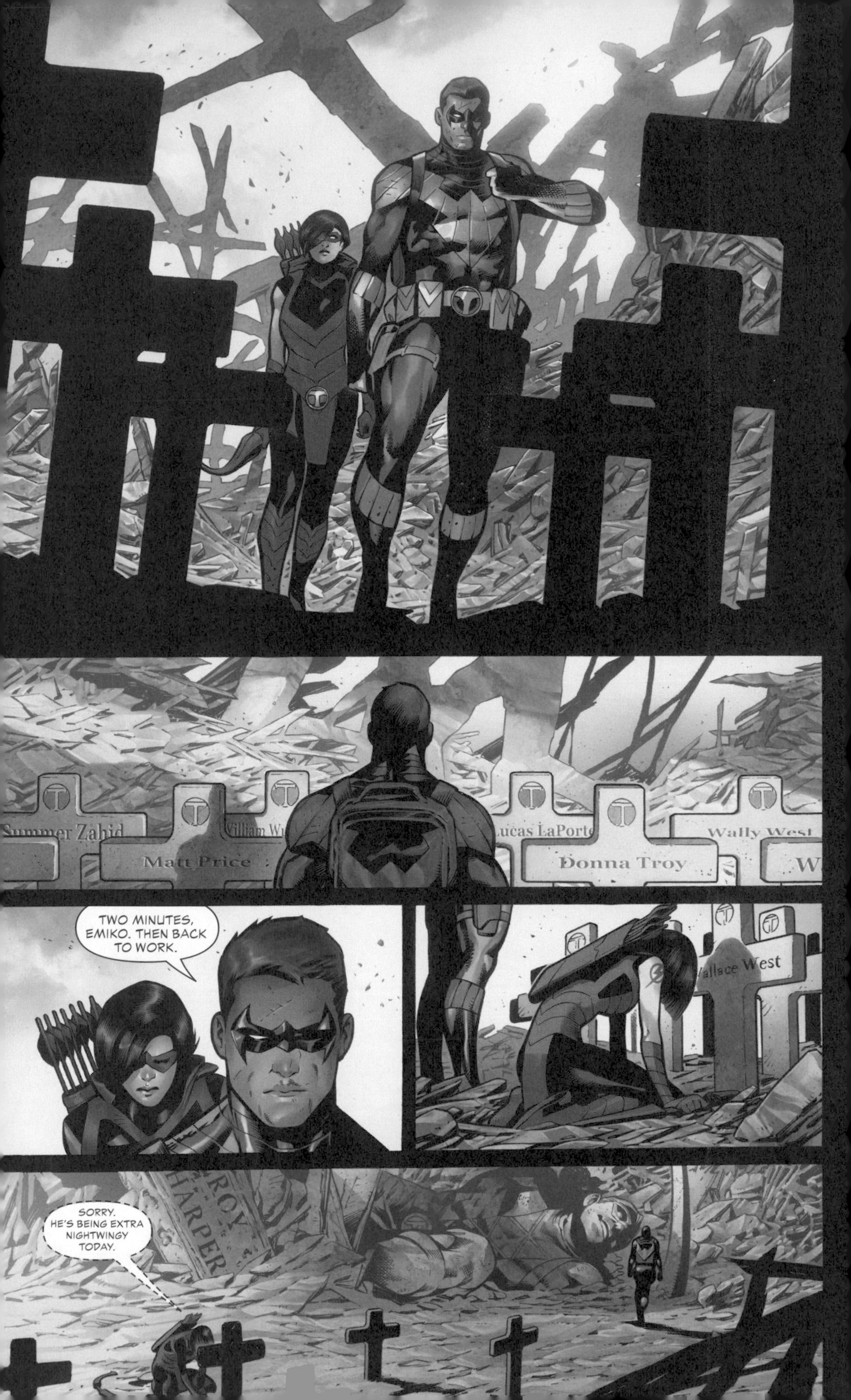
Matt Price
Lucas LaPorte
Donna Troy
Wally West
TWO MINUTES, EMIKO. THEN BACK TO WORK.
Wallace West
HARPER
SORRY. HE'S BEING EXTRA NIGHTWINGY TODAY.

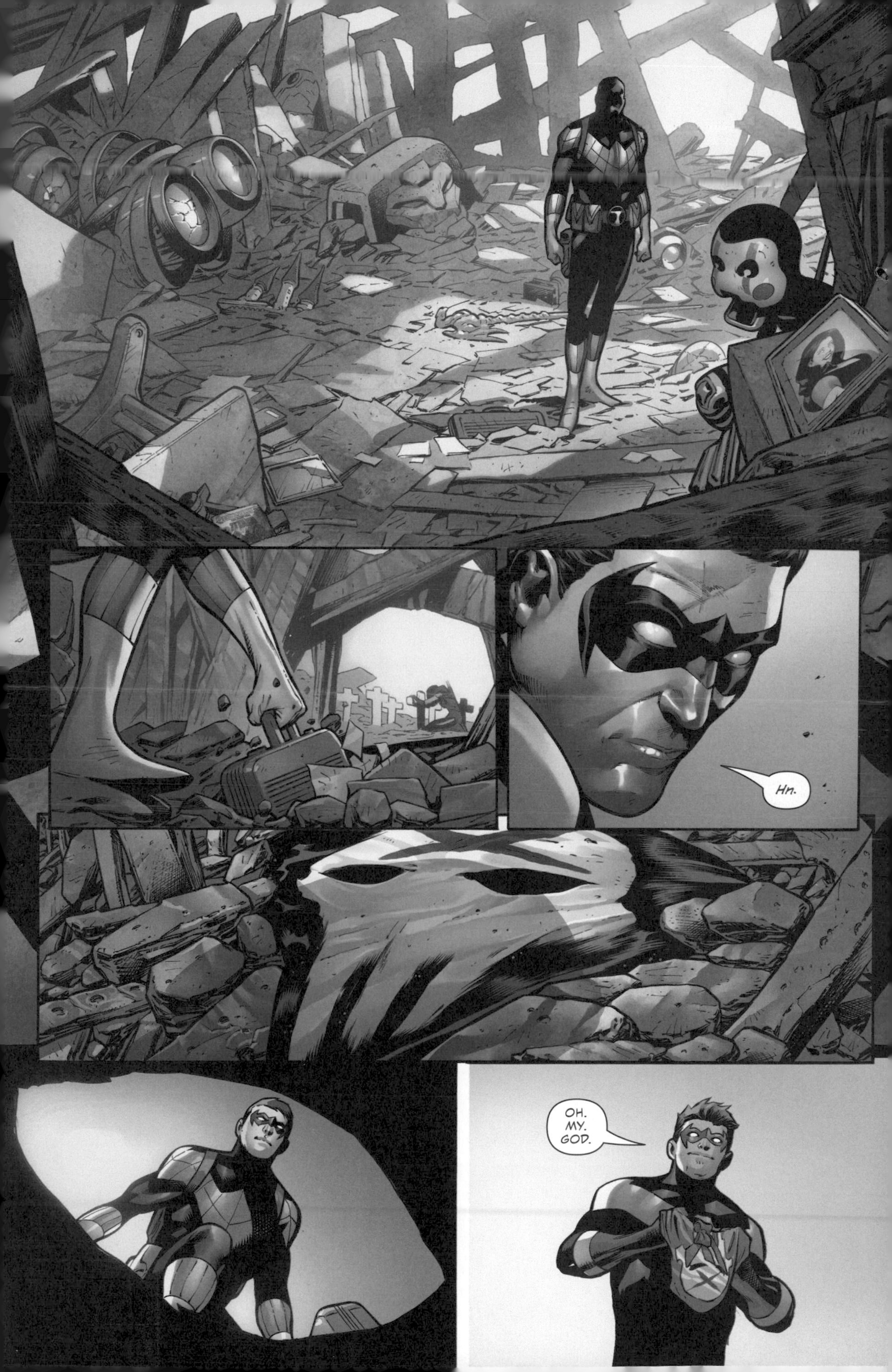
Hn.
OH. MY. GOD.

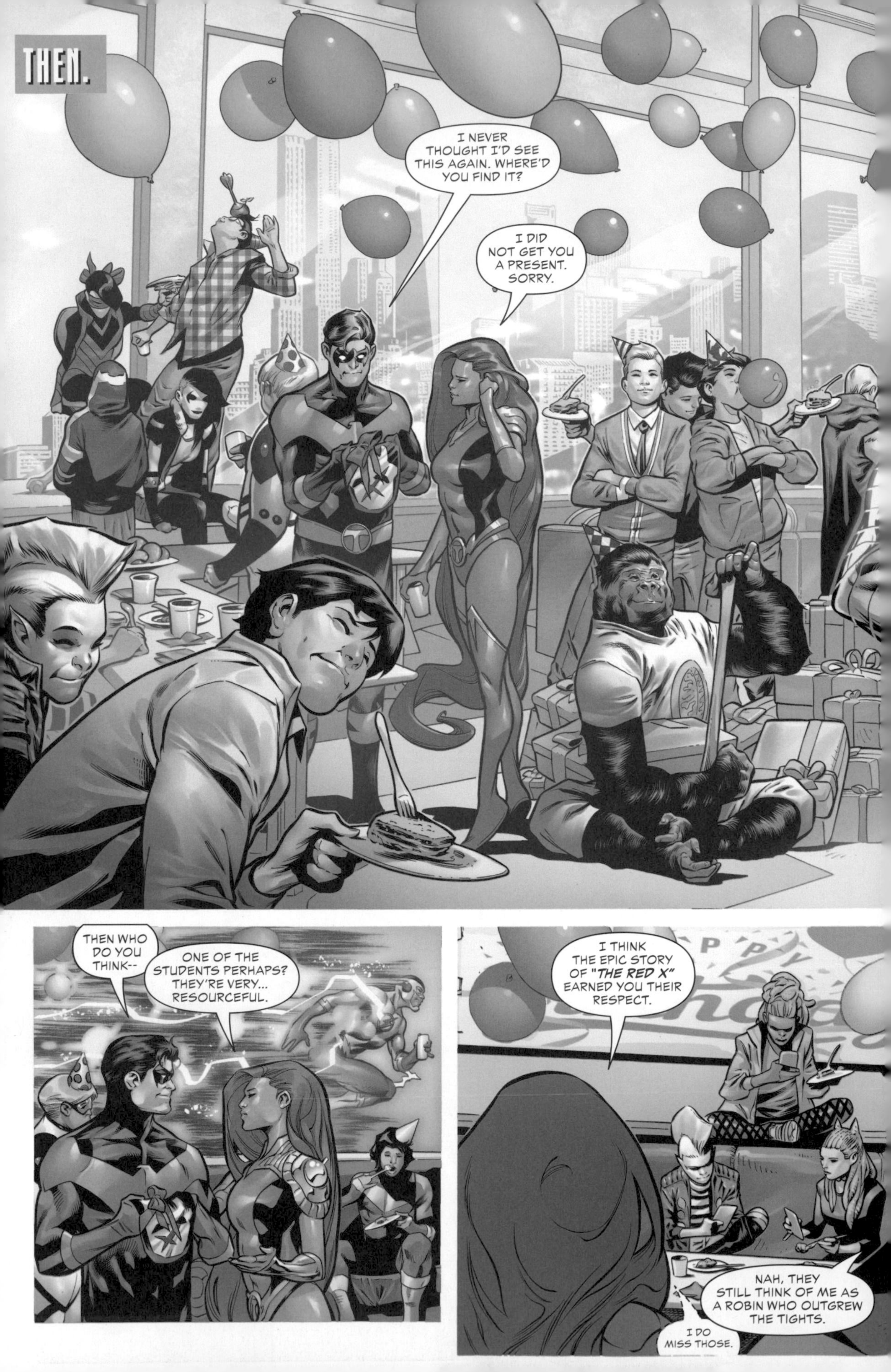
THEN.
I NEVER THOUGHT I'D SEE THIS AGAIN. WHERE'D YOU FIND IT?
I DID NOT GET YOU A PRESENT. SORRY.
THEN WHO DO YOU THINK--
ONE OF THE STUDENTS PERHAPS? THEY'RE VERY... RESOURCEFUL.
I THINK THE EPIC STORY OF "THE RED X" EARNED YOU THEIR RESPECT.
NAH, THEY STILL THINK OF ME AS A ROBIN WHO OUTGREW THE TIGHTS.
I DO MISS THOSE.

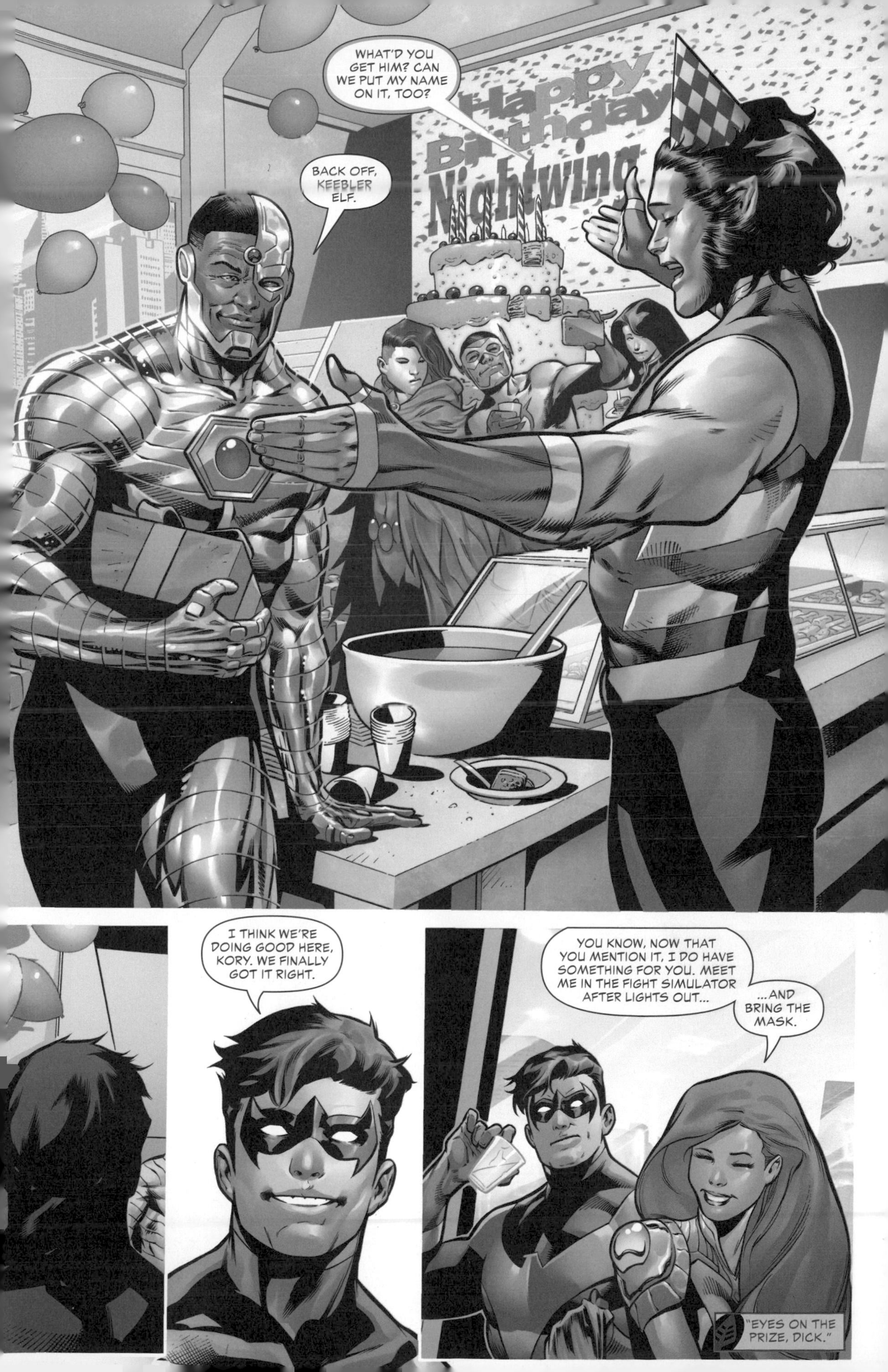
WHAT'D YOU GET HIM? CAN WE PUT MY NAME ON IT, TOO?
Happy Birthday Nightwing
BACK OFF, KEEBLER ELF.
I THINK WE'RE DOING GOOD HERE, KORY. WE FINALLY GOT IT RIGHT.
YOU KNOW, NOW THAT YOU MENTION IT, I DO HAVE SOMETHING FOR YOU. MEET ME IN THE FIGHT SIMULATOR AFTER LIGHTS OUT...
...AND BRING THE MASK.
"EYES ON THE PRIZE, DICK."

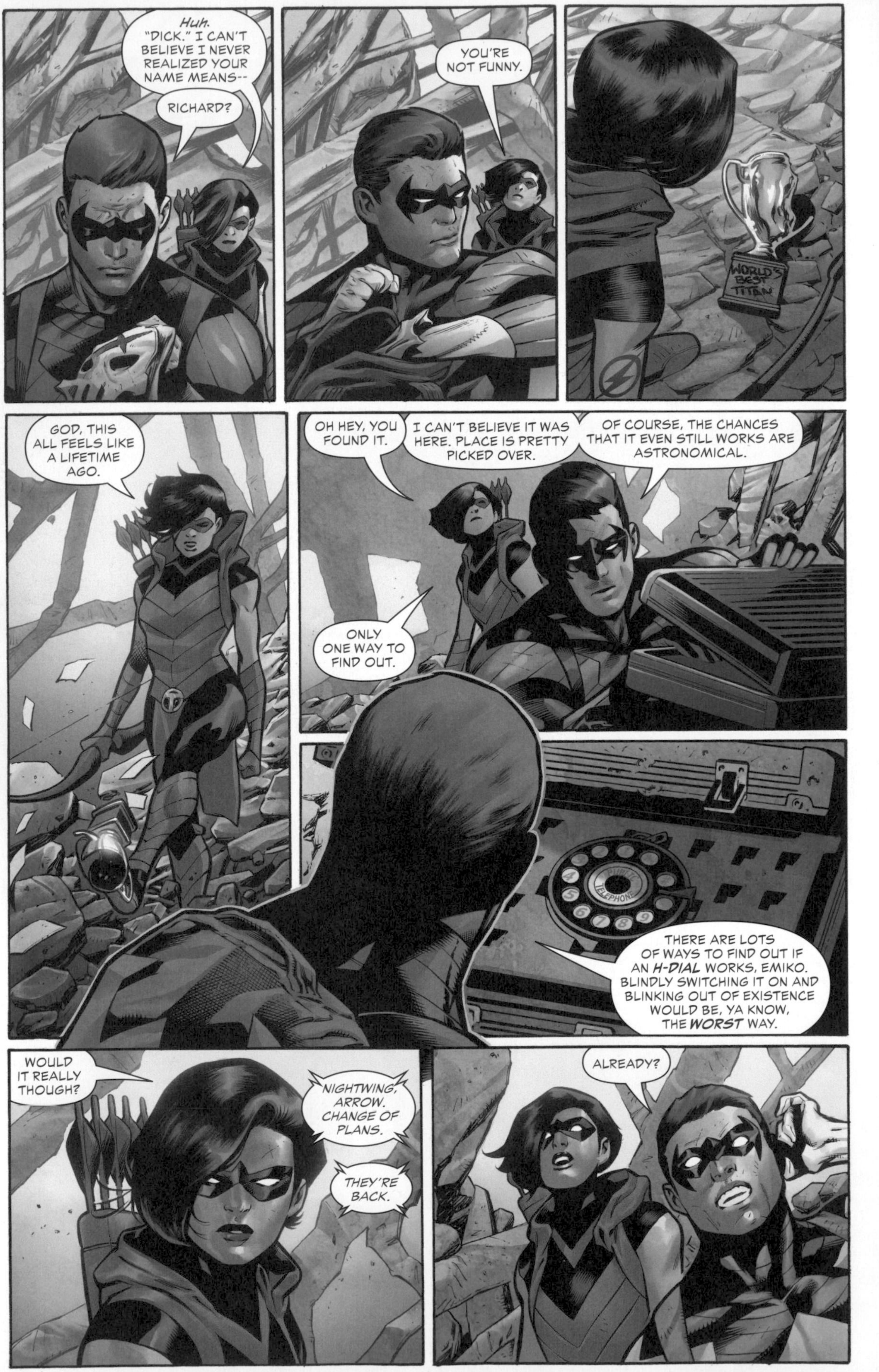
Huh.
"DICK." I CAN'T BELIEVE I NEVER REALIZED YOUR NAME MEANS--
RICHARD?
YOU'RE NOT FUNNY.
WORLD'S BEST TITAN
GOD, THIS ALL FEELS LIKE A LIFETIME AGO.
OH HEY, YOU FOUND IT.
I CAN'T BELIEVE IT WAS HERE. PLACE IS PRETTY PICKED OVER.
OF COURSE, THE CHANCES THAT IT EVEN STILL WORKS ARE ASTRONOMICAL.
ONLY ONE WAY TO FIND OUT.
THERE ARE LOTS OF WAYS TO FIND OUT IF AN H-DIAL WORKS, EMIKO. BLINDLY SWITCHING IT ON AND BLINKING OUT OF EXISTENCE WOULD BE, YA KNOW, THE WORST WAY.
WOULD IT REALLY THOUGH?
NIGHTWING, ARROW. CHANGE OF PLANS.
THEY'RE BACK.
ALREADY?

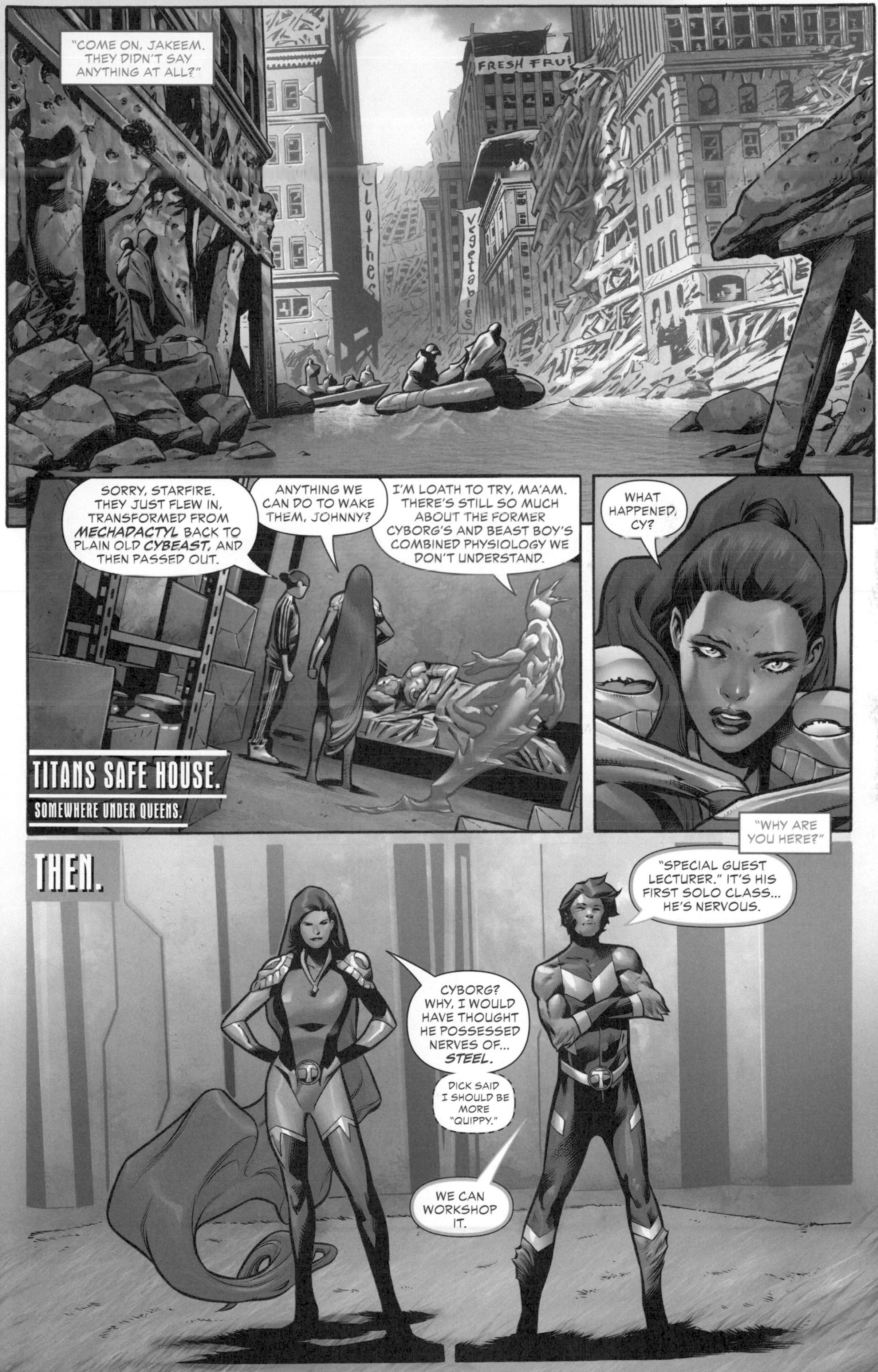
"COME ON, JAKEEM. THEY DIDN'T SAY ANYTHING AT ALL?"
FRESH FRUI
Clothes
Vegetables
SORRY, STARFIRE. THEY JUST FLEW IN, TRANSFORMED FROM MECHADACTYL BACK TO PLAIN OLD CYBEAST, AND THEN PASSED OUT.
ANYTHING WE CAN DO TO WAKE THEM, JOHNNY?
I'M LOATH TO TRY, MA'AM. THERE'S STILL SO MUCH ABOUT THE FORMER CYBORG'S AND BEAST BOY'S COMBINED PHYSIOLOGY WE DON'T UNDERSTAND.
TITANS SAFE HOUSE.
SOMEWHERE UNDER QUEENS.
WHAT HAPPENED, CY?
"WHY ARE YOU HERE?"
THEN.
"SPECIAL GUEST LECTURER." IT'S HIS FIRST SOLO CLASS... HE'S NERVOUS.
CYBORG? WHY, I WOULD HAVE THOUGHT HE POSSESSED NERVES OF... STEEL.
DICK SAID I SHOULD BE MORE "QUIPPY."
WE CAN WORKSHOP IT.

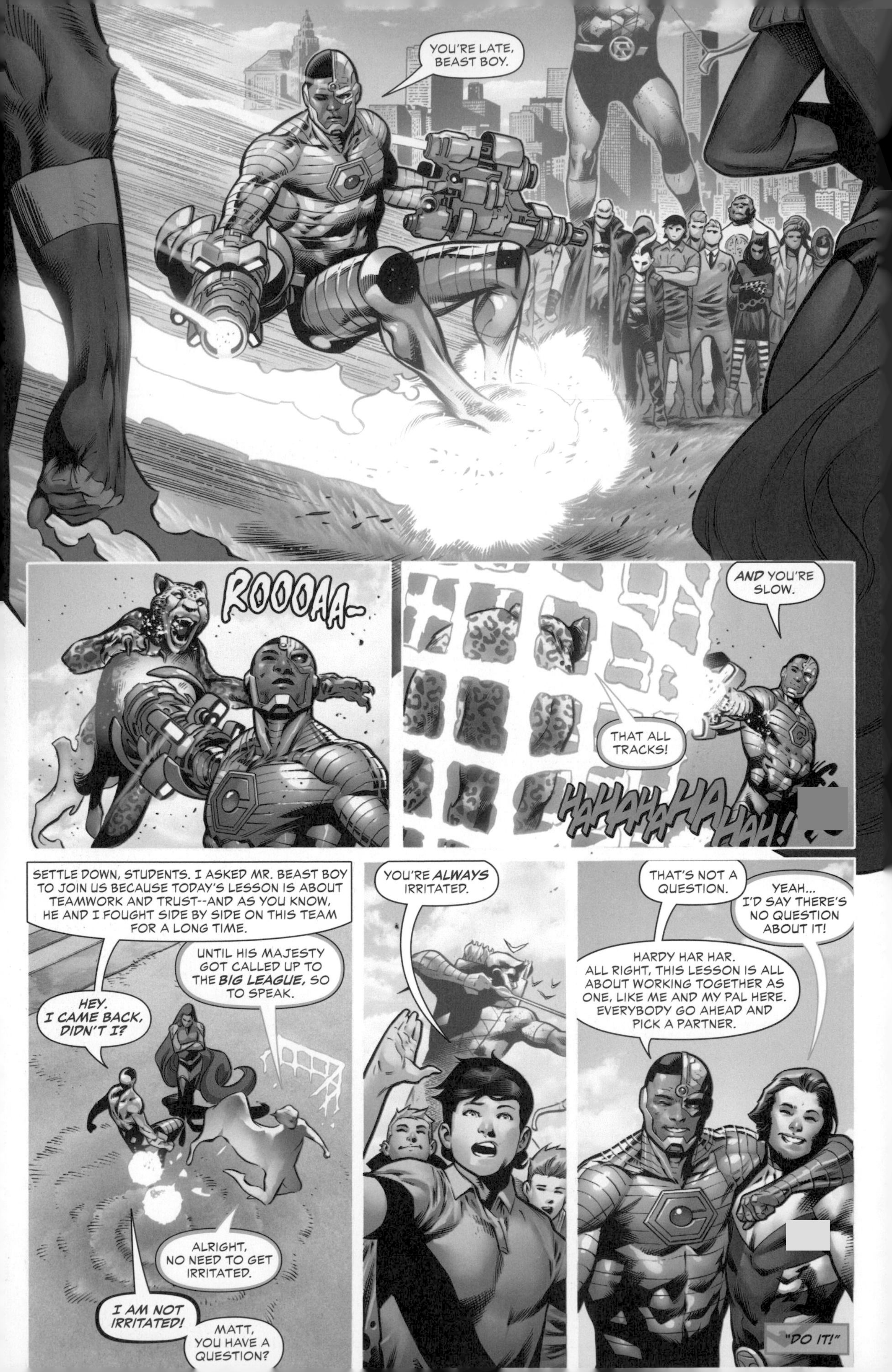
YOU'RE LATE, BEAST BOY.
ROOOAA-
AND YOU'RE SLOW.
THAT ALL TRACKS!
HAHAHAHAHAHAH!
SETTLE DOWN, STUDENTS. I ASKED MR. BEAST BOY TO JOIN US BECAUSE TODAY'S LESSON IS ABOUT TEAMWORK AND TRUST--AND AS YOU KNOW, HE AND I FOUGHT SIDE BY SIDE ON THIS TEAM FOR A LONG TIME.
UNTIL HIS MAJESTY GOT CALLED UP TO THE BIG LEAGUE, SO TO SPEAK.
HEY. I CAME BACK, DIDN'T I?
ALRIGHT, NO NEED TO GET IRRITATED.
I AM NOT IRRITATED!
MATT, YOU HAVE A QUESTION?
YOU'RE ALWAYS IRRITATED.
THAT'S NOT A QUESTION.
YEAH... I'D SAY THERE'S NO QUESTION ABOUT IT!
HARDY HAR HAR. ALL RIGHT, THIS LESSON IS ALL ABOUT WORKING TOGETHER AS ONE, LIKE ME AND MY PAL HERE. EVERYBODY GO AHEAD AND PICK A PARTNER.
"DO IT!"

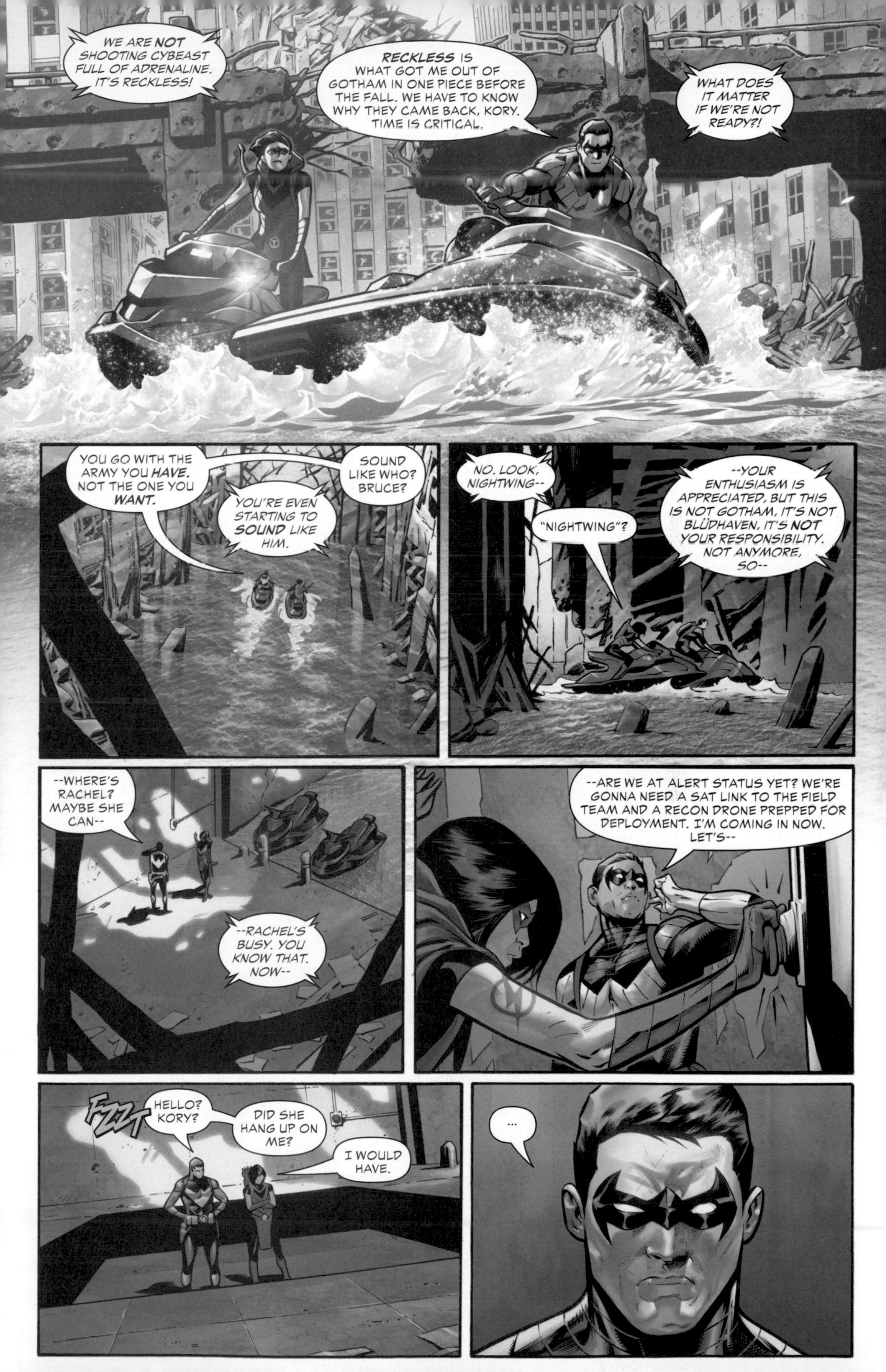
WE ARE NOT SHOOTING CYBEAST FULL OF ADRENALINE. IT'S RECKLESS!
RECKLESS IS WHAT GOT ME OUT OF GOTHAM IN ONE PIECE BEFORE THE FALL. WE HAVE TO KNOW WHY THEY CAME BACK, KORY. TIME IS CRITICAL.
WHAT DOES IT MATTER IF WE'RE NOT READY?!
YOU GO WITH THE ARMY YOU HAVE. NOT THE ONE YOU WANT.
YOU'RE EVEN STARTING TO SOUND LIKE HIM.
SOUND LIKE WHO? BRUCE?
NO. LOOK, NIGHTWING--
"NIGHTWING"?
--YOUR ENTHUSIASM IS APPRECIATED, BUT THIS IS NOT GOTHAM, IT'S NOT BLÜDHAVEN, IT'S NOT YOUR RESPONSIBILITY. NOT ANYMORE, SO--
--WHERE'S RACHEL? MAYBE SHE CAN--
--RACHEL'S BUSY. YOU KNOW THAT. NOW--
--ARE WE AT ALERT STATUS YET? WE'RE GONNA NEED A SAT LINK TO THE FIELD TEAM AND A RECON DRONE PREPPED FOR DEPLOYMENT. I'M COMING IN NOW. LET'S--
FZZT
HELLO? KORY?
DID SHE HANG UP ON ME?
I WOULD HAVE.
...

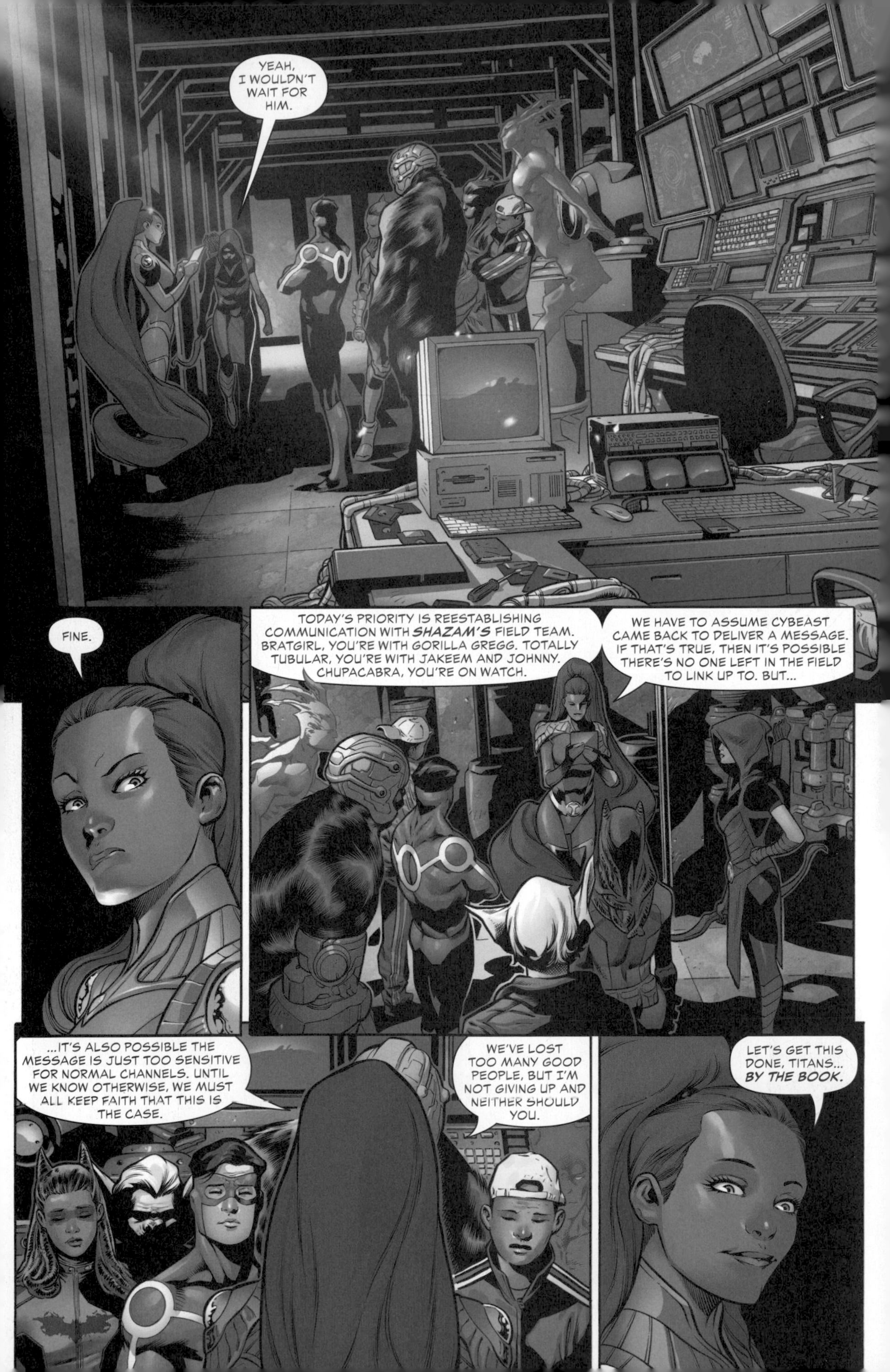

YEAH, I WOULDN'T WAIT FOR HIM.
FINE.
TODAY'S PRIORITY IS REESTABLISHING COMMUNICATION WITH SHAZAM'S FIELD TEAM. BRATGIRL, YOU'RE WITH GORILLA GREGG. TOTALLY TUBULAR, YOU'RE WITH JAKEEM AND JOHNNY. CHUPACABRA, YOU'RE ON WATCH.
WE HAVE TO ASSUME CYBEAST CAME BACK TO DELIVER A MESSAGE. IF THAT'S TRUE, THEN IT'S POSSIBLE THERE'S NO ONE LEFT IN THE FIELD TO LINK UP TO. BUT...
...IT'S ALSO POSSIBLE THE MESSAGE IS JUST TOO SENSITIVE FOR NORMAL CHANNELS. UNTIL WE KNOW OTHERWISE, WE MUST ALL KEEP FAITH THAT THIS IS THE CASE.
WE'VE LOST TOO MANY GOOD PEOPLE, BUT I'M NOT GIVING UP AND NEITHER SHOULD YOU.
LET'S GET THIS DONE, TITANS... BY THE BOOK.

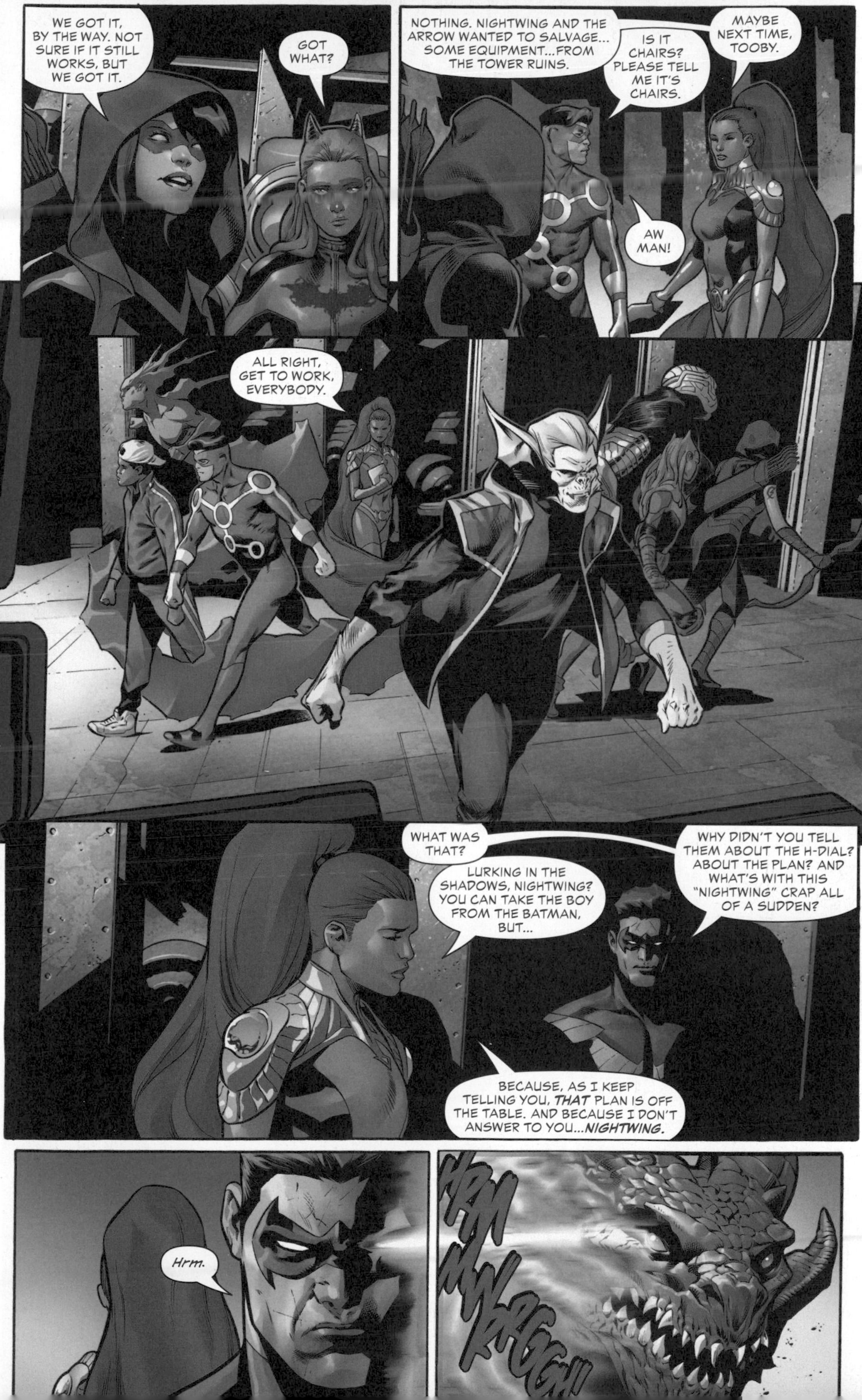

WE GOT IT, BY THE WAY. NOT SURE IF IT STILL WORKS, BUT WE GOT IT.
GOT WHAT?
NOTHING. NIGHTWING AND THE ARROW WANTED TO SALVAGE... SOME EQUIPMENT...FROM THE TOWER RUINS.
IS IT CHAIRS? PLEASE TELL ME IT'S CHAIRS.
MAYBE NEXT TIME, TOOBY.
AW MAN!
ALL RIGHT, GET TO WORK, EVERYBODY.
WHAT WAS THAT?
LURKING IN THE SHADOWS, NIGHTWING? YOU CAN TAKE THE BOY FROM THE BATMAN, BUT...
WHY DIDN'T YOU TELL THEM ABOUT THE H-DIAL? ABOUT THE PLAN? AND WHAT'S WITH THIS "NIGHTWING" CRAP ALL OF A SUDDEN?
BECAUSE, AS I KEEP TELLING YOU, *THAT* PLAN IS OFF THE TABLE. AND BECAUSE I DON'T ANSWER TO YOU...*NIGHTWING.*
Hrm.

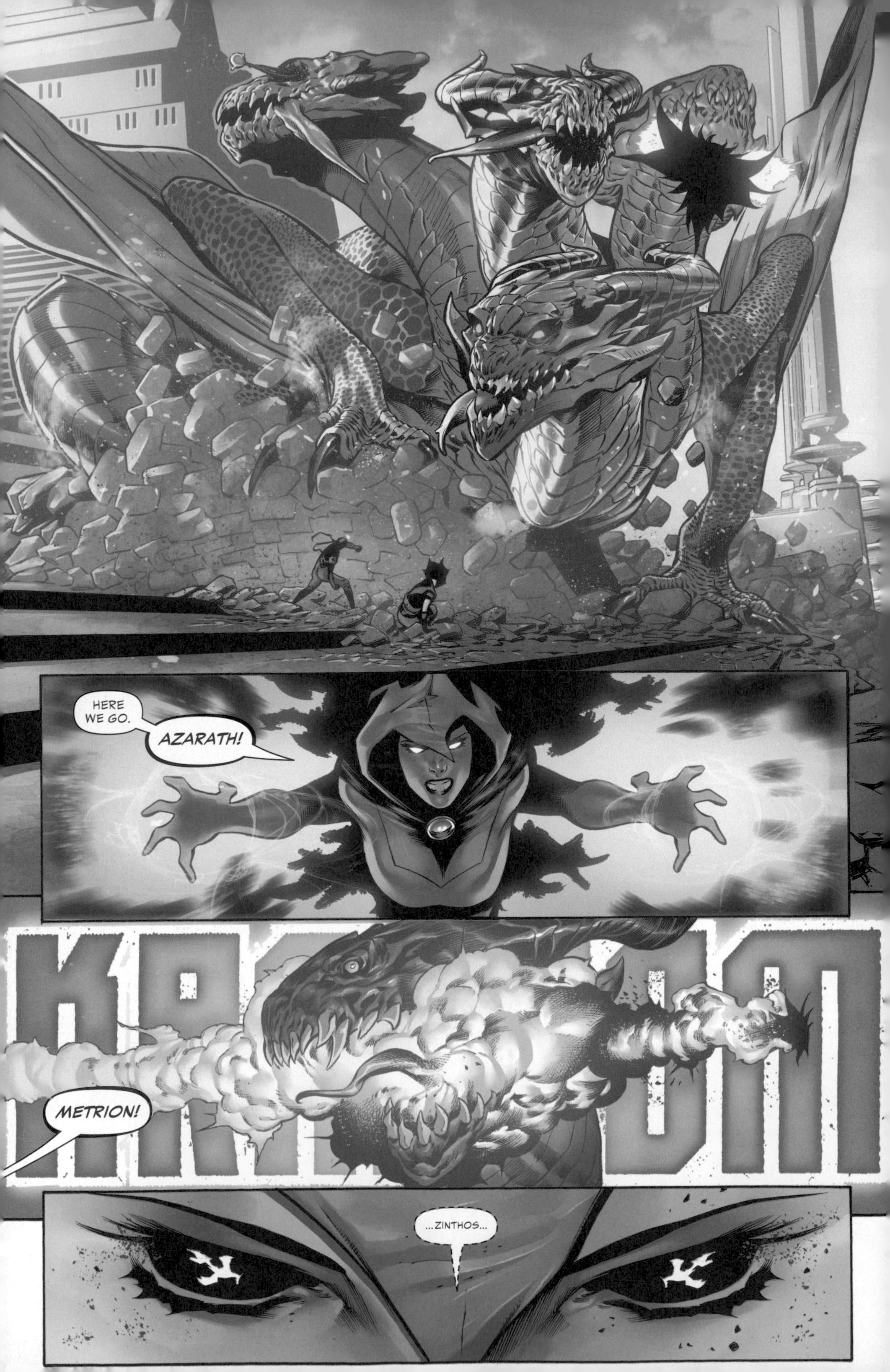
HERE WE GO.
AZARATH!
METRION!
...ZINTHOS...

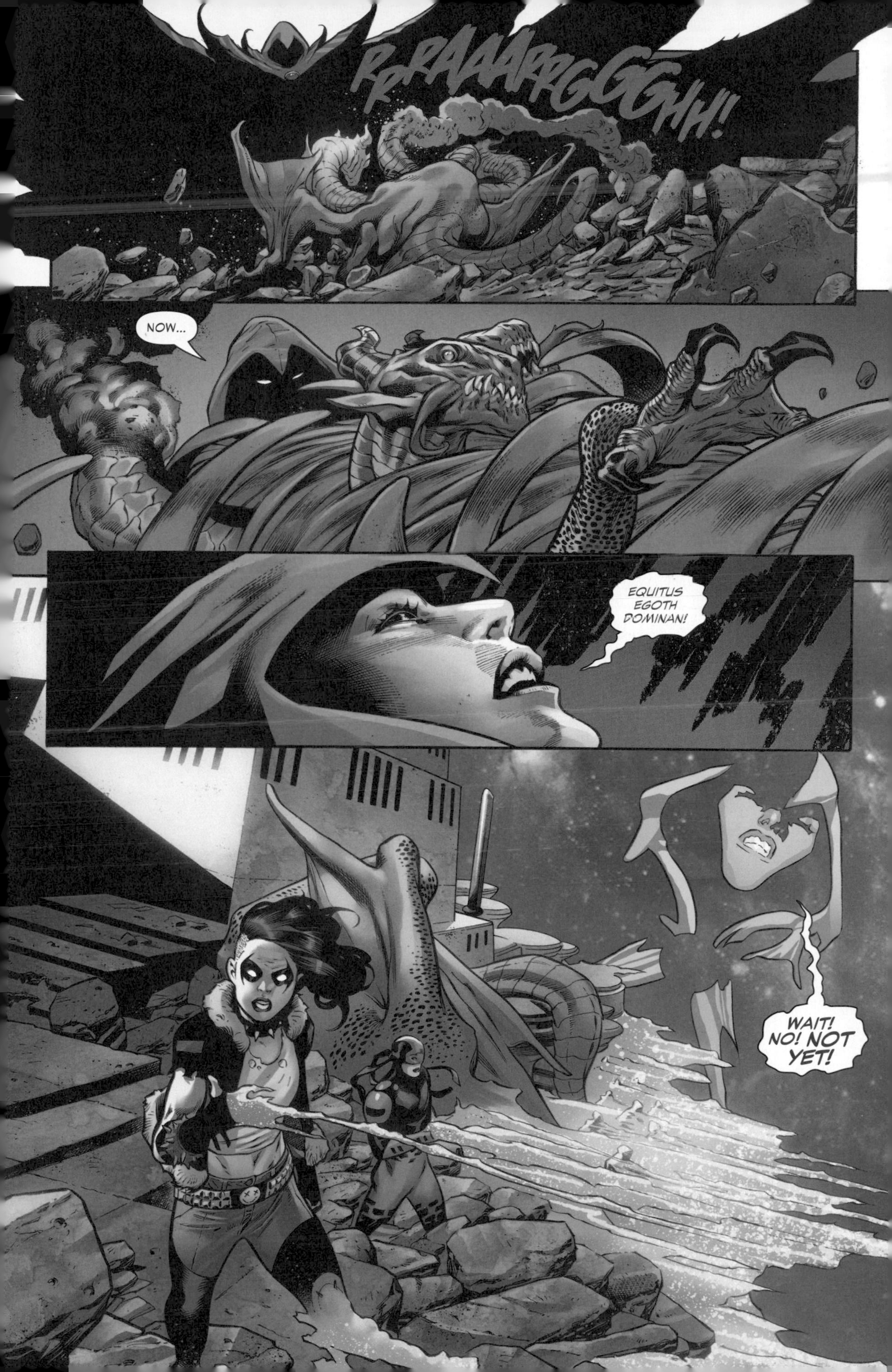
RRRAAAARRGGGGHH!
NOW...
EQUITUS EGOTH DOMINAN!
WAIT! NO! NOT YET!

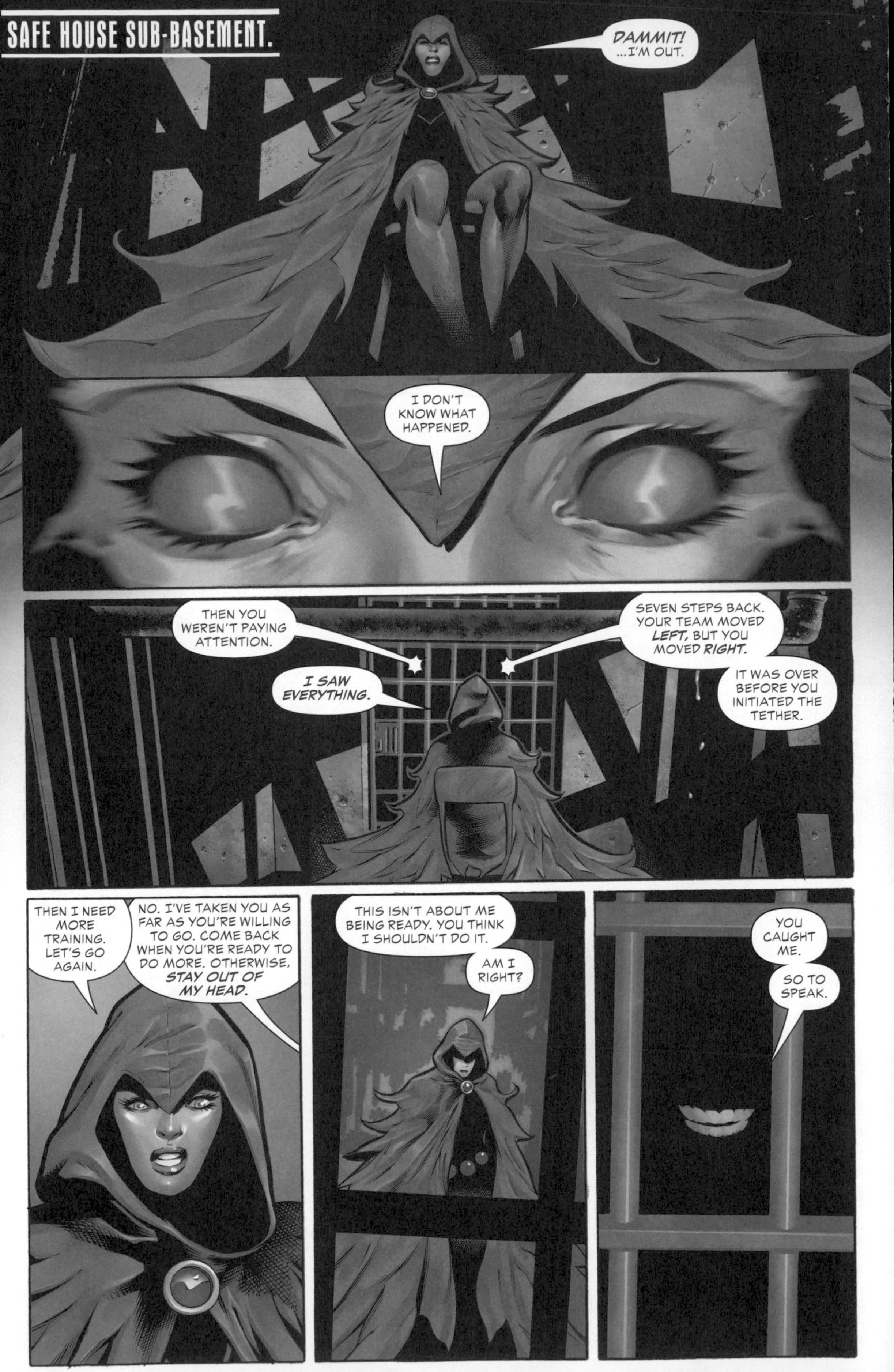
SAFE HOUSE SUB-BASEMENT.
DAMMIT! ...I'M OUT.
I DON'T KNOW WHAT HAPPENED.
THEN YOU WEREN'T PAYING ATTENTION.
I SAW EVERYTHING.
SEVEN STEPS BACK. YOUR TEAM MOVED LEFT, BUT YOU MOVED RIGHT.
IT WAS OVER BEFORE YOU INITIATED THE TETHER.
THEN I NEED MORE TRAINING. LET'S GO AGAIN.
NO. I'VE TAKEN YOU AS FAR AS YOU'RE WILLING TO GO. COME BACK WHEN YOU'RE READY TO DO MORE. OTHERWISE, STAY OUT OF MY HEAD.
THIS ISN'T ABOUT ME BEING READY. YOU THINK I SHOULDN'T DO IT.
AM I RIGHT?
YOU CAUGHT ME.
SO TO SPEAK.

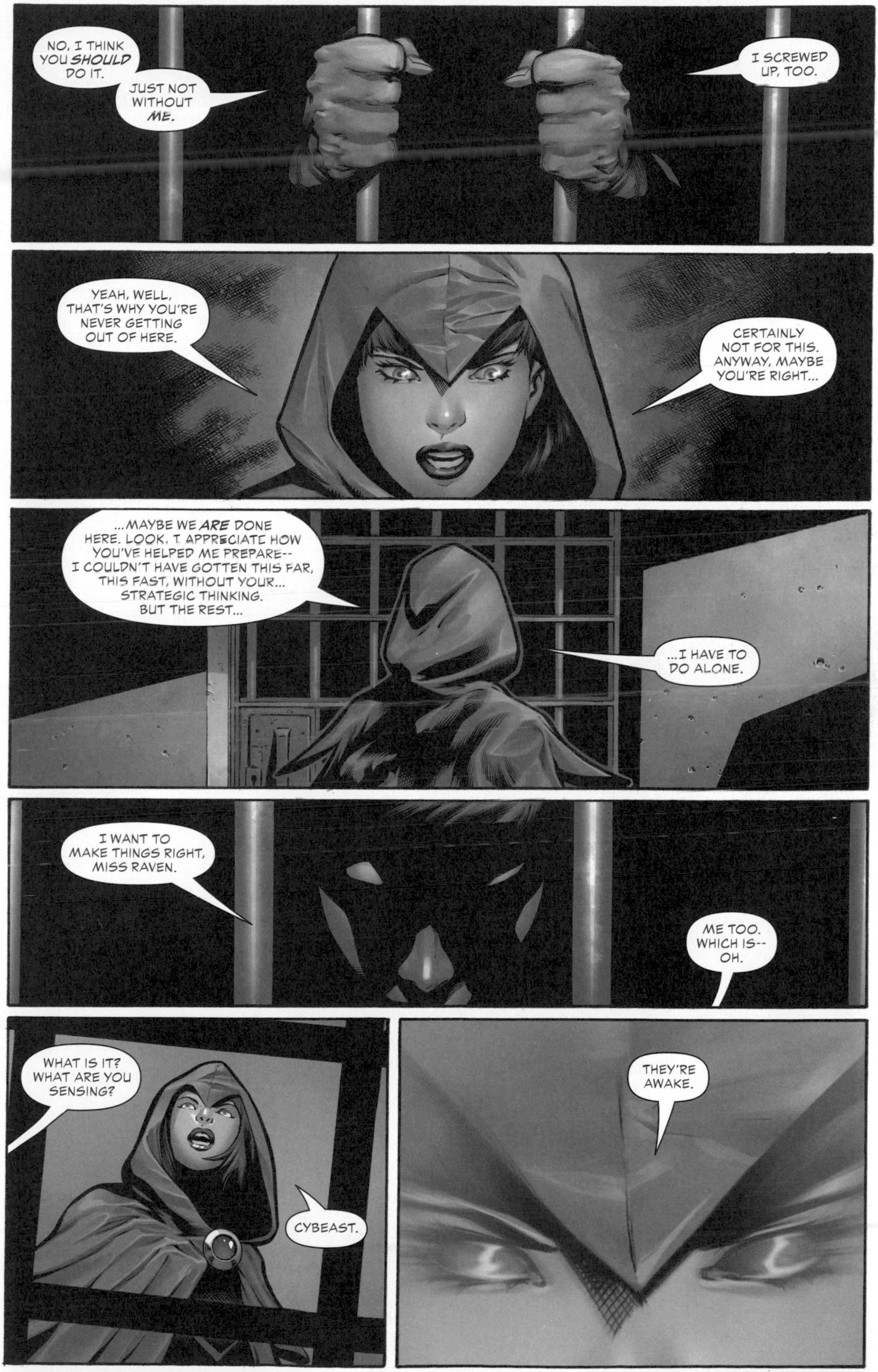
NO, I THINK YOU SHOULD DO IT.
JUST NOT WITHOUT ME.
I SCREWED UP, TOO.
YEAH, WELL, THAT'S WHY YOU'RE NEVER GETTING OUT OF HERE.
CERTAINLY NOT FOR THIS. ANYWAY, MAYBE YOU'RE RIGHT...
...MAYBE WE ARE DONE HERE. LOOK. I APPRECIATE HOW YOU'VE HELPED ME PREPARE-- I COULDN'T HAVE GOTTEN THIS FAR, THIS FAST, WITHOUT YOUR... STRATEGIC THINKING. BUT THE REST...
...I HAVE TO DO ALONE.
I WANT TO MAKE THINGS RIGHT, MISS RAVEN.
ME TOO. WHICH IS-- OH.
WHAT IS IT? WHAT ARE YOU SENSING?
CYBEAST.
THEY'RE AWAKE.

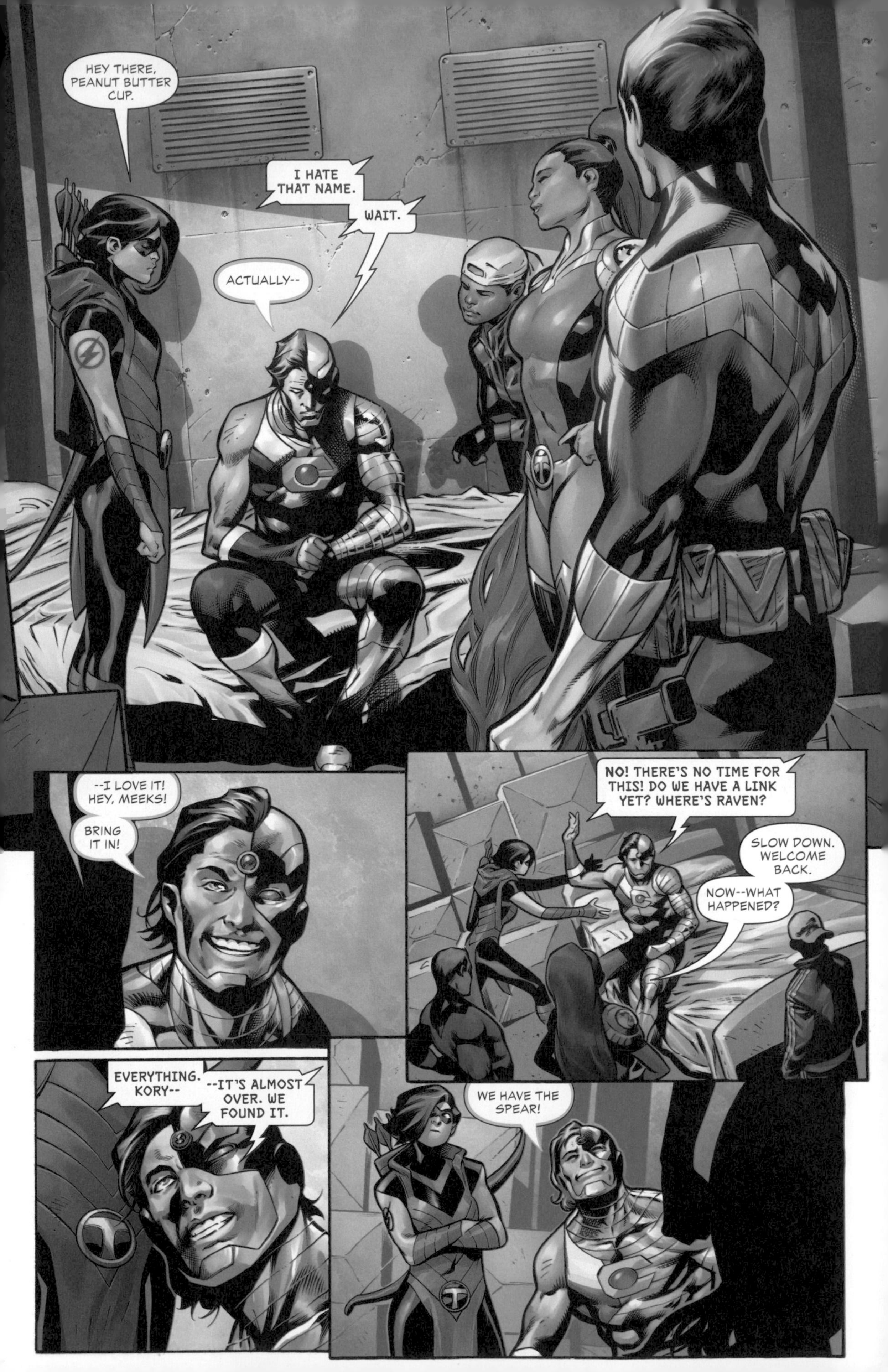
HEY THERE, PEANUT BUTTER CUP.
I HATE THAT NAME.
WAIT.
ACTUALLY--
--I LOVE IT! HEY, MEEKS!
BRING IT IN!
NO! THERE'S NO TIME FOR THIS! DO WE HAVE A LINK YET? WHERE'S RAVEN?
SLOW DOWN. WELCOME BACK.
NOW--WHAT HAPPENED?
EVERYTHING. KORY--
--IT'S ALMOST OVER. WE FOUND IT.
WE HAVE THE SPEAR!

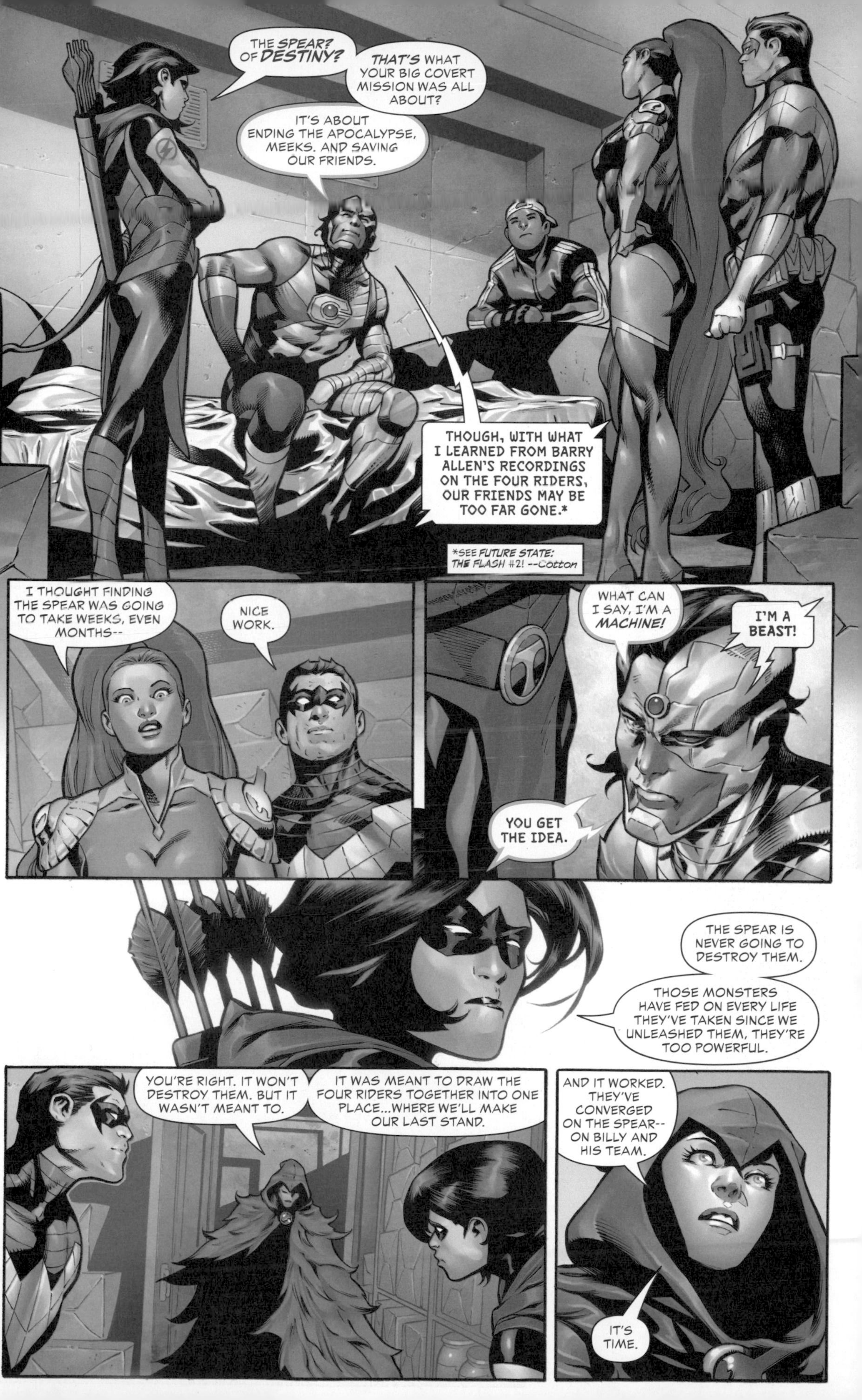
THE SPEAR? OF DESTINY?
THAT'S WHAT YOUR BIG COVERT MISSION WAS ALL ABOUT?
IT'S ABOUT ENDING THE APOCALYPSE, MEEKS. AND SAVING OUR FRIENDS.
THOUGH, WITH WHAT I LEARNED FROM BARRY ALLEN'S RECORDINGS ON THE FOUR RIDERS, OUR FRIENDS MAY BE TOO FAR GONE.*
*SEE FUTURE STATE: THE FLASH #2! --Cotton
I THOUGHT FINDING THE SPEAR WAS GOING TO TAKE WEEKS, EVEN MONTHS--
NICE WORK.
WHAT CAN I SAY, I'M A MACHINE!
I'M A BEAST!
YOU GET THE IDEA.
THE SPEAR IS NEVER GOING TO DESTROY THEM.
THOSE MONSTERS HAVE FED ON EVERY LIFE THEY'VE TAKEN SINCE WE UNLEASHED THEM, THEY'RE TOO POWERFUL.
YOU'RE RIGHT. IT WON'T DESTROY THEM. BUT IT WASN'T MEANT TO.
IT WAS MEANT TO DRAW THE FOUR RIDERS TOGETHER INTO ONE PLACE...WHERE WE'LL MAKE OUR LAST STAND.
AND IT WORKED. THEY'VE CONVERGED ON THE SPEAR-- ON BILLY AND HIS TEAM.
IT'S TIME.

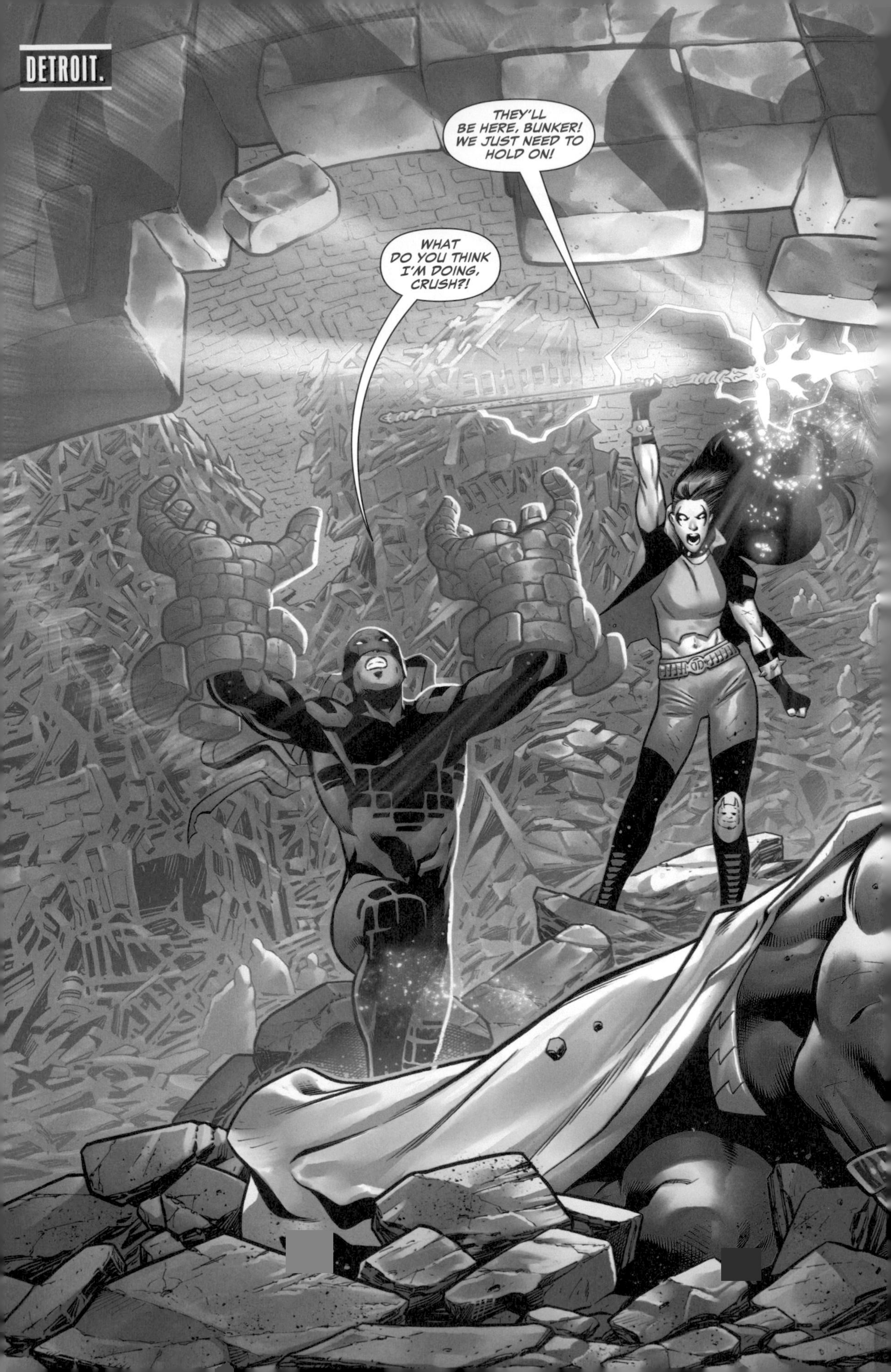
DETROIT.
THEY'LL BE HERE, BUNKER! WE JUST NEED TO HOLD ON!
WHAT DO YOU THINK I'M DOING, CRUSH?!

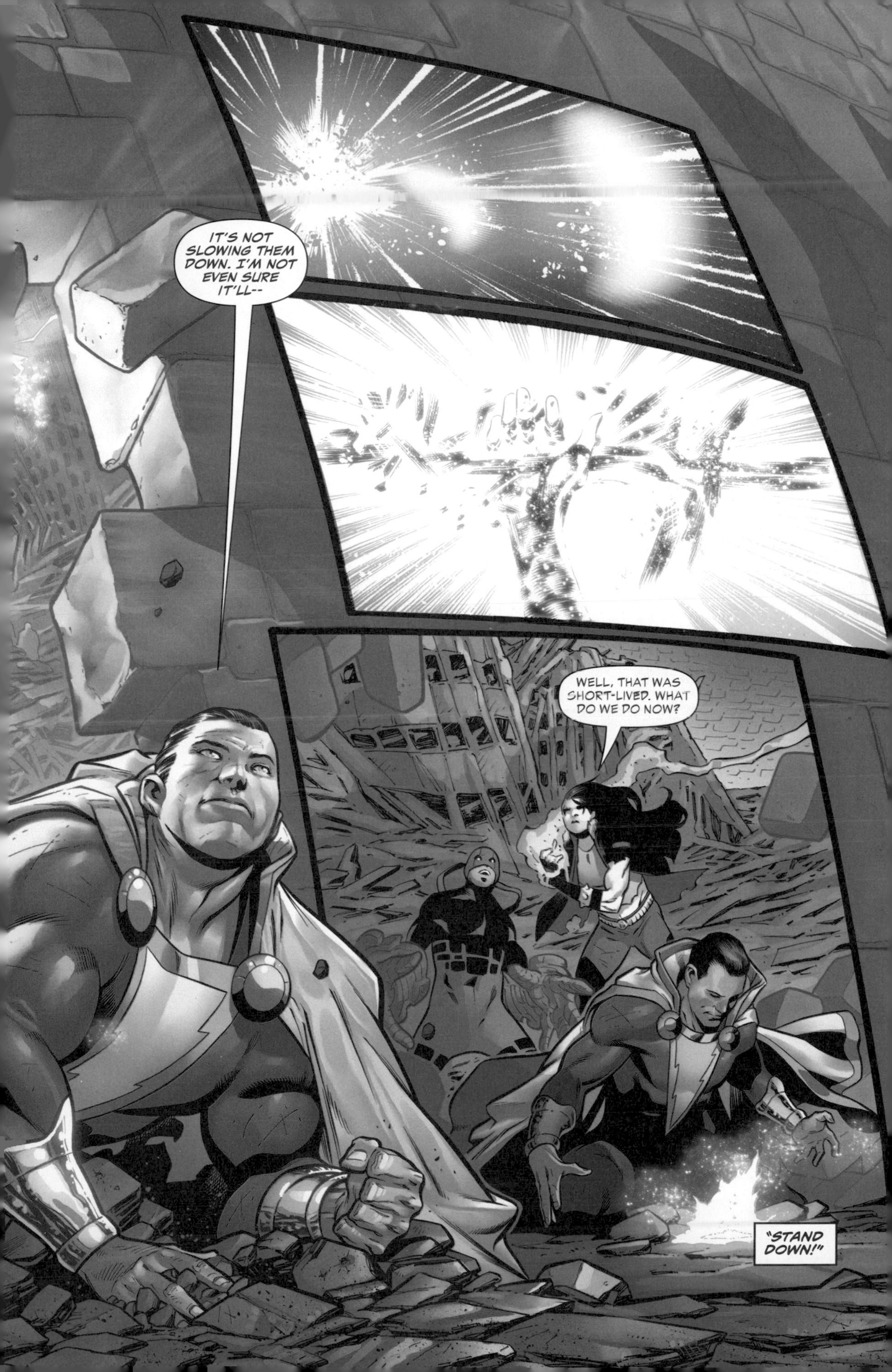
IT'S NOT SLOWING THEM DOWN. I'M NOT EVEN SURE IT'LL--
WELL, THAT WAS SHORT-LIVED. WHAT DO WE DO NOW?
"STAND DOWN!"

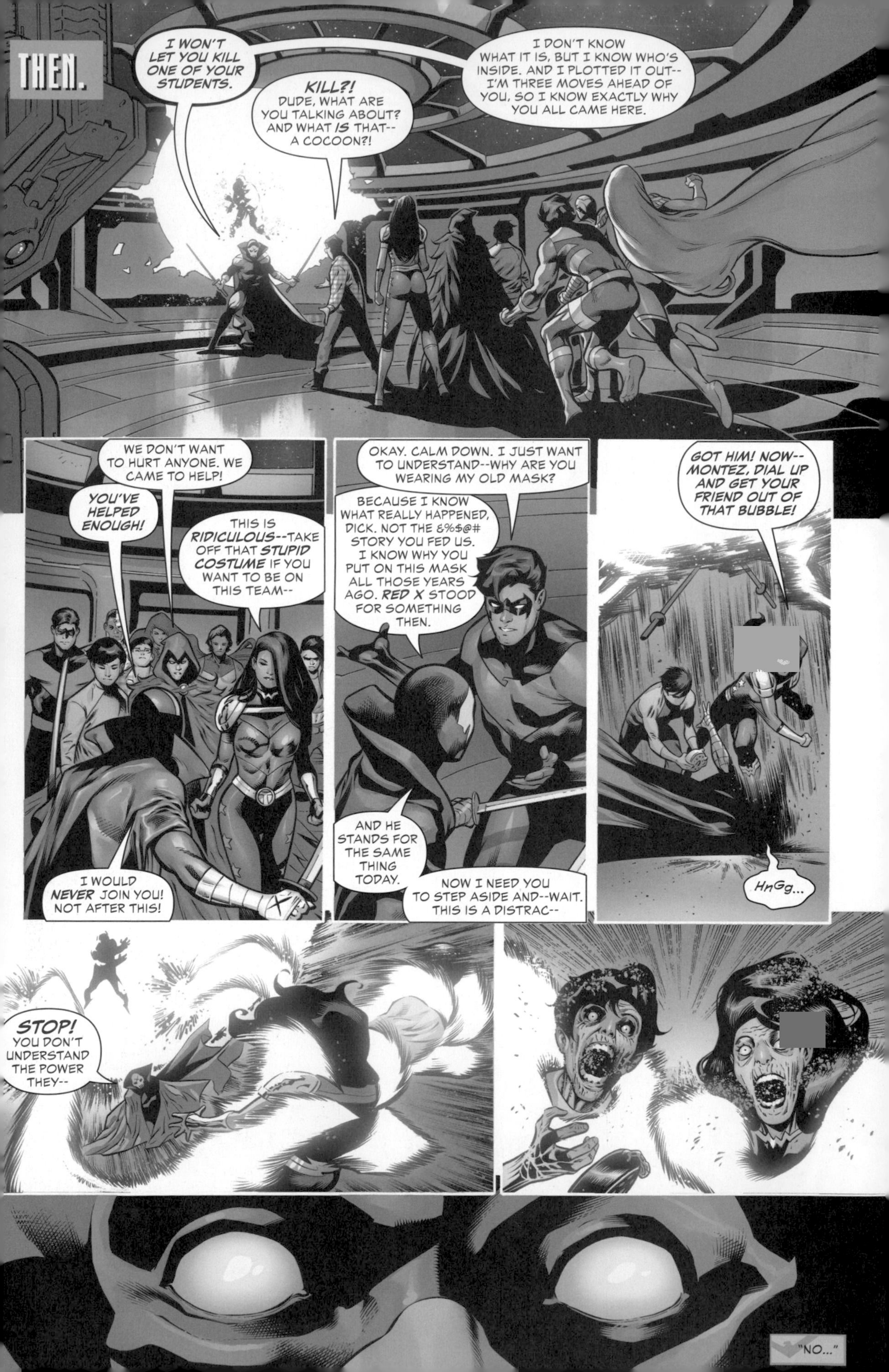

THEN.
I WON'T LET YOU KILL ONE OF YOUR STUDENTS.
KILL?! DUDE, WHAT ARE YOU TALKING ABOUT? AND WHAT IS THAT-- A COCOON?!
I DON'T KNOW WHAT IT IS, BUT I KNOW WHO'S INSIDE. AND I PLOTTED IT OUT-- I'M THREE MOVES AHEAD OF YOU, SO I KNOW EXACTLY WHY YOU ALL CAME HERE.
WE DON'T WANT TO HURT ANYONE. WE CAME TO HELP!
YOU'VE HELPED ENOUGH!
THIS IS RIDICULOUS--TAKE OFF THAT STUPID COSTUME IF YOU WANT TO BE ON THIS TEAM--
I WOULD NEVER JOIN YOU! NOT AFTER THIS!
OKAY. CALM DOWN. I JUST WANT TO UNDERSTAND--WHY ARE YOU WEARING MY OLD MASK?
BECAUSE I KNOW WHAT REALLY HAPPENED, DICK. NOT THE &%$@# STORY YOU FED US. I KNOW WHY YOU PUT ON THIS MASK ALL THOSE YEARS AGO. RED X STOOD FOR SOMETHING THEN.
AND HE STANDS FOR THE SAME THING TODAY.
NOW I NEED YOU TO STEP ASIDE AND--WAIT. THIS IS A DISTRAC--
GOT HIM! NOW-- MONTEZ, DIAL UP AND GET YOUR FRIEND OUT OF THAT BUBBLE!
HnGg...
STOP! YOU DON'T UNDERSTAND THE POWER THEY--
"NO..."

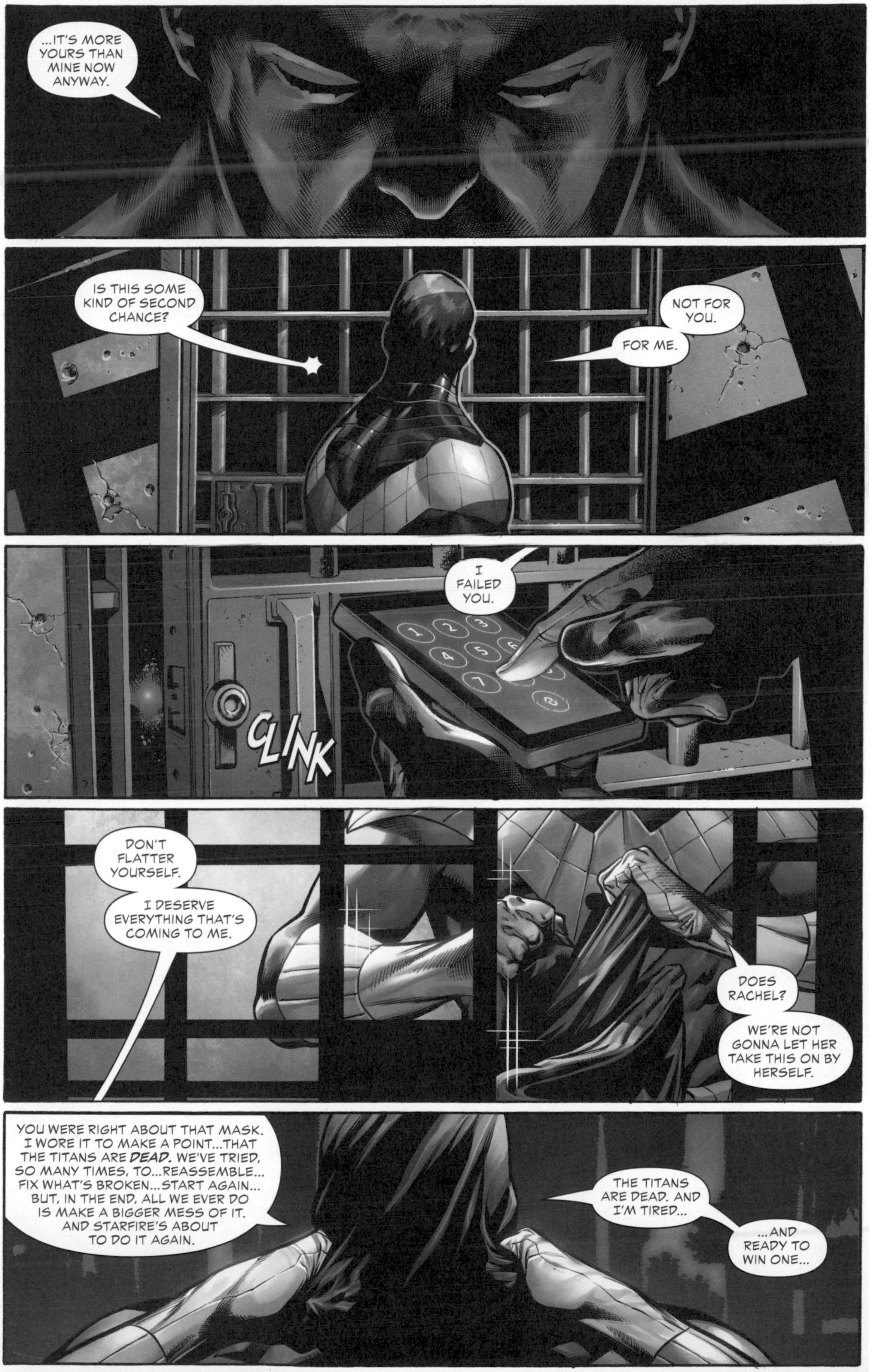
...IT'S MORE YOURS THAN MINE NOW ANYWAY.
IS THIS SOME KIND OF SECOND CHANCE?
NOT FOR YOU.
FOR ME.
I FAILED YOU.
CLINK
DON'T FLATTER YOURSELF.
I DESERVE EVERYTHING THAT'S COMING TO ME.
DOES RACHEL?
WE'RE NOT GONNA LET HER TAKE THIS ON BY HERSELF.
YOU WERE RIGHT ABOUT THAT MASK. I WORE IT TO MAKE A POINT...THAT THE TITANS ARE DEAD. WE'VE TRIED, SO MANY TIMES, TO...REASSEMBLE... FIX WHAT'S BROKEN...START AGAIN... BUT, IN THE END, ALL WE EVER DO IS MAKE A BIGGER MESS OF IT. AND STARFIRE'S ABOUT TO DO IT AGAIN.
THE TITANS ARE DEAD. AND I'M TIRED...
...AND READY TO WIN ONE...

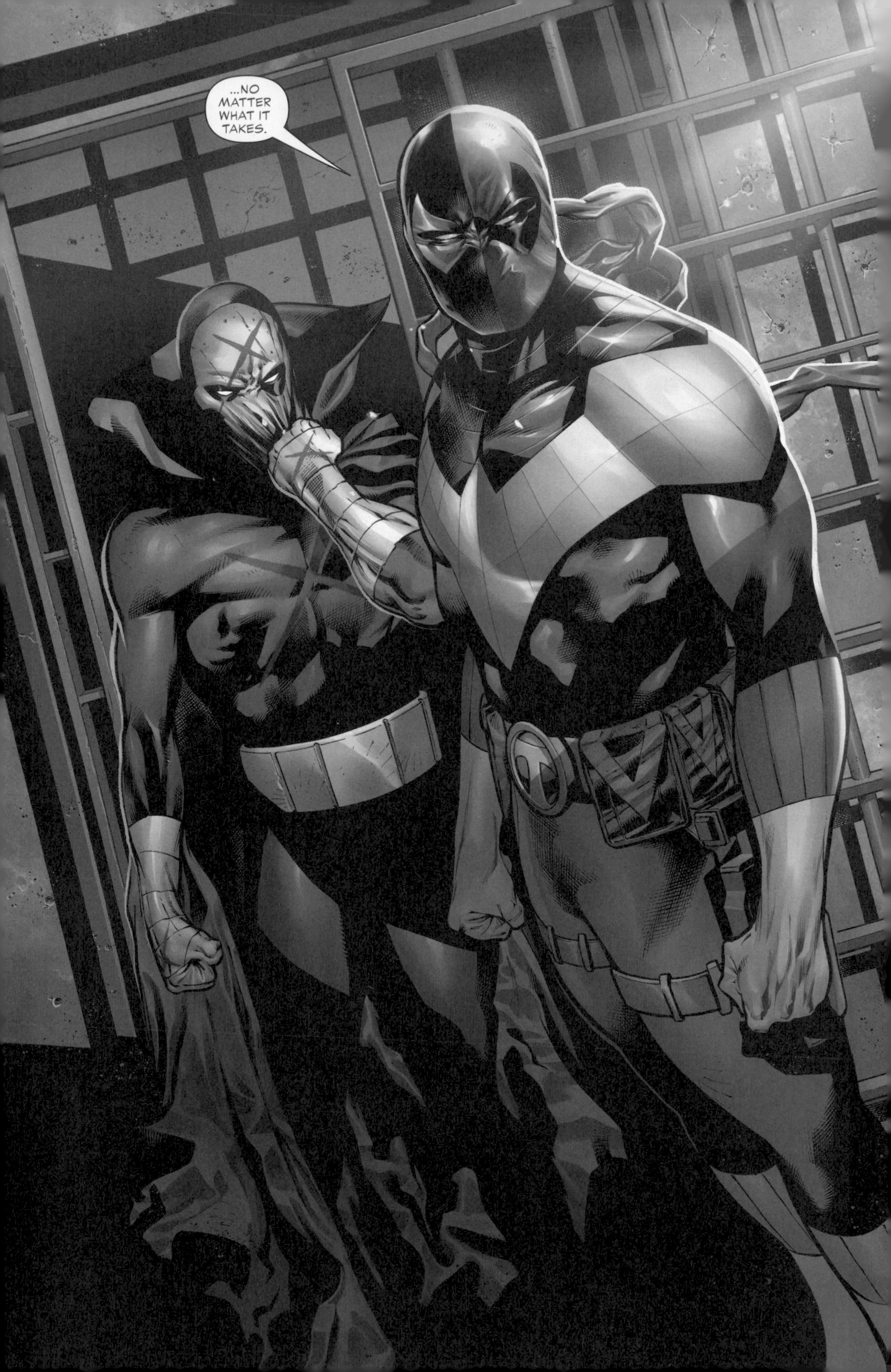
...NO MATTER WHAT IT TAKES.

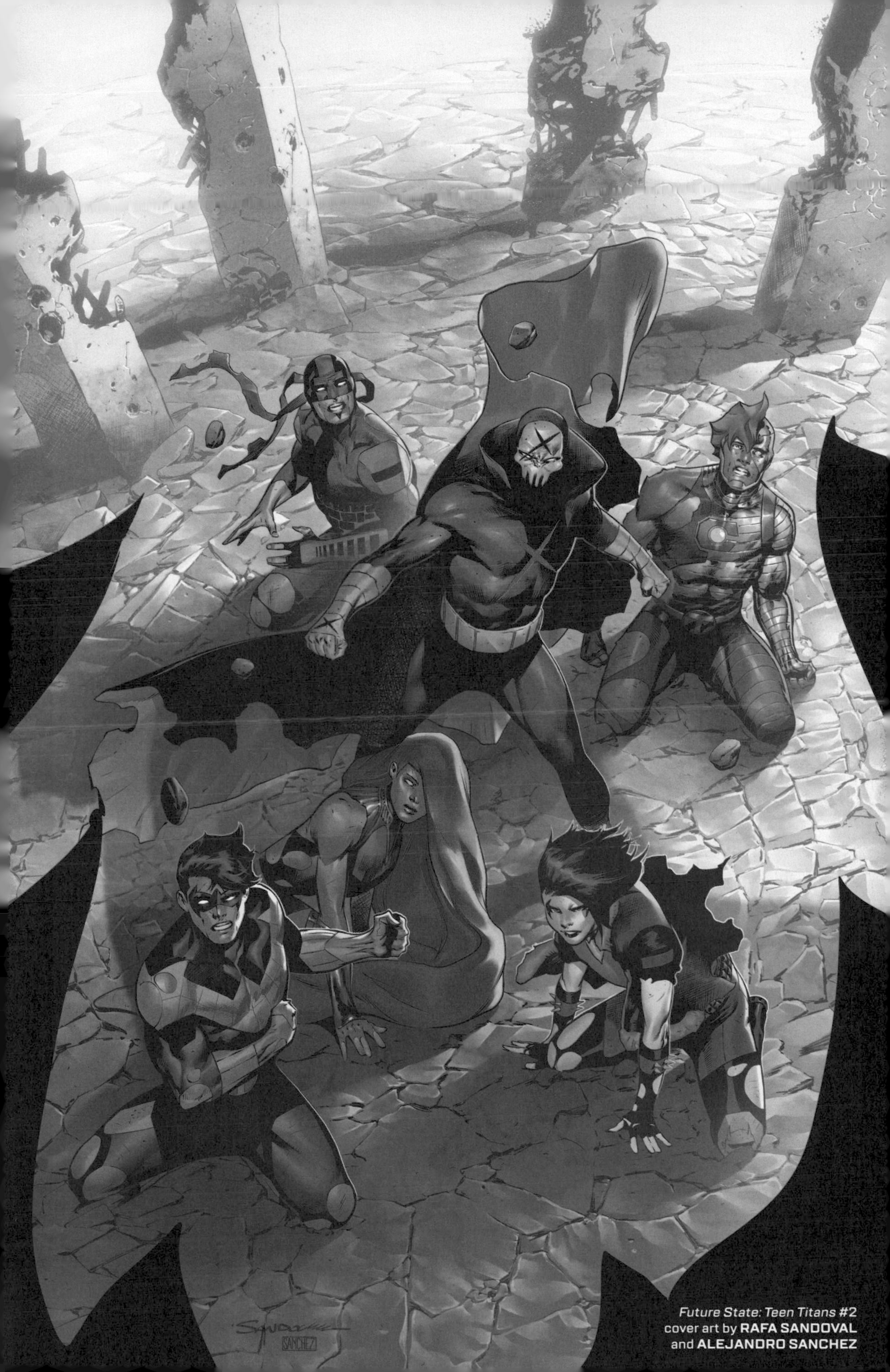

Future State: Teen Titans #2
cover art by **RAFA SANDOVAL**
and **ALEJANDRO SANCHEZ**

Future State: Teen Titans #2
variant cover art by **DUSTIN NGUYEN**

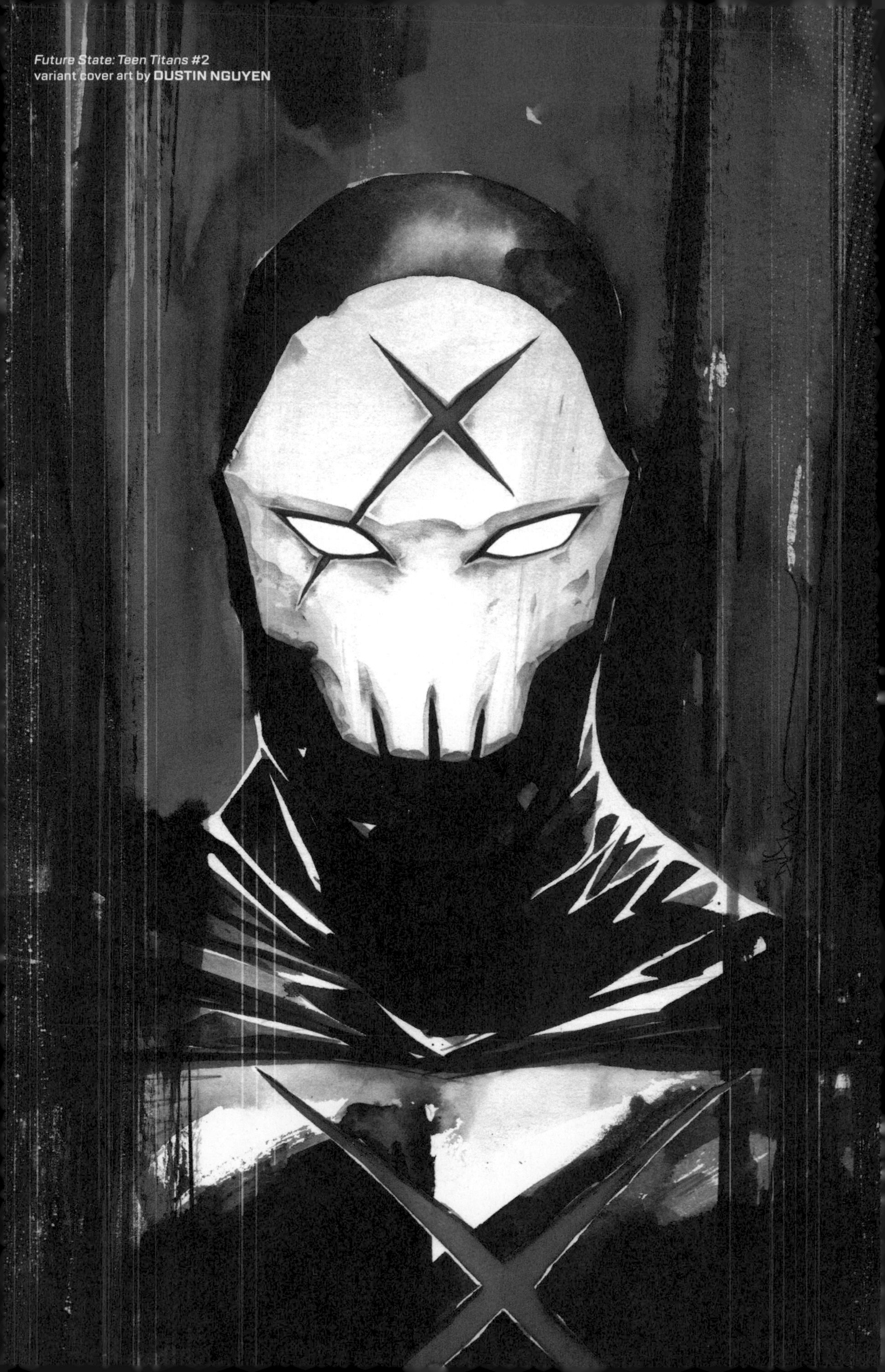

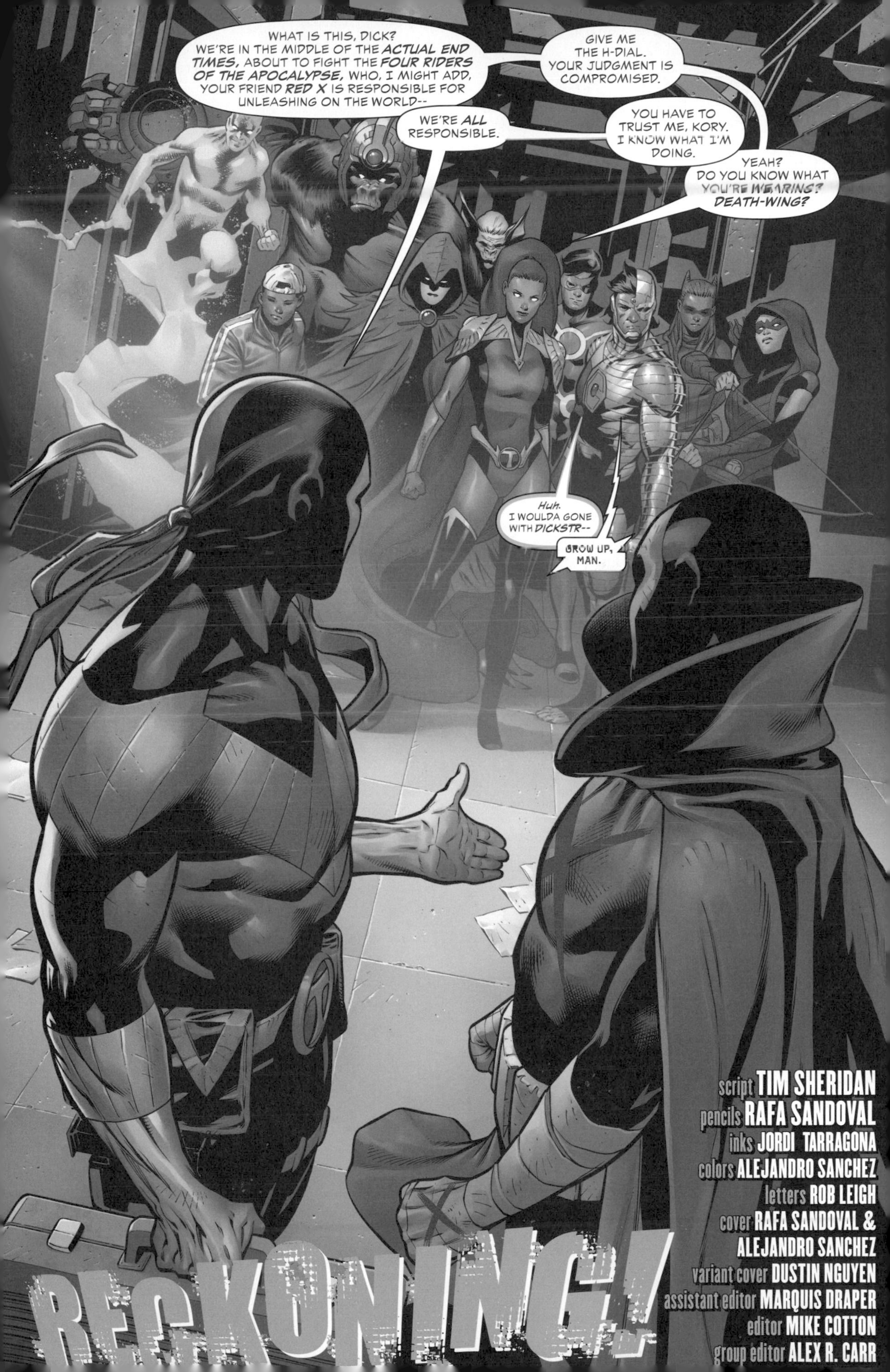
WHAT IS THIS, DICK? WE'RE IN THE MIDDLE OF THE ACTUAL END TIMES, ABOUT TO FIGHT THE FOUR RIDERS OF THE APOCALYPSE, WHO, I MIGHT ADD, YOUR FRIEND RED X IS RESPONSIBLE FOR UNLEASHING ON THE WORLD--
WE'RE ALL RESPONSIBLE.
GIVE ME THE H-DIAL. YOUR JUDGMENT IS COMPROMISED.
YOU HAVE TO TRUST ME, KORY. I KNOW WHAT I'M DOING.
YEAH? DO YOU KNOW WHAT YOU'RE WEARING? DEATH-WING?
Huh. I WOULDA GONE WITH DICKSTR--
GROW UP, MAN.
RECKONING!
script TIM SHERIDAN
pencils RAFA SANDOVAL
inks JORDI TARRAGONA
colors ALEJANDRO SANCHEZ
letters ROB LEIGH
cover RAFA SANDOVAL & ALEJANDRO SANCHEZ
variant cover DUSTIN NGUYEN
assistant editor MARQUIS DRAPER
editor MIKE COTTON
group editor ALEX R. CARR

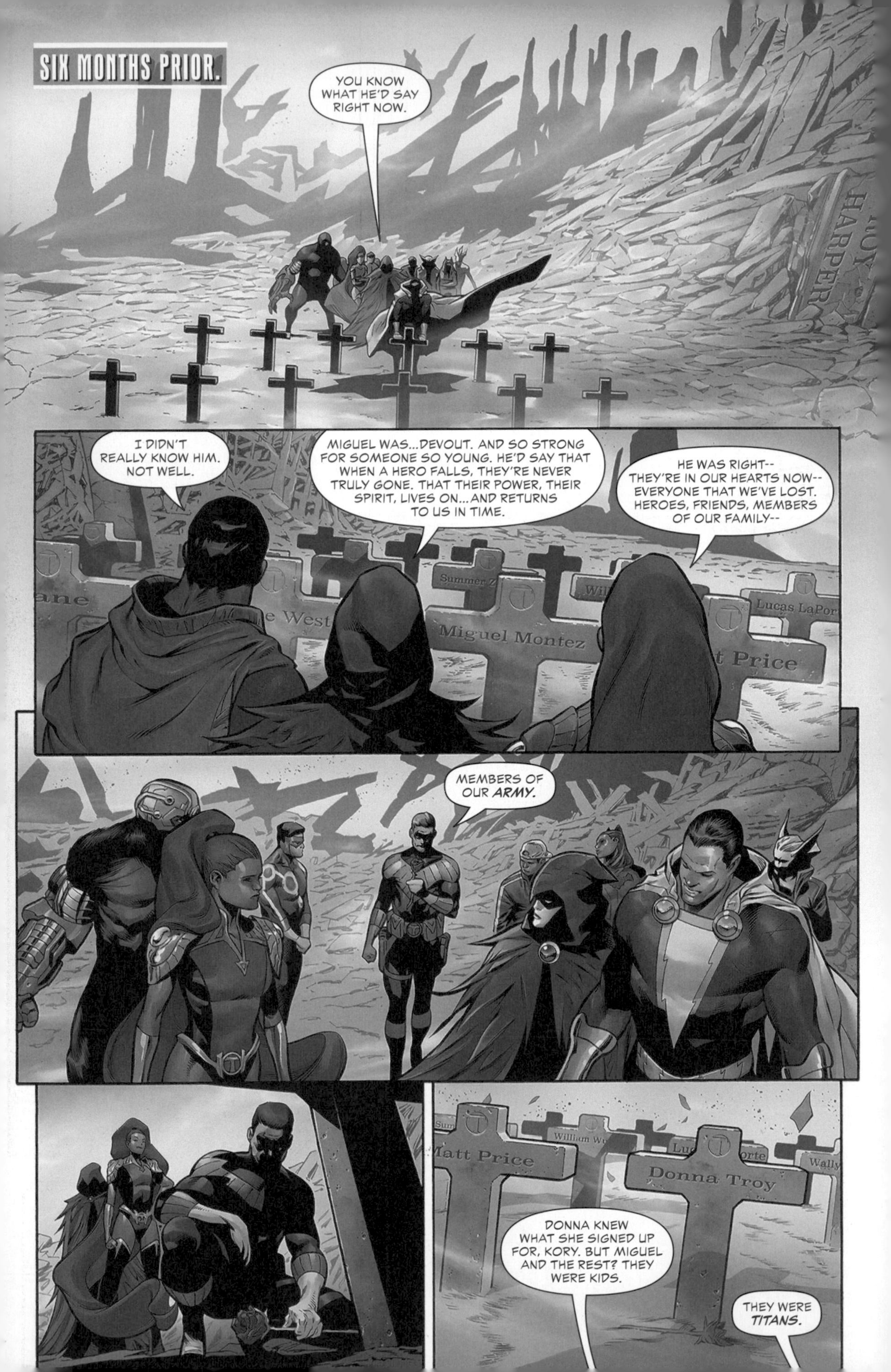
SIX MONTHS PRIOR.
YOU KNOW WHAT HE'D SAY RIGHT NOW.
I DIDN'T REALLY KNOW HIM. NOT WELL.
MIGUEL WAS...DEVOUT. AND SO STRONG FOR SOMEONE SO YOUNG. HE'D SAY THAT WHEN A HERO FALLS, THEY'RE NEVER TRULY GONE. THAT THEIR POWER, THEIR SPIRIT, LIVES ON...AND RETURNS TO US IN TIME.
HE WAS RIGHT-- THEY'RE IN OUR HEARTS NOW-- EVERYONE THAT WE'VE LOST. HEROES, FRIENDS, MEMBERS OF OUR FAMILY--
Miguel Montez
MEMBERS OF OUR *ARMY.*
Matt Price
Donna Troy
DONNA KNEW WHAT SHE SIGNED UP FOR, KORY. BUT MIGUEL AND THE REST? THEY WERE KIDS.
THEY WERE *TITANS.*

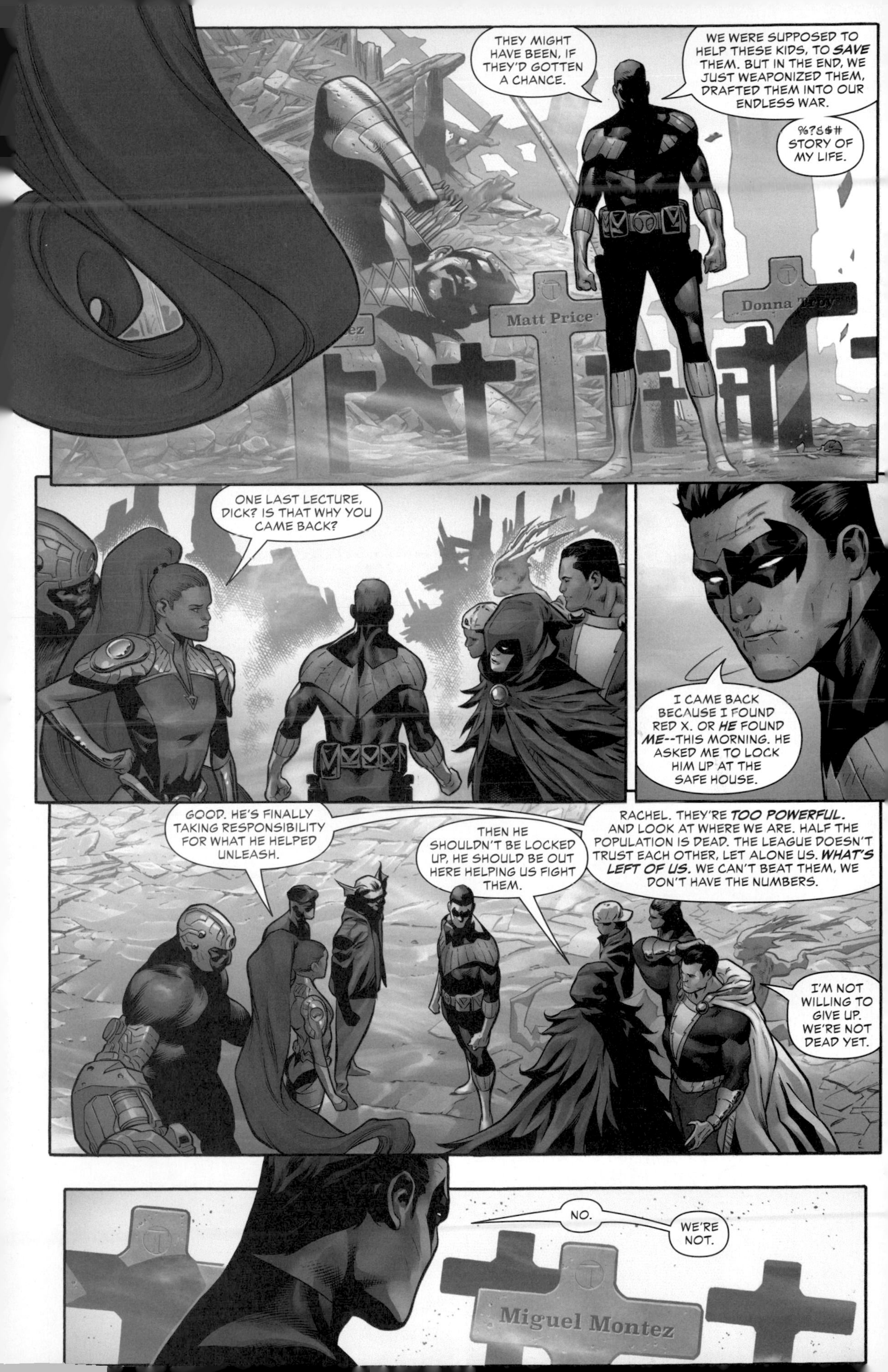
THEY MIGHT HAVE BEEN, IF THEY'D GOTTEN A CHANCE.
WE WERE SUPPOSED TO HELP THESE KIDS, TO *SAVE* THEM. BUT IN THE END, WE JUST WEAPONIZED THEM, DRAFTED THEM INTO OUR ENDLESS WAR.
%?$$# STORY OF MY LIFE.
Matt Price
Donna Troy
ONE LAST LECTURE, DICK? IS THAT WHY YOU CAME BACK?
I CAME BACK BECAUSE I FOUND RED X. OR *HE* FOUND *ME*--THIS MORNING. HE ASKED ME TO LOCK HIM UP AT THE SAFE HOUSE.
GOOD. HE'S FINALLY TAKING RESPONSIBILITY FOR WHAT HE HELPED UNLEASH.
THEN HE SHOULDN'T BE LOCKED UP, HE SHOULD BE OUT HERE HELPING US FIGHT THEM.
RACHEL. THEY'RE *TOO POWERFUL.* AND LOOK AT WHERE WE ARE. HALF THE POPULATION IS DEAD. THE LEAGUE DOESN'T TRUST EACH OTHER, LET ALONE US. *WHAT'S LEFT OF US.* WE CAN'T BEAT THEM, WE DON'T HAVE THE NUMBERS.
I'M NOT WILLING TO GIVE UP. WE'RE NOT DEAD YET.
NO.
WE'RE NOT.
Miguel Montez

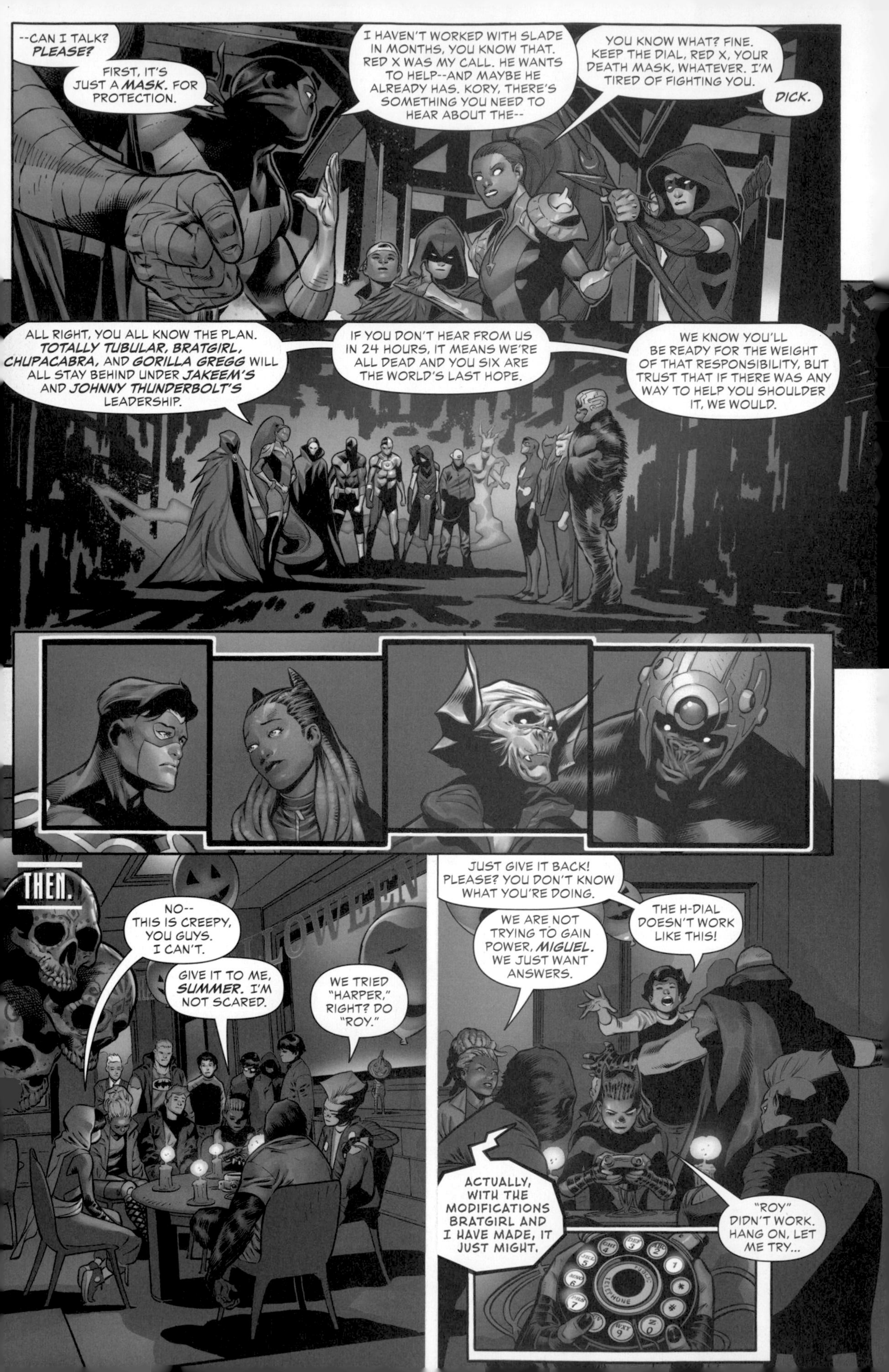
--CAN I TALK? PLEASE?
FIRST, IT'S JUST A MASK. FOR PROTECTION.
I HAVEN'T WORKED WITH SLADE IN MONTHS, YOU KNOW THAT. RED X WAS MY CALL. HE WANTS TO HELP--AND MAYBE HE ALREADY HAS. KORY, THERE'S SOMETHING YOU NEED TO HEAR ABOUT THE--
YOU KNOW WHAT? FINE. KEEP THE DIAL, RED X, YOUR DEATH MASK, WHATEVER. I'M TIRED OF FIGHTING YOU.
DICK.
ALL RIGHT, YOU ALL KNOW THE PLAN. TOTALLY TUBULAR, BRATGIRL, CHUPACABRA, AND GORILLA GREGG WILL ALL STAY BEHIND UNDER JAKEEM'S AND JOHNNY THUNDERBOLT'S LEADERSHIP.
IF YOU DON'T HEAR FROM US IN 24 HOURS, IT MEANS WE'RE ALL DEAD AND YOU SIX ARE THE WORLD'S LAST HOPE.
WE KNOW YOU'LL BE READY FOR THE WEIGHT OF THAT RESPONSIBILITY, BUT TRUST THAT IF THERE WAS ANY WAY TO HELP YOU SHOULDER IT, WE WOULD.
THEN.
NO-- THIS IS CREEPY, YOU GUYS. I CAN'T.
GIVE IT TO ME, SUMMER. I'M NOT SCARED.
WE TRIED "HARPER," RIGHT? DO "ROY."
JUST GIVE IT BACK! PLEASE? YOU DON'T KNOW WHAT YOU'RE DOING.
THE H-DIAL DOESN'T WORK LIKE THIS!
WE ARE NOT TRYING TO GAIN POWER, MIGUEL. WE JUST WANT ANSWERS.
ACTUALLY, WITH THE MODIFICATIONS BRATGIRL AND I HAVE MADE, IT JUST MIGHT.
"ROY" DIDN'T WORK. HANG ON, LET ME TRY...

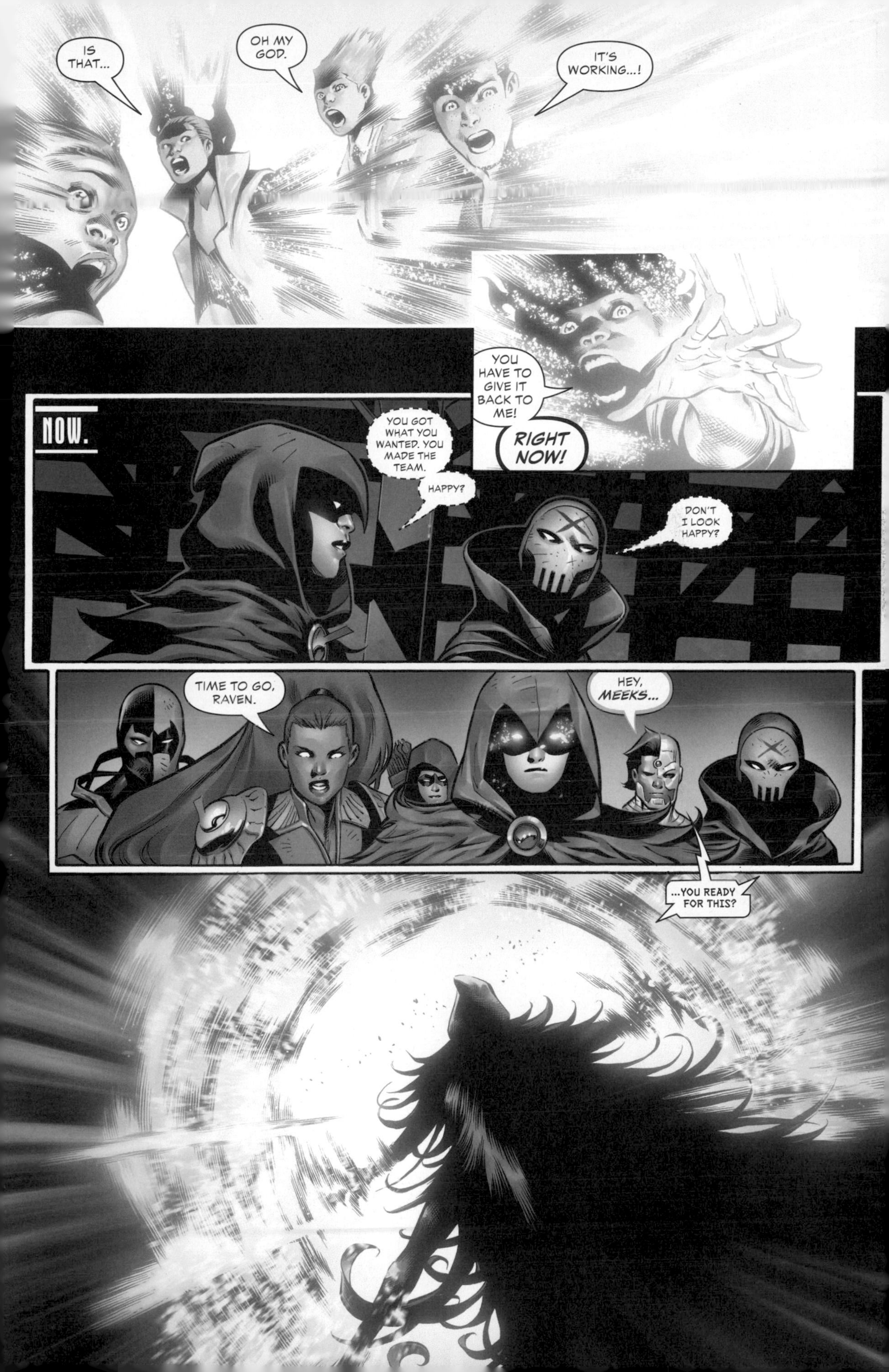
IS THAT...
OH MY GOD.
IT'S WORKING...!
YOU HAVE TO GIVE IT BACK TO ME!
RIGHT NOW!
NOW.
YOU GOT WHAT YOU WANTED. YOU MADE THE TEAM.
HAPPY?
DON'T I LOOK HAPPY?
TIME TO GO, RAVEN.
HEY, MEEKS...
...YOU READY FOR THIS?

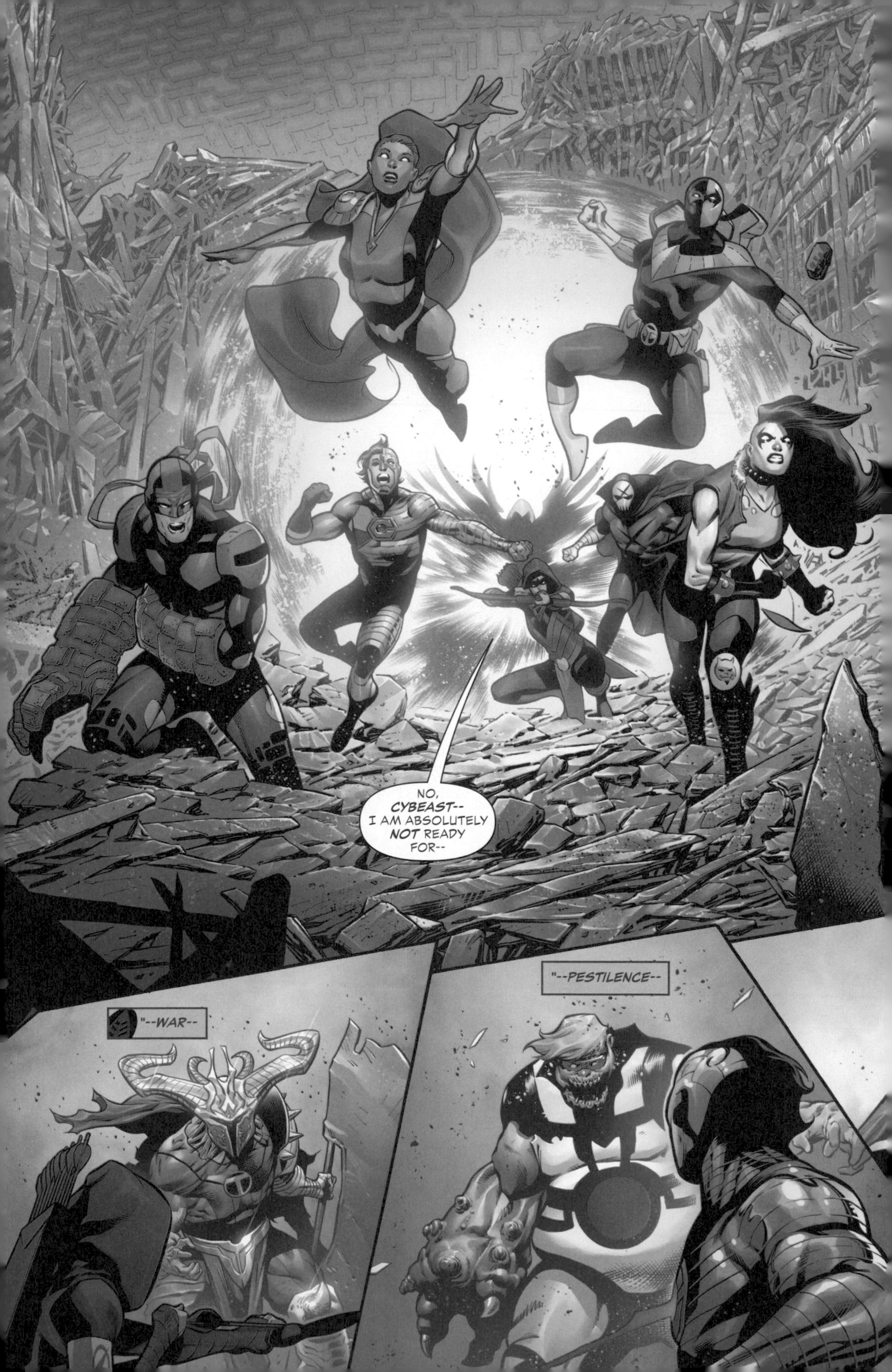
NO, CYBEAST-- I AM ABSOLUTELY NOT READY FOR--
"--WAR--
"--PESTILENCE--

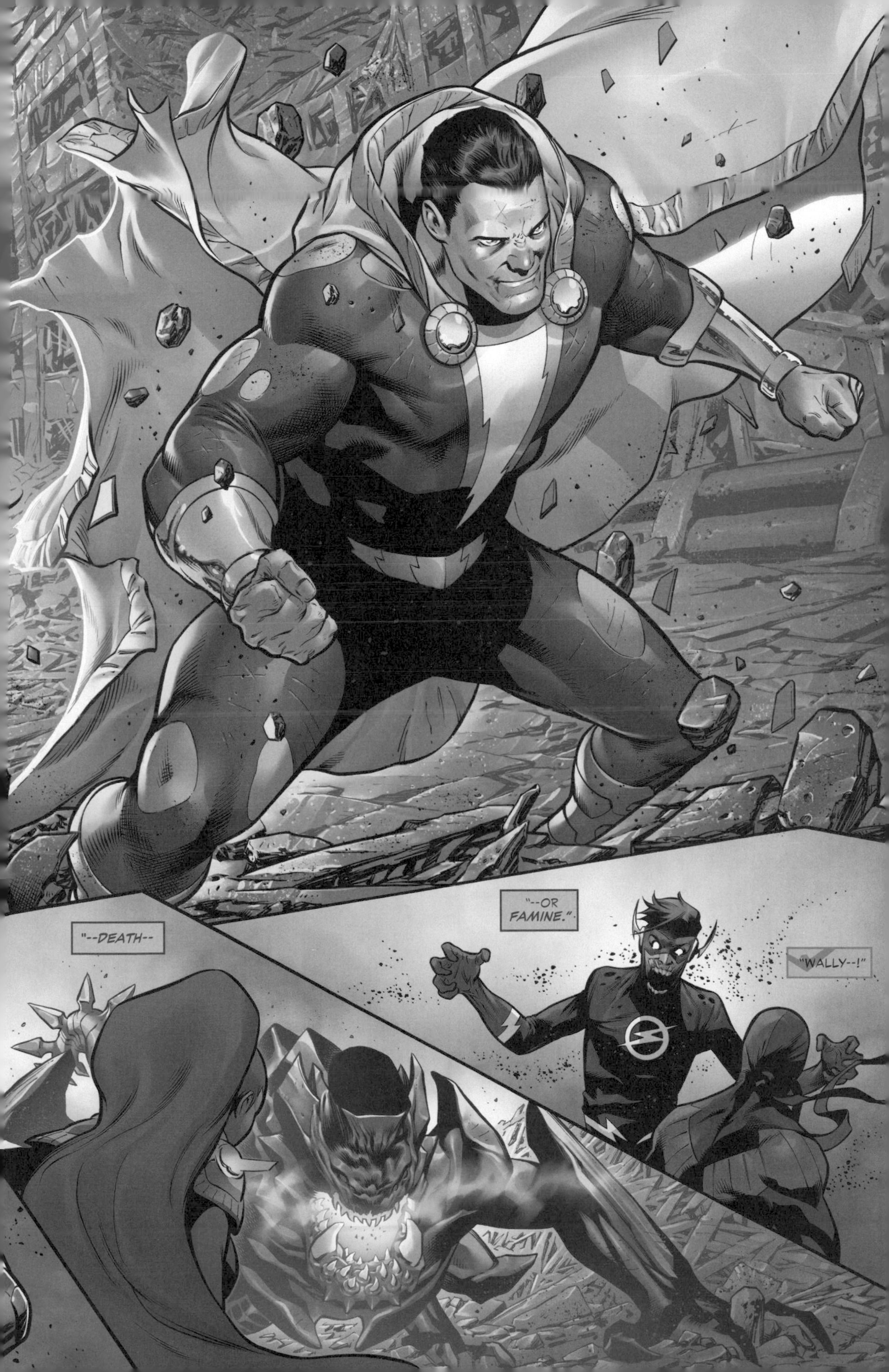
"--DEATH--
"--OR FAMINE."
"WALLY--!"

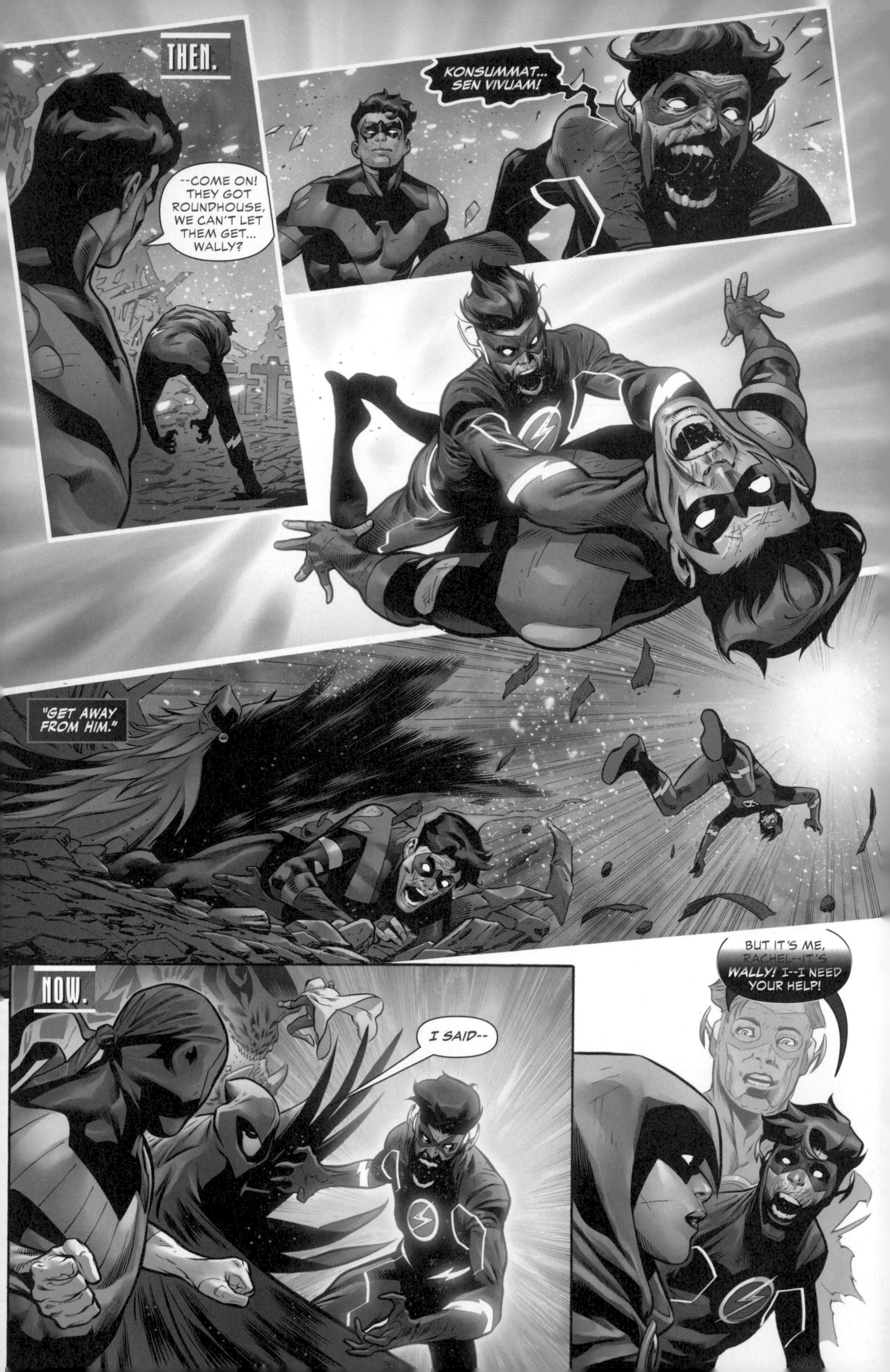
THEN.
--COME ON! THEY GOT ROUNDHOUSE, WE CAN'T LET THEM GET... WALLY?
KONSUMMAT... SEN VIVUAM!
"GET AWAY FROM HIM."
NOW.
I SAID--
BUT IT'S ME, RACHEL--IT'S WALLY! I--I NEED YOUR HELP!

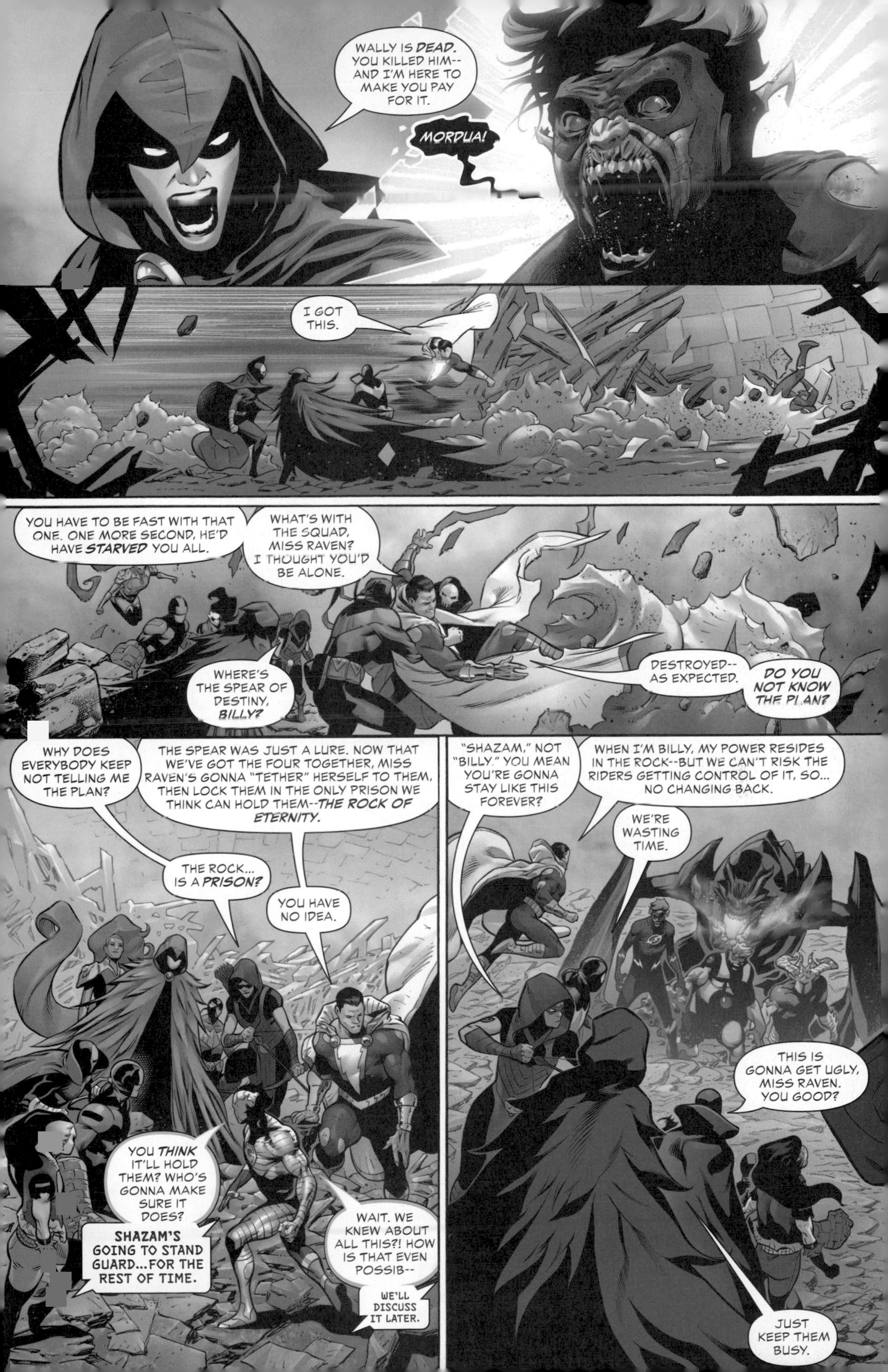
WALLY IS *DEAD.* YOU KILLED HIM-- AND I'M HERE TO MAKE YOU PAY FOR IT.
MORDUA!
I GOT THIS.
YOU HAVE TO BE FAST WITH THAT ONE. ONE MORE SECOND, HE'D HAVE *STARVED* YOU ALL.
WHAT'S WITH THE SQUAD, MISS RAVEN? I THOUGHT YOU'D BE ALONE.
WHERE'S THE SPEAR OF DESTINY, *BILLY?*
DESTROYED-- AS EXPECTED.
DO YOU NOT KNOW THE PLAN?
WHY DOES EVERYBODY KEEP NOT TELLING ME THE PLAN?
THE SPEAR WAS JUST A LURE. NOW THAT WE'VE GOT THE FOUR TOGETHER, MISS RAVEN'S GONNA "TETHER" HERSELF TO THEM, THEN LOCK THEM IN THE ONLY PRISON WE THINK CAN HOLD THEM--*THE ROCK OF ETERNITY.*
THE ROCK... IS A *PRISON?*
YOU HAVE NO IDEA.
YOU *THINK* IT'LL HOLD THEM? WHO'S GONNA MAKE SURE IT DOES?
SHAZAM'S GOING TO STAND GUARD...FOR THE REST OF TIME.
WAIT. WE KNEW ABOUT ALL THIS?! HOW IS THAT EVEN POSSIB--
WE'LL DISCUSS IT LATER.
"SHAZAM," NOT "BILLY." YOU MEAN YOU'RE GONNA STAY LIKE THIS FOREVER?
WHEN I'M BILLY, MY POWER RESIDES IN THE ROCK--BUT WE CAN'T RISK THE RIDERS GETTING CONTROL OF IT, SO... NO CHANGING BACK.
WE'RE WASTING TIME.
THIS IS GONNA GET UGLY, MISS RAVEN. YOU GOOD?
JUST KEEP THEM BUSY.

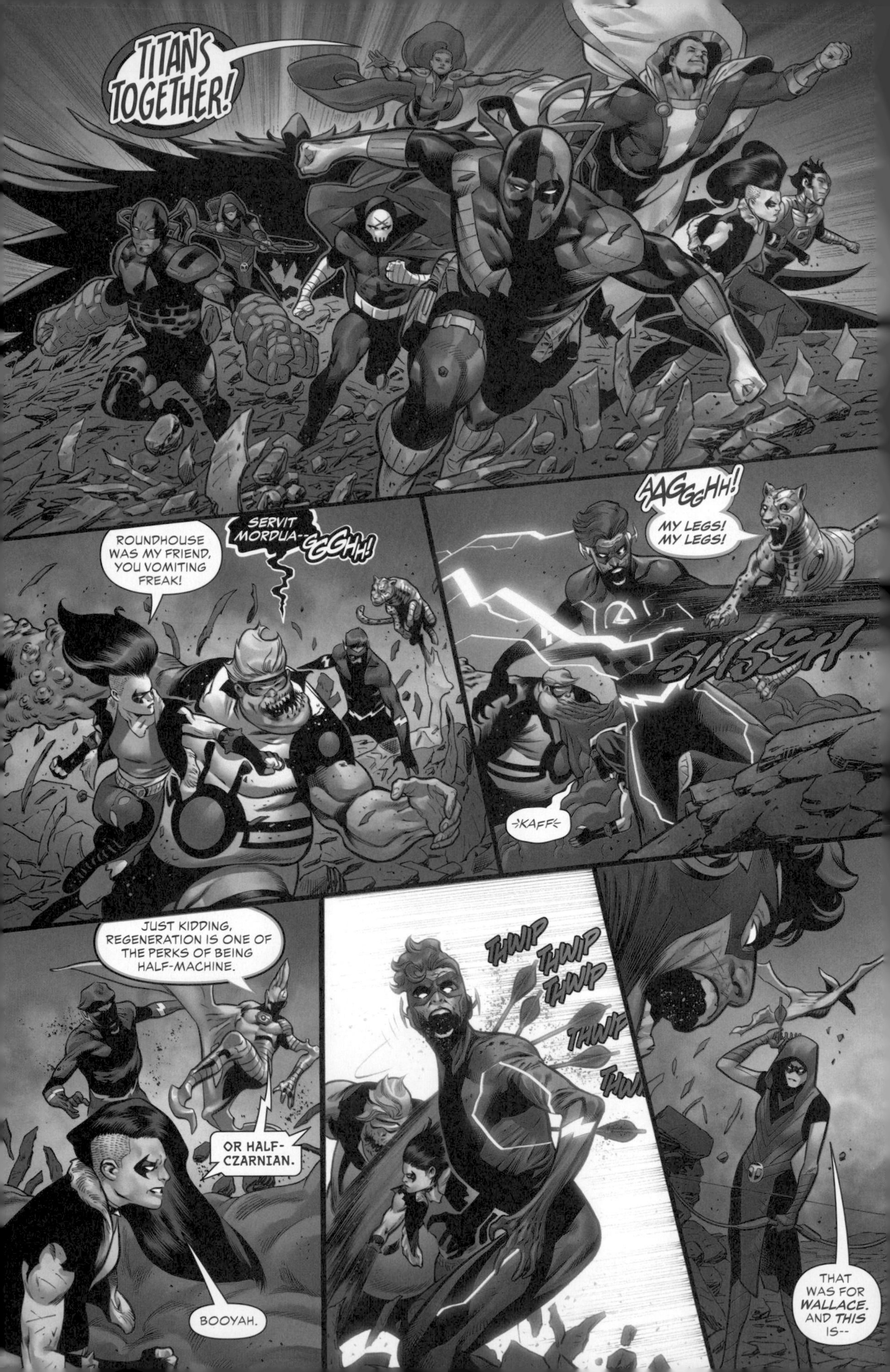
TITANS TOGETHER!
ROUNDHOUSE WAS MY FRIEND, YOU VOMITING FREAK!
SERVIT MORDUA--GGHH!
AAGGGHH!
MY LEGS! MY LEGS!
SLISSH
-KAFF-
JUST KIDDING, REGENERATION IS ONE OF THE PERKS OF BEING HALF-MACHINE.
OR HALF-CZARNIAN.
BOOYAH.
THWIP THWIP THWIP THWIP THWIP
THAT WAS FOR WALLACE. AND THIS IS--

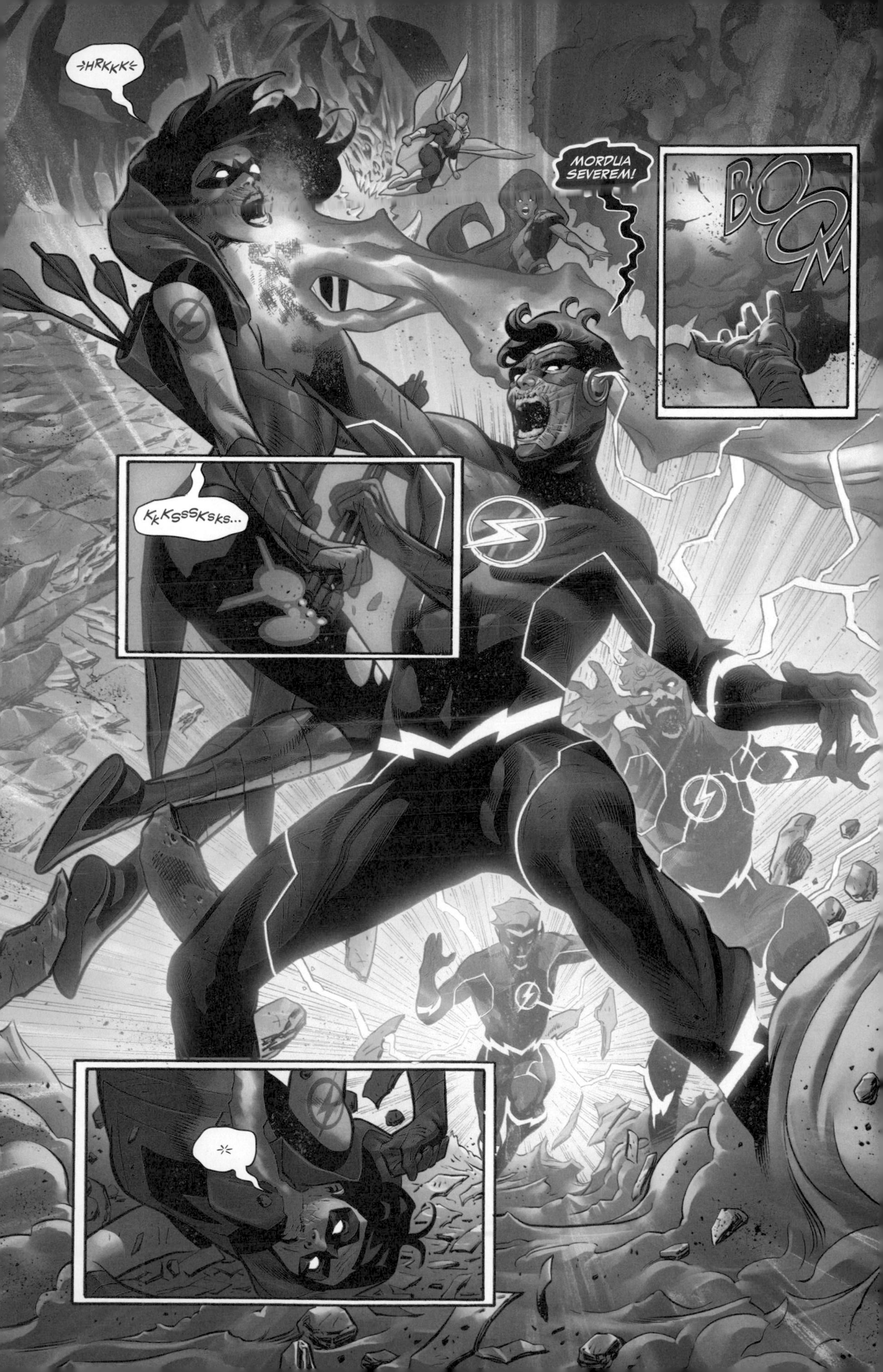

HRKKK
MORDUA SEVEREM!
BOOM
KKKSSSKSKS...

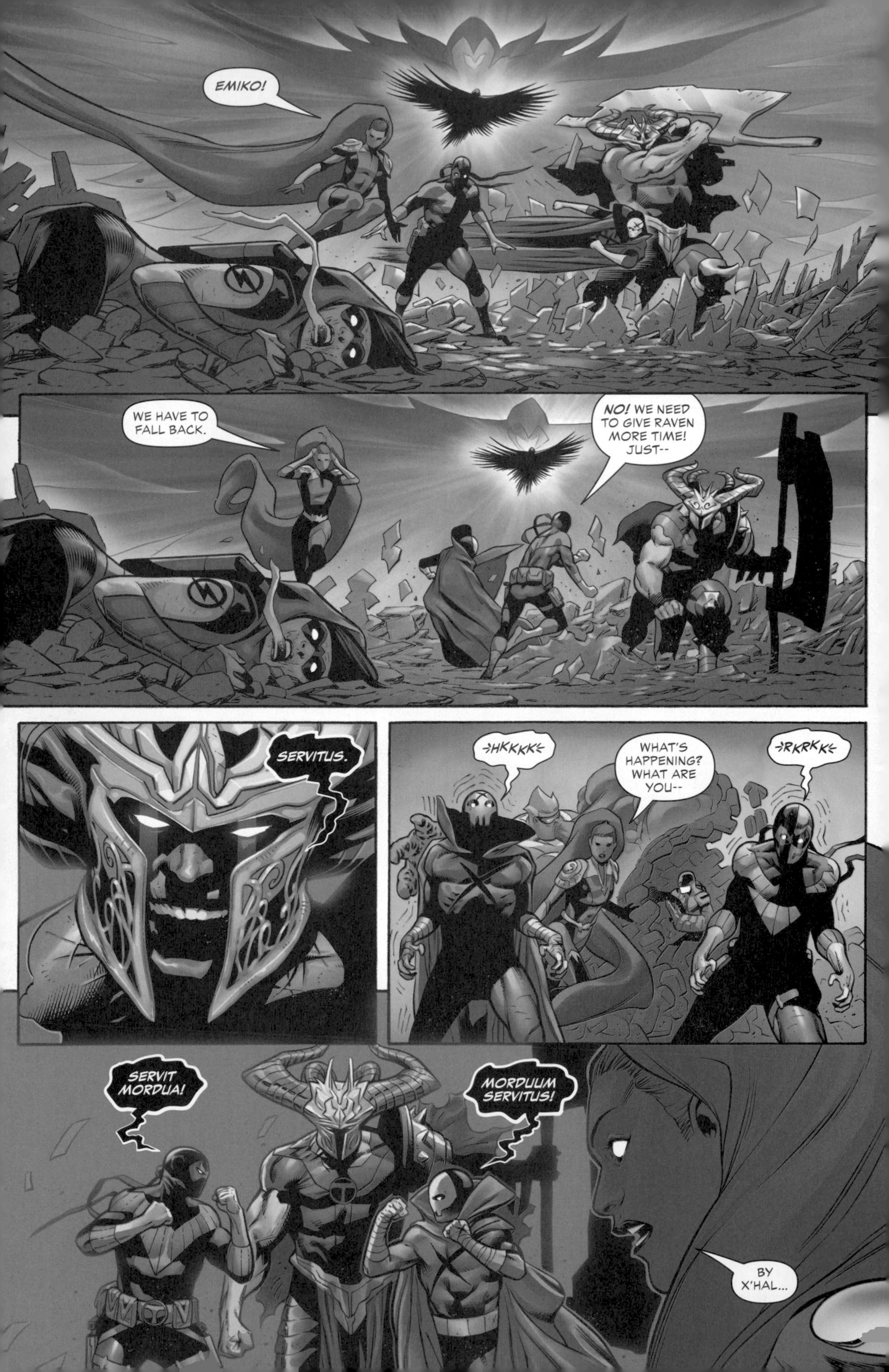
EMIKO!
WE HAVE TO FALL BACK.
NO! WE NEED TO GIVE RAVEN MORE TIME! JUST--
SERVITUS.
HKKKK
WHAT'S HAPPENING? WHAT ARE YOU--
RKRKK
SERVIT MORDUA!
MORDUUM SERVITUS!
BY X'HAL...

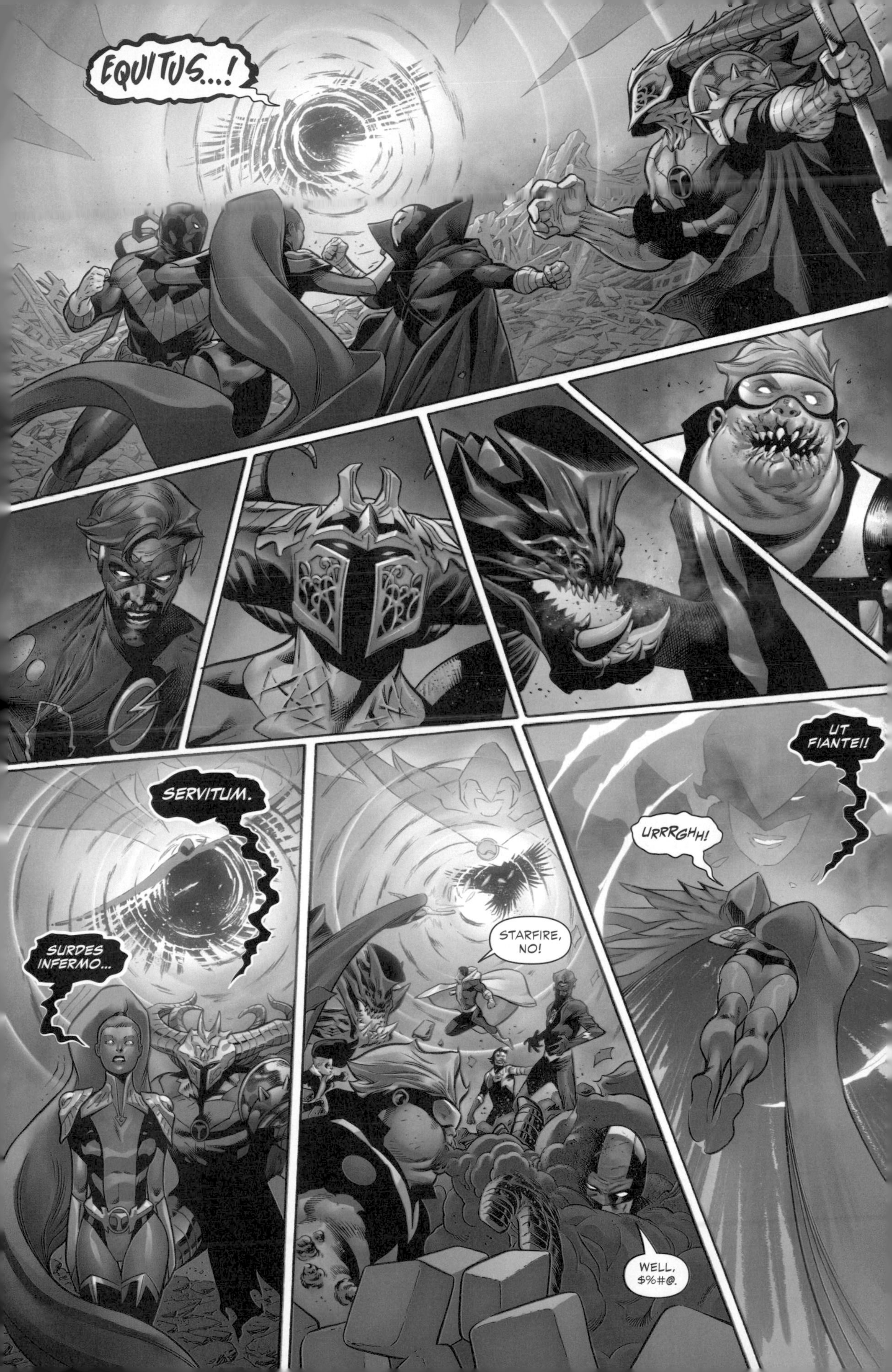
EQUITUS...!
SERVITUM.
SURDES INFERMO...
STARFIRE, NO!
WELL, $%#@.
UT FIANTE!!
URRRGHH!

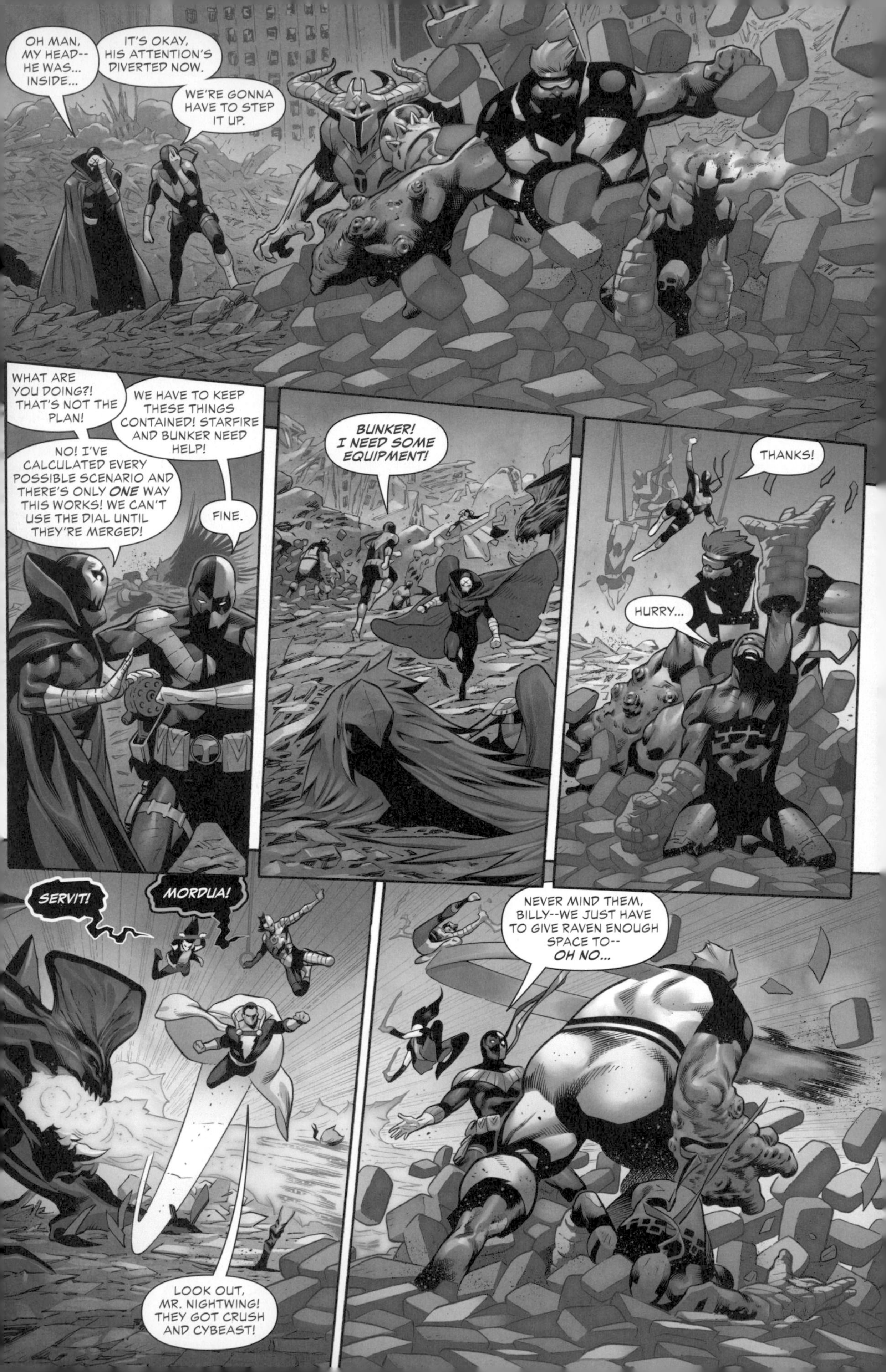
OH MAN, MY HEAD-- HE WAS... INSIDE...
IT'S OKAY, HIS ATTENTION'S DIVERTED NOW.
WE'RE GONNA HAVE TO STEP IT UP.
WHAT ARE YOU DOING?! THAT'S NOT THE PLAN!
WE HAVE TO KEEP THESE THINGS CONTAINED! STARFIRE AND BUNKER NEED HELP!
NO! I'VE CALCULATED EVERY POSSIBLE SCENARIO AND THERE'S ONLY ONE WAY THIS WORKS! WE CAN'T USE THE DIAL UNTIL THEY'RE MERGED!
FINE.
BUNKER! I NEED SOME EQUIPMENT!
THANKS!
HURRY...
SERVIT!
MORDUA!
NEVER MIND THEM, BILLY--WE JUST HAVE TO GIVE RAVEN ENOUGH SPACE TO-- OH NO...
LOOK OUT, MR. NIGHTWING! THEY GOT CRUSH AND CYBEAST!

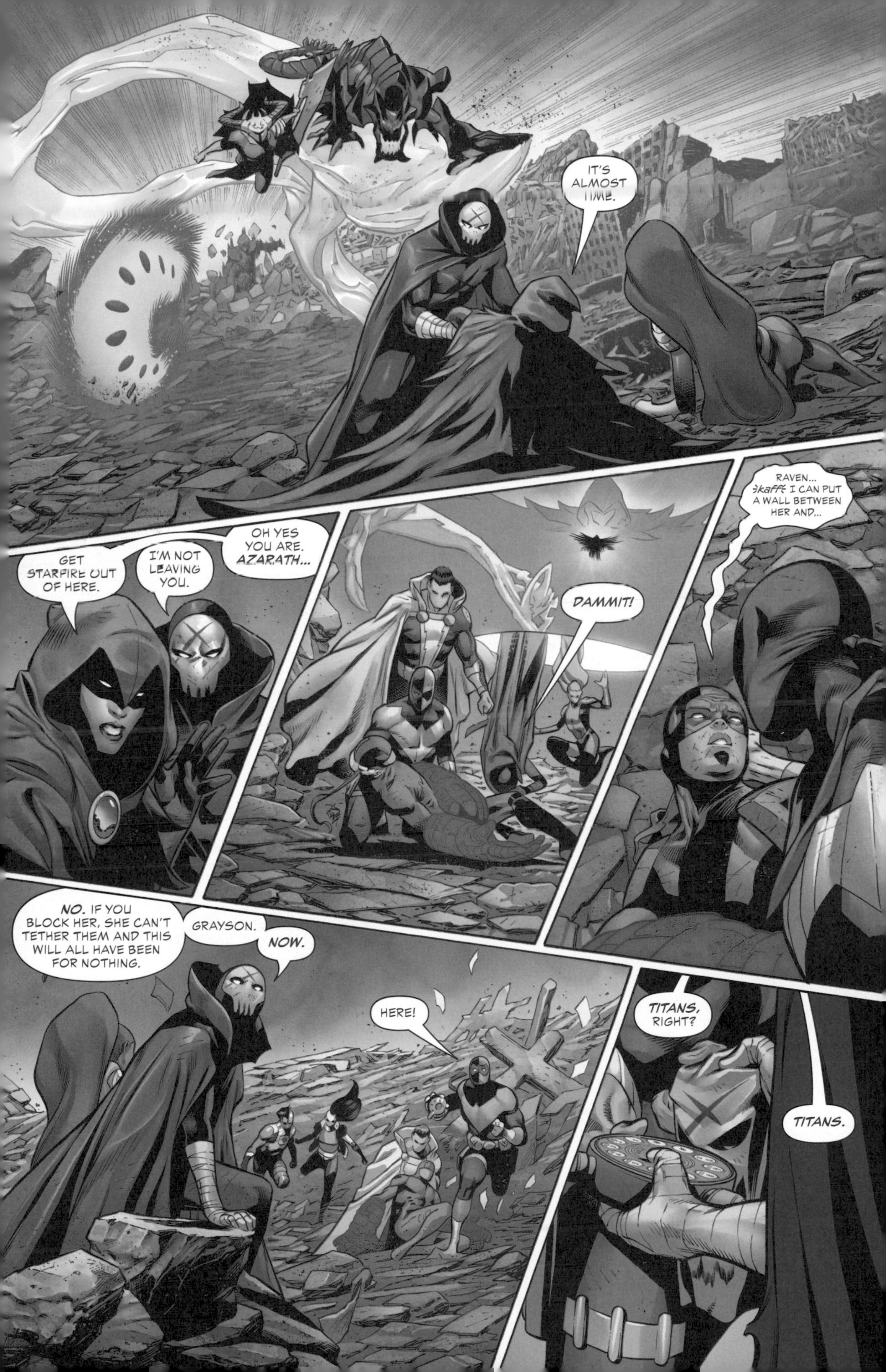
IT'S ALMOST TIME.
GET STARFIRE OUT OF HERE.
I'M NOT LEAVING YOU.
OH YES YOU ARE. AZARATH...
DAMMIT!
RAVEN... *kaff* I CAN PUT A WALL BETWEEN HER AND...
NO. IF YOU BLOCK HER, SHE CAN'T TETHER THEM AND THIS WILL ALL HAVE BEEN FOR NOTHING.
GRAYSON.
NOW.
HERE!
TITANS, RIGHT?
TITANS.

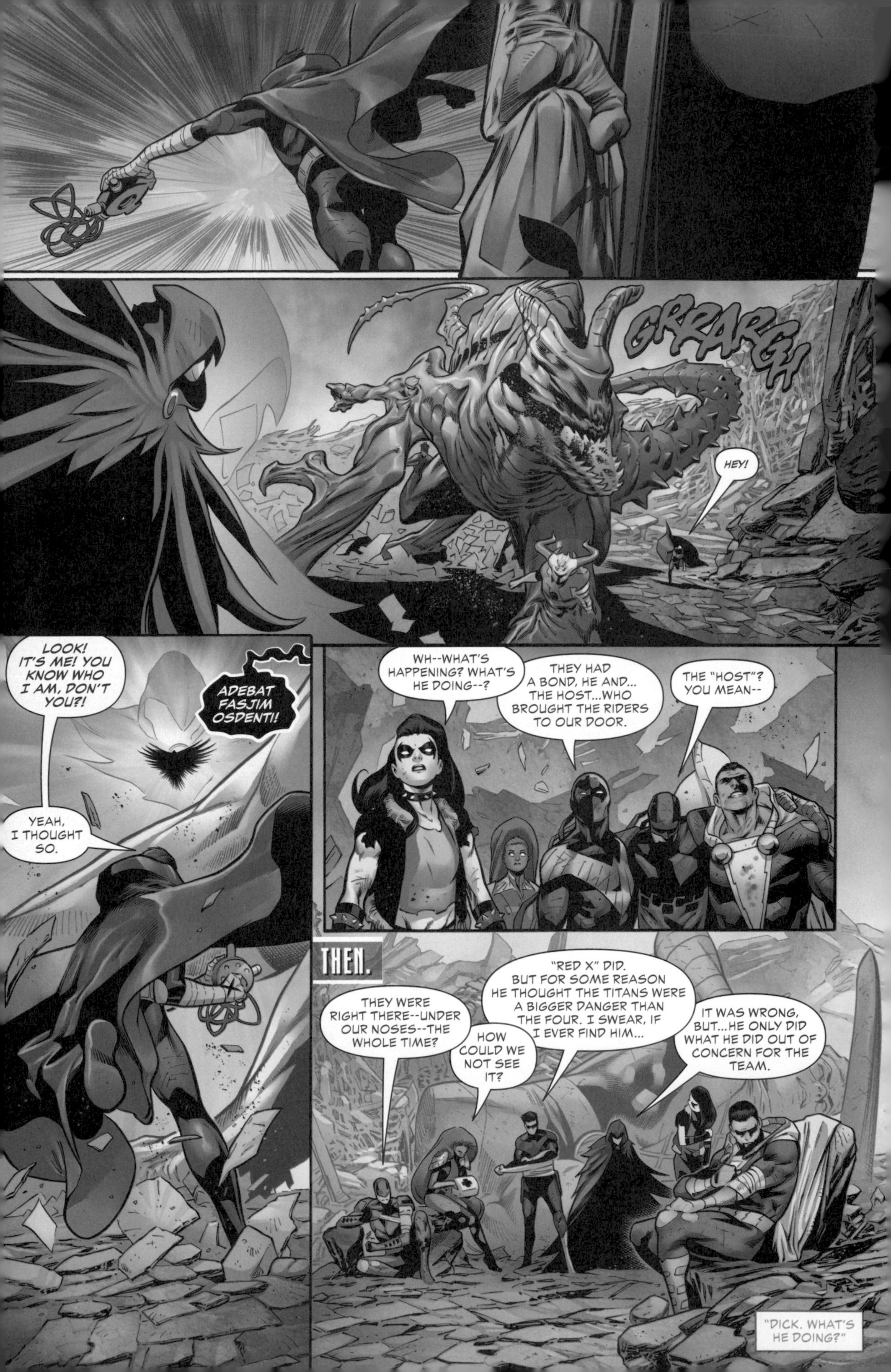
GRRARGH
HEY!
LOOK! IT'S ME! YOU KNOW WHO I AM, DON'T YOU?!
ADEBAT FASJIM OSDENTI!
YEAH, I THOUGHT SO.
WH--WHAT'S HAPPENING? WHAT'S HE DOING--?
THEY HAD A BOND, HE AND... THE HOST...WHO BROUGHT THE RIDERS TO OUR DOOR.
THE "HOST"? YOU MEAN--
THEN.
THEY WERE RIGHT THERE--UNDER OUR NOSES--THE WHOLE TIME?
HOW COULD WE NOT SEE IT?
"RED X" DID. BUT FOR SOME REASON HE THOUGHT THE TITANS WERE A BIGGER DANGER THAN THE FOUR. I SWEAR, IF I EVER FIND HIM...
IT WAS WRONG, BUT...HE ONLY DID WHAT HE DID OUT OF CONCERN FOR THE TEAM.
"DICK. WHAT'S HE DOING?"

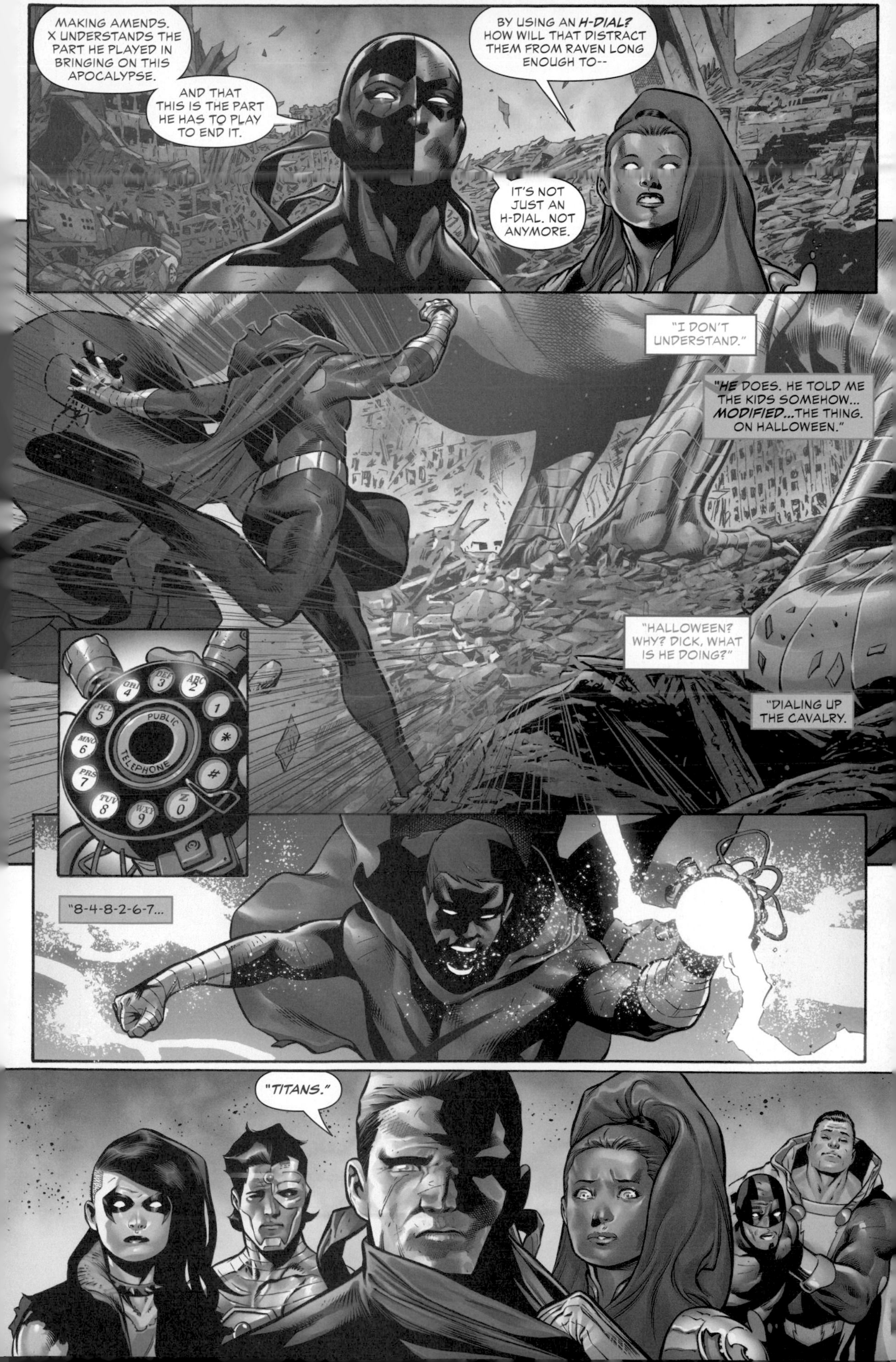
MAKING AMENDS. X UNDERSTANDS THE PART HE PLAYED IN BRINGING ON THIS APOCALYPSE.
AND THAT THIS IS THE PART HE HAS TO PLAY TO END IT.
BY USING AN *H-DIAL?* HOW WILL THAT DISTRACT THEM FROM RAVEN LONG ENOUGH TO--
IT'S NOT JUST AN H-DIAL. NOT ANYMORE.
"I DON'T UNDERSTAND."
"*HE* DOES. HE TOLD ME THE KIDS SOMEHOW... *MODIFIED...* THE THING. ON HALLOWEEN."
"HALLOWEEN? WHY? DICK, WHAT IS HE DOING?"
"DIALING UP THE CAVALRY.
PUBLIC TELEPHONE
"8-4-8-2-6-7...
"*TITANS.*"

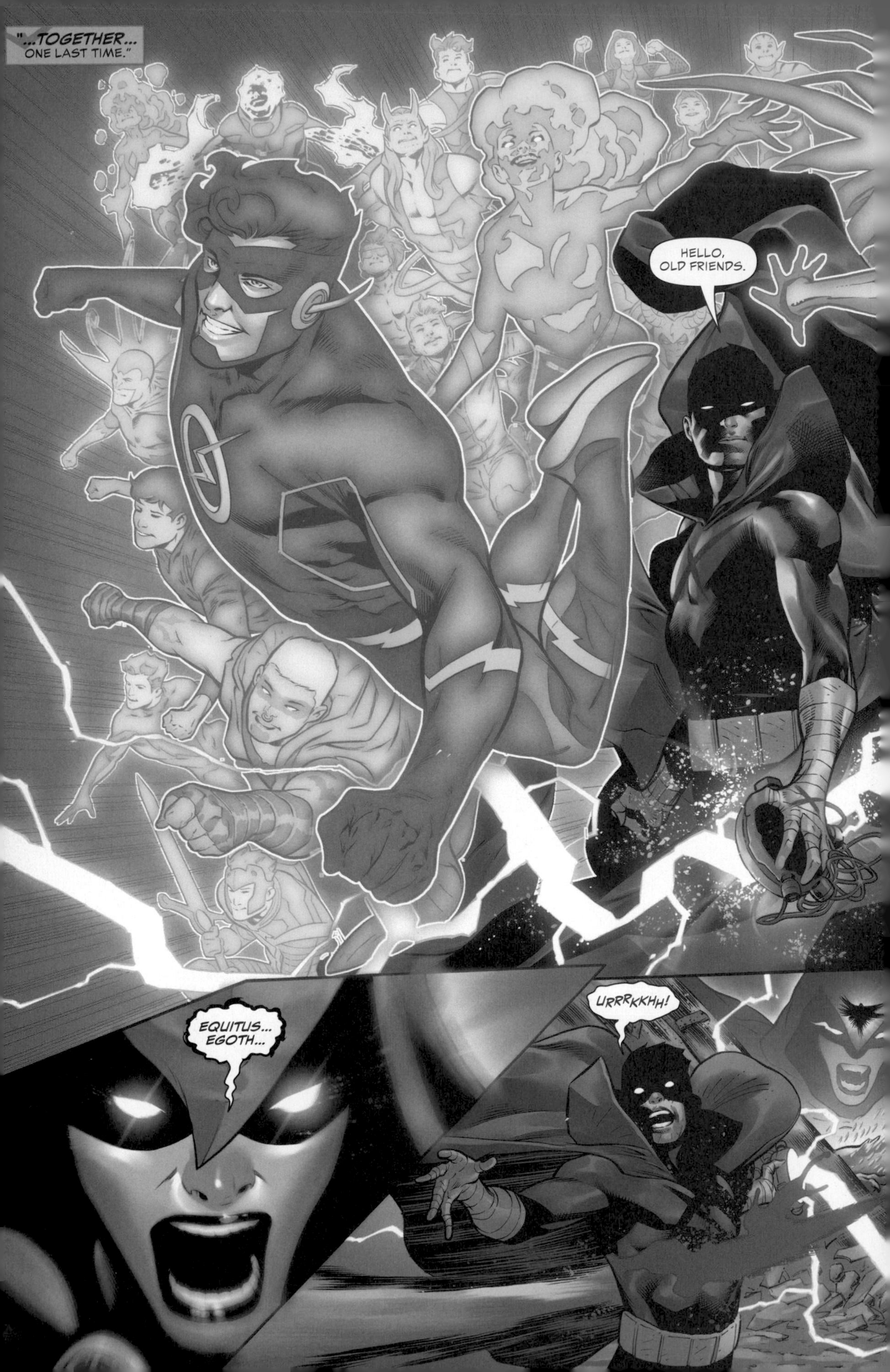
"...TOGETHER...
ONE LAST TIME."
HELLO, OLD FRIENDS.
EQUITUS... EGOTH...
URRRKKHH!

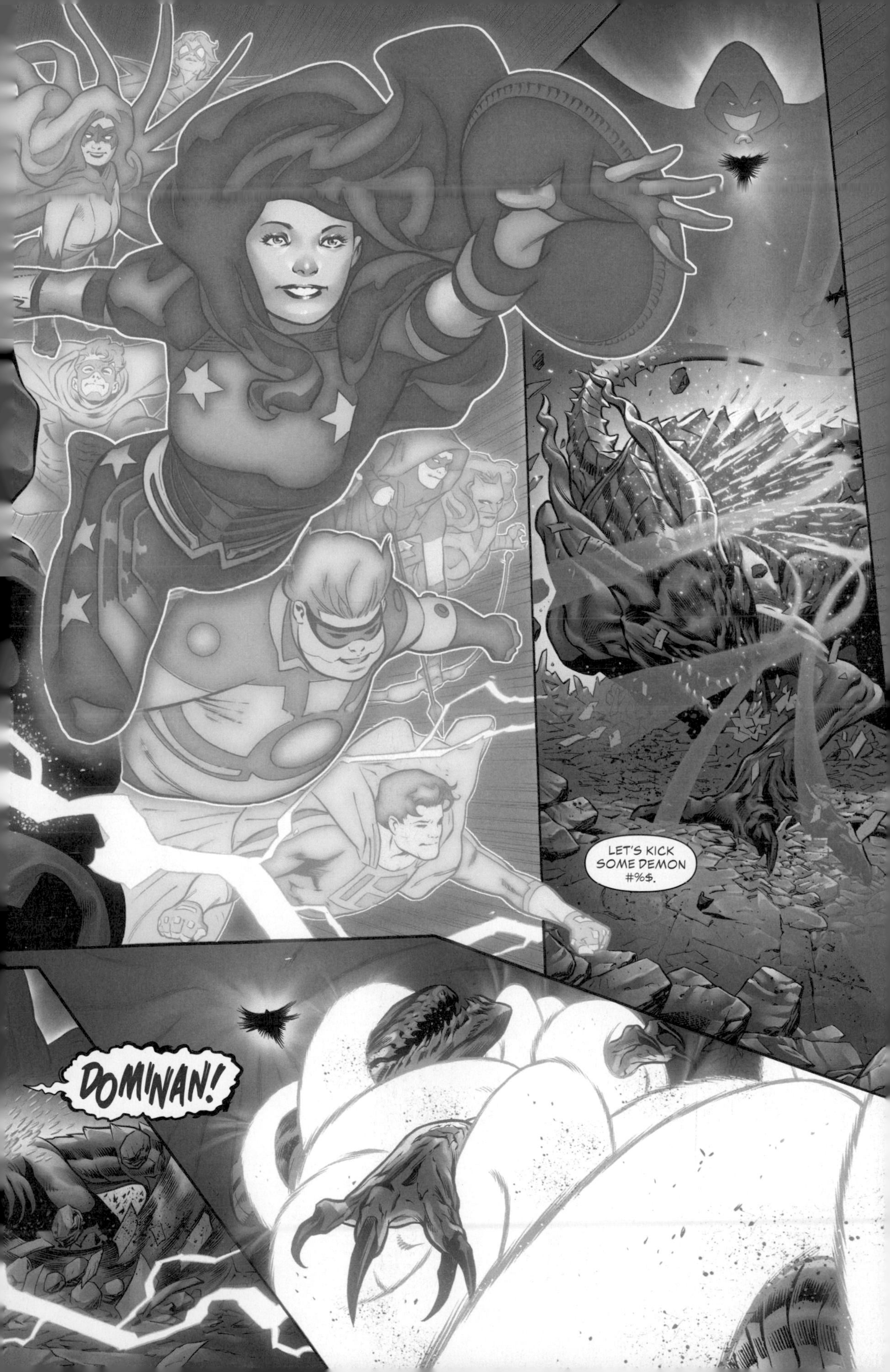
LET'S KICK SOME DEMON #%$.
DOMINAN!

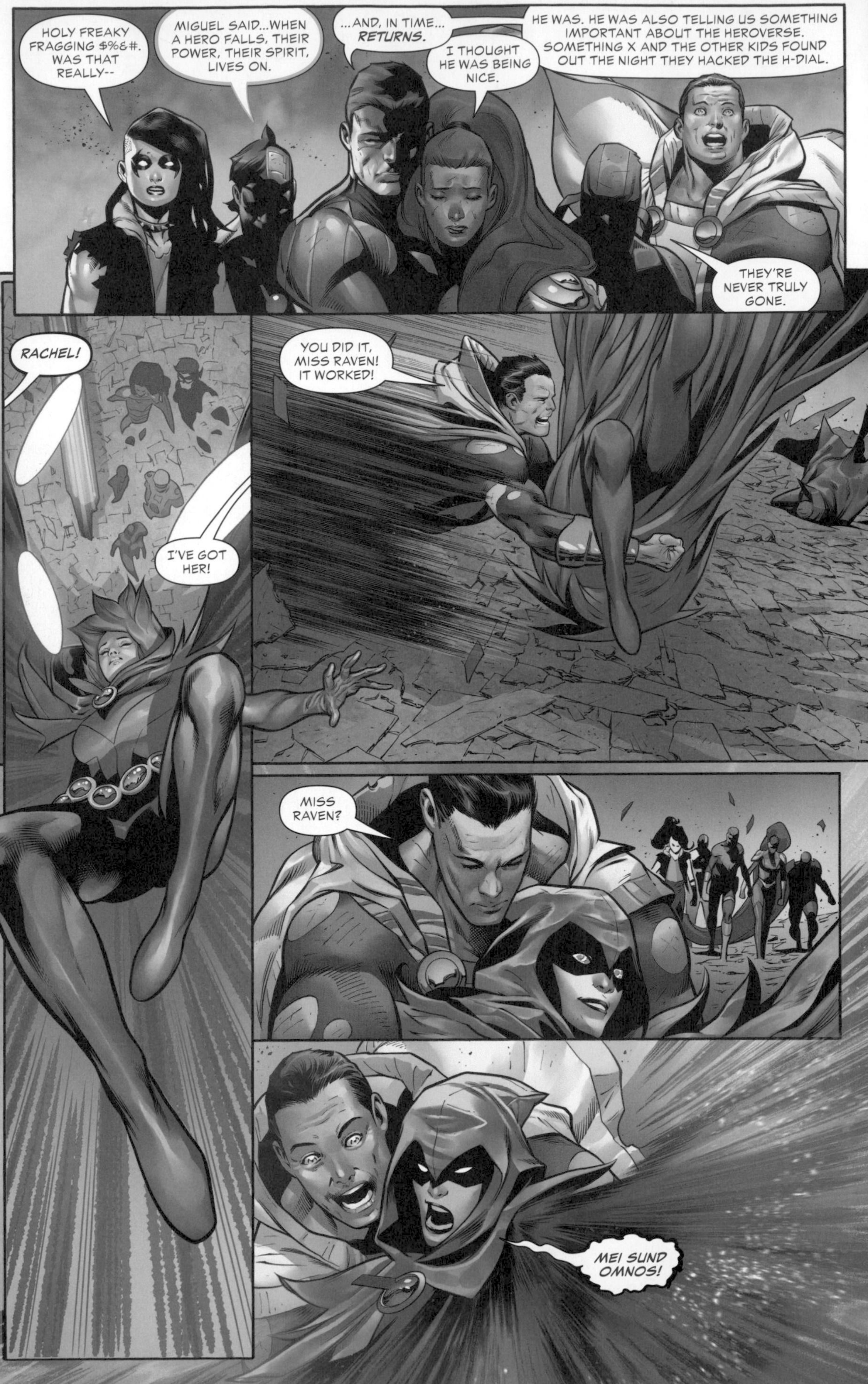
HOLY FREAKY FRAGGING $%&#. WAS THAT REALLY--
MIGUEL SAID...WHEN A HERO FALLS, THEIR POWER, THEIR SPIRIT, LIVES ON.
...AND, IN TIME... RETURNS.
I THOUGHT HE WAS BEING NICE.
HE WAS. HE WAS ALSO TELLING US SOMETHING IMPORTANT ABOUT THE HEROVERSE. SOMETHING X AND THE OTHER KIDS FOUND OUT THE NIGHT THEY HACKED THE H-DIAL.
THEY'RE NEVER TRULY GONE.
RACHEL!
YOU DID IT, MISS RAVEN! IT WORKED!
I'VE GOT HER!
MISS RAVEN?
MEI SUND OMNOS!

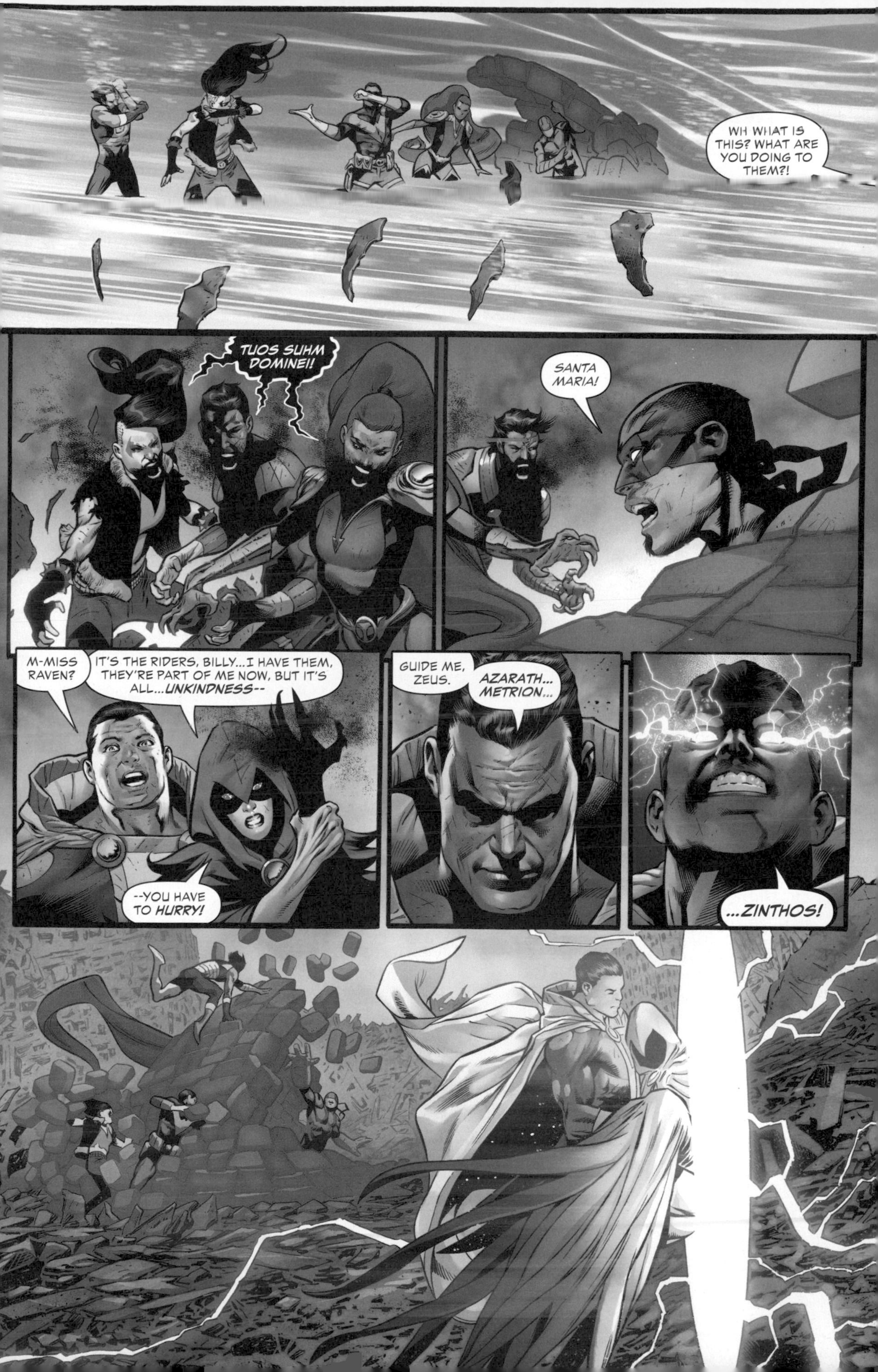
WH WHAT IS THIS? WHAT ARE YOU DOING TO THEM?!
TUOS SUHM DOMINEI!
SANTA MARIA!
M-MISS RAVEN?
IT'S THE RIDERS, BILLY...I HAVE THEM, THEY'RE PART OF ME NOW, BUT IT'S ALL...UNKINDNESS--
--YOU HAVE TO HURRY!
GUIDE ME, ZEUS.
AZARATH... METRION...
...ZINTHOS!

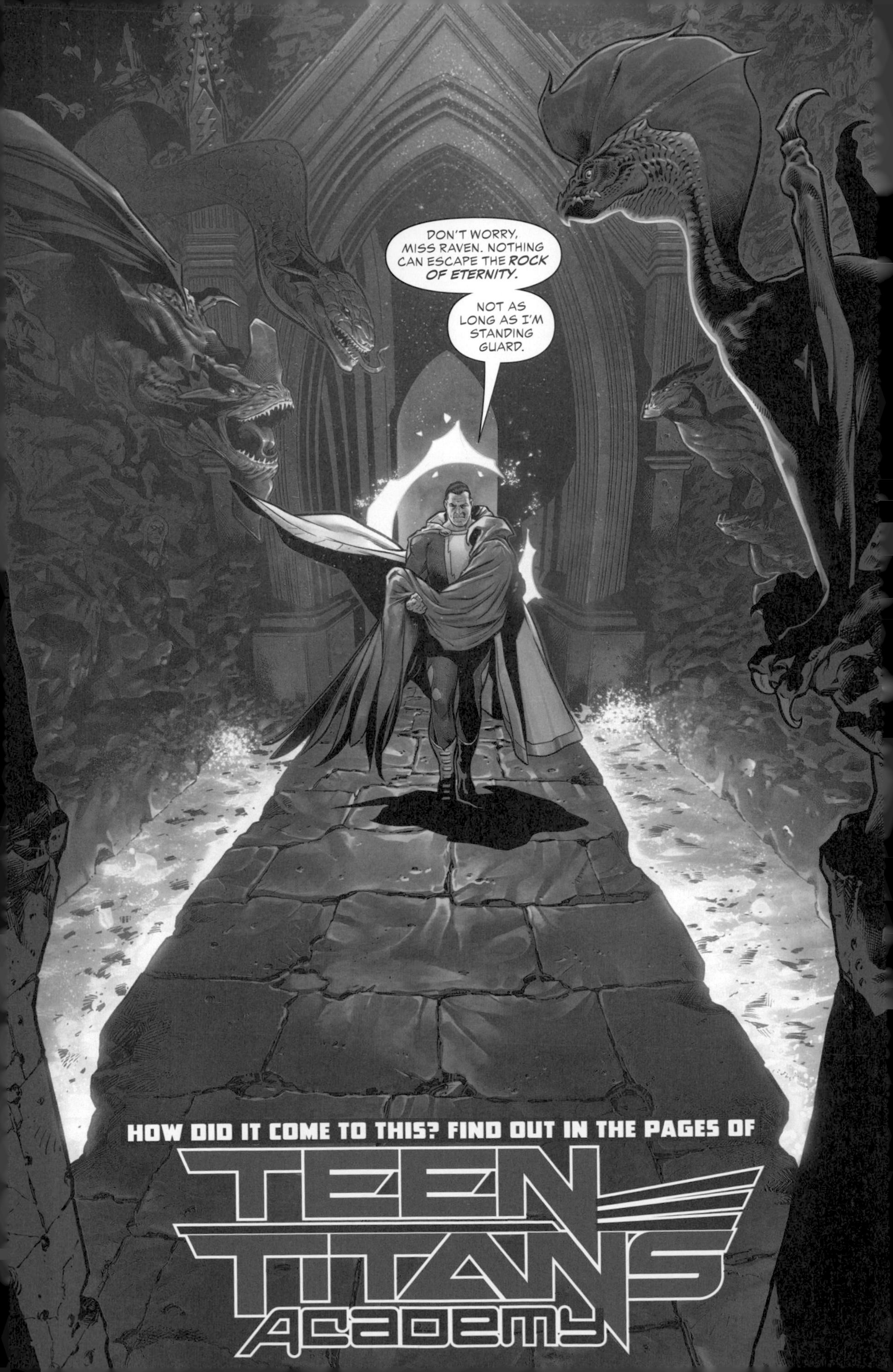
DON'T WORRY, MISS RAVEN. NOTHING CAN ESCAPE THE *ROCK OF ETERNITY.*
NOT AS LONG AS I'M STANDING GUARD.
HOW DID IT COME TO THIS? FIND OUT IN THE PAGES OF
TEEN TITANS ACADEMY

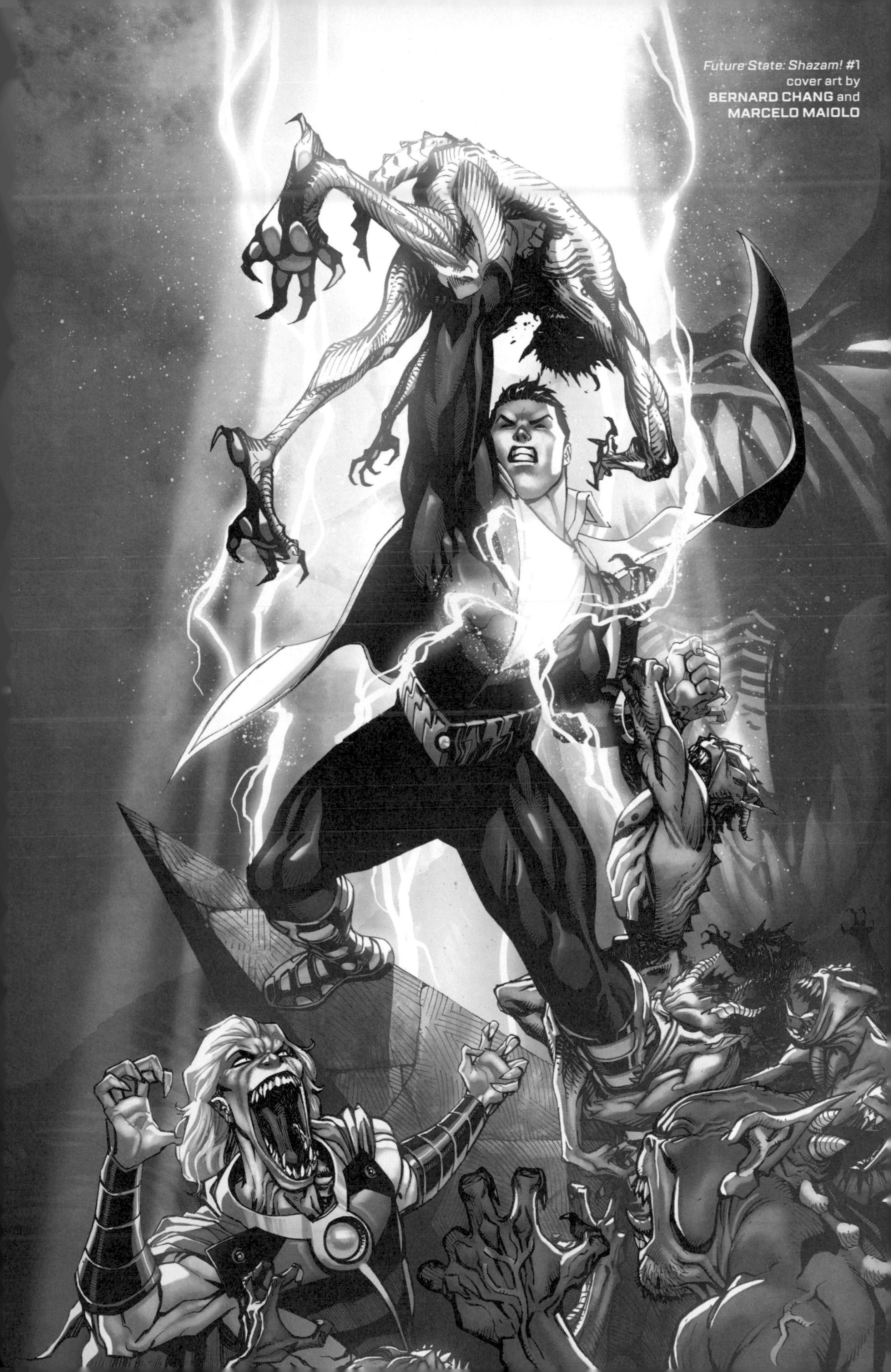

Future State: Shazam! #1
cover art by
BERNARD CHANG and
MARCELO MAIOLO

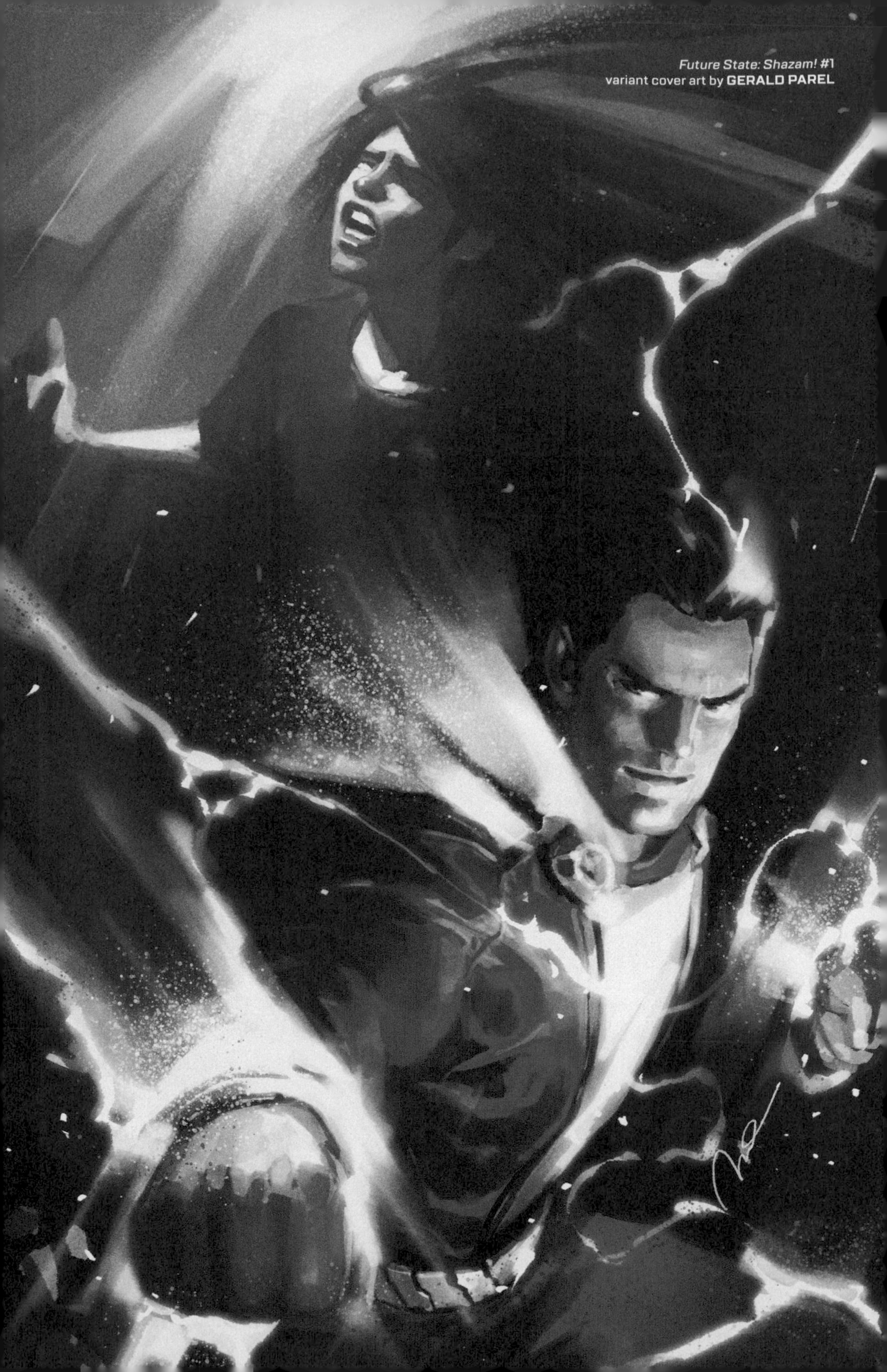

Future State: Shazam! #1
variant cover art by **GERALD PAREL**

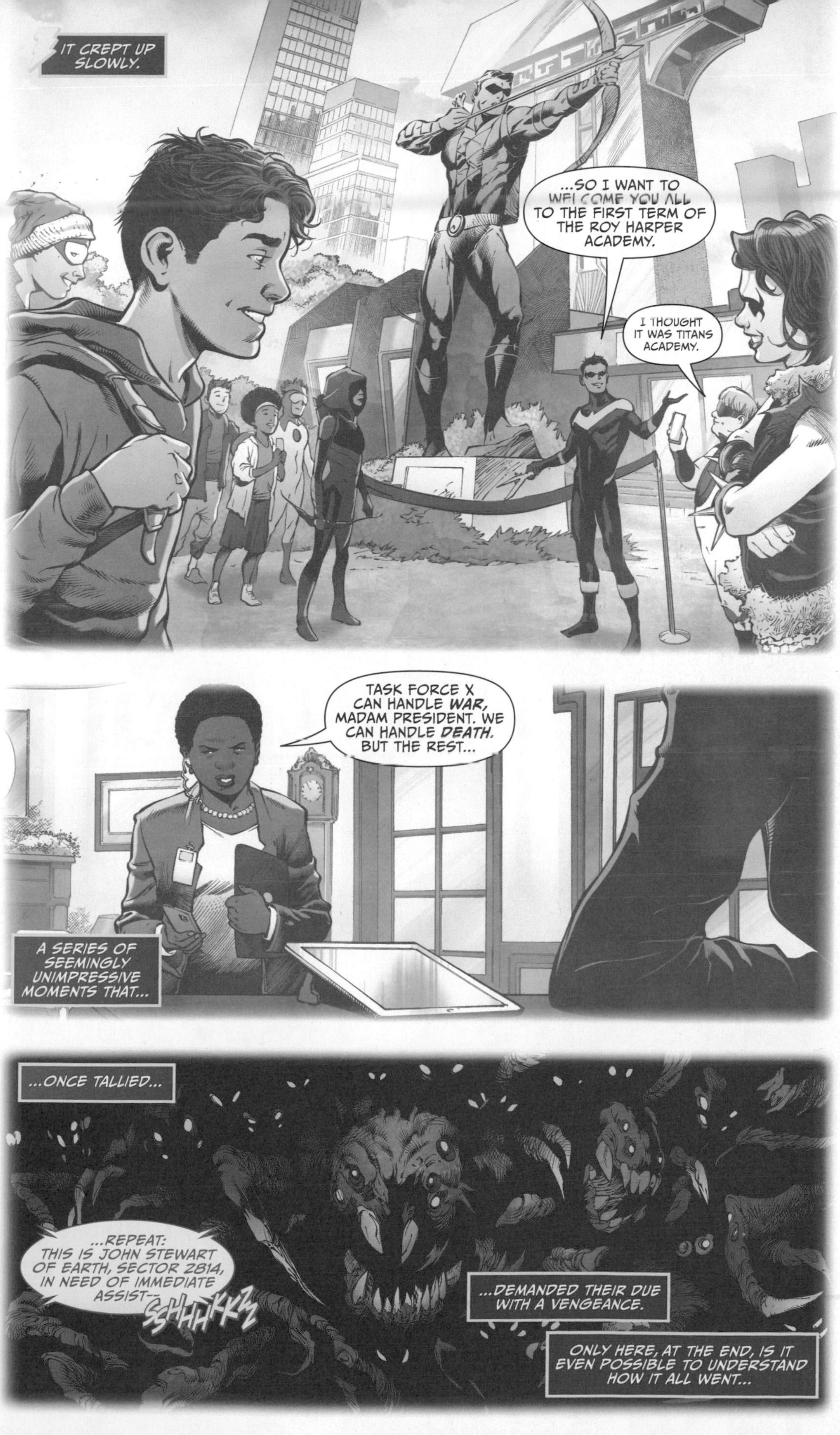
IT CREPT UP SLOWLY.
...SO I WANT TO WELCOME YOU ALL TO THE FIRST TERM OF THE ROY HARPER ACADEMY.
I THOUGHT IT WAS TITANS ACADEMY.
TASK FORCE X CAN HANDLE WAR, MADAM PRESIDENT. WE CAN HANDLE DEATH. BUT THE REST...
A SERIES OF SEEMINGLY UNIMPRESSIVE MOMENTS THAT...
...ONCE TALLIED...
...REPEAT: THIS IS JOHN STEWART OF EARTH, SECTOR 2814, IN NEED OF IMMEDIATE ASSIST--
SSHHHKKZ
...DEMANDED THEIR DUE WITH A VENGEANCE.
ONLY HERE, AT THE END, IS IT EVEN POSSIBLE TO UNDERSTAND HOW IT ALL WENT...

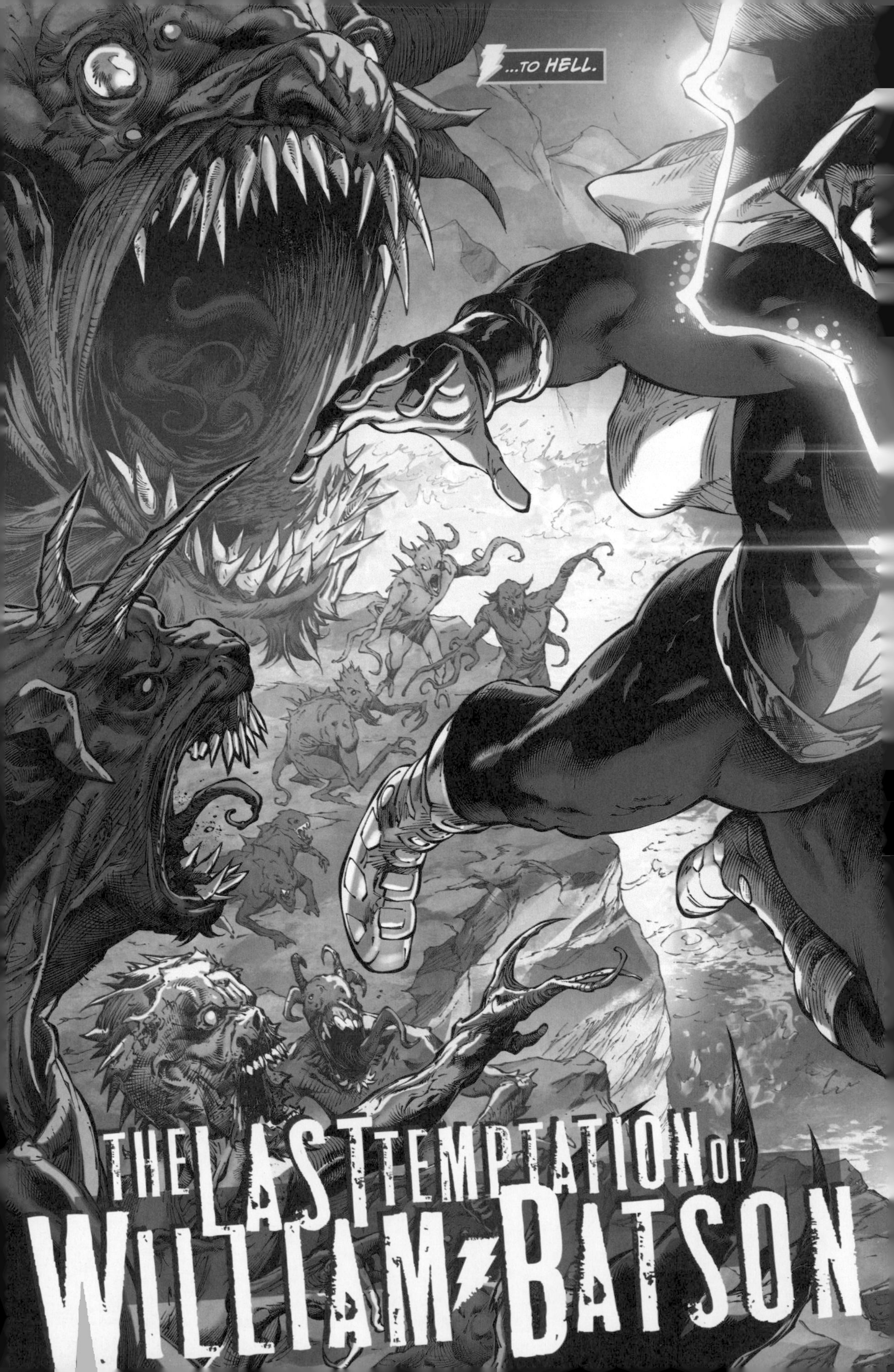
...TO HELL.
THE LAST TEMPTATION OF
WILLIAM BATSON

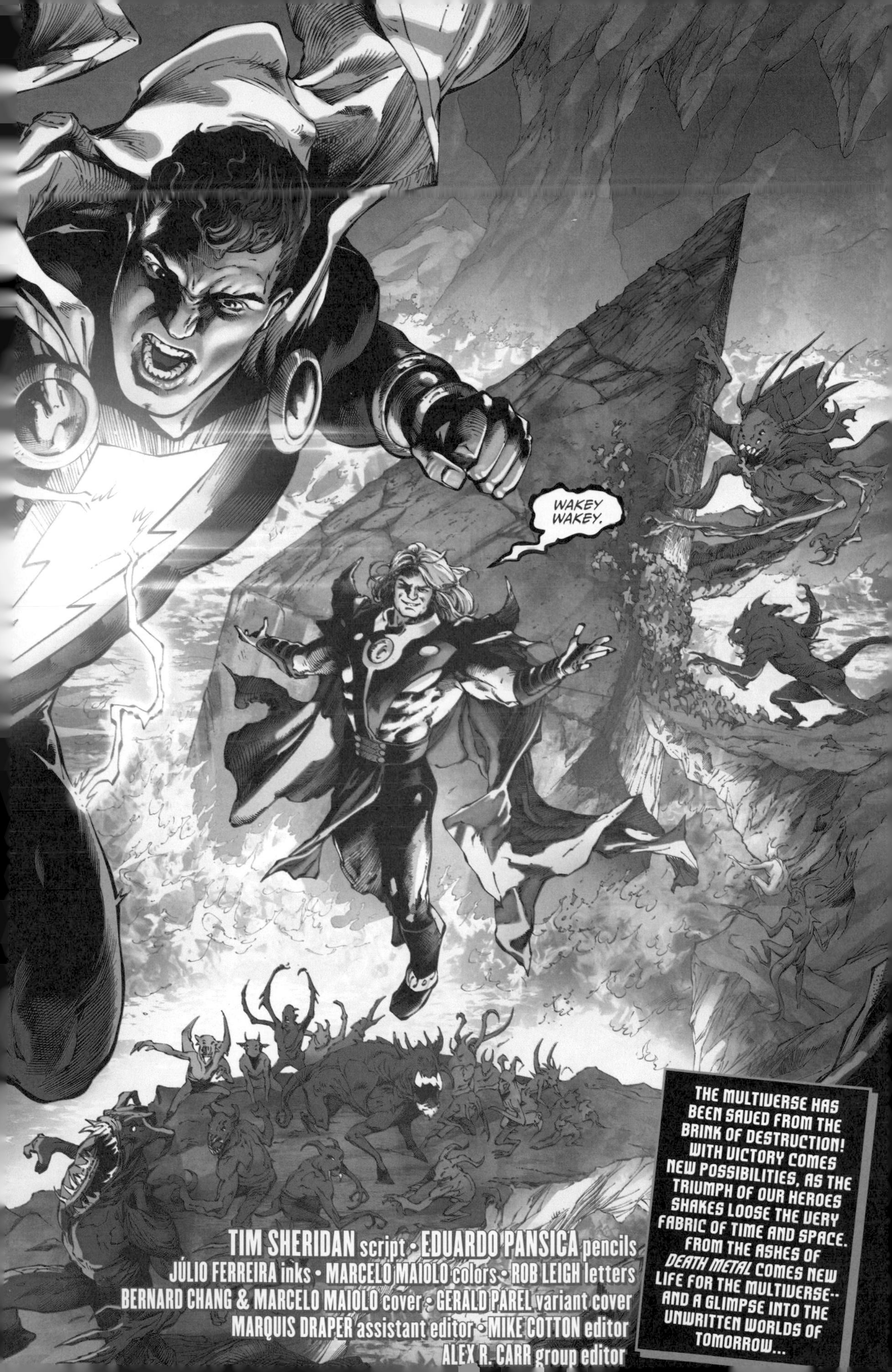
WAKEY WAKEY.
THE MULTIVERSE HAS BEEN SAVED FROM THE BRINK OF DESTRUCTION! WITH VICTORY COMES NEW POSSIBILITIES, AS THE TRIUMPH OF OUR HEROES SHAKES LOOSE THE VERY FABRIC OF TIME AND SPACE. FROM THE ASHES OF DEATH METAL COMES NEW LIFE FOR THE MULTIVERSE-- AND A GLIMPSE INTO THE UNWRITTEN WORLDS OF TOMORROW...
TIM SHERIDAN script • EDUARDO PANSICA pencils
JÚLIO FERREIRA inks • MARCELO MAIOLO colors • ROB LEIGH letters
BERNARD CHANG & MARCELO MAIOLO cover • GERALD PAREL variant cover
MARQUIS DRAPER assistant editor • MIKE COTTON editor
ALEX R. CARR group editor

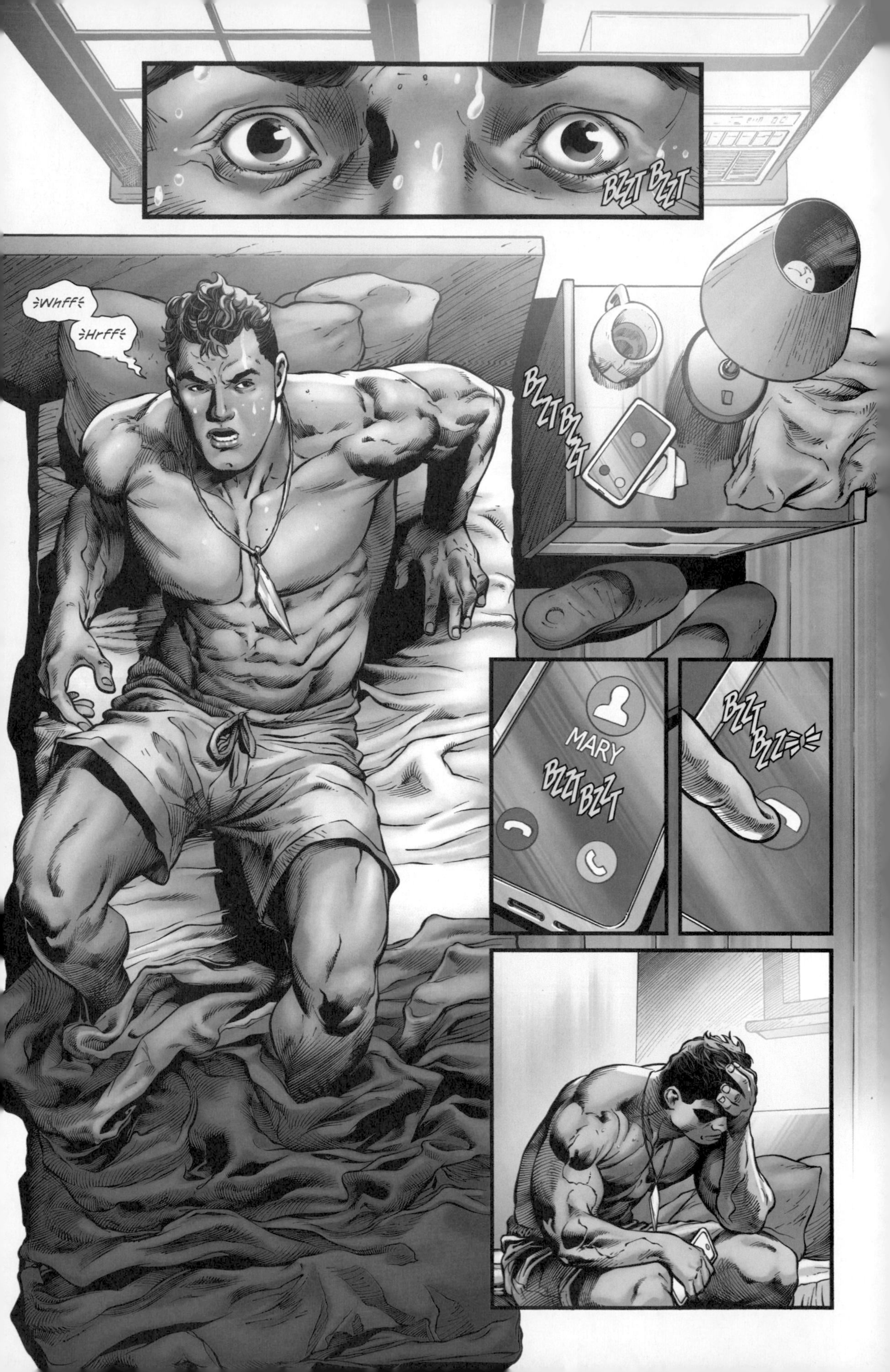
BZZT BZZT
Whff
Hrff
BZZT BZZT
MARY
BZZT BZZT
BZZT BZZ

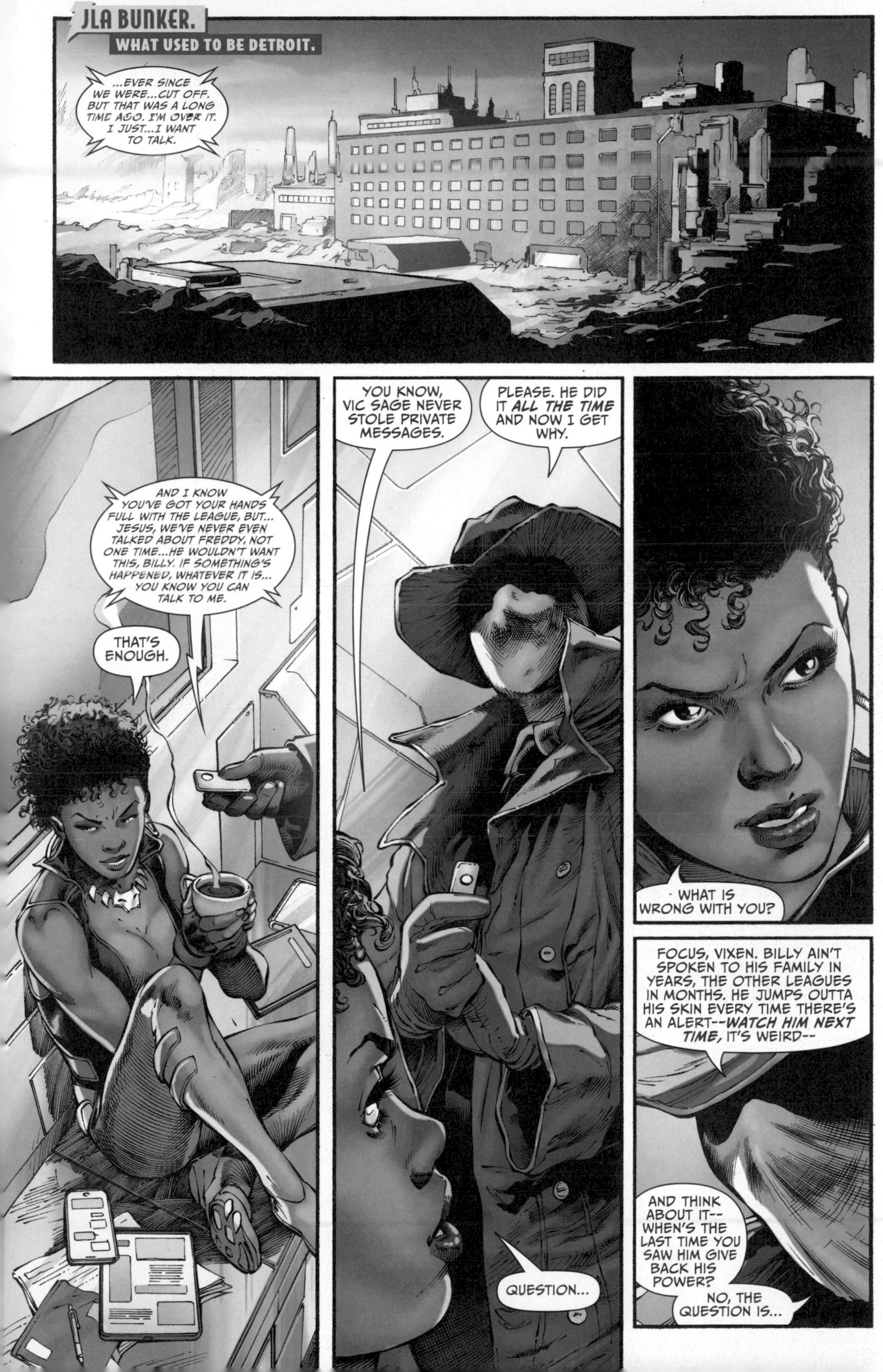
JLA BUNKER.
WHAT USED TO BE DETROIT.
...EVER SINCE WE WERE...CUT OFF. BUT THAT WAS A LONG TIME AGO. I'M OVER IT. I JUST...I WANT TO TALK.
AND I KNOW YOU'VE GOT YOUR HANDS FULL WITH THE LEAGUE, BUT... JESUS, WE'VE NEVER EVEN TALKED ABOUT FREDDY, NOT ONE TIME...HE WOULDN'T WANT THIS, BILLY. IF SOMETHING'S HAPPENED, WHATEVER IT IS... YOU KNOW YOU CAN TALK TO ME.
THAT'S ENOUGH.
YOU KNOW, VIC SAGE NEVER STOLE PRIVATE MESSAGES.
PLEASE. HE DID IT ALL THE TIME AND NOW I GET WHY.
QUESTION...
WHAT IS WRONG WITH YOU?
FOCUS, VIXEN. BILLY AIN'T SPOKEN TO HIS FAMILY IN YEARS, THE OTHER LEAGUES IN MONTHS. HE JUMPS OUTTA HIS SKIN EVERY TIME THERE'S AN ALERT--WATCH HIM NEXT TIME, IT'S WEIRD--
AND THINK ABOUT IT-- WHEN'S THE LAST TIME YOU SAW HIM GIVE BACK HIS POWER?
NO, THE QUESTION IS...

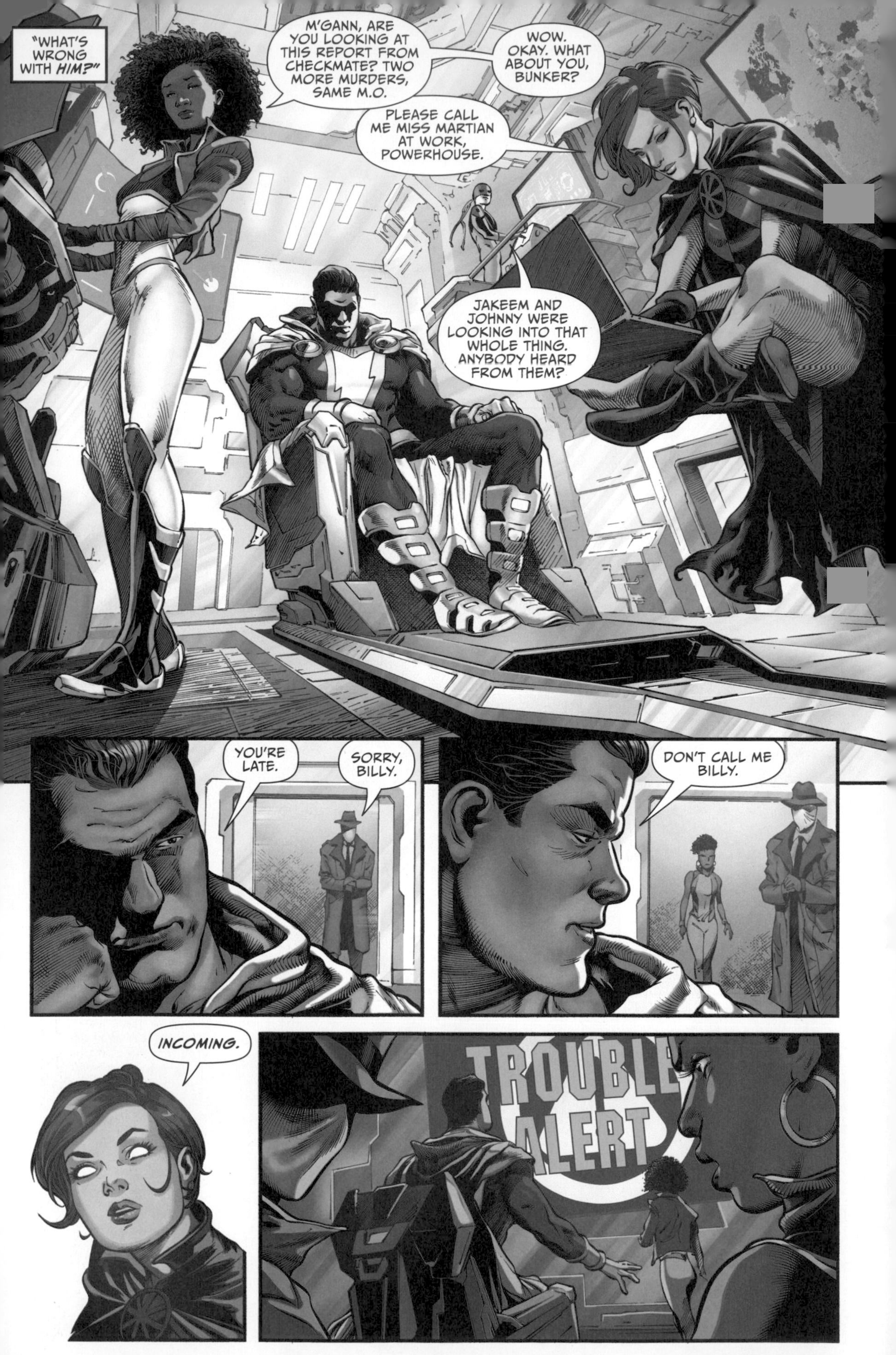

"WHAT'S WRONG WITH *HIM?*"
M'GANN, ARE YOU LOOKING AT THIS REPORT FROM CHECKMATE? TWO MORE MURDERS, SAME M.O.
WOW. OKAY. WHAT ABOUT YOU, BUNKER?
PLEASE CALL ME MISS MARTIAN AT WORK, POWERHOUSE.
JAKEEM AND JOHNNY WERE LOOKING INTO THAT WHOLE THING. ANYBODY HEARD FROM THEM?
YOU'RE LATE.
SORRY, BILLY.
DON'T CALL ME BILLY.
INCOMING.
TROUBLE ALERT

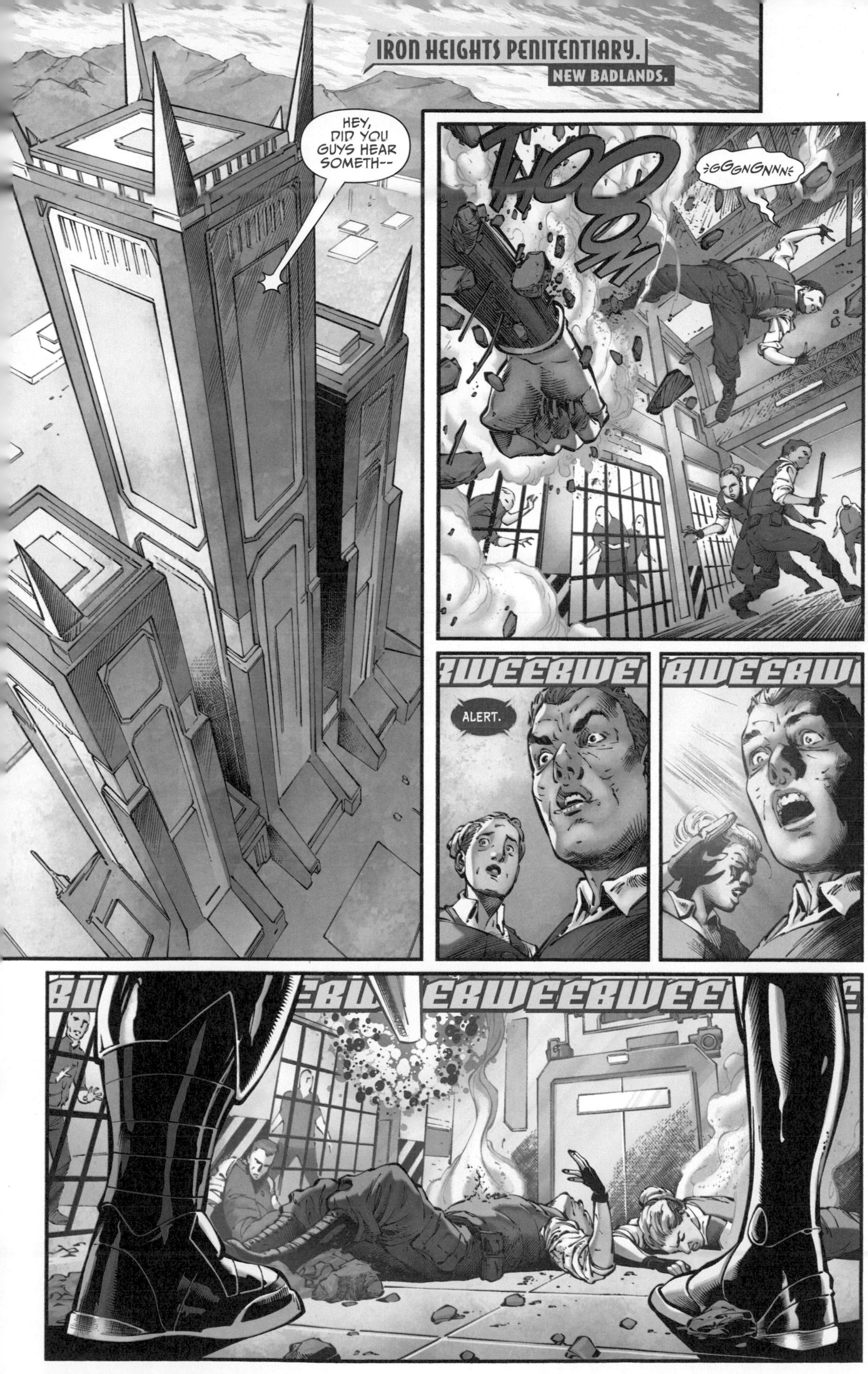
IRON HEIGHTS PENITENTIARY.
NEW BADLANDS.
HEY, DID YOU GUYS HEAR SOMETH--
THOOOM
GGGNGNNN
BWEEBWE
ALERT.
BWEEBW
BWEEBWEEBWEEBWEE

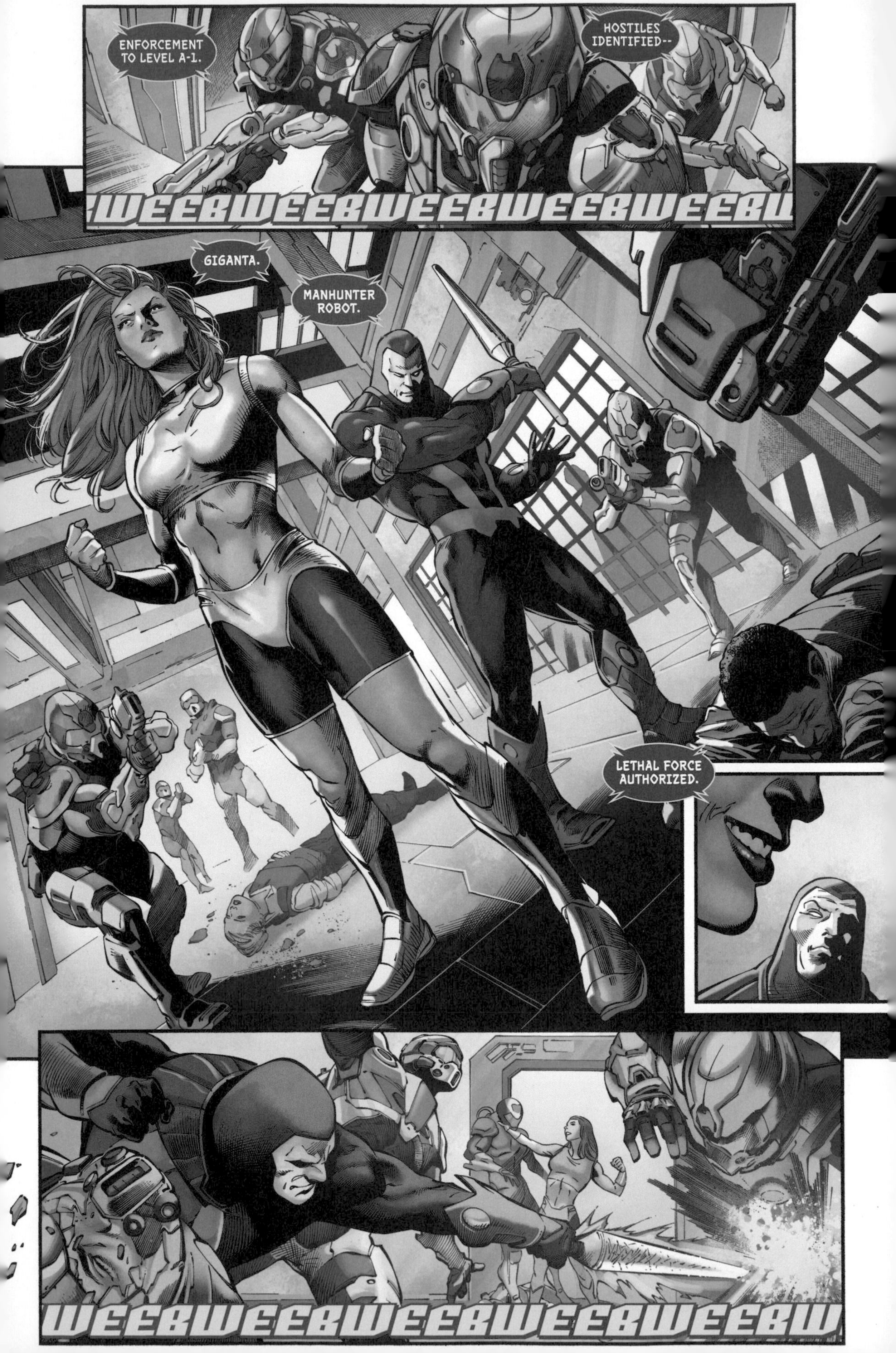
ENFORCEMENT TO LEVEL A-1.
HOSTILES IDENTIFIED--
WEEBWEEBWEEBWEEBWEEBW
GIGANTA.
MANHUNTER ROBOT.
LETHAL FORCE AUTHORIZED.
WEEBWEEBWEEBWEEBWEEBW

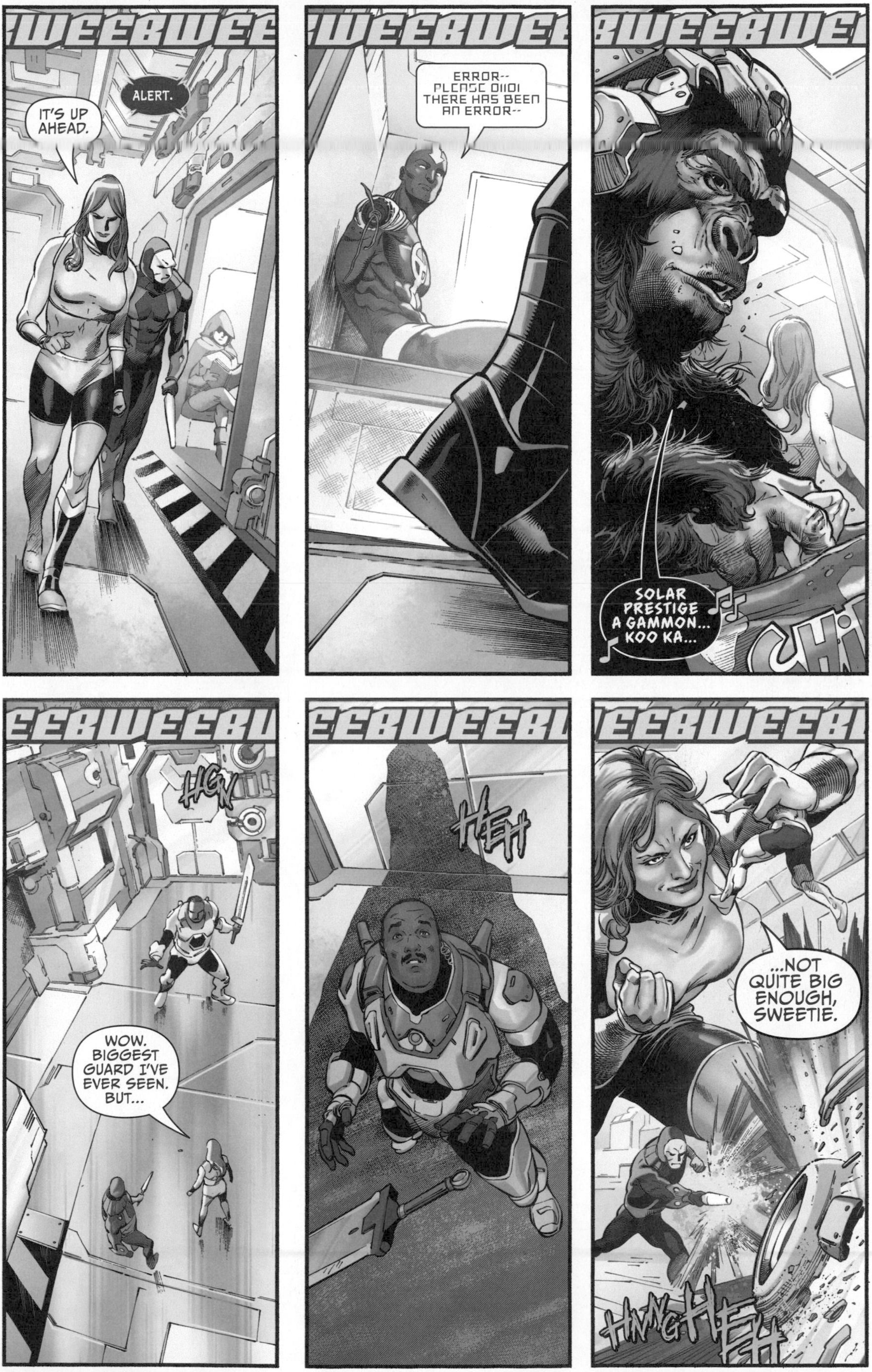
ALERT.
IT'S UP AHEAD.
ERROR-- PLEASE 01101 THERE HAS BEEN AN ERROR--
SOLAR PRESTIGE A GAMMON... KOO KA...
HGN
WOW. BIGGEST GUARD I'VE EVER SEEN. BUT...
HEH
...NOT QUITE BIG ENOUGH, SWEETIE.
HNNG HEH

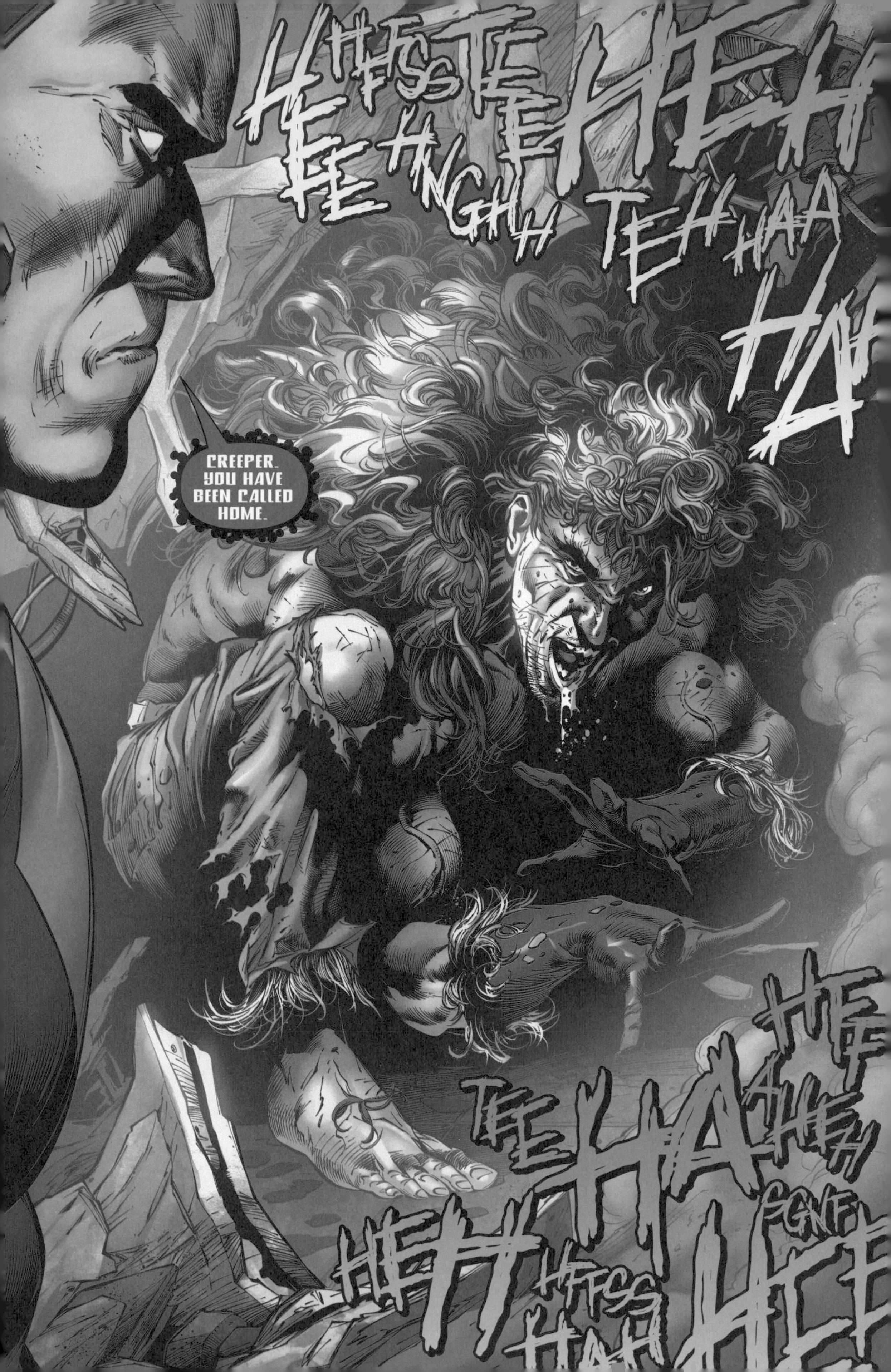
CREEPER. YOU HAVE BEEN CALLED HOME.

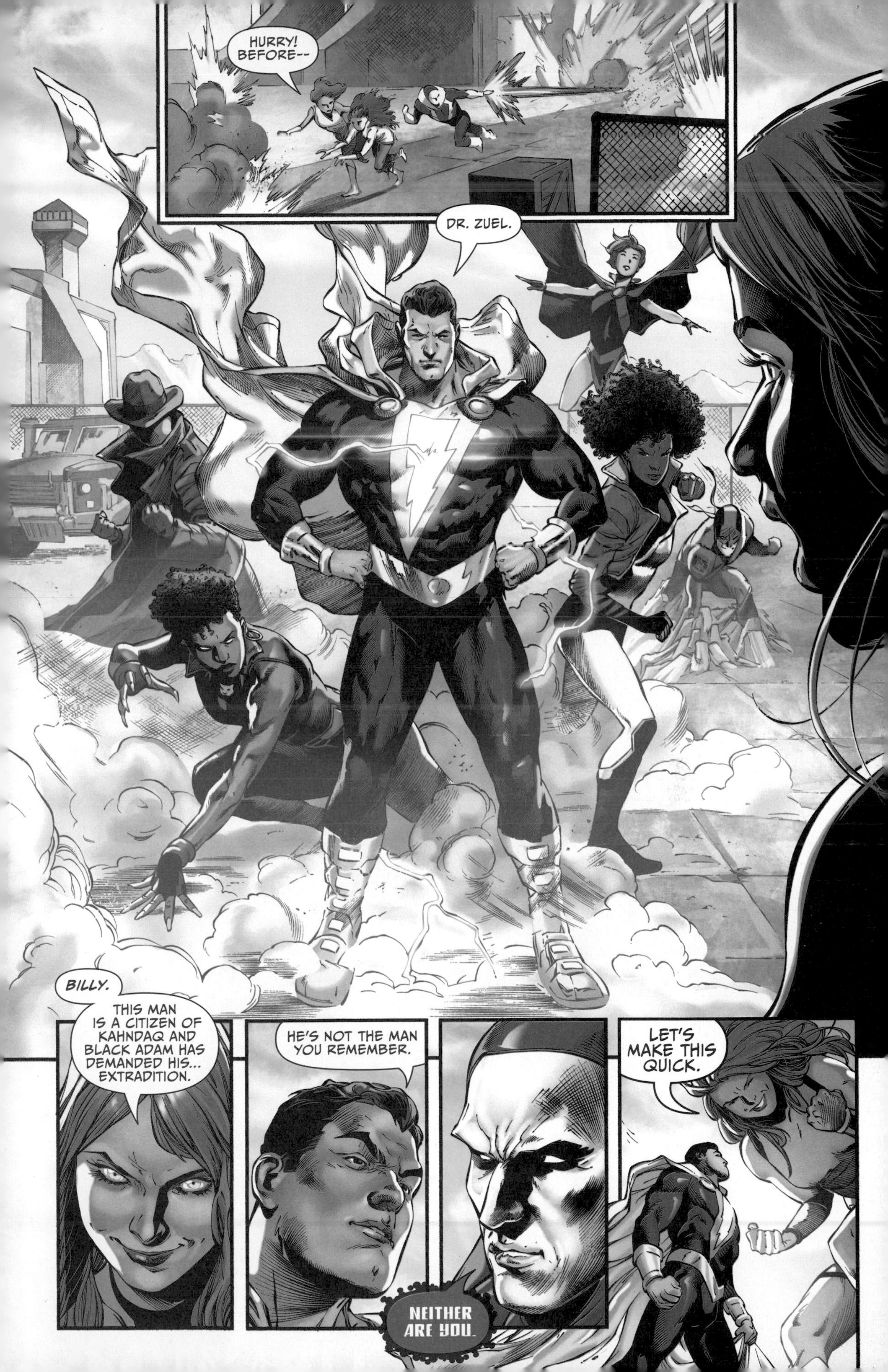
HURRY! BEFORE--
DR. ZUEL.
BILLY.
THIS MAN IS A CITIZEN OF KAHNDAQ AND BLACK ADAM HAS DEMANDED HIS... EXTRADITION.
HE'S NOT THE MAN YOU REMEMBER.
LET'S MAKE THIS QUICK.
NEITHER ARE YOU.

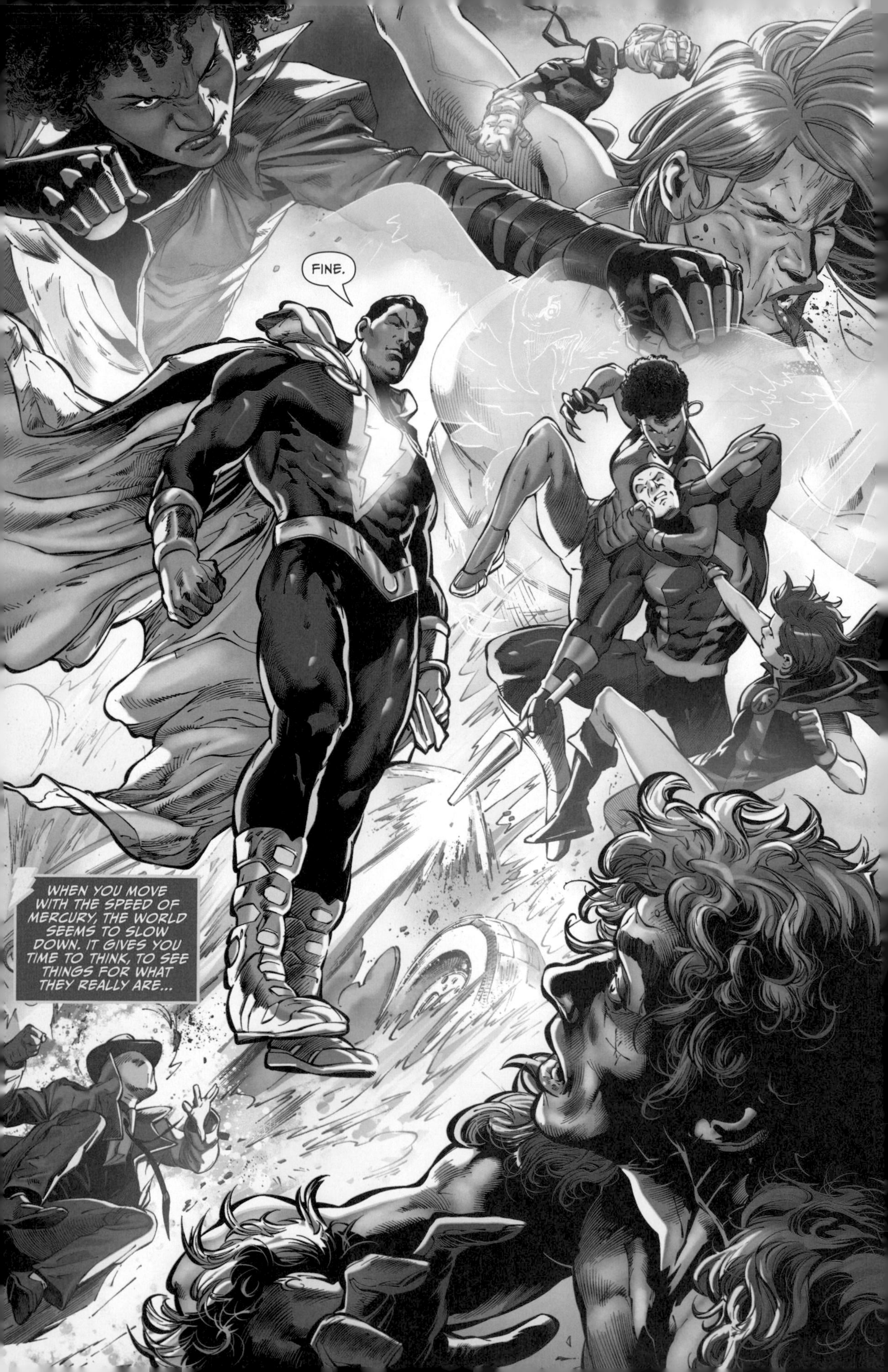
FINE.
WHEN YOU MOVE WITH THE SPEED OF MERCURY, THE WORLD SEEMS TO SLOW DOWN. IT GIVES YOU TIME TO THINK, TO SEE THINGS FOR WHAT THEY REALLY ARE...

...AND TO DEAL WITH THEM QUICKLY...

GOOD WORK. WAIT, WHERE'S--

CREEPER? I DON'T--

I DO.

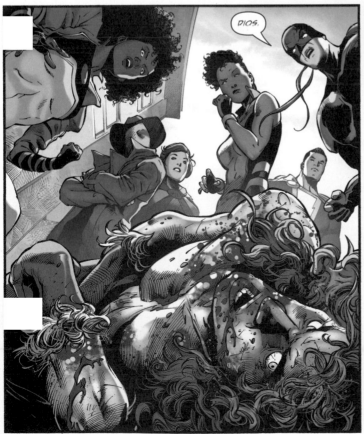

DIOS.

...AND ACCORDINGLY.

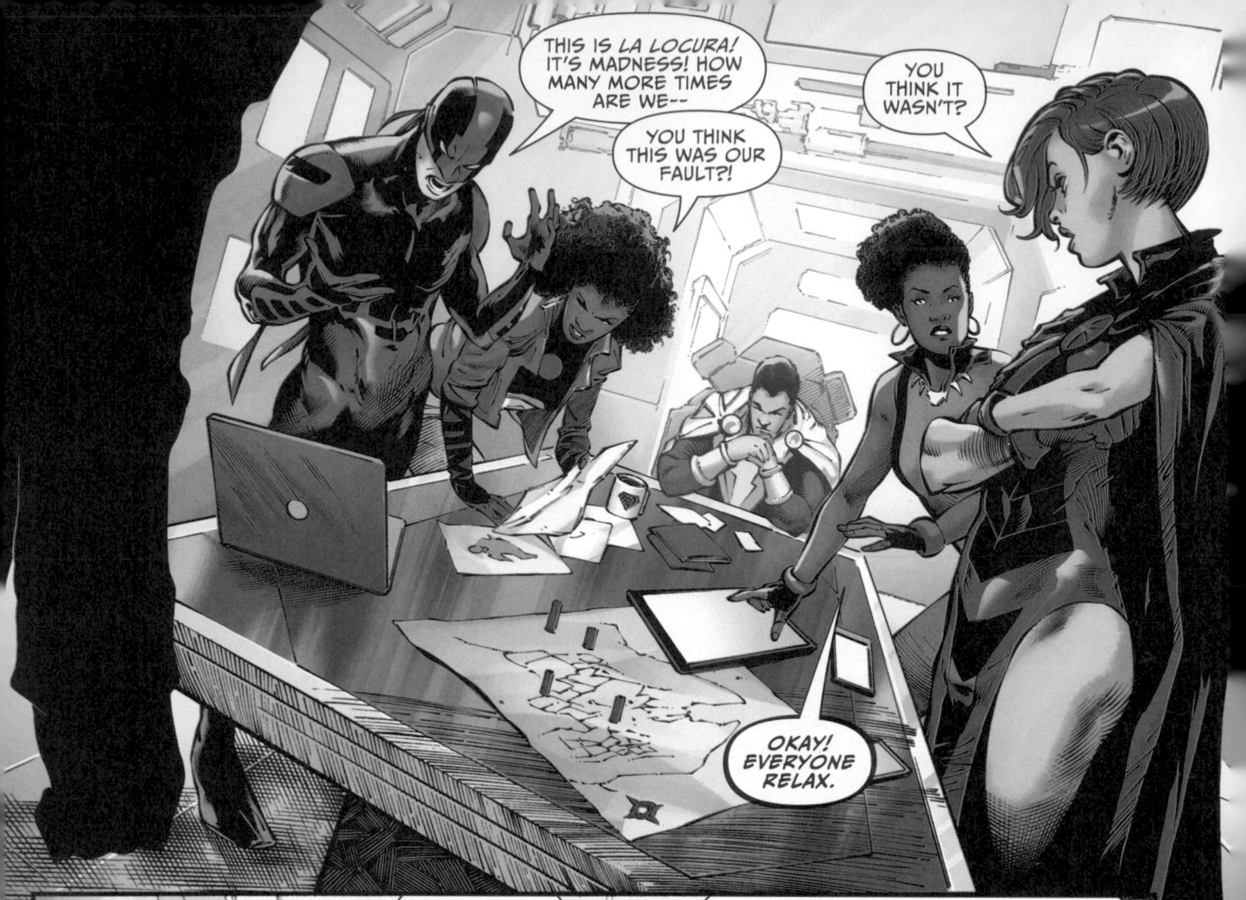
THIS IS LA LOCURA! IT'S MADNESS! HOW MANY MORE TIMES ARE WE--
YOU THINK THIS WAS OUR FAULT?!
YOU THINK IT WASN'T?
OKAY! EVERYONE RELAX.

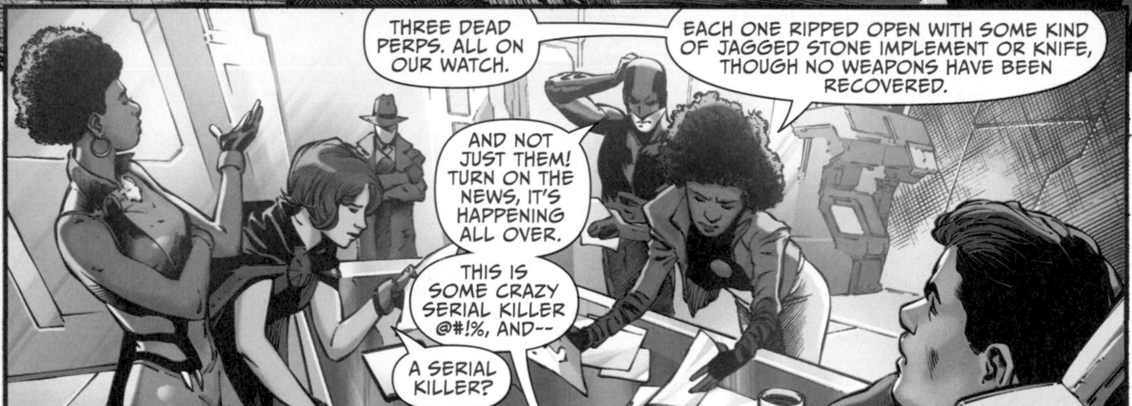
THREE DEAD PERPS. ALL ON OUR WATCH.
EACH ONE RIPPED OPEN WITH SOME KIND OF JAGGED STONE IMPLEMENT OR KNIFE, THOUGH NO WEAPONS HAVE BEEN RECOVERED.
AND NOT JUST THEM! TURN ON THE NEWS, IT'S HAPPENING ALL OVER.
THIS IS SOME CRAZY SERIAL KILLER @#!%, AND--
A SERIAL KILLER?
--AND IT'S HAPPENING RIGHT UNDER OUR NOSES.
WHERE THE HELL IS JAKEEM?

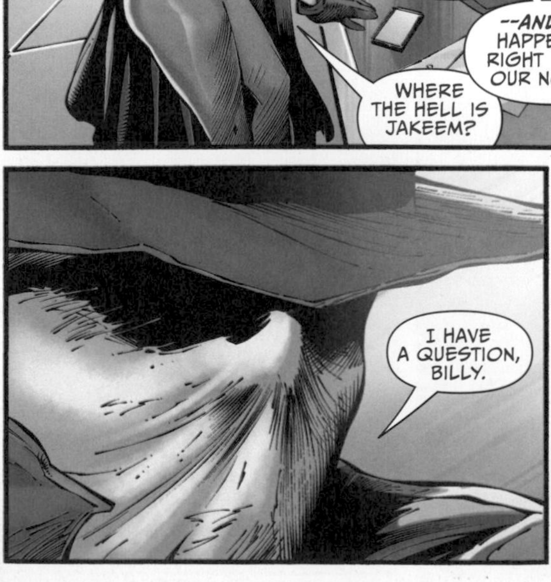
I HAVE A QUESTION, BILLY.

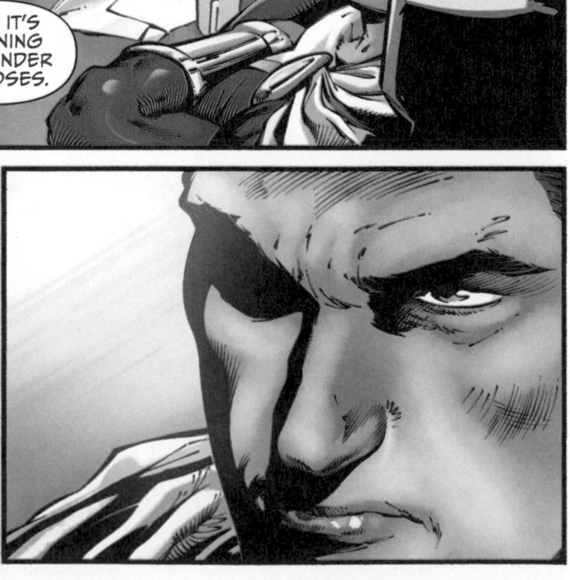

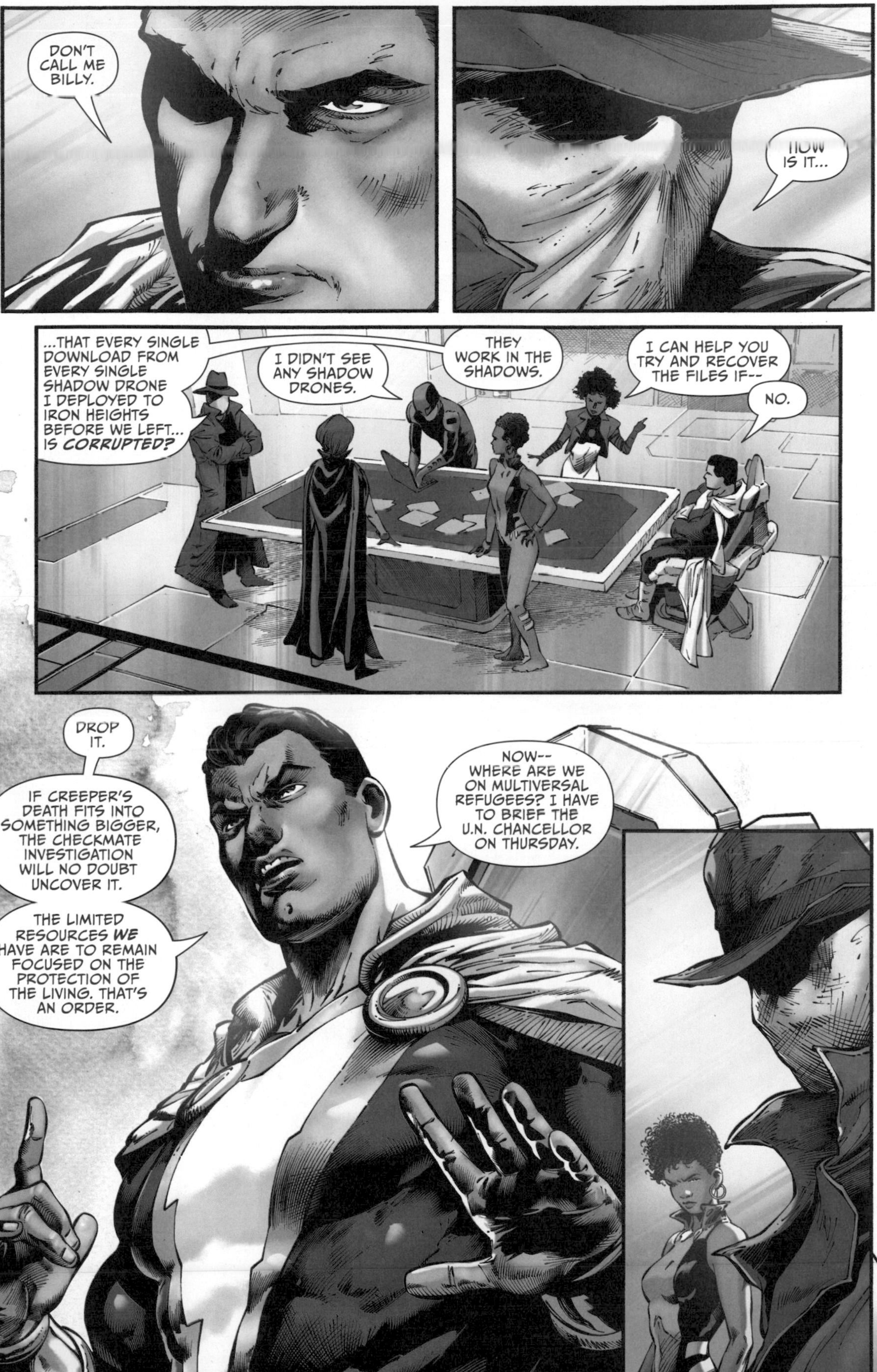
DON'T CALL ME BILLY.
HOW IS IT...
...THAT EVERY SINGLE DOWNLOAD FROM EVERY SINGLE SHADOW DRONE I DEPLOYED TO IRON HEIGHTS BEFORE WE LEFT... IS CORRUPTED?
I DIDN'T SEE ANY SHADOW DRONES.
THEY WORK IN THE SHADOWS.
I CAN HELP YOU TRY AND RECOVER THE FILES IF--
NO.
DROP IT.
IF CREEPER'S DEATH FITS INTO SOMETHING BIGGER, THE CHECKMATE INVESTIGATION WILL NO DOUBT UNCOVER IT.
THE LIMITED RESOURCES WE HAVE ARE TO REMAIN FOCUSED ON THE PROTECTION OF THE LIVING. THAT'S AN ORDER.
NOW-- WHERE ARE WE ON MULTIVERSAL REFUGEES? I HAVE TO BRIEF THE U.N. CHANCELLOR ON THURSDAY.

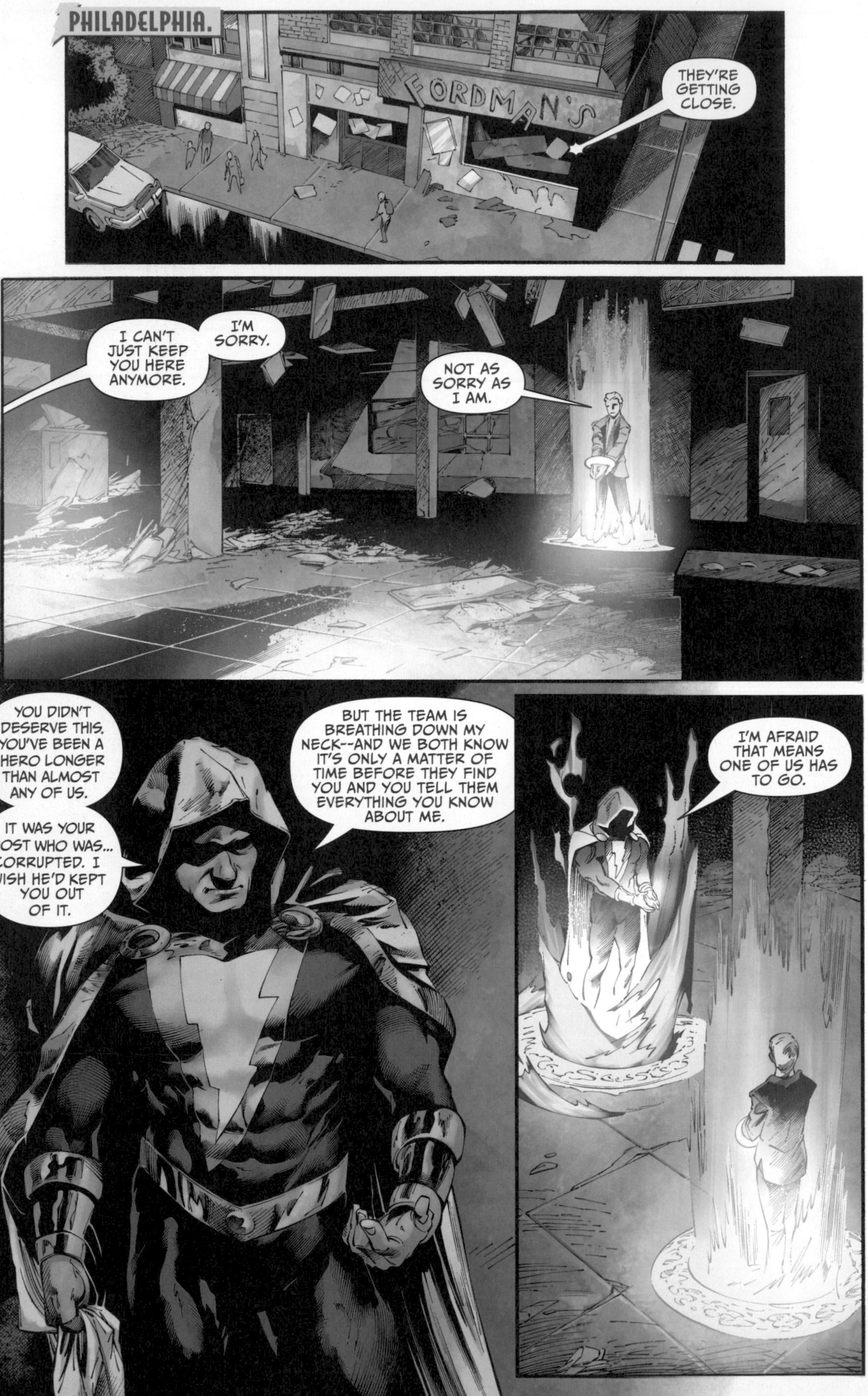
PHILADELPHIA.
FORDMAN'S
THEY'RE GETTING CLOSE.
I CAN'T JUST KEEP YOU HERE ANYMORE.
I'M SORRY.
NOT AS SORRY AS I AM.
YOU DIDN'T DESERVE THIS. YOU'VE BEEN A HERO LONGER THAN ALMOST ANY OF US.
IT WAS YOUR HOST WHO WAS... CORRUPTED. I WISH HE'D KEPT YOU OUT OF IT.
BUT THE TEAM IS BREATHING DOWN MY NECK--AND WE BOTH KNOW IT'S ONLY A MATTER OF TIME BEFORE THEY FIND YOU AND YOU TELL THEM EVERYTHING YOU KNOW ABOUT ME.
I'M AFRAID THAT MEANS ONE OF US HAS TO GO.

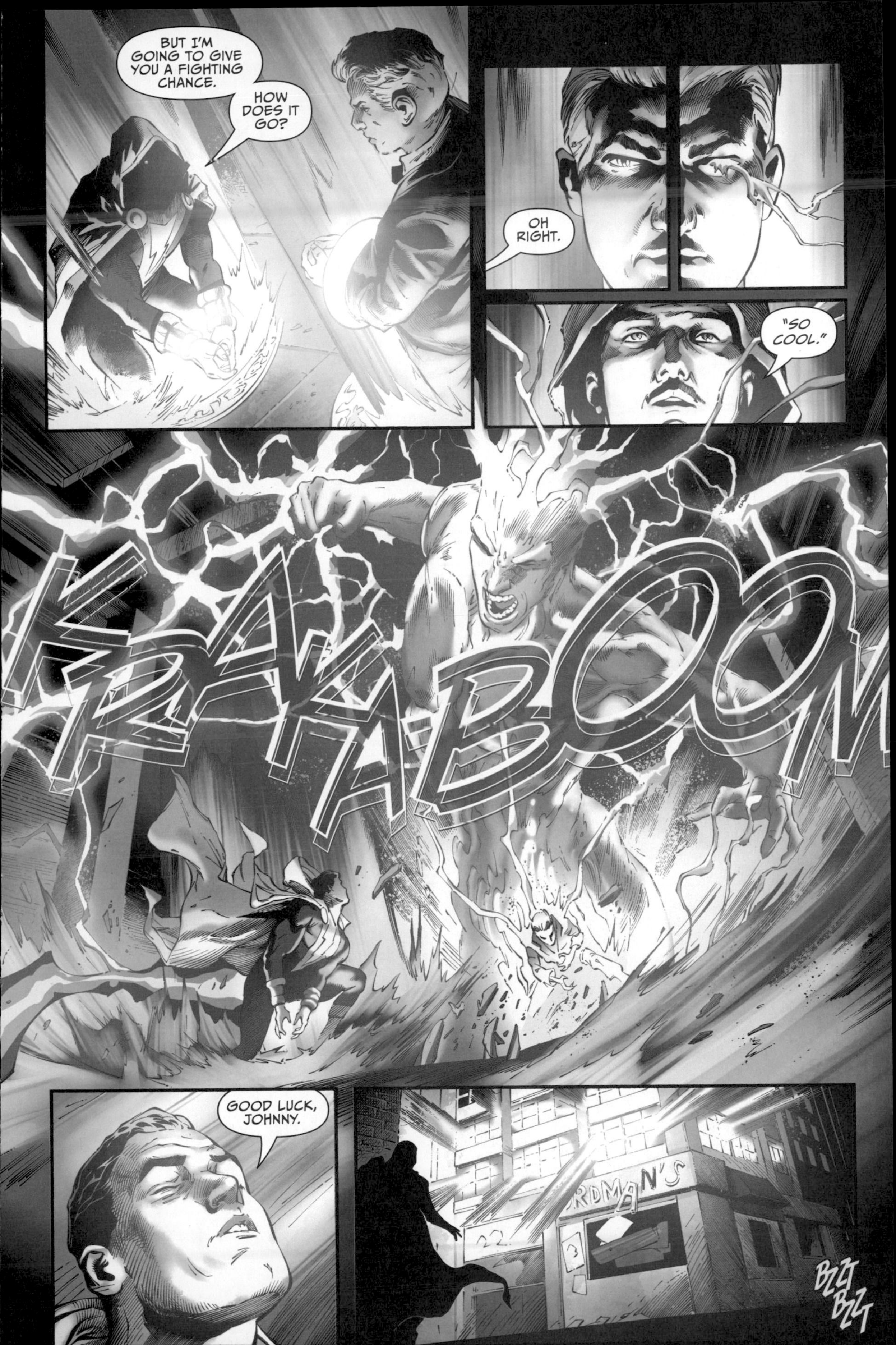
BUT I'M GOING TO GIVE YOU A FIGHTING CHANCE.
HOW DOES IT GO?
OH RIGHT.
"SO COOL."
KA-KA-BOOM
GOOD LUCK, JOHNNY.
RDMAN'S
BZZT BZZT

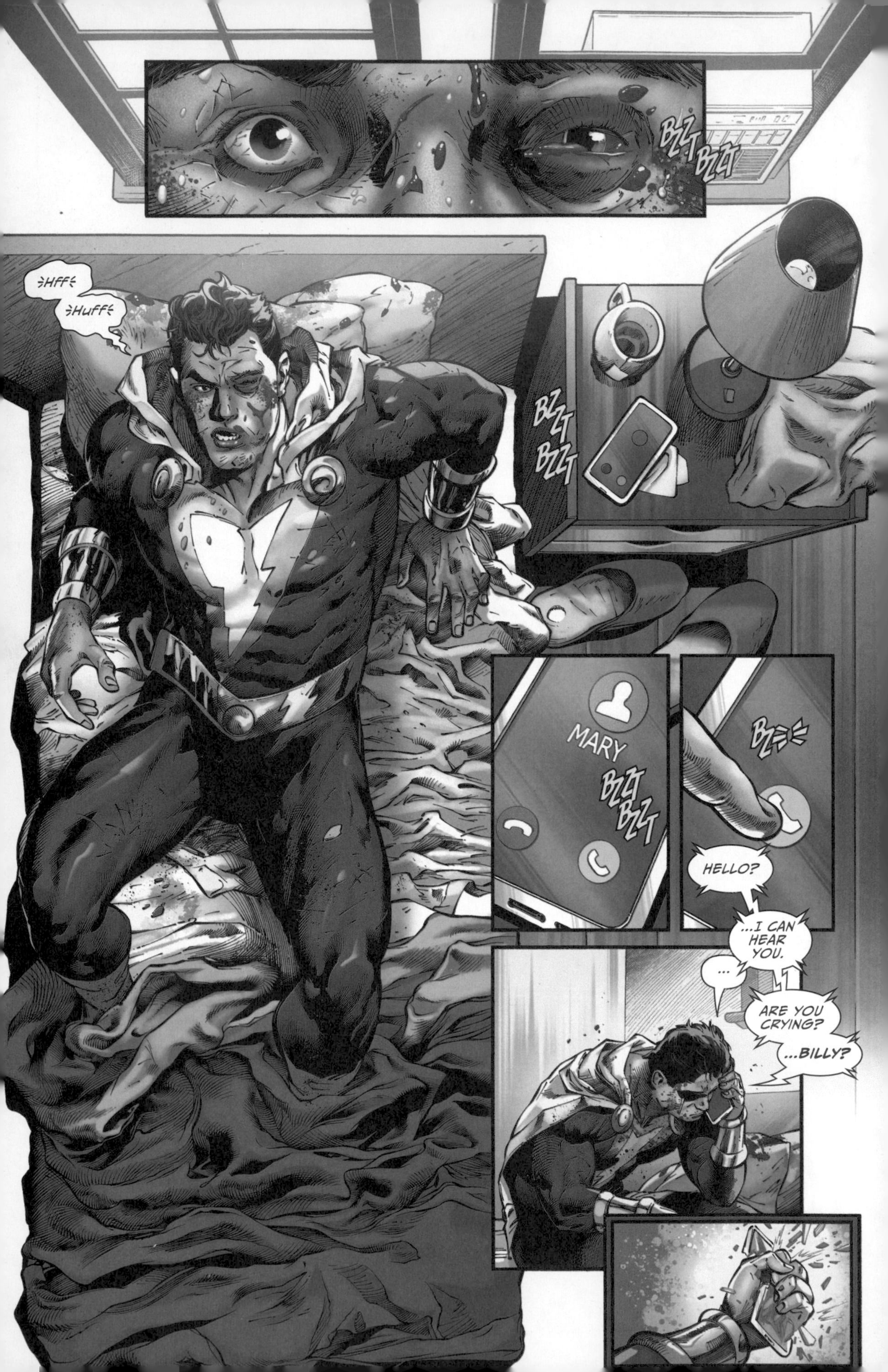
BZZT BZZT
HFF
HUFF
BZZT BZZT
MARY
BZZT BZZT
BZ
HELLO?
...I CAN HEAR YOU.
...
ARE YOU CRYING?
...BILLY?

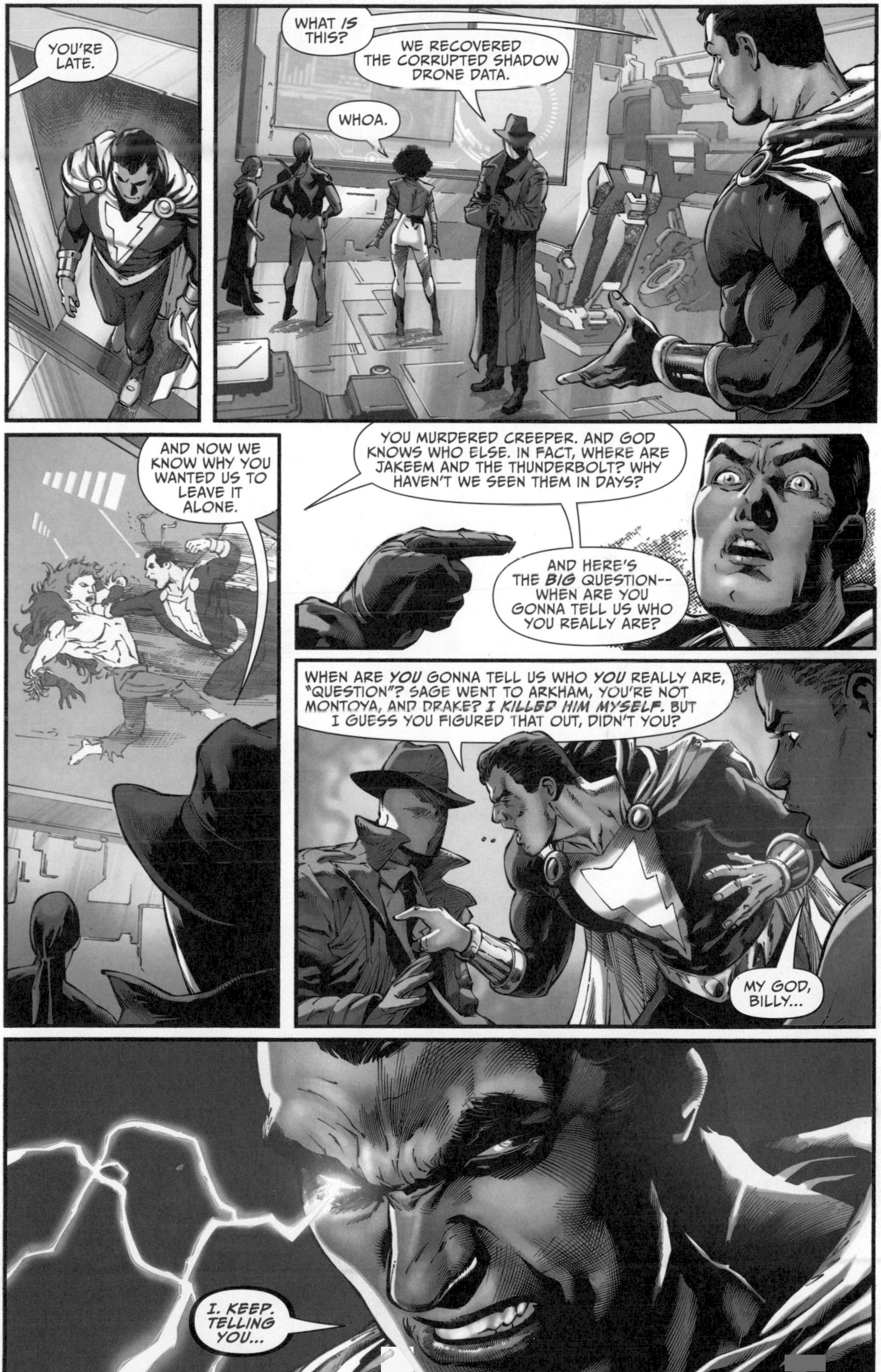
YOU'RE LATE.
WHAT IS THIS?
WE RECOVERED THE CORRUPTED SHADOW DRONE DATA.
WHOA.
AND NOW WE KNOW WHY YOU WANTED US TO LEAVE IT ALONE.
YOU MURDERED CREEPER. AND GOD KNOWS WHO ELSE. IN FACT, WHERE ARE JAKEEM AND THE THUNDERBOLT? WHY HAVEN'T WE SEEN THEM IN DAYS?
AND HERE'S THE BIG QUESTION-- WHEN ARE YOU GONNA TELL US WHO YOU REALLY ARE?
WHEN ARE YOU GONNA TELL US WHO YOU REALLY ARE, "QUESTION"? SAGE WENT TO ARKHAM, YOU'RE NOT MONTOYA, AND DRAKE? I KILLED HIM MYSELF. BUT I GUESS YOU FIGURED THAT OUT, DIDN'T YOU?
MY GOD, BILLY...
I. KEEP. TELLING YOU...

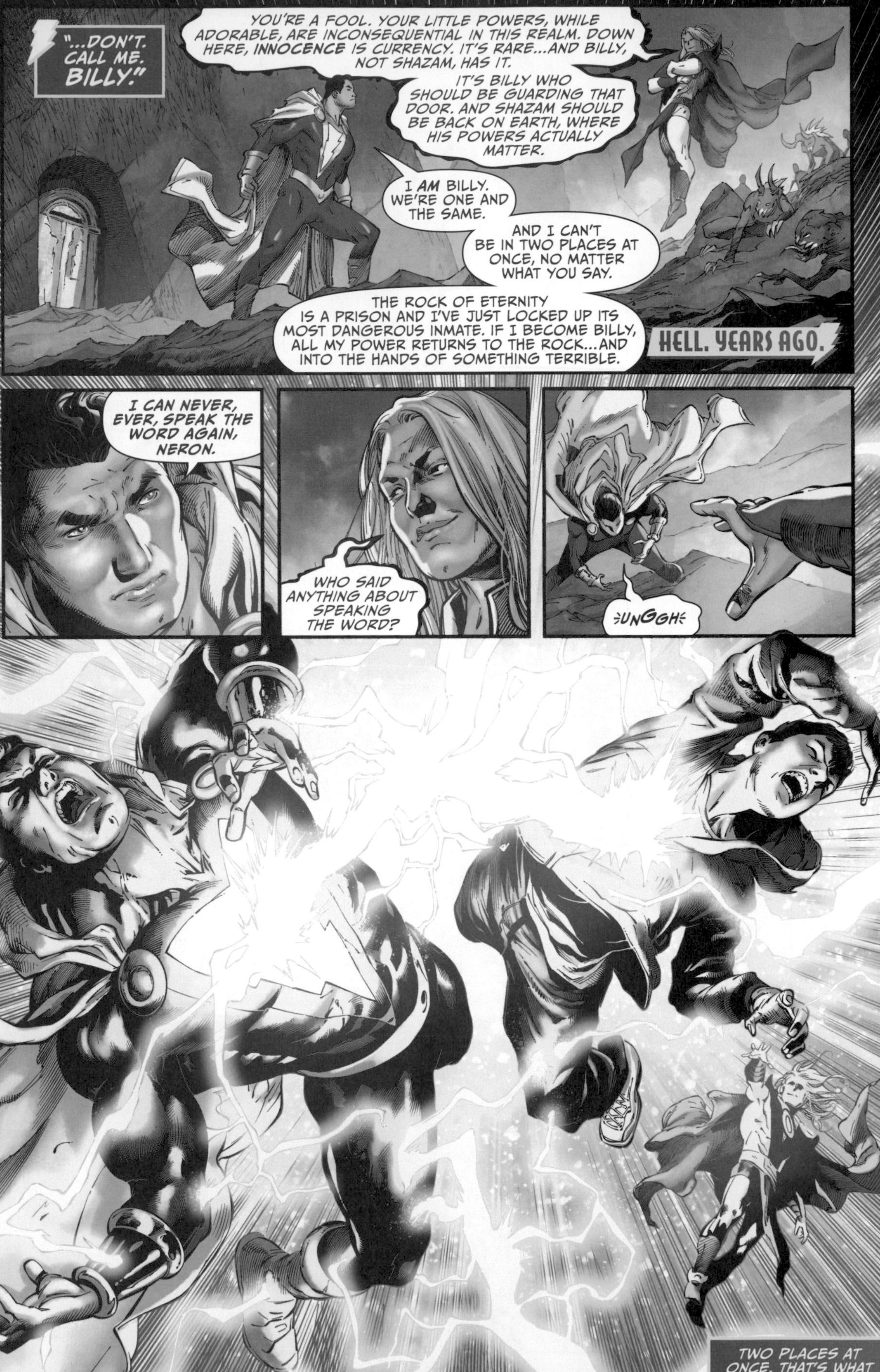
"...DON'T. CALL ME. BILLY!"
YOU'RE A FOOL. YOUR LITTLE POWERS, WHILE ADORABLE, ARE INCONSEQUENTIAL IN THIS REALM. DOWN HERE, INNOCENCE IS CURRENCY. IT'S RARE...AND BILLY, NOT SHAZAM, HAS IT.
IT'S BILLY WHO SHOULD BE GUARDING THAT DOOR. AND SHAZAM SHOULD BE BACK ON EARTH, WHERE HIS POWERS ACTUALLY MATTER.
I AM BILLY. WE'RE ONE AND THE SAME.
AND I CAN'T BE IN TWO PLACES AT ONCE, NO MATTER WHAT YOU SAY.
THE ROCK OF ETERNITY IS A PRISON AND I'VE JUST LOCKED UP ITS MOST DANGEROUS INMATE. IF I BECOME BILLY, ALL MY POWER RETURNS TO THE ROCK...AND INTO THE HANDS OF SOMETHING TERRIBLE.
HELL. YEARS AGO.
I CAN NEVER, EVER, SPEAK THE WORD AGAIN, NERON.
WHO SAID ANYTHING ABOUT SPEAKING THE WORD?
UNGGH
TWO PLACES AT ONCE. THAT'S WHAT THE DEVIL PROMISED.

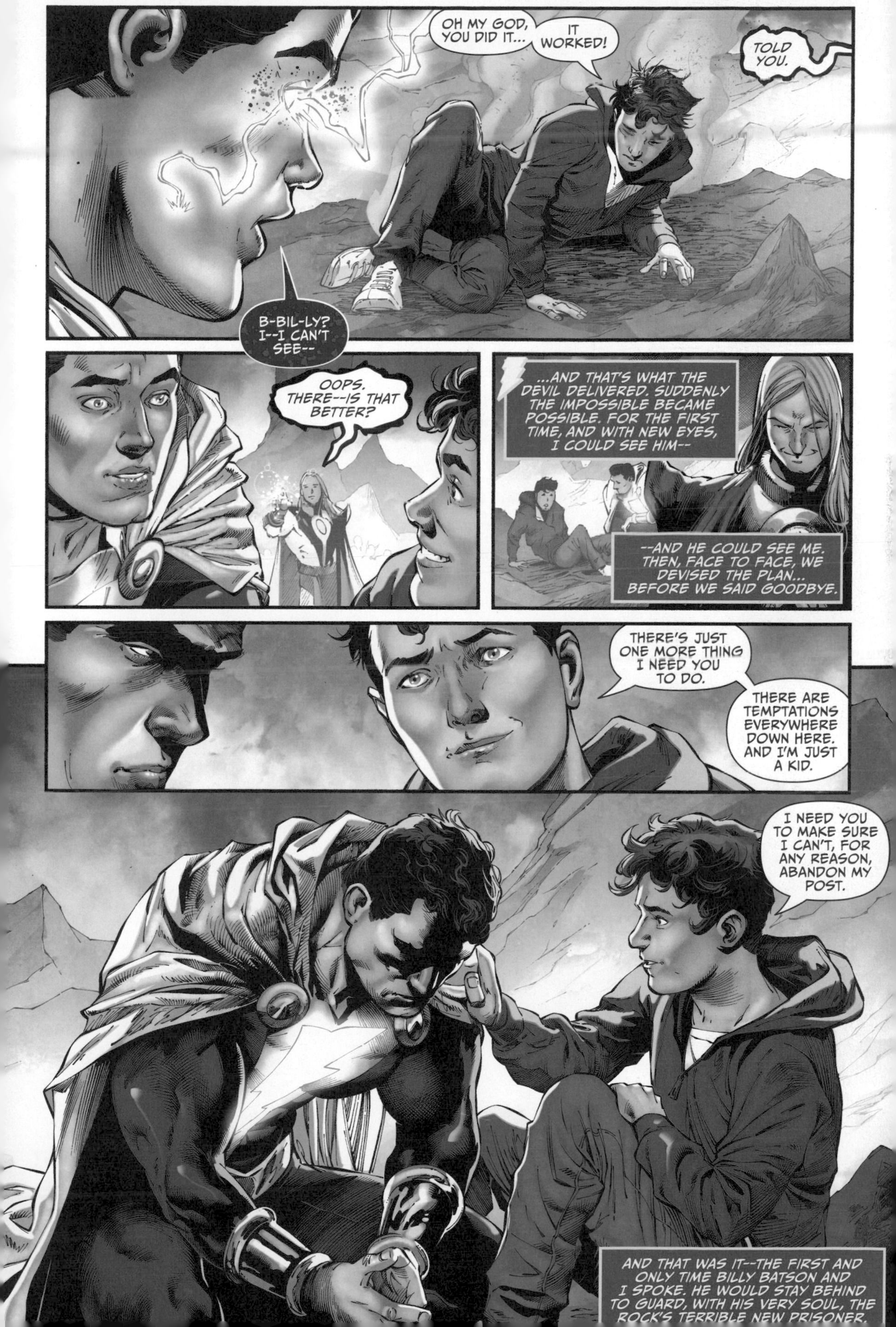
OH MY GOD, YOU DID IT...
IT WORKED!
TOLD YOU.
B-BIL-LY? I--I CAN'T SEE--
OOPS. THERE--IS THAT BETTER?
...AND THAT'S WHAT THE DEVIL DELIVERED. SUDDENLY THE IMPOSSIBLE BECAME POSSIBLE. FOR THE FIRST TIME, AND WITH NEW EYES, I COULD SEE HIM--
--AND HE COULD SEE ME. THEN, FACE TO FACE, WE DEVISED THE PLAN... BEFORE WE SAID GOODBYE.
THERE'S JUST ONE MORE THING I NEED YOU TO DO.
THERE ARE TEMPTATIONS EVERYWHERE DOWN HERE. AND I'M JUST A KID.
I NEED YOU TO MAKE SURE I CAN'T, FOR ANY REASON, ABANDON MY POST.
AND THAT WAS IT--THE FIRST AND ONLY TIME BILLY BATSON AND I SPOKE. HE WOULD STAY BEHIND TO GUARD, WITH HIS VERY SOUL, THE ROCK'S TERRIBLE NEW PRISONER.

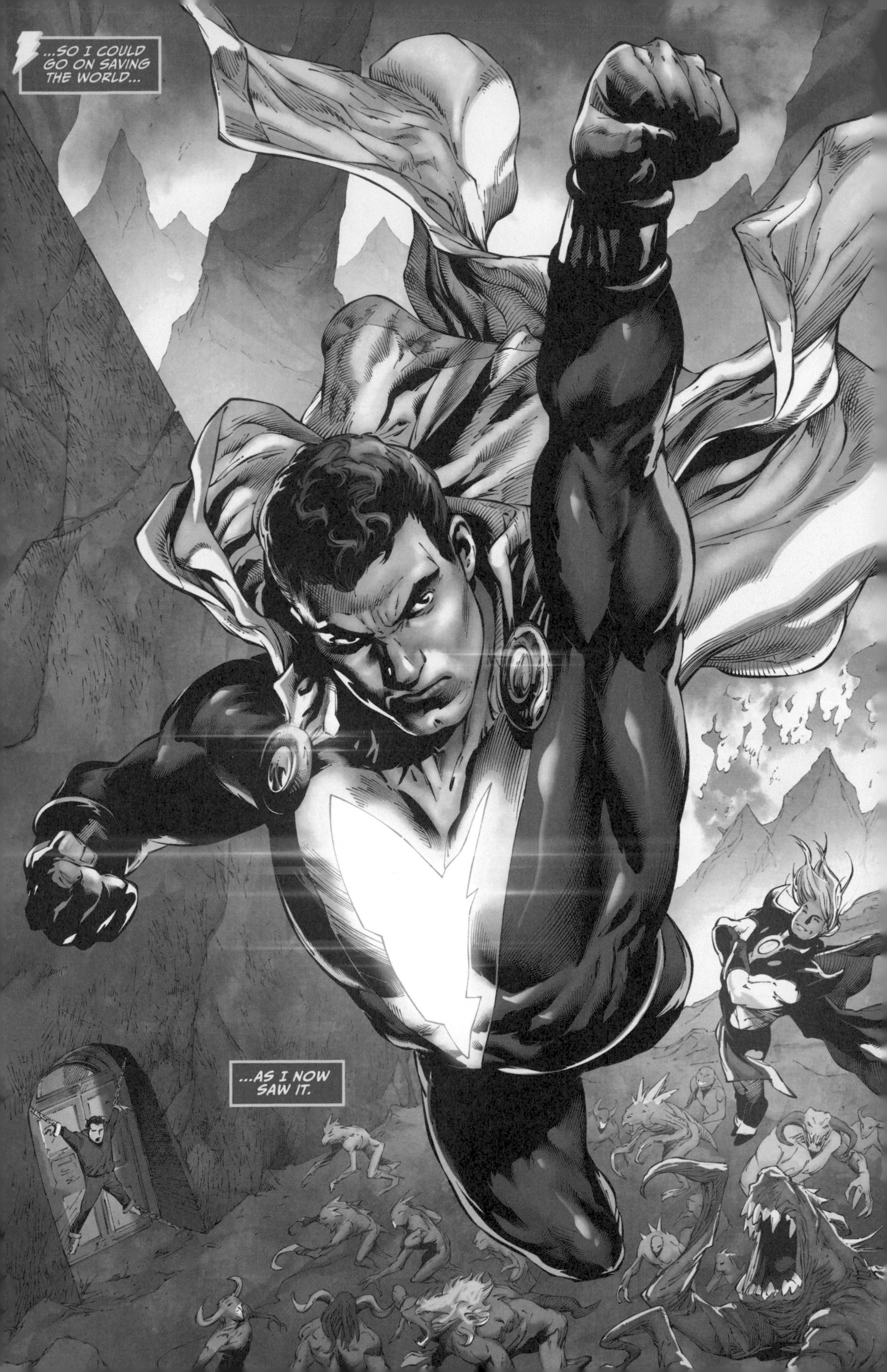
...SO I COULD GO ON SAVING THE WORLD...
...AS I NOW SAW IT.

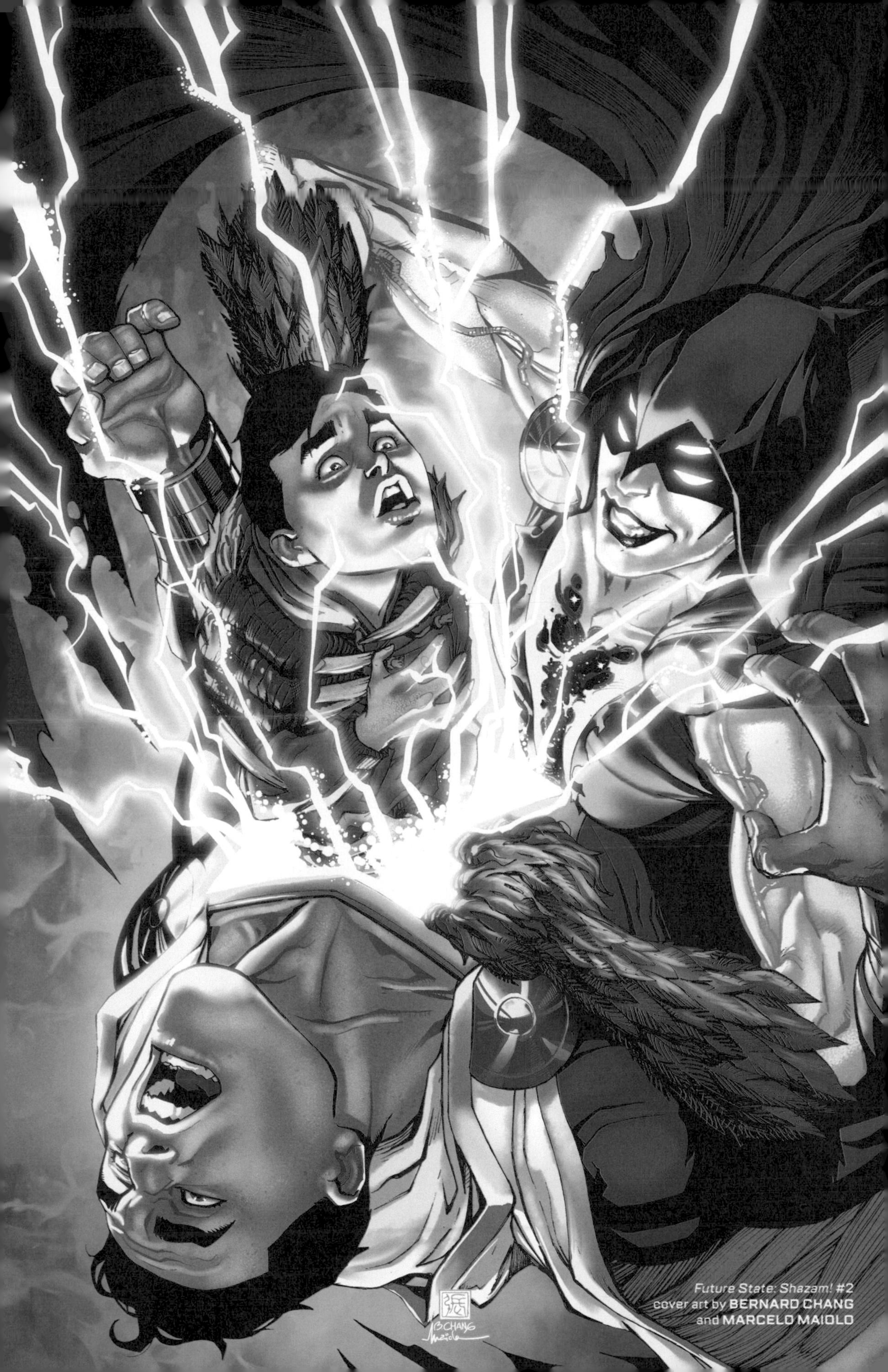

Future State: Shazam! #2
cover art by **BERNARD CHANG**
and **MARCELO MAIOLO**

Future State: Shazam! **#2**
variant cover art by **GERALD PAREL**

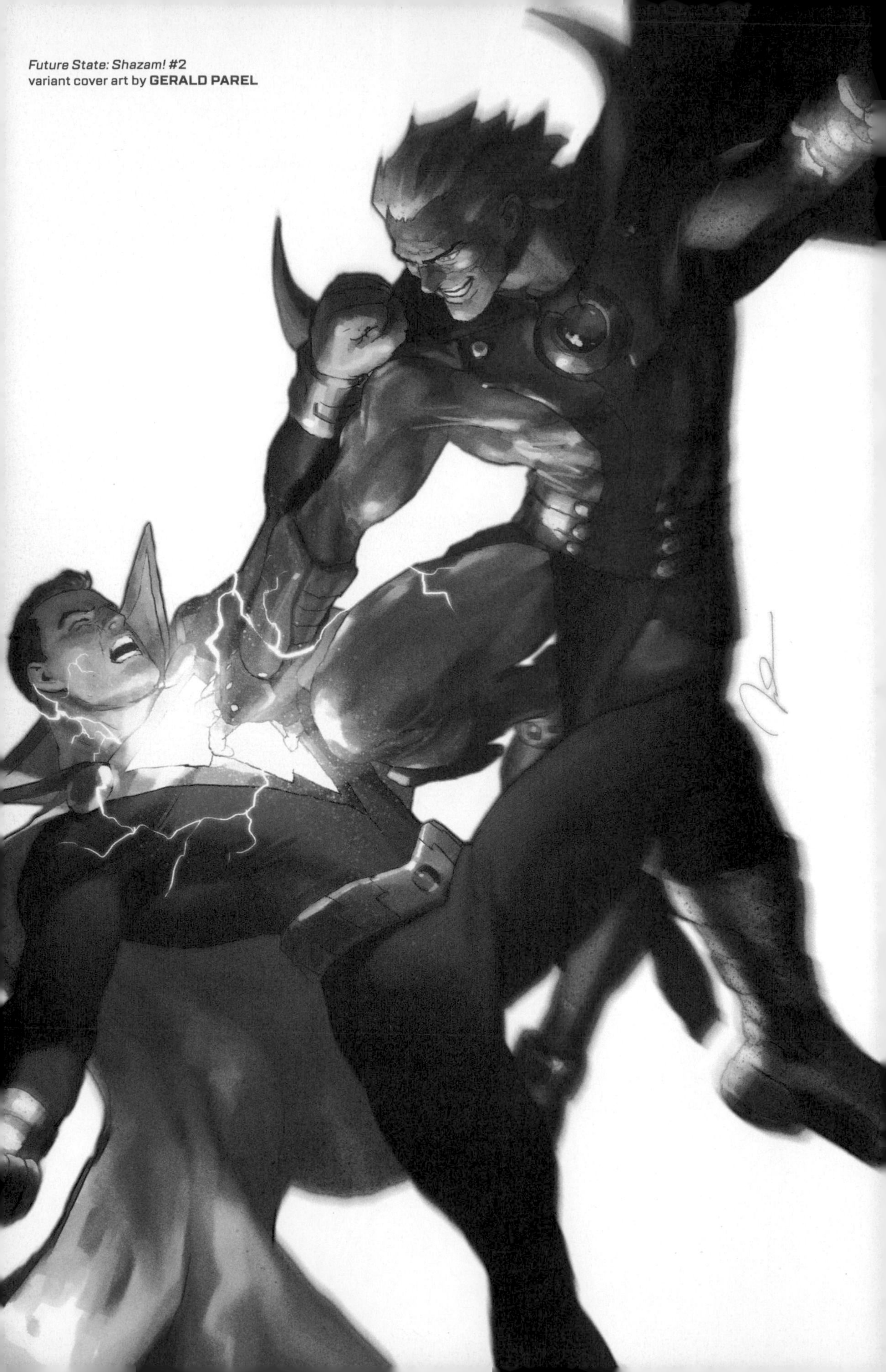

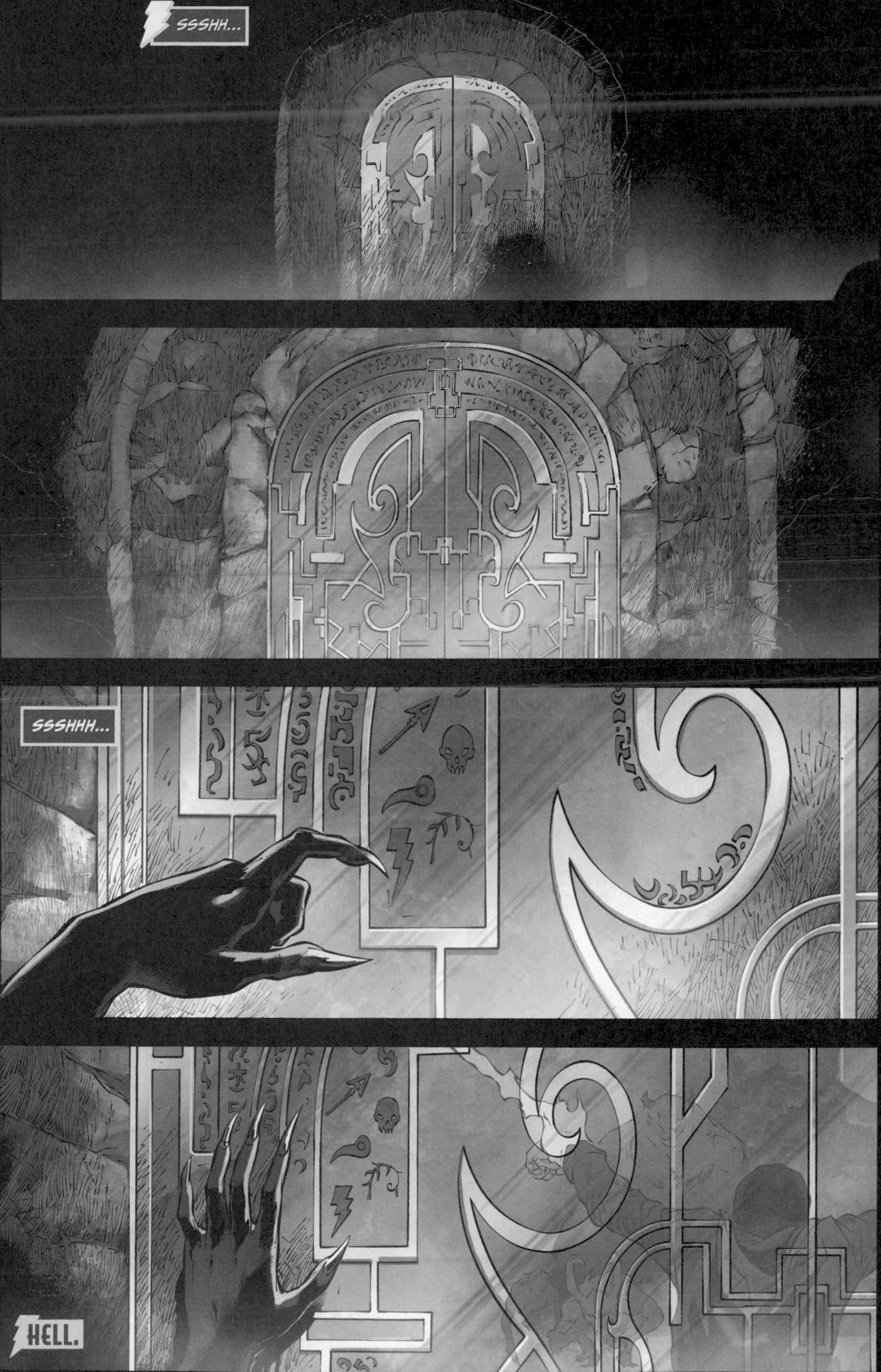
SSSHH...
SSSHHH...
HELL.

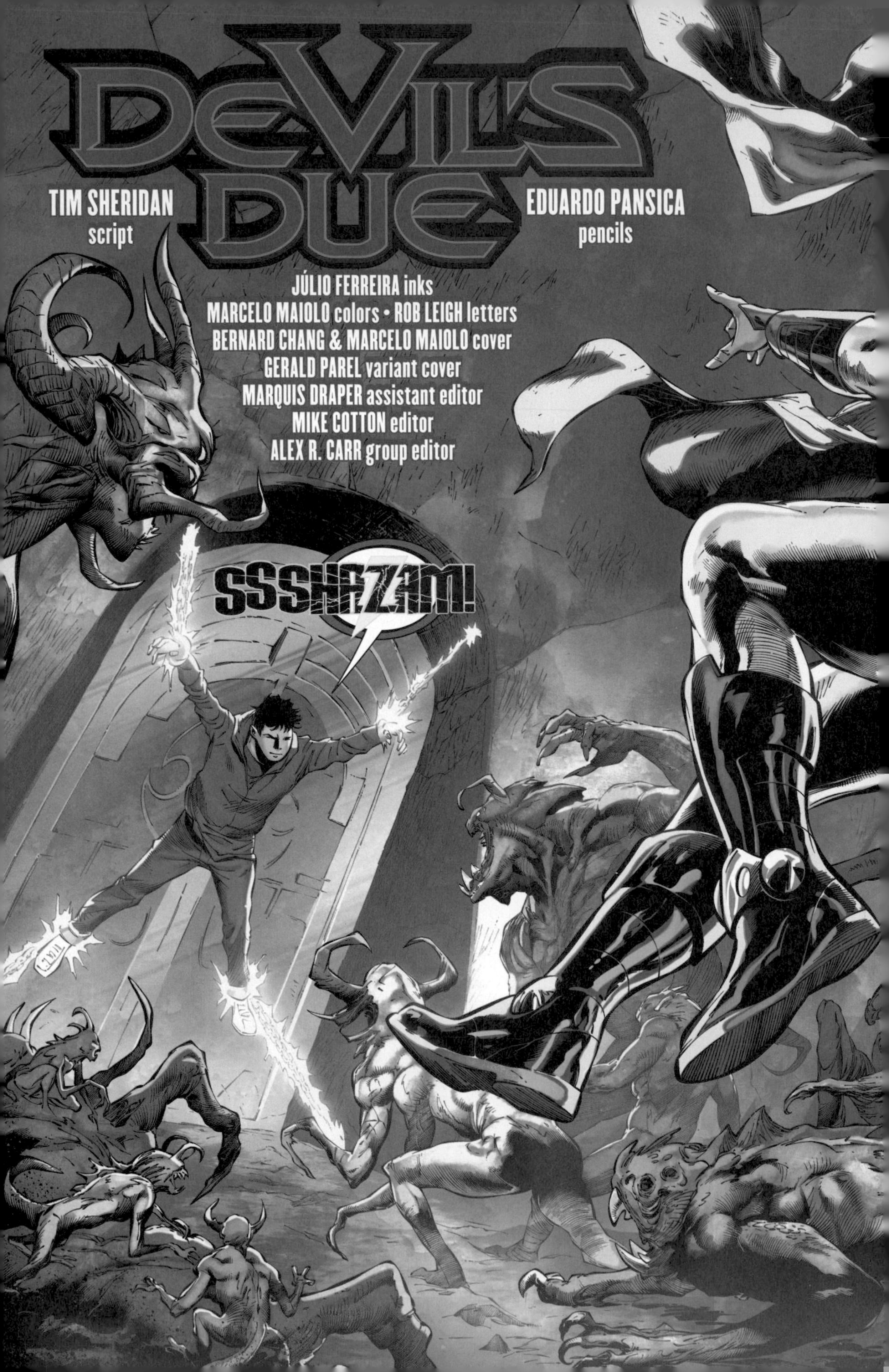
DEVIL'S DUE
TIM SHERIDAN script
EDUARDO PANSICA pencils
JÚLIO FERREIRA inks
MARCELO MAIOLO colors • ROB LEIGH letters
BERNARD CHANG & MARCELO MAIOLO cover
GERALD PAREL variant cover
MARQUIS DRAPER assistant editor
MIKE COTTON editor
ALEX R. CARR group editor
SSSHAZAM!

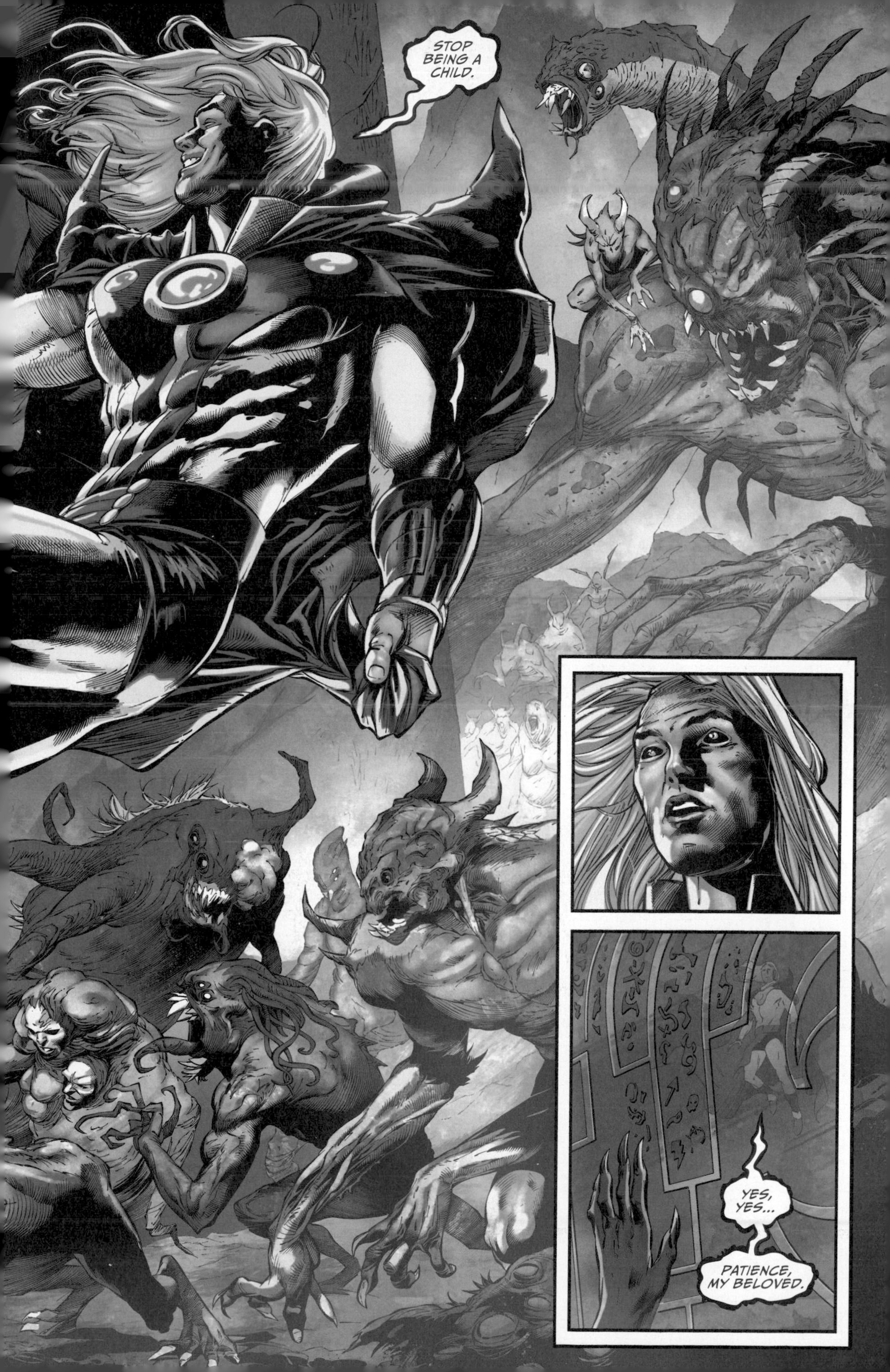
STOP BEING A CHILD.
YES, YES...
PATIENCE, MY BELOVED.

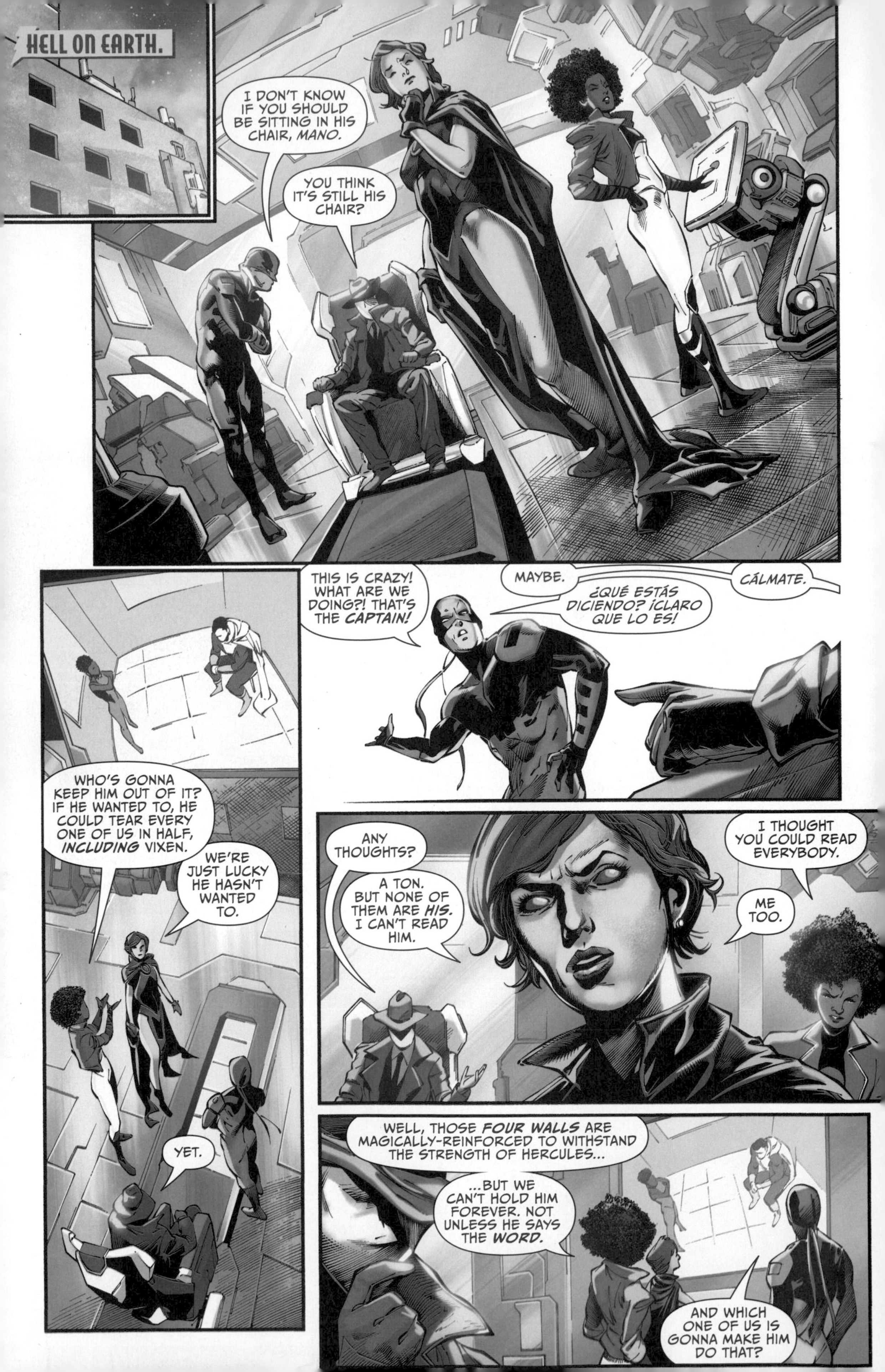
HELL ON EARTH.
I DON'T KNOW IF YOU SHOULD BE SITTING IN HIS CHAIR, MANO.
YOU THINK IT'S STILL HIS CHAIR?
THIS IS CRAZY! WHAT ARE WE DOING?! THAT'S THE CAPTAIN!
MAYBE.
¿QUÉ ESTÁS DICIENDO? ¡CLARO QUE LO ES!
CÁLMATE.
WHO'S GONNA KEEP HIM OUT OF IT? IF HE WANTED TO, HE COULD TEAR EVERY ONE OF US IN HALF, INCLUDING VIXEN.
WE'RE JUST LUCKY HE HASN'T WANTED TO.
YET.
ANY THOUGHTS?
A TON. BUT NONE OF THEM ARE HIS. I CAN'T READ HIM.
I THOUGHT YOU COULD READ EVERYBODY.
ME TOO.
WELL, THOSE FOUR WALLS ARE MAGICALLY-REINFORCED TO WITHSTAND THE STRENGTH OF HERCULES...
...BUT WE CAN'T HOLD HIM FOREVER. NOT UNLESS HE SAYS THE WORD.
AND WHICH ONE OF US IS GONNA MAKE HIM DO THAT?

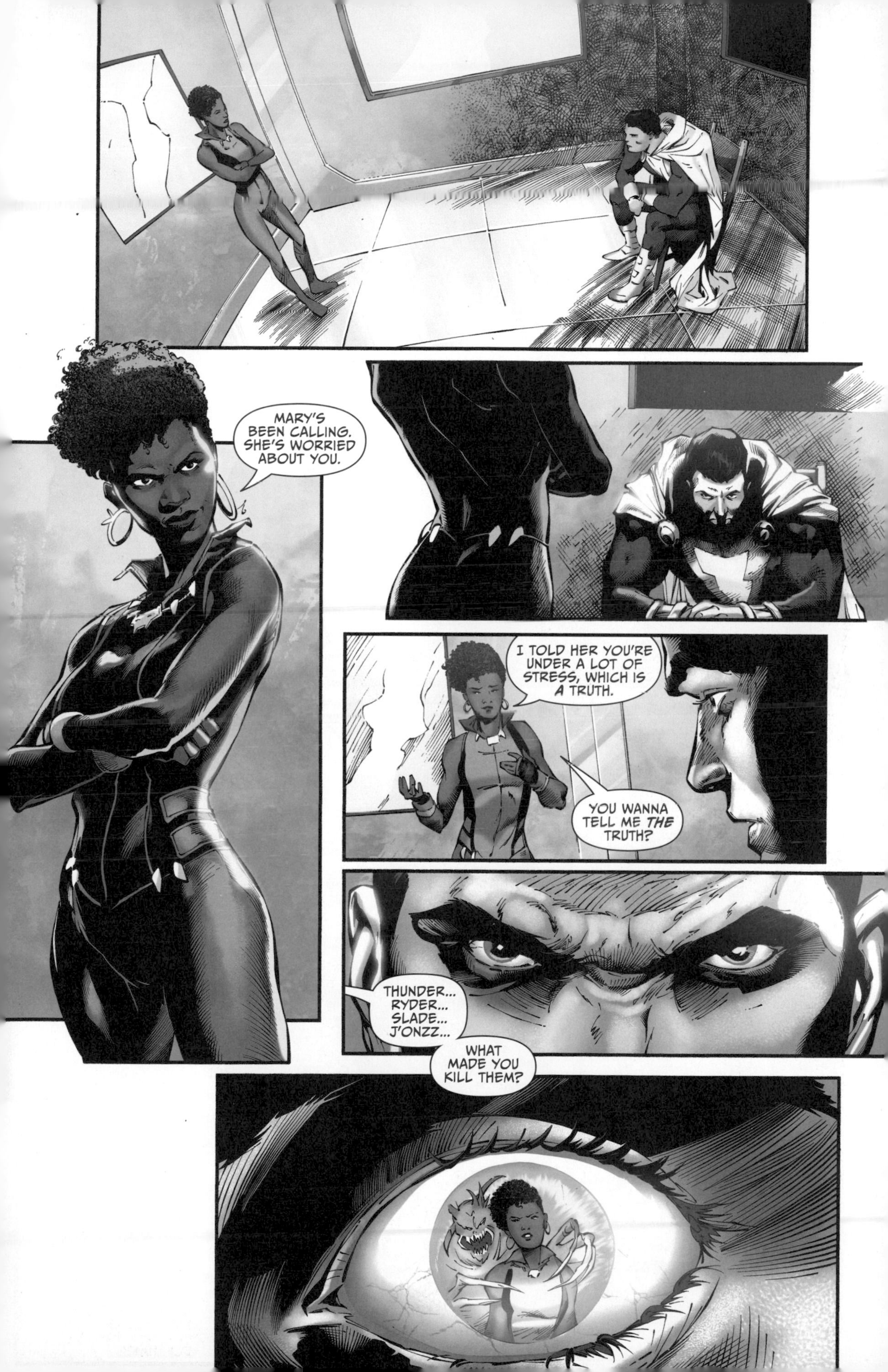

MARY'S BEEN CALLING. SHE'S WORRIED ABOUT YOU.
I TOLD HER YOU'RE UNDER A LOT OF STRESS, WHICH IS A TRUTH.
YOU WANNA TELL ME THE TRUTH?
THUNDER... RYDER... SLADE... J'ONZZ...
WHAT MADE YOU KILL THEM?

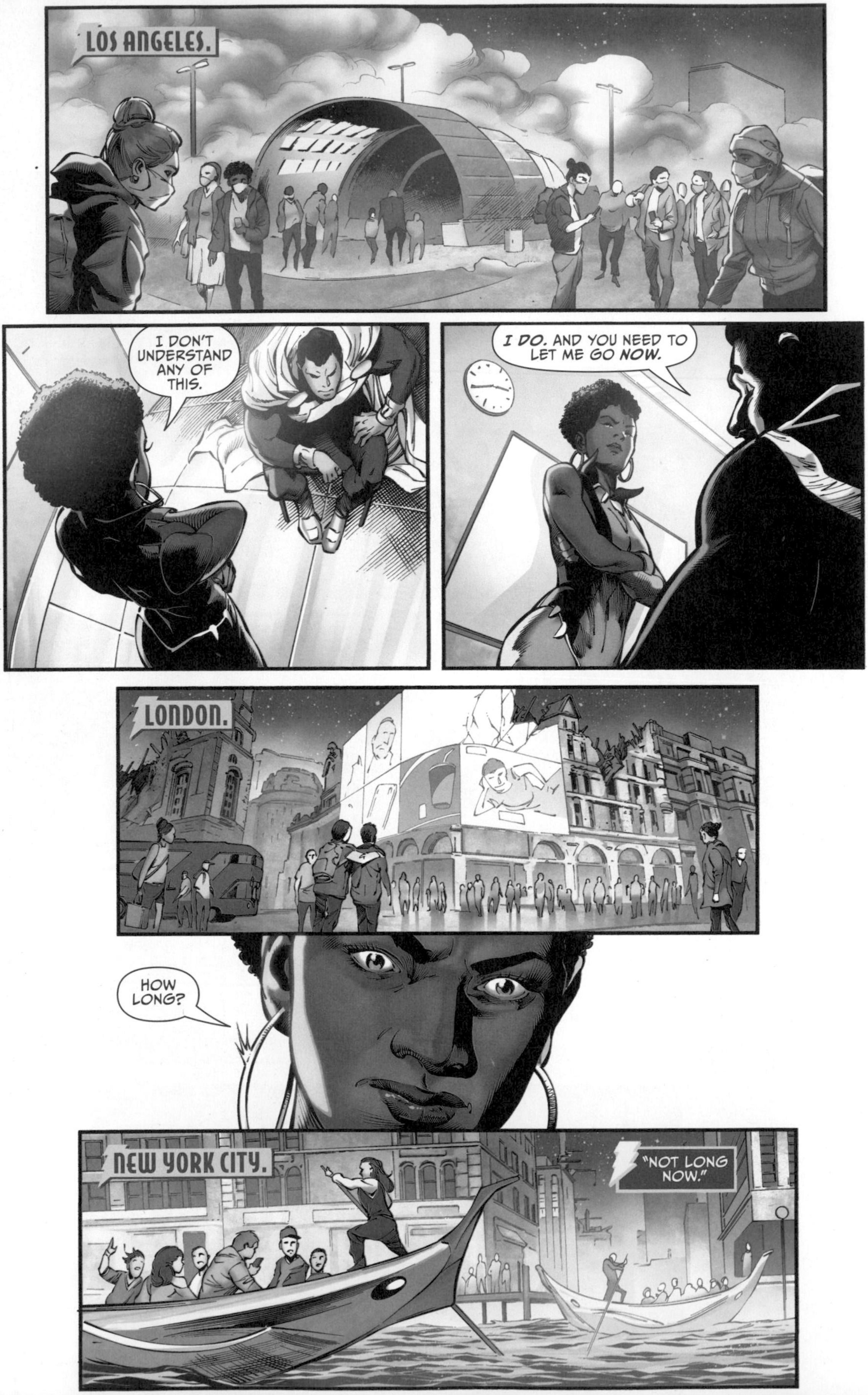
LOS ANGELES.
I DON'T UNDERSTAND ANY OF THIS.
I DO. AND YOU NEED TO LET ME GO NOW.
LONDON.
HOW LONG?
NEW YORK CITY.
"NOT LONG NOW."

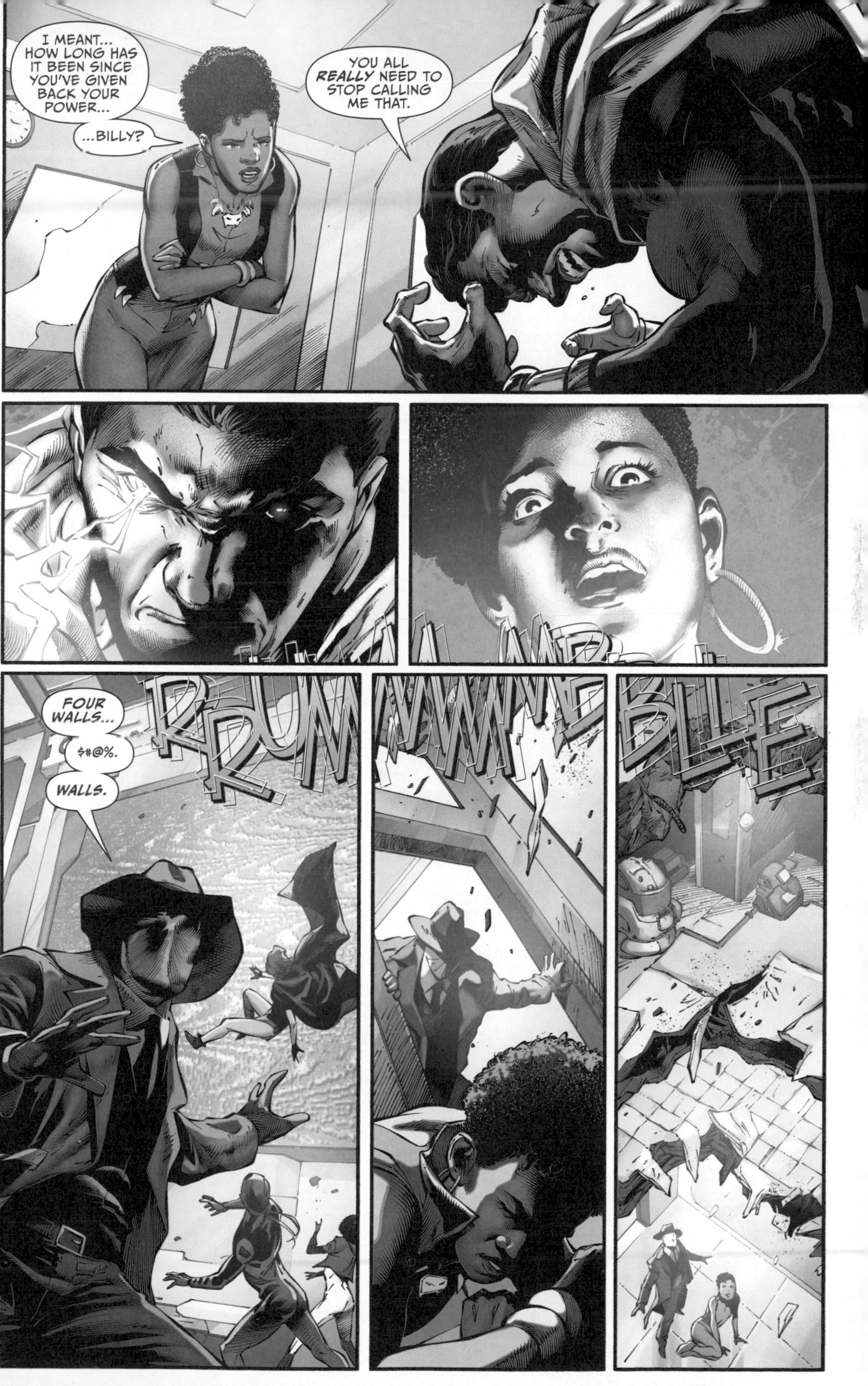

I MEANT... HOW LONG HAS IT BEEN SINCE YOU'VE GIVEN BACK YOUR POWER...
...BILLY?
YOU ALL *REALLY* NEED TO STOP CALLING ME THAT.
RRUMMMMMBBLLE
FOUR WALLS...
$#@%.
WALLS.

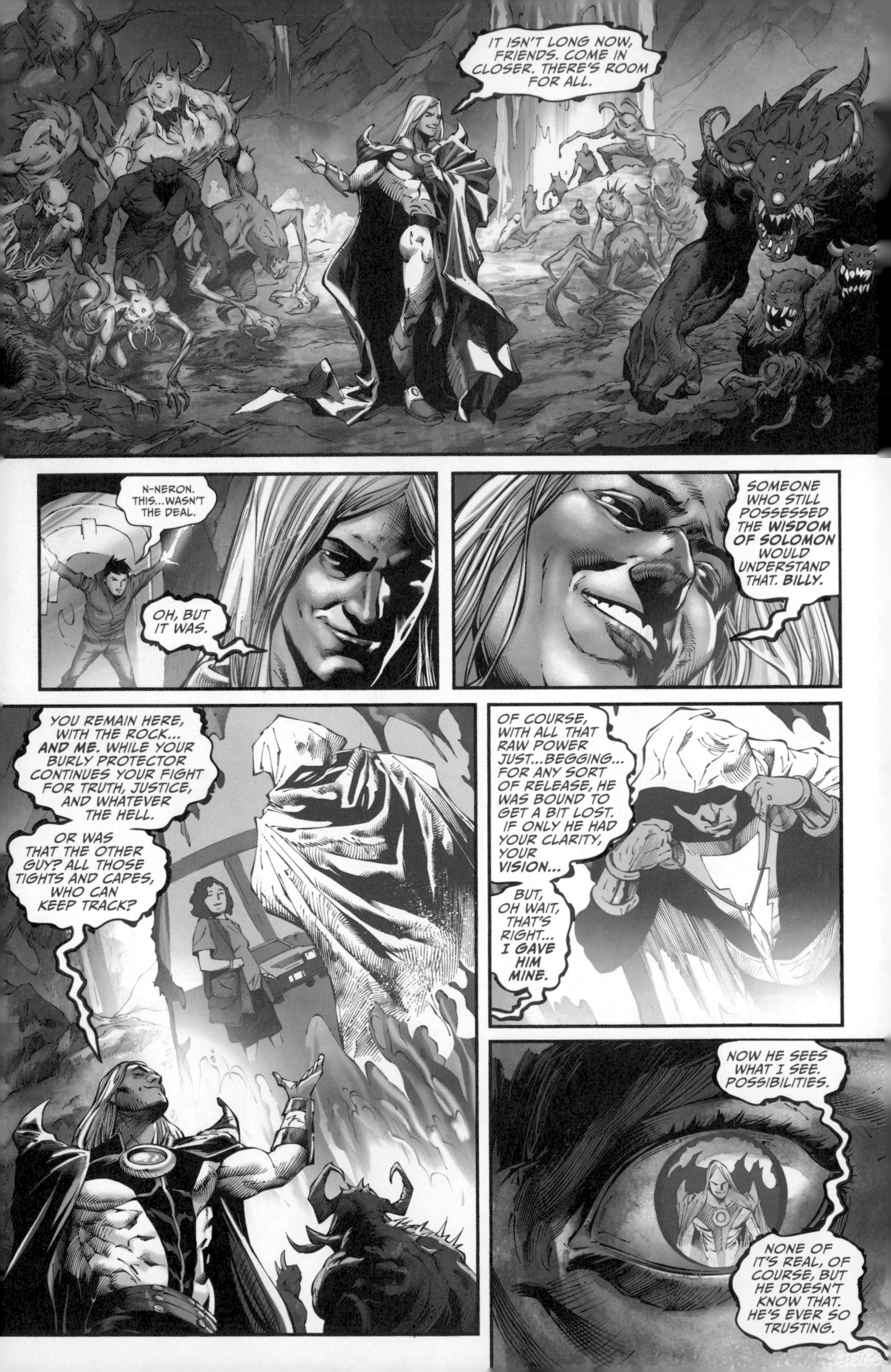
IT ISN'T LONG NOW, FRIENDS. COME IN CLOSER. THERE'S ROOM FOR ALL.
N-NERON. THIS...WASN'T THE DEAL.
OH, BUT IT WAS.
SOMEONE WHO STILL POSSESSED THE WISDOM OF SOLOMON WOULD UNDERSTAND THAT. BILLY.
YOU REMAIN HERE, WITH THE ROCK... AND ME. WHILE YOUR BURLY PROTECTOR CONTINUES YOUR FIGHT FOR TRUTH, JUSTICE, AND WHATEVER THE HELL.
OR WAS THAT THE OTHER GUY? ALL THOSE TIGHTS AND CAPES, WHO CAN KEEP TRACK?
OF COURSE, WITH ALL THAT RAW POWER JUST...BEGGING... FOR ANY SORT OF RELEASE, HE WAS BOUND TO GET A BIT LOST. IF ONLY HE HAD YOUR CLARITY, YOUR VISION...
BUT, OH WAIT, THAT'S RIGHT... I GAVE HIM MINE.
NOW HE SEES WHAT I SEE. POSSIBILITIES.
NONE OF IT'S REAL, OF COURSE, BUT HE DOESN'T KNOW THAT. HE'S EVER SO TRUSTING.

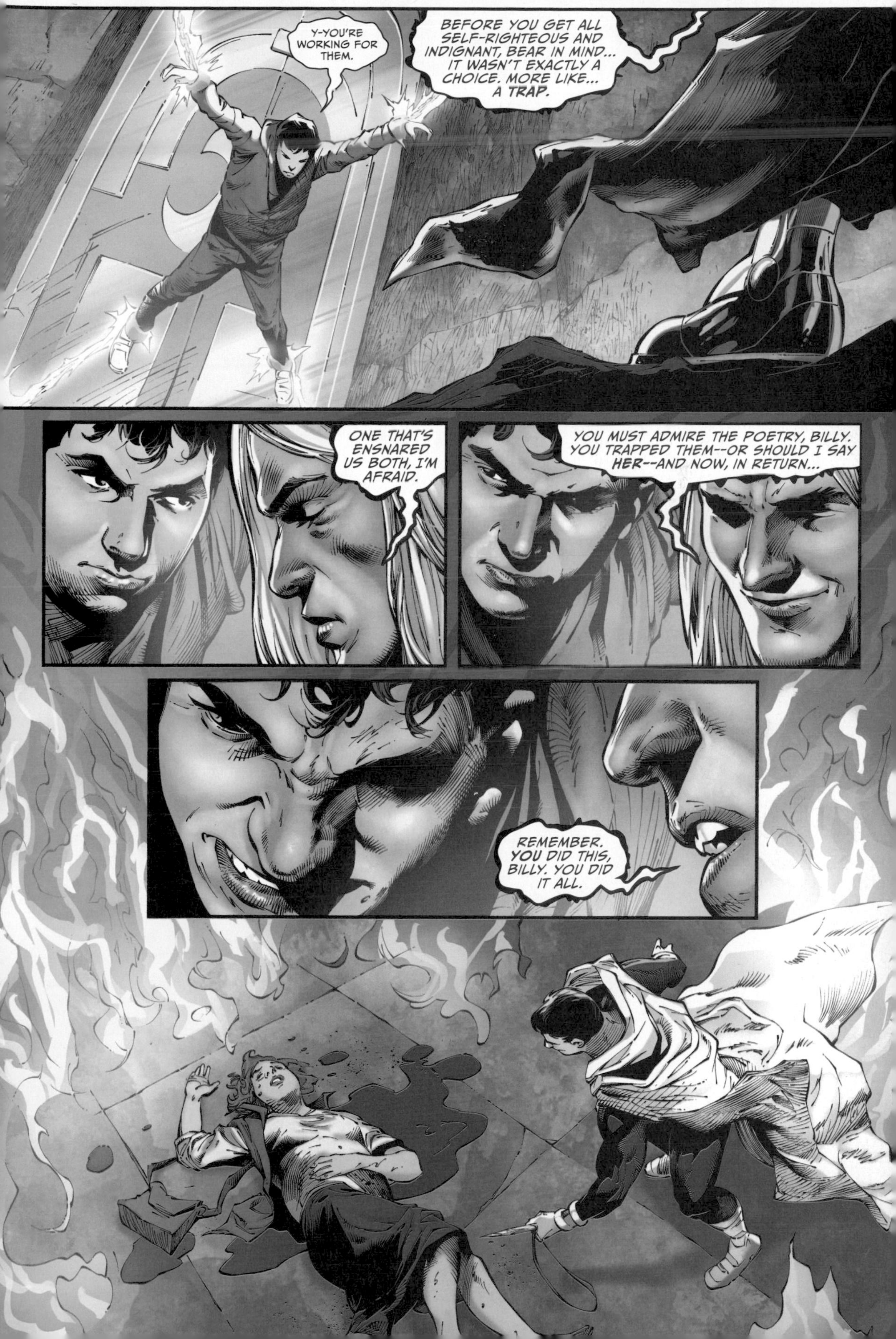
Y-YOU'RE WORKING FOR THEM.
BEFORE YOU GET ALL SELF-RIGHTEOUS AND INDIGNANT, BEAR IN MIND... IT WASN'T EXACTLY A CHOICE. MORE LIKE... A **TRAP**.
ONE THAT'S ENSNARED US BOTH, I'M AFRAID.
YOU MUST ADMIRE THE POETRY, BILLY. YOU TRAPPED THEM--OR SHOULD I SAY **HER**--AND NOW, IN RETURN...
REMEMBER. **YOU** DID THIS, BILLY. YOU DID IT ALL.

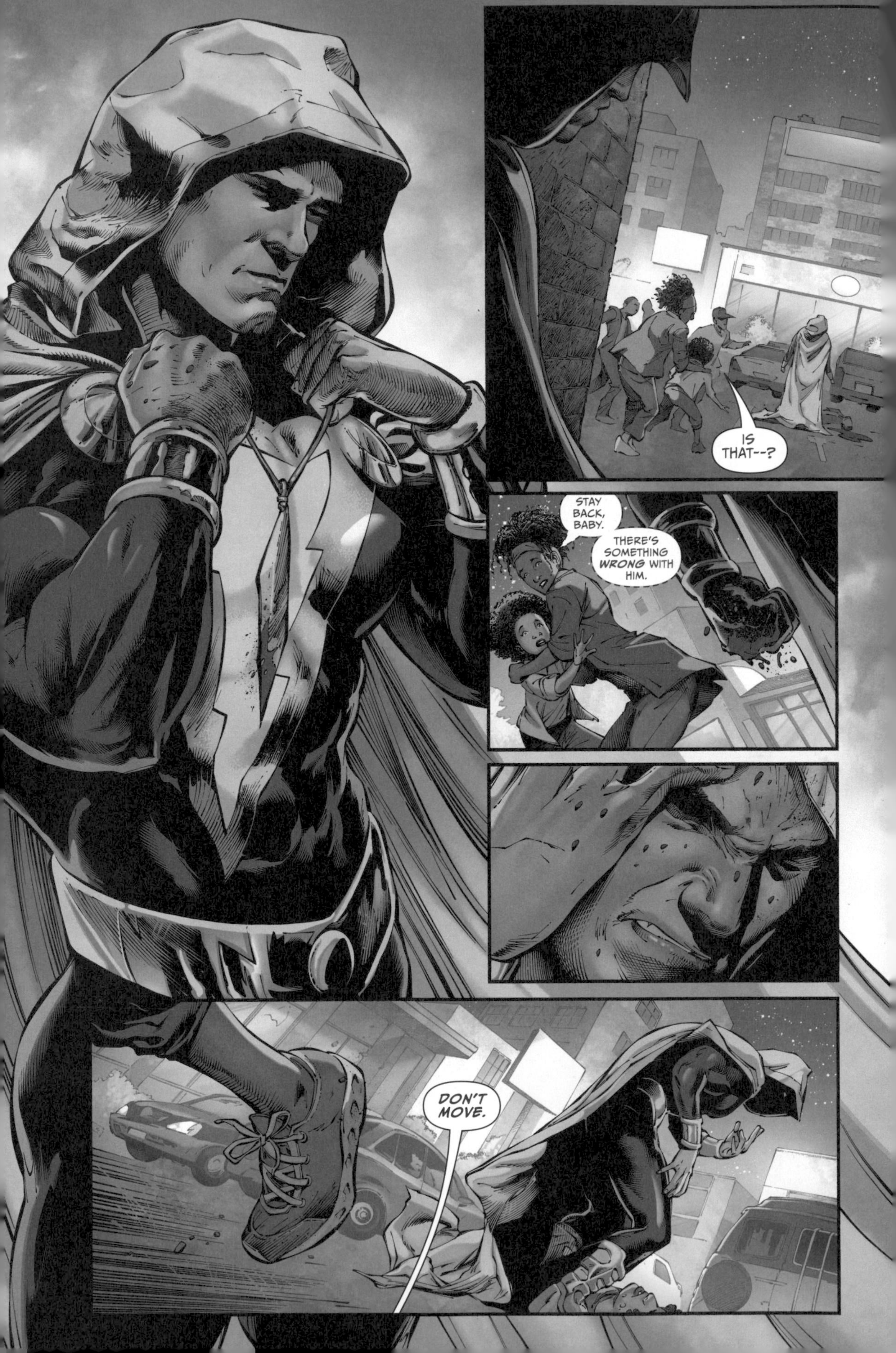
IS THAT--?
STAY BACK, BABY.
THERE'S SOMETHING WRONG WITH HIM.
DON'T MOVE.

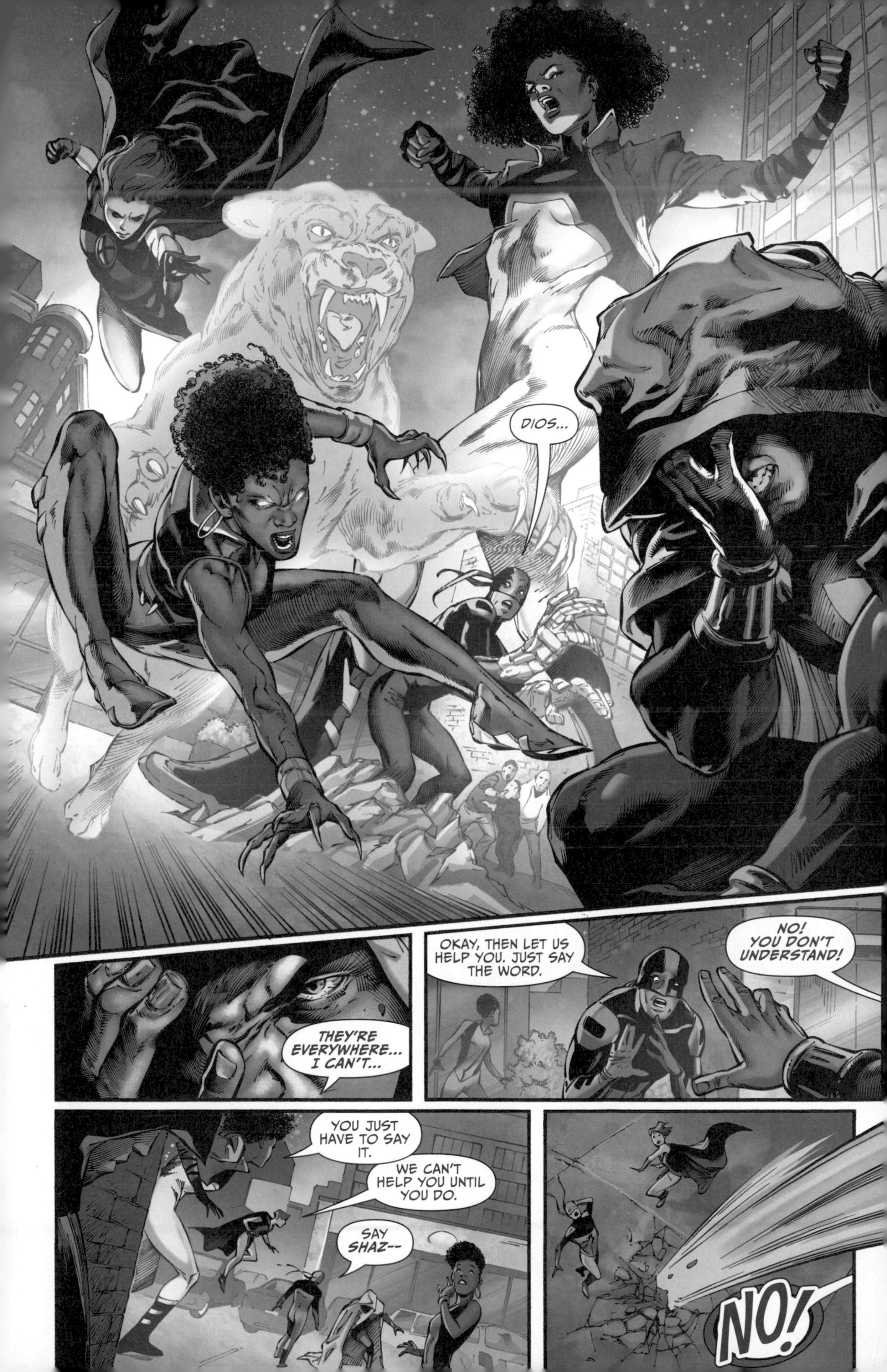
DIOS...
THEY'RE EVERYWHERE... I CAN'T...
OKAY, THEN LET US HELP YOU. JUST SAY THE WORD.
NO! YOU DON'T UNDERSTAND!
YOU JUST HAVE TO SAY IT.
WE CAN'T HELP YOU UNTIL YOU DO.
SAY SHAZ--
NO!

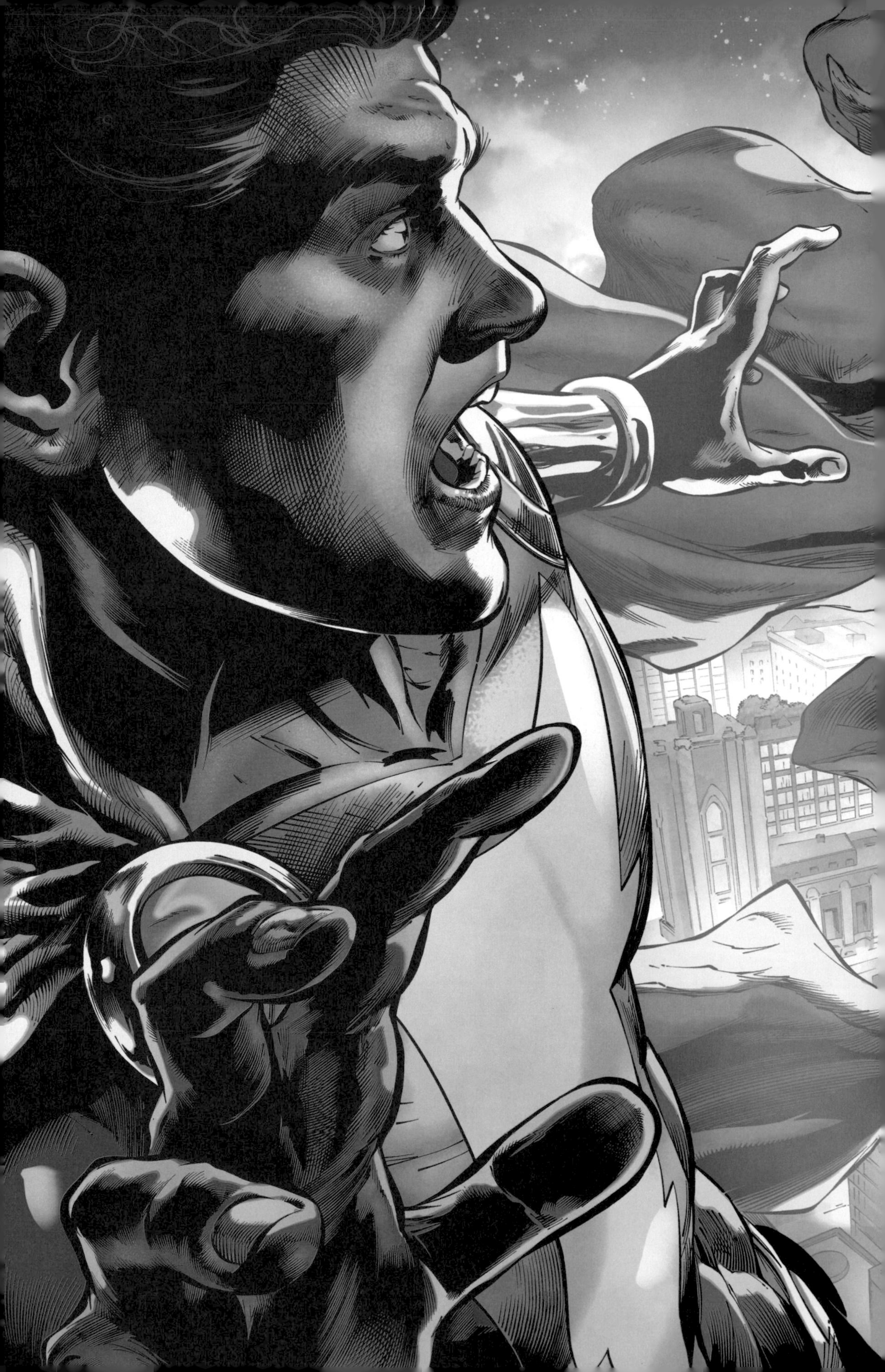

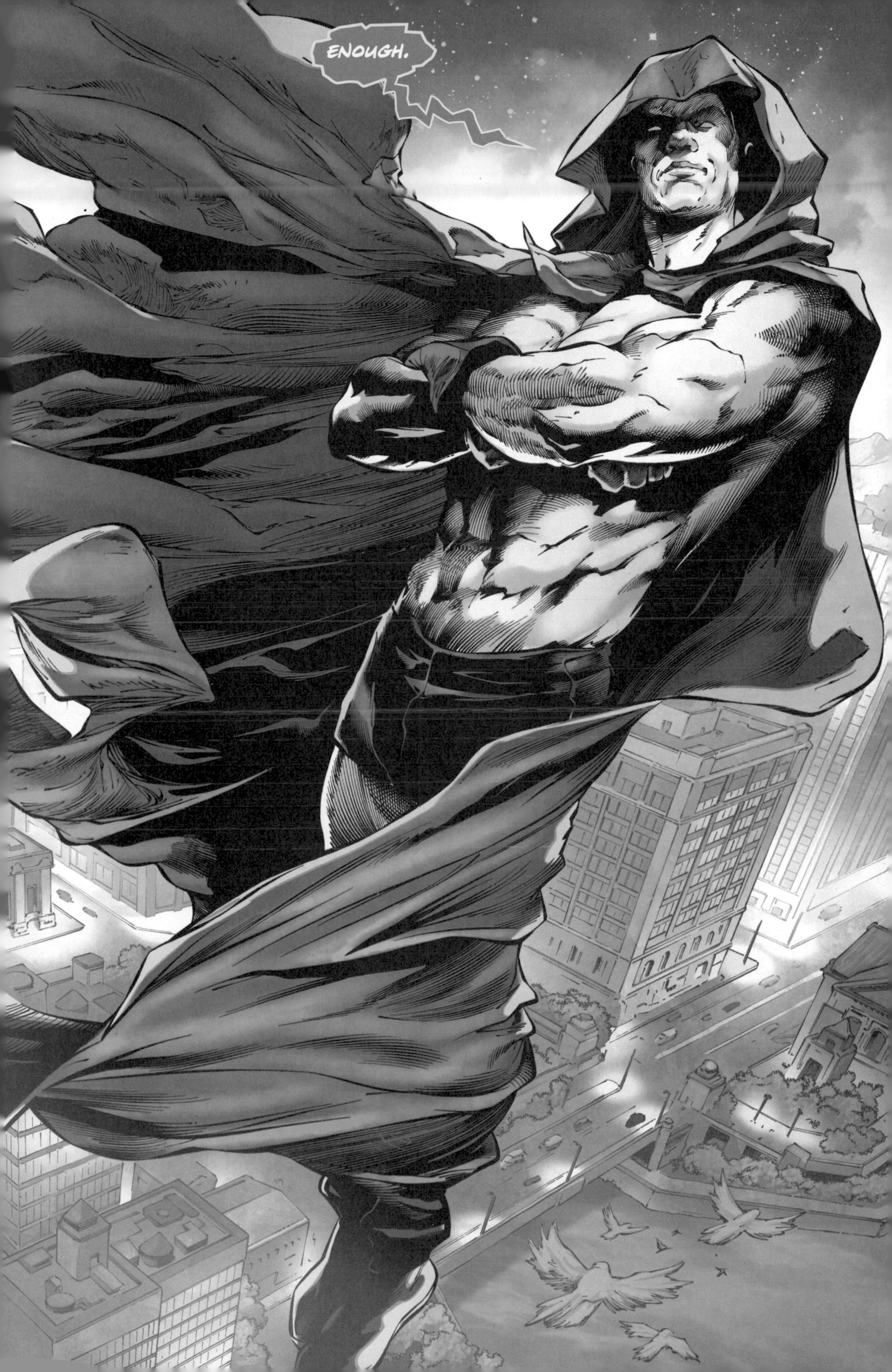
ENOUGH.

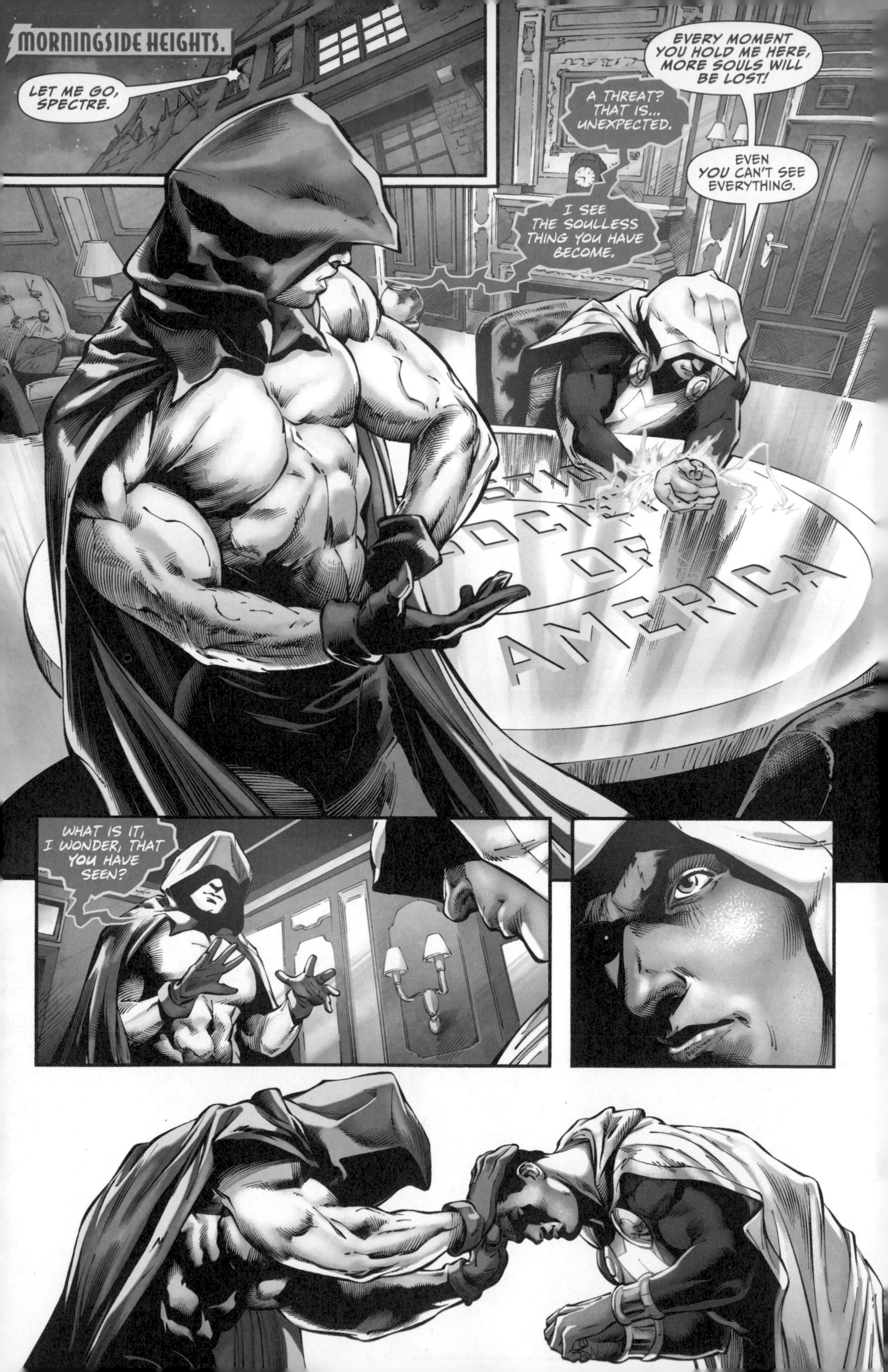
MORNINGSIDE HEIGHTS.
LET ME GO, SPECTRE.
EVERY MOMENT YOU HOLD ME HERE, MORE SOULS WILL BE LOST!
A THREAT? THAT IS... UNEXPECTED.
EVEN YOU CAN'T SEE EVERYTHING.
I SEE THE SOULLESS THING YOU HAVE BECOME.
AMERICA
WHAT IS IT, I WONDER, THAT YOU HAVE SEEN?

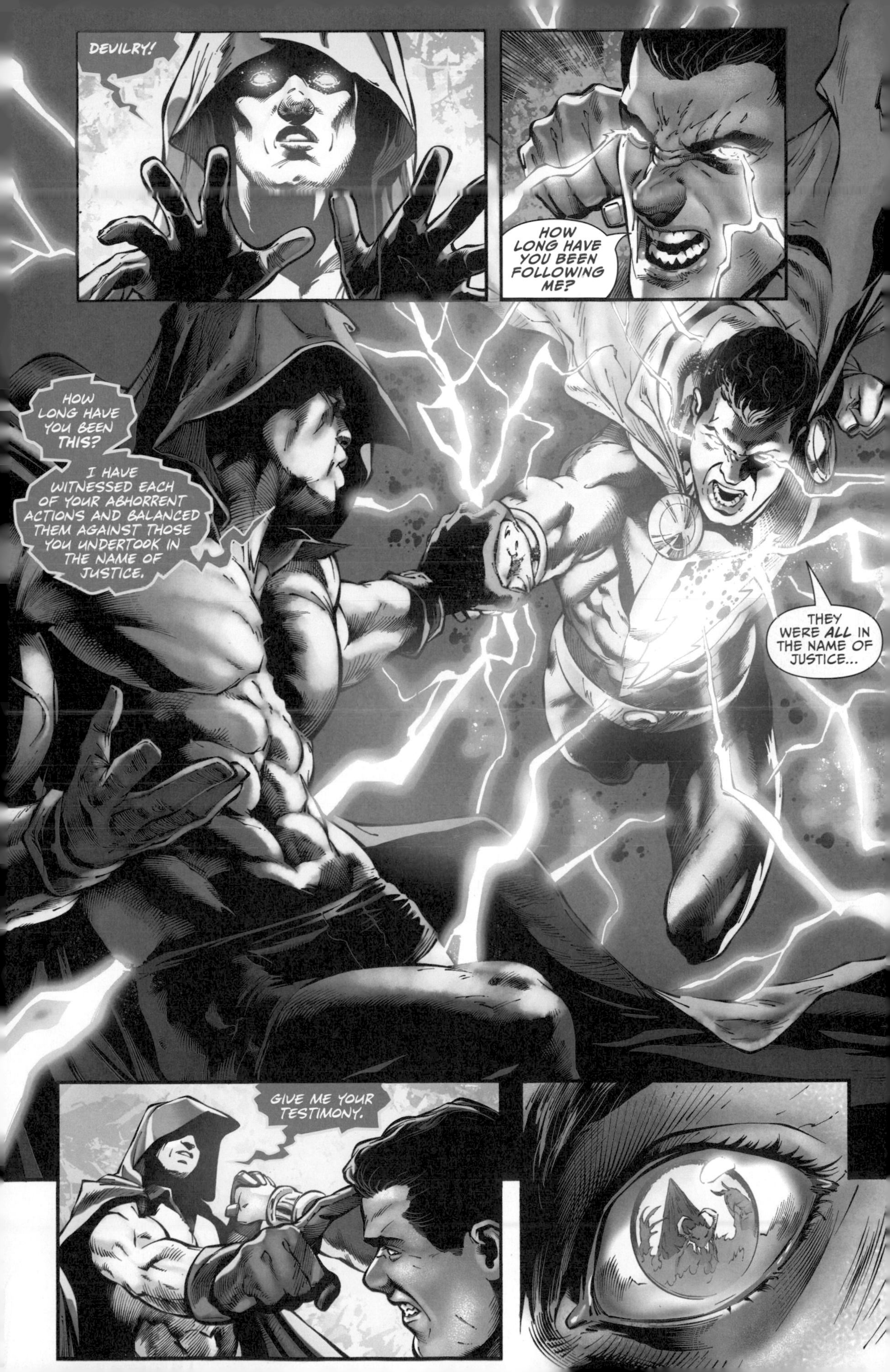
DEVILRY!
HOW LONG HAVE YOU BEEN FOLLOWING ME?
HOW LONG HAVE YOU BEEN THIS?
I HAVE WITNESSED EACH OF YOUR ABHORRENT ACTIONS AND BALANCED THEM AGAINST THOSE YOU UNDERTOOK IN THE NAME OF JUSTICE.
THEY WERE ALL IN THE NAME OF JUSTICE...
GIVE ME YOUR TESTIMONY.

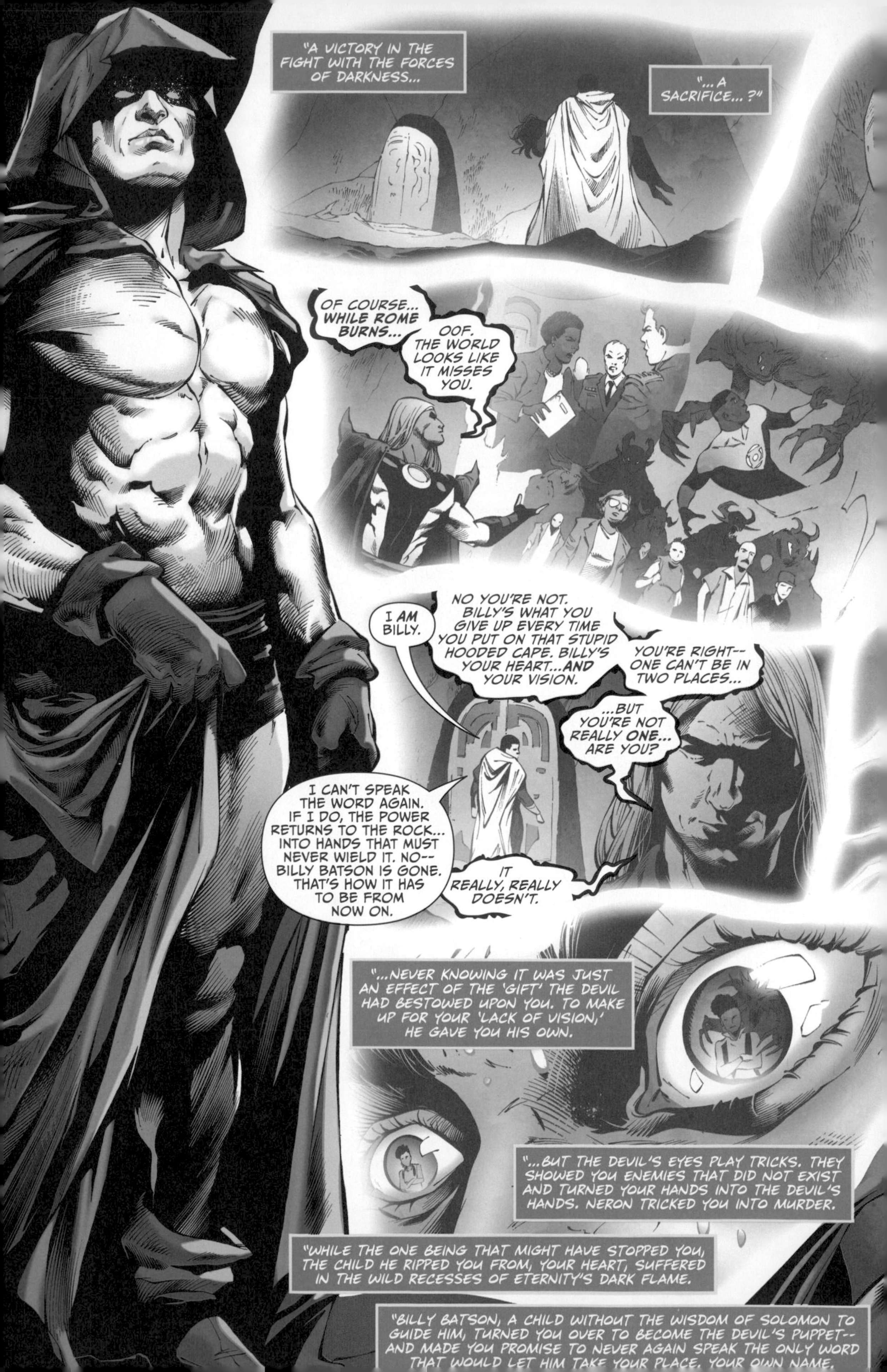
"A VICTORY IN THE FIGHT WITH THE FORCES OF DARKNESS...
"...A SACRIFICE...?"
OF COURSE... WHILE ROME BURNS...
OOF. THE WORLD LOOKS LIKE IT MISSES YOU.
I AM BILLY.
NO YOU'RE NOT. BILLY'S WHAT YOU GIVE UP EVERY TIME YOU PUT ON THAT STUPID HOODED CAPE. BILLY'S YOUR HEART...AND YOUR VISION.
YOU'RE RIGHT-- ONE CAN'T BE IN TWO PLACES...
...BUT YOU'RE NOT REALLY ONE... ARE YOU?
I CAN'T SPEAK THE WORD AGAIN. IF I DO, THE POWER RETURNS TO THE ROCK... INTO HANDS THAT MUST NEVER WIELD IT. NO-- BILLY BATSON IS GONE. THAT'S HOW IT HAS TO BE FROM NOW ON.
IT REALLY, REALLY DOESN'T.
"...NEVER KNOWING IT WAS JUST AN EFFECT OF THE 'GIFT' THE DEVIL HAD BESTOWED UPON YOU. TO MAKE UP FOR YOUR 'LACK OF VISION,' HE GAVE YOU HIS OWN.
"...BUT THE DEVIL'S EYES PLAY TRICKS. THEY SHOWED YOU ENEMIES THAT DID NOT EXIST AND TURNED YOUR HANDS INTO THE DEVIL'S HANDS. NERON TRICKED YOU INTO MURDER.
"WHILE THE ONE BEING THAT MIGHT HAVE STOPPED YOU, THE CHILD HE RIPPED YOU FROM, YOUR HEART, SUFFERED IN THE WILD RECESSES OF ETERNITY'S DARK FLAME.
"BILLY BATSON, A CHILD WITHOUT THE WISDOM OF SOLOMON TO GUIDE HIM, TURNED YOU OVER TO BECOME THE DEVIL'S PUPPET-- AND MADE YOU PROMISE TO NEVER AGAIN SPEAK THE ONLY WORD THAT WOULD LET HIM TAKE YOUR PLACE. YOUR OWN NAME.

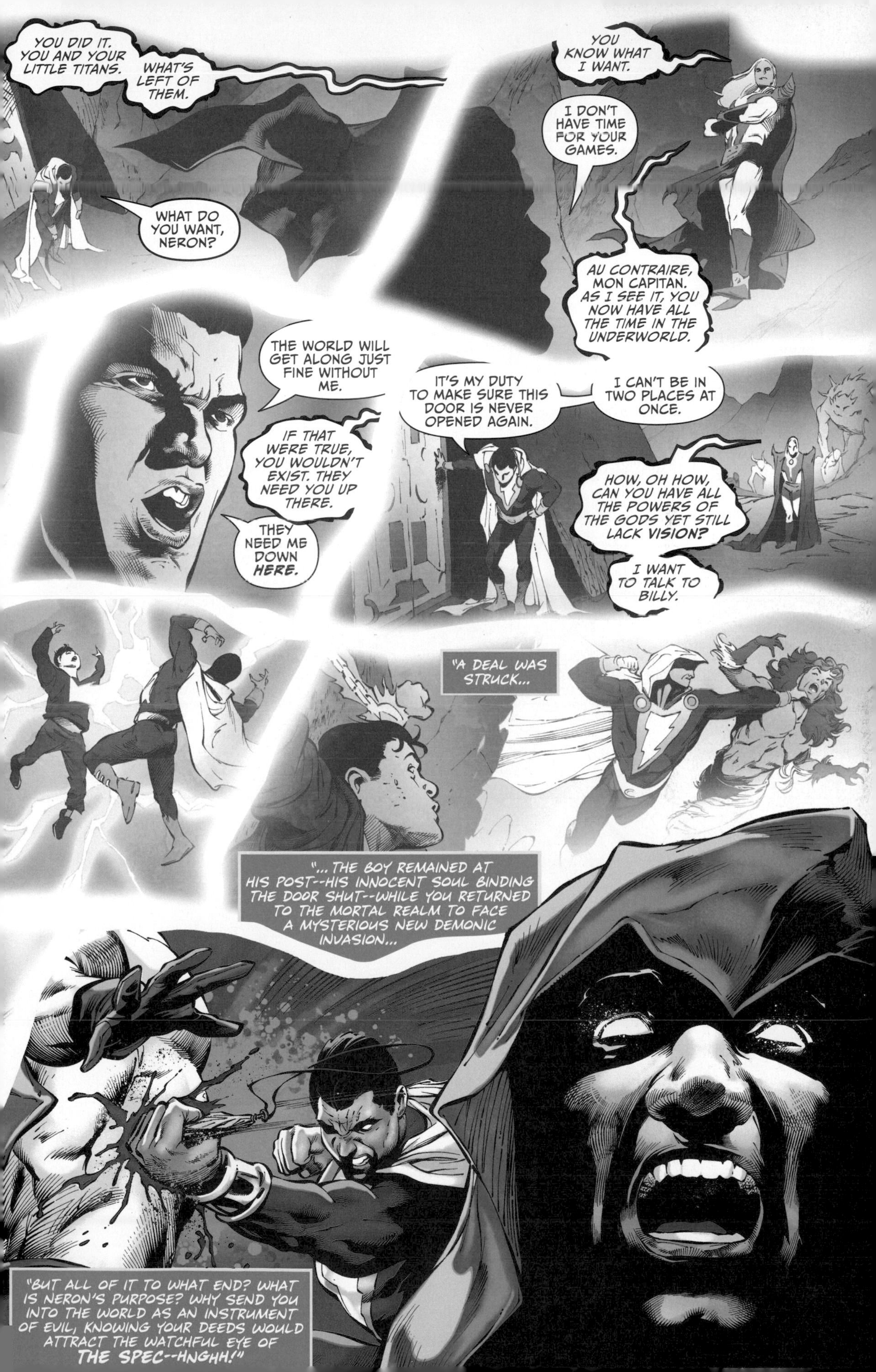

YOU DID IT. YOU AND YOUR LITTLE TITANS.
WHAT'S LEFT OF THEM.
WHAT DO YOU WANT, NERON?
YOU KNOW WHAT I WANT.
I DON'T HAVE TIME FOR YOUR GAMES.
AU CONTRAIRE, MON CAPITAN. AS I SEE IT, YOU NOW HAVE ALL THE TIME IN THE UNDERWORLD.
THE WORLD WILL GET ALONG JUST FINE WITHOUT ME.
IF THAT WERE TRUE, YOU WOULDN'T EXIST. THEY NEED YOU UP THERE.
THEY NEED ME DOWN HERE.
IT'S MY DUTY TO MAKE SURE THIS DOOR IS NEVER OPENED AGAIN.
I CAN'T BE IN TWO PLACES AT ONCE.
HOW, OH HOW, CAN YOU HAVE ALL THE POWERS OF THE GODS YET STILL LACK VISION?
I WANT TO TALK TO BILLY.
"A DEAL WAS STRUCK...
"...THE BOY REMAINED AT HIS POST--HIS INNOCENT SOUL BINDING THE DOOR SHUT--WHILE YOU RETURNED TO THE MORTAL REALM TO FACE A MYSTERIOUS NEW DEMONIC INVASION...
"BUT ALL OF IT TO WHAT END? WHAT IS NERON'S PURPOSE? WHY SEND YOU INTO THE WORLD AS AN INSTRUMENT OF EVIL, KNOWING YOUR DEEDS WOULD ATTRACT THE WATCHFUL EYE OF THE SPEC--HNGHH!"

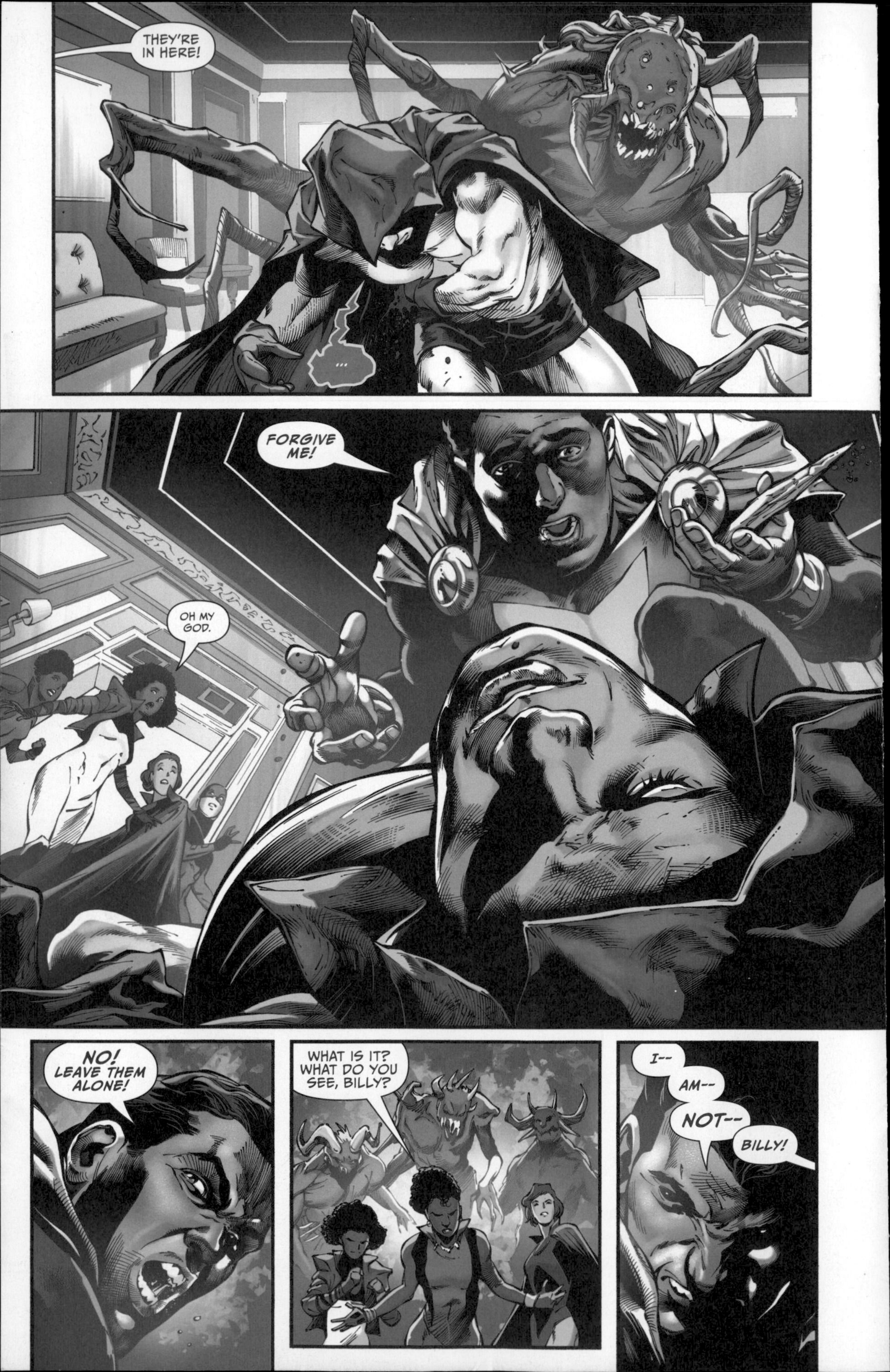
THEY'RE IN HERE!
...
FORGIVE ME!
OH MY GOD.
NO! LEAVE THEM ALONE!
WHAT IS IT? WHAT DO YOU SEE, BILLY?
I--
AM--
NOT--
BILLY!

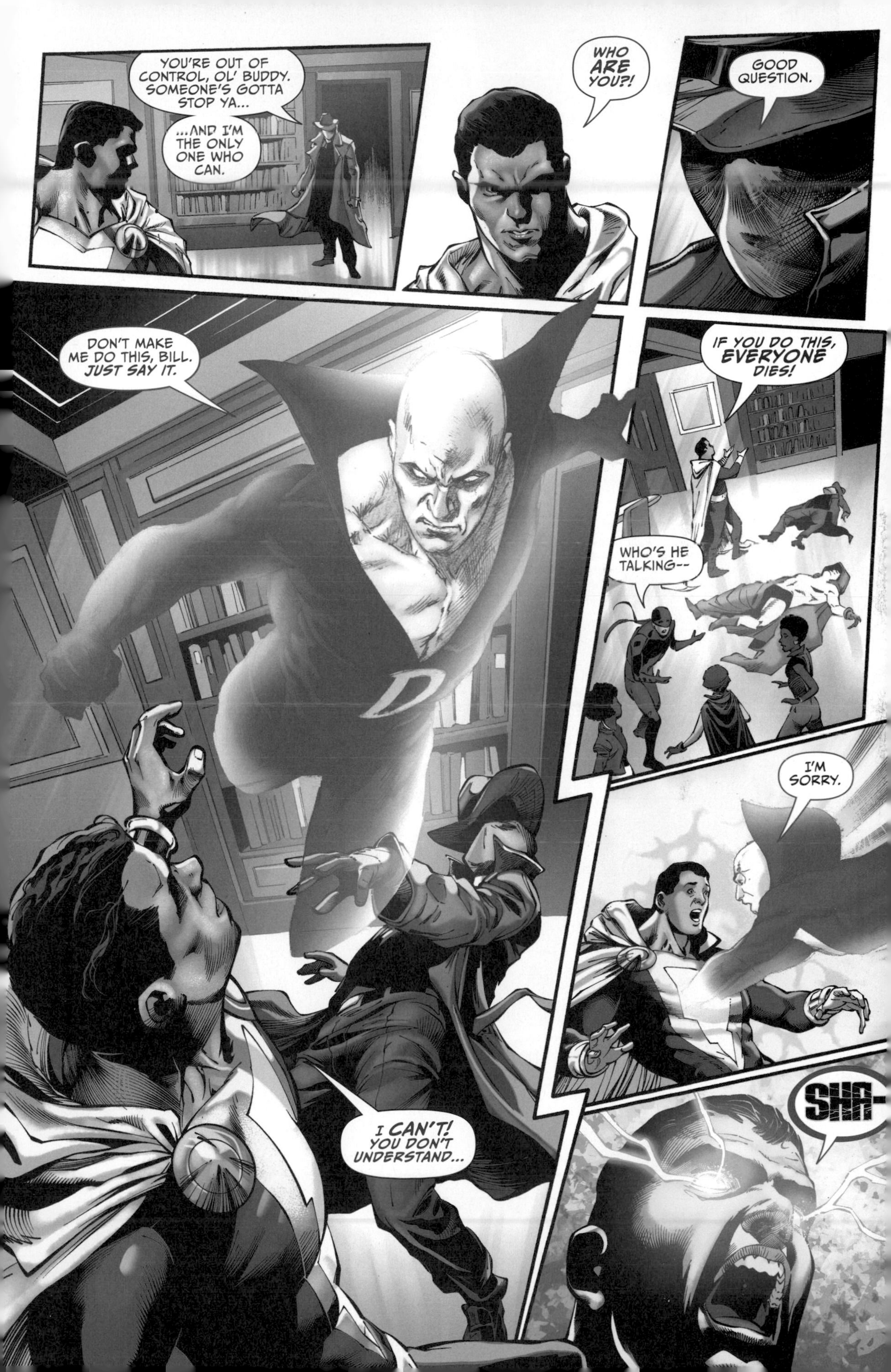
YOU'RE OUT OF CONTROL, OL' BUDDY. SOMEONE'S GOTTA STOP YA...
...AND I'M THE ONLY ONE WHO CAN.
WHO ARE YOU?!
GOOD QUESTION.
DON'T MAKE ME DO THIS, BILL. JUST SAY IT.
I CAN'T! YOU DON'T UNDERSTAND...
IF YOU DO THIS, EVERYONE DIES!
WHO'S HE TALKING--
I'M SORRY.
SHA-

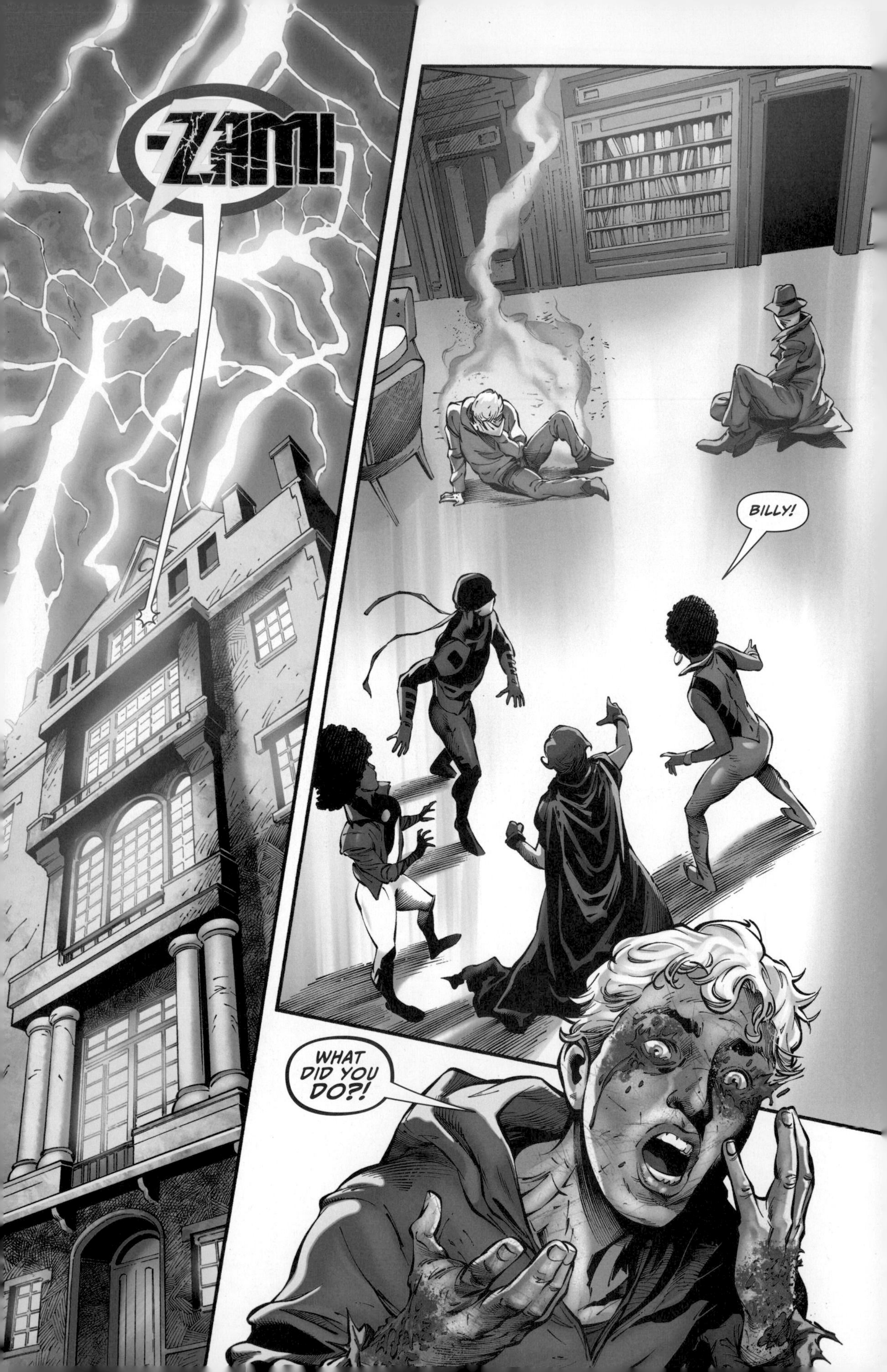

-SZAM!
BILLY!
WHAT DID YOU DO?!

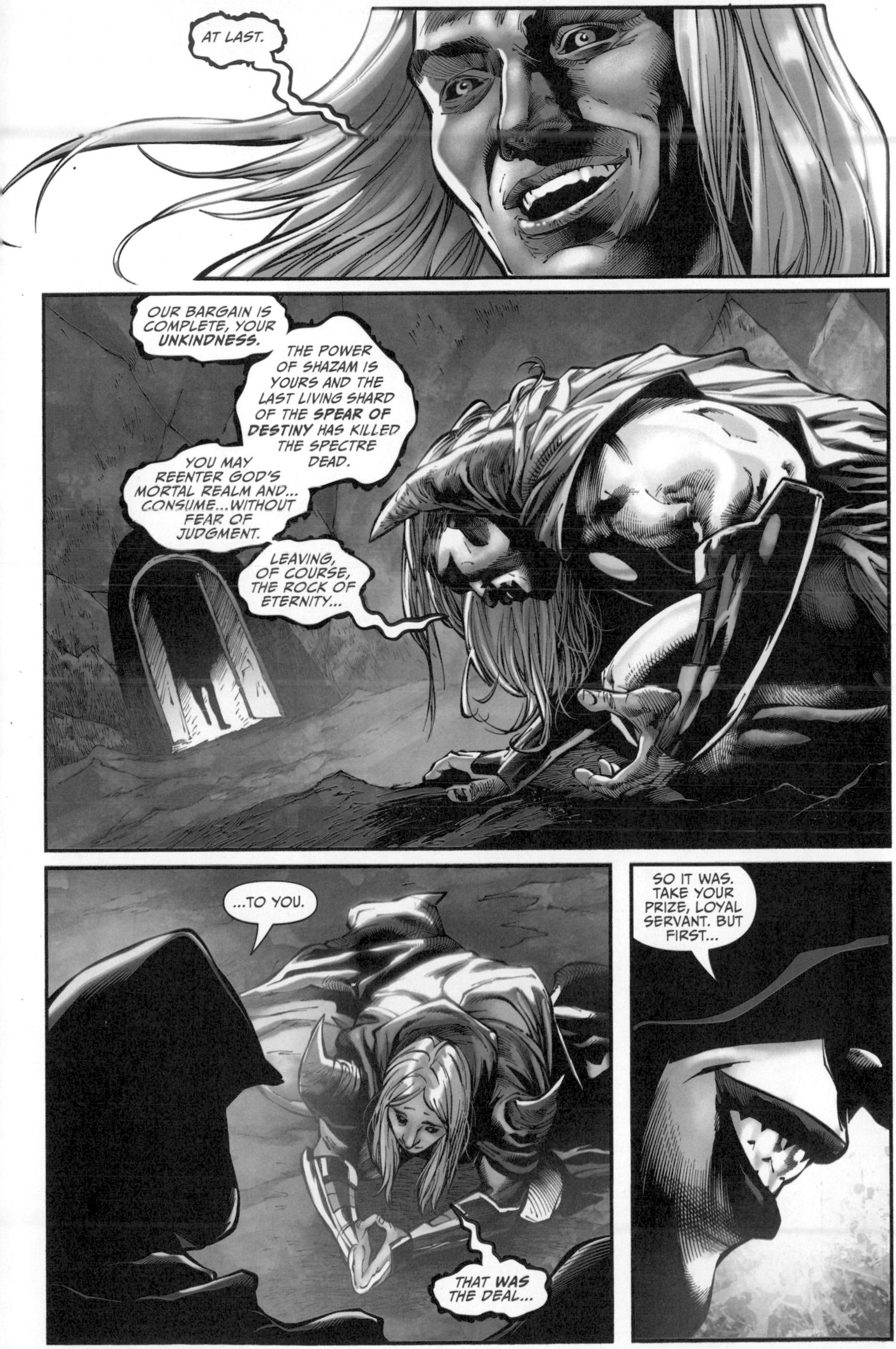
AT LAST.
OUR BARGAIN IS COMPLETE, YOUR UNKINDNESS.
THE POWER OF SHAZAM IS YOURS AND THE LAST LIVING SHARD OF THE SPEAR OF DESTINY HAS KILLED THE SPECTRE DEAD.
YOU MAY REENTER GOD'S MORTAL REALM AND... CONSUME...WITHOUT FEAR OF JUDGMENT.
LEAVING, OF COURSE, THE ROCK OF ETERNITY...
...TO YOU.
THAT WAS THE DEAL...
SO IT WAS. TAKE YOUR PRIZE, LOYAL SERVANT. BUT FIRST...

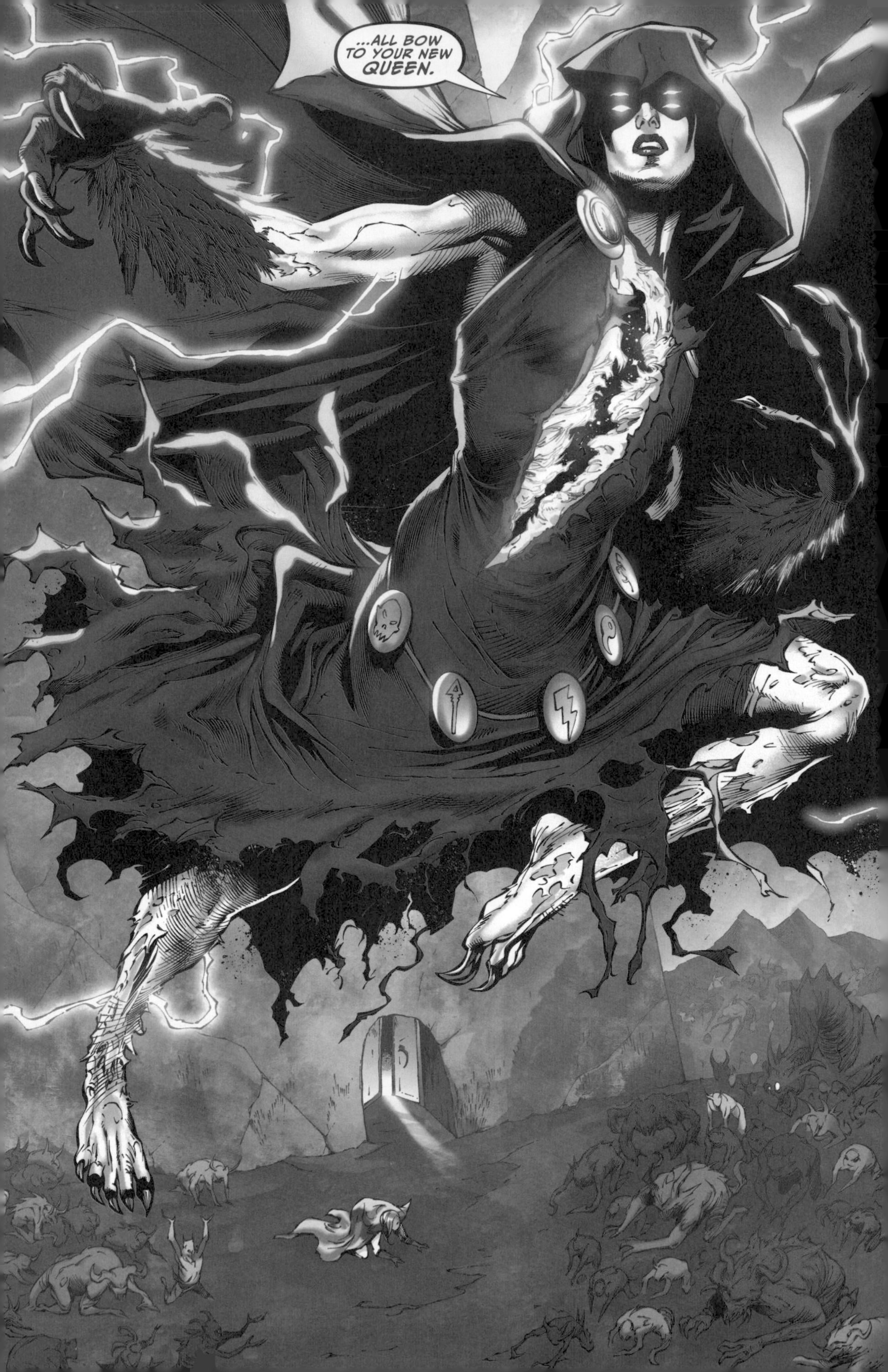
...ALL BOW TO YOUR NEW QUEEN.

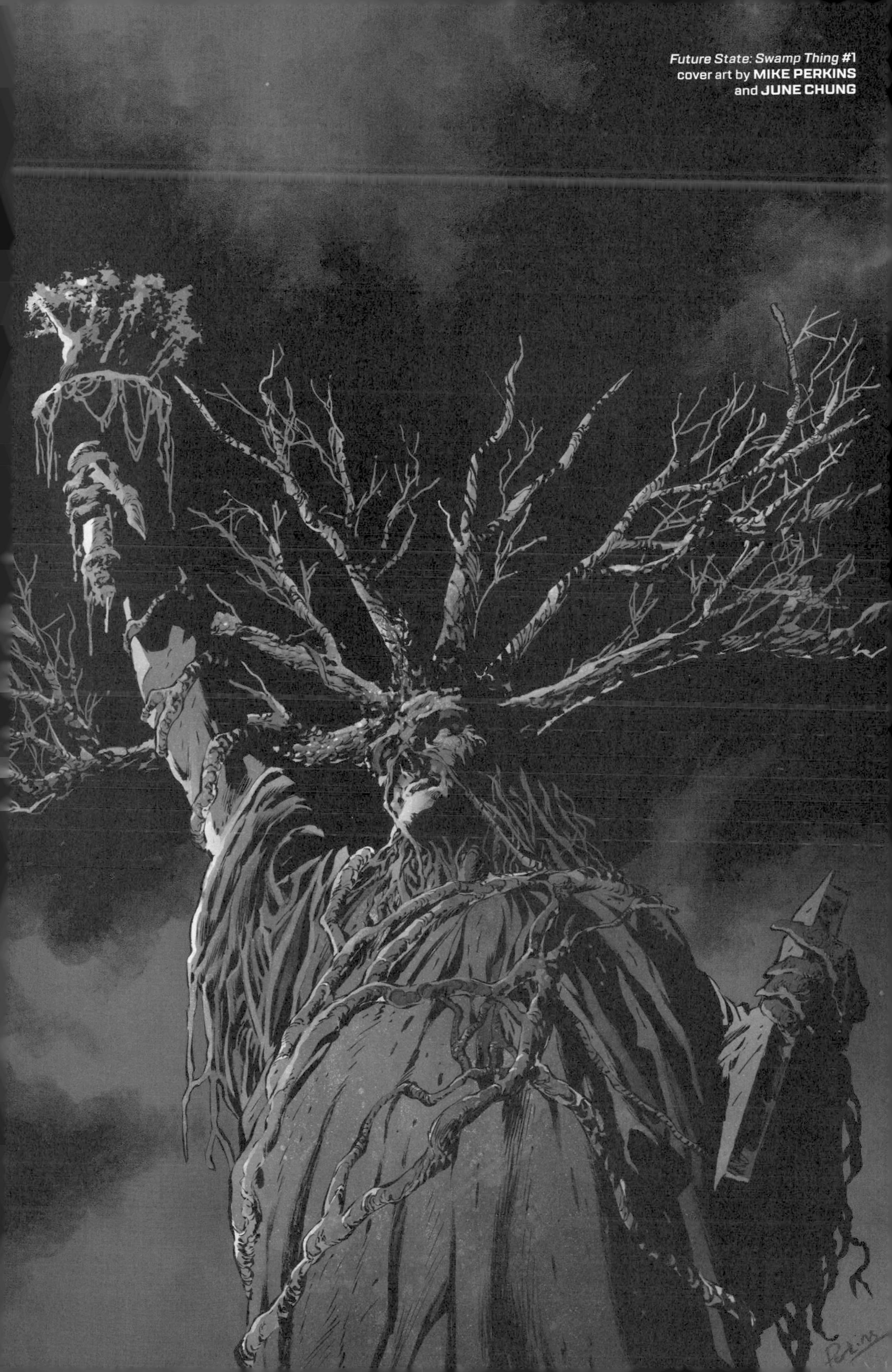

Future State: Swamp Thing #1
cover art by **MIKE PERKINS**
and **JUNE CHUNG**

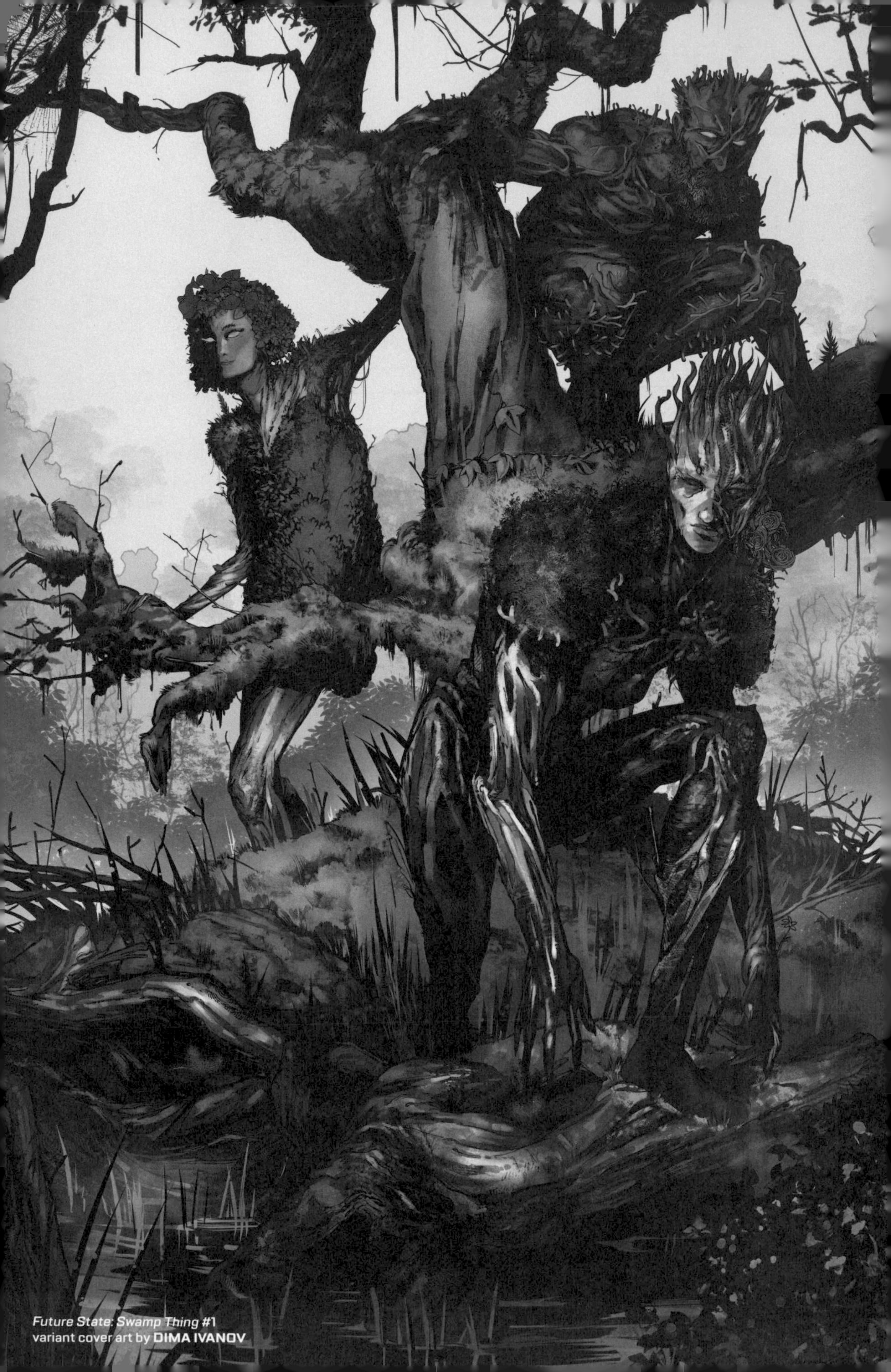

Future State: Swamp Thing #1
variant cover art by **DIMA IVANOV**

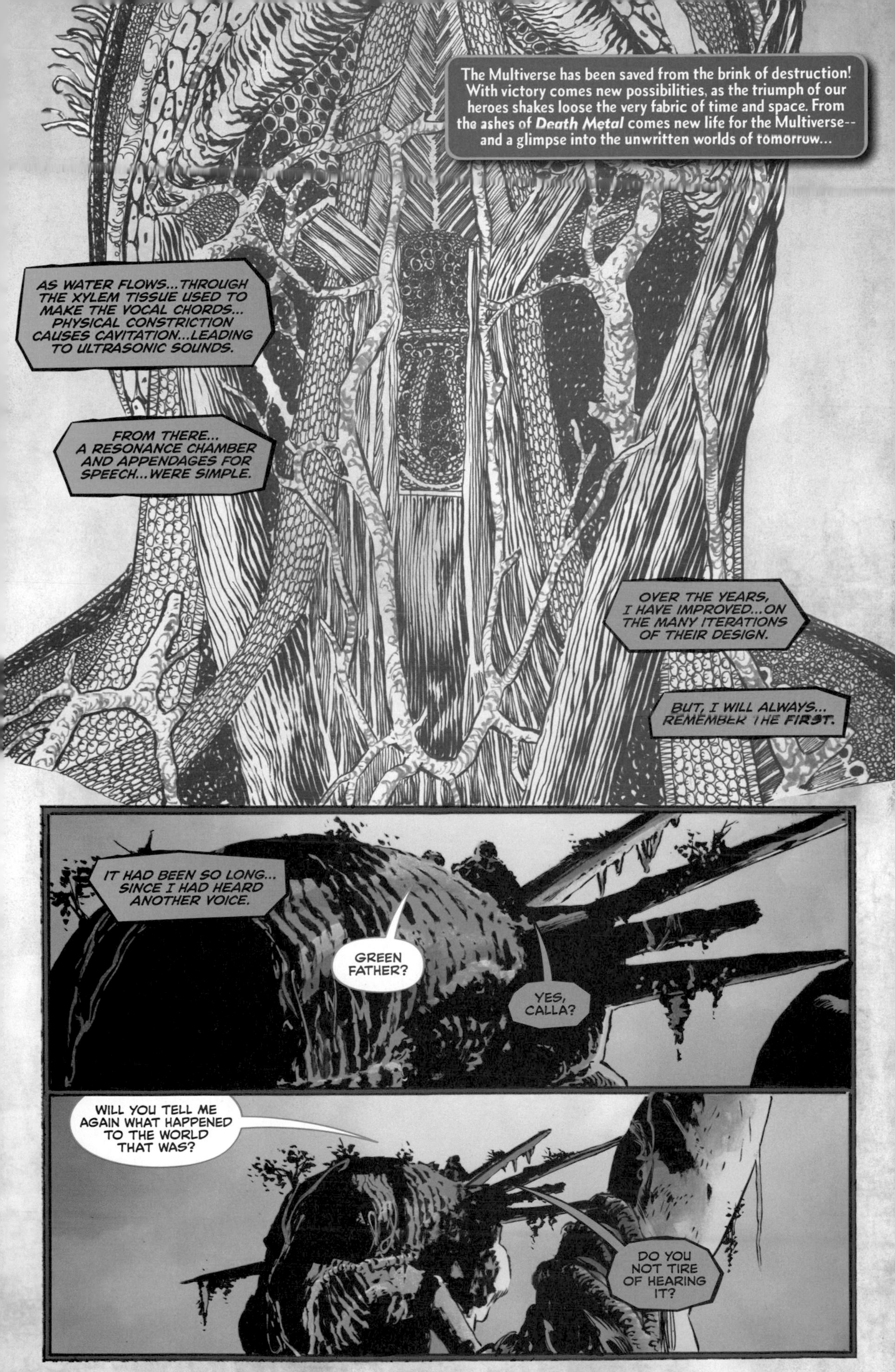
The Multiverse has been saved from the brink of destruction! With victory comes new possibilities, as the triumph of our heroes shakes loose the very fabric of time and space. From the ashes of *Death Metal* comes new life for the Multiverse--and a glimpse into the unwritten worlds of tomorrow...
AS WATER FLOWS...THROUGH THE XYLEM TISSUE USED TO MAKE THE VOCAL CHORDS... PHYSICAL CONSTRICTION CAUSES CAVITATION...LEADING TO ULTRASONIC SOUNDS.
FROM THERE... A RESONANCE CHAMBER AND APPENDAGES FOR SPEECH...WERE SIMPLE.
OVER THE YEARS, I HAVE IMPROVED...ON THE MANY ITERATIONS OF THEIR DESIGN.
BUT, I WILL ALWAYS... REMEMBER THE FIRST.
IT HAD BEEN SO LONG... SINCE I HAD HEARD ANOTHER VOICE.
GREEN FATHER?
YES, CALLA?
WILL YOU TELL ME AGAIN WHAT HAPPENED TO THE WORLD THAT WAS?
DO YOU NOT TIRE OF HEARING IT?

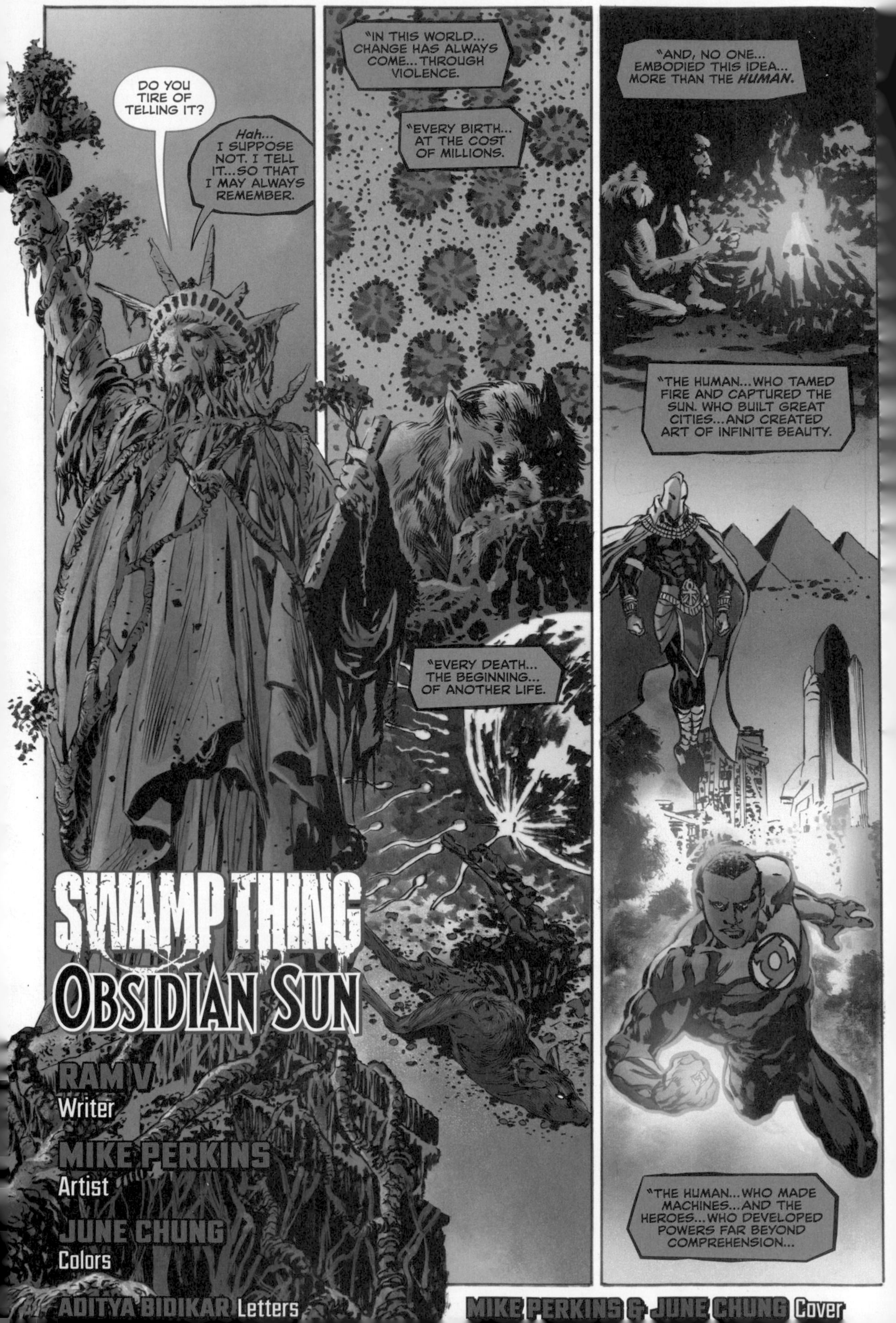

DO YOU TIRE OF TELLING IT?
Hah... I SUPPOSE NOT. I TELL IT...SO THAT I MAY ALWAYS REMEMBER.
"IN THIS WORLD... CHANGE HAS ALWAYS COME...THROUGH VIOLENCE.
"EVERY BIRTH... AT THE COST OF MILLIONS.
"EVERY DEATH... THE BEGINNING... OF ANOTHER LIFE.
"AND, NO ONE... EMBODIED THIS IDEA... MORE THAN THE HUMAN.
"THE HUMAN...WHO TAMED FIRE AND CAPTURED THE SUN. WHO BUILT GREAT CITIES...AND CREATED ART OF INFINITE BEAUTY.
"THE HUMAN...WHO MADE MACHINES...AND THE HEROES...WHO DEVELOPED POWERS FAR BEYOND COMPREHENSION...
SWAMP THING
OBSIDIAN SUN
RAM V Writer
MIKE PERKINS Artist
JUNE CHUNG Colors
ADITYA BIDIKAR Letters
MIKE PERKINS & JUNE CHUNG Cover

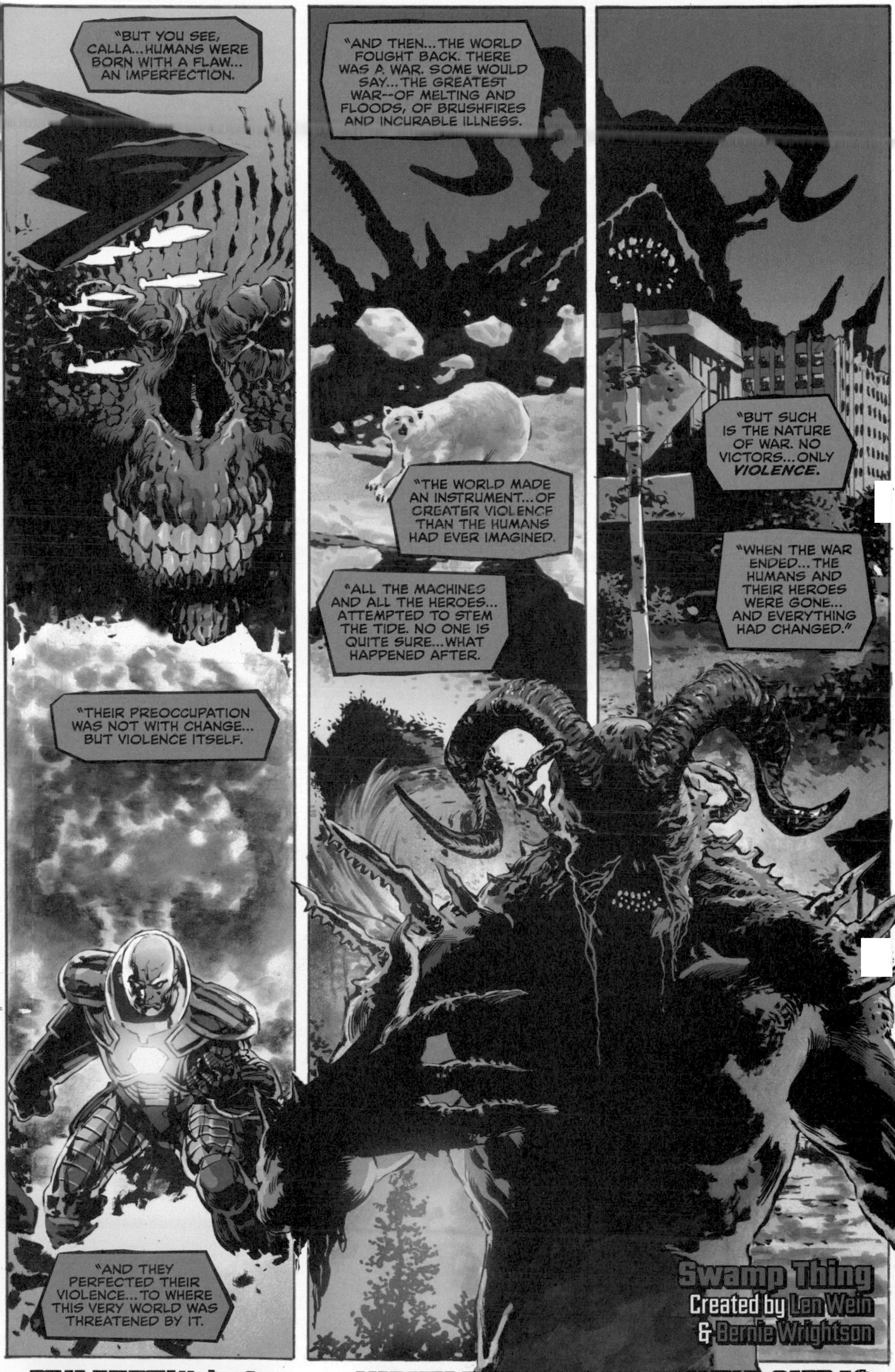
"BUT YOU SEE, CALLA...HUMANS WERE BORN WITH A FLAW... AN IMPERFECTION.
"THEIR PREOCCUPATION WAS NOT WITH CHANGE... BUT VIOLENCE ITSELF.
"AND THEY PERFECTED THEIR VIOLENCE...TO WHERE THIS VERY WORLD WAS THREATENED BY IT.
"AND THEN...THE WORLD FOUGHT BACK. THERE WAS A WAR. SOME WOULD SAY...THE GREATEST WAR--OF MELTING AND FLOODS, OF BRUSHFIRES AND INCURABLE ILLNESS.
"THE WORLD MADE AN INSTRUMENT...OF GREATER VIOLENCE THAN THE HUMANS HAD EVER IMAGINED.
"ALL THE MACHINES AND ALL THE HEROES... ATTEMPTED TO STEM THE TIDE. NO ONE IS QUITE SURE...WHAT HAPPENED AFTER.
"BUT SUCH IS THE NATURE OF WAR. NO VICTORS...ONLY VIOLENCE.
"WHEN THE WAR ENDED...THE HUMANS AND THEIR HEROES WERE GONE... AND EVERYTHING HAD CHANGED."
Swamp Thing
Created by Len Wein
& Bernie Wrightson

DIMA IVANOV Variant Cover MARQUIS DRAPER Asst. Ed. ALEX R. CARR Editor

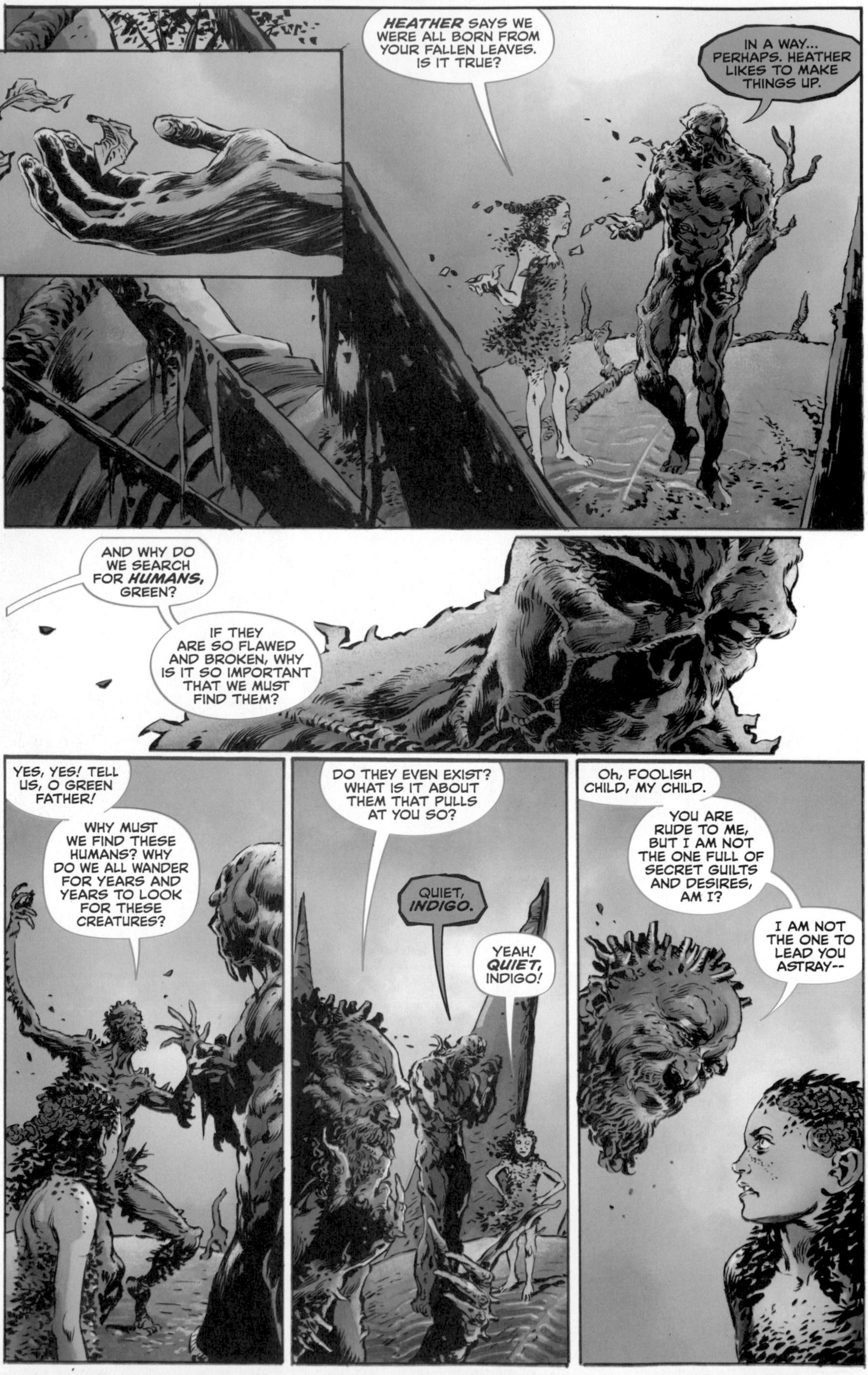
HEATHER SAYS WE WERE ALL BORN FROM YOUR FALLEN LEAVES. IS IT TRUE?
IN A WAY... PERHAPS. HEATHER LIKES TO MAKE THINGS UP.
AND WHY DO WE SEARCH FOR HUMANS, GREEN?
IF THEY ARE SO FLAWED AND BROKEN, WHY IS IT SO IMPORTANT THAT WE MUST FIND THEM?
YES, YES! TELL US, O GREEN FATHER!
WHY MUST WE FIND THESE HUMANS? WHY DO WE ALL WANDER FOR YEARS AND YEARS TO LOOK FOR THESE CREATURES?
DO THEY EVEN EXIST? WHAT IS IT ABOUT THEM THAT PULLS AT YOU SO?
QUIET, INDIGO.
YEAH! QUIET, INDIGO!
Oh, FOOLISH CHILD, MY CHILD.
YOU ARE RUDE TO ME, BUT I AM NOT THE ONE FULL OF SECRET GUILTS AND DESIRES, AM I?
I AM NOT THE ONE TO LEAD YOU ASTRAY--

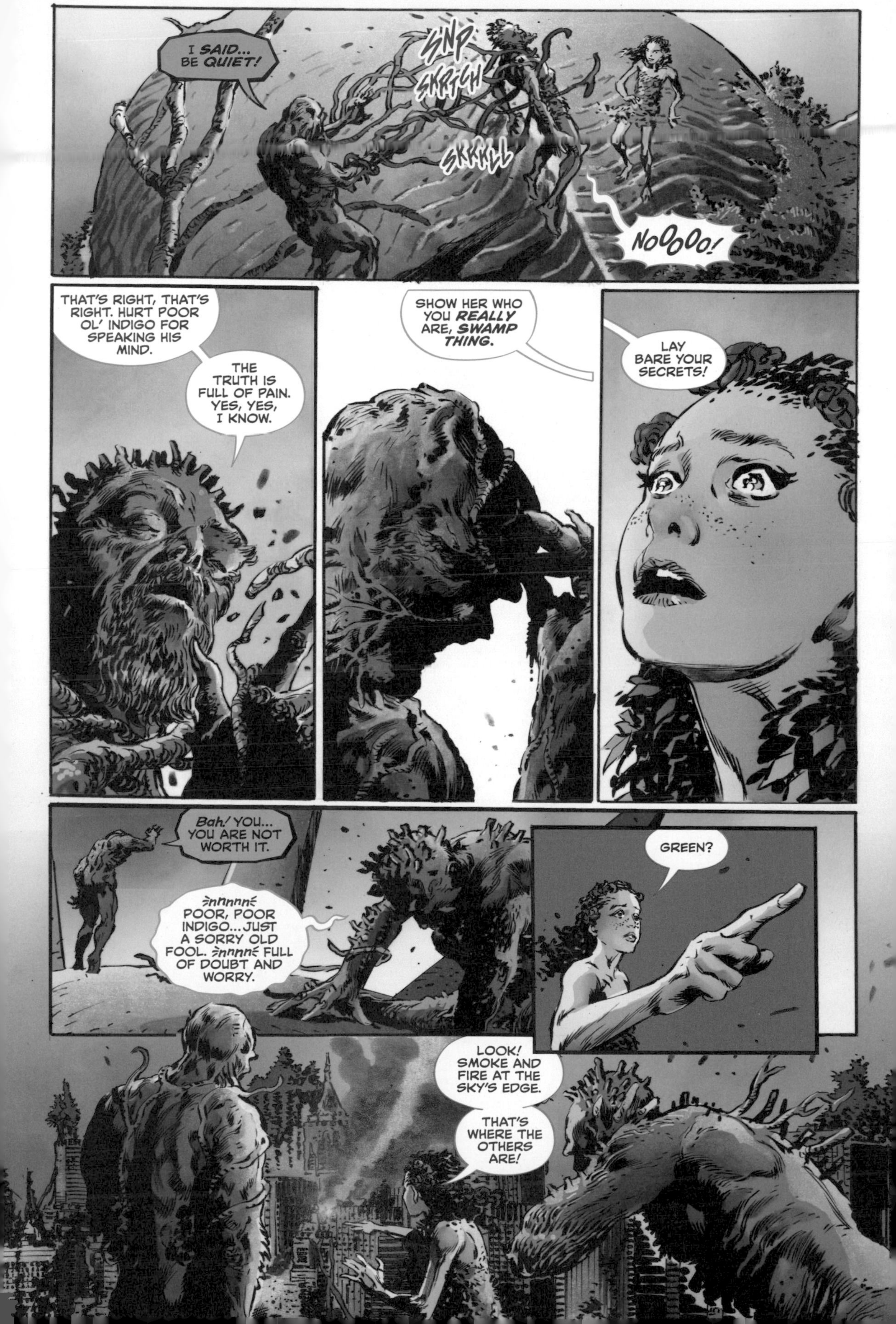

I SAID... BE QUIET!
SNP
SKRTCH
SKKKLL
NOOOOO!
THAT'S RIGHT, THAT'S RIGHT. HURT POOR OL' INDIGO FOR SPEAKING HIS MIND.
THE TRUTH IS FULL OF PAIN. YES, YES, I KNOW.
SHOW HER WHO YOU REALLY ARE, SWAMP THING.
LAY BARE YOUR SECRETS!
Bah! YOU... YOU ARE NOT WORTH IT.
nnnnn POOR, POOR INDIGO... JUST A SORRY OLD FOOL. nnnnn FULL OF DOUBT AND WORRY.
GREEN?
LOOK! SMOKE AND FIRE AT THE SKY'S EDGE.
THAT'S WHERE THE OTHERS ARE!

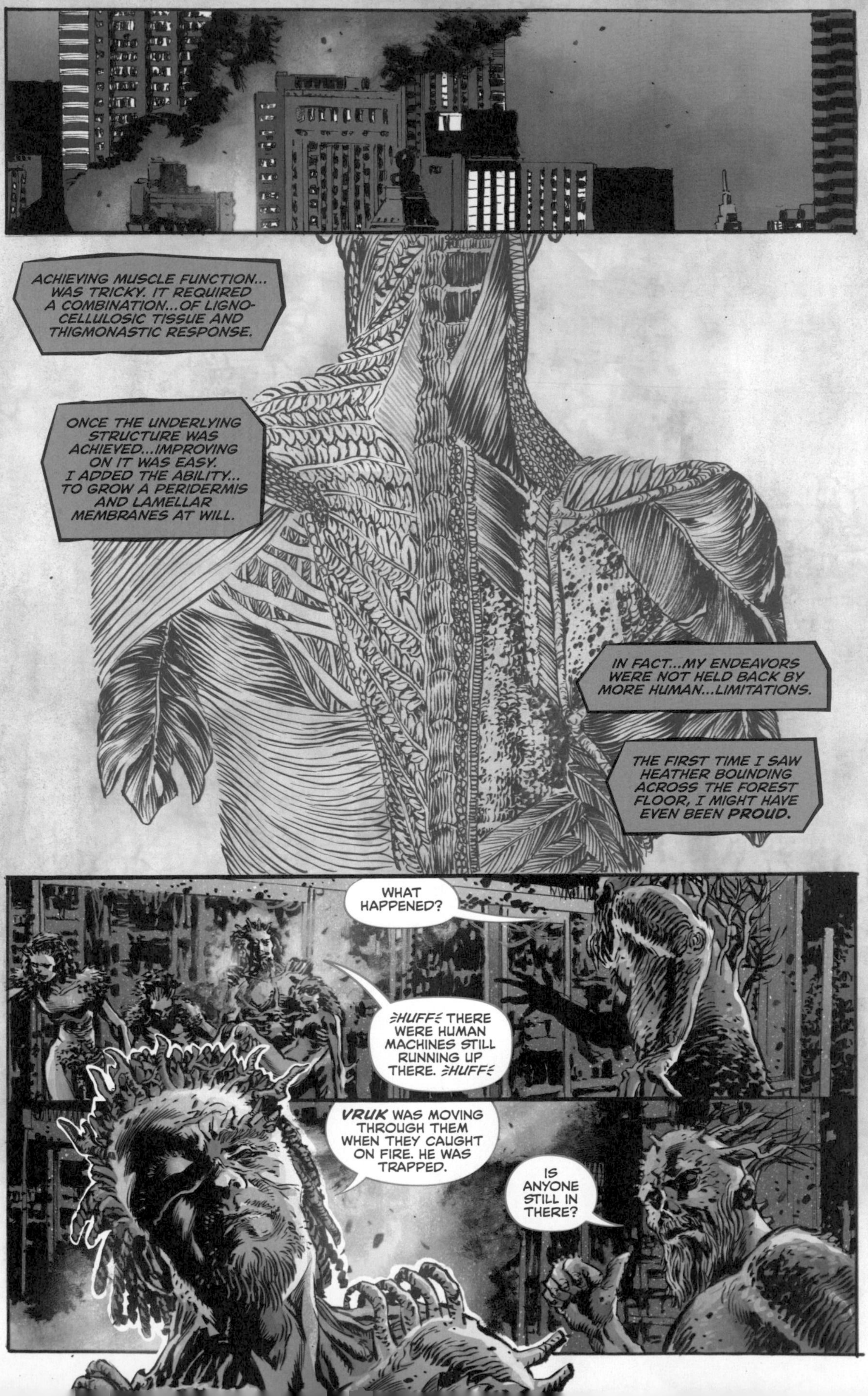
ACHIEVING MUSCLE FUNCTION... WAS TRICKY. IT REQUIRED A COMBINATION...OF LIGNO-CELLULOSIC TISSUE AND THIGMONASTIC RESPONSE.
ONCE THE UNDERLYING STRUCTURE WAS ACHIEVED...IMPROVING ON IT WAS EASY. I ADDED THE ABILITY... TO GROW A PERIDERMIS AND LAMELLAR MEMBRANES AT WILL.
IN FACT...MY ENDEAVORS WERE NOT HELD BACK BY MORE HUMAN...LIMITATIONS.
THE FIRST TIME I SAW HEATHER BOUNDING ACROSS THE FOREST FLOOR, I MIGHT HAVE EVEN BEEN PROUD.
WHAT HAPPENED?
HUFF THERE WERE HUMAN MACHINES STILL RUNNING UP THERE. HUFF
VRUK WAS MOVING THROUGH THEM WHEN THEY CAUGHT ON FIRE. HE WAS TRAPPED.
IS ANYONE STILL IN THERE?

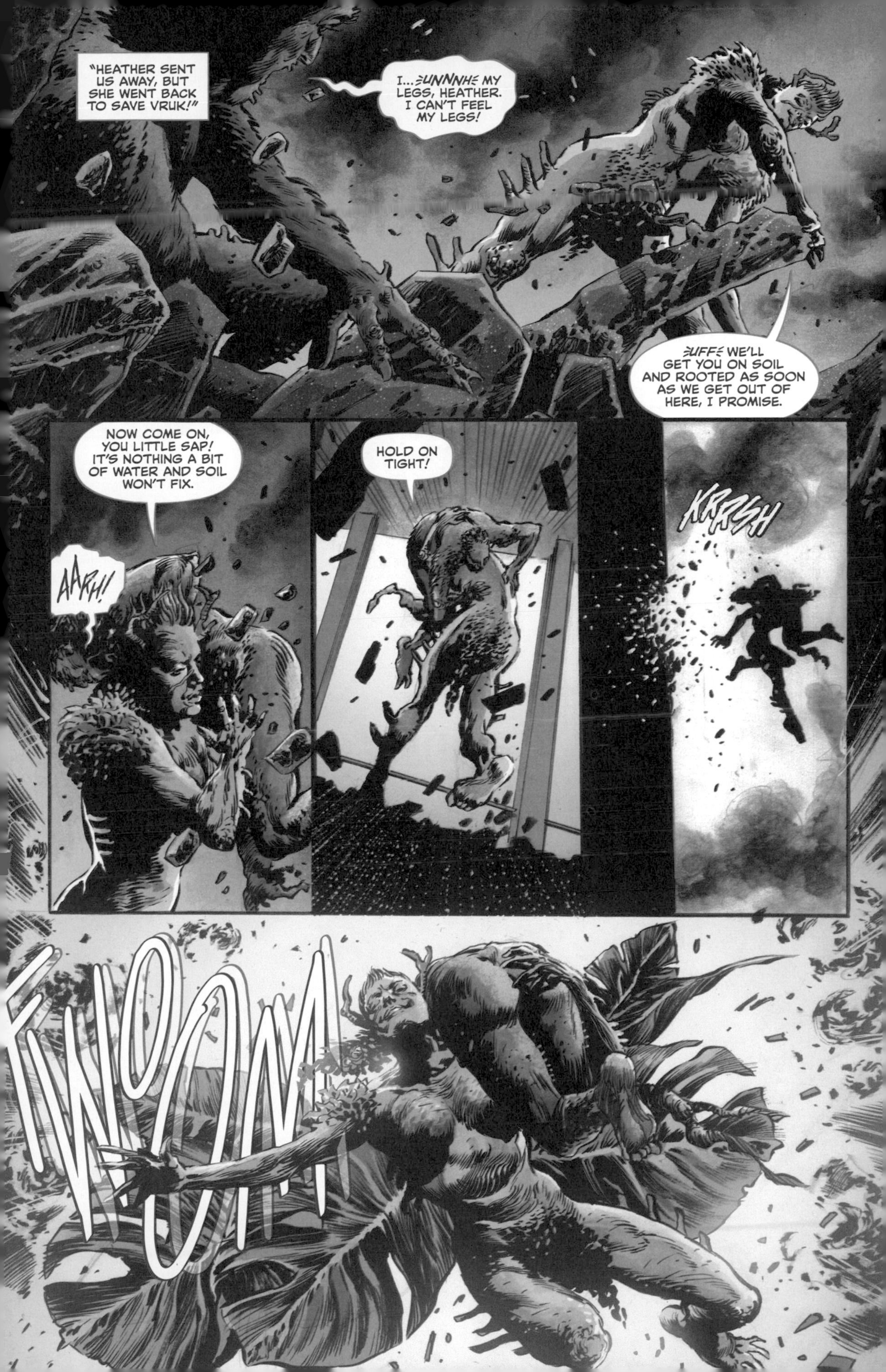
"HEATHER SENT US AWAY, BUT SHE WENT BACK TO SAVE VRUK!"
I... UNNNH MY LEGS, HEATHER. I CAN'T FEEL MY LEGS!
UFF WE'LL GET YOU ON SOIL AND ROOTED AS SOON AS WE GET OUT OF HERE, I PROMISE.
NOW COME ON, YOU LITTLE SAP! IT'S NOTHING A BIT OF WATER AND SOIL WON'T FIX.
AARH!
HOLD ON TIGHT!
KRRSH
FWOOM

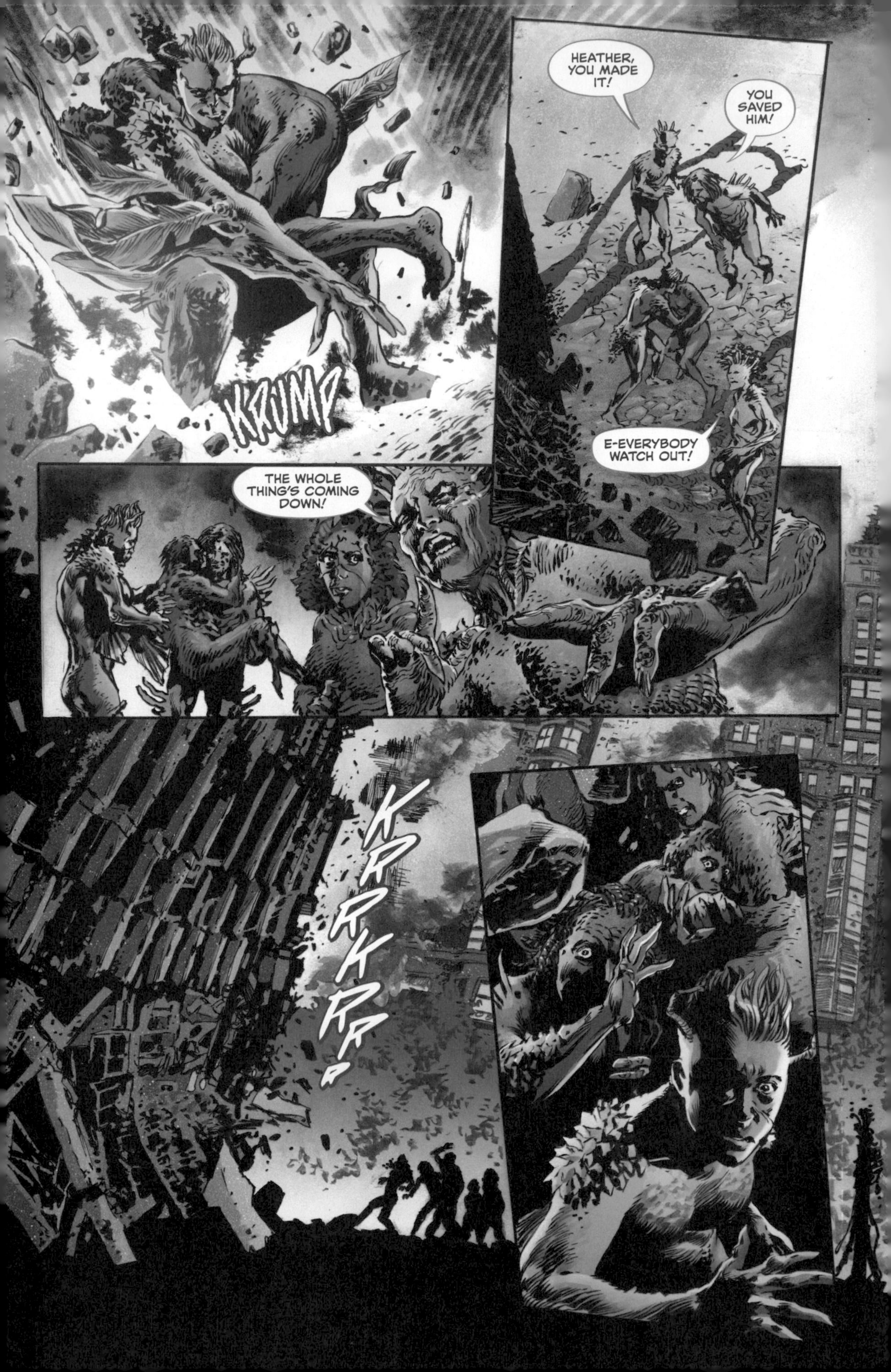
KRUMP
HEATHER, YOU MADE IT!
YOU SAVED HIM!
E-EVERYBODY WATCH OUT!
THE WHOLE THING'S COMING DOWN!
KRRKRRR

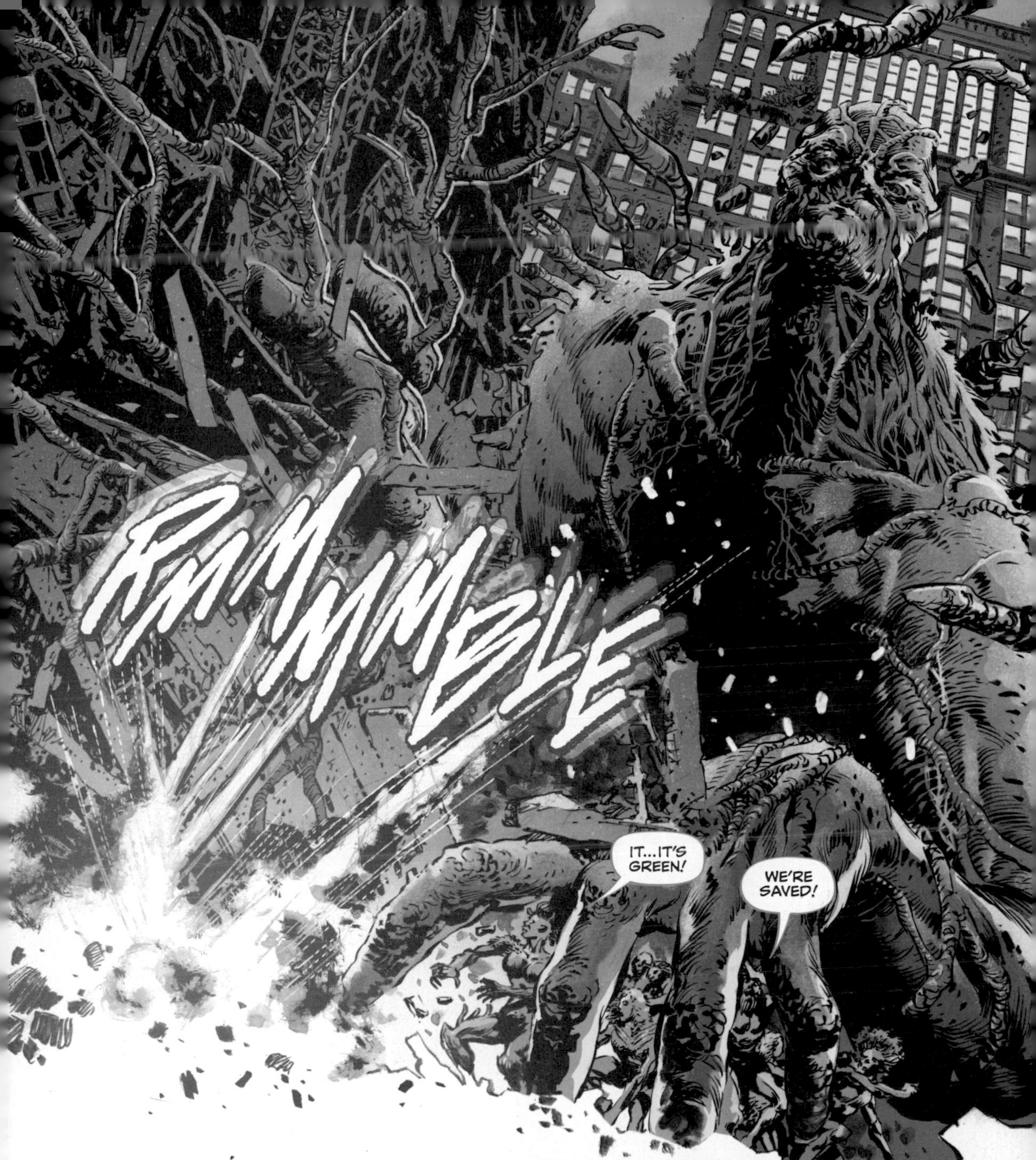
RMMMMBLE
IT...IT'S GREEN!
WE'RE SAVED!

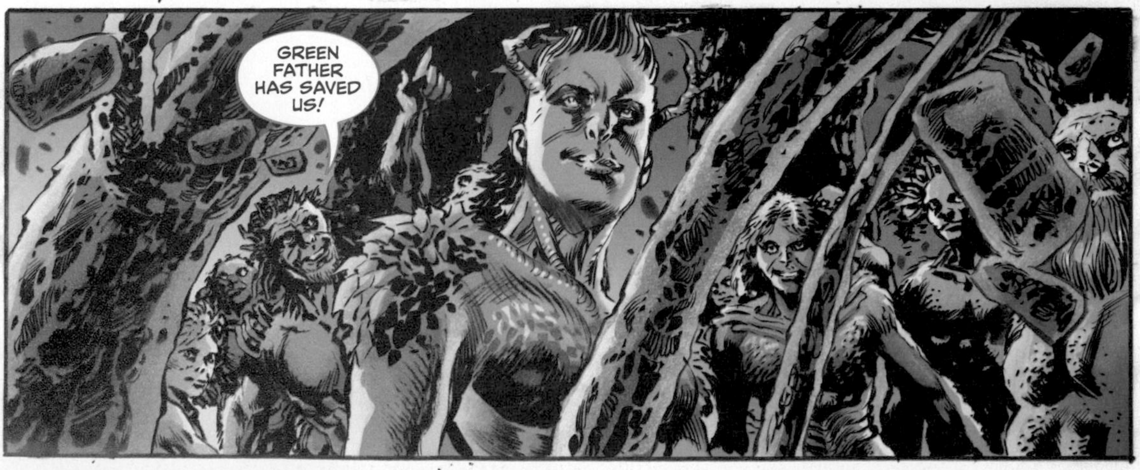
GREEN FATHER HAS SAVED US!

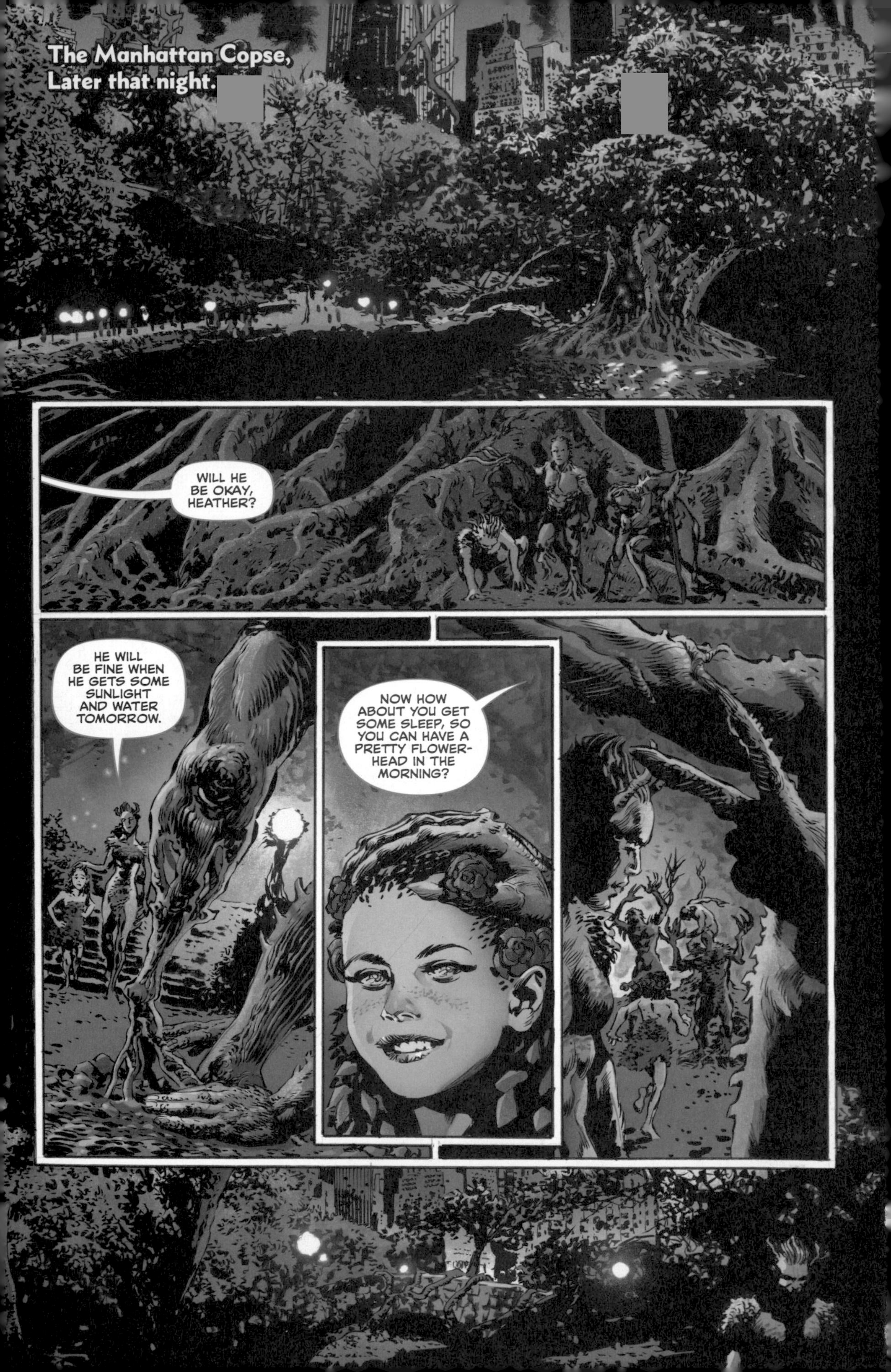

The Manhattan Copse,
Later that night.
WILL HE BE OKAY, HEATHER?
HE WILL BE FINE WHEN HE GETS SOME SUNLIGHT AND WATER TOMORROW.
NOW HOW ABOUT YOU GET SOME SLEEP, SO YOU CAN HAVE A PRETTY FLOWER-HEAD IN THE MORNING?

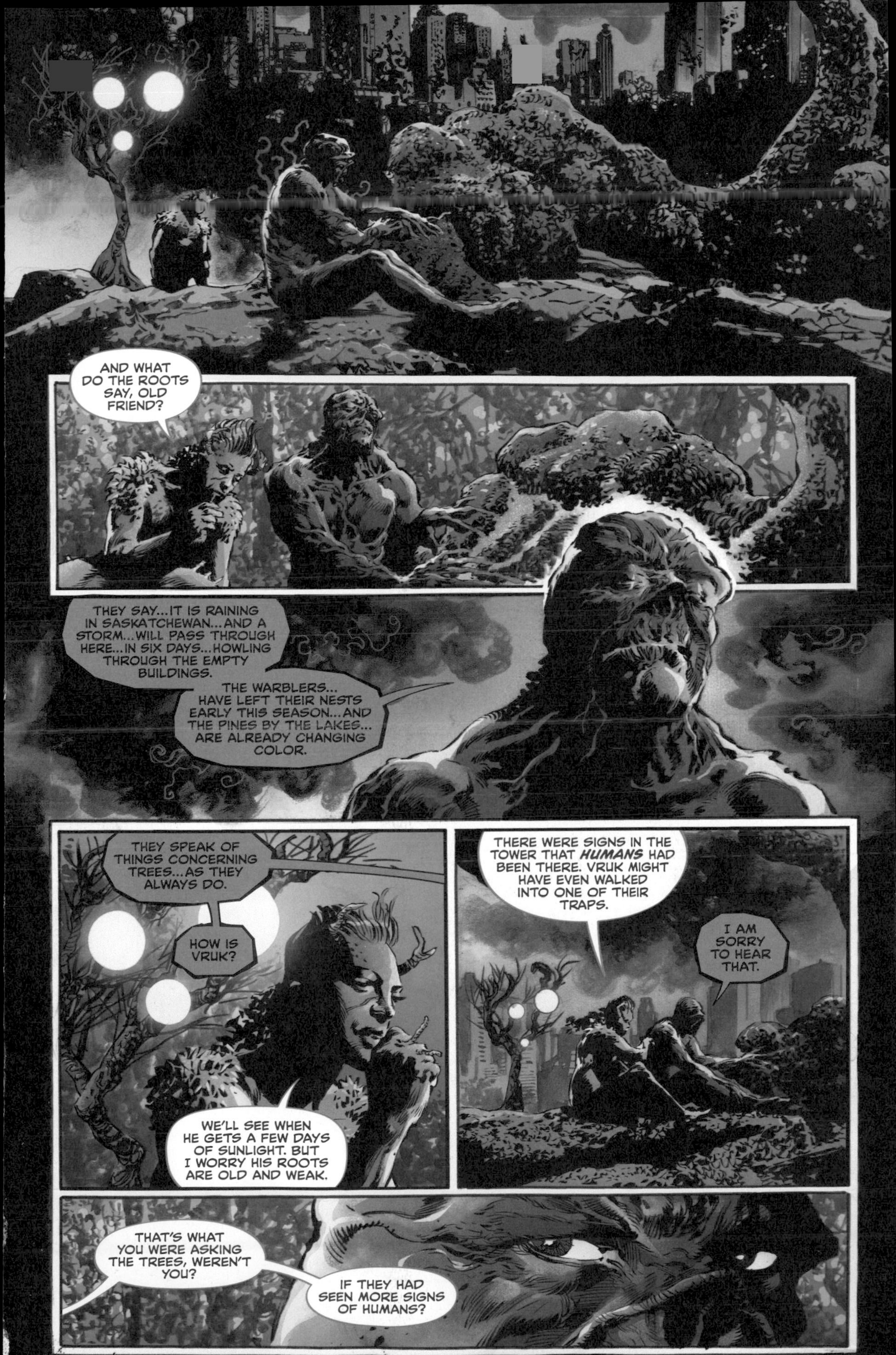
AND WHAT DO THE ROOTS SAY, OLD FRIEND?
THEY SAY...IT IS RAINING IN SASKATCHEWAN...AND A STORM...WILL PASS THROUGH HERE...IN SIX DAYS...HOWLING THROUGH THE EMPTY BUILDINGS.
THE WARBLERS... HAVE LEFT THEIR NESTS EARLY THIS SEASON...AND THE PINES BY THE LAKES... ARE ALREADY CHANGING COLOR.
THEY SPEAK OF THINGS CONCERNING TREES...AS THEY ALWAYS DO.
HOW IS VRUK?
WE'LL SEE WHEN HE GETS A FEW DAYS OF SUNLIGHT. BUT I WORRY HIS ROOTS ARE OLD AND WEAK.
THERE WERE SIGNS IN THE TOWER THAT HUMANS HAD BEEN THERE. VRUK MIGHT HAVE EVEN WALKED INTO ONE OF THEIR TRAPS.
I AM SORRY TO HEAR THAT.
THAT'S WHAT YOU WERE ASKING THE TREES, WEREN'T YOU?
IF THEY HAD SEEN MORE SIGNS OF HUMANS?

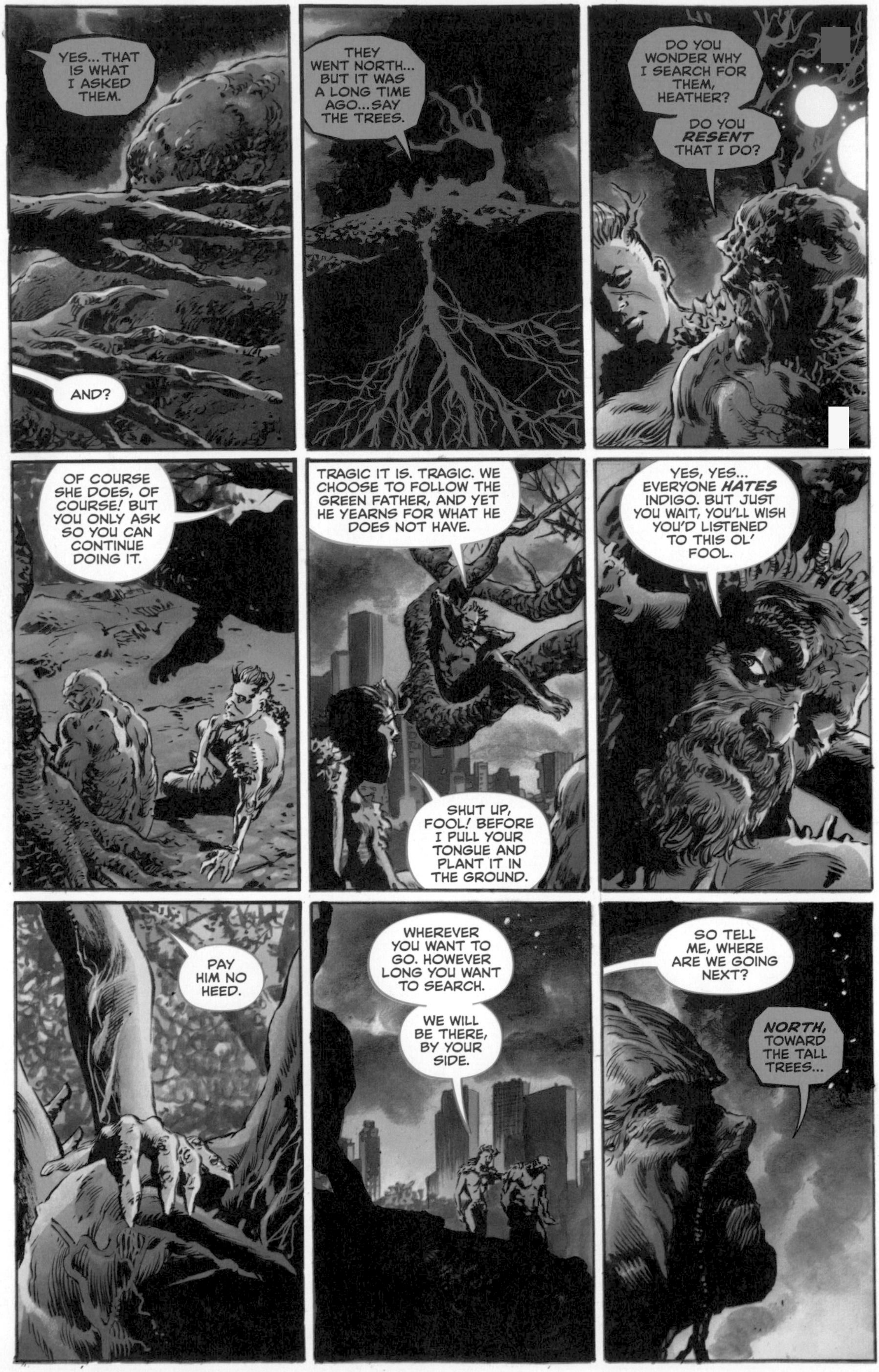
YES... THAT IS WHAT I ASKED THEM.
AND?
THEY WENT NORTH... BUT IT WAS A LONG TIME AGO...SAY THE TREES.
DO YOU WONDER WHY I SEARCH FOR THEM, HEATHER?
DO YOU *RESENT* THAT I DO?
OF COURSE SHE DOES, OF COURSE! BUT YOU ONLY ASK SO YOU CAN CONTINUE DOING IT.
TRAGIC IT IS. TRAGIC. WE CHOOSE TO FOLLOW THE GREEN FATHER, AND YET HE YEARNS FOR WHAT HE DOES NOT HAVE.
SHUT UP, FOOL! BEFORE I PULL YOUR TONGUE AND PLANT IT IN THE GROUND.
YES, YES... EVERYONE *HATES* INDIGO. BUT JUST YOU WAIT, YOU'LL WISH YOU'D LISTENED TO THIS OL' FOOL.
PAY HIM NO HEED.
WHEREVER YOU WANT TO GO. HOWEVER LONG YOU WANT TO SEARCH.
WE WILL BE THERE, BY YOUR SIDE.
SO TELL ME, WHERE ARE WE GOING NEXT?
NORTH, TOWARD THE TALL TREES...

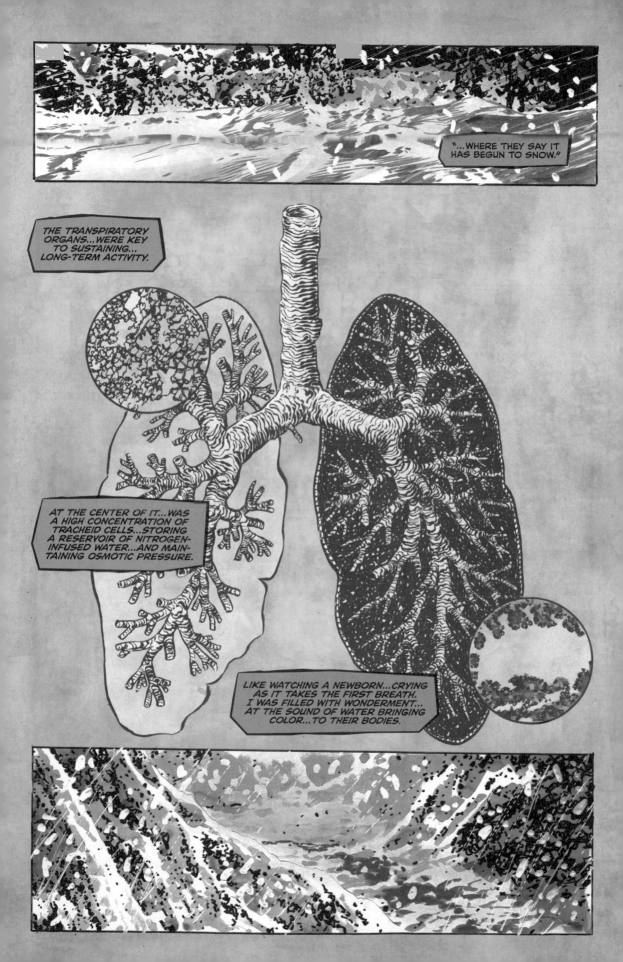

"...WHERE THEY SAY IT HAS BEGUN TO SNOW."

THE TRANSPIRATORY ORGANS...WERE KEY TO SUSTAINING... LONG-TERM ACTIVITY.

AT THE CENTER OF IT...WAS A HIGH CONCENTRATION OF TRACHEID CELLS...STORING A RESERVOIR OF NITROGEN-INFUSED WATER...AND MAINTAINING OSMOTIC PRESSURE.

LIKE WATCHING A NEWBORN...CRYING AS IT TAKES THE FIRST BREATH. I WAS FILLED WITH WONDERMENT... AT THE SOUND OF WATER BRINGING COLOR...TO THEIR BODIES.

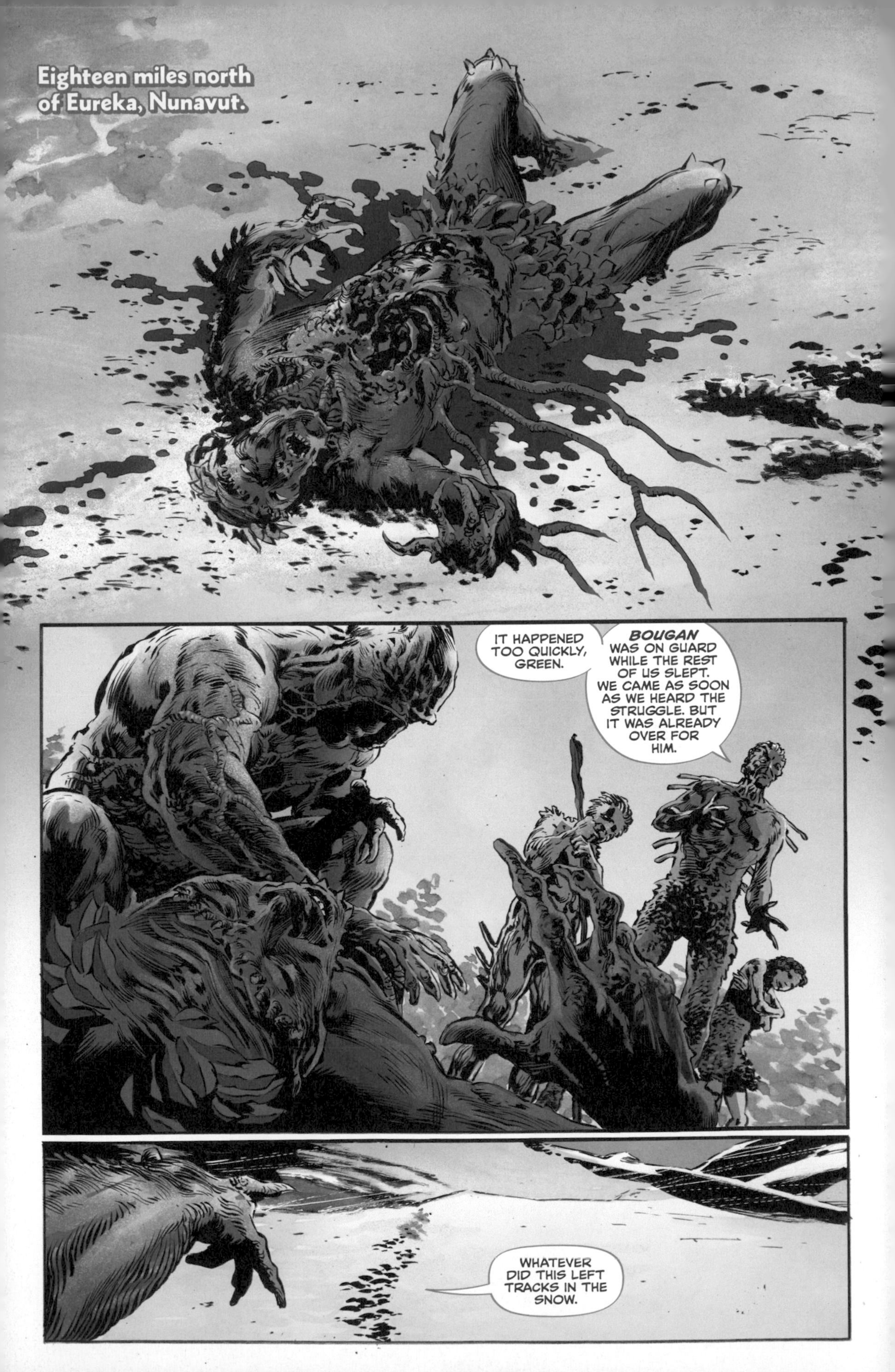
Eighteen miles north of Eureka, Nunavut.
IT HAPPENED TOO QUICKLY, GREEN.
BOUGAN WAS ON GUARD WHILE THE REST OF US SLEPT. WE CAME AS SOON AS WE HEARD THE STRUGGLE. BUT IT WAS ALREADY OVER FOR HIM.
WHATEVER DID THIS LEFT TRACKS IN THE SNOW.

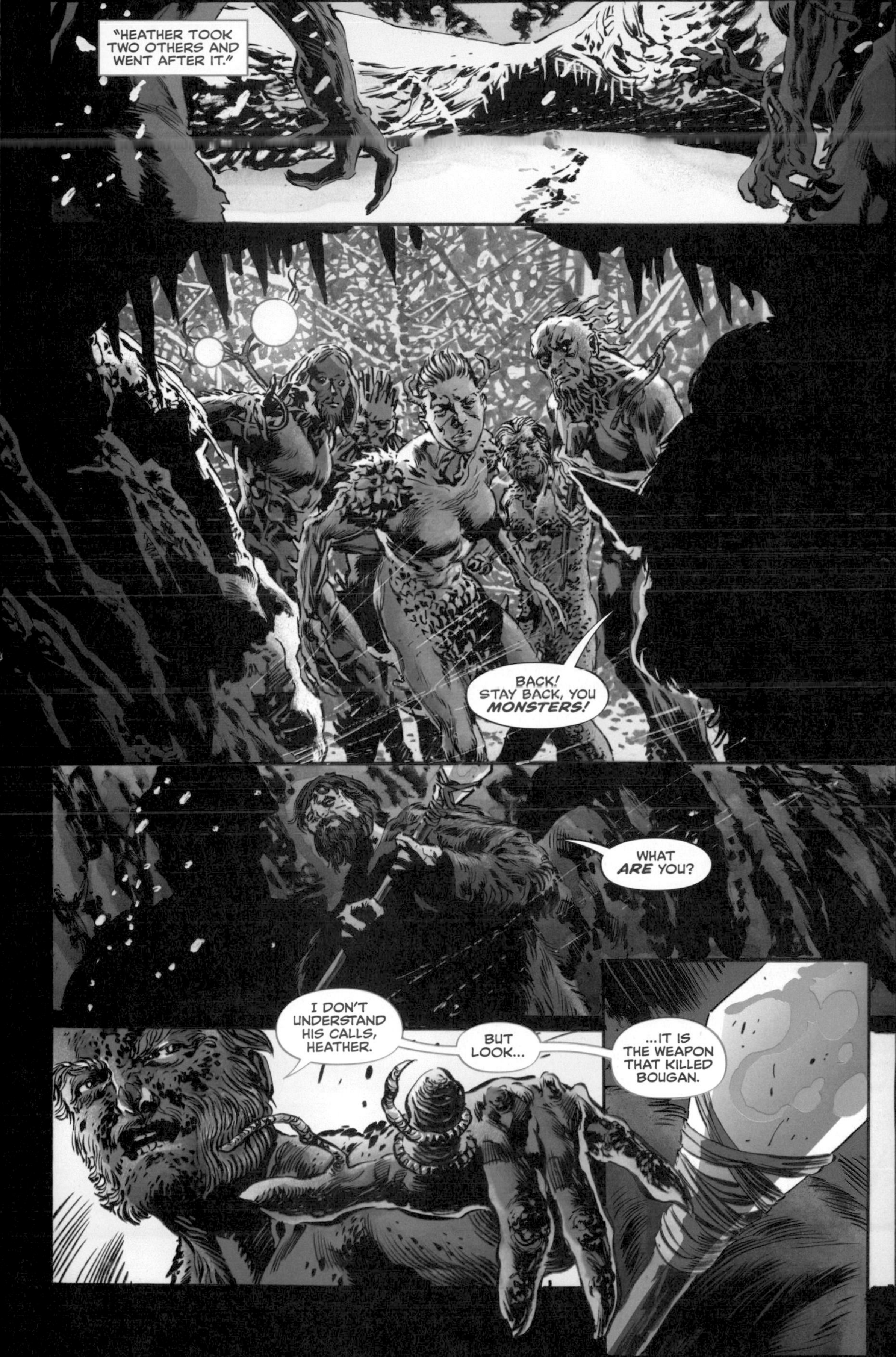

"HEATHER TOOK TWO OTHERS AND WENT AFTER IT."
BACK! STAY BACK, YOU *MONSTERS!*
WHAT *ARE* YOU?
I DON'T UNDERSTAND HIS CALLS, HEATHER.
BUT LOOK...
...IT IS THE WEAPON THAT KILLED BOUGAN.

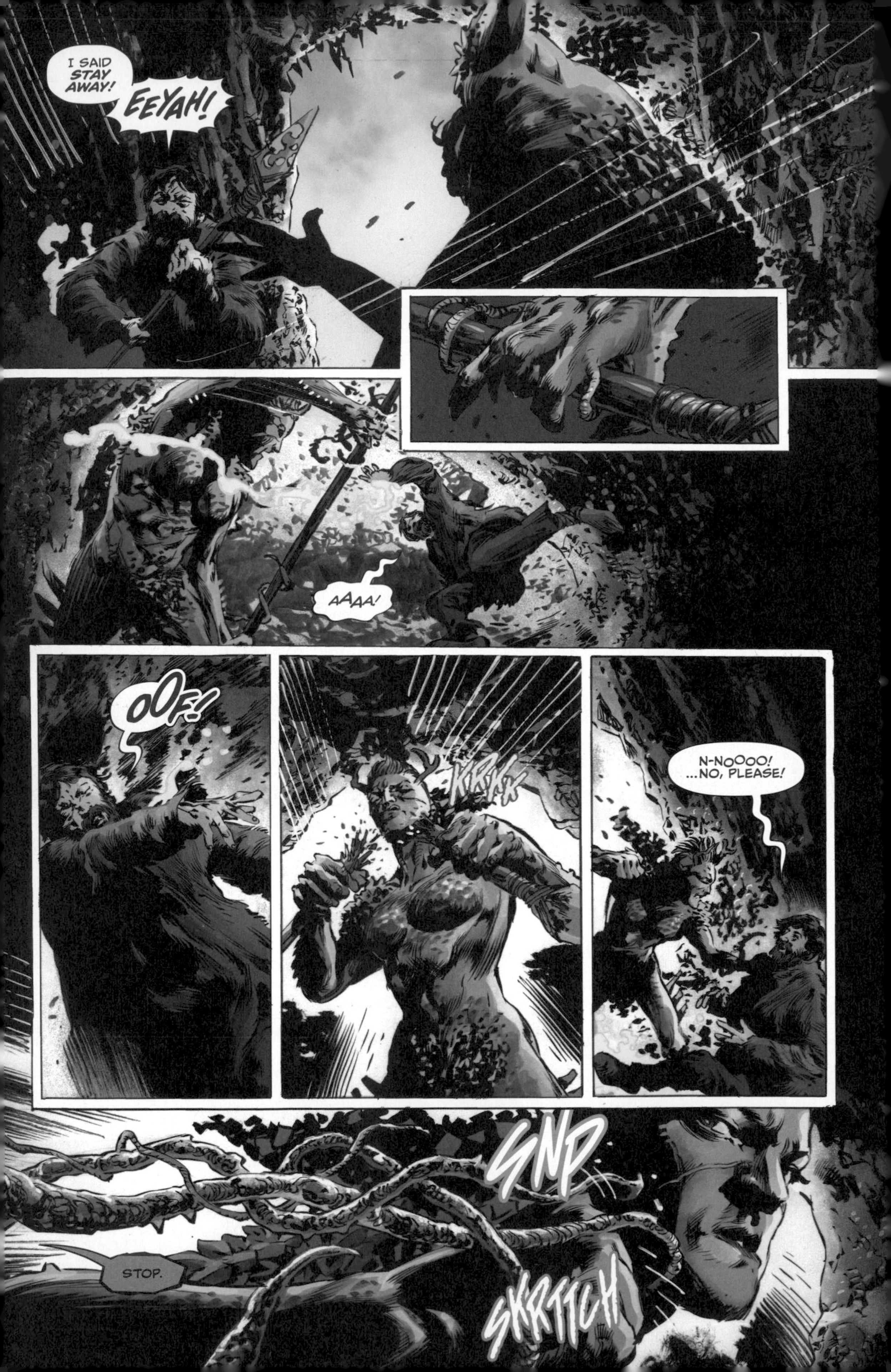
I SAID STAY AWAY!
EEYAH!
AAAA!
OOF!
KRKK
N-NOOOO! ...NO, PLEASE!
SNP
STOP.
SKRTCH

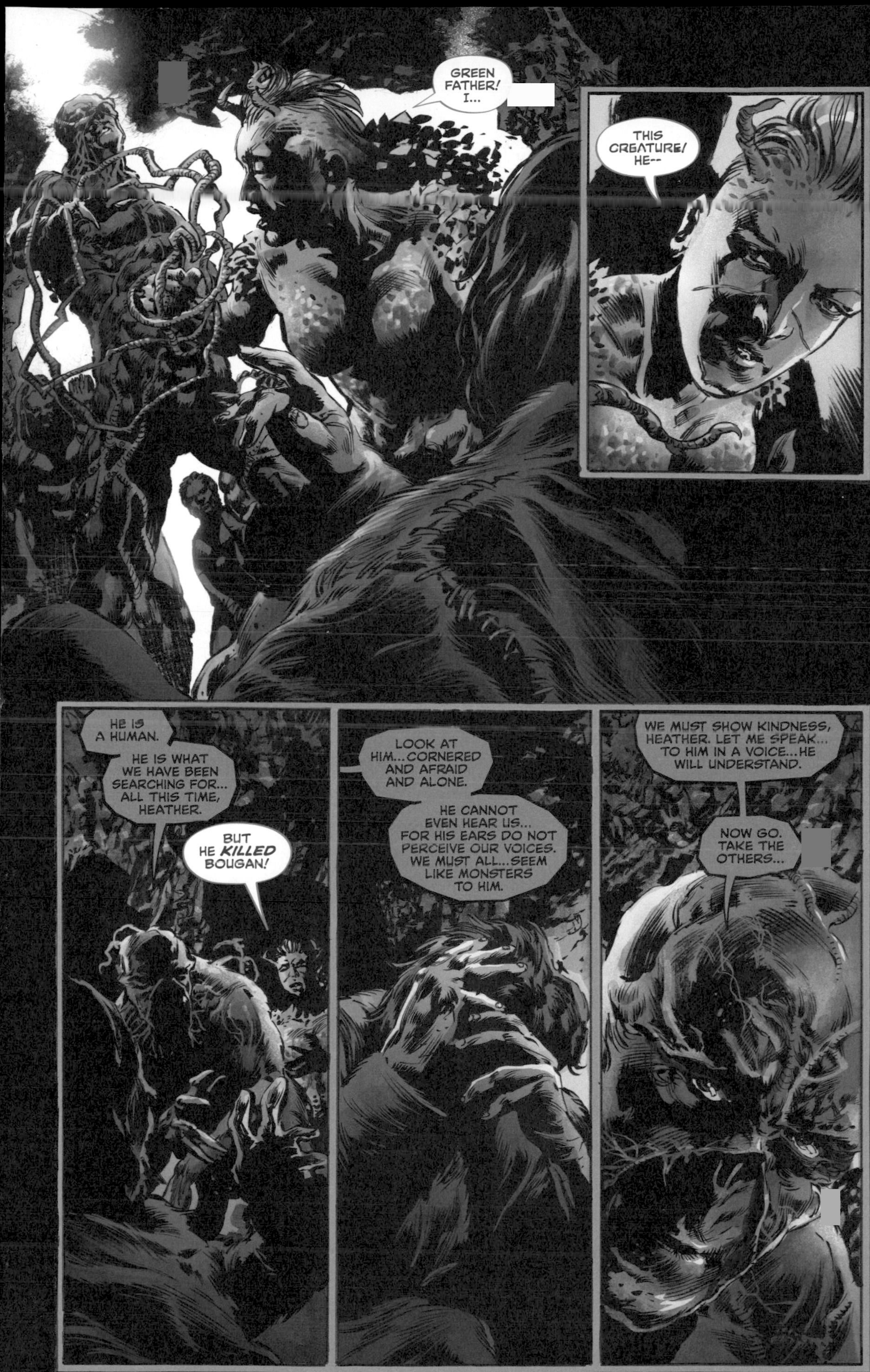
GREEN FATHER! I...
THIS CREATURE! HE--
HE IS A HUMAN.
HE IS WHAT WE HAVE BEEN SEARCHING FOR... ALL THIS TIME, HEATHER.
BUT HE *KILLED* BOUGAN!
LOOK AT HIM...CORNERED AND AFRAID AND ALONE.
HE CANNOT EVEN HEAR US... FOR HIS EARS DO NOT PERCEIVE OUR VOICES. WE MUST ALL...SEEM LIKE MONSTERS TO HIM.
WE MUST SHOW KINDNESS, HEATHER. LET ME SPEAK... TO HIM IN A VOICE...HE WILL UNDERSTAND.
NOW GO. TAKE THE OTHERS...

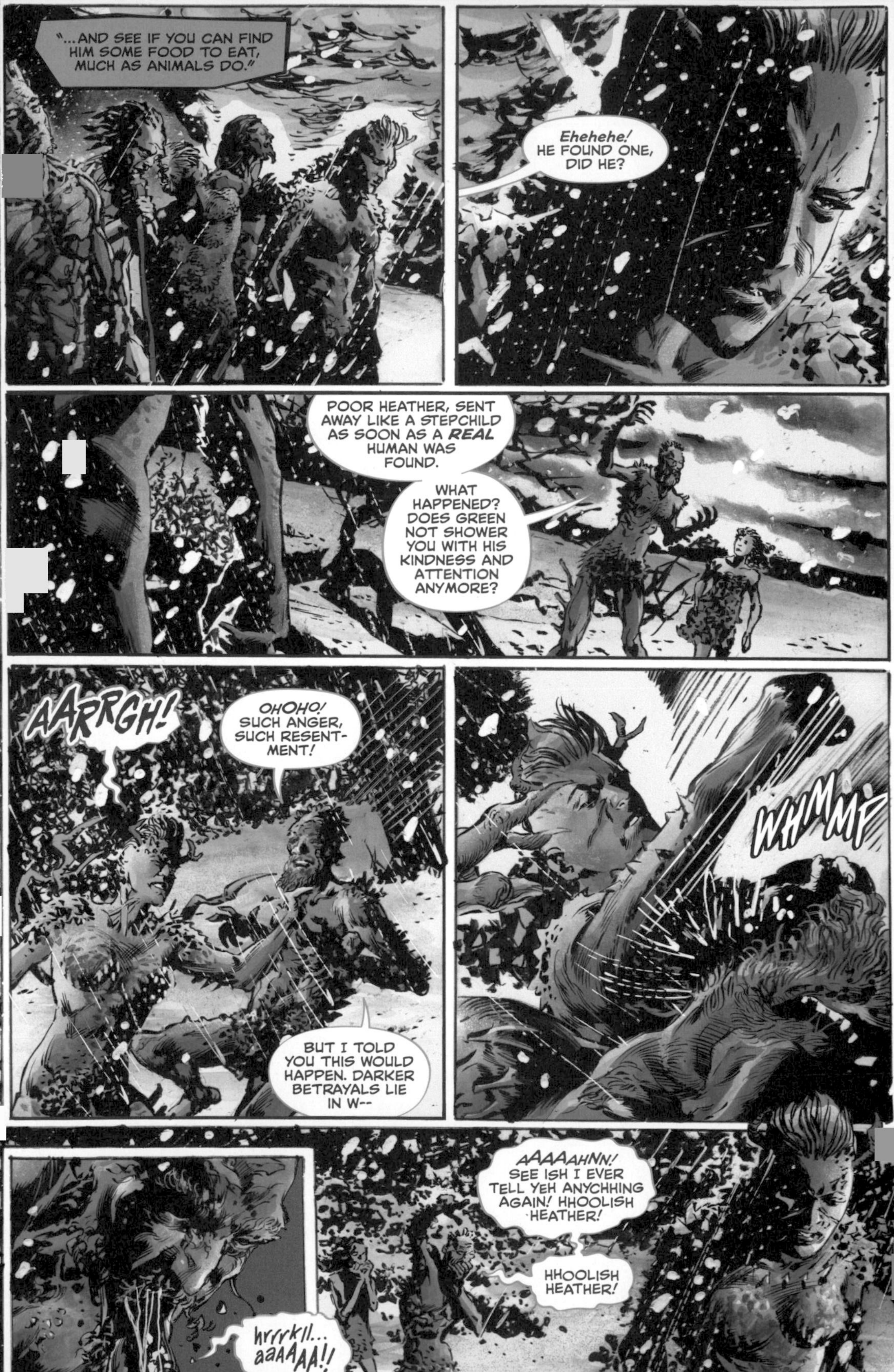
"...AND SEE IF YOU CAN FIND HIM SOME FOOD TO EAT, MUCH AS ANIMALS DO."
Ehehehe! HE FOUND ONE, DID HE?
POOR HEATHER, SENT AWAY LIKE A STEPCHILD AS SOON AS A **REAL** HUMAN WAS FOUND.
WHAT HAPPENED? DOES GREEN NOT SHOWER YOU WITH HIS KINDNESS AND ATTENTION ANYMORE?
AARRGH!
OHOHO! SUCH ANGER, SUCH RESENTMENT!
BUT I TOLD YOU THIS WOULD HAPPEN. DARKER BETRAYALS LIE IN W--
WHMMF
hrrrkll... aaaAAA!!
AAAAAHNN! SEE ISH I EVER TELL YEH ANYCHHING AGAIN! HHOOLISH HEATHER!
HHOOLISH HEATHER!

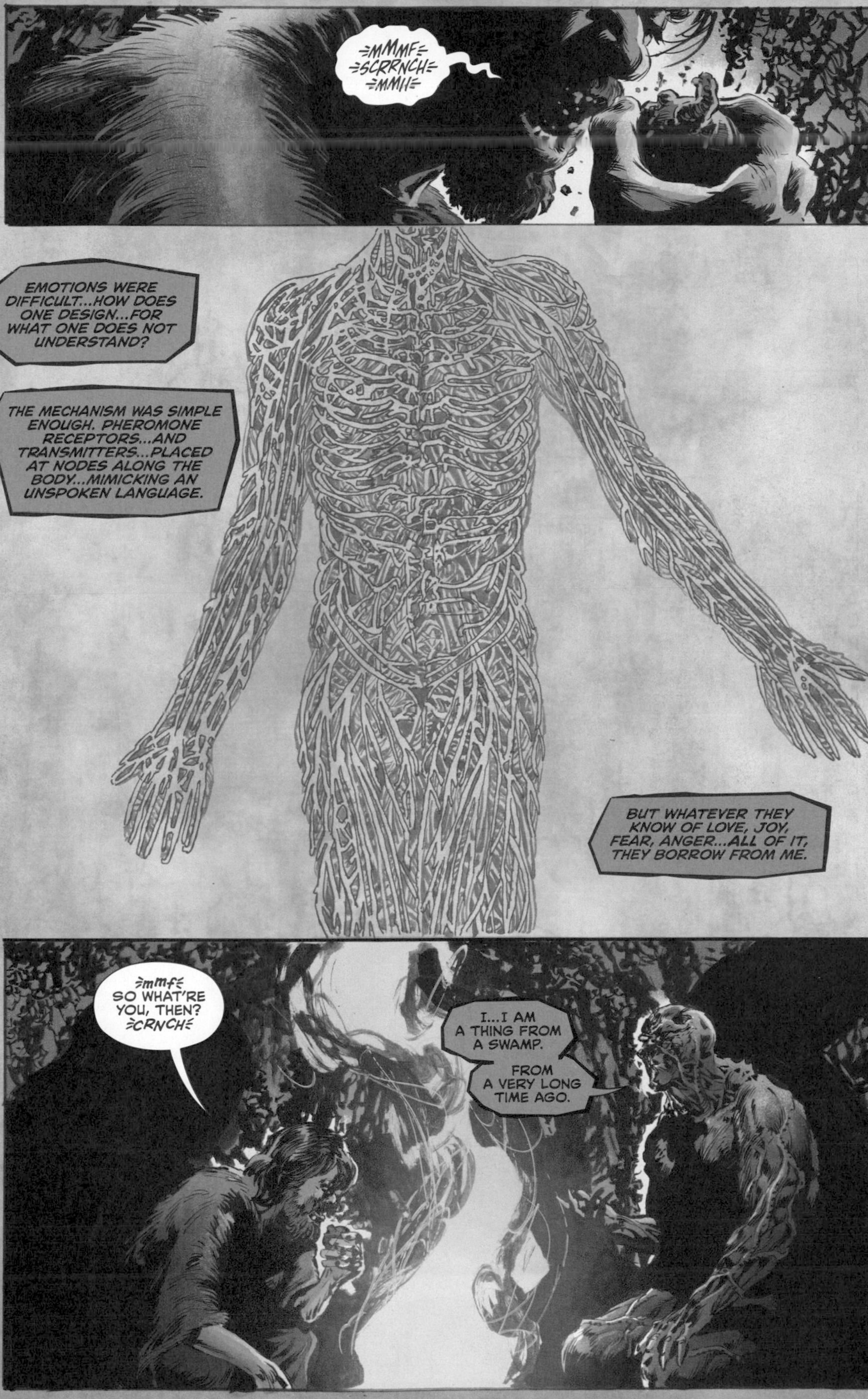
MMMF SCRRNCH MMM
EMOTIONS WERE DIFFICULT...HOW DOES ONE DESIGN...FOR WHAT ONE DOES NOT UNDERSTAND?
THE MECHANISM WAS SIMPLE ENOUGH. PHEROMONE RECEPTORS...AND TRANSMITTERS...PLACED AT NODES ALONG THE BODY...MIMICKING AN UNSPOKEN LANGUAGE.
BUT WHATEVER THEY KNOW OF LOVE, JOY, FEAR, ANGER...ALL OF IT, THEY BORROW FROM ME.
mmf SO WHAT'RE YOU, THEN? CRNCH
I...I AM A THING FROM A SWAMP.
FROM A VERY LONG TIME AGO.

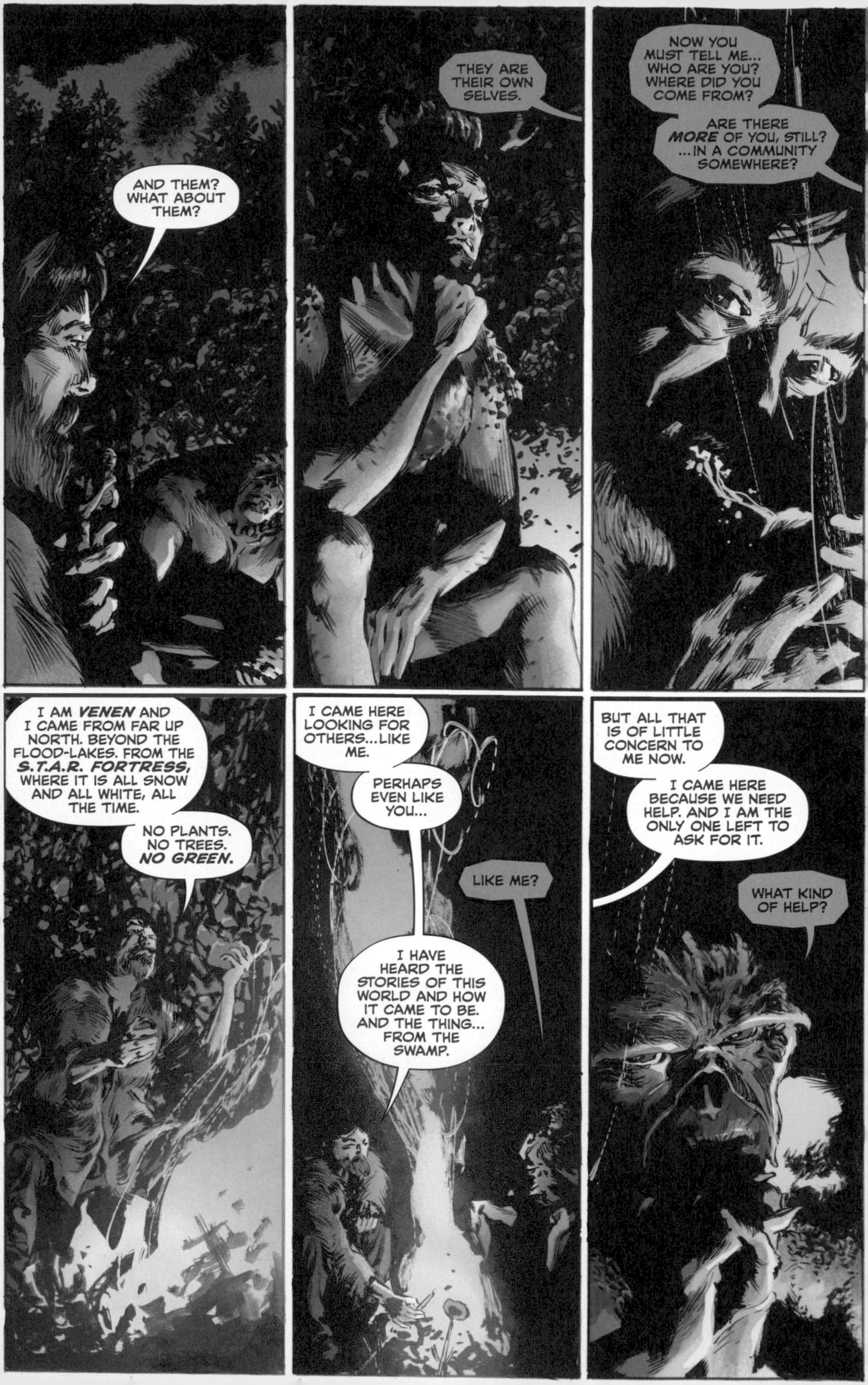
AND THEM? WHAT ABOUT THEM?
THEY ARE THEIR OWN SELVES.
NOW YOU MUST TELL ME... WHO ARE YOU? WHERE DID YOU COME FROM?
ARE THERE MORE OF YOU, STILL? ...IN A COMMUNITY SOMEWHERE?
I AM VENEN AND I CAME FROM FAR UP NORTH. BEYOND THE FLOOD-LAKES. FROM THE S.T.A.R. FORTRESS, WHERE IT IS ALL SNOW AND ALL WHITE, ALL THE TIME.
NO PLANTS. NO TREES. NO GREEN.
I CAME HERE LOOKING FOR OTHERS...LIKE ME.
PERHAPS EVEN LIKE YOU...
LIKE ME?
I HAVE HEARD THE STORIES OF THIS WORLD AND HOW IT CAME TO BE. AND THE THING... FROM THE SWAMP.
BUT ALL THAT IS OF LITTLE CONCERN TO ME NOW.
I CAME HERE BECAUSE WE NEED HELP. AND I AM THE ONLY ONE LEFT TO ASK FOR IT.
WHAT KIND OF HELP?

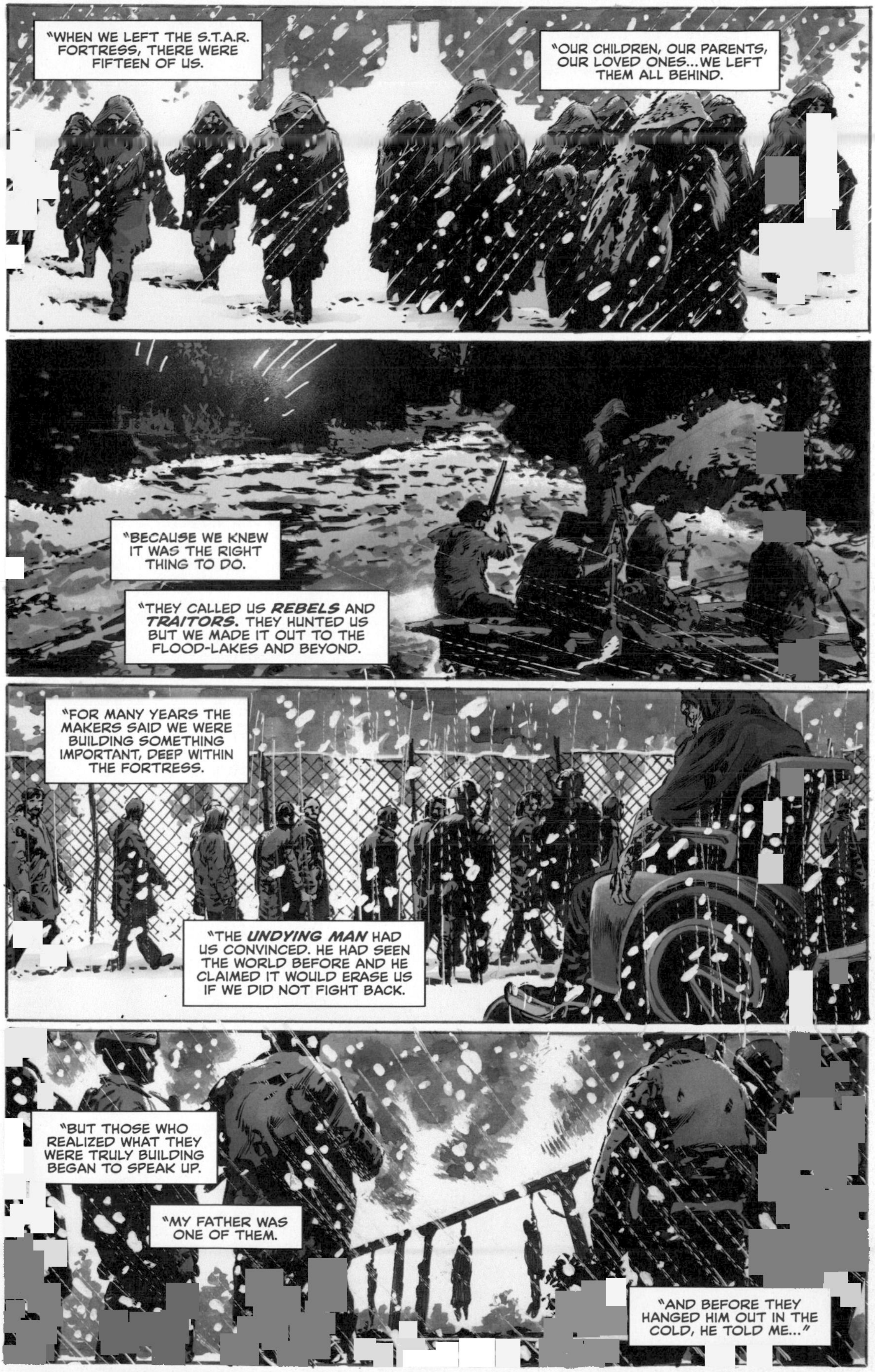
"WHEN WE LEFT THE S.T.A.R. FORTRESS, THERE WERE FIFTEEN OF US.
"OUR CHILDREN, OUR PARENTS, OUR LOVED ONES...WE LEFT THEM ALL BEHIND.
"BECAUSE WE KNEW IT WAS THE RIGHT THING TO DO.
"THEY CALLED US REBELS AND TRAITORS. THEY HUNTED US BUT WE MADE IT OUT TO THE FLOOD-LAKES AND BEYOND.
"FOR MANY YEARS THE MAKERS SAID WE WERE BUILDING SOMETHING IMPORTANT, DEEP WITHIN THE FORTRESS.
"THE UNDYING MAN HAD US CONVINCED. HE HAD SEEN THE WORLD BEFORE AND HE CLAIMED IT WOULD ERASE US IF WE DID NOT FIGHT BACK.
"BUT THOSE WHO REALIZED WHAT THEY WERE TRULY BUILDING BEGAN TO SPEAK UP.
"MY FATHER WAS ONE OF THEM.
"AND BEFORE THEY HANGED HIM OUT IN THE COLD, HE TOLD ME..."

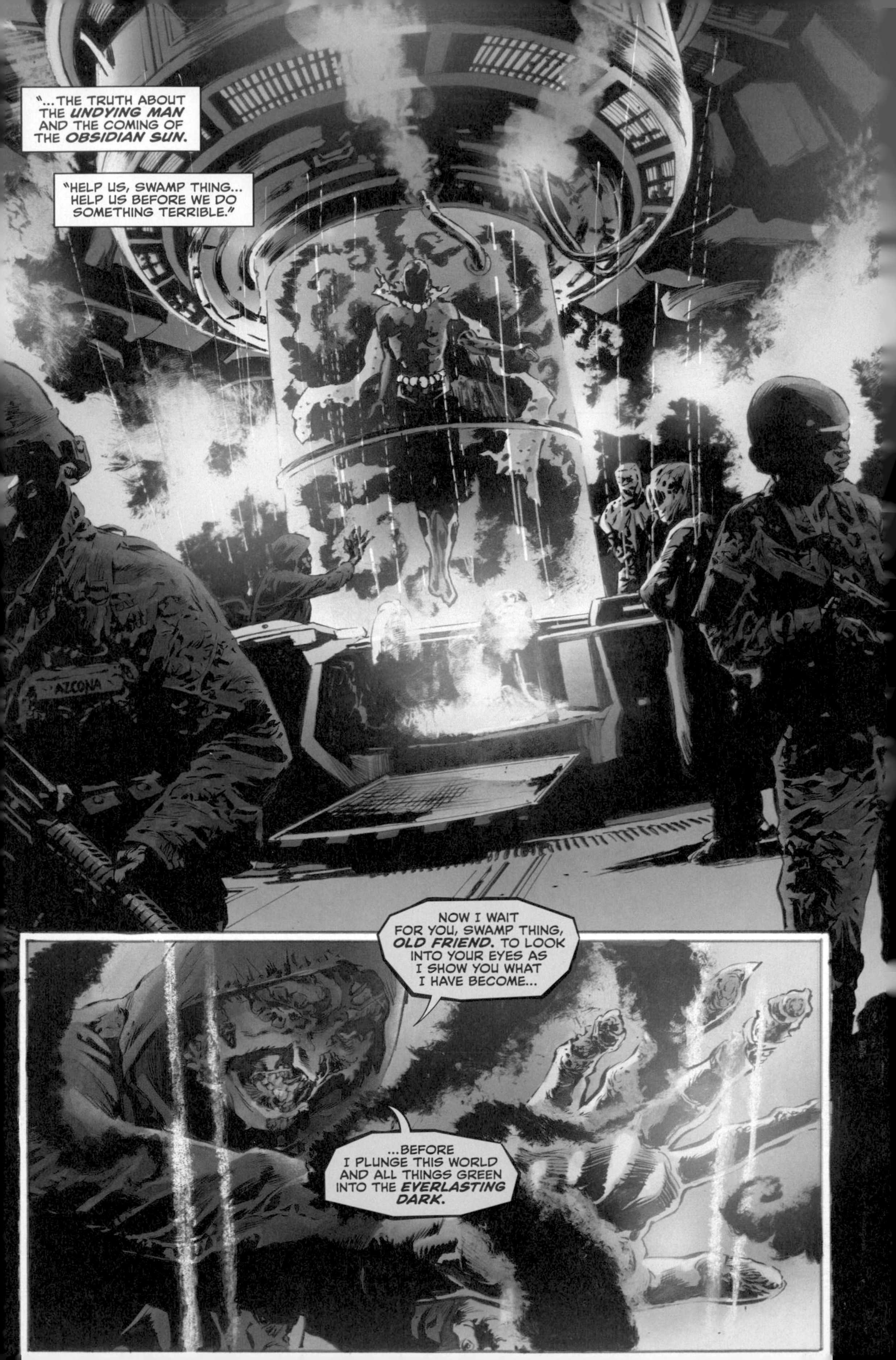
"...THE TRUTH ABOUT THE UNDYING MAN AND THE COMING OF THE OBSIDIAN SUN.
"HELP US, SWAMP THING... HELP US BEFORE WE DO SOMETHING TERRIBLE."
AZCONA
NOW I WAIT FOR YOU, SWAMP THING, OLD FRIEND. TO LOOK INTO YOUR EYES AS I SHOW YOU WHAT I HAVE BECOME...
...BEFORE I PLUNGE THIS WORLD AND ALL THINGS GREEN INTO THE EVERLASTING DARK.

Future State: Swamp Thing #2
cover art by **MIKE PERKINS**
and **JUNE CHUNG**

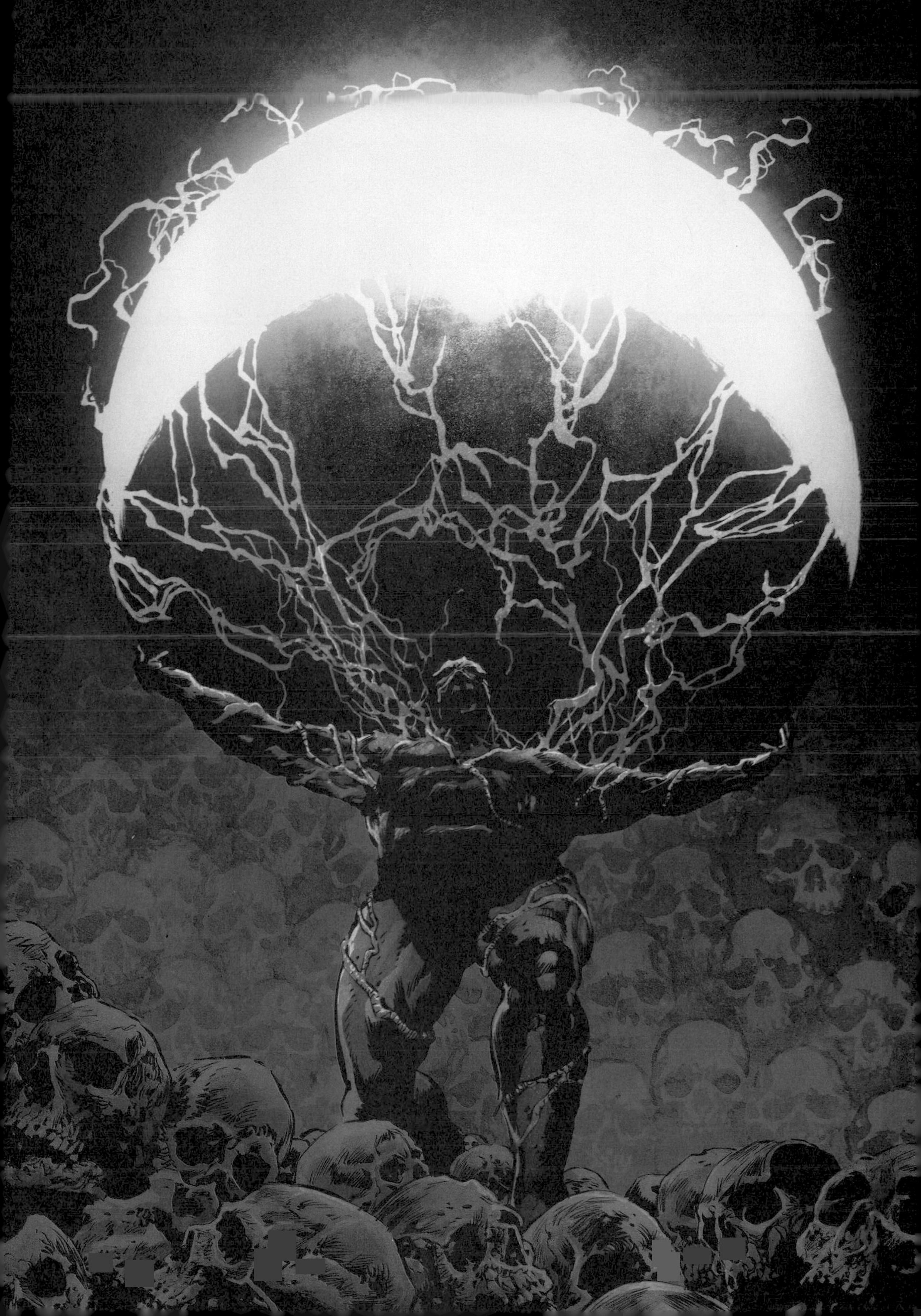

Future State: Swamp Thing #2
variant cover art by **DIMA IVANOV**

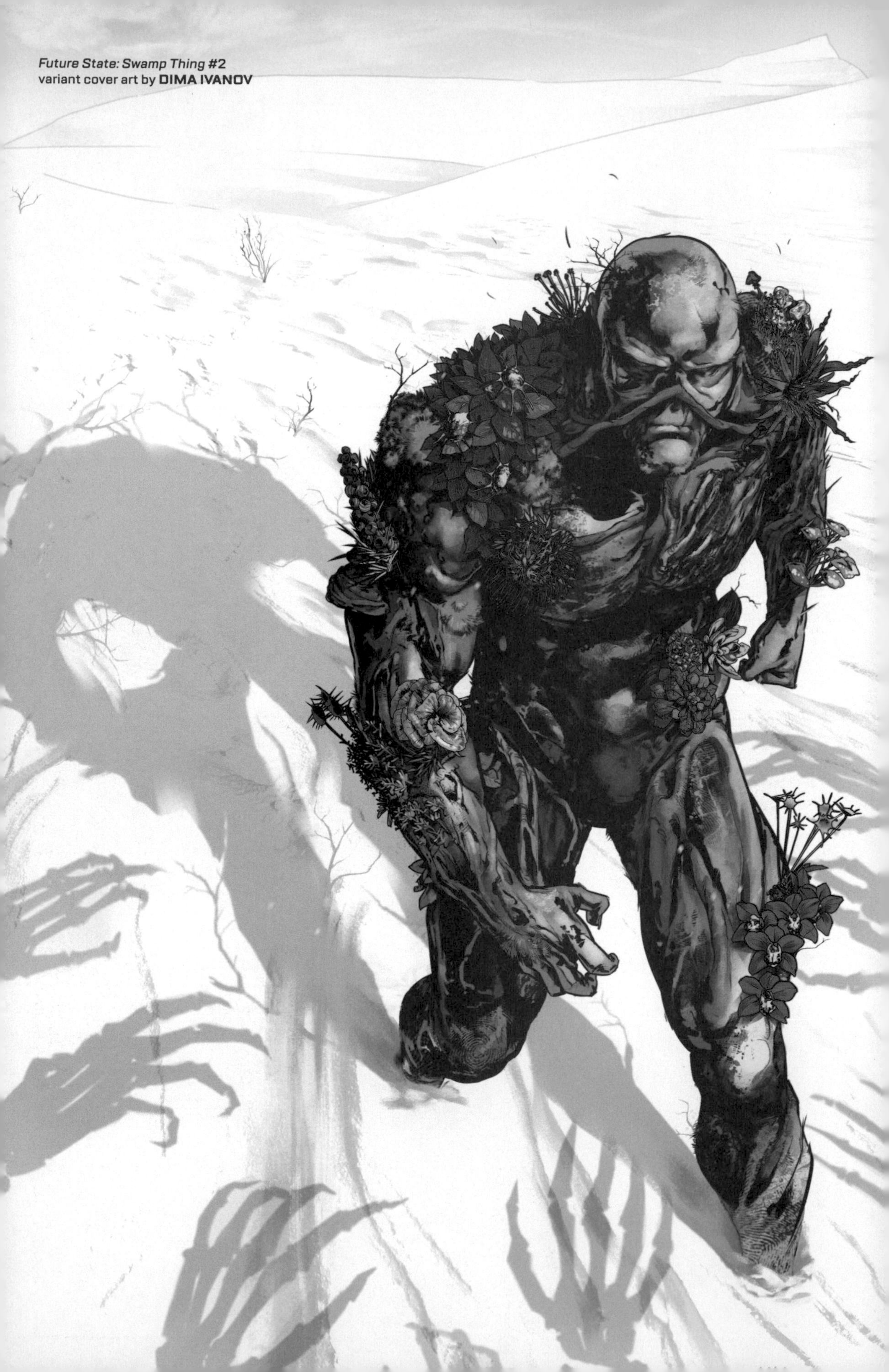

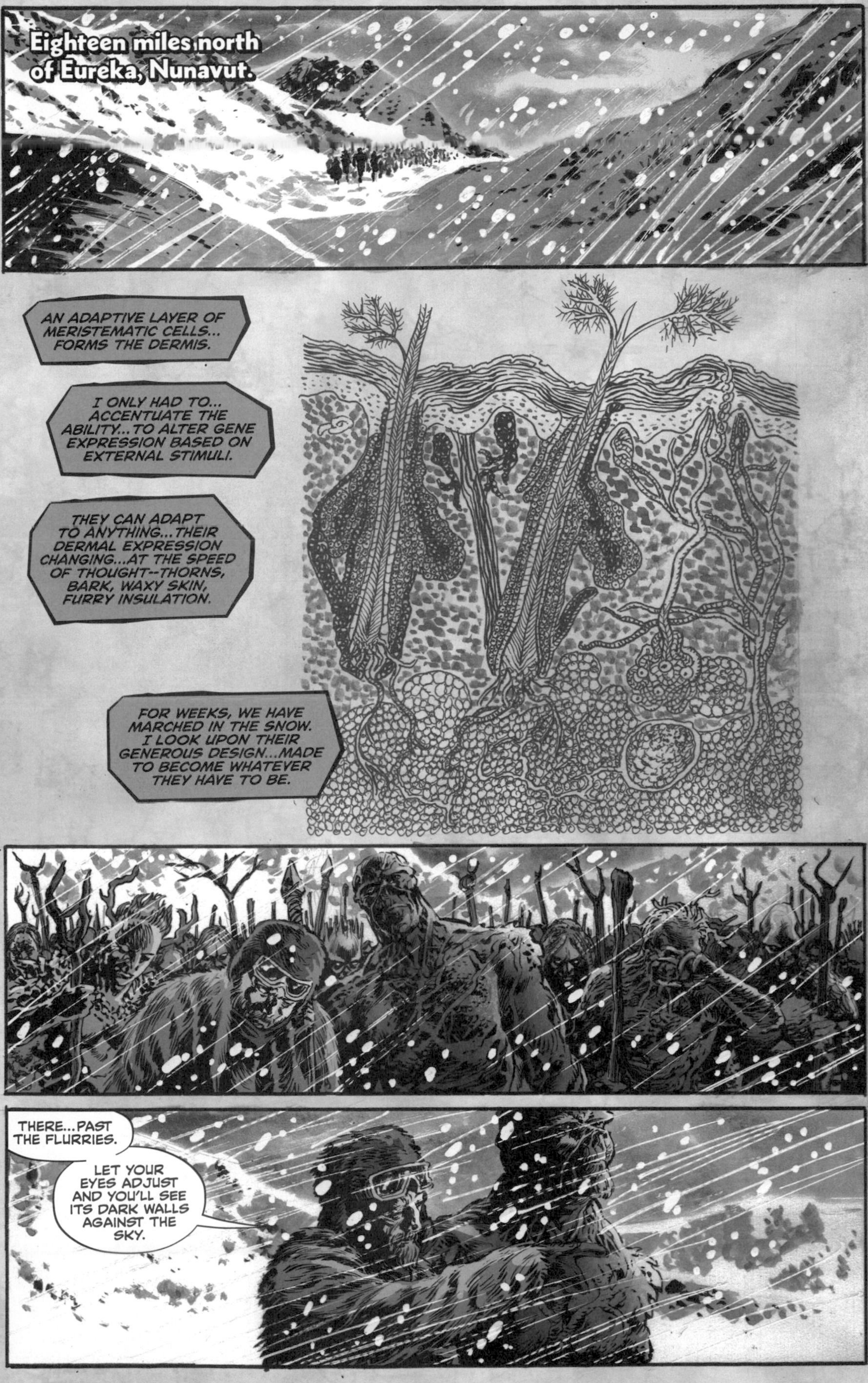
Eighteen miles north of Eureka, Nunavut.
AN ADAPTIVE LAYER OF MERISTEMATIC CELLS... FORMS THE DERMIS.
I ONLY HAD TO... ACCENTUATE THE ABILITY...TO ALTER GENE EXPRESSION BASED ON EXTERNAL STIMULI.
THEY CAN ADAPT TO ANYTHING...THEIR DERMAL EXPRESSION CHANGING...AT THE SPEED OF THOUGHT--THORNS, BARK, WAXY SKIN, FURRY INSULATION.
FOR WEEKS, WE HAVE MARCHED IN THE SNOW. I LOOK UPON THEIR GENEROUS DESIGN...MADE TO BECOME WHATEVER THEY HAVE TO BE.
THERE...PAST THE FLURRIES.
LET YOUR EYES ADJUST AND YOU'LL SEE ITS DARK WALLS AGAINST THE SKY.

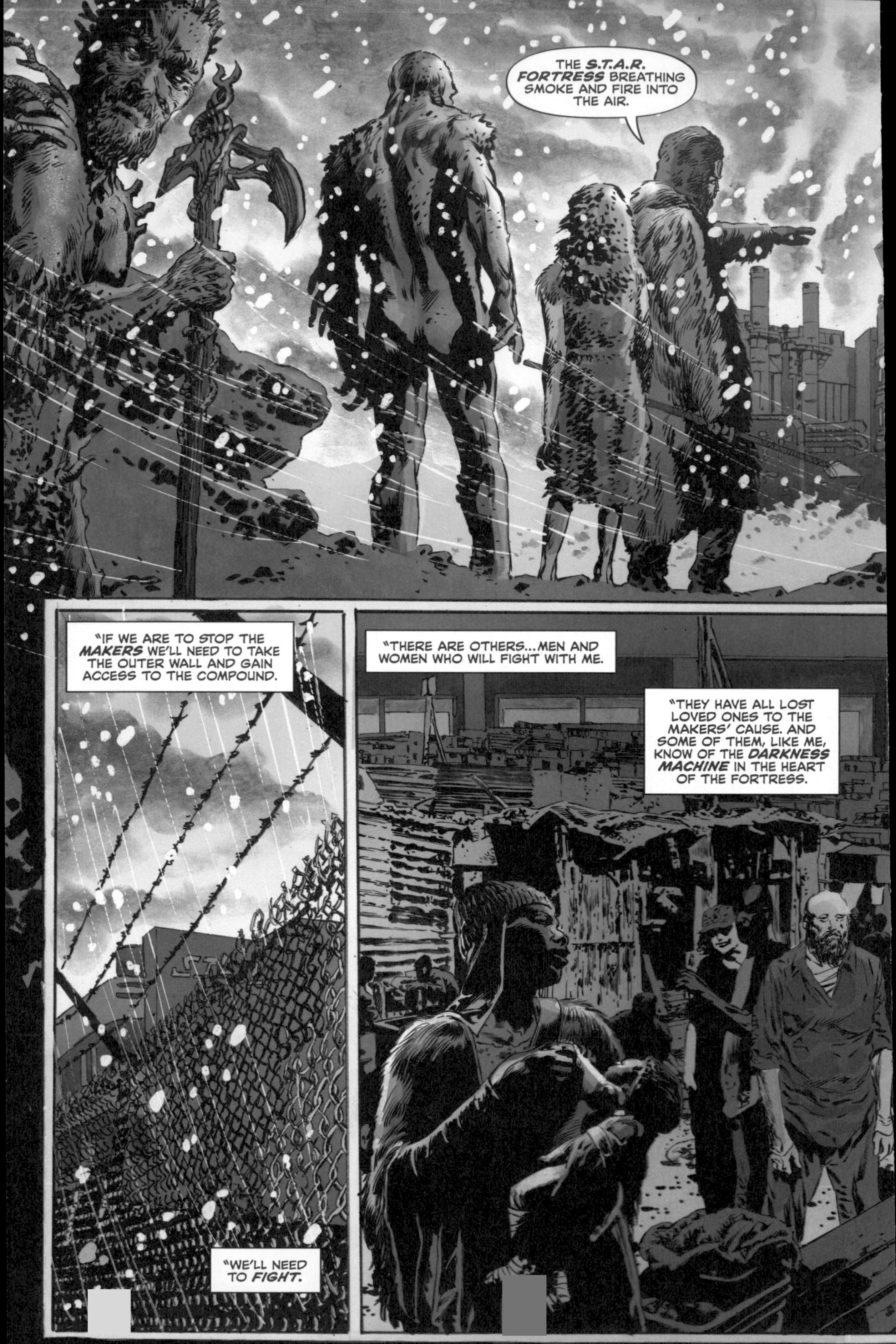
THE S.T.A.R. FORTRESS BREATHING SMOKE AND FIRE INTO THE AIR.
"IF WE ARE TO STOP THE MAKERS WE'LL NEED TO TAKE THE OUTER WALL AND GAIN ACCESS TO THE COMPOUND.
"WE'LL NEED TO FIGHT.
"THERE ARE OTHERS...MEN AND WOMEN WHO WILL FIGHT WITH ME.
"THEY HAVE ALL LOST LOVED ONES TO THE MAKERS' CAUSE. AND SOME OF THEM, LIKE ME, KNOW OF THE DARKNESS MACHINE IN THE HEART OF THE FORTRESS.

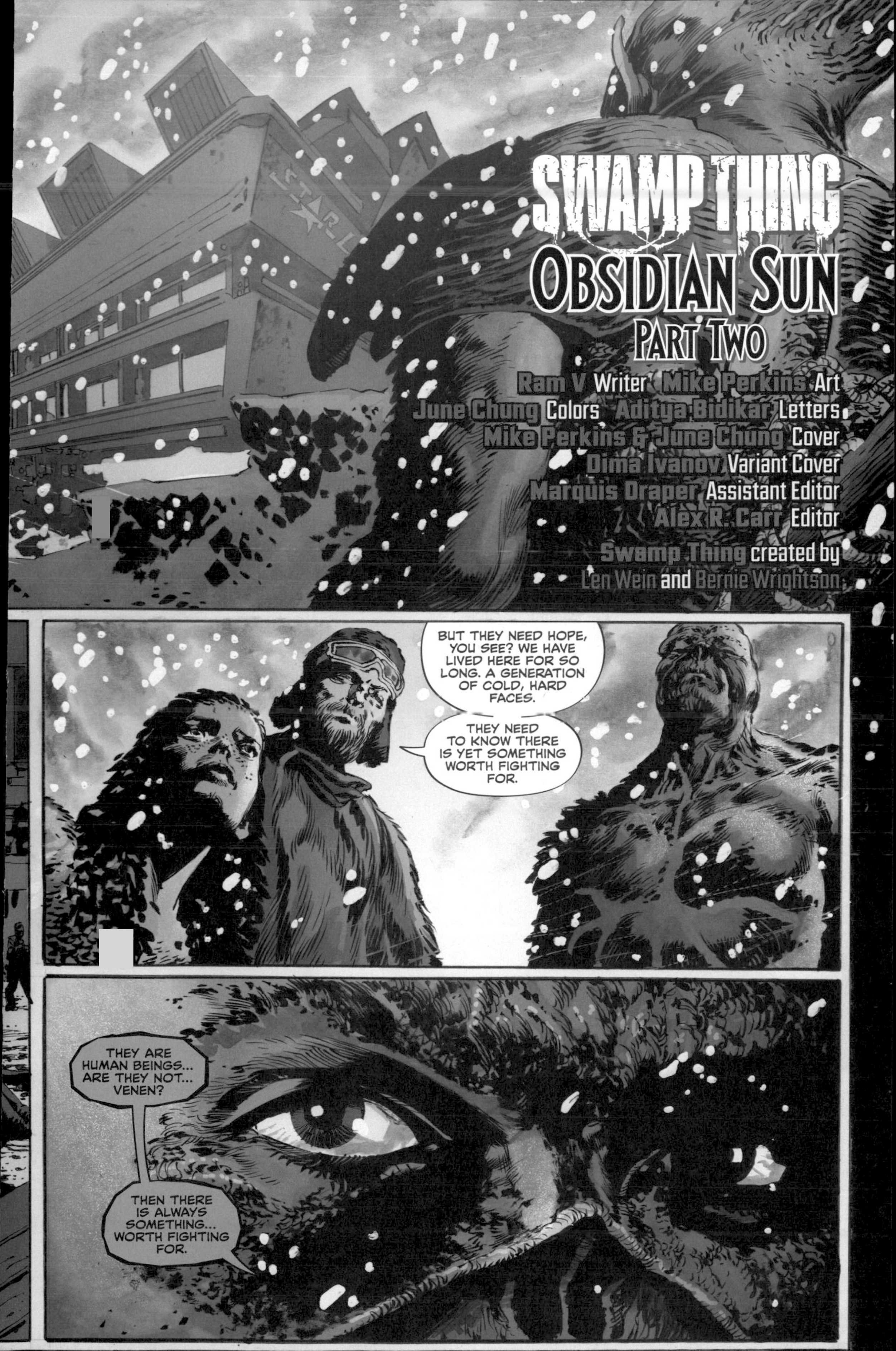
SWAMP THING
OBSIDIAN SUN
PART TWO
Ram V Writer Mike Perkins Art
June Chung Colors Aditya Bidikar Letters
Mike Perkins & June Chung Cover
Dima Ivanov Variant Cover
Marquis Draper Assistant Editor
Alex R. Carr Editor
Swamp Thing created by
Len Wein and Bernie Wrightson
BUT THEY NEED HOPE, YOU SEE? WE HAVE LIVED HERE FOR SO LONG. A GENERATION OF COLD, HARD FACES.
THEY NEED TO KNOW THERE IS YET SOMETHING WORTH FIGHTING FOR.
THEY ARE HUMAN BEINGS... ARE THEY NOT... VENEN?
THEN THERE IS ALWAYS SOMETHING... WORTH FIGHTING FOR.

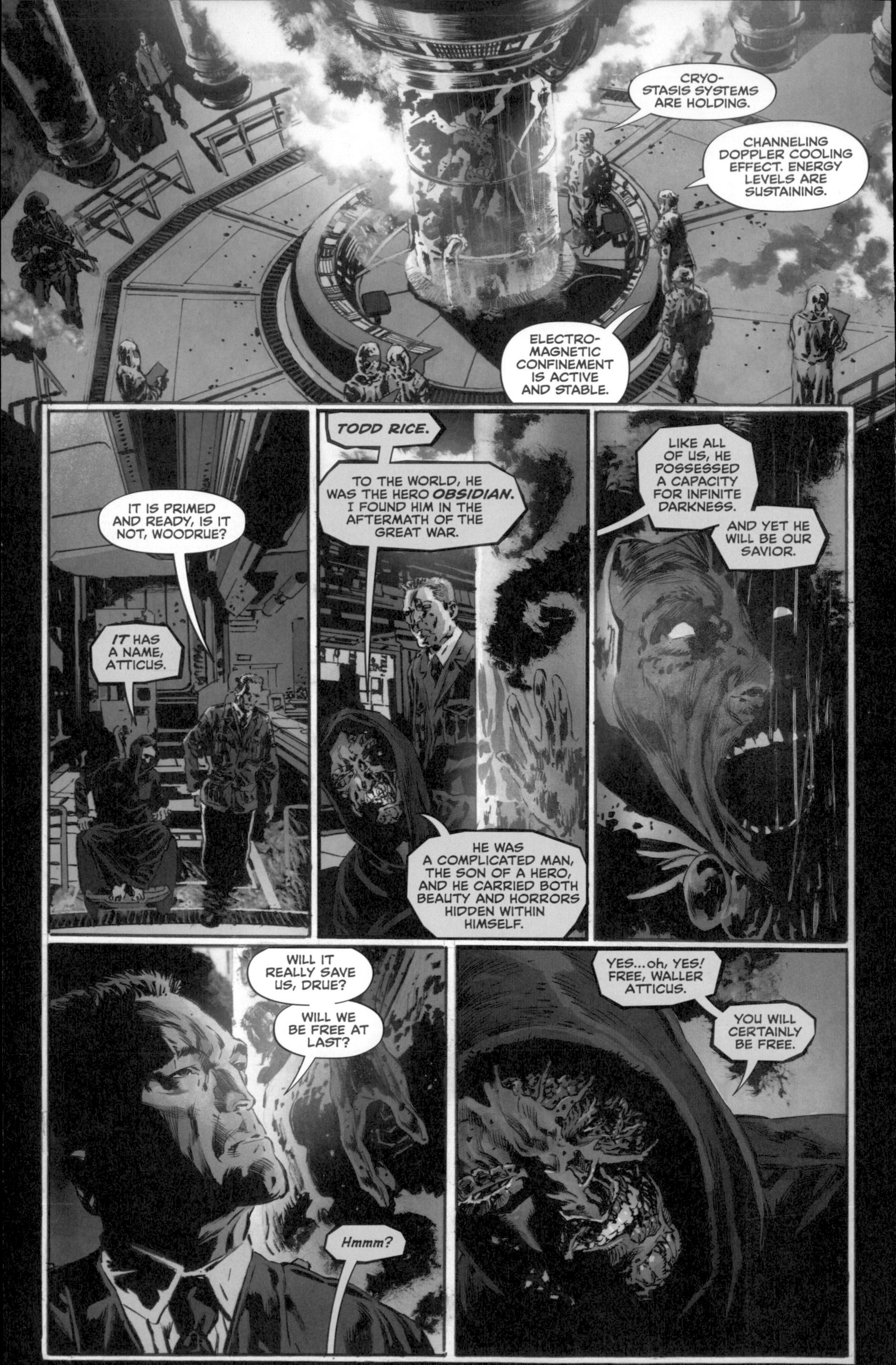
CRYO-STASIS SYSTEMS ARE HOLDING.
CHANNELING DOPPLER COOLING EFFECT. ENERGY LEVELS ARE SUSTAINING.
ELECTRO-MAGNETIC CONFINEMENT IS ACTIVE AND STABLE.
IT IS PRIMED AND READY, IS IT NOT, WOODRUE?
IT HAS A NAME, ATTICUS.
TODD RICE.
TO THE WORLD, HE WAS THE HERO *OBSIDIAN*. I FOUND HIM IN THE AFTERMATH OF THE GREAT WAR.
HE WAS A COMPLICATED MAN, THE SON OF A HERO, AND HE CARRIED BOTH BEAUTY AND HORRORS HIDDEN WITHIN HIMSELF.
LIKE ALL OF US, HE POSSESSED A CAPACITY FOR INFINITE DARKNESS.
AND YET HE WILL BE OUR SAVIOR.
WILL IT REALLY SAVE US, DRUE?
WILL WE BE FREE AT LAST?
Hmmm?
YES...oh, YES! FREE, WALLER ATTICUS.
YOU WILL CERTAINLY BE FREE.

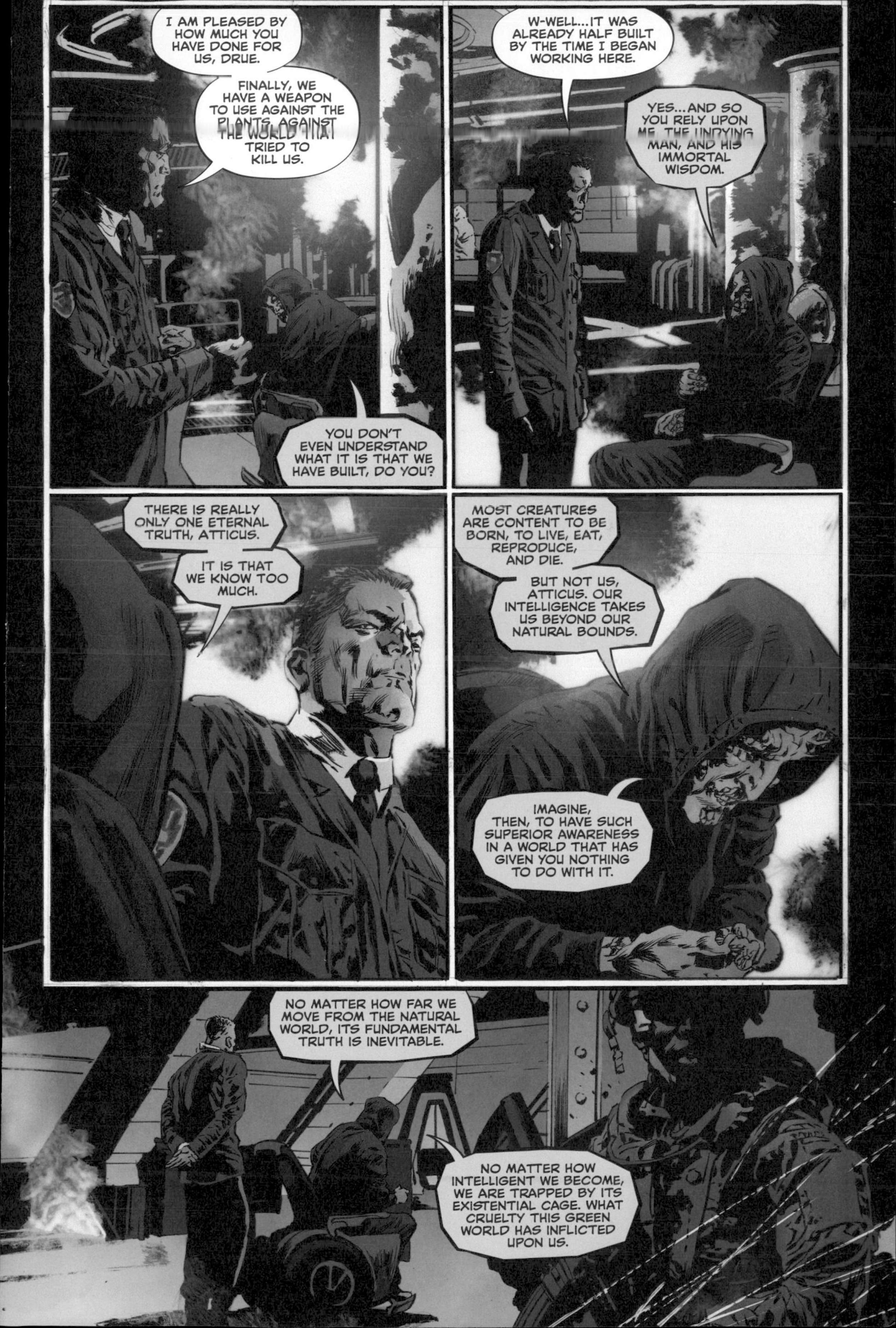
I AM PLEASED BY HOW MUCH YOU HAVE DONE FOR US, DRUE.
FINALLY, WE HAVE A WEAPON TO USE AGAINST THE PLANTS, AGAINST THE WORLD THAT TRIED TO KILL US.
YOU DON'T EVEN UNDERSTAND WHAT IT IS THAT WE HAVE BUILT, DO YOU?
W-WELL...IT WAS ALREADY HALF BUILT BY THE TIME I BEGAN WORKING HERE.
YES...AND SO YOU RELY UPON ME, THE UNDYING MAN, AND HIS IMMORTAL WISDOM.
THERE IS REALLY ONLY ONE ETERNAL TRUTH, ATTICUS.
IT IS THAT WE KNOW TOO MUCH.
MOST CREATURES ARE CONTENT TO BE BORN, TO LIVE, EAT, REPRODUCE, AND DIE.
BUT NOT US, ATTICUS. OUR INTELLIGENCE TAKES US BEYOND OUR NATURAL BOUNDS.
IMAGINE, THEN, TO HAVE SUCH SUPERIOR AWARENESS IN A WORLD THAT HAS GIVEN YOU NOTHING TO DO WITH IT.
NO MATTER HOW FAR WE MOVE FROM THE NATURAL WORLD, ITS FUNDAMENTAL TRUTH IS INEVITABLE.
NO MATTER HOW INTELLIGENT WE BECOME, WE ARE TRAPPED BY ITS EXISTENTIAL CAGE. WHAT CRUELTY THIS GREEN WORLD HAS INFLICTED UPON US.

I REVERED IT ONCE. NOW I SHALL END IT. AND YOU SHALL BE FREE.

I WILL BREAK US OUT OF THIS COMEDY OF LIFE AND DEATH WITH *DARKNESS*.

THE LONGEST NIGHTS ON THE EARTH OCCUR IN THIS PLACE.

IF NO ONE CAN SEE US...DO WE EVEN EXIST? TRUE FREEDOM FROM EXISTENCE IS ONLY IN ABSOLUTE DARKNESS.

WALLER ATTICUS! THE REBELS ARE AT THE WALLS.

AND THEY'VE FOUND SOME SORT OF PLANT CREATURES TO HELP THEM, SIR.

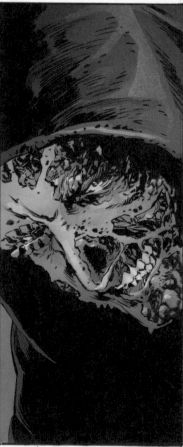

CLOSE DOWN ALL LEVEL TWO ACCESS.

SCRAMBLE DEFENSES TO THE OUTER WALLS.

ARM THE INSIDE GROUPS WITH *INCENDIARIES*.

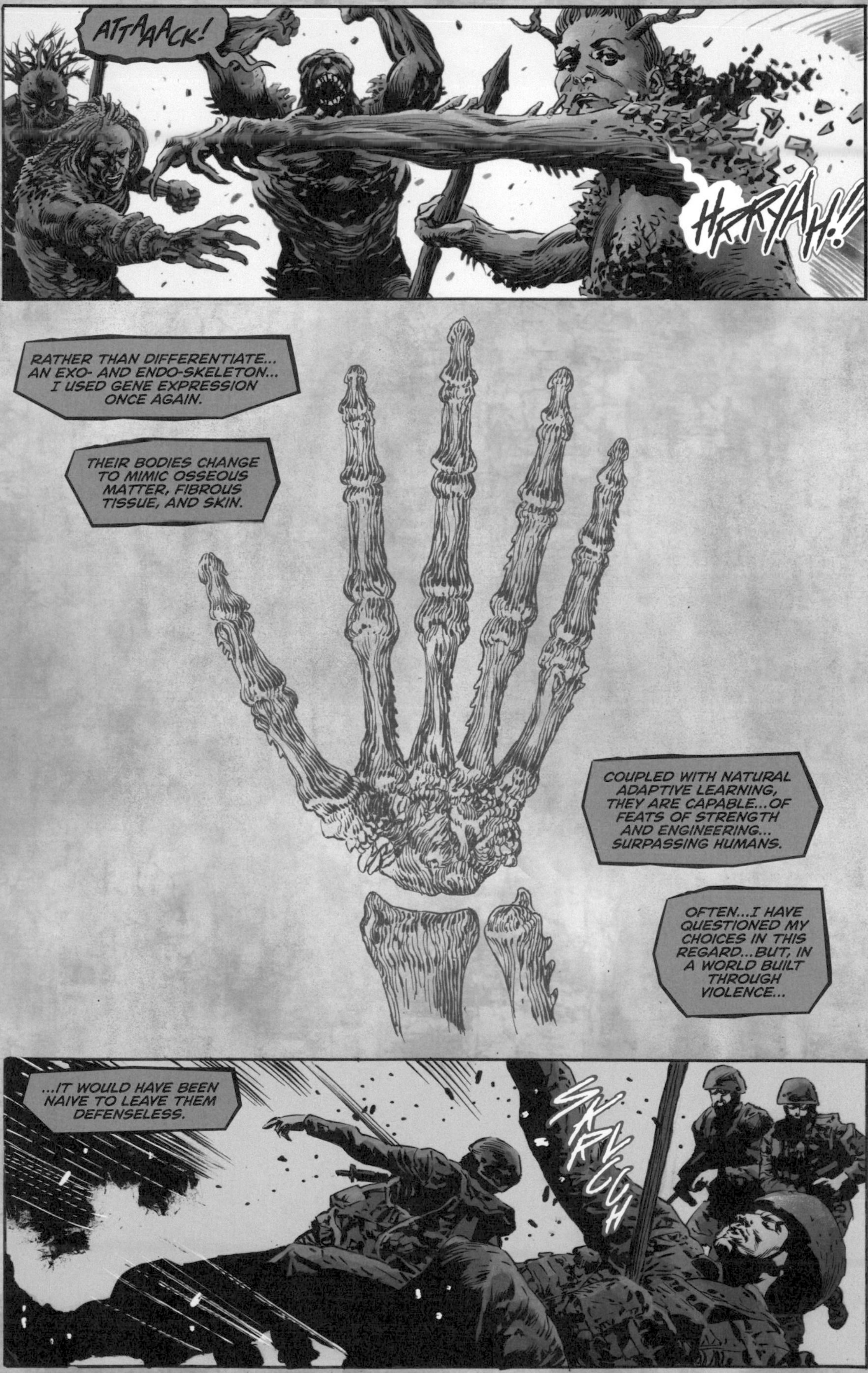
ATTAAACK!
HRRYAH!!
RATHER THAN DIFFERENTIATE... AN EXO- AND ENDO-SKELETON... I USED GENE EXPRESSION ONCE AGAIN.
THEIR BODIES CHANGE TO MIMIC OSSEOUS MATTER, FIBROUS TISSUE, AND SKIN.
COUPLED WITH NATURAL ADAPTIVE LEARNING, THEY ARE CAPABLE...OF FEATS OF STRENGTH AND ENGINEERING... SURPASSING HUMANS.
OFTEN...I HAVE QUESTIONED MY CHOICES IN THIS REGARD...BUT, IN A WORLD BUILT THROUGH VIOLENCE...
...IT WOULD HAVE BEEN NAIVE TO LEAVE THEM DEFENSELESS.

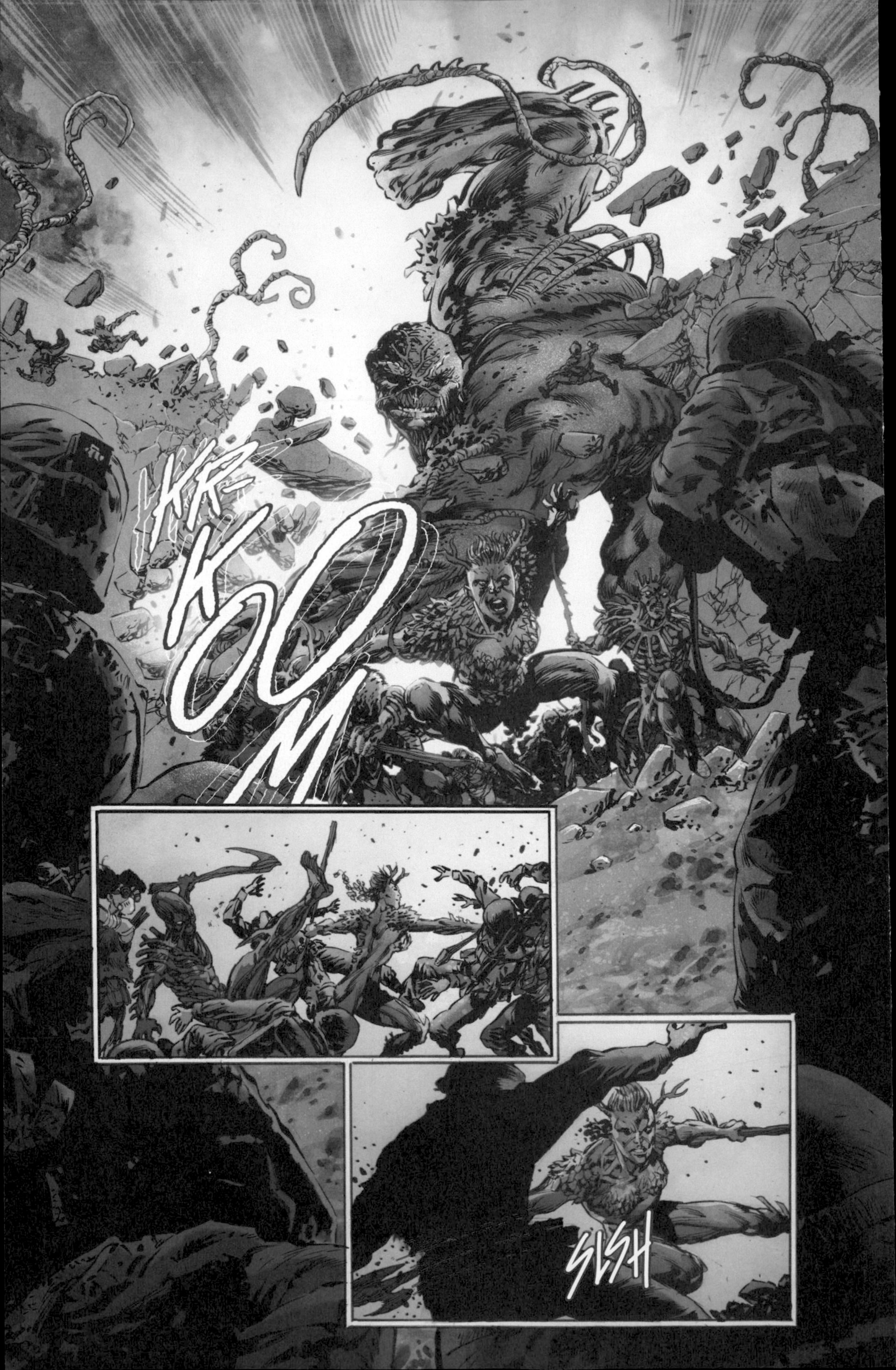
KR-K-BOOM
SLSH

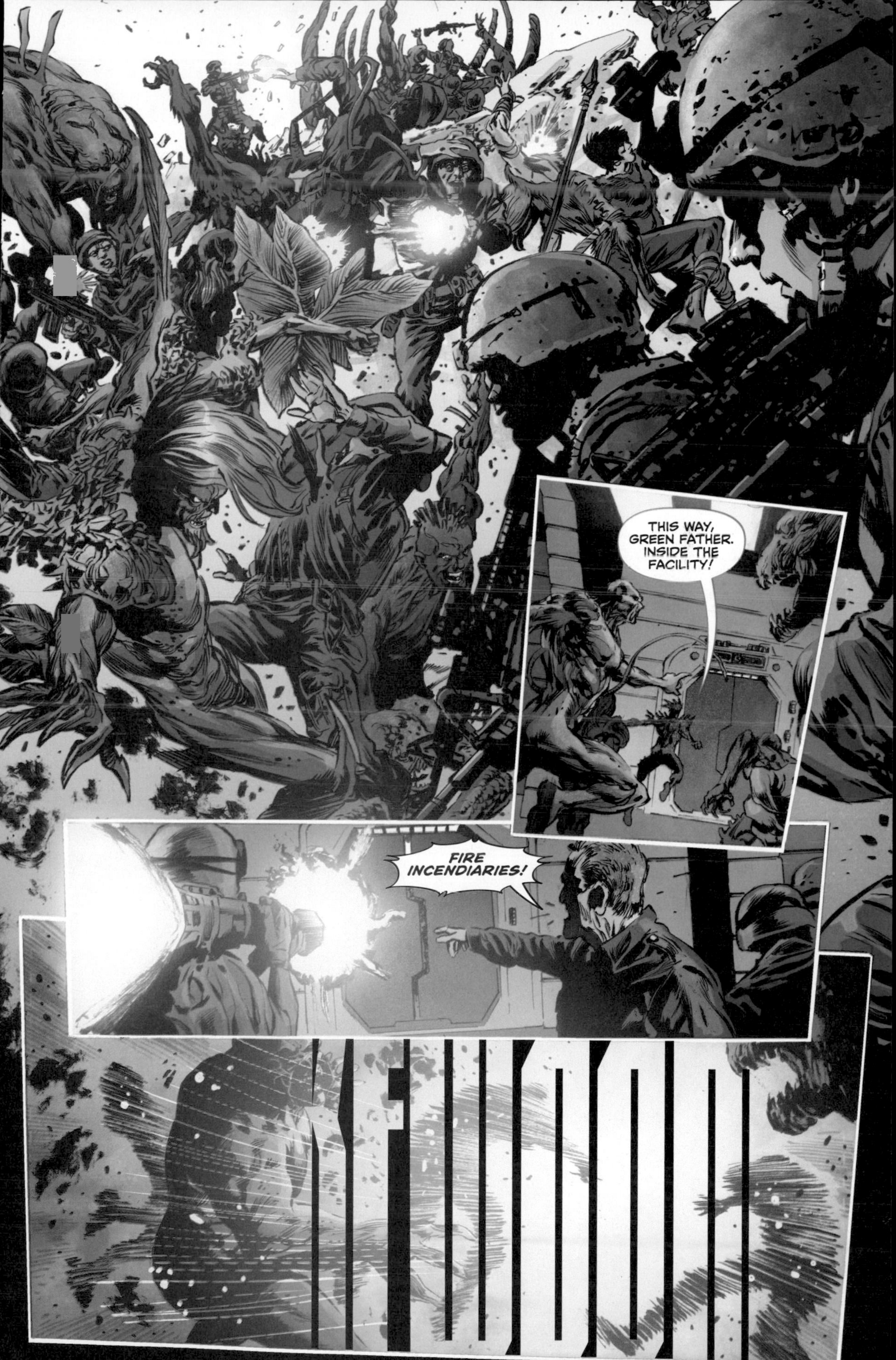
THIS WAY, GREEN FATHER. INSIDE THE FACILITY!
FIRE INCENDIARIES!

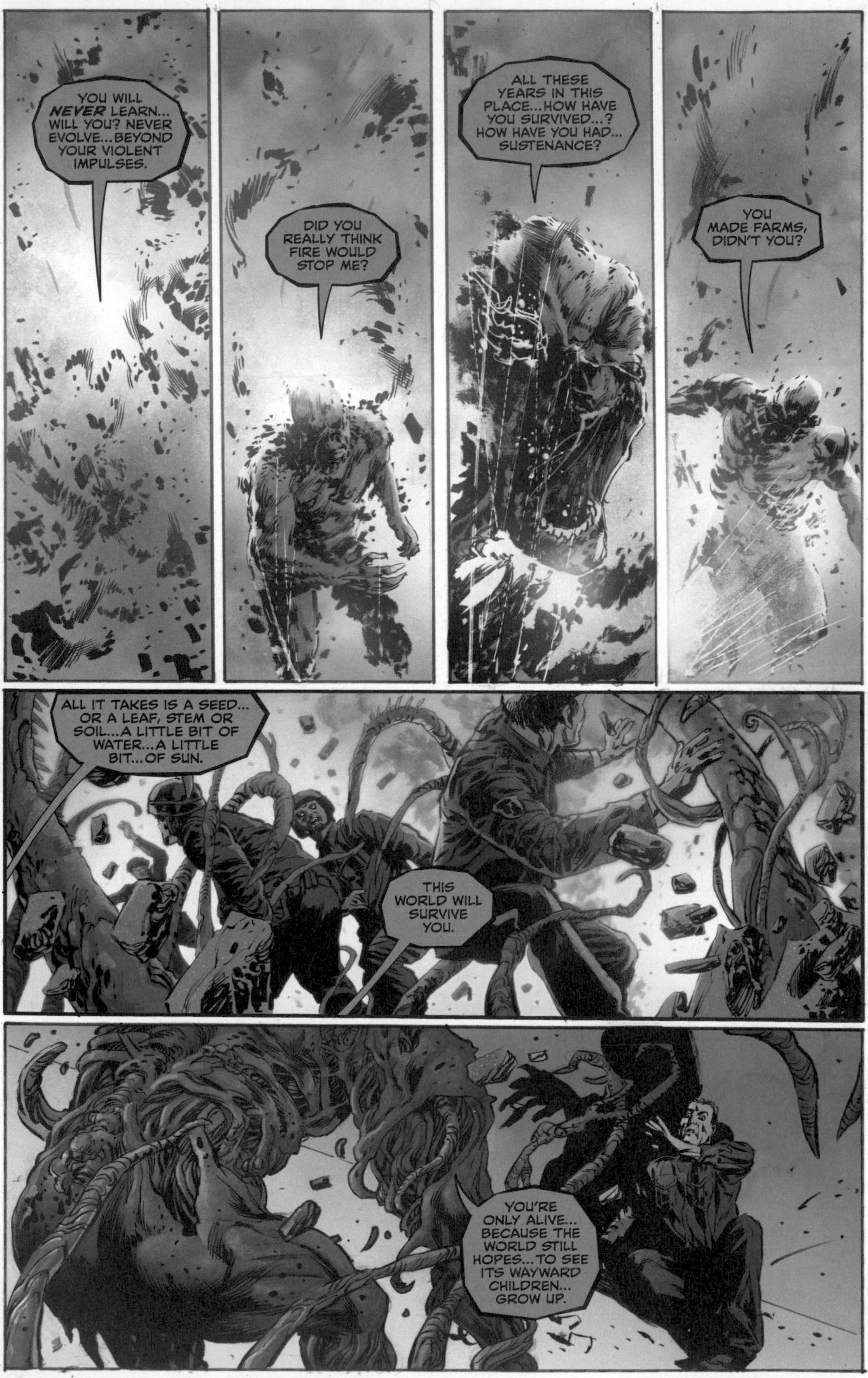
YOU WILL *NEVER* LEARN... WILL YOU? NEVER EVOLVE...BEYOND YOUR VIOLENT IMPULSES.
DID YOU REALLY THINK FIRE WOULD STOP ME?
ALL THESE YEARS IN THIS PLACE...HOW HAVE YOU SURVIVED...? HOW HAVE YOU HAD... SUSTENANCE?
YOU MADE FARMS, DIDN'T YOU?
ALL IT TAKES IS A SEED... OR A LEAF, STEM OR SOIL...A LITTLE BIT OF WATER...A LITTLE BIT...OF SUN.
THIS WORLD WILL SURVIVE YOU.
YOU'RE ONLY ALIVE... BECAUSE THE WORLD STILL HOPES...TO SEE ITS WAYWARD CHILDREN... GROW UP.

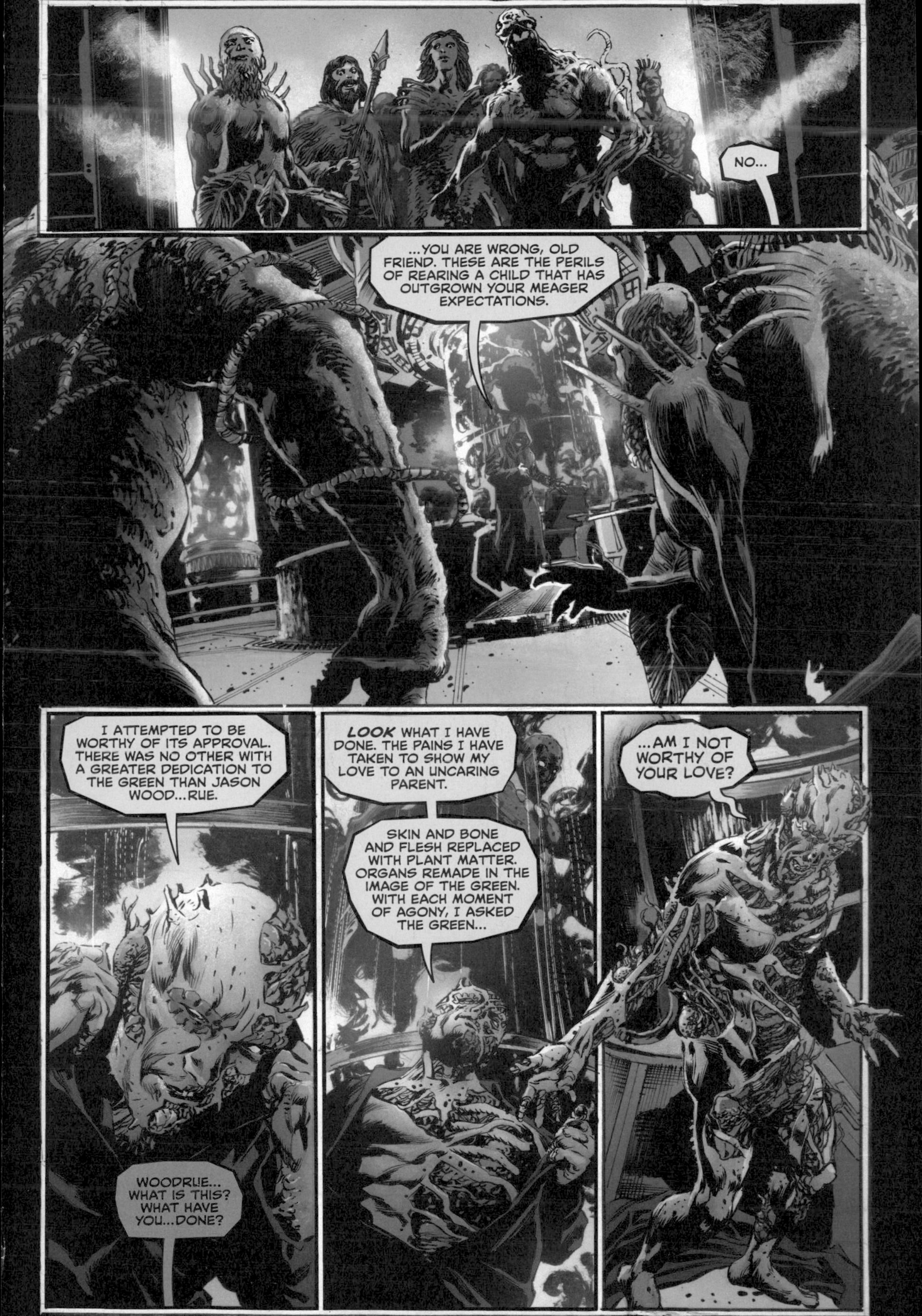
NO...
...YOU ARE WRONG, OLD FRIEND. THESE ARE THE PERILS OF REARING A CHILD THAT HAS OUTGROWN YOUR MEAGER EXPECTATIONS.
I ATTEMPTED TO BE WORTHY OF ITS APPROVAL. THERE WAS NO OTHER WITH A GREATER DEDICATION TO THE GREEN THAN JASON WOOD...RUE.
WOODRUE... WHAT IS THIS? WHAT HAVE YOU...DONE?
LOOK WHAT I HAVE DONE. THE PAINS I HAVE TAKEN TO SHOW MY LOVE TO AN UNCARING PARENT.
SKIN AND BONE AND FLESH REPLACED WITH PLANT MATTER. ORGANS REMADE IN THE IMAGE OF THE GREEN. WITH EACH MOMENT OF AGONY, I ASKED THE GREEN...
...AM I NOT WORTHY OF YOUR LOVE?

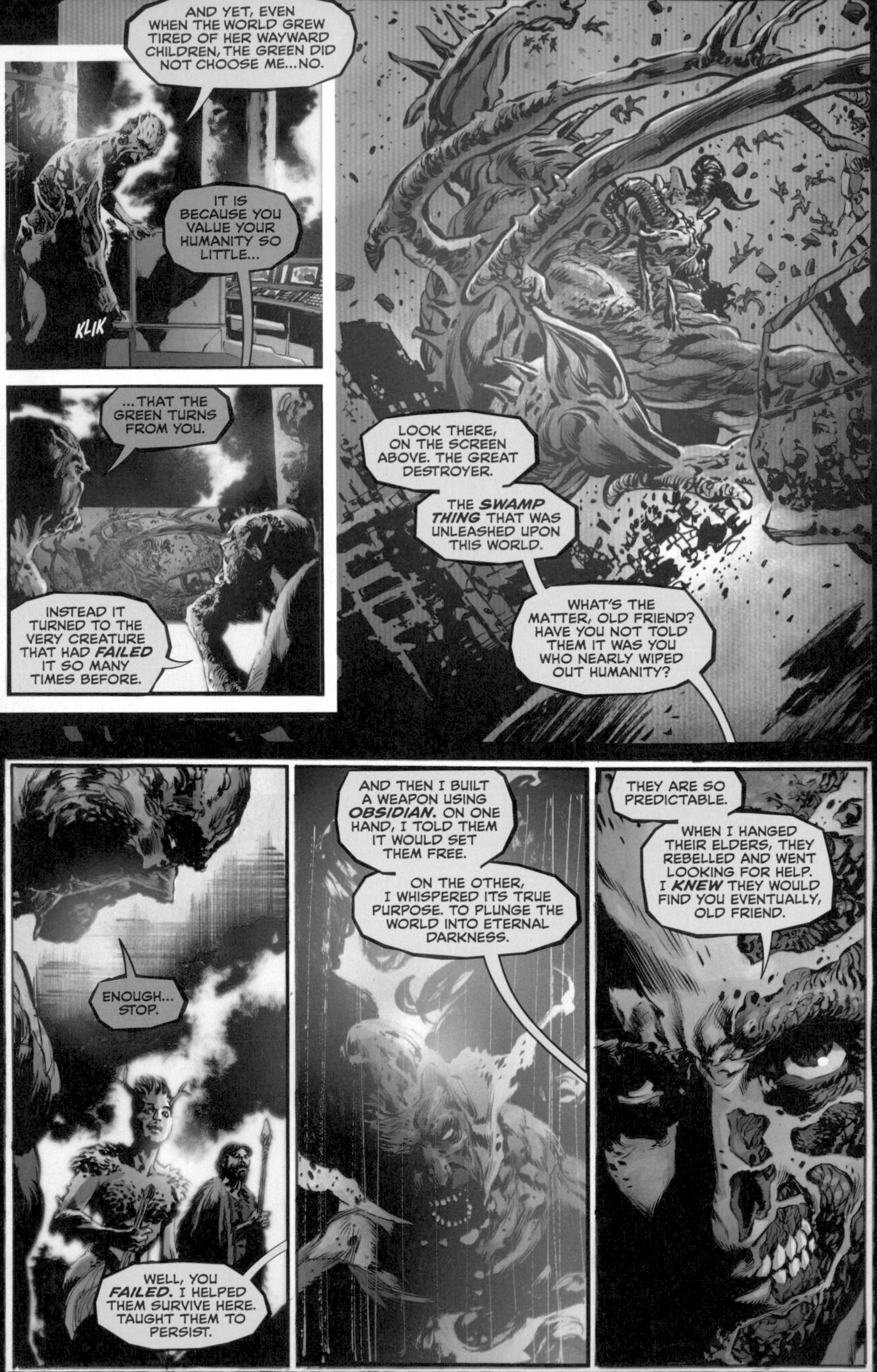
AND YET, EVEN WHEN THE WORLD GREW TIRED OF HER WAYWARD CHILDREN, THE GREEN DID NOT CHOOSE ME...NO.
IT IS BECAUSE YOU VALUE YOUR HUMANITY SO LITTLE...
KLIK
...THAT THE GREEN TURNS FROM YOU.
INSTEAD IT TURNED TO THE VERY CREATURE THAT HAD FAILED IT SO MANY TIMES BEFORE.
LOOK THERE, ON THE SCREEN ABOVE. THE GREAT DESTROYER.
THE SWAMP THING THAT WAS UNLEASHED UPON THIS WORLD.
WHAT'S THE MATTER, OLD FRIEND? HAVE YOU NOT TOLD THEM IT WAS YOU WHO NEARLY WIPED OUT HUMANITY?
ENOUGH... STOP.
WELL, YOU FAILED. I HELPED THEM SURVIVE HERE. TAUGHT THEM TO PERSIST.
AND THEN I BUILT A WEAPON USING OBSIDIAN. ON ONE HAND, I TOLD THEM IT WOULD SET THEM FREE.
ON THE OTHER, I WHISPERED ITS TRUE PURPOSE. TO PLUNGE THE WORLD INTO ETERNAL DARKNESS.
THEY ARE SO PREDICTABLE.
WHEN I HANGED THEIR ELDERS, THEY REBELLED AND WENT LOOKING FOR HELP. I KNEW THEY WOULD FIND YOU EVENTUALLY, OLD FRIEND.

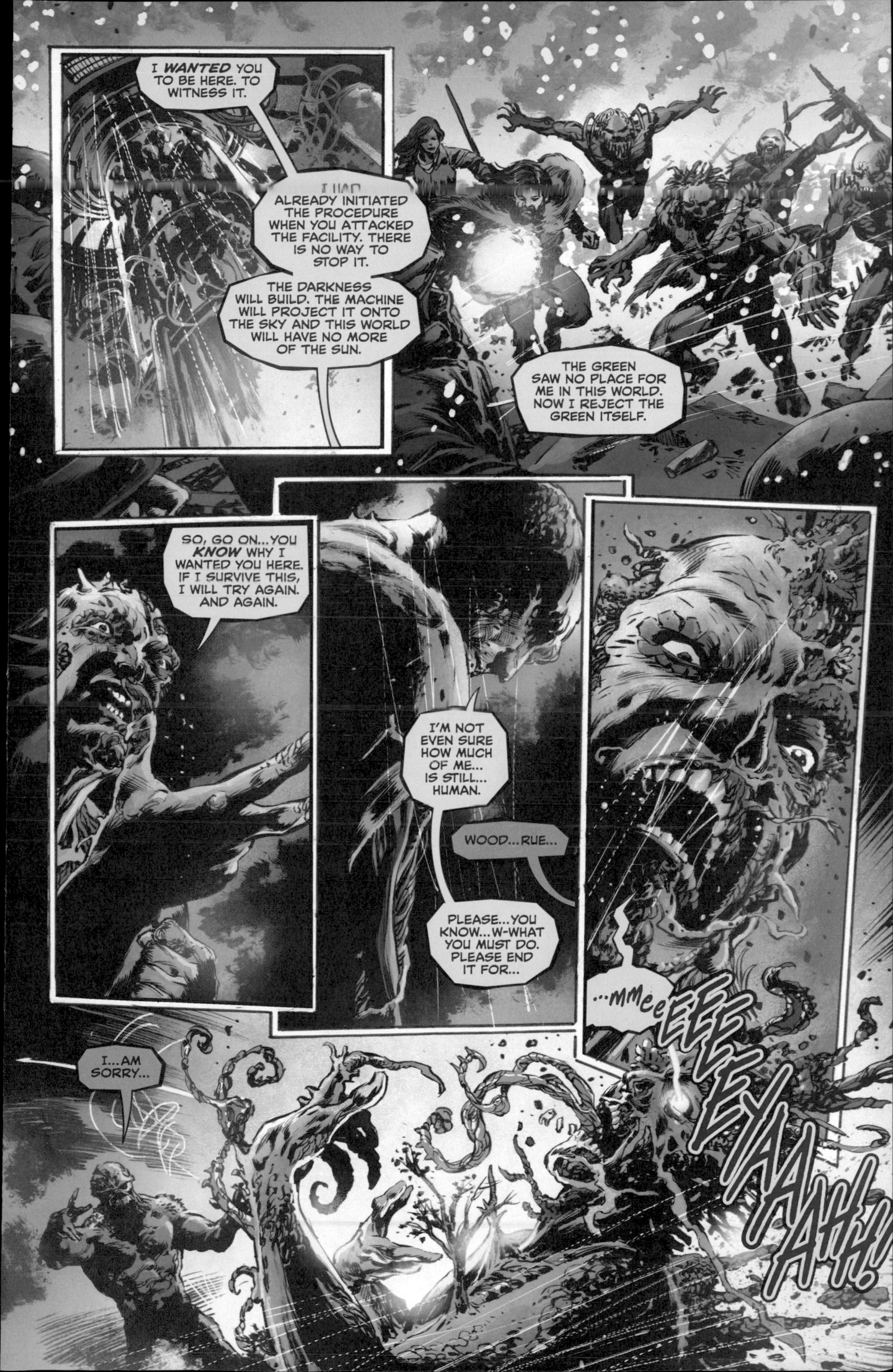
I WANTED YOU TO BE HERE. TO WITNESS IT.
I HAD ALREADY INITIATED THE PROCEDURE WHEN YOU ATTACKED THE FACILITY. THERE IS NO WAY TO STOP IT.
THE DARKNESS WILL BUILD. THE MACHINE WILL PROJECT IT ONTO THE SKY AND THIS WORLD WILL HAVE NO MORE OF THE SUN.
THE GREEN SAW NO PLACE FOR ME IN THIS WORLD. NOW I REJECT THE GREEN ITSELF.
SO, GO ON...YOU KNOW WHY I WANTED YOU HERE. IF I SURVIVE THIS, I WILL TRY AGAIN. AND AGAIN.
I'M NOT EVEN SURE HOW MUCH OF ME... IS STILL... HUMAN.
WOOD...RUE...
PLEASE...YOU KNOW...W-WHAT YOU MUST DO. PLEASE END IT FOR...
...MMeeEEEEYAAAHH!
I...AM SORRY...

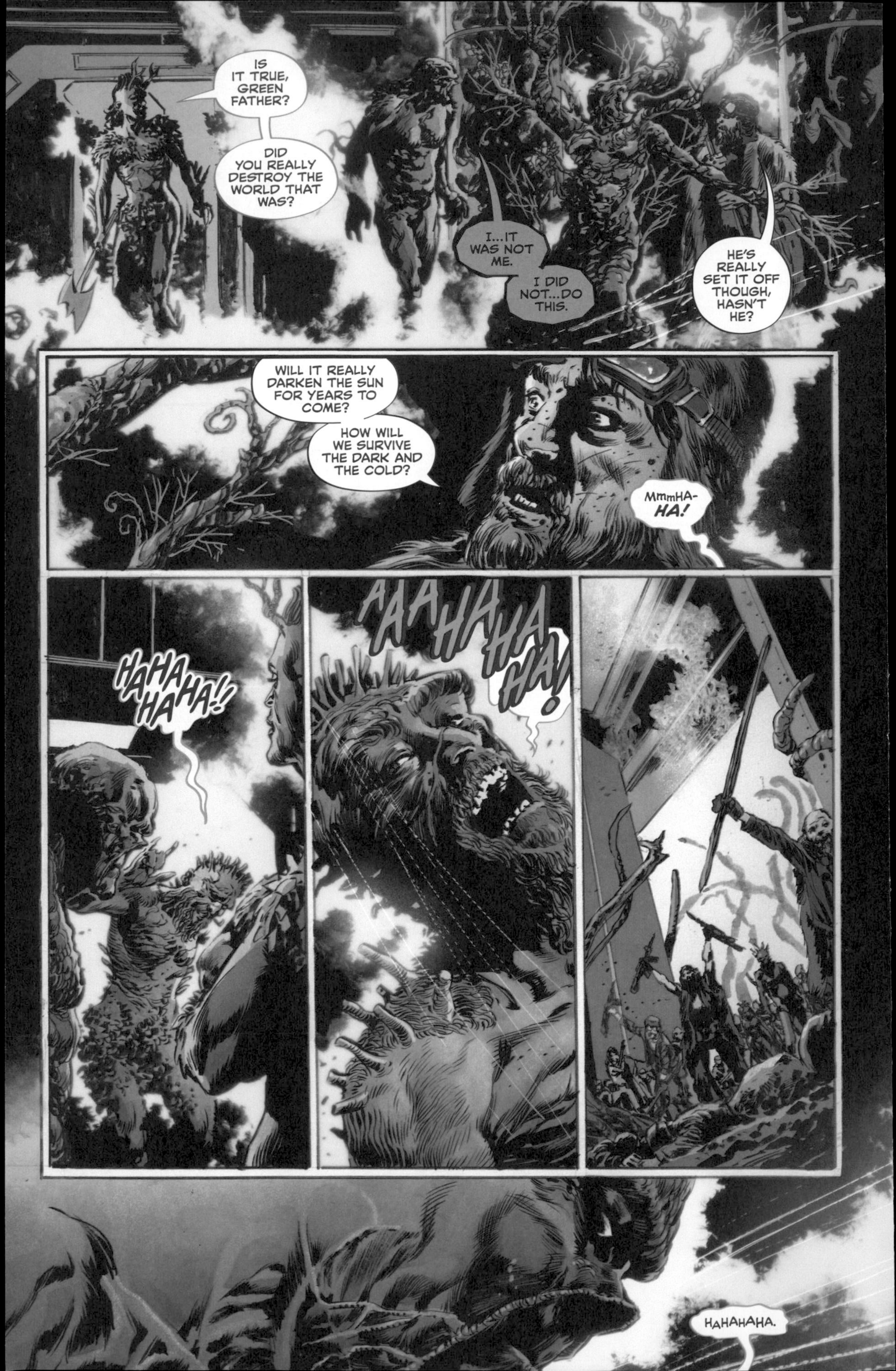
IS IT TRUE, GREEN FATHER?
DID YOU REALLY DESTROY THE WORLD THAT WAS?
I...IT WAS NOT ME.
I DID NOT...DO THIS.
HE'S REALLY SET IT OFF THOUGH, HASN'T HE?
WILL IT REALLY DARKEN THE SUN FOR YEARS TO COME?
HOW WILL WE SURVIVE THE DARK AND THE COLD?
MmmHA-HA!
HAHAHAHA!!
AAAHAHAHAHA!
HAHAHAHA.

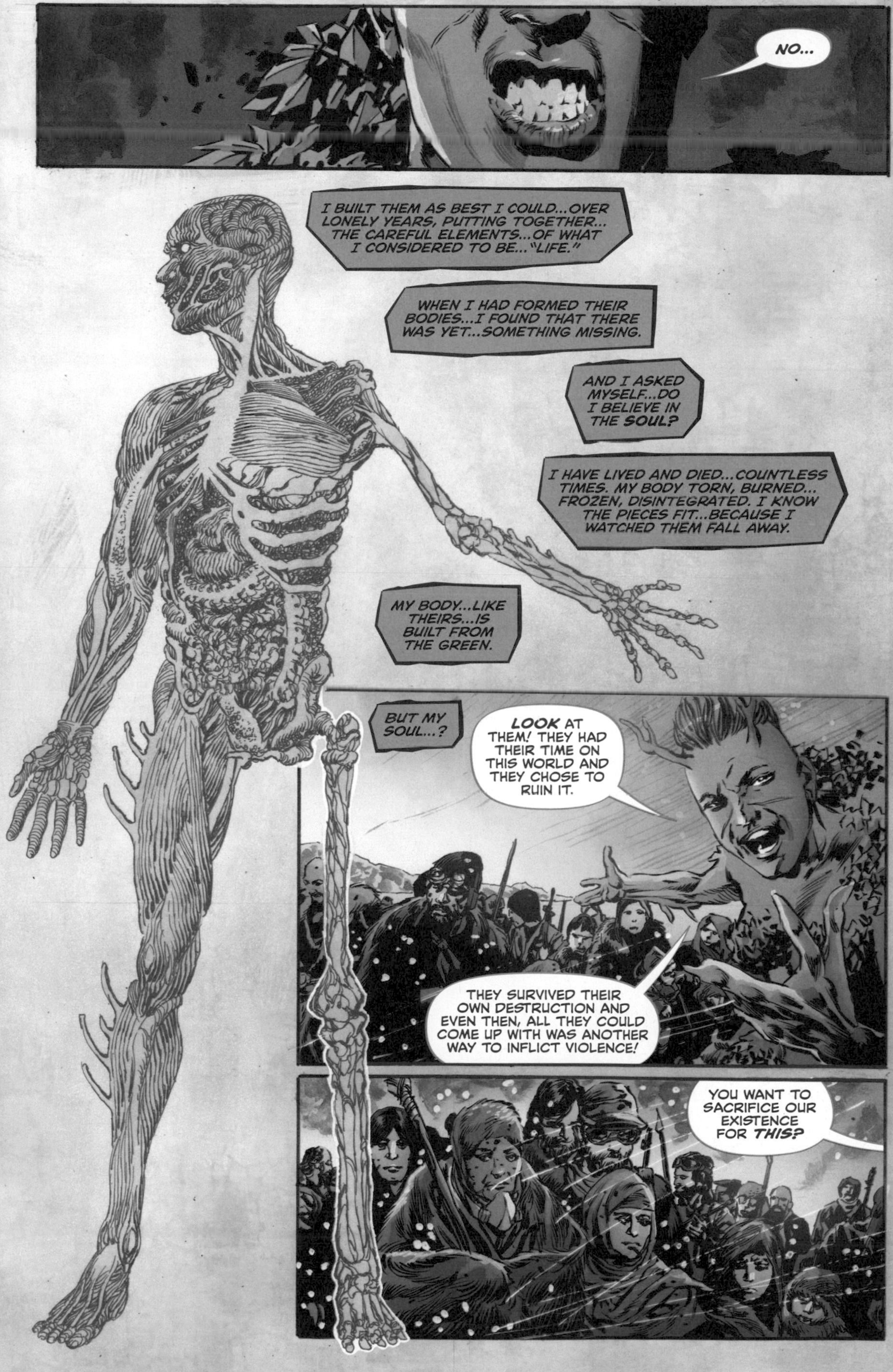
NO...
I BUILT THEM AS BEST I COULD...OVER LONELY YEARS, PUTTING TOGETHER... THE CAREFUL ELEMENTS...OF WHAT I CONSIDERED TO BE..."LIFE."
WHEN I HAD FORMED THEIR BODIES...I FOUND THAT THERE WAS YET...SOMETHING MISSING.
AND I ASKED MYSELF...DO I BELIEVE IN THE SOUL?
I HAVE LIVED AND DIED...COUNTLESS TIMES. MY BODY TORN, BURNED... FROZEN, DISINTEGRATED. I KNOW THE PIECES FIT...BECAUSE I WATCHED THEM FALL AWAY.
MY BODY...LIKE THEIRS...IS BUILT FROM THE GREEN.
BUT MY SOUL...?
LOOK AT THEM! THEY HAD THEIR TIME ON THIS WORLD AND THEY CHOSE TO RUIN IT.
THEY SURVIVED THEIR OWN DESTRUCTION AND EVEN THEN, ALL THEY COULD COME UP WITH WAS ANOTHER WAY TO INFLICT VIOLENCE!
YOU WANT TO SACRIFICE OUR EXISTENCE FOR THIS?

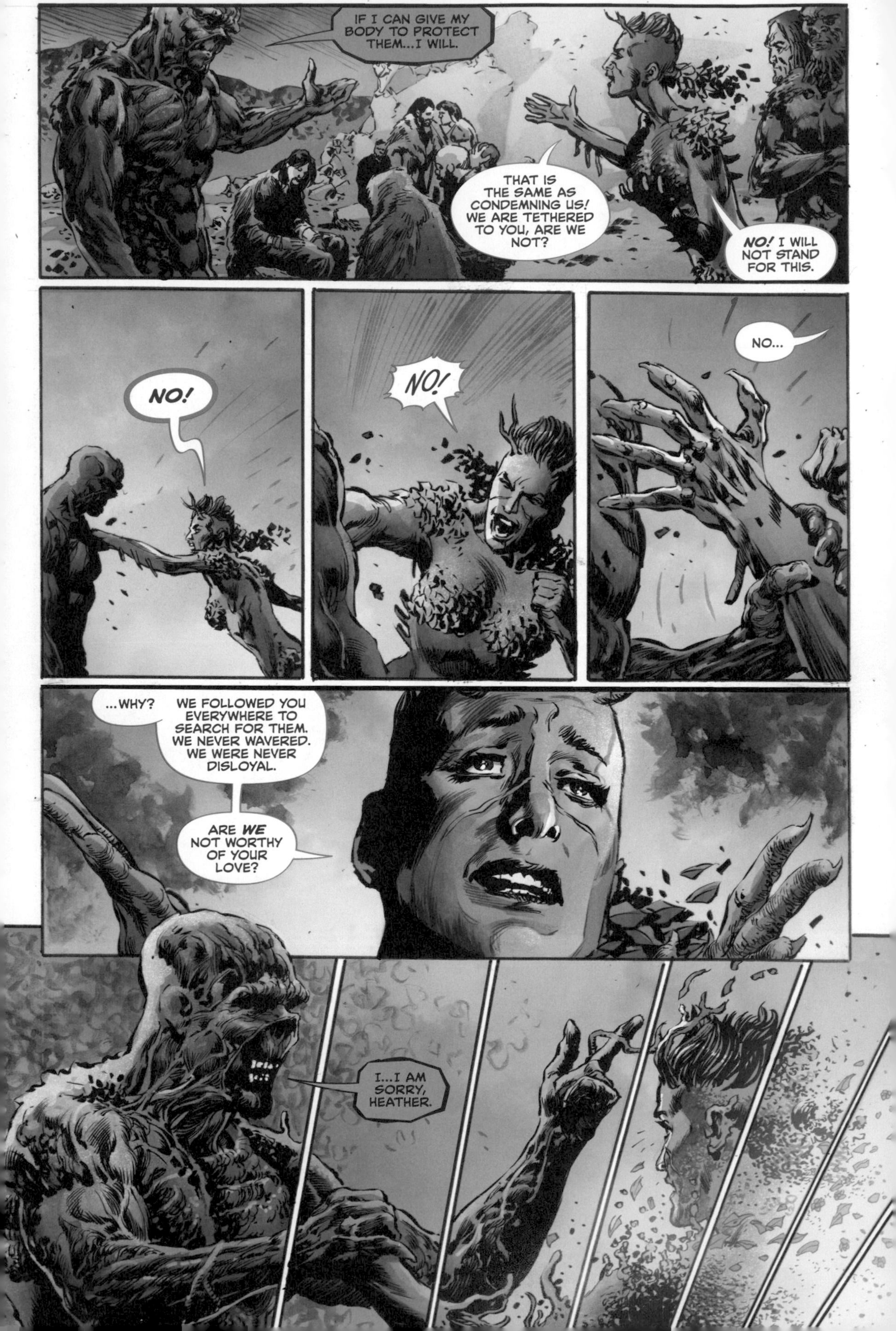
IF I CAN GIVE MY BODY TO PROTECT THEM...I WILL.
THAT IS THE SAME AS CONDEMNING US! WE ARE TETHERED TO YOU, ARE WE NOT?
NO! I WILL NOT STAND FOR THIS.
NO!
NO!
NO...
...WHY?
WE FOLLOWED YOU EVERYWHERE TO SEARCH FOR THEM. WE NEVER WAVERED. WE WERE NEVER DISLOYAL.
ARE WE NOT WORTHY OF YOUR LOVE?
I...I AM SORRY, HEATHER.

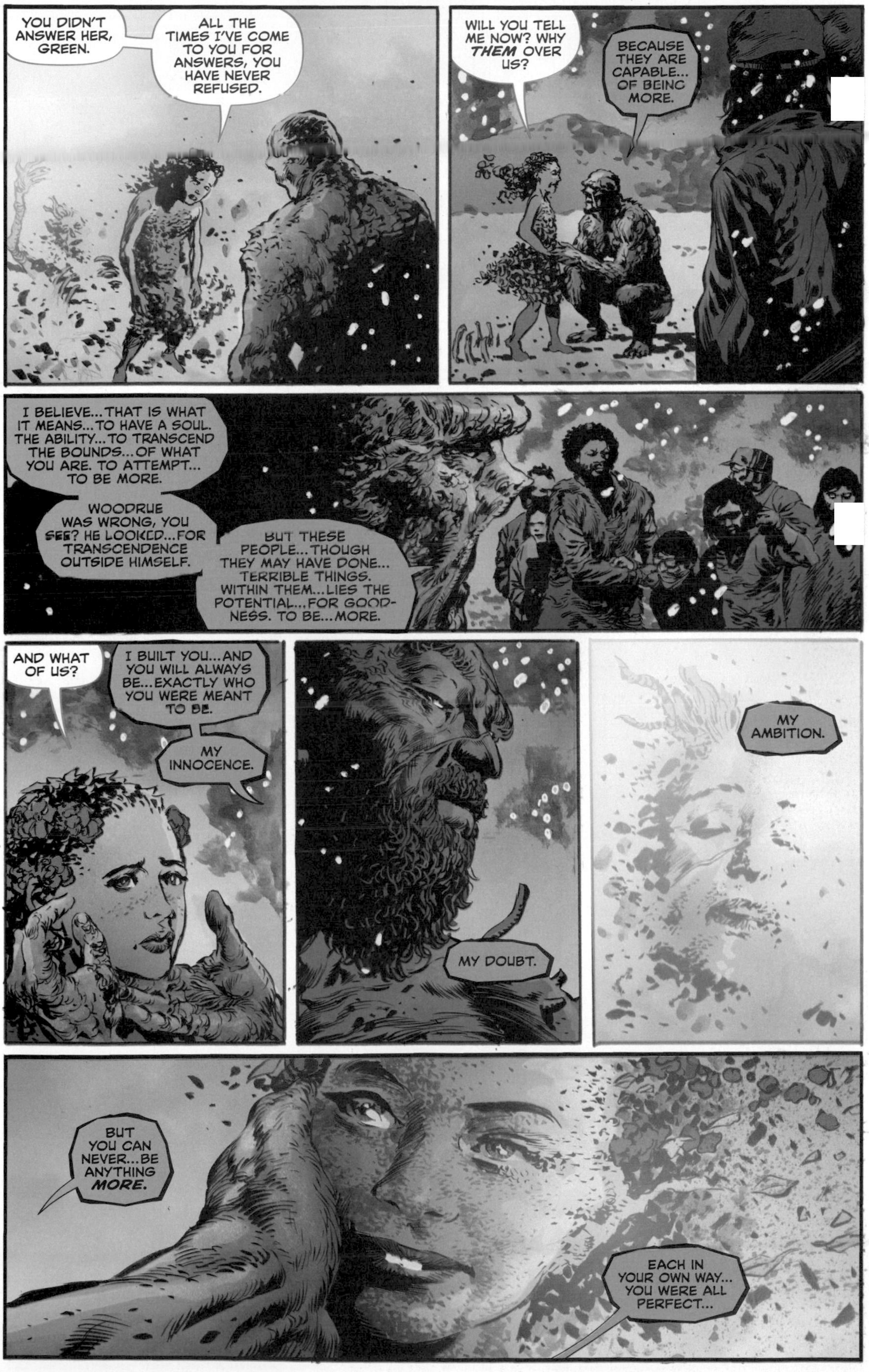
YOU DIDN'T ANSWER HER, GREEN.
ALL THE TIMES I'VE COME TO YOU FOR ANSWERS, YOU HAVE NEVER REFUSED.
WILL YOU TELL ME NOW? WHY *THEM* OVER US?
BECAUSE THEY ARE CAPABLE... OF BEING MORE.
I BELIEVE...THAT IS WHAT IT MEANS...TO HAVE A SOUL. THE ABILITY...TO TRANSCEND THE BOUNDS...OF WHAT YOU ARE. TO ATTEMPT... TO BE MORE.
WOODRUE WAS WRONG, YOU SEE? HE LOOKED...FOR TRANSCENDENCE OUTSIDE HIMSELF.
BUT THESE PEOPLE...THOUGH THEY MAY HAVE DONE... TERRIBLE THINGS. WITHIN THEM...LIES THE POTENTIAL...FOR GOODNESS. TO BE...MORE.
AND WHAT OF US?
I BUILT YOU...AND YOU WILL ALWAYS BE...EXACTLY WHO YOU WERE MEANT TO BE.
MY INNOCENCE.
MY DOUBT.
MY AMBITION.
BUT YOU CAN NEVER...BE ANYTHING *MORE*.
EACH IN YOUR OWN WAY... YOU WERE ALL PERFECT...

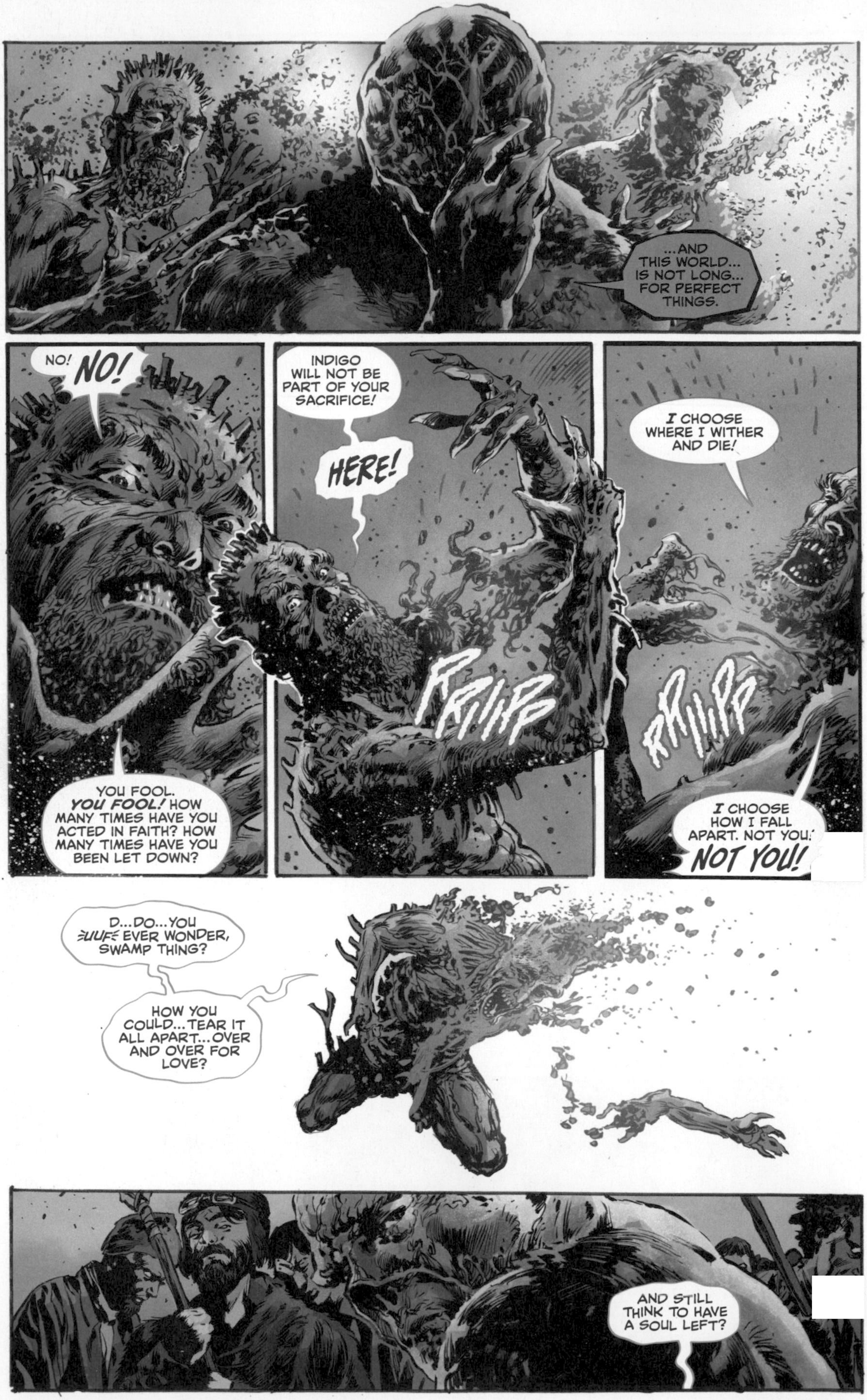
...AND THIS WORLD... IS NOT LONG... FOR PERFECT THINGS.
NO! NO!
YOU FOOL. YOU FOOL! HOW MANY TIMES HAVE YOU ACTED IN FAITH? HOW MANY TIMES HAVE YOU BEEN LET DOWN?
INDIGO WILL NOT BE PART OF YOUR SACRIFICE!
HERE!
RRIPP
I CHOOSE WHERE I WITHER AND DIE!
RRIPP
I CHOOSE HOW I FALL APART. NOT YOU! NOT YOU!
D...DO...YOU HUFF EVER WONDER, SWAMP THING?
HOW YOU COULD...TEAR IT ALL APART...OVER AND OVER FOR LOVE?
AND STILL THINK TO HAVE A SOUL LEFT?

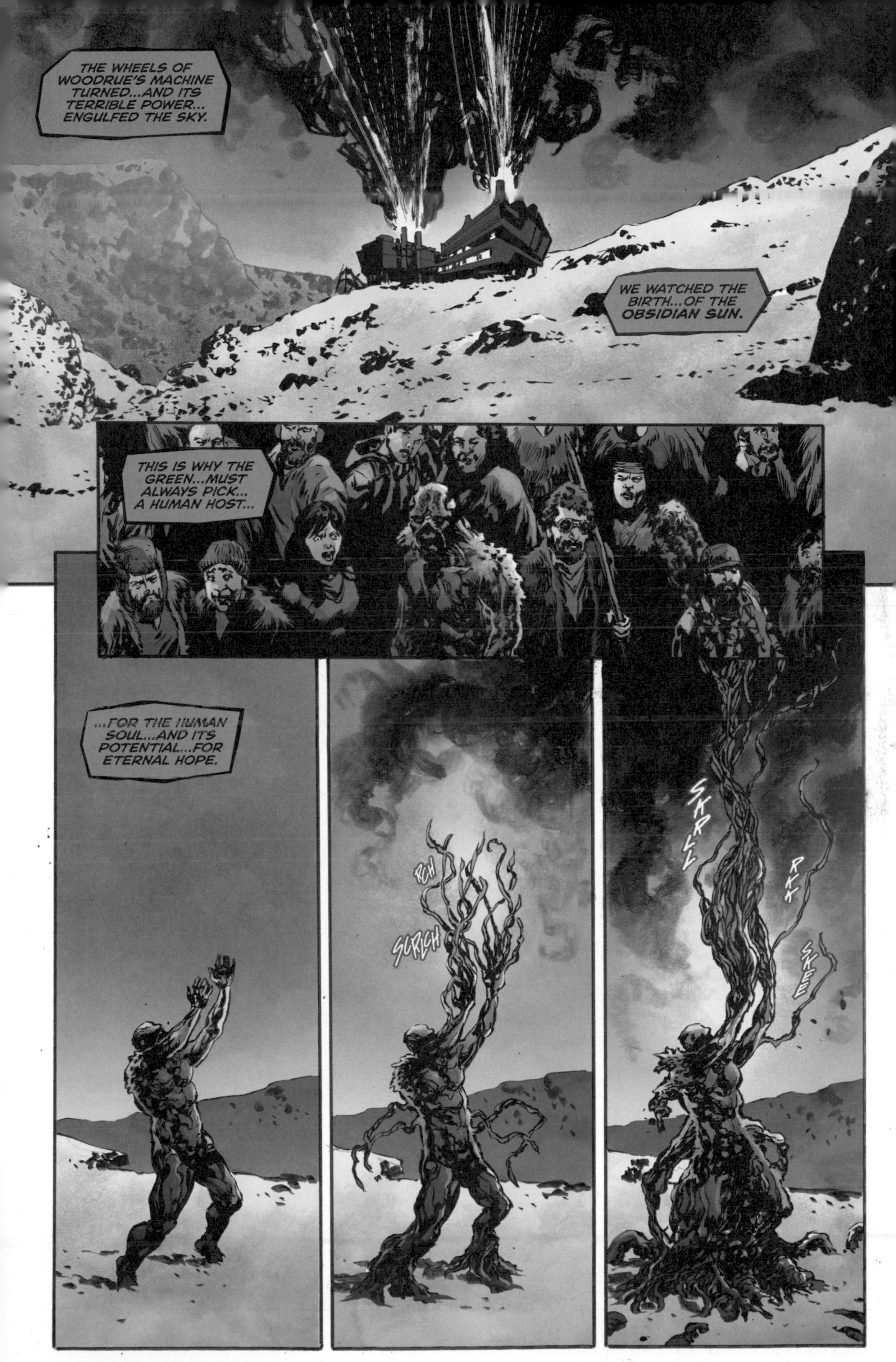
THE WHEELS OF WOODRUE'S MACHINE TURNED...AND ITS TERRIBLE POWER... ENGULFED THE SKY.
WE WATCHED THE BIRTH...OF THE OBSIDIAN SUN.
THIS IS WHY THE GREEN...MUST ALWAYS PICK... A HUMAN HOST...
...FOR THE HUMAN SOUL...AND ITS POTENTIAL...FOR ETERNAL HOPE.
RCH
SCRCH
SKRLL
RKK
SKEE

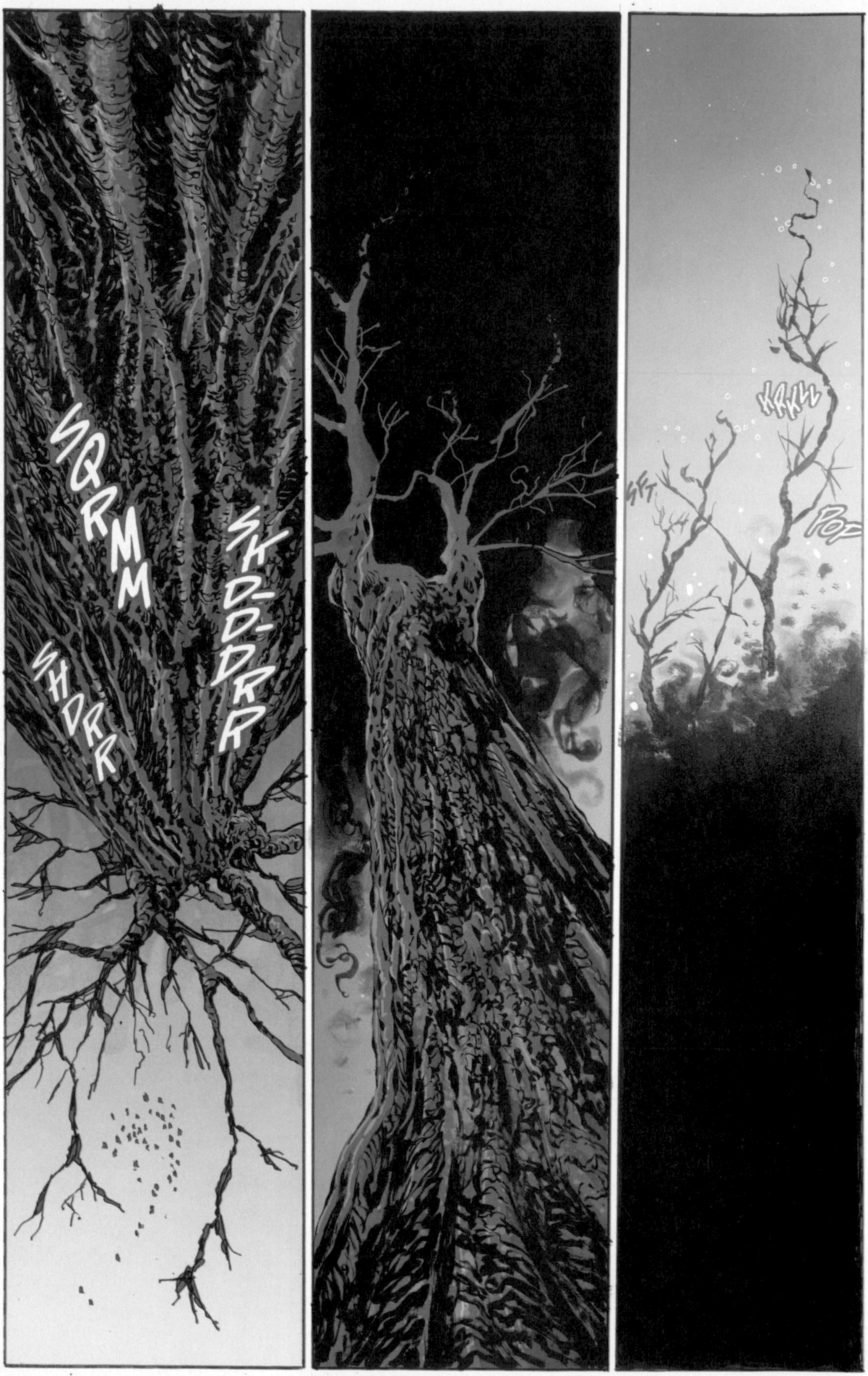
SQRMM
SKD-D-DRR
SHDRR
SFT
POP

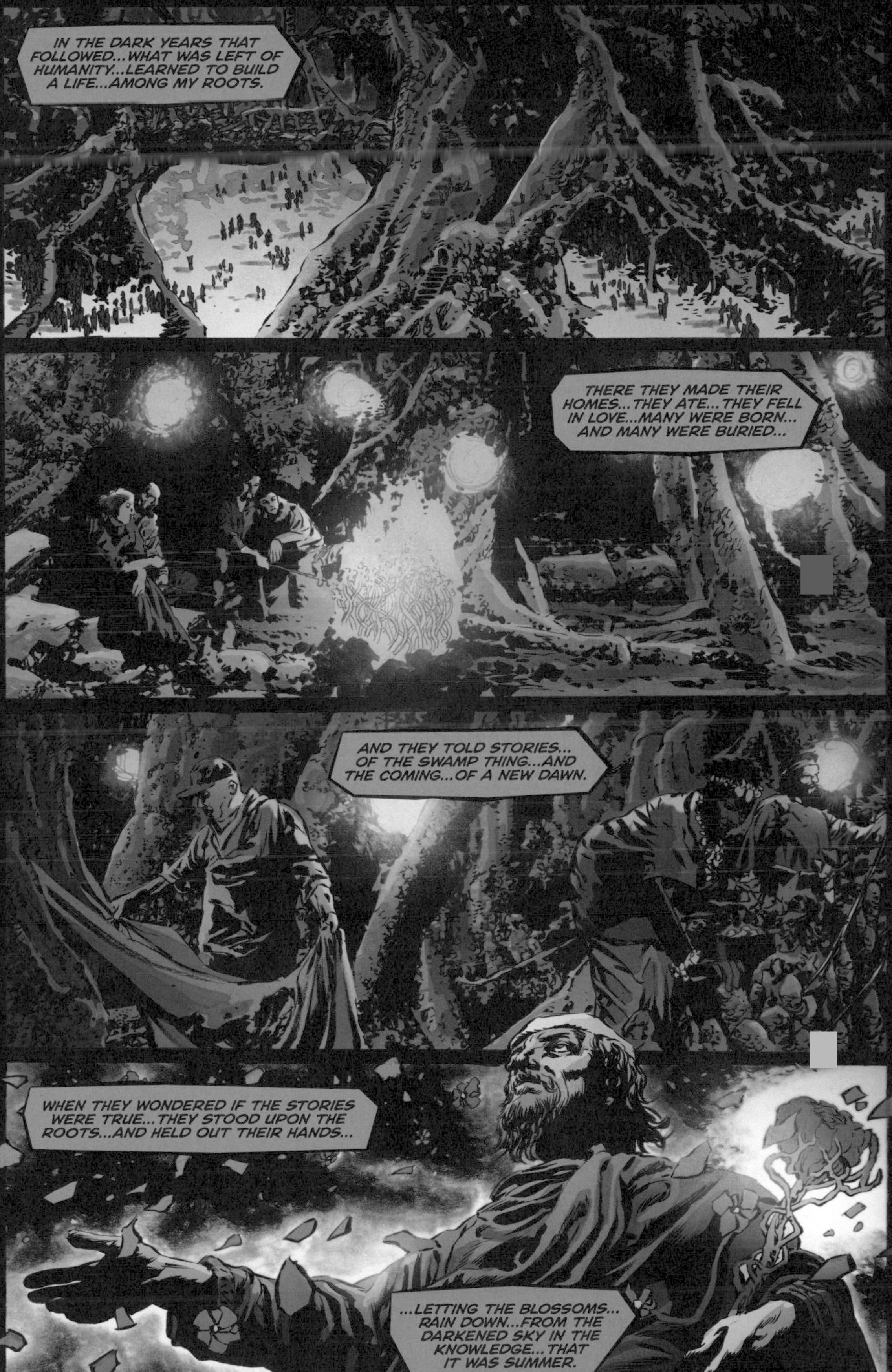
IN THE DARK YEARS THAT FOLLOWED...WHAT WAS LEFT OF HUMANITY...LEARNED TO BUILD A LIFE...AMONG MY ROOTS.
THERE THEY MADE THEIR HOMES...THEY ATE...THEY FELL IN LOVE...MANY WERE BORN... AND MANY WERE BURIED...
AND THEY TOLD STORIES... OF THE SWAMP THING...AND THE COMING...OF A NEW DAWN.
WHEN THEY WONDERED IF THE STORIES WERE TRUE...THEY STOOD UPON THE ROOTS...AND HELD OUT THEIR HANDS...
...LETTING THE BLOSSOMS... RAIN DOWN...FROM THE DARKENED SKY IN THE KNOWLEDGE...THAT IT WAS SUMMER.

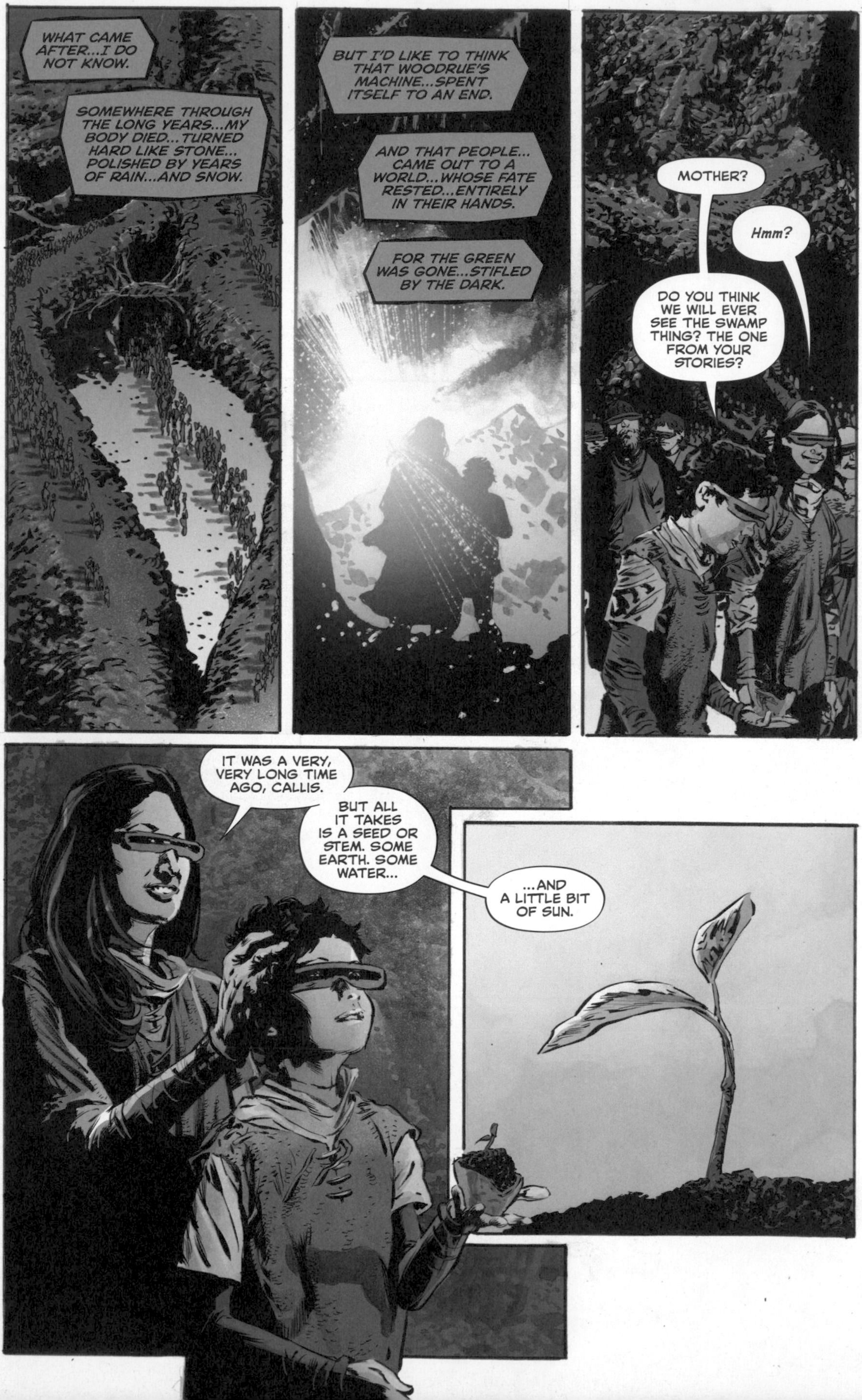
WHAT CAME AFTER...I DO NOT KNOW.
SOMEWHERE THROUGH THE LONG YEARS...MY BODY DIED...TURNED HARD LIKE STONE... POLISHED BY YEARS OF RAIN...AND SNOW.
BUT I'D LIKE TO THINK THAT WOODRUE'S MACHINE...SPENT ITSELF TO AN END.
AND THAT PEOPLE... CAME OUT TO A WORLD...WHOSE FATE RESTED...ENTIRELY IN THEIR HANDS.
FOR THE GREEN WAS GONE...STIFLED BY THE DARK.
MOTHER?
Hmm?
DO YOU THINK WE WILL EVER SEE THE SWAMP THING? THE ONE FROM YOUR STORIES?
IT WAS A VERY, VERY LONG TIME AGO, CALLIS.
BUT ALL IT TAKES IS A SEED OR STEM. SOME EARTH. SOME WATER...
...AND A LITTLE BIT OF SUN.

FUTURE STATE: BLACK ADAM CHAPTER 1

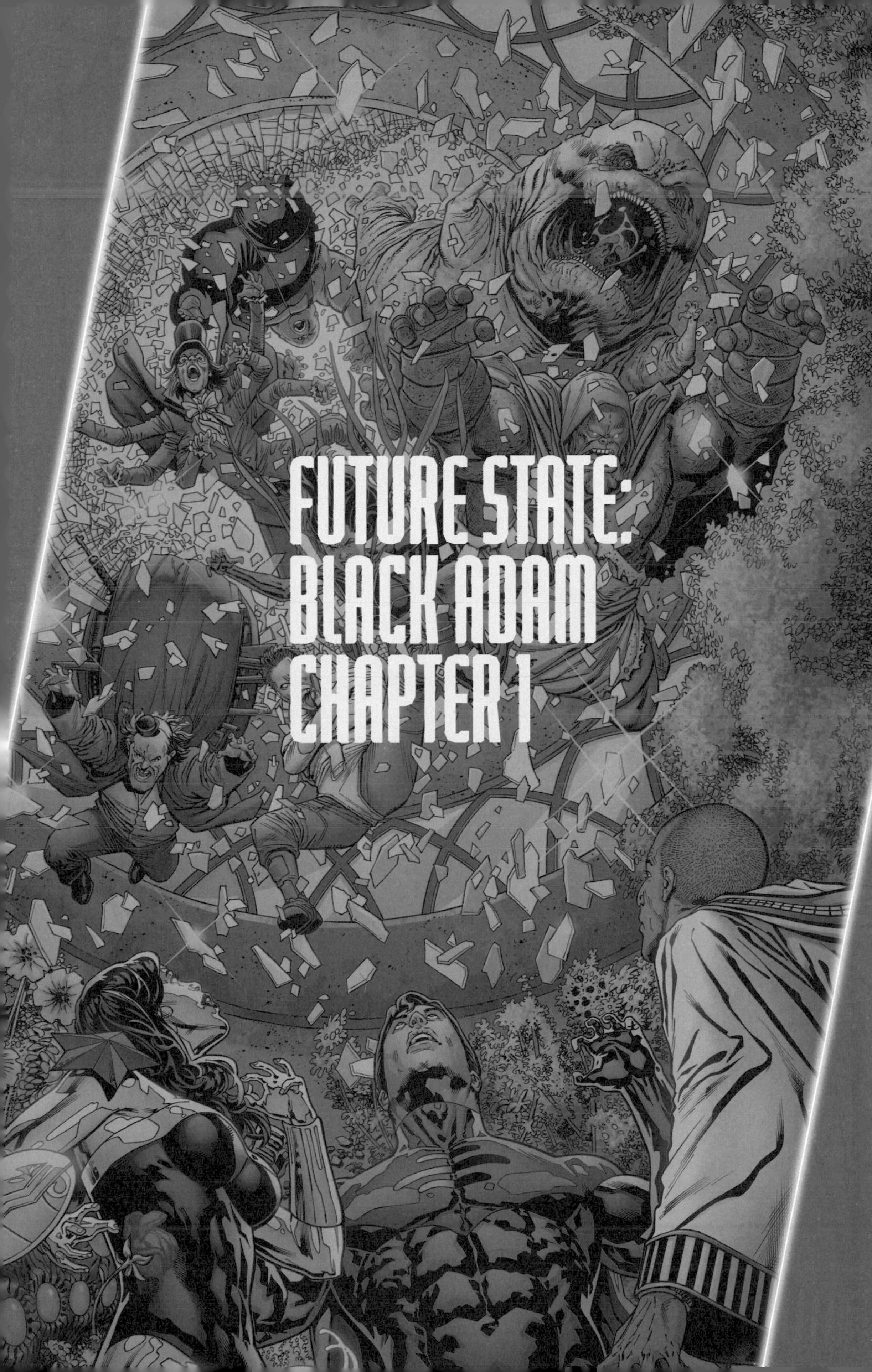

FUTURE STATE

YEARS FROM NOW, AFTER MAGIC SLIPPED SILENTLY AWAY FROM THE COSMOS...

AND THE BEINGS OF THE UNIVERSE LEANED ON THE POWERS OF TECHNOLOGY...

THE MULTI-DIMENSIONS WERE AT PEACE...*ORDERED*... UNTIL NOW...

TRANSDIMENSIONAL SHIFT-VARIABLE QUANTUM FIELD...GALACTIC ALERT... UNKNOWN OBJECT MOVING THROUGH OAN GRAVEYARD, SECTOR *ZERO*.

DC COMICS™ PROUDLY PRESENTS:

FUTURE STATE: **BLACK ADAM**

CHAPTER ONE:

THE BEGINNING OF THE END

JEREMY ADAMS *writer* FERNANDO PASARIN *penciller* OCLAIR ALBERT *inker* JEROMY COX *colors*

WES ABBOTT *letters* MARQUIS DRAPER *assistant editor* MIKE COTTON *editor* ALEX R. CARR *group editor*

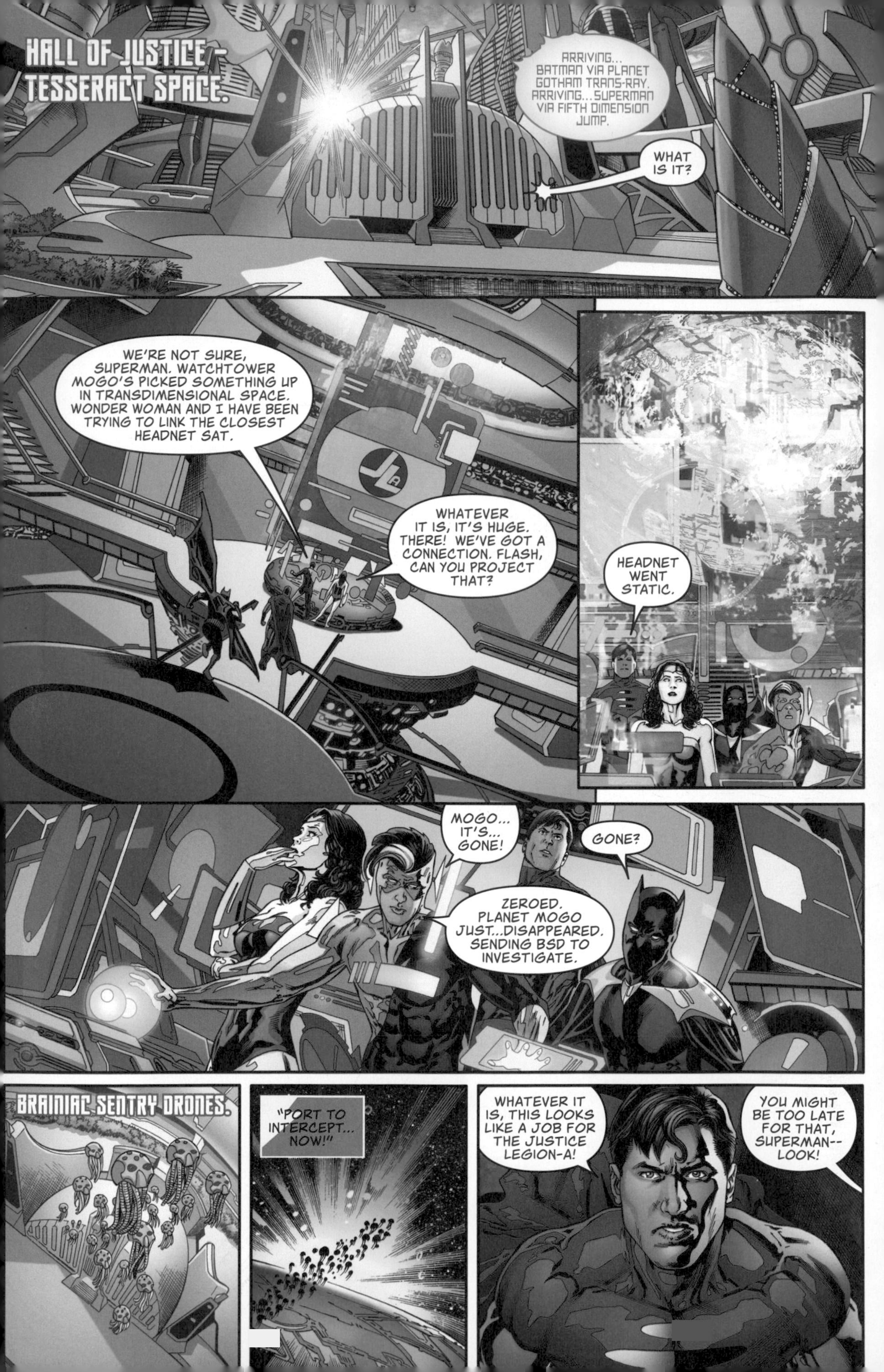
HALL OF JUSTICE - TESSERACT SPACE.
ARRIVING... BATMAN VIA PLANET GOTHAM TRANS-RAY. ARRIVING... SUPERMAN VIA FIFTH DIMENSION JUMP.
WHAT IS IT?
WE'RE NOT SURE, SUPERMAN. WATCHTOWER MOGO'S PICKED SOMETHING UP IN TRANSDIMENSIONAL SPACE. WONDER WOMAN AND I HAVE BEEN TRYING TO LINK THE CLOSEST HEADNET SAT.
WHATEVER IT IS, IT'S HUGE. THERE! WE'VE GOT A CONNECTION. FLASH, CAN YOU PROJECT THAT?
HEADNET WENT STATIC.
MOGO... IT'S... GONE!
GONE?
ZEROED. PLANET MOGO JUST...DISAPPEARED. SENDING BSD TO INVESTIGATE.
BRAINIAC SENTRY DRONES.
"PORT TO INTERCEPT... NOW!"
WHATEVER IT IS, THIS LOOKS LIKE A JOB FOR THE JUSTICE LEGION-A!
YOU MIGHT BE TOO LATE FOR THAT, SUPERMAN-- LOOK!

LEAVING HIS FORTRESS OF SOLITUDE AT THE CENTER OF A SUN, THE ORPHAN FROM KRYPTON, NOW CALLED **SUPERMAN PRIME**, REAPPEARS IN THE UNIVERSE'S DARKEST HOUR.

FOR A TIME, THIS CHAMPION OF THE OMNIVERSE WAS ABSENT FROM HUMANITY.

BUT, AFTER DEFEATING SOLARIS THE LIVING SUN, THE MAN NAMED KAL-EL RECOMMITS TO FIGHT FOR TRUTH AND JUSTICE...

HIS LIFE'S MISSION. ONE THAT BRINGS HIM PEACE AND JOY...

BUT...AS HE PEERS INTO THE INKY BLACKNESS OF SPACE WITH HIS ULTRASCOPIC VISION...THE SMILE DISAPPEARS, AND HE STOPS...

SUPERMAN EXPERIENCES A FEELING HE HASN'T FELT SINCE...

HE STRUGGLES TO REMEMBER THE NAME... DOOM SOMETHING? IT HAS BEEN TENS OF THOUSANDS OF YEARS SINCE HIS FIRST DEATH...

HE REMEMBERS THE NAME-- DOOMSDAY. AND AT THAT MOMENT, HE KNOWS FEAR ONCE AGAIN BECAUSE...

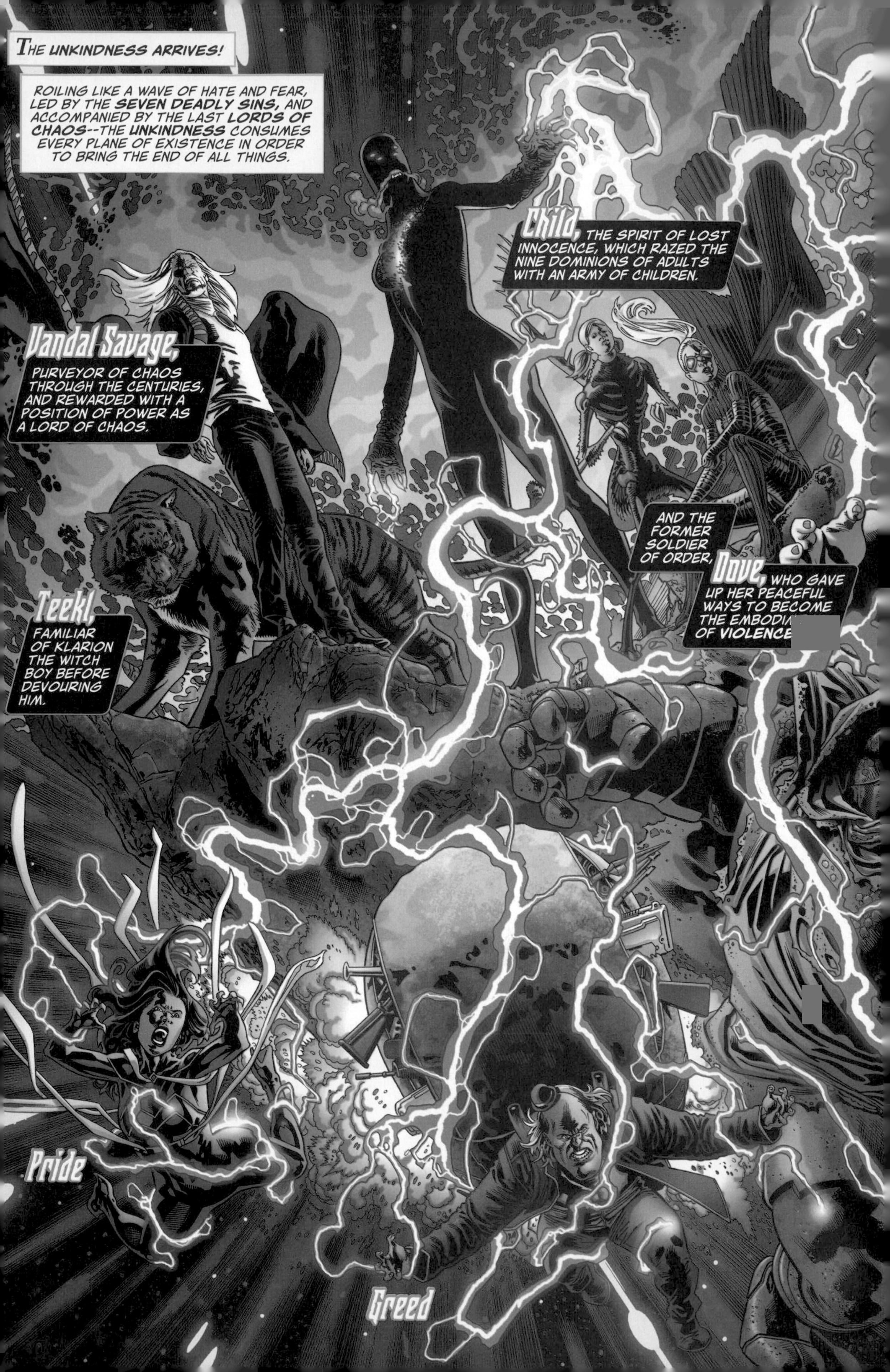
THE UNKINDNESS ARRIVES!
ROILING LIKE A WAVE OF HATE AND FEAR, LED BY THE SEVEN DEADLY SINS, AND ACCOMPANIED BY THE LAST LORDS OF CHAOS--THE UNKINDNESS CONSUMES EVERY PLANE OF EXISTENCE IN ORDER TO BRING THE END OF ALL THINGS.
Child, THE SPIRIT OF LOST INNOCENCE, WHICH RAZED THE NINE DOMINIONS OF ADULTS WITH AN ARMY OF CHILDREN.
Vandal Savage, PURVEYOR OF CHAOS THROUGH THE CENTURIES, AND REWARDED WITH A POSITION OF POWER AS A LORD OF CHAOS.
AND THE FORMER SOLDIER OF ORDER,
Dove, WHO GAVE UP HER PEACEFUL WAYS TO BECOME THE EMBODI OF VIOLENCE
Teekl, FAMILIAR OF KLARION THE WITCH BOY BEFORE DEVOURING HIM.
Pride
Greed

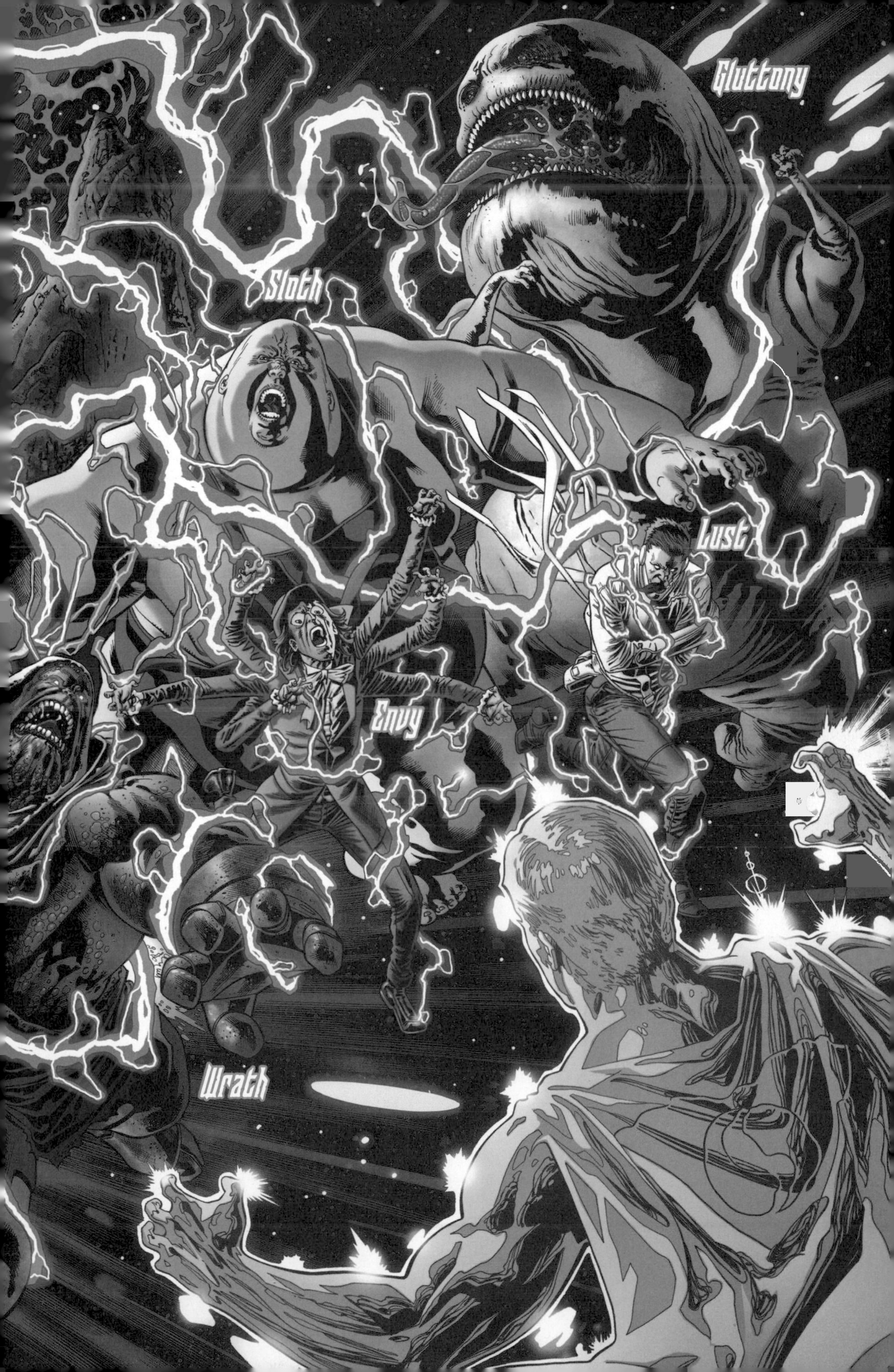
Gluttony
Sloth
Lust
Envy
Wrath

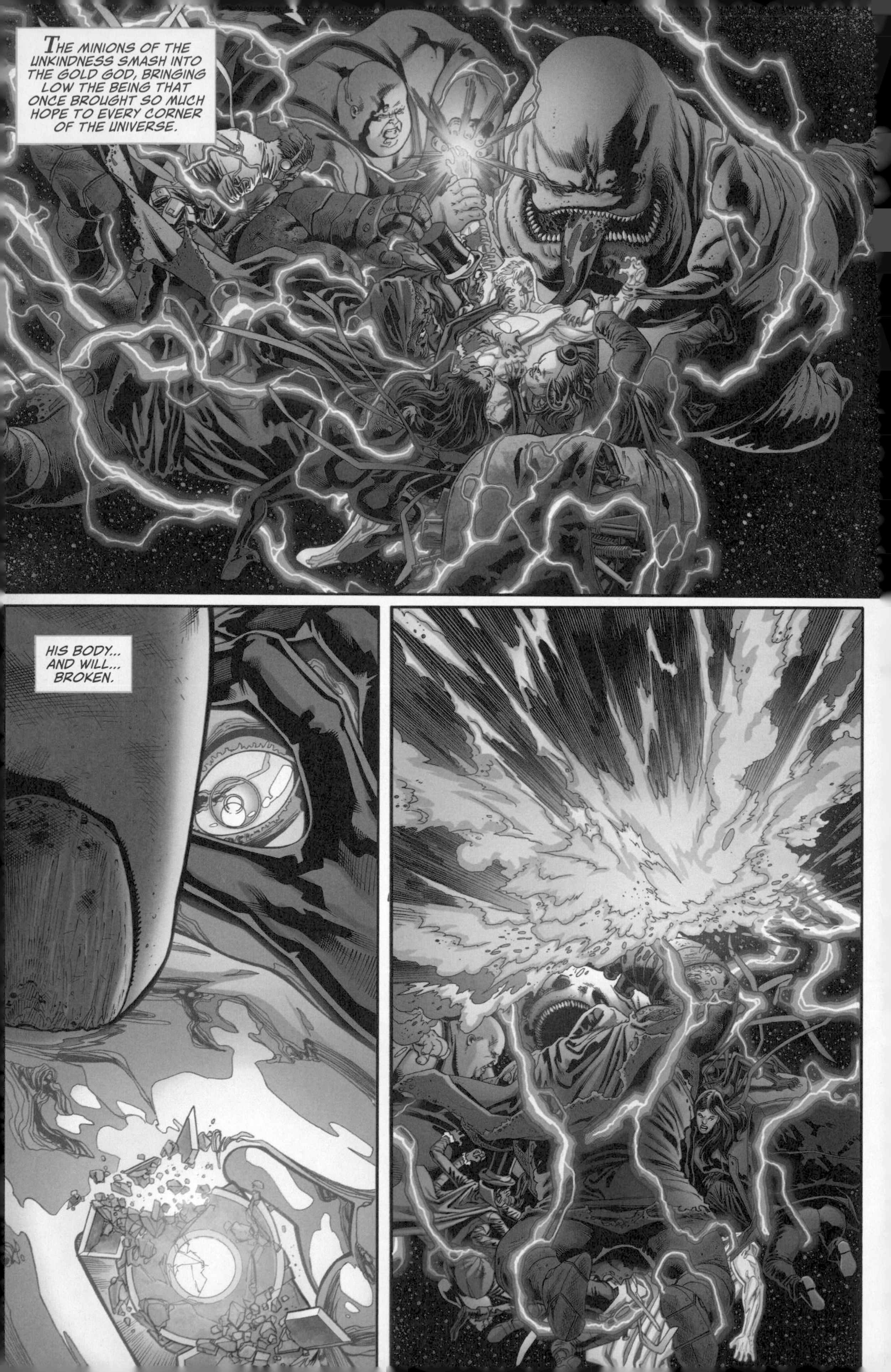
THE MINIONS OF THE UNKINDNESS SMASH INTO THE GOLD GOD, BRINGING LOW THE BEING THAT ONCE BROUGHT SO MUCH HOPE TO EVERY CORNER OF THE UNIVERSE.
HIS BODY... AND WILL... BROKEN.

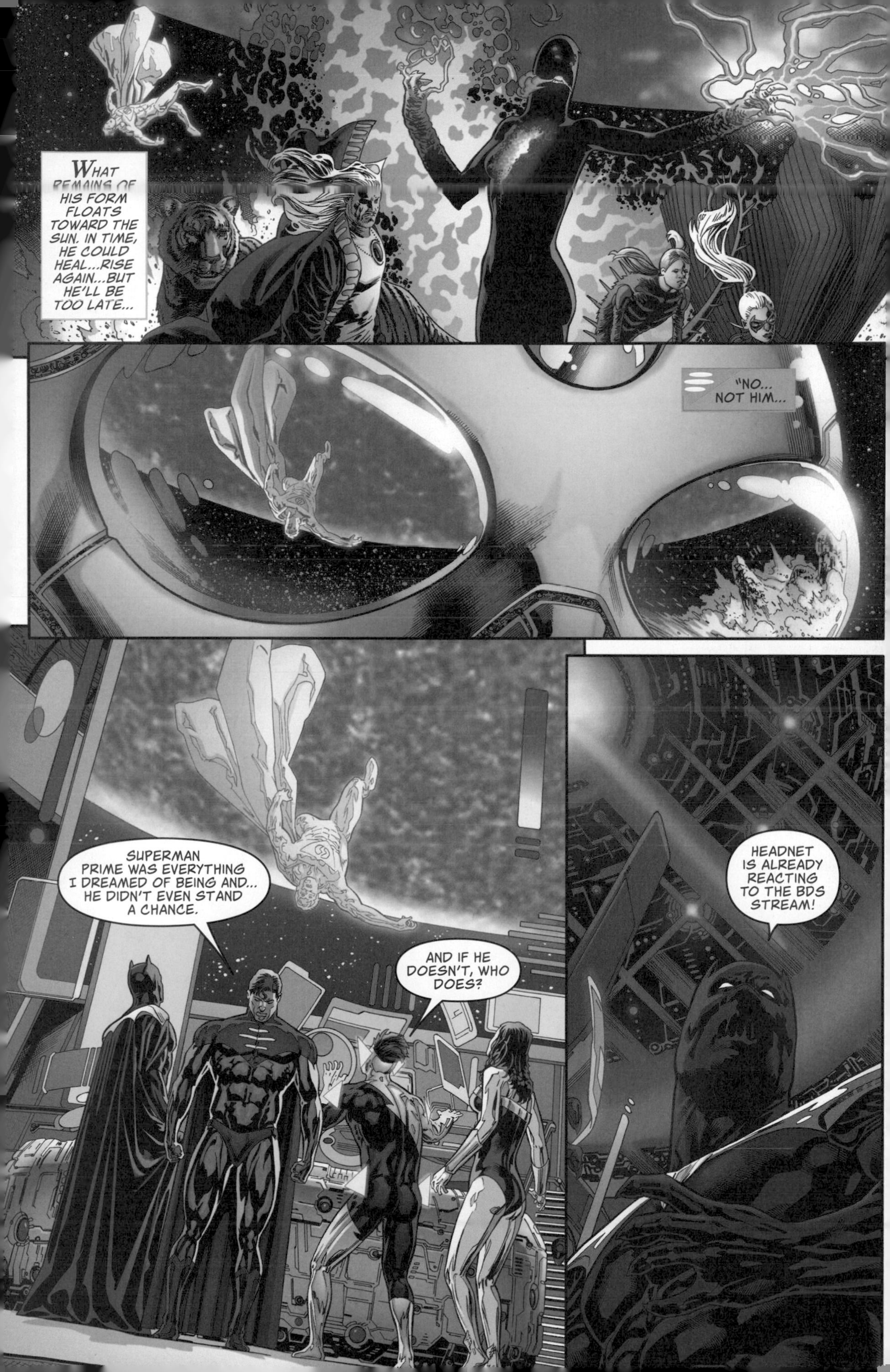
WHAT REMAINS OF HIS FORM FLOATS TOWARD THE SUN. IN TIME, HE COULD HEAL...RISE AGAIN...BUT HE'LL BE TOO LATE...
"NO... NOT HIM...
SUPERMAN PRIME WAS EVERYTHING I DREAMED OF BEING AND... HE DIDN'T EVEN STAND A CHANCE.
AND IF HE DOESN'T, WHO DOES?
HEADNET IS ALREADY REACTING TO THE BDS STREAM!

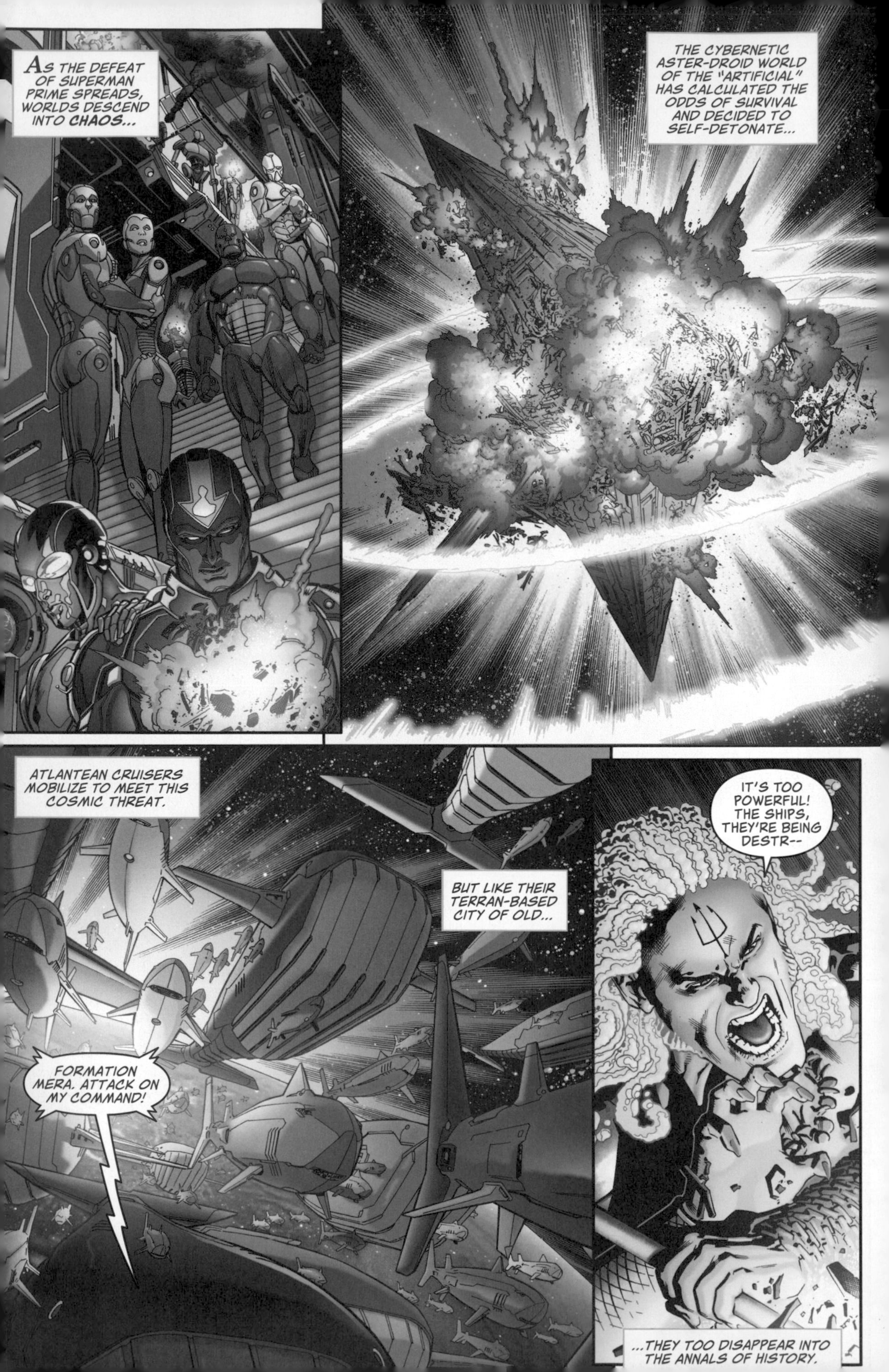
AS THE DEFEAT OF SUPERMAN PRIME SPREADS, WORLDS DESCEND INTO CHAOS...
THE CYBERNETIC ASTER-DROID WORLD OF THE "ARTIFICIAL" HAS CALCULATED THE ODDS OF SURVIVAL AND DECIDED TO SELF-DETONATE...
ATLANTEAN CRUISERS MOBILIZE TO MEET THIS COSMIC THREAT.
FORMATION MERA. ATTACK ON MY COMMAND!
BUT LIKE THEIR TERRAN-BASED CITY OF OLD...
IT'S TOO POWERFUL! THE SHIPS, THEY'RE BEING DESTR--
...THEY TOO DISAPPEAR INTO THE ANNALS OF HISTORY.

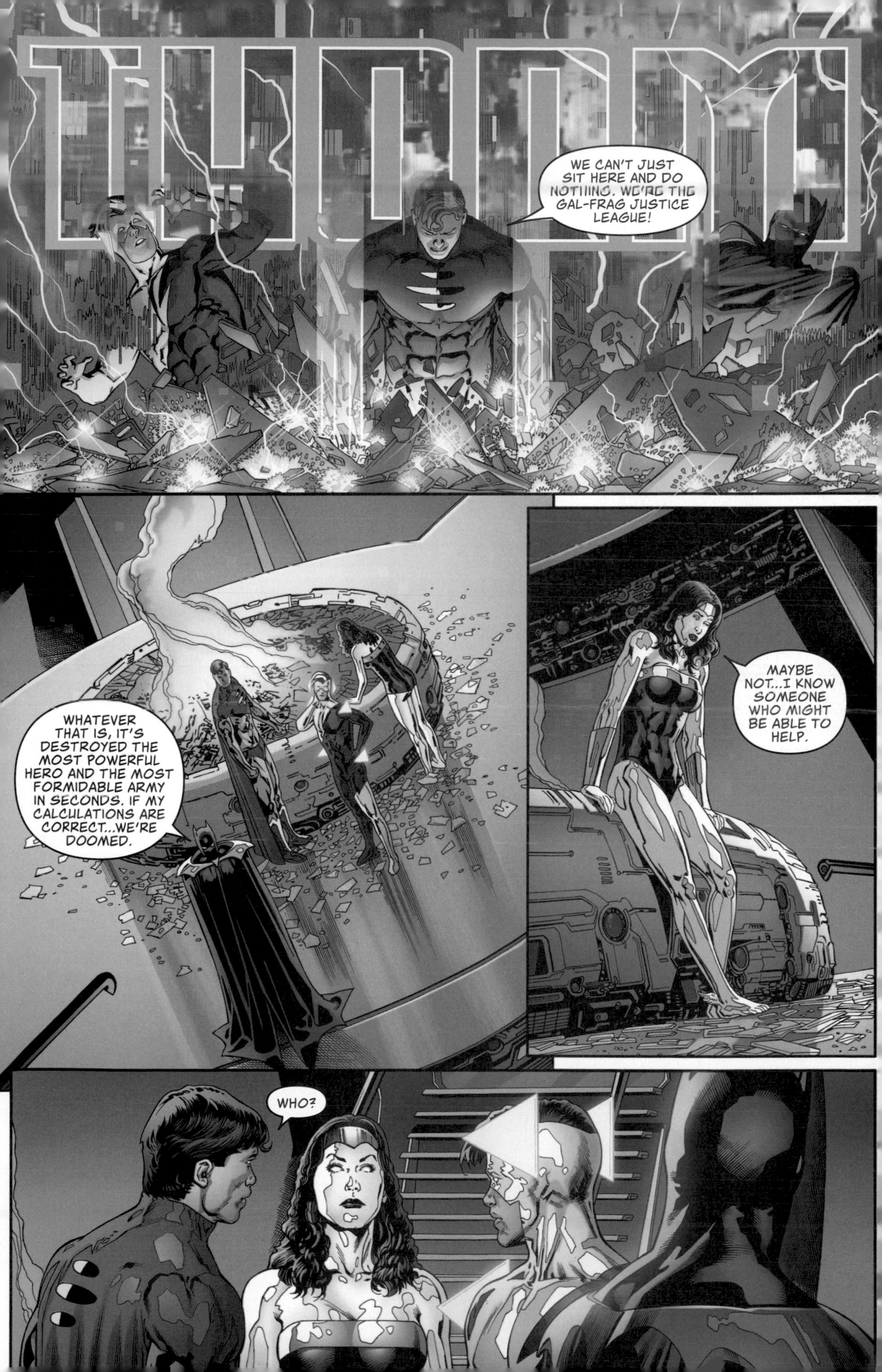
THOOM
WE CAN'T JUST SIT HERE AND DO NOTHING. WE'RE THE GAL-FRAG JUSTICE LEAGUE!
WHATEVER THAT IS, IT'S DESTROYED THE MOST POWERFUL HERO AND THE MOST FORMIDABLE ARMY IN SECONDS. IF MY CALCULATIONS ARE CORRECT...WE'RE DOOMED.
MAYBE NOT...I KNOW SOMEONE WHO MIGHT BE ABLE TO HELP.
WHO?

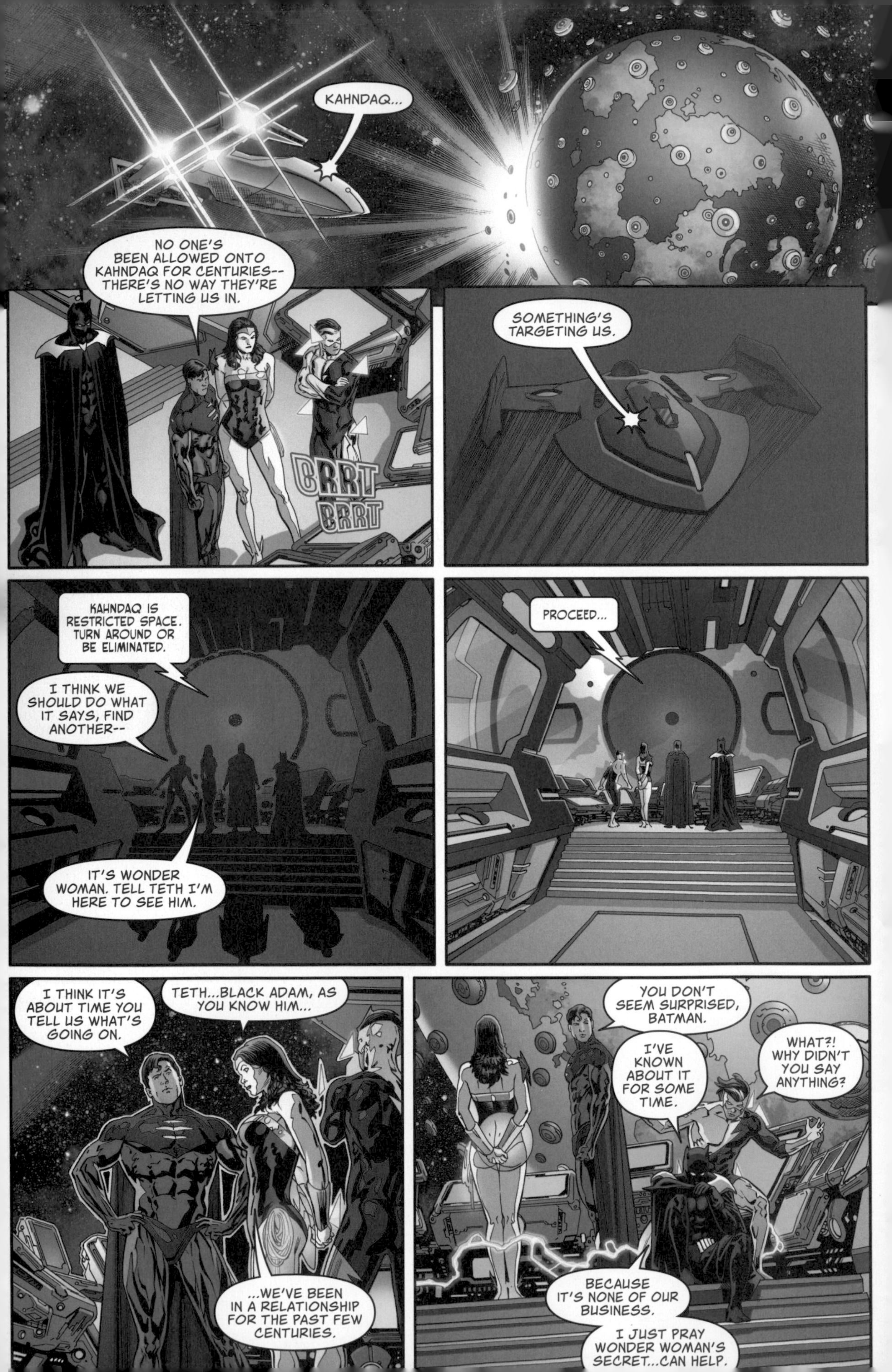
KAHNDAQ...
NO ONE'S BEEN ALLOWED ONTO KAHNDAQ FOR CENTURIES-- THERE'S NO WAY THEY'RE LETTING US IN.
CRRRT
CRRRT
SOMETHING'S TARGETING US.
KAHNDAQ IS RESTRICTED SPACE. TURN AROUND OR BE ELIMINATED.
I THINK WE SHOULD DO WHAT IT SAYS, FIND ANOTHER--
IT'S WONDER WOMAN. TELL TETH I'M HERE TO SEE HIM.
PROCEED...
I THINK IT'S ABOUT TIME YOU TELL US WHAT'S GOING ON.
TETH...BLACK ADAM, AS YOU KNOW HIM...
...WE'VE BEEN IN A RELATIONSHIP FOR THE PAST FEW CENTURIES.
YOU DON'T SEEM SURPRISED, BATMAN.
I'VE KNOWN ABOUT IT FOR SOME TIME.
WHAT?! WHY DIDN'T YOU SAY ANYTHING?
BECAUSE IT'S NONE OF OUR BUSINESS.
I JUST PRAY WONDER WOMAN'S SECRET...CAN HELP.

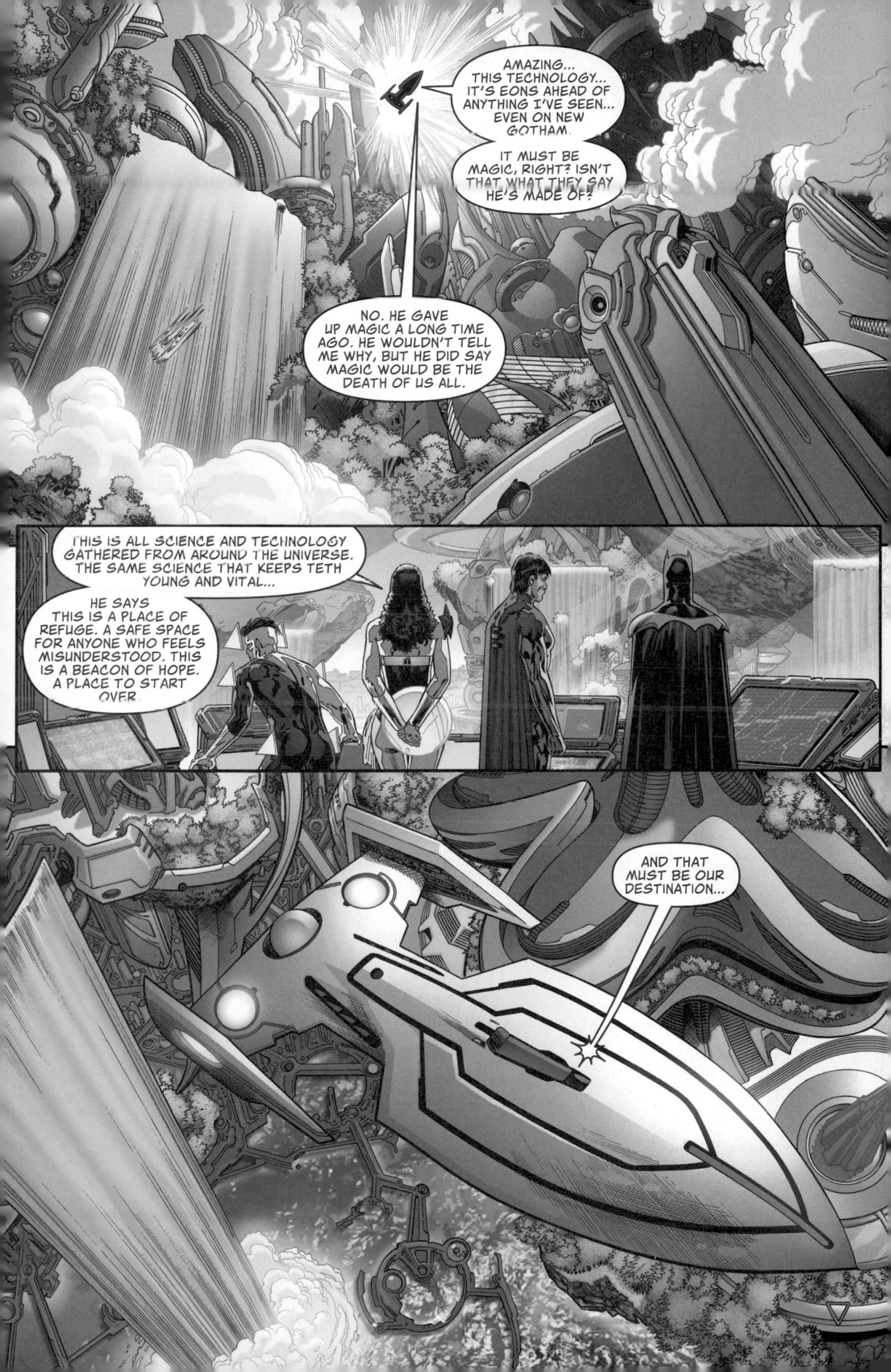
AMAZING... THIS TECHNOLOGY... IT'S EONS AHEAD OF ANYTHING I'VE SEEN... EVEN ON NEW GOTHAM.
IT MUST BE MAGIC, RIGHT? ISN'T THAT WHAT THEY SAY HE'S MADE OF?
NO. HE GAVE UP MAGIC A LONG TIME AGO. HE WOULDN'T TELL ME WHY, BUT HE DID SAY MAGIC WOULD BE THE DEATH OF US ALL.
THIS IS ALL SCIENCE AND TECHNOLOGY GATHERED FROM AROUND THE UNIVERSE. THE SAME SCIENCE THAT KEEPS TETH YOUNG AND VITAL...
HE SAYS THIS IS A PLACE OF REFUGE. A SAFE SPACE FOR ANYONE WHO FEELS MISUNDERSTOOD. THIS IS A BEACON OF HOPE. A PLACE TO START OVER.
AND THAT MUST BE OUR DESTINATION...

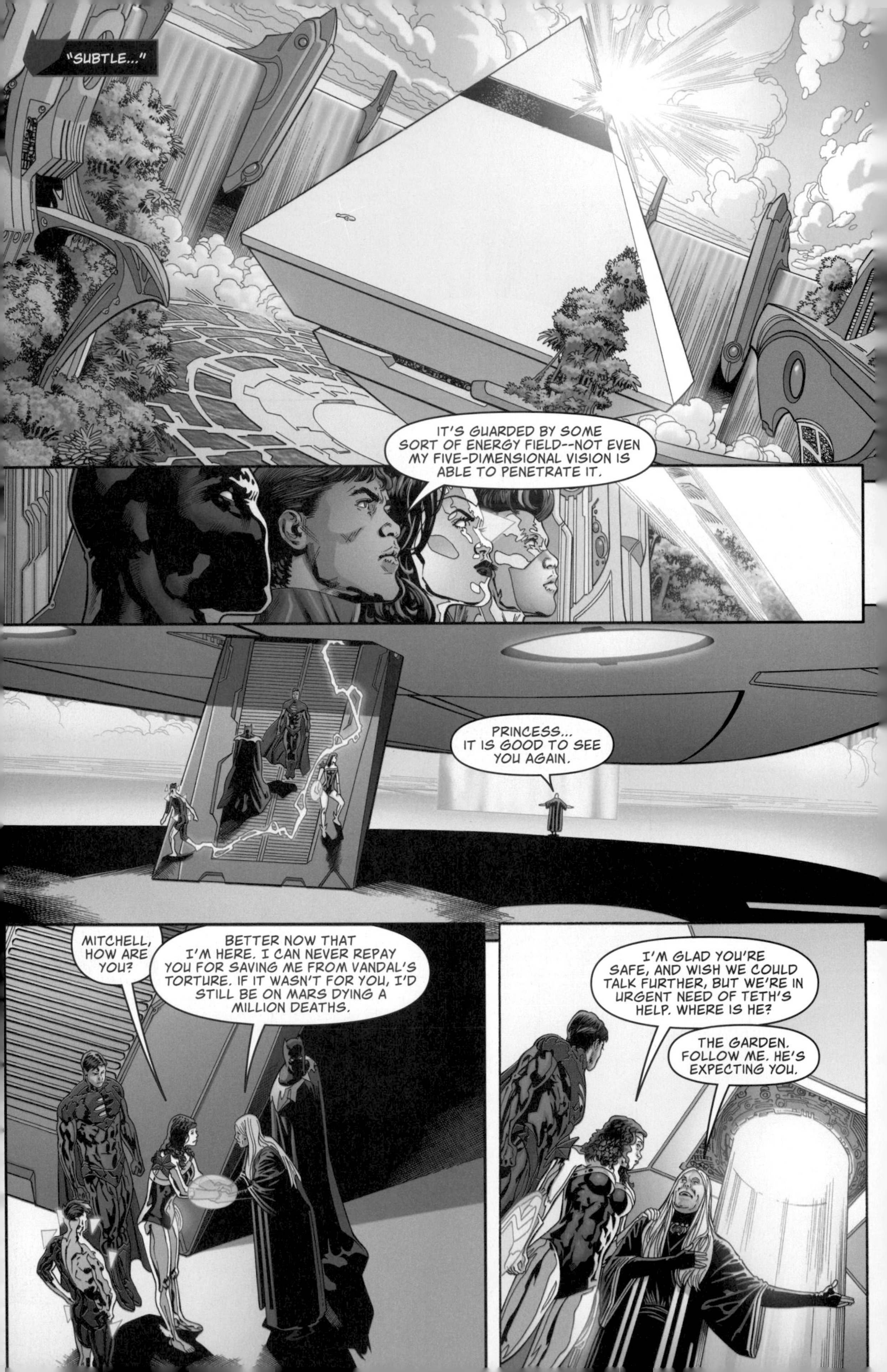
"SUBTLE..."
IT'S GUARDED BY SOME SORT OF ENERGY FIELD--NOT EVEN MY FIVE-DIMENSIONAL VISION IS ABLE TO PENETRATE IT.
PRINCESS... IT IS GOOD TO SEE YOU AGAIN.
MITCHELL, HOW ARE YOU?
BETTER NOW THAT I'M HERE. I CAN NEVER REPAY YOU FOR SAVING ME FROM VANDAL'S TORTURE. IF IT WASN'T FOR YOU, I'D STILL BE ON MARS DYING A MILLION DEATHS.
I'M GLAD YOU'RE SAFE, AND WISH WE COULD TALK FURTHER, BUT WE'RE IN URGENT NEED OF TETH'S HELP. WHERE IS HE?
THE GARDEN. FOLLOW ME. HE'S EXPECTING YOU.

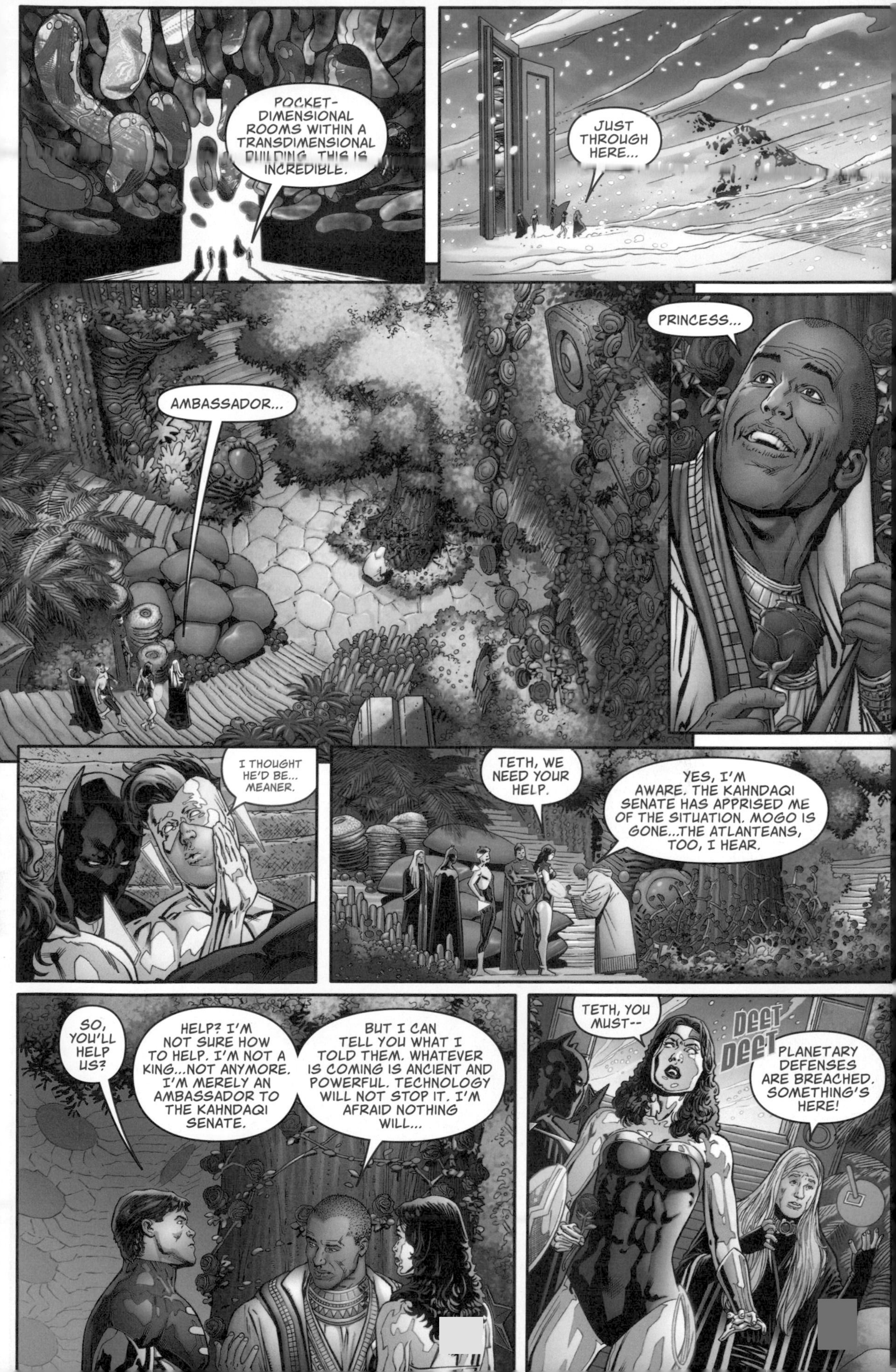
POCKET-DIMENSIONAL ROOMS WITHIN A TRANSDIMENSIONAL BUILDING. THIS IS INCREDIBLE.
JUST THROUGH HERE...
AMBASSADOR...
PRINCESS...
I THOUGHT HE'D BE... MEANER.
TETH, WE NEED YOUR HELP.
YES, I'M AWARE. THE KAHNDAQI SENATE HAS APPRISED ME OF THE SITUATION. MOGO IS GONE...THE ATLANTEANS, TOO, I HEAR.
SO, YOU'LL HELP US?
HELP? I'M NOT SURE HOW TO HELP. I'M NOT A KING...NOT ANYMORE. I'M MERELY AN AMBASSADOR TO THE KAHNDAQI SENATE.
BUT I CAN TELL YOU WHAT I TOLD THEM. WHATEVER IS COMING IS ANCIENT AND POWERFUL. TECHNOLOGY WILL NOT STOP IT. I'M AFRAID NOTHING WILL...
TETH, YOU MUST--
DEET DEET
PLANETARY DEFENSES ARE BREACHED. SOMETHING'S HERE!

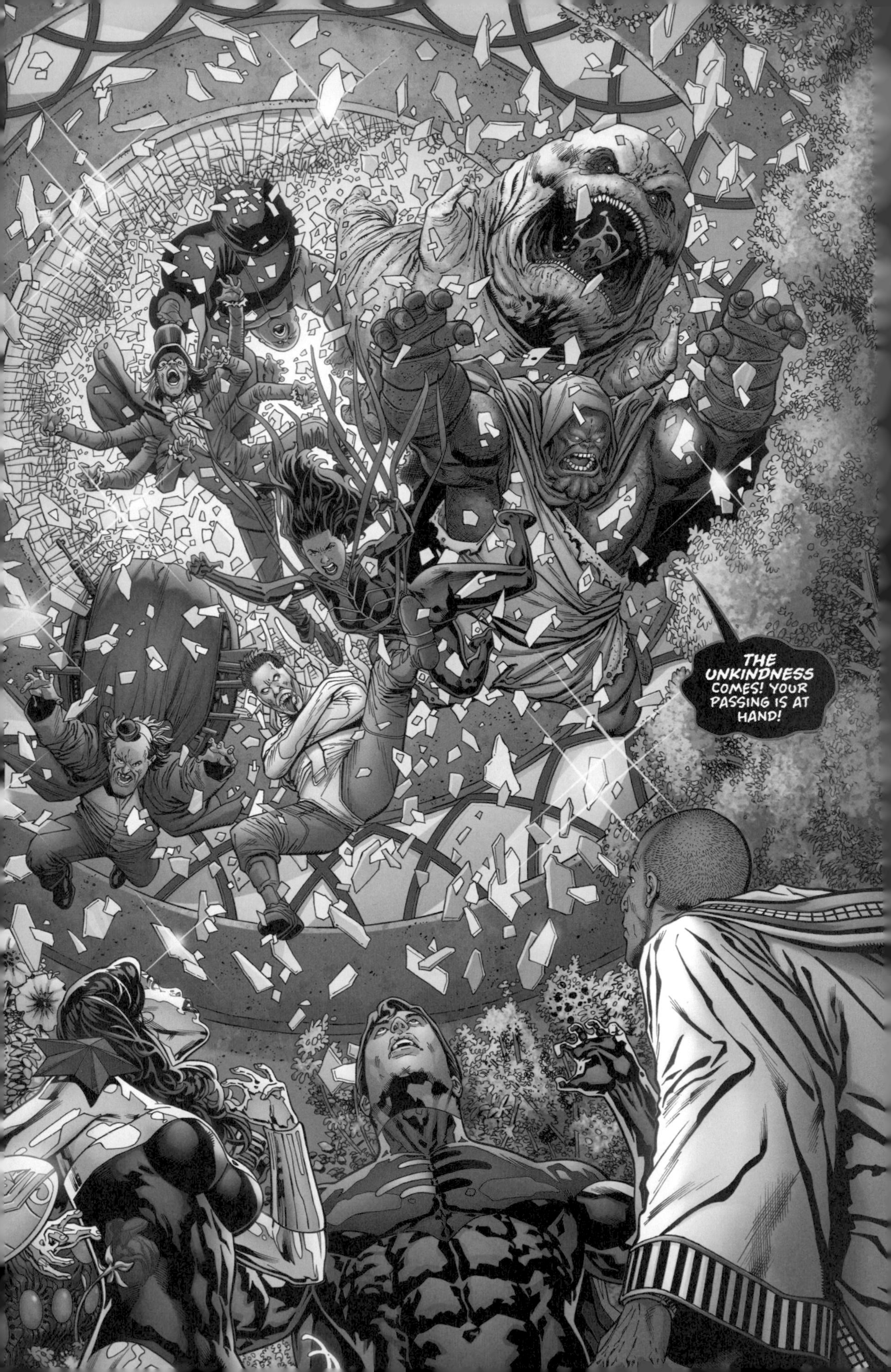
THE UNKINDNESS COMES! YOUR PASSING IS AT HAND!

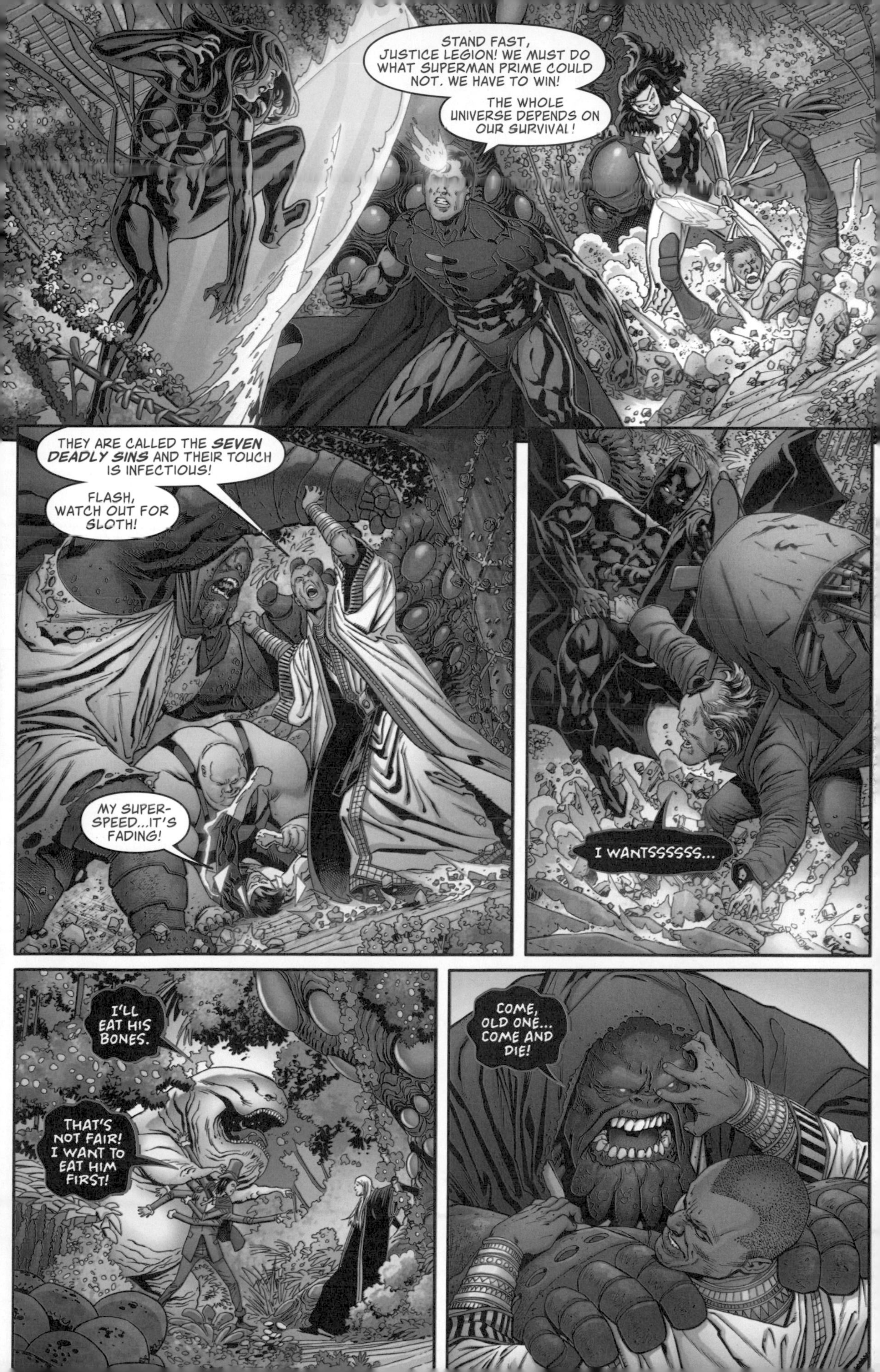
STAND FAST, JUSTICE LEGION! WE MUST DO WHAT SUPERMAN PRIME COULD NOT. WE HAVE TO WIN!
THE WHOLE UNIVERSE DEPENDS ON OUR SURVIVAL!
THEY ARE CALLED THE SEVEN DEADLY SINS AND THEIR TOUCH IS INFECTIOUS!
FLASH, WATCH OUT FOR SLOTH!
MY SUPER-SPEED...IT'S FADING!
I WANTSSSSSS...
I'LL EAT HIS BONES.
THAT'S NOT FAIR! I WANT TO EAT HIM FIRST!
COME, OLD ONE... COME AND DIE!

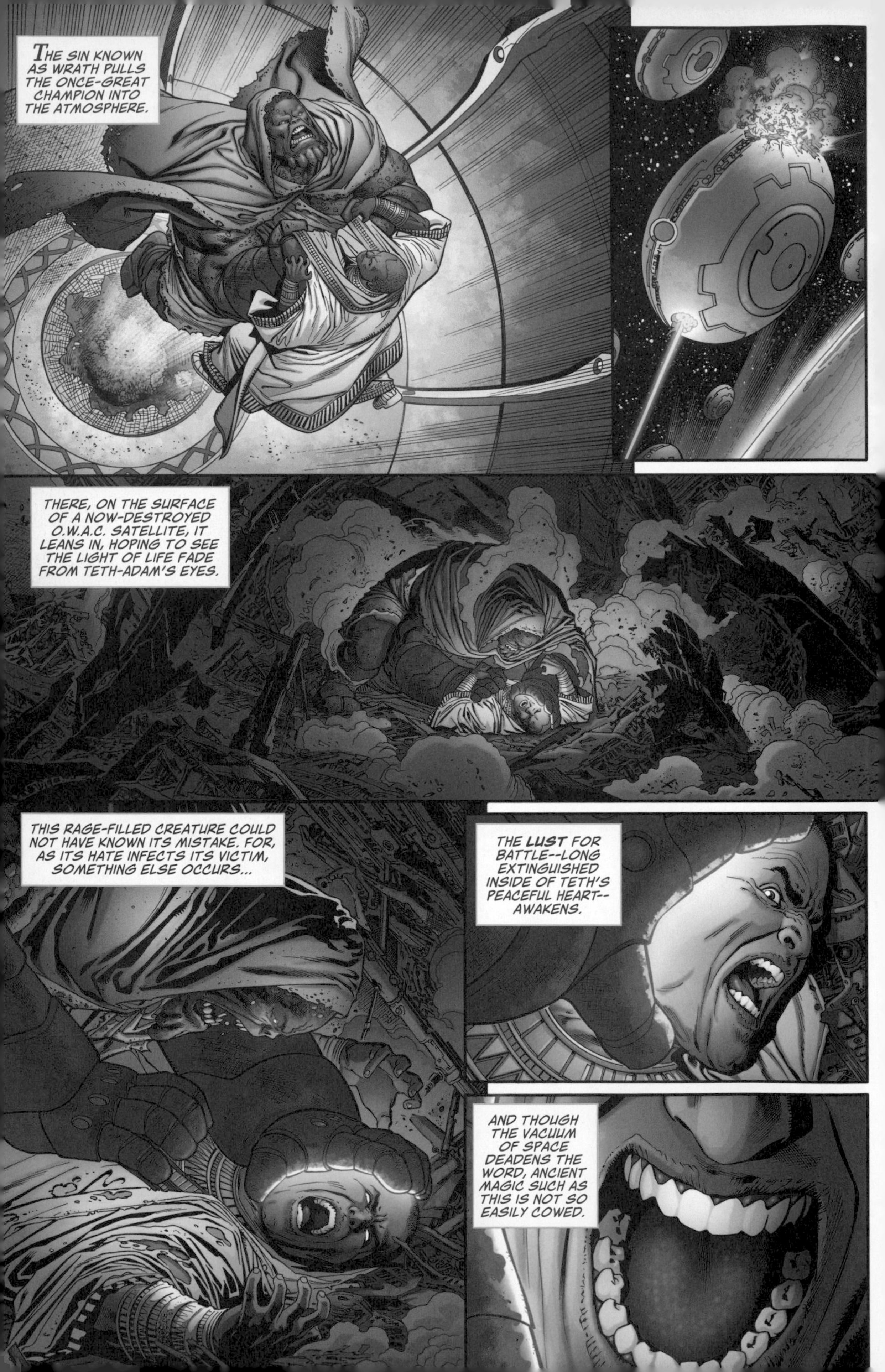
THE SIN KNOWN AS WRATH PULLS THE ONCE-GREAT CHAMPION INTO THE ATMOSPHERE.
THERE, ON THE SURFACE OF A NOW-DESTROYED O.W.A.C. SATELLITE, IT LEANS IN, HOPING TO SEE THE LIGHT OF LIFE FADE FROM TETH-ADAM'S EYES.
THIS RAGE-FILLED CREATURE COULD NOT HAVE KNOWN ITS MISTAKE. FOR, AS ITS HATE INFECTS ITS VICTIM, SOMETHING ELSE OCCURS...
THE LUST FOR BATTLE--LONG EXTINGUISHED INSIDE OF TETH'S PEACEFUL HEART--AWAKENS.
AND THOUGH THE VACUUM OF SPACE DEADENS THE WORD, ANCIENT MAGIC SUCH AS THIS IS NOT SO EASILY COWED.

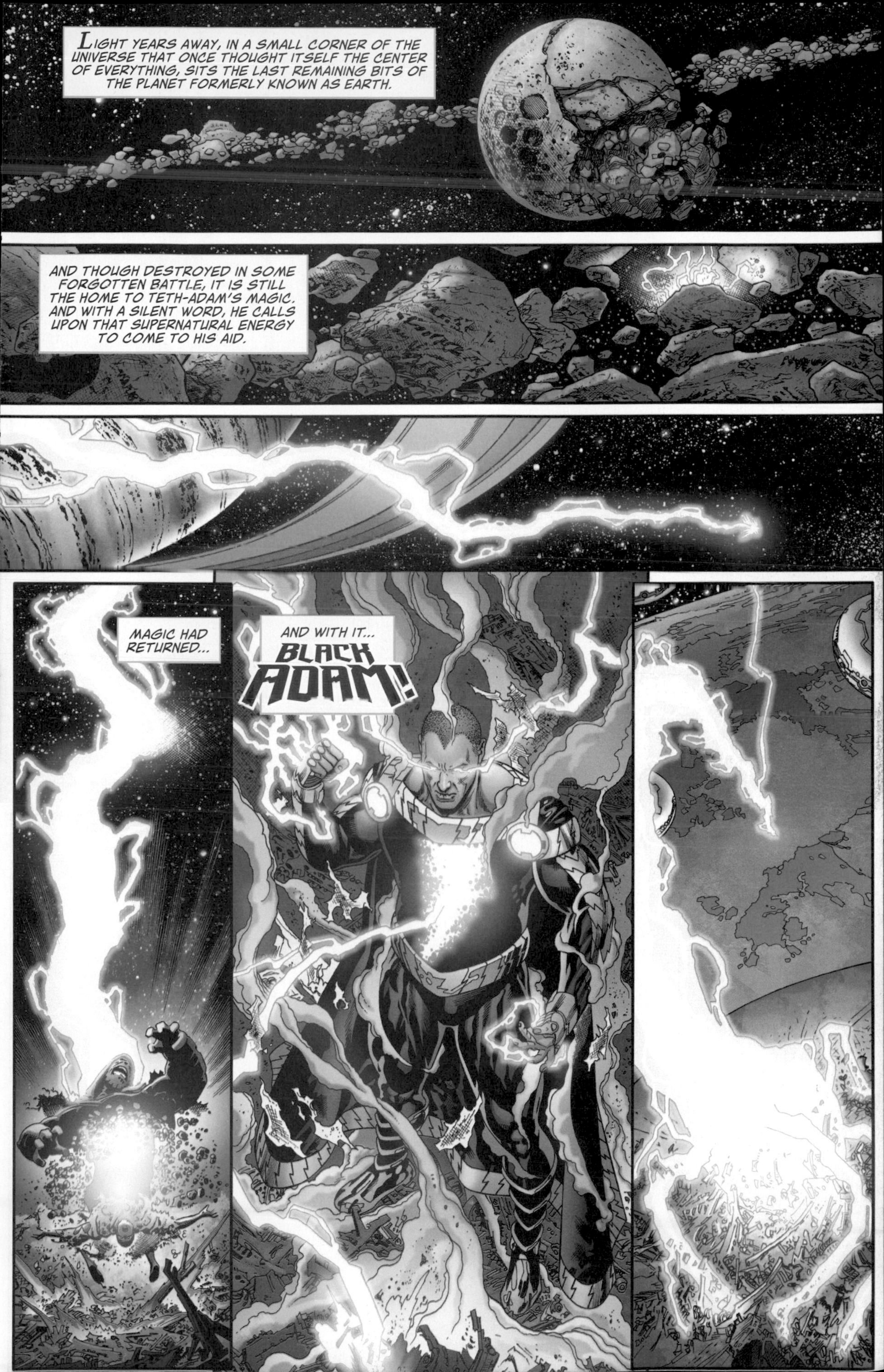
LIGHT YEARS AWAY, IN A SMALL CORNER OF THE UNIVERSE THAT ONCE THOUGHT ITSELF THE CENTER OF EVERYTHING, SITS THE LAST REMAINING BITS OF THE PLANET FORMERLY KNOWN AS EARTH.
AND THOUGH DESTROYED IN SOME FORGOTTEN BATTLE, IT IS STILL THE HOME TO TETH-ADAM'S MAGIC. AND WITH A SILENT WORD, HE CALLS UPON THAT SUPERNATURAL ENERGY TO COME TO HIS AID.
MAGIC HAD RETURNED...
AND WITH IT... BLACK ADAM!

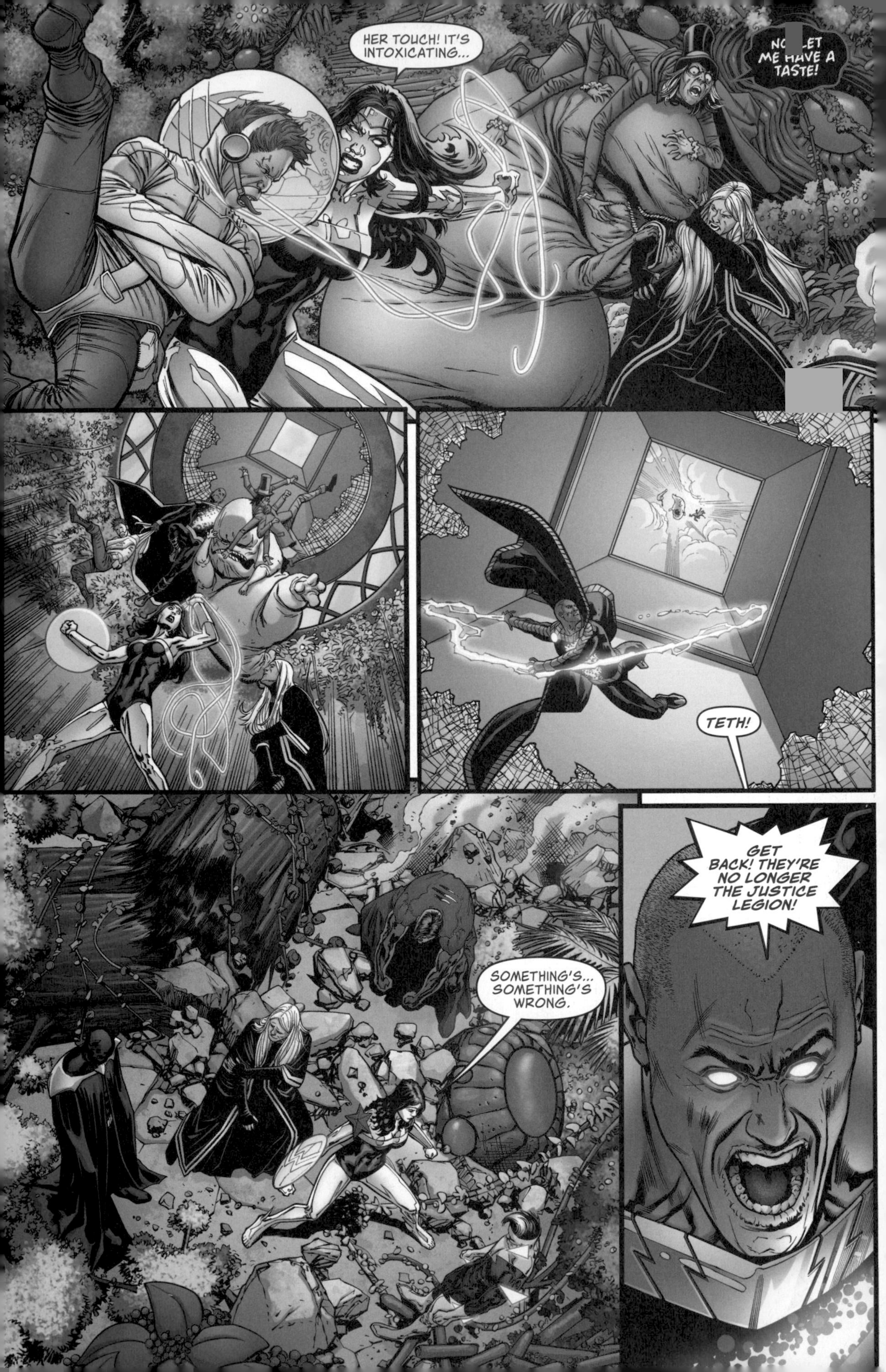
HER TOUCH! IT'S INTOXICATING...
NO—LET ME HAVE A TASTE!
TETH!
SOMETHING'S... SOMETHING'S WRONG.
GET BACK! THEY'RE NO LONGER THE JUSTICE LEGION!

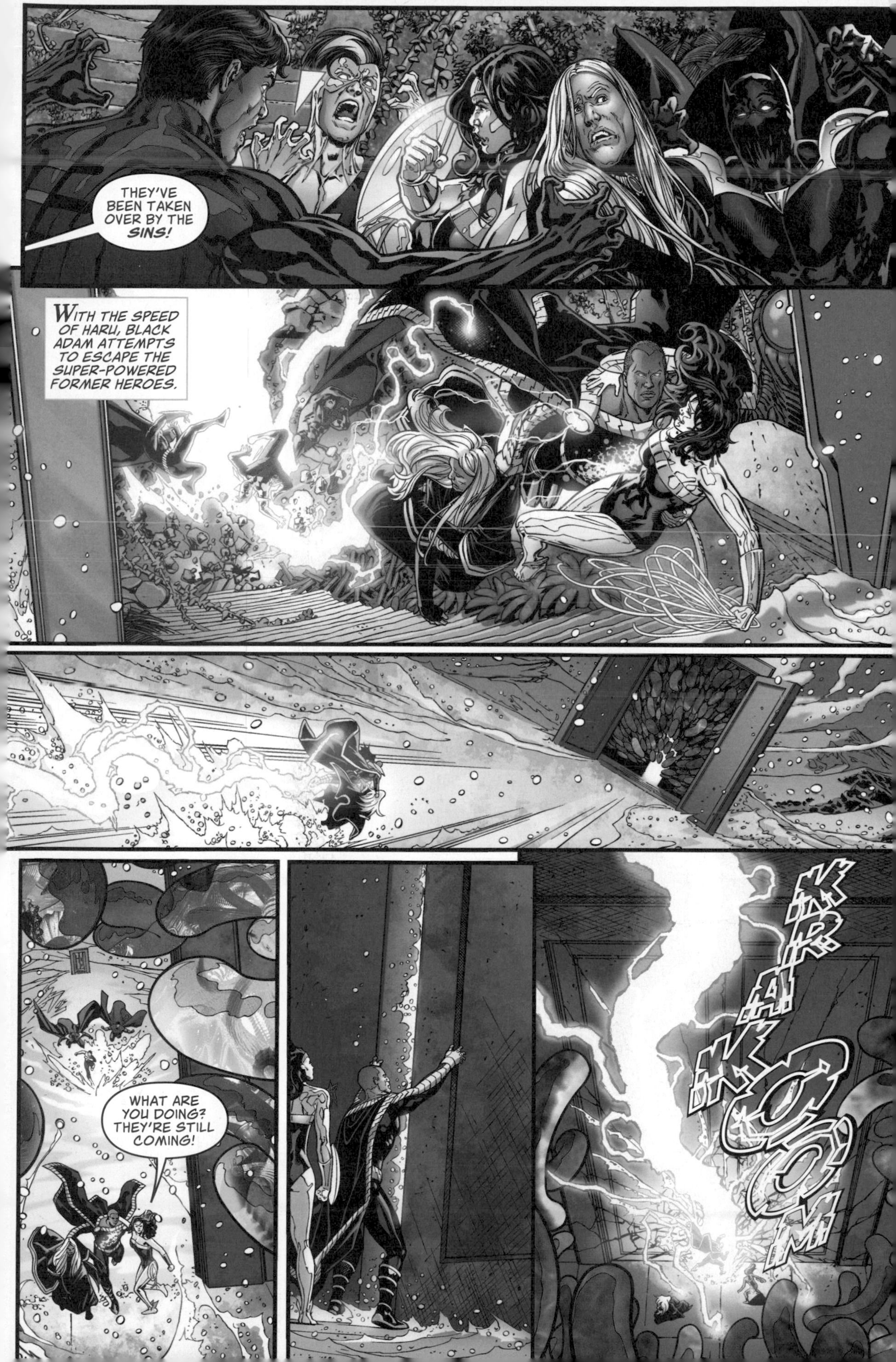
THEY'VE BEEN TAKEN OVER BY THE SINS!
WITH THE SPEED OF HARU, BLACK ADAM ATTEMPTS TO ESCAPE THE SUPER-POWERED FORMER HEROES.
WHAT ARE YOU DOING? THEY'RE STILL COMING!
KRAKOOOM

ARE WE SAFE?

NO...ALL THE ROOMS IN THE PYRAMID ARE DIMENSIONALLY LINKED. IT WILL TAKE THEM A MOMENT, BUT THEY WILL FIND A WAY IN.

THEN WE HAVE TO BE READY. SURELY, KAHNDAQ HAS SOMETHING THAT CAN DESTROY THESE BEINGS.

NO, MY SWEET. THERE IS NOTHING THAT CAN DESTROY THEM. THEY ARE ETERNAL, AND CAN ONLY BE CONTAINED.

KAHNDAQ, LIKE THE REST OF THE UNIVERSE, HAS FORGOTTEN THE MAGIC IT WOULD TAKE TO CONTAIN THESE SPIRITS. THEY WILL COME...AND WE...

WE WILL WHAT, ADAM?

WE WILL DIE...

YOU WOULD GIVE UP? YOU WELCOME YOUR DEATH? MITCHELL'S? MINE?

"SWEET ONE... THIS IS NOT NEW.

"ONCE, A LONG TIME AGO, A WIZARD IMPRISONED ME WITHIN THE ROCK OF ETERNITY FOR TENS OF THOUSANDS OF YEARS, WITH ONLY A SMALL GOLD BRAZIER TO GIVE ME LIGHT. ENOUGH TO SHOW ME HOW ALONE I WAS. IT WAS TORTURE...AND I PRAYED FOR DEATH.

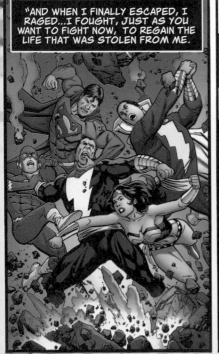

"AND WHEN I FINALLY ESCAPED, I RAGED...I FOUGHT, JUST AS YOU WANT TO FIGHT NOW, TO REGAIN THE LIFE THAT WAS STOLEN FROM ME.

BUT... IT WAS ALL FOR NAUGHT.

LIFE IS CRUEL. THE GARDEN YOU FOUND ME IN... EACH FLOWER WAS PLANTED FOR PAST RELATIONSHIPS... FRIENDS...LOVERS...EACH ONE DIED IN FRONT OF ME.

I SOMETIMES WONDER WHICH WAS WORSE...THOUSANDS OF YEARS IMPRISONED IN THE DARK...OR THE THOUSANDS AFTER, WATCHING THOSE I LOVE DIE IN FRONT OF ME.

BUT NOW... WITH THIS *BEING* THAT SEEKS TO DESTROY OUR UNIVERSE...WE CAN END THE FUTILITY OF LIVING... TOGETHER.

TETH... YOU CAN'T GIVE UP.

THERE IS NO CHOICE...

NO...TETH... WE HAVE TO LIVE. IF NOT FOR ME...FOR OUR CHILD.

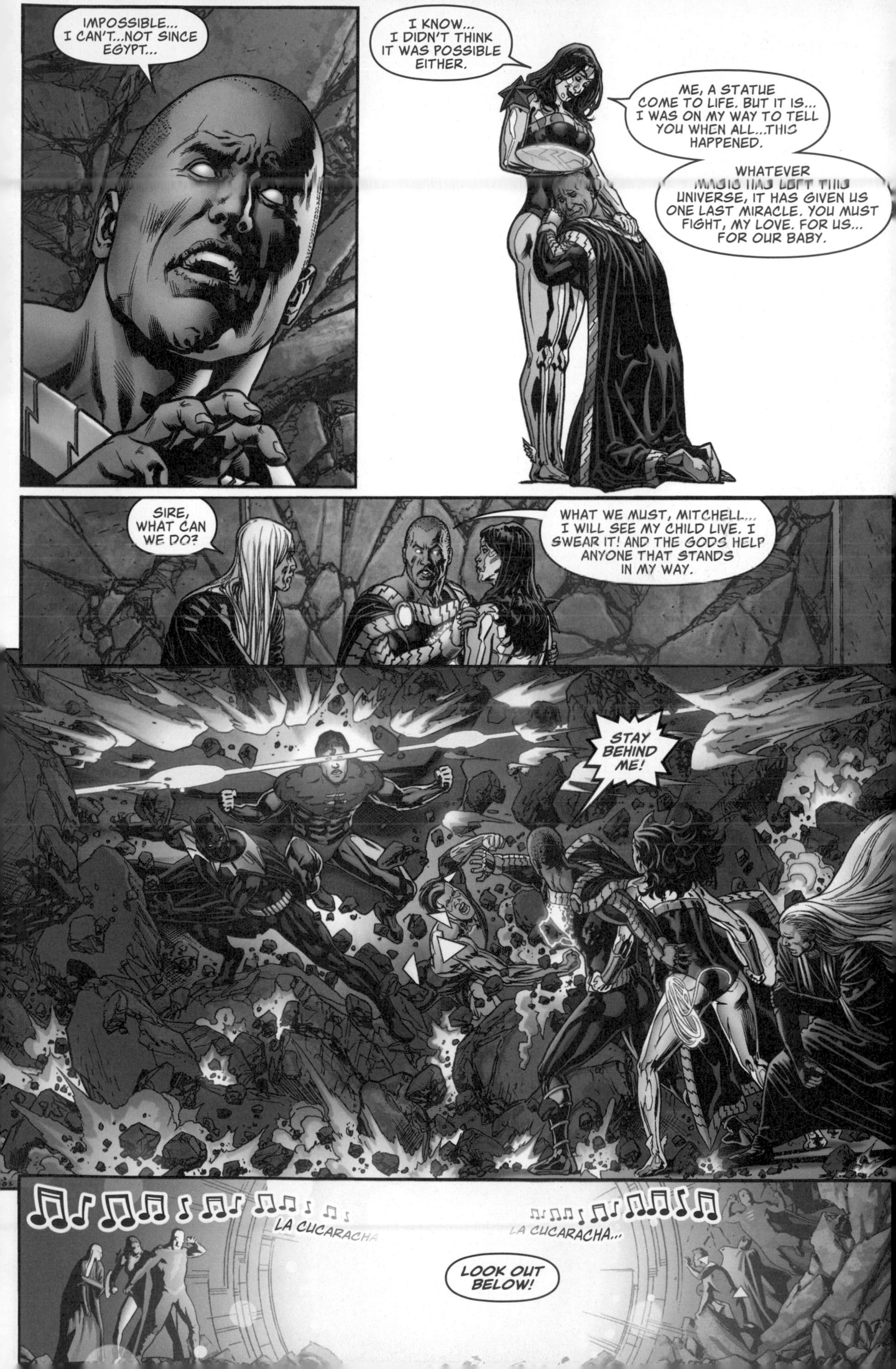
IMPOSSIBLE... I CAN'T...NOT SINCE EGYPT...
I KNOW... I DIDN'T THINK IT WAS POSSIBLE EITHER.
ME, A STATUE COME TO LIFE. BUT IT IS... I WAS ON MY WAY TO TELL YOU WHEN ALL...THIS HAPPENED.
WHATEVER MAGIC HAS LEFT THIS UNIVERSE, IT HAS GIVEN US ONE LAST MIRACLE. YOU MUST FIGHT, MY LOVE. FOR US... FOR OUR BABY.
SIRE, WHAT CAN WE DO?
WHAT WE MUST, MITCHELL... I WILL SEE MY CHILD LIVE. I SWEAR IT! AND THE GODS HELP ANYONE THAT STANDS IN MY WAY.
STAY BEHIND ME!
LA CUCARACHA
LA CUCARACHA...
LOOK OUT BELOW!

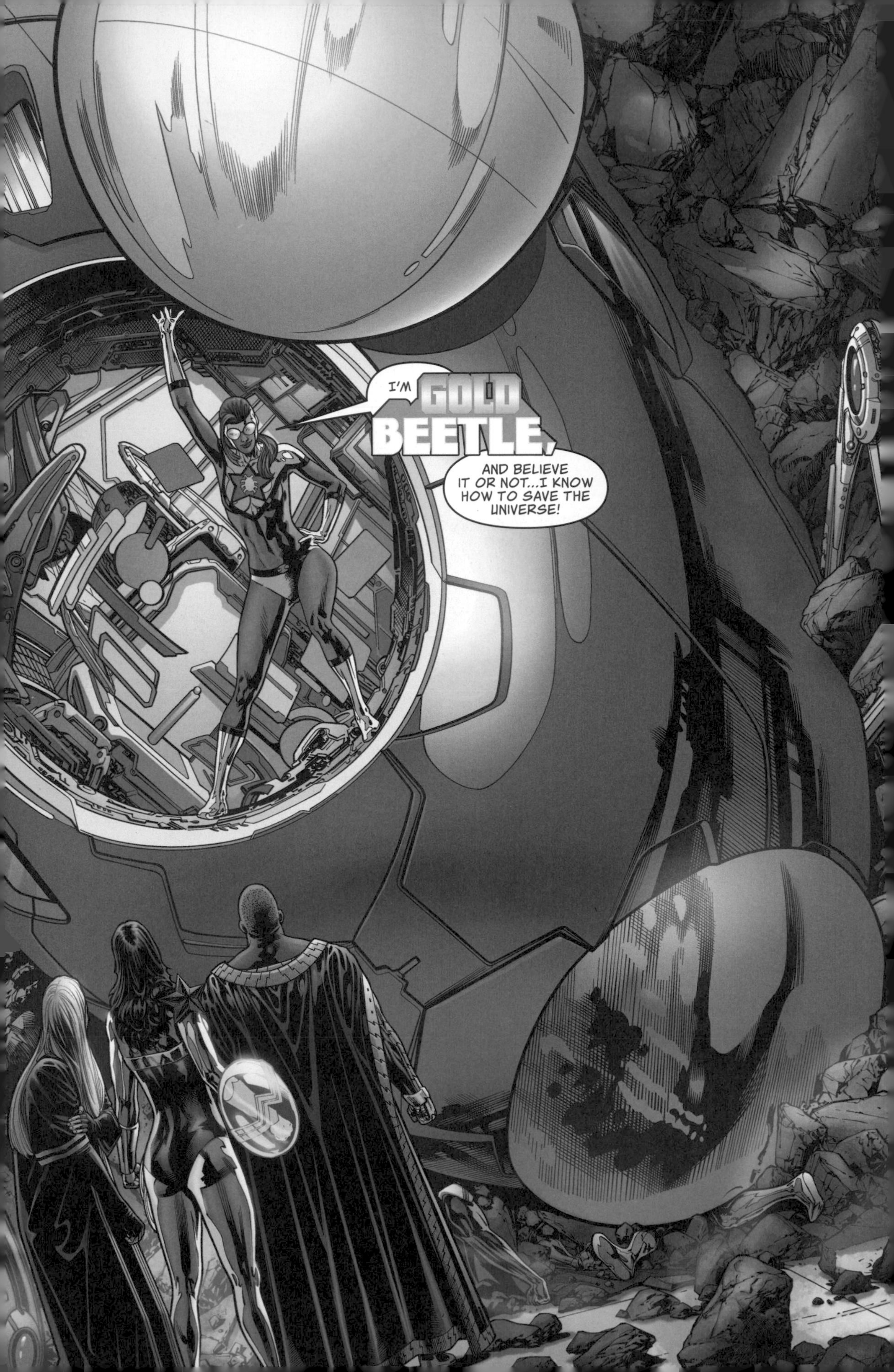
I'M GOLD BEETLE,
AND BELIEVE IT OR NOT...I KNOW HOW TO SAVE THE UNIVERSE!

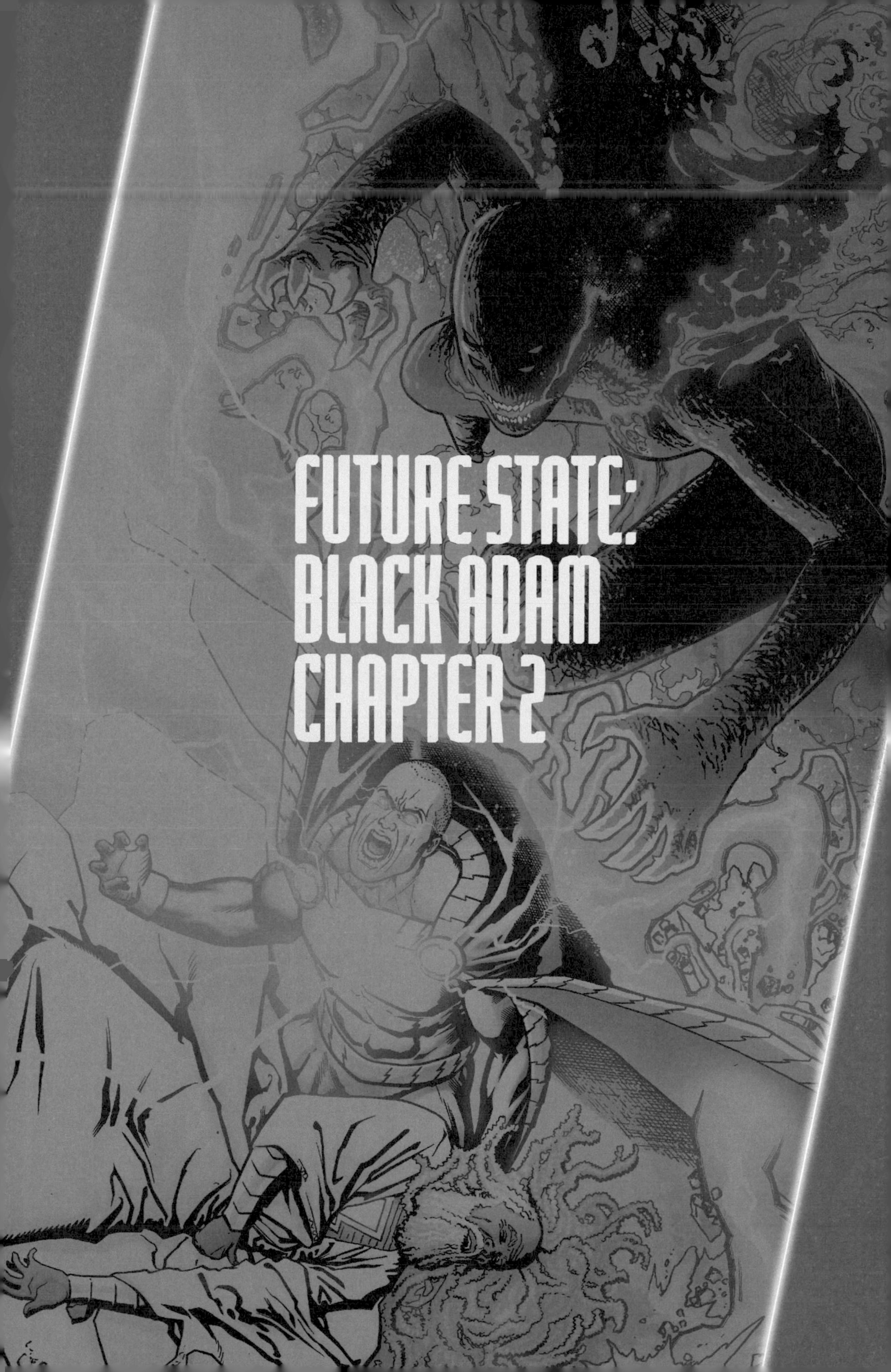
FUTURE STATE:
BLACK ADAM
CHAPTER 2

FUTURE STATE

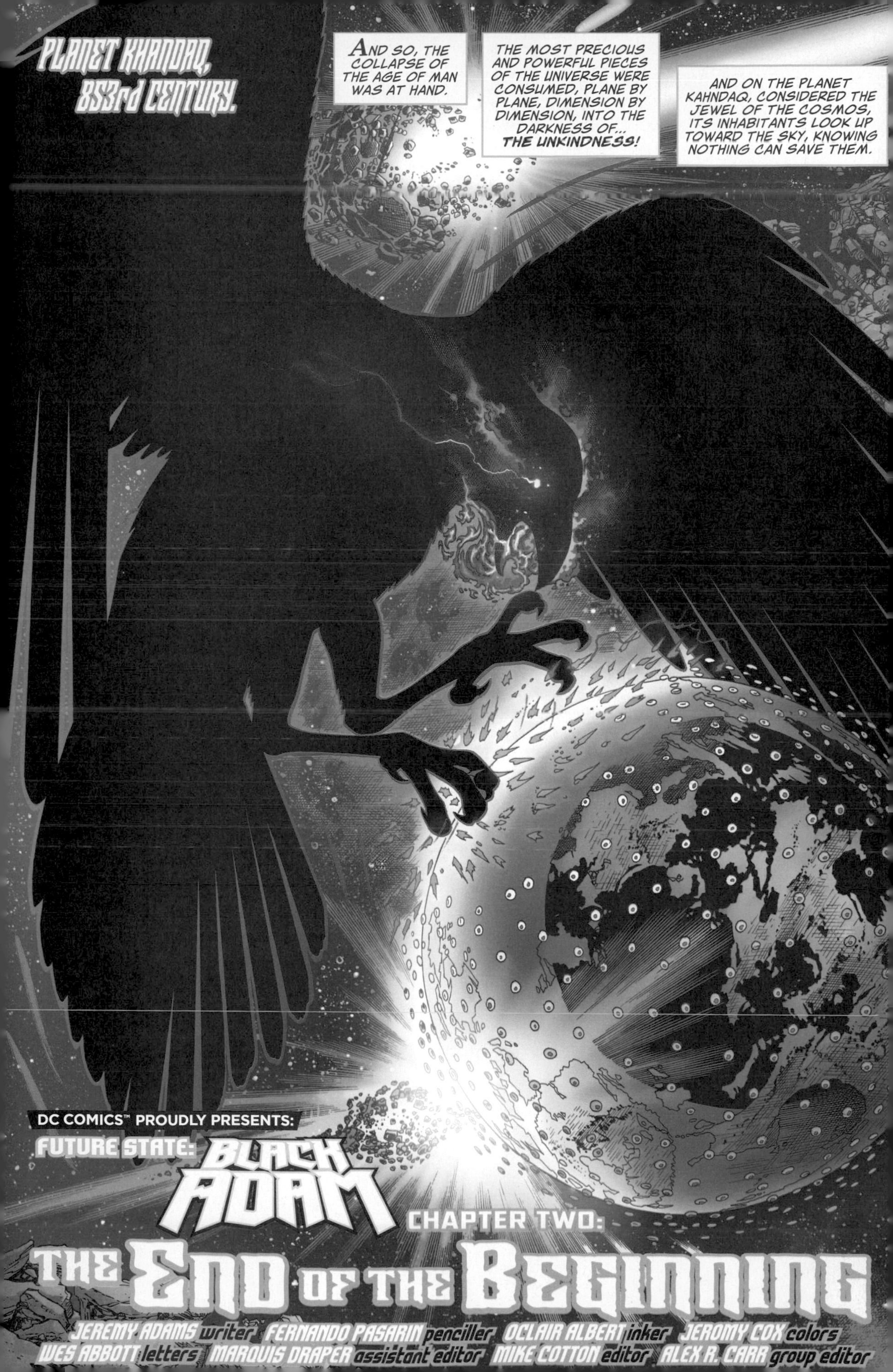
PLANET KHANDAQ, 853rd CENTURY.
AND SO, THE COLLAPSE OF THE AGE OF MAN WAS AT HAND.
THE MOST PRECIOUS AND POWERFUL PIECES OF THE UNIVERSE WERE CONSUMED, PLANE BY PLANE, DIMENSION BY DIMENSION, INTO THE DARKNESS OF... THE UNKINDNESS!
AND ON THE PLANET KAHNDAQ, CONSIDERED THE JEWEL OF THE COSMOS, ITS INHABITANTS LOOK UP TOWARD THE SKY, KNOWING NOTHING CAN SAVE THEM.
DC COMICS™ PROUDLY PRESENTS:
FUTURE STATE: BLACK ADAM
CHAPTER TWO:
THE END OF THE BEGINNING
JEREMY ADAMS writer FERNANDO PASARIN penciller OCLAIR ALBERT inker JEROMY COX colors
WES ABBOTT letters MARQUIS DRAPER assistant editor MIKE COTTON editor ALEX R. CARR group editor

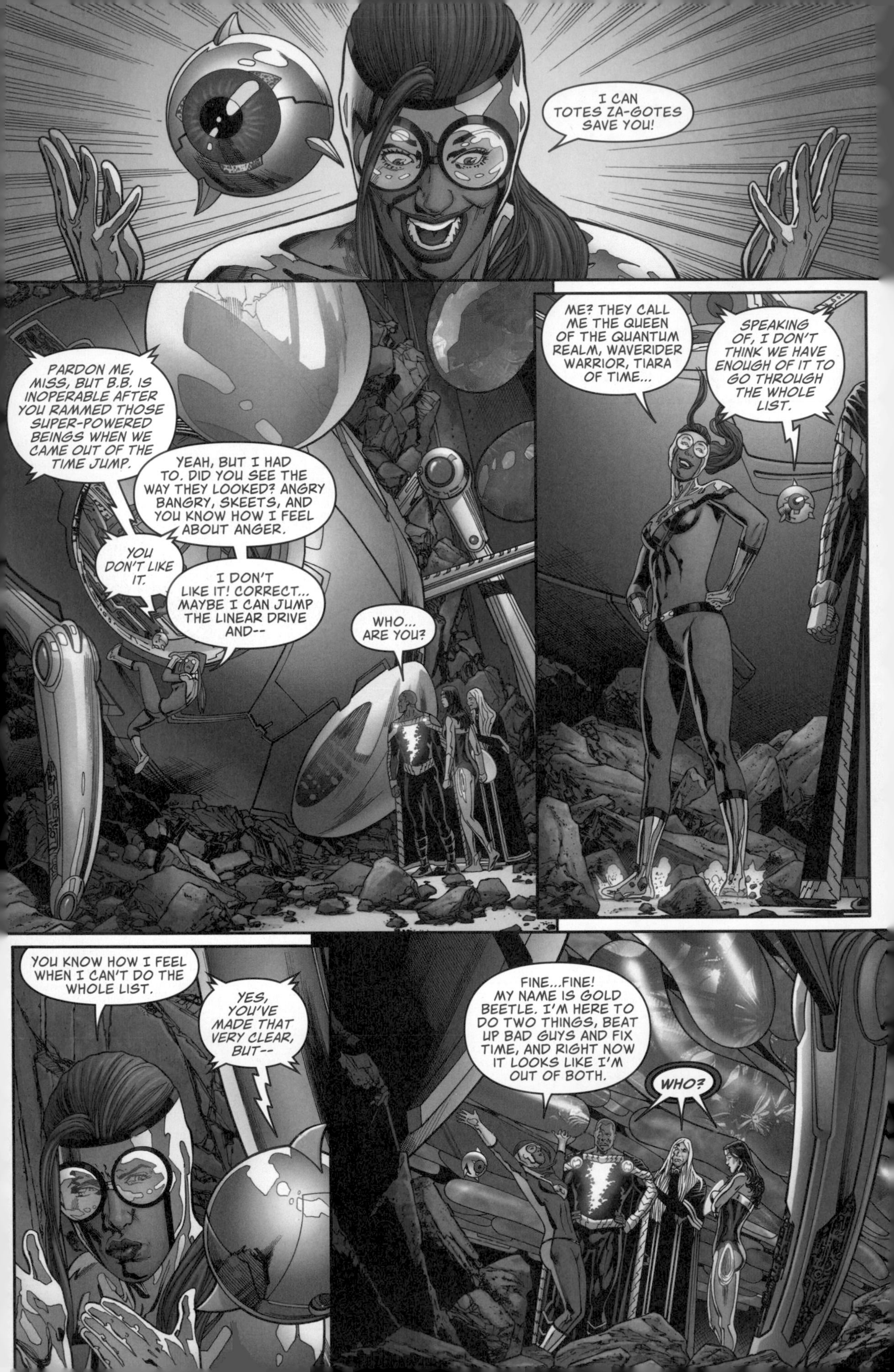
I CAN TOTES ZA-GOTES SAVE YOU!
PARDON ME, MISS, BUT B.B. IS INOPERABLE AFTER YOU RAMMED THOSE SUPER-POWERED BEINGS WHEN WE CAME OUT OF THE TIME JUMP.
YEAH, BUT I HAD TO. DID YOU SEE THE WAY THEY LOOKED? ANGRY BANGRY, SKEETS, AND YOU KNOW HOW I FEEL ABOUT ANGER.
YOU DON'T LIKE IT.
I DON'T LIKE IT! CORRECT... MAYBE I CAN JUMP THE LINEAR DRIVE AND--
WHO... ARE YOU?
ME? THEY CALL ME THE QUEEN OF THE QUANTUM REALM, WAVERIDER WARRIOR, TIARA OF TIME...
SPEAKING OF, I DON'T THINK WE HAVE ENOUGH OF IT TO GO THROUGH THE WHOLE LIST.
YOU KNOW HOW I FEEL WHEN I CAN'T DO THE WHOLE LIST.
YES, YOU'VE MADE THAT VERY CLEAR, BUT--
FINE...FINE! MY NAME IS GOLD BEETLE. I'M HERE TO DO TWO THINGS, BEAT UP BAD GUYS AND FIX TIME, AND RIGHT NOW IT LOOKS LIKE I'M OUT OF BOTH.
WHO?

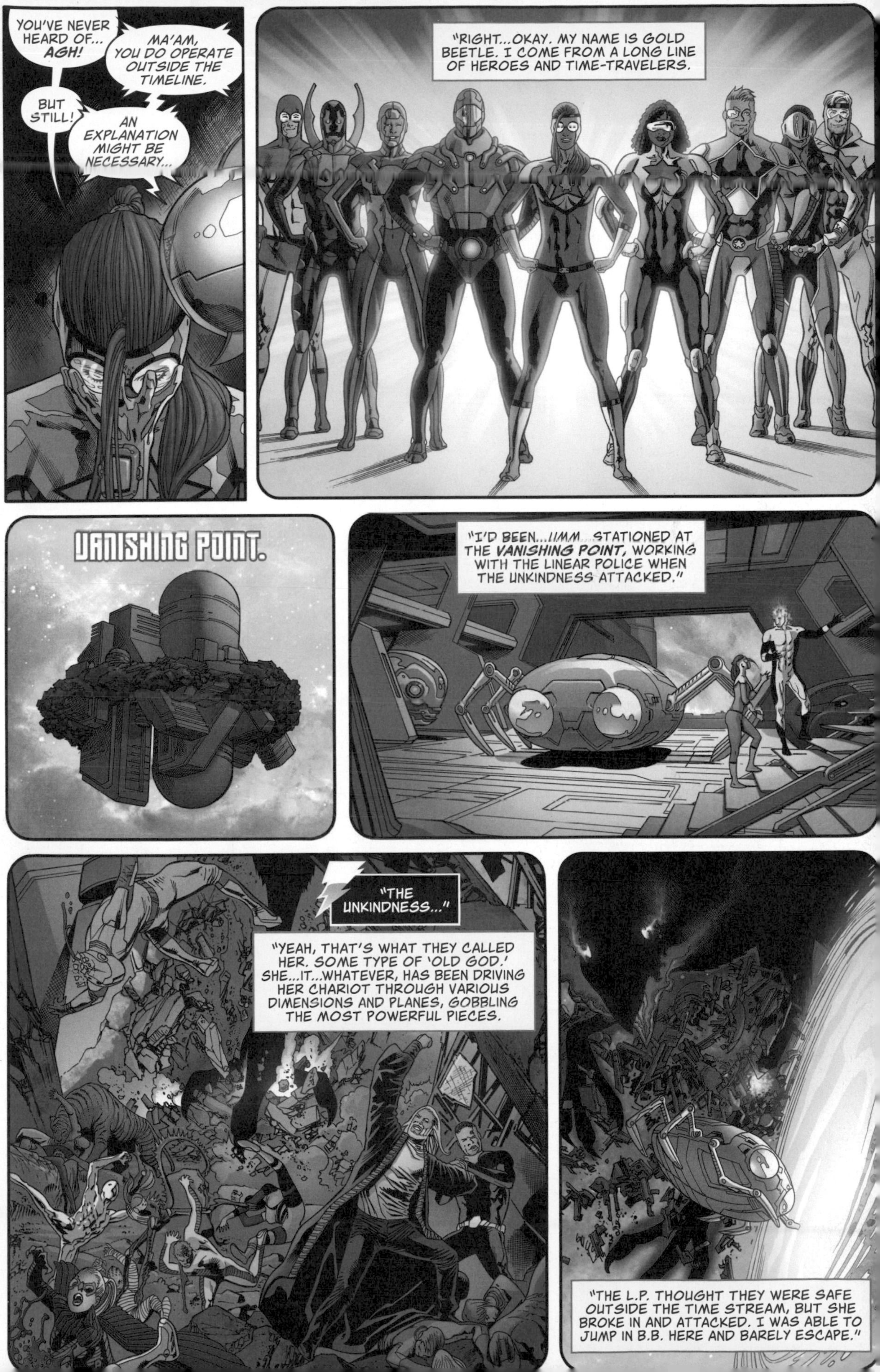
YOU'VE NEVER HEARD OF... AGH!
MA'AM, YOU DO OPERATE OUTSIDE THE TIMELINE.
BUT STILL!
AN EXPLANATION MIGHT BE NECESSARY...
"RIGHT...OKAY. MY NAME IS GOLD BEETLE. I COME FROM A LONG LINE OF HEROES AND TIME-TRAVELERS.
VANISHING POINT.
"I'D BEEN...UMM...STATIONED AT THE VANISHING POINT, WORKING WITH THE LINEAR POLICE WHEN THE UNKINDNESS ATTACKED."
"THE UNKINDNESS..."
"YEAH, THAT'S WHAT THEY CALLED HER. SOME TYPE OF 'OLD GOD.' SHE...IT...WHATEVER, HAS BEEN DRIVING HER CHARIOT THROUGH VARIOUS DIMENSIONS AND PLANES, GOBBLING THE MOST POWERFUL PIECES.
"THE L.P. THOUGHT THEY WERE SAFE OUTSIDE THE TIME STREAM, BUT SHE BROKE IN AND ATTACKED. I WAS ABLE TO JUMP IN B.B. HERE AND BARELY ESCAPE."

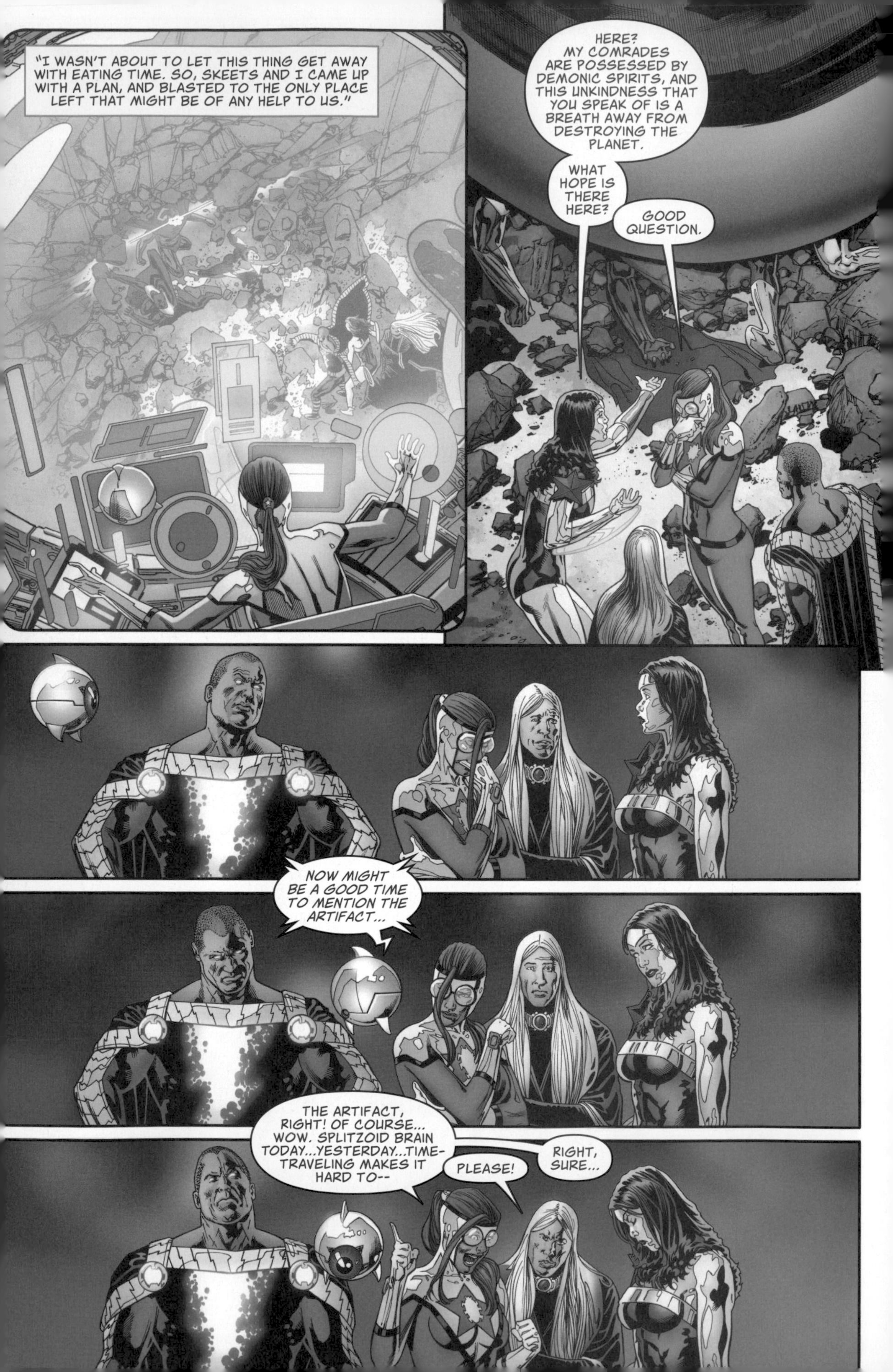
"I WASN'T ABOUT TO LET THIS THING GET AWAY WITH EATING TIME. SO, SKEETS AND I CAME UP WITH A PLAN, AND BLASTED TO THE ONLY PLACE LEFT THAT MIGHT BE OF ANY HELP TO US."
HERE? MY COMRADES ARE POSSESSED BY DEMONIC SPIRITS, AND THIS UNKINDNESS THAT YOU SPEAK OF IS A BREATH AWAY FROM DESTROYING THE PLANET.
WHAT HOPE IS THERE HERE?
GOOD QUESTION.
NOW MIGHT BE A GOOD TIME TO MENTION THE ARTIFACT...
THE ARTIFACT, RIGHT! OF COURSE... WOW. SPLITZOID BRAIN TODAY...YESTERDAY...TIME-TRAVELING MAKES IT HARD TO--
PLEASE!
RIGHT, SURE...

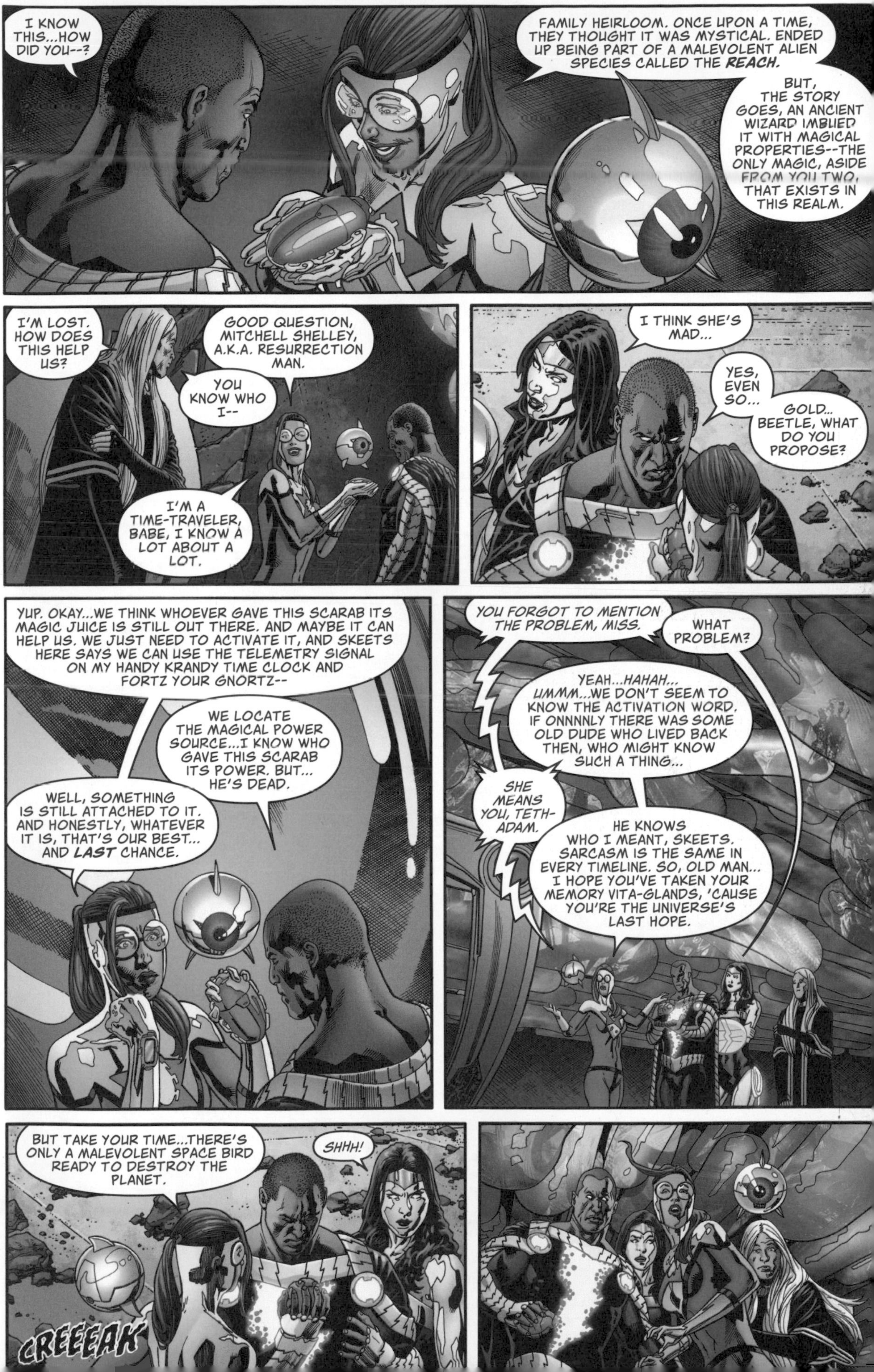
I KNOW THIS...HOW DID YOU--?
FAMILY HEIRLOOM. ONCE UPON A TIME, THEY THOUGHT IT WAS MYSTICAL. ENDED UP BEING PART OF A MALEVOLENT ALIEN SPECIES CALLED THE REACH.
BUT, THE STORY GOES, AN ANCIENT WIZARD IMBUED IT WITH MAGICAL PROPERTIES--THE ONLY MAGIC, ASIDE FROM YOU TWO, THAT EXISTS IN THIS REALM.
I'M LOST. HOW DOES THIS HELP US?
GOOD QUESTION, MITCHELL SHELLEY, A.K.A. RESURRECTION MAN.
YOU KNOW WHO I--
I'M A TIME-TRAVELER, BABE, I KNOW A LOT ABOUT A LOT.
I THINK SHE'S MAD...
YES, EVEN SO...
GOLD... BEETLE, WHAT DO YOU PROPOSE?
YUP. OKAY...WE THINK WHOEVER GAVE THIS SCARAB ITS MAGIC JUICE IS STILL OUT THERE. AND MAYBE IT CAN HELP US. WE JUST NEED TO ACTIVATE IT, AND SKEETS HERE SAYS WE CAN USE THE TELEMETRY SIGNAL ON MY HANDY KRANDY TIME CLOCK AND FORTZ YOUR GNORTZ--
WE LOCATE THE MAGICAL POWER SOURCE...I KNOW WHO GAVE THIS SCARAB ITS POWER. BUT... HE'S DEAD.
WELL, SOMETHING IS STILL ATTACHED TO IT. AND HONESTLY, WHATEVER IT IS, THAT'S OUR BEST... AND LAST CHANCE.
YOU FORGOT TO MENTION THE PROBLEM, MISS.
WHAT PROBLEM?
YEAH...HAHAH... UMMM...WE DON'T SEEM TO KNOW THE ACTIVATION WORD. IF ONNNNLY THERE WAS SOME OLD DUDE WHO LIVED BACK THEN, WHO MIGHT KNOW SUCH A THING...
SHE MEANS YOU, TETH-ADAM.
HE KNOWS WHO I MEANT, SKEETS. SARCASM IS THE SAME IN EVERY TIMELINE. SO, OLD MAN... I HOPE YOU'VE TAKEN YOUR MEMORY VITA-GLANDS, 'CAUSE YOU'RE THE UNIVERSE'S LAST HOPE.
BUT TAKE YOUR TIME...THERE'S ONLY A MALEVOLENT SPACE BIRD READY TO DESTROY THE PLANET.
SHHH!
CREEEAK

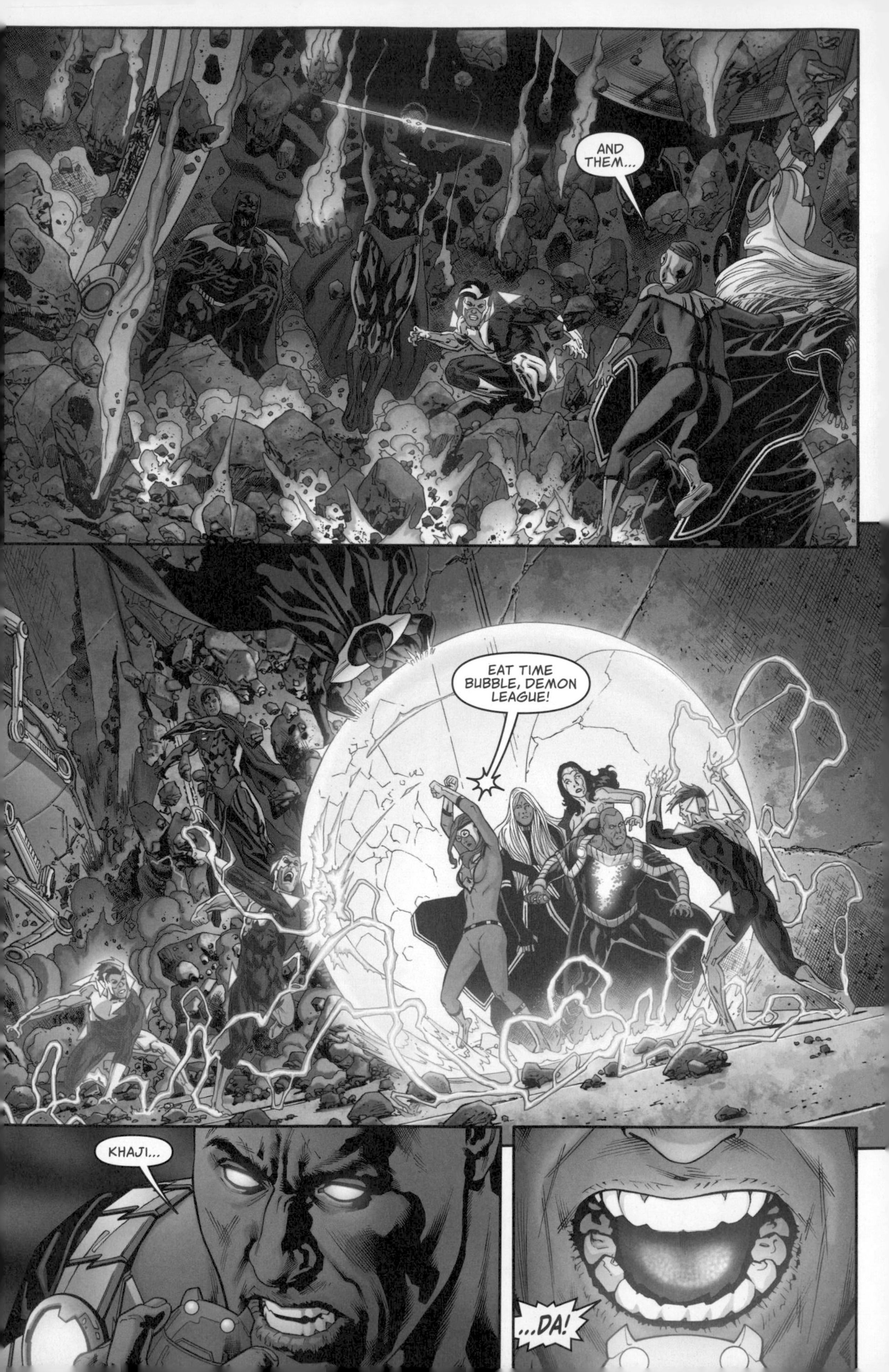
AND THEM...
EAT TIME BUBBLE, DEMON LEAGUE!
KHAJI...
...DA!

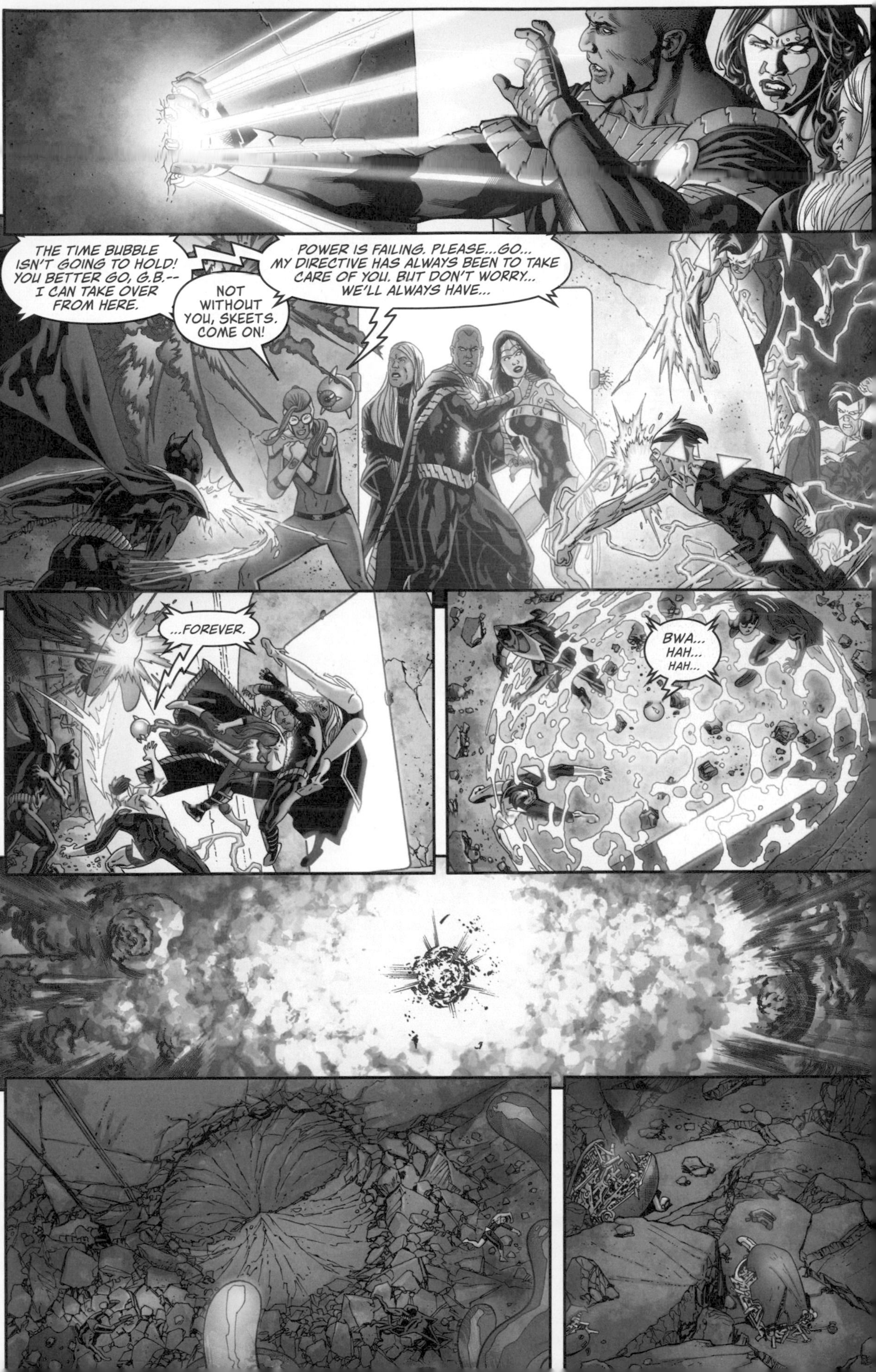
THE TIME BUBBLE ISN'T GOING TO HOLD! YOU BETTER GO, G.B.-- I CAN TAKE OVER FROM HERE.
NOT WITHOUT YOU, SKEETS. COME ON!
POWER IS FAILING. PLEASE...GO... MY DIRECTIVE HAS ALWAYS BEEN TO TAKE CARE OF YOU. BUT DON'T WORRY... WE'LL ALWAYS HAVE...
...FOREVER.
BWA... HAH... HAH...

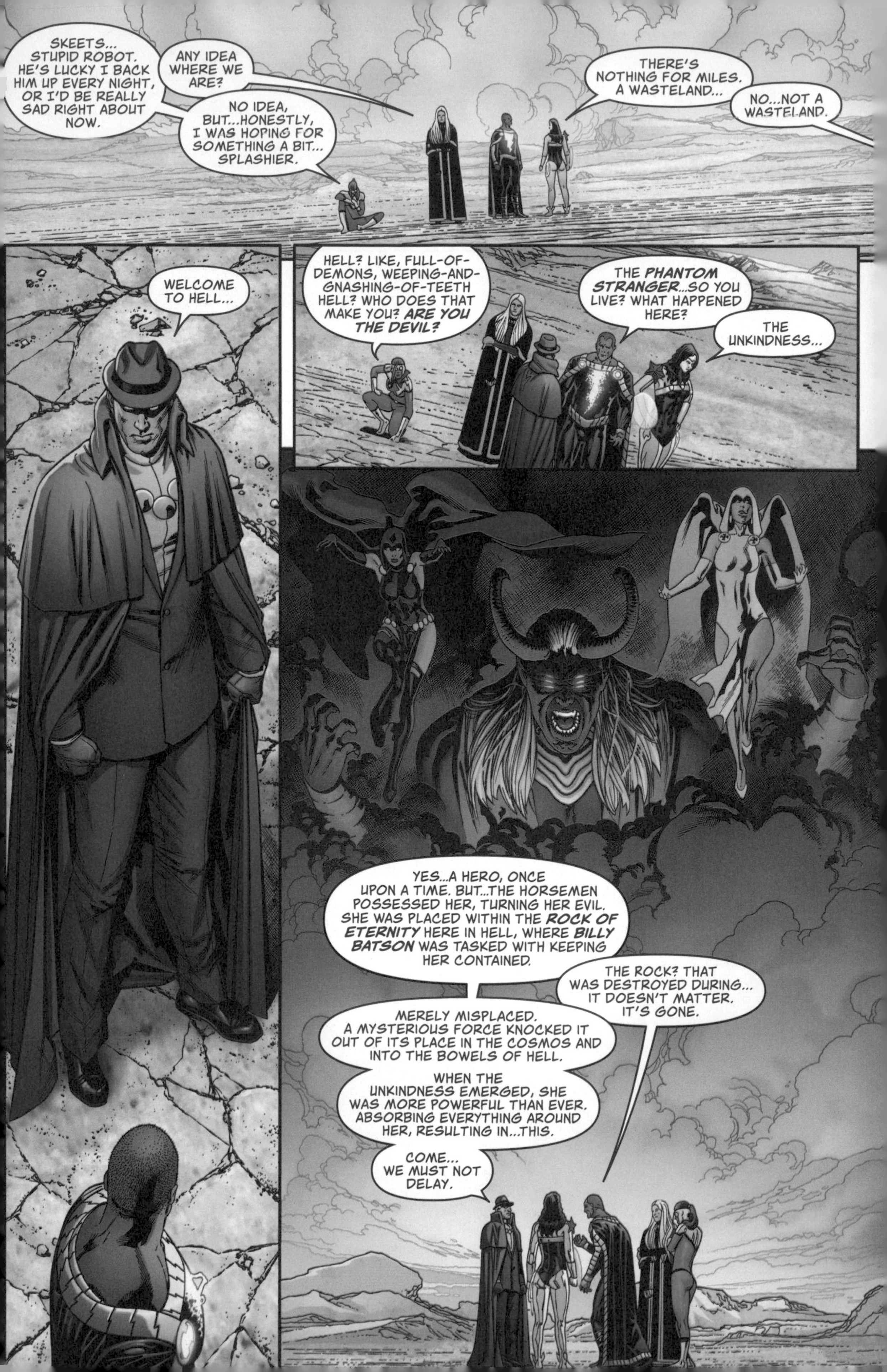
SKEETS... STUPID ROBOT. HE'S LUCKY I BACK HIM UP EVERY NIGHT, OR I'D BE REALLY SAD RIGHT ABOUT NOW.
ANY IDEA WHERE WE ARE?
NO IDEA, BUT...HONESTLY, I WAS HOPING FOR SOMETHING A BIT... SPLASHIER.
THERE'S NOTHING FOR MILES. A WASTELAND...
NO...NOT A WASTELAND.
WELCOME TO HELL...
HELL? LIKE, FULL-OF-DEMONS, WEEPING-AND-GNASHING-OF-TEETH HELL? WHO DOES THAT MAKE YOU? ARE YOU THE DEVIL?
THE PHANTOM STRANGER...SO YOU LIVE? WHAT HAPPENED HERE?
THE UNKINDNESS...
YES...A HERO, ONCE UPON A TIME. BUT...THE HORSEMEN POSSESSED HER, TURNING HER EVIL. SHE WAS PLACED WITHIN THE ROCK OF ETERNITY HERE IN HELL, WHERE BILLY BATSON WAS TASKED WITH KEEPING HER CONTAINED.
THE ROCK? THAT WAS DESTROYED DURING... IT DOESN'T MATTER. IT'S GONE.
MERELY MISPLACED. A MYSTERIOUS FORCE KNOCKED IT OUT OF ITS PLACE IN THE COSMOS AND INTO THE BOWELS OF HELL.
WHEN THE UNKINDNESS EMERGED, SHE WAS MORE POWERFUL THAN EVER. ABSORBING EVERYTHING AROUND HER, RESULTING IN...THIS.
COME... WE MUST NOT DELAY.

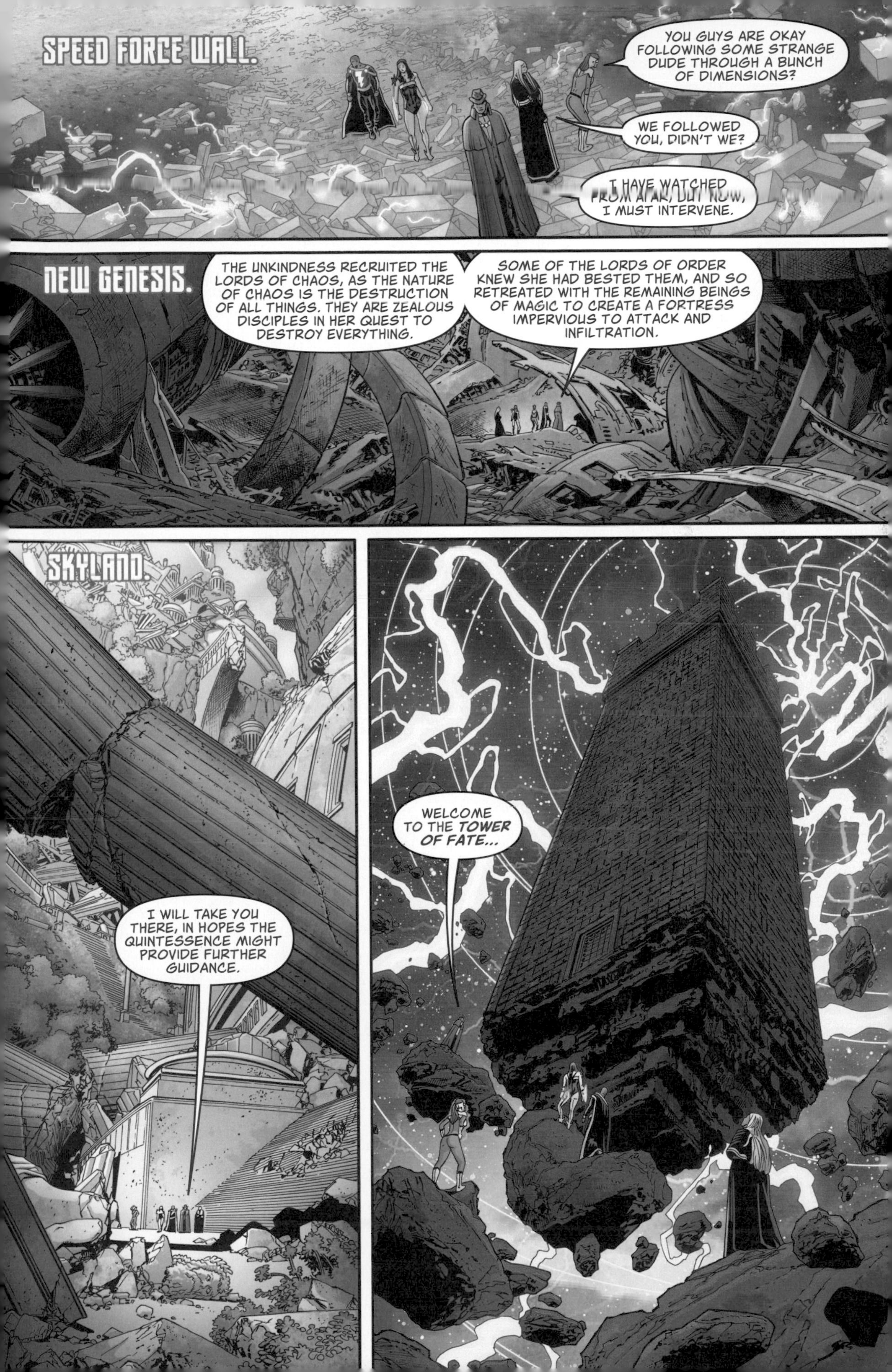
SPEED FORCE WALL.
YOU GUYS ARE OKAY FOLLOWING SOME STRANGE DUDE THROUGH A BUNCH OF DIMENSIONS?
WE FOLLOWED YOU, DIDN'T WE?
I HAVE WATCHED FROM AFAR, BUT NOW, I MUST INTERVENE.
NEW GENESIS.
THE UNKINDNESS RECRUITED THE LORDS OF CHAOS, AS THE NATURE OF CHAOS IS THE DESTRUCTION OF ALL THINGS. THEY ARE ZEALOUS DISCIPLES IN HER QUEST TO DESTROY EVERYTHING.
SOME OF THE LORDS OF ORDER KNEW SHE HAD BESTED THEM, AND SO RETREATED WITH THE REMAINING BEINGS OF MAGIC TO CREATE A FORTRESS IMPERVIOUS TO ATTACK AND INFILTRATION.
SKYLAND.
I WILL TAKE YOU THERE, IN HOPES THE QUINTESSENCE MIGHT PROVIDE FURTHER GUIDANCE.
WELCOME TO THE TOWER OF FATE...

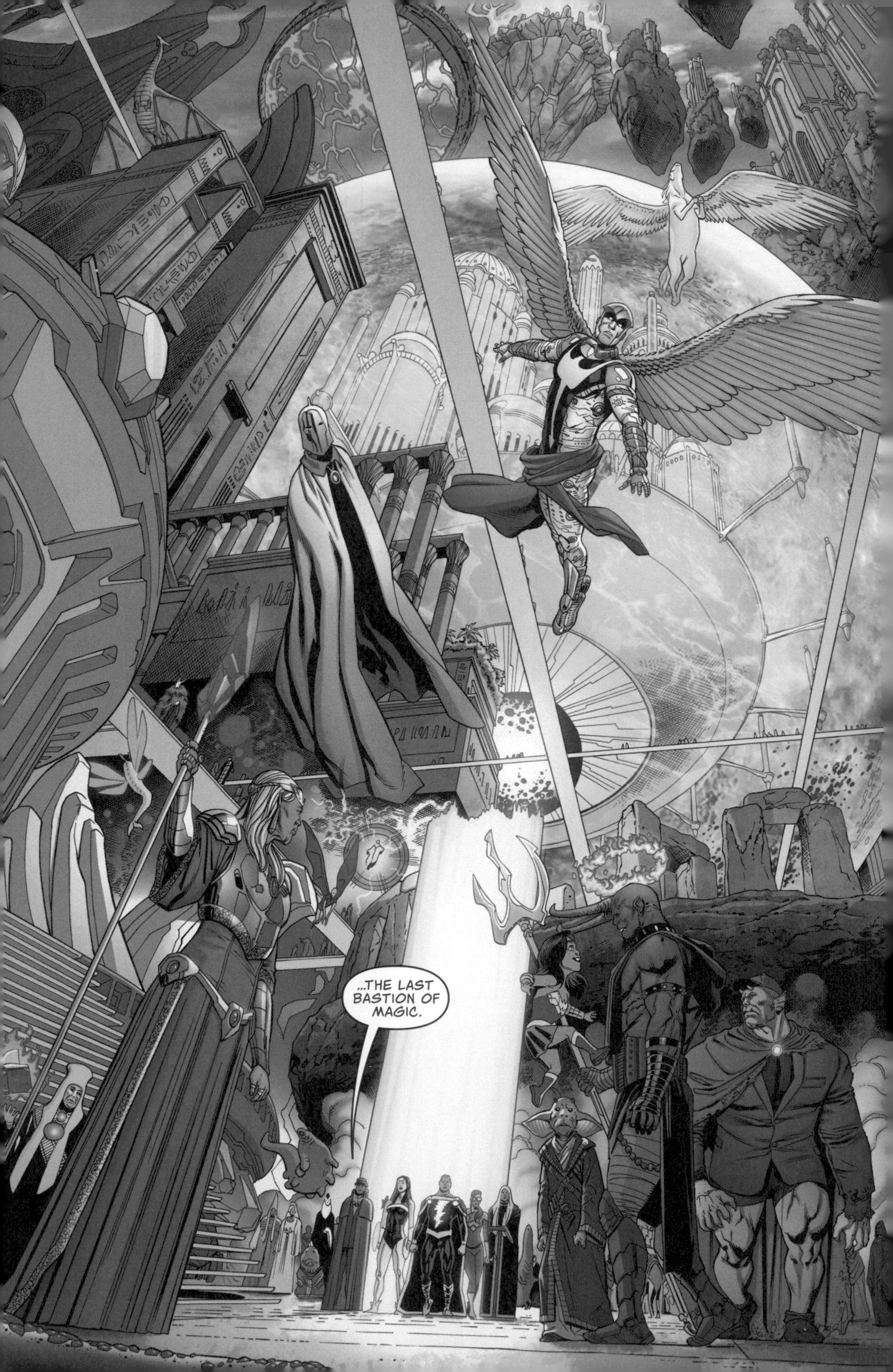
...THE LAST BASTION OF MAGIC.

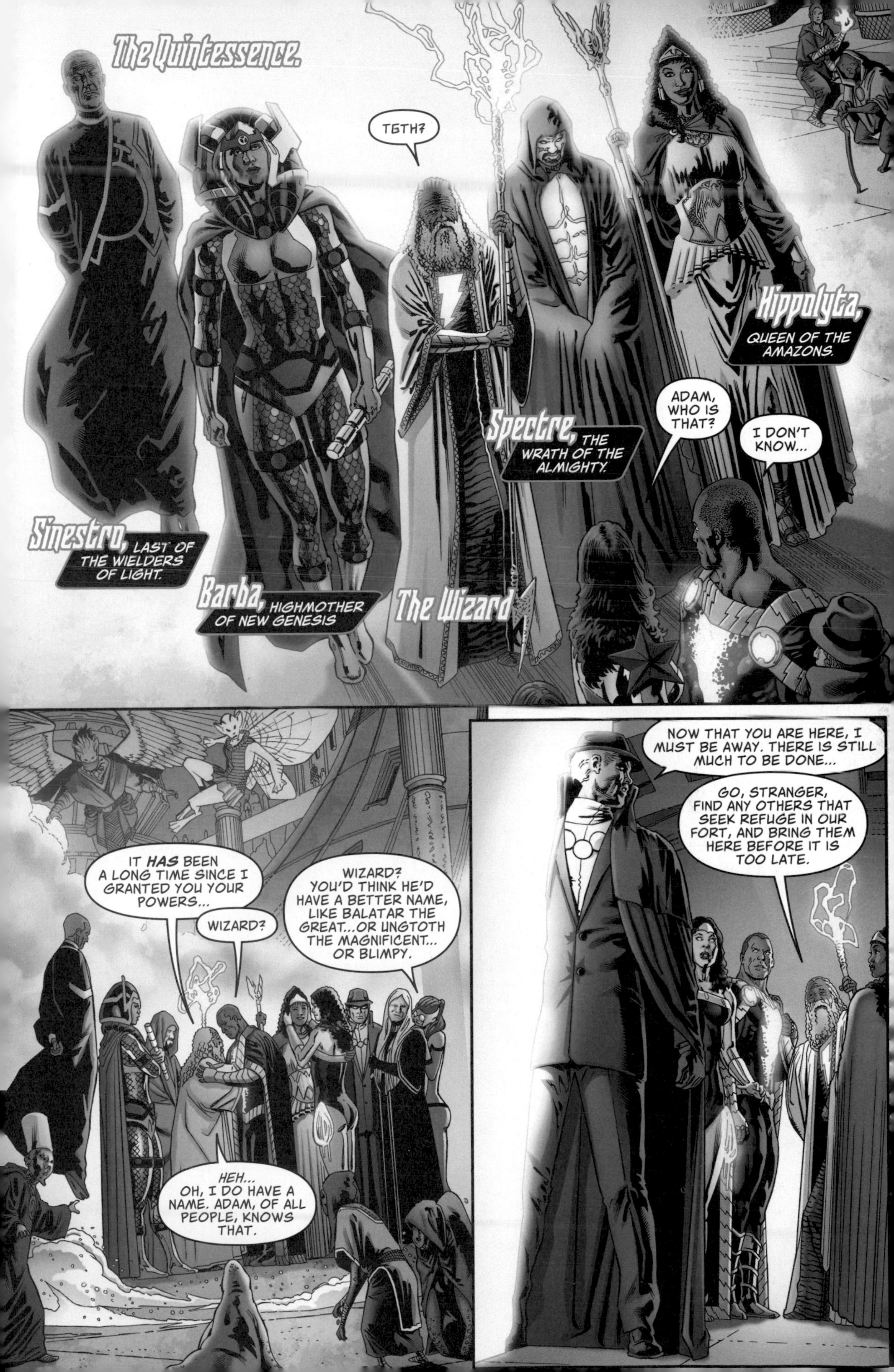
The Quintessence.
TETH?
Hippolyta, QUEEN OF THE AMAZONS.
Spectre, THE WRATH OF THE ALMIGHTY.
ADAM, WHO IS THAT?
I DON'T KNOW...
Sinestro, LAST OF THE WIELDERS OF LIGHT.
Barba, HIGHMOTHER OF NEW GENESIS
The Wizard
IT HAS BEEN A LONG TIME SINCE I GRANTED YOU YOUR POWERS...
WIZARD?
WIZARD? YOU'D THINK HE'D HAVE A BETTER NAME, LIKE BALATAR THE GREAT...OR UNGTOTH THE MAGNIFICENT... OR BLIMPY.
HEH... OH, I DO HAVE A NAME. ADAM, OF ALL PEOPLE, KNOWS THAT.
NOW THAT YOU ARE HERE, I MUST BE AWAY. THERE IS STILL MUCH TO BE DONE...
GO, STRANGER, FIND ANY OTHERS THAT SEEK REFUGE IN OUR FORT, AND BRING THEM HERE BEFORE IT IS TOO LATE.

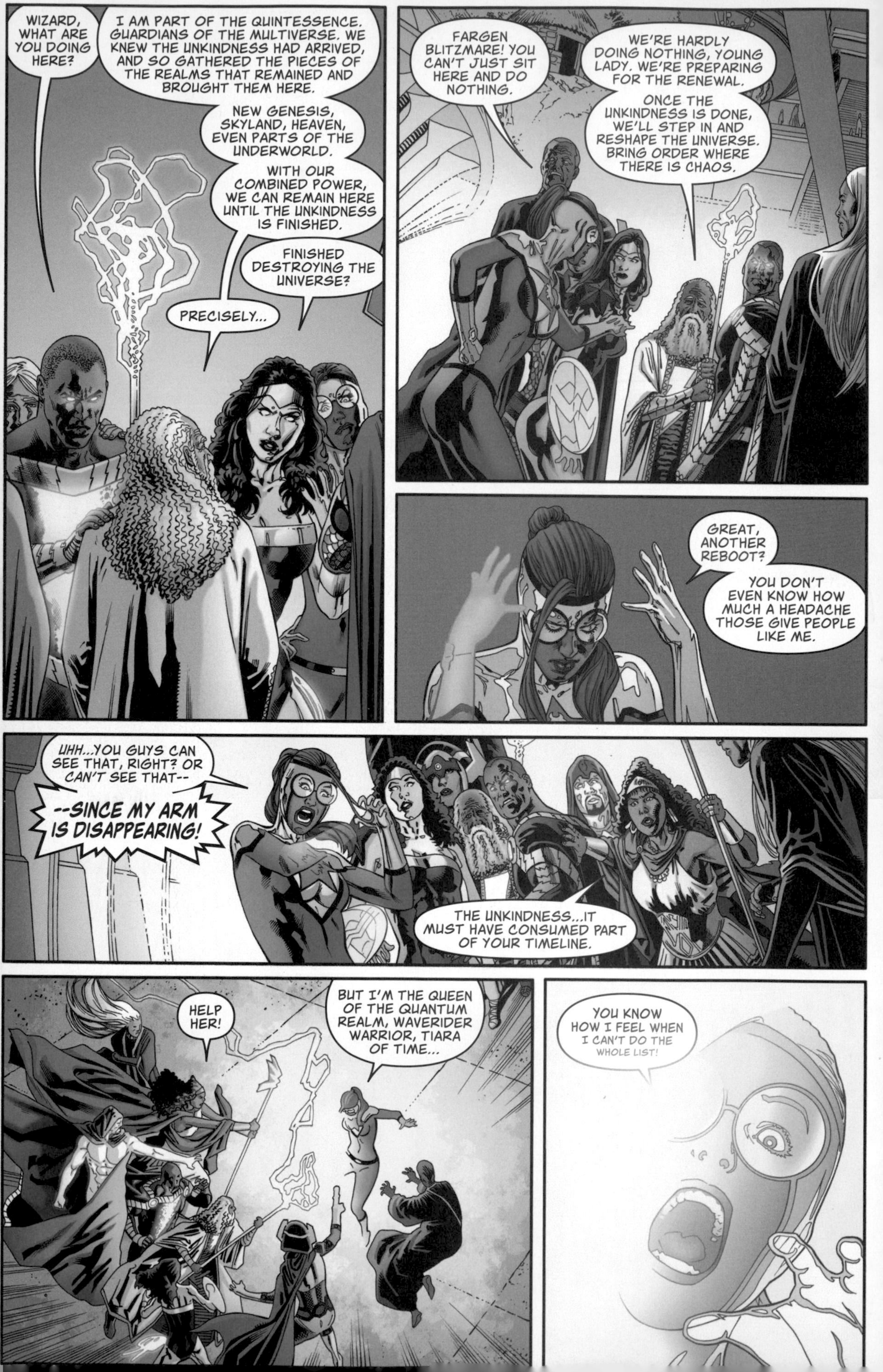

WIZARD, WHAT ARE YOU DOING HERE?
I AM PART OF THE QUINTESSENCE. GUARDIANS OF THE MULTIVERSE. WE KNEW THE UNKINDNESS HAD ARRIVED, AND SO GATHERED THE PIECES OF THE REALMS THAT REMAINED AND BROUGHT THEM HERE.
NEW GENESIS, SKYLAND, HEAVEN, EVEN PARTS OF THE UNDERWORLD.
WITH OUR COMBINED POWER, WE CAN REMAIN HERE UNTIL THE UNKINDNESS IS FINISHED.
FINISHED DESTROYING THE UNIVERSE?
PRECISELY...
FARGEN BLITZMARE! YOU CAN'T JUST SIT HERE AND DO NOTHING.
WE'RE HARDLY DOING NOTHING, YOUNG LADY. WE'RE PREPARING FOR THE RENEWAL.
ONCE THE UNKINDNESS IS DONE, WE'LL STEP IN AND RESHAPE THE UNIVERSE. BRING ORDER WHERE THERE IS CHAOS.
GREAT, ANOTHER REBOOT?
YOU DON'T EVEN KNOW HOW MUCH A HEADACHE THOSE GIVE PEOPLE LIKE ME.
UHH...YOU GUYS CAN SEE THAT, RIGHT? OR CAN'T SEE THAT--
--SINCE MY ARM IS DISAPPEARING!
THE UNKINDNESS...IT MUST HAVE CONSUMED PART OF YOUR TIMELINE.
HELP HER!
BUT I'M THE QUEEN OF THE QUANTUM REALM, WAVERIDER WARRIOR, TIARA OF TIME...
YOU KNOW HOW I FEEL WHEN I CAN'T DO THE WHOLE LIST!

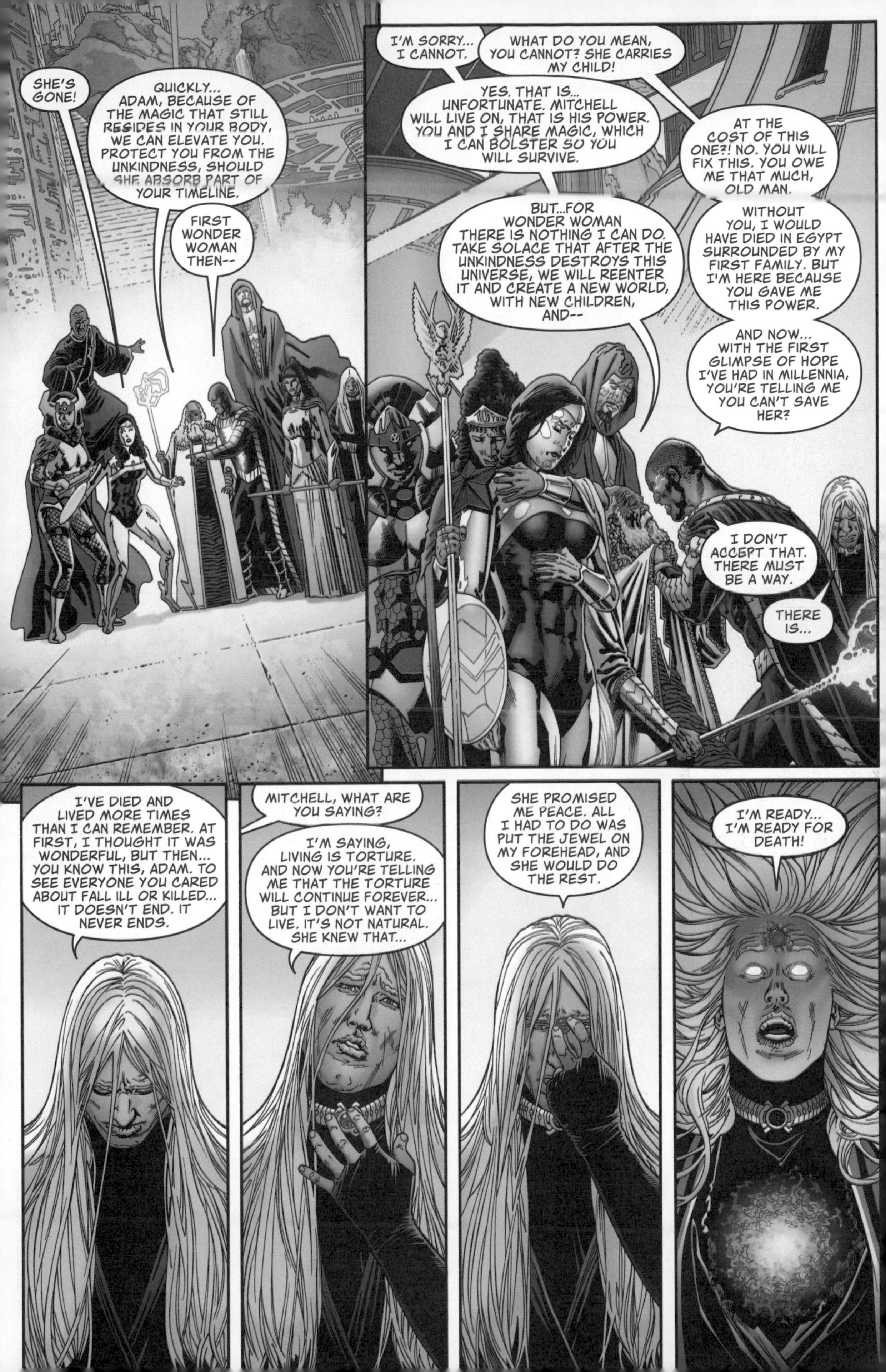
SHE'S GONE!
QUICKLY... ADAM, BECAUSE OF THE MAGIC THAT STILL RESIDES IN YOUR BODY, WE CAN ELEVATE YOU. PROTECT YOU FROM THE UNKINDNESS, SHOULD SHE ABSORB PART OF YOUR TIMELINE.
FIRST WONDER WOMAN THEN--
I'M SORRY... I CANNOT.
WHAT DO YOU MEAN, YOU CANNOT? SHE CARRIES MY CHILD!
YES. THAT IS... UNFORTUNATE. MITCHELL WILL LIVE ON, THAT IS HIS POWER. YOU AND I SHARE MAGIC, WHICH I CAN BOLSTER SO YOU WILL SURVIVE.
AT THE COST OF THIS ONE?! NO. YOU WILL FIX THIS. YOU OWE ME THAT MUCH, OLD MAN.
BUT...FOR WONDER WOMAN THERE IS NOTHING I CAN DO. TAKE SOLACE THAT AFTER THE UNKINDNESS DESTROYS THIS UNIVERSE, WE WILL REENTER IT AND CREATE A NEW WORLD, WITH NEW CHILDREN, AND--
WITHOUT YOU, I WOULD HAVE DIED IN EGYPT SURROUNDED BY MY FIRST FAMILY. BUT I'M HERE BECAUSE YOU GAVE ME THIS POWER.
AND NOW... WITH THE FIRST GLIMPSE OF HOPE I'VE HAD IN MILLENNIA, YOU'RE TELLING ME YOU CAN'T SAVE HER?
I DON'T ACCEPT THAT. THERE MUST BE A WAY.
THERE IS...
I'VE DIED AND LIVED MORE TIMES THAN I CAN REMEMBER. AT FIRST, I THOUGHT IT WAS WONDERFUL, BUT THEN... YOU KNOW THIS, ADAM. TO SEE EVERYONE YOU CARED ABOUT FALL ILL OR KILLED... IT DOESN'T END. IT NEVER ENDS.
MITCHELL, WHAT ARE YOU SAYING?
I'M SAYING, LIVING IS TORTURE. AND NOW YOU'RE TELLING ME THAT THE TORTURE WILL CONTINUE FOREVER... BUT I DON'T WANT TO LIVE. IT'S NOT NATURAL. SHE KNEW THAT...
SHE PROMISED ME PEACE. ALL I HAD TO DO WAS PUT THE JEWEL ON MY FOREHEAD, AND SHE WOULD DO THE REST.
I'M READY... I'M READY FOR DEATH!

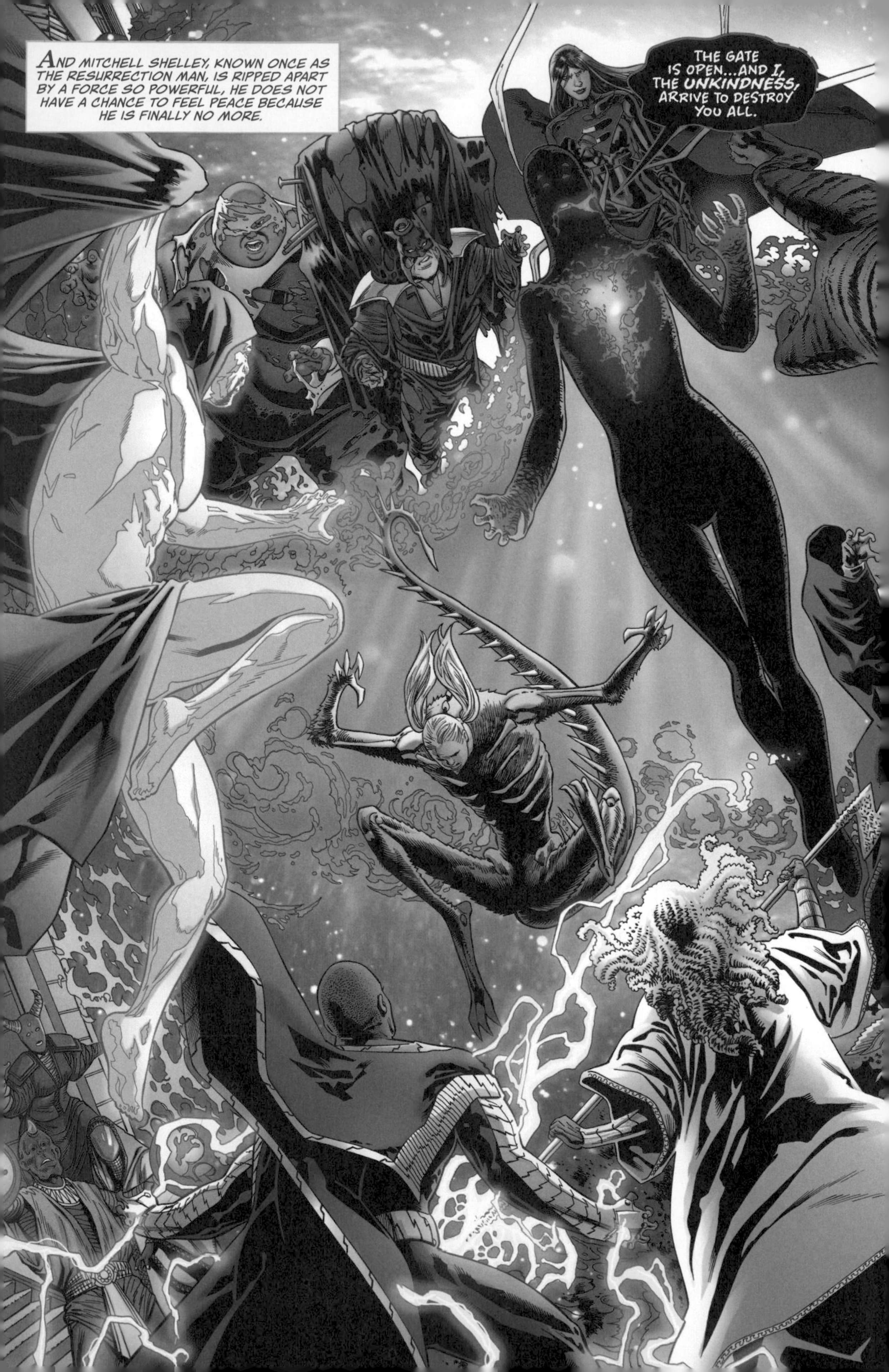
AND MITCHELL SHELLEY, KNOWN ONCE AS THE RESURRECTION MAN, IS RIPPED APART BY A FORCE SO POWERFUL, HE DOES NOT HAVE A CHANCE TO FEEL PEACE BECAUSE HE IS FINALLY NO MORE.
THE GATE IS OPEN...AND I, THE UNKINDNESS, ARRIVE TO DESTROY YOU ALL.

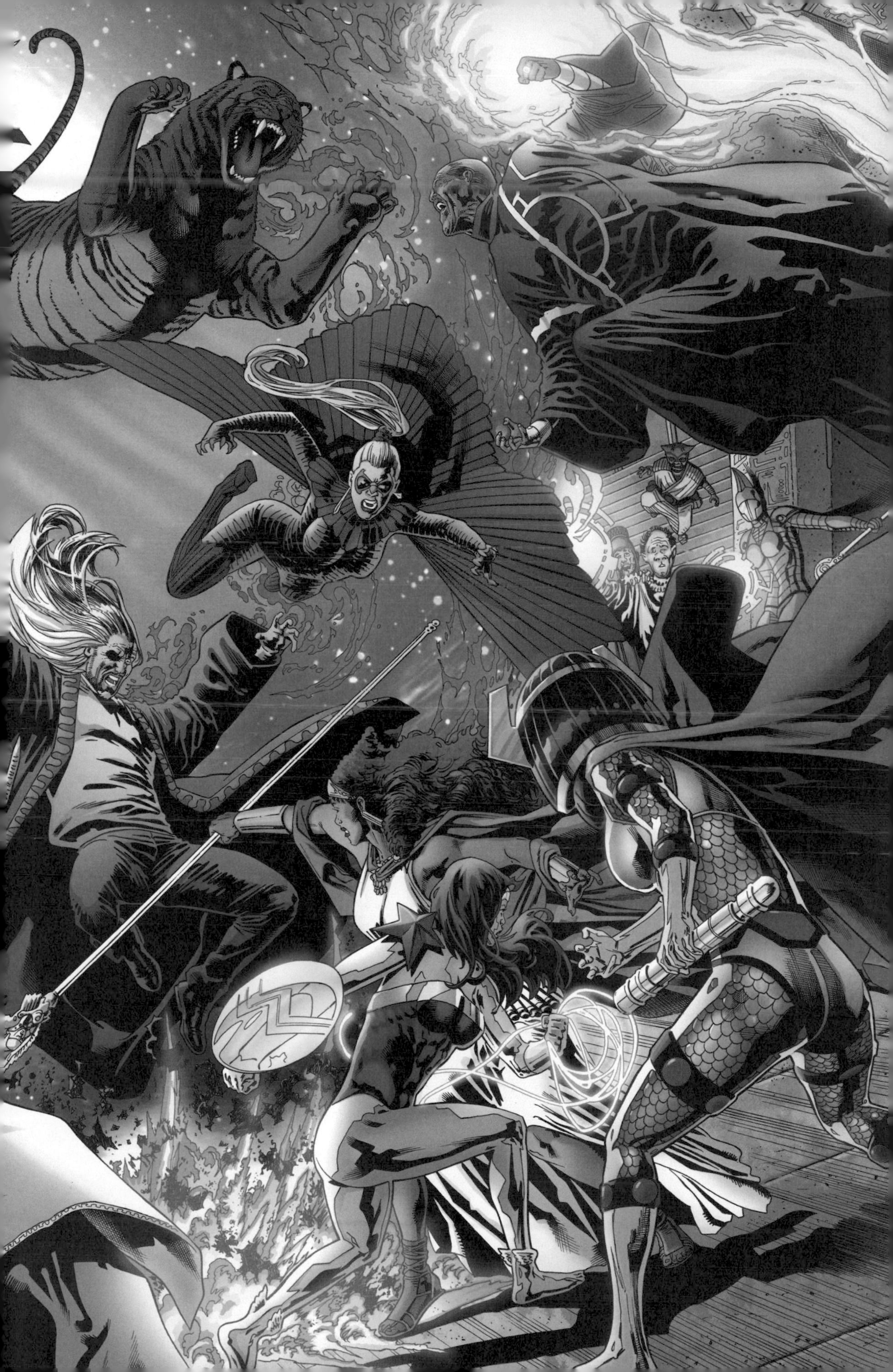

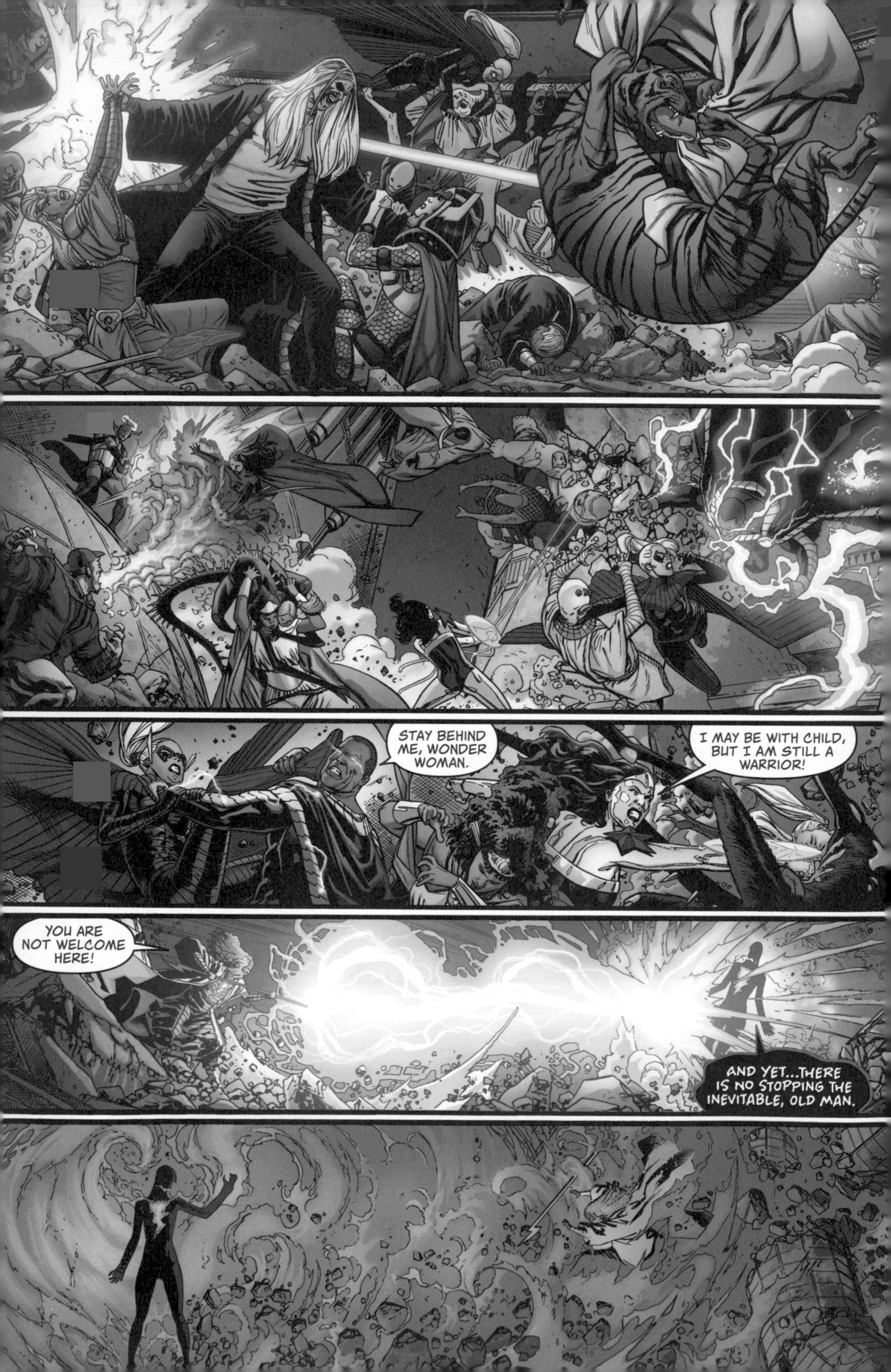
STAY BEHIND ME, WONDER WOMAN.
I MAY BE WITH CHILD, BUT I AM STILL A WARRIOR!
YOU ARE NOT WELCOME HERE!
AND YET...THERE IS NO STOPPING THE INEVITABLE, OLD MAN.

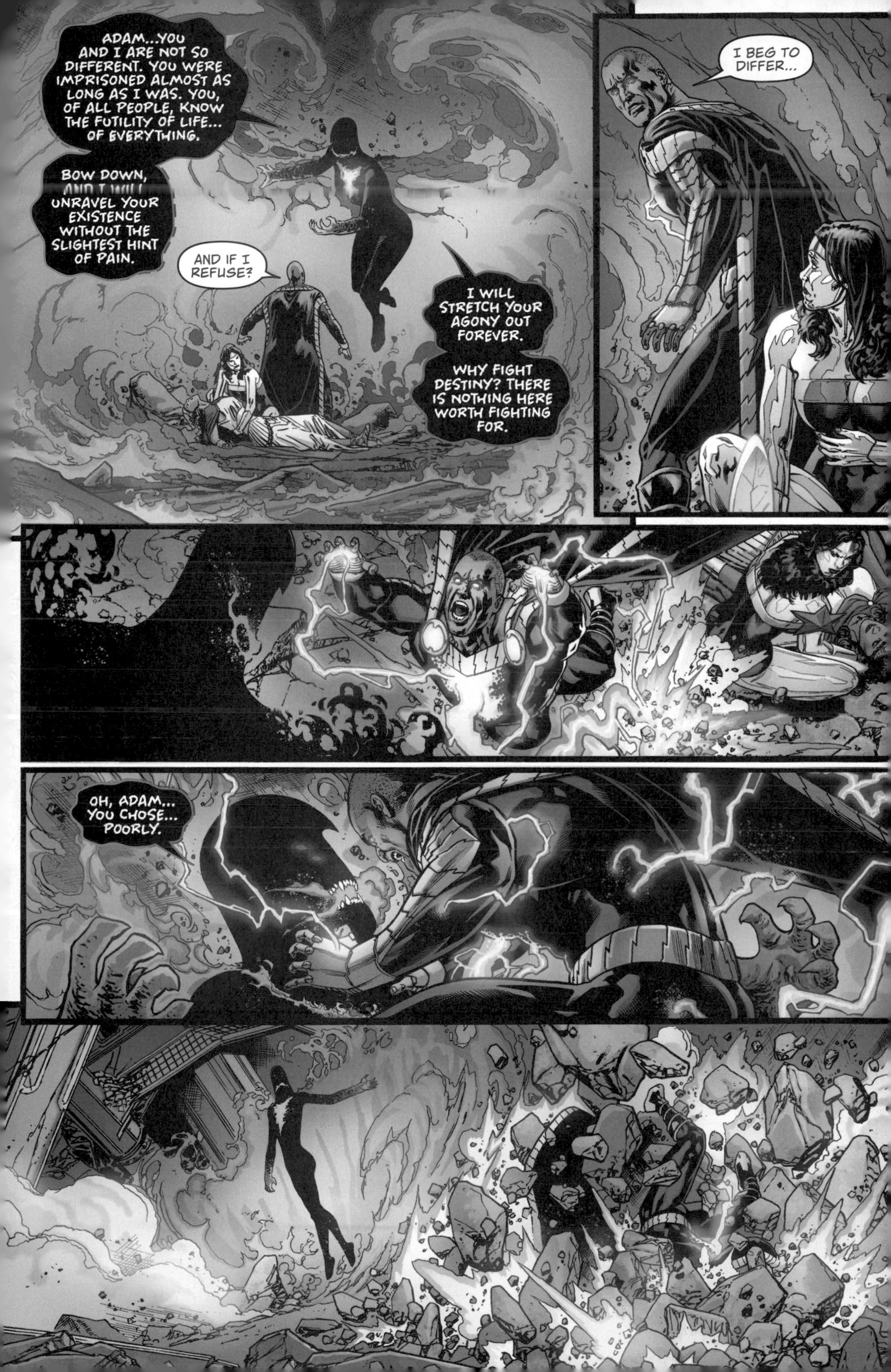
ADAM...YOU AND I ARE NOT SO DIFFERENT. YOU WERE IMPRISONED ALMOST AS LONG AS I WAS. YOU, OF ALL PEOPLE, KNOW THE FUTILITY OF LIFE... OF EVERYTHING.
BOW DOWN, AND I WILL UNRAVEL YOUR EXISTENCE WITHOUT THE SLIGHTEST HINT OF PAIN.
AND IF I REFUSE?
I WILL STRETCH YOUR AGONY OUT FOREVER.
WHY FIGHT DESTINY? THERE IS NOTHING HERE WORTH FIGHTING FOR.
I BEG TO DIFFER...
OH, ADAM... YOU CHOSE... POORLY.

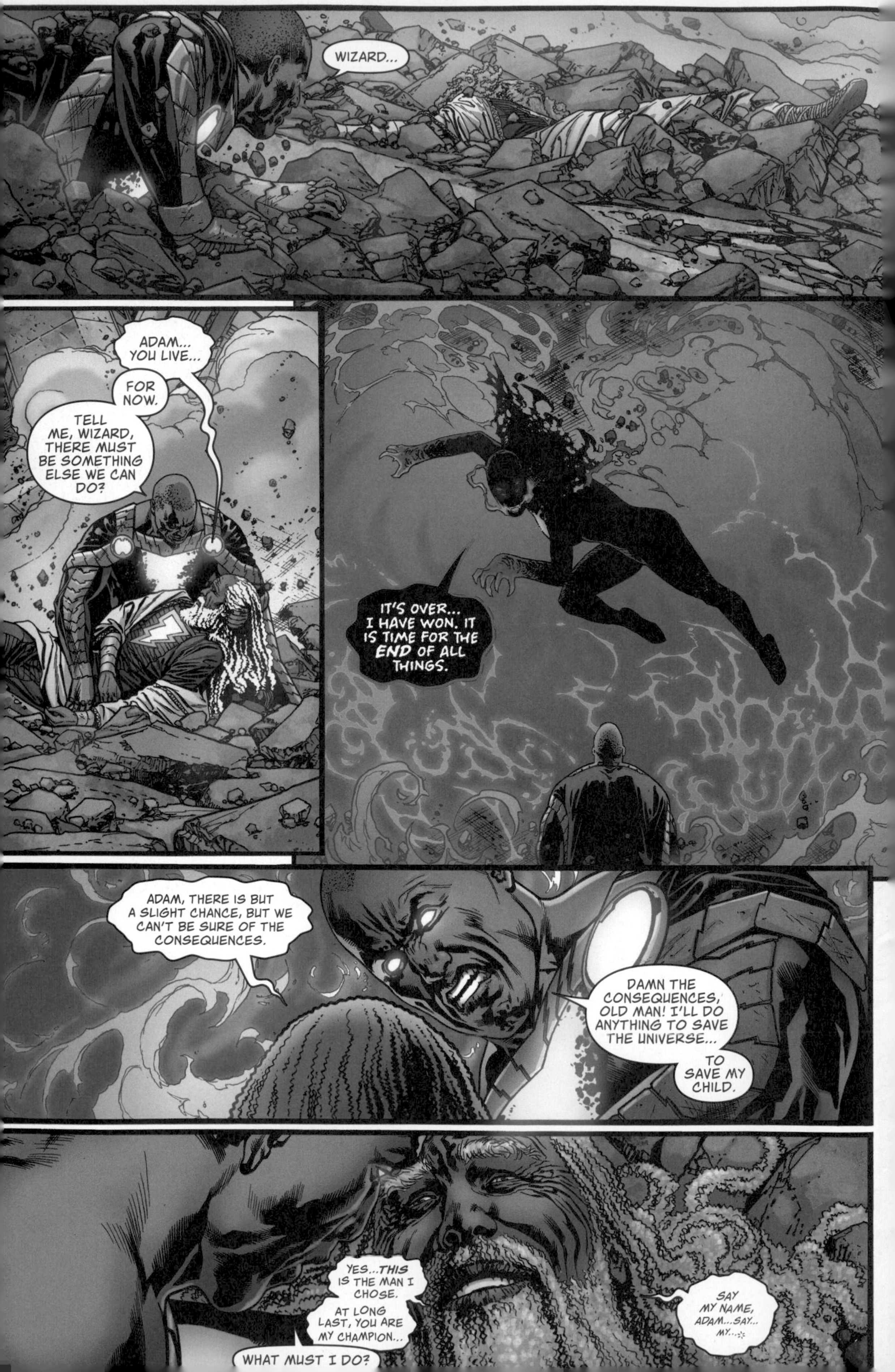
WIZARD...
ADAM... YOU LIVE...
FOR NOW.
TELL ME, WIZARD, THERE MUST BE SOMETHING ELSE WE CAN DO?
IT'S OVER... I HAVE WON. IT IS TIME FOR THE END OF ALL THINGS.
ADAM, THERE IS BUT A SLIGHT CHANCE, BUT WE CAN'T BE SURE OF THE CONSEQUENCES.
DAMN THE CONSEQUENCES, OLD MAN! I'LL DO ANYTHING TO SAVE THE UNIVERSE...
TO SAVE MY CHILD.
YES...THIS IS THE MAN I CHOSE.
AT LONG LAST, YOU ARE MY CHAMPION...
WHAT MUST I DO?
SAY MY NAME, ADAM...SAY... MY...

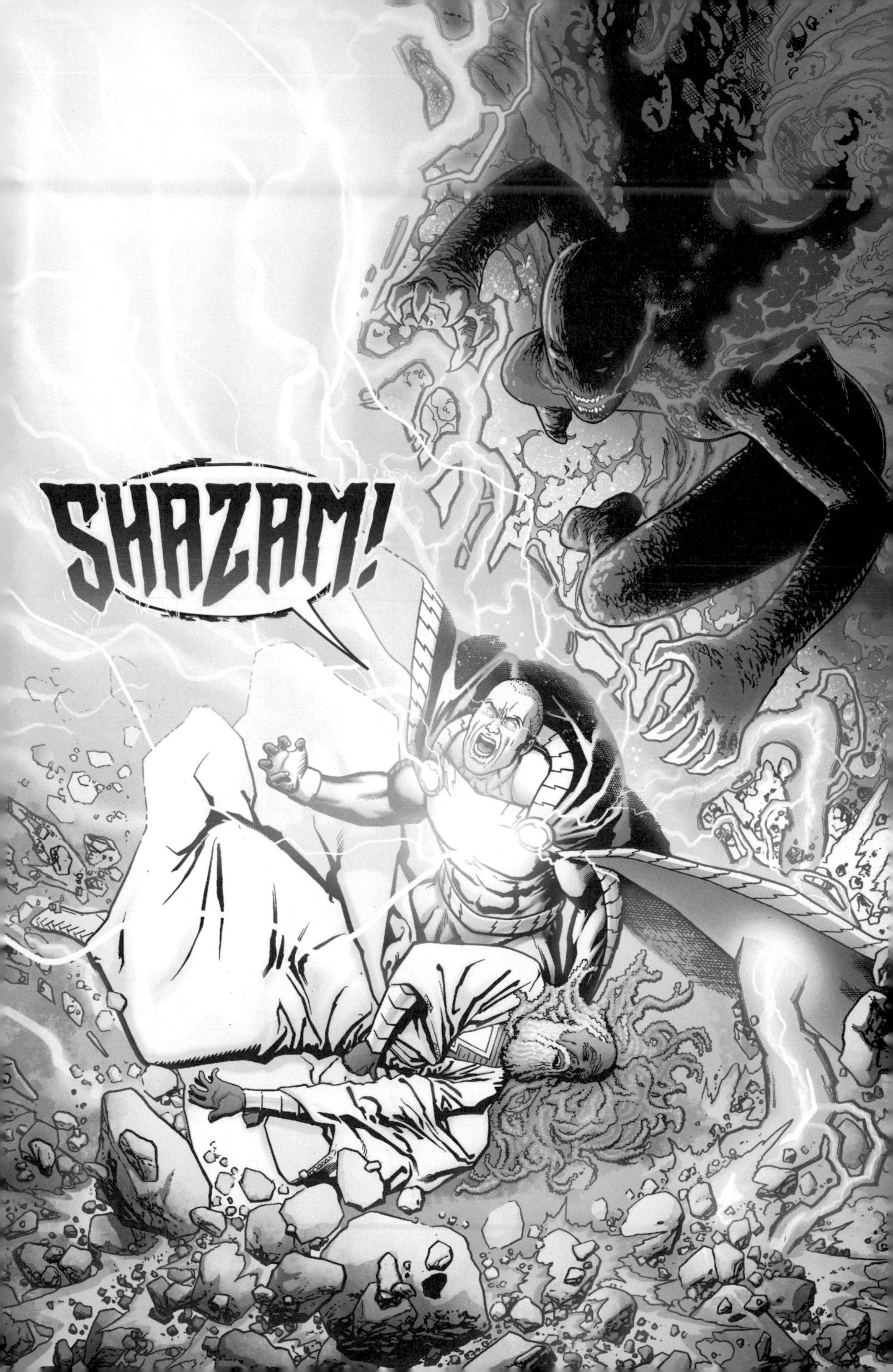
SHAZAM!

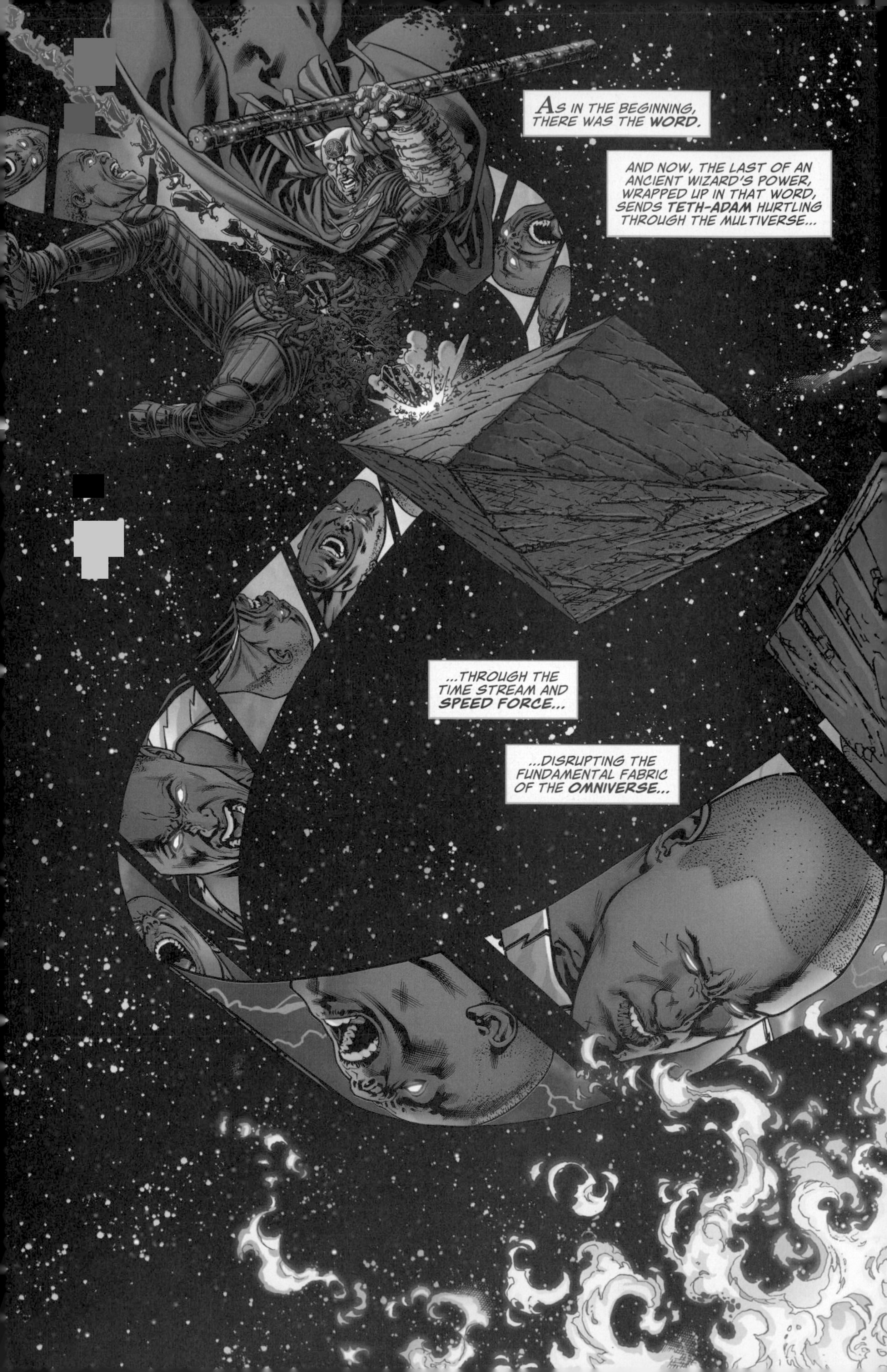
AS IN THE BEGINNING, THERE WAS THE WORD.
AND NOW, THE LAST OF AN ANCIENT WIZARD'S POWER, WRAPPED UP IN THAT WORD, SENDS TETH-ADAM HURTLING THROUGH THE MULTIVERSE...
...THROUGH THE TIME STREAM AND SPEED FORCE...
...DISRUPTING THE FUNDAMENTAL FABRIC OF THE OMNIVERSE...

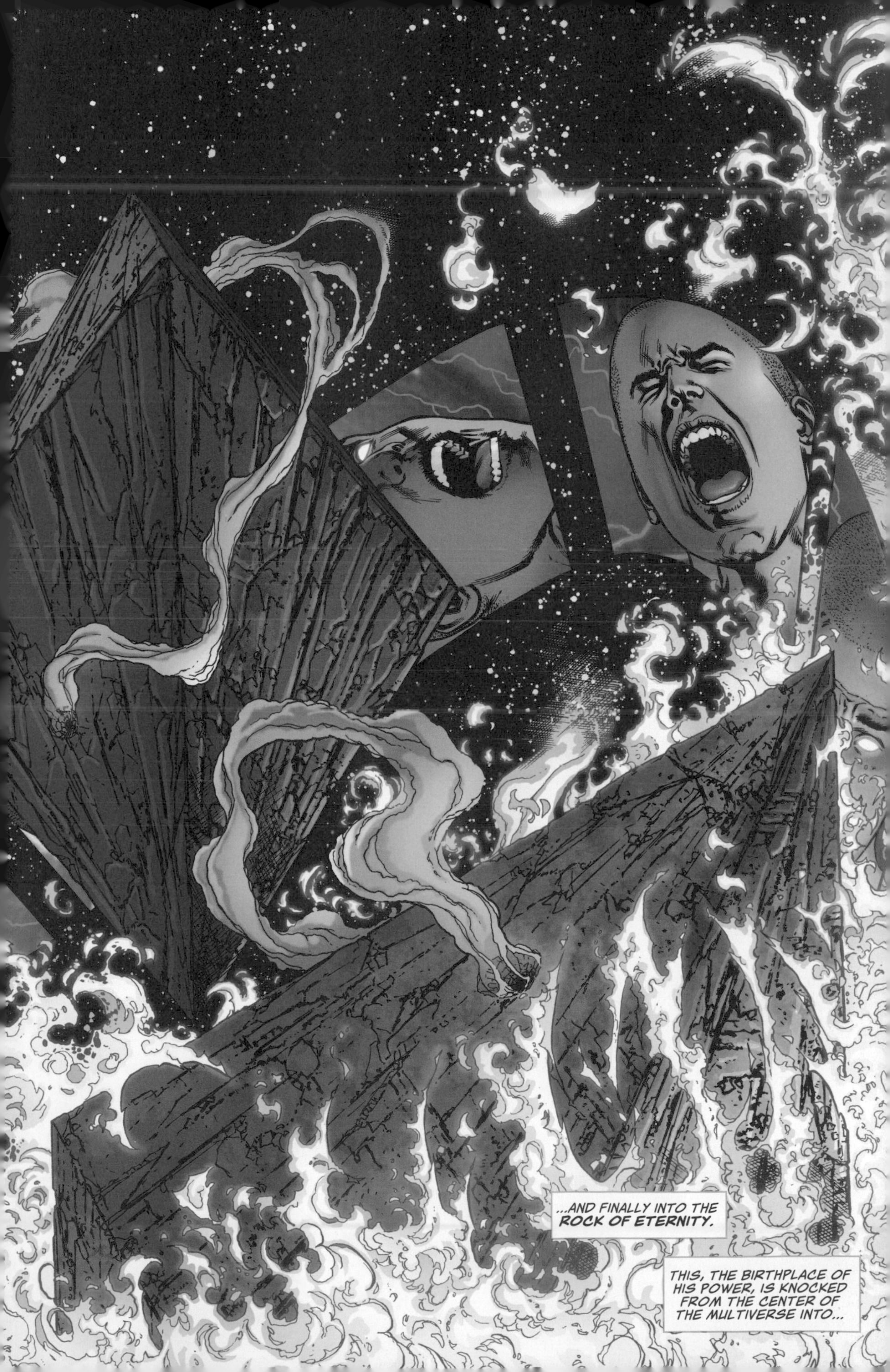

...AND FINALLY INTO THE ROCK OF ETERNITY.
THIS, THE BIRTHPLACE OF HIS POWER, IS KNOCKED FROM THE CENTER OF THE MULTIVERSE INTO...

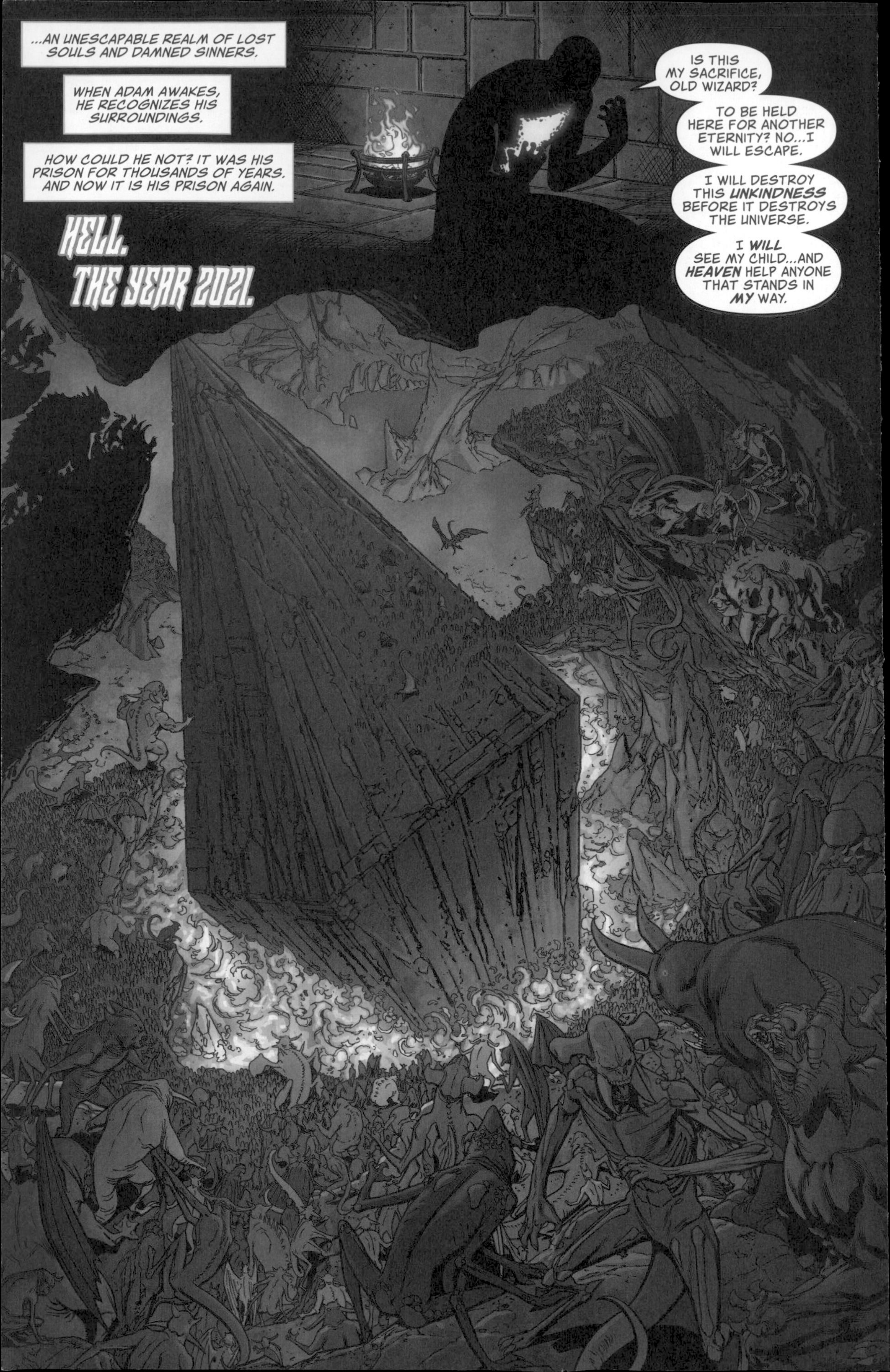
...AN UNESCAPABLE REALM OF LOST SOULS AND DAMNED SINNERS.
WHEN ADAM AWAKES, HE RECOGNIZES HIS SURROUNDINGS.
HOW COULD HE NOT? IT WAS HIS PRISON FOR THOUSANDS OF YEARS. AND NOW IT IS HIS PRISON AGAIN.
IS THIS MY SACRIFICE, OLD WIZARD?
TO BE HELD HERE FOR ANOTHER ETERNITY? NO...I WILL ESCAPE.
I WILL DESTROY THIS UNKINDNESS BEFORE IT DESTROYS THE UNIVERSE.
I WILL SEE MY CHILD...AND HEAVEN HELP ANYONE THAT STANDS IN MY WAY.
HELL. THE YEAR 2021.

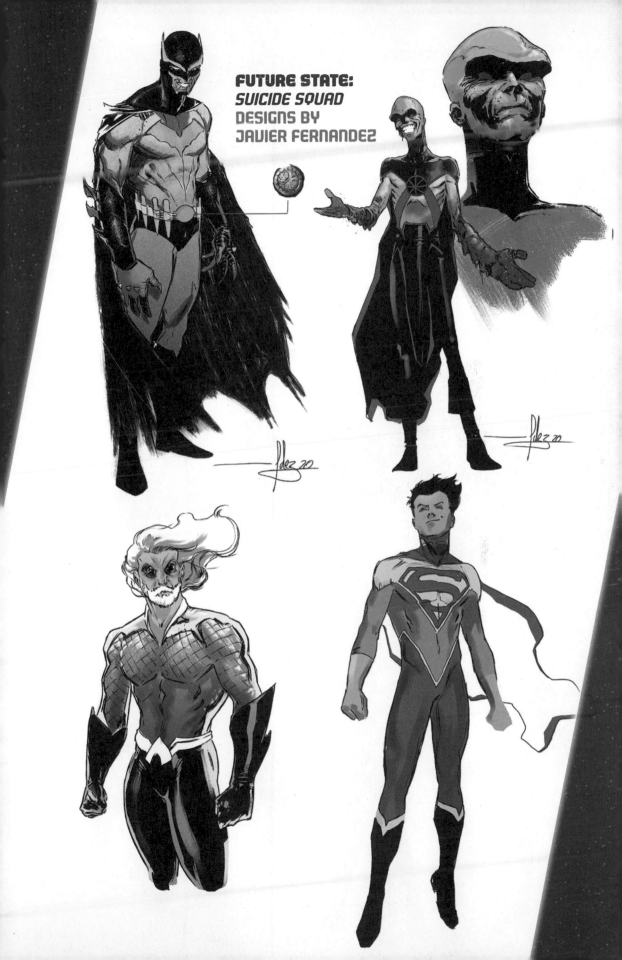

FUTURE STATE: *SUICIDE SQUAD* DESIGNS BY JAVIER FERNANDEZ

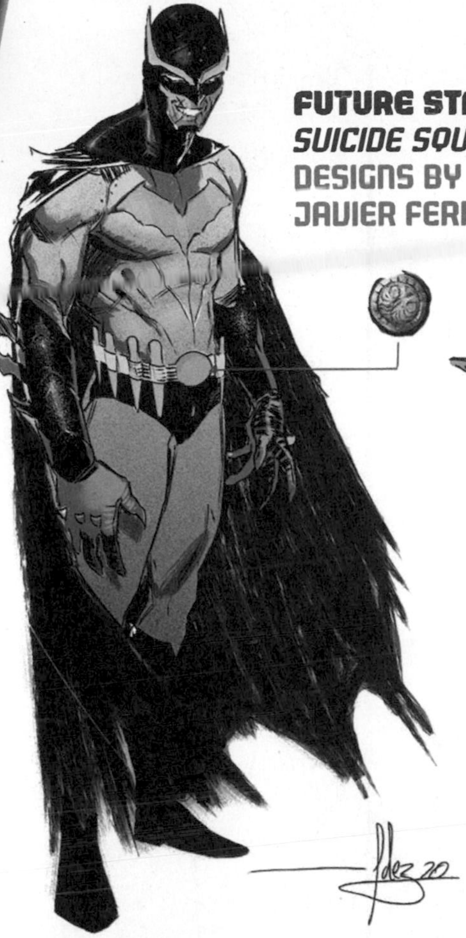

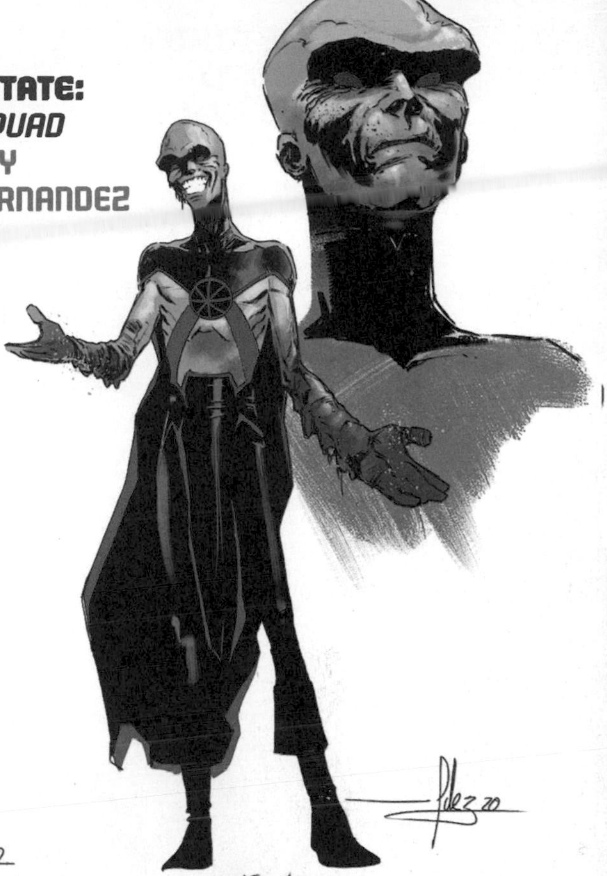

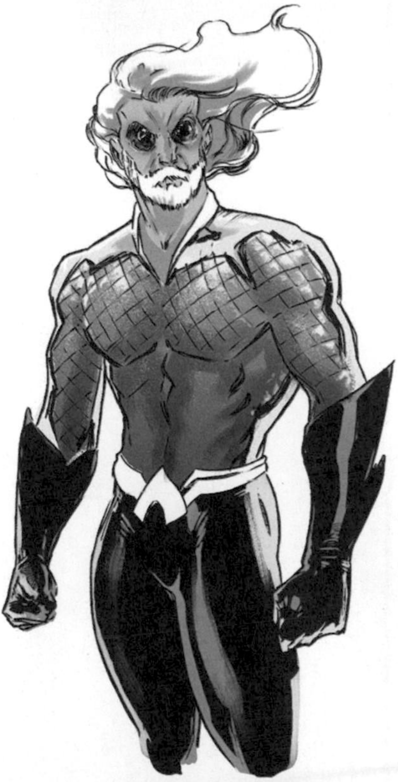

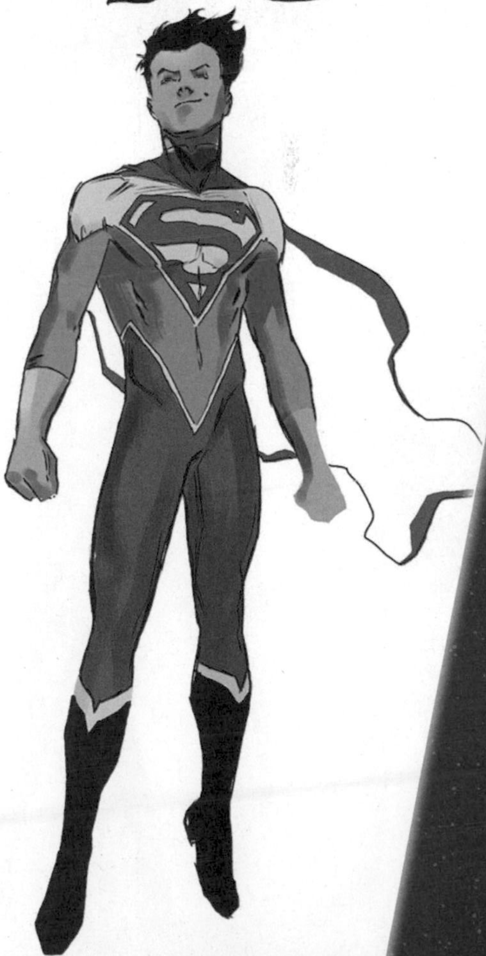

FUTURE STATE: *TEEN TITANS* DESIGNS BY RAFA SANDOVAL

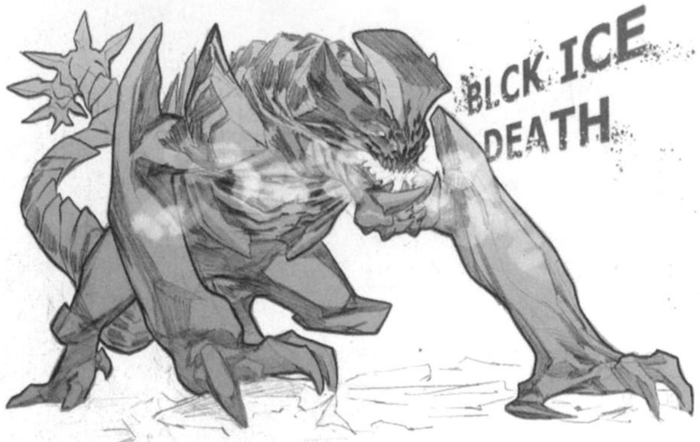
BLCK ICE
DEATH

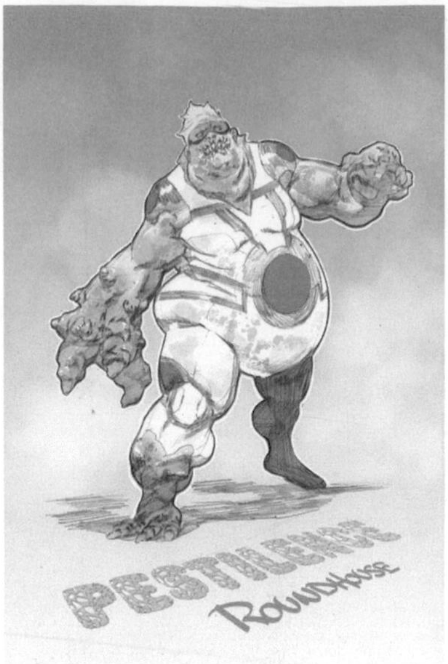
PESTILENCE
ROUNDHOUSE

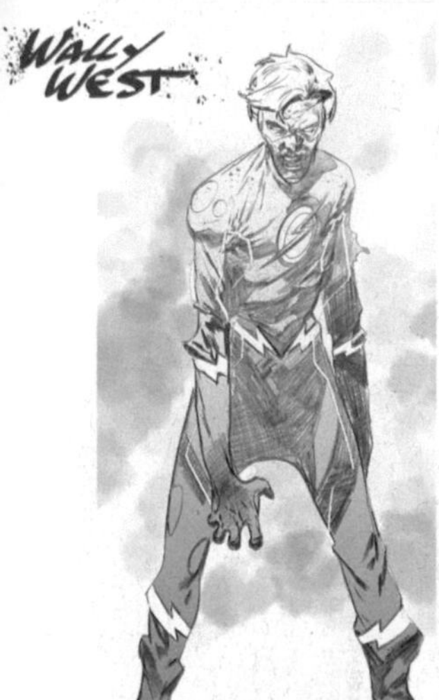
WALLY WEST

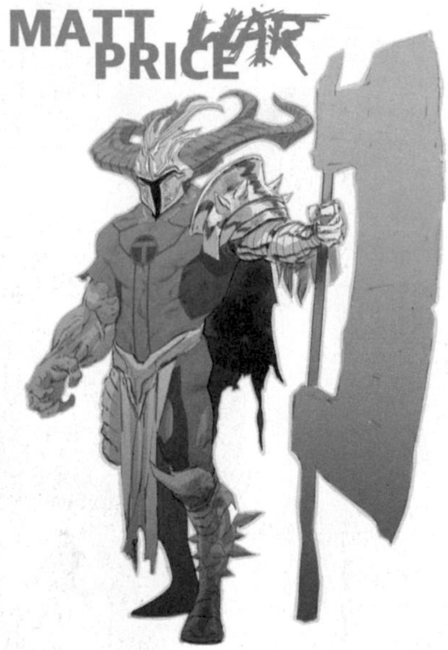
MATT PRICE
WAR

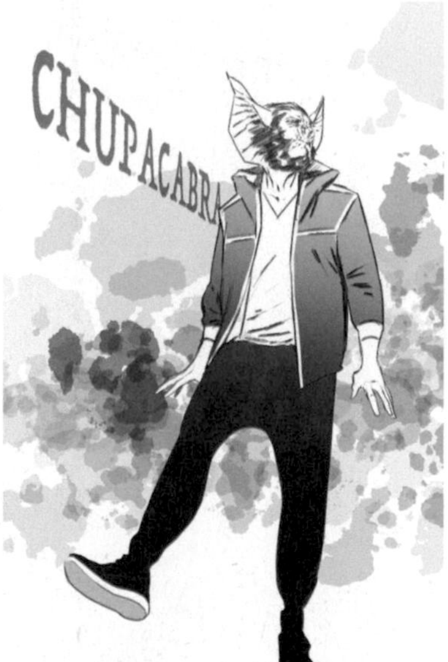
CHUPACABRA

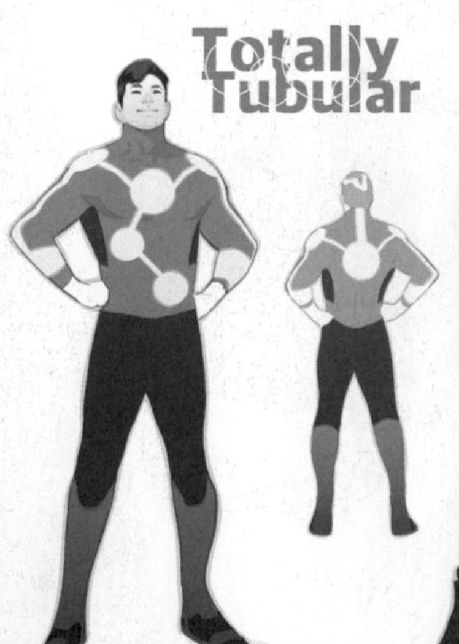
Totally Tubular

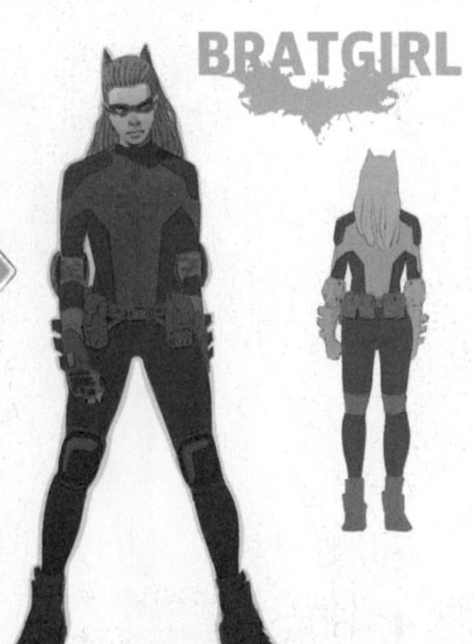
BRATGIRL

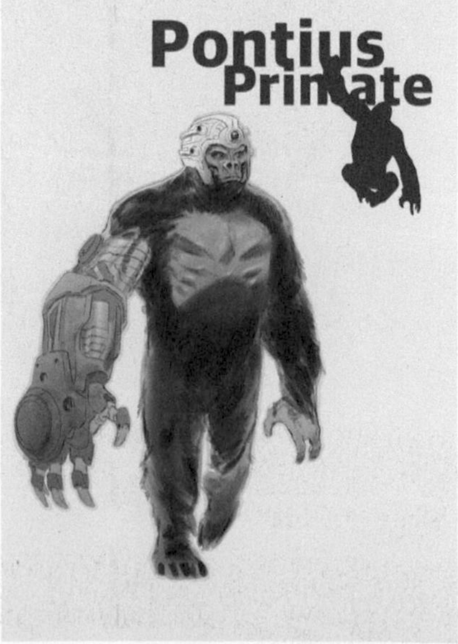
Pontius Primate

FUTURE STATE: ***SWAMP THING***
DESIGNS BY MIKE PERKINS

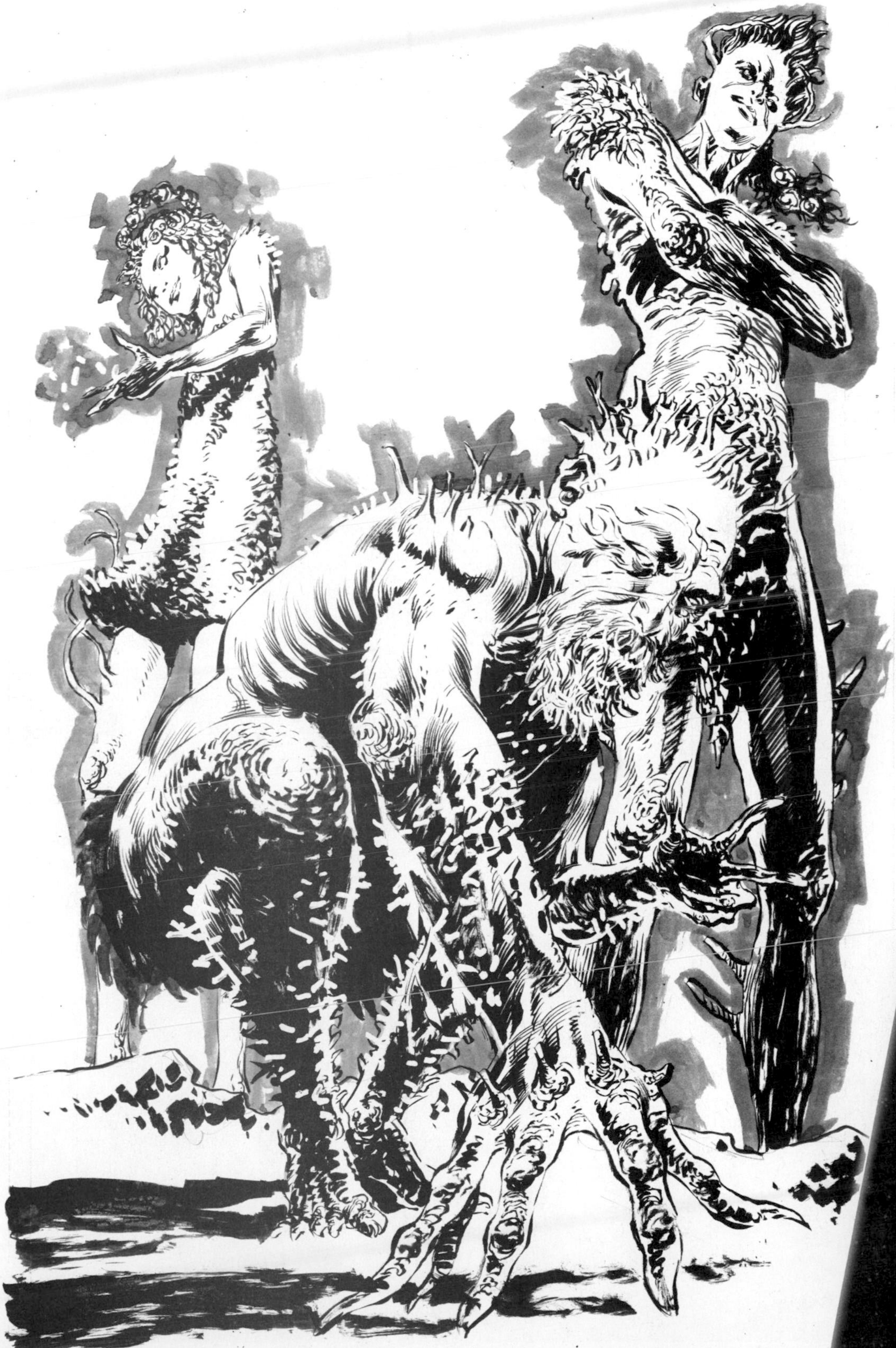

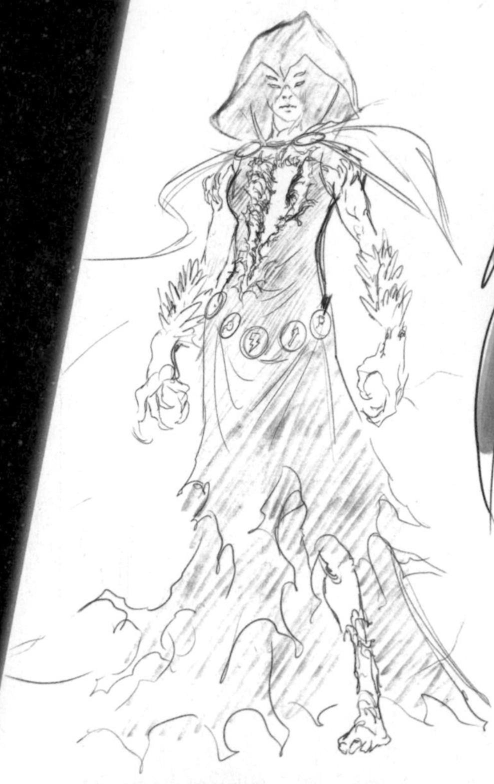

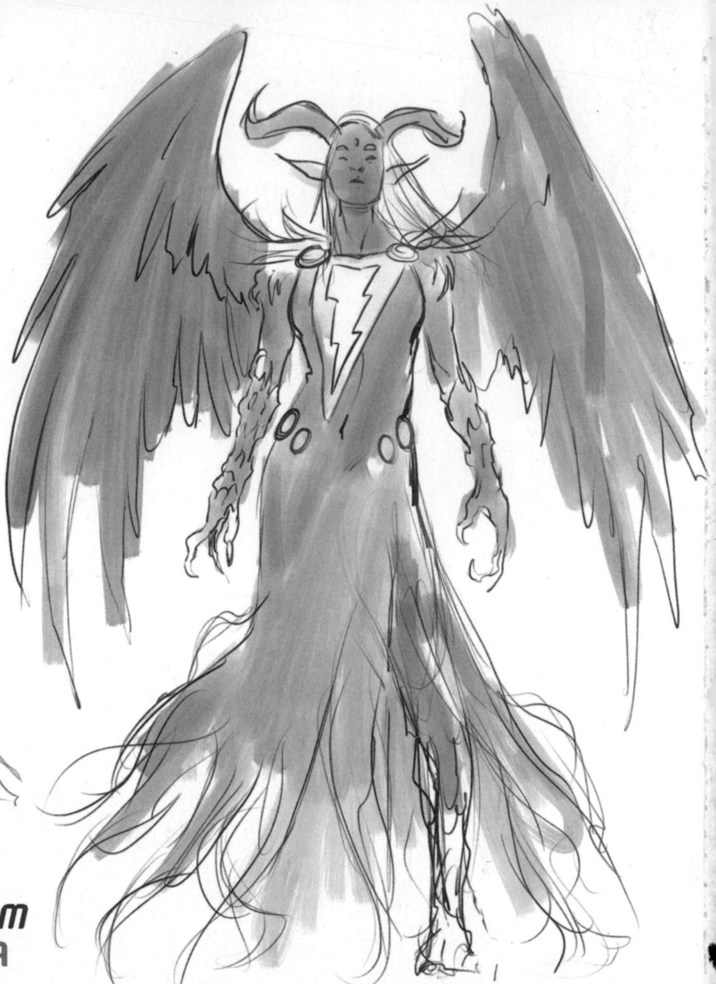

FUTURE STATE: ***SHAZAM!***
& FUTURE STATE: ***BLACK ADAM***
DESIGNS BY EDUARDO PANSICA
& FERNANDO PASARIN

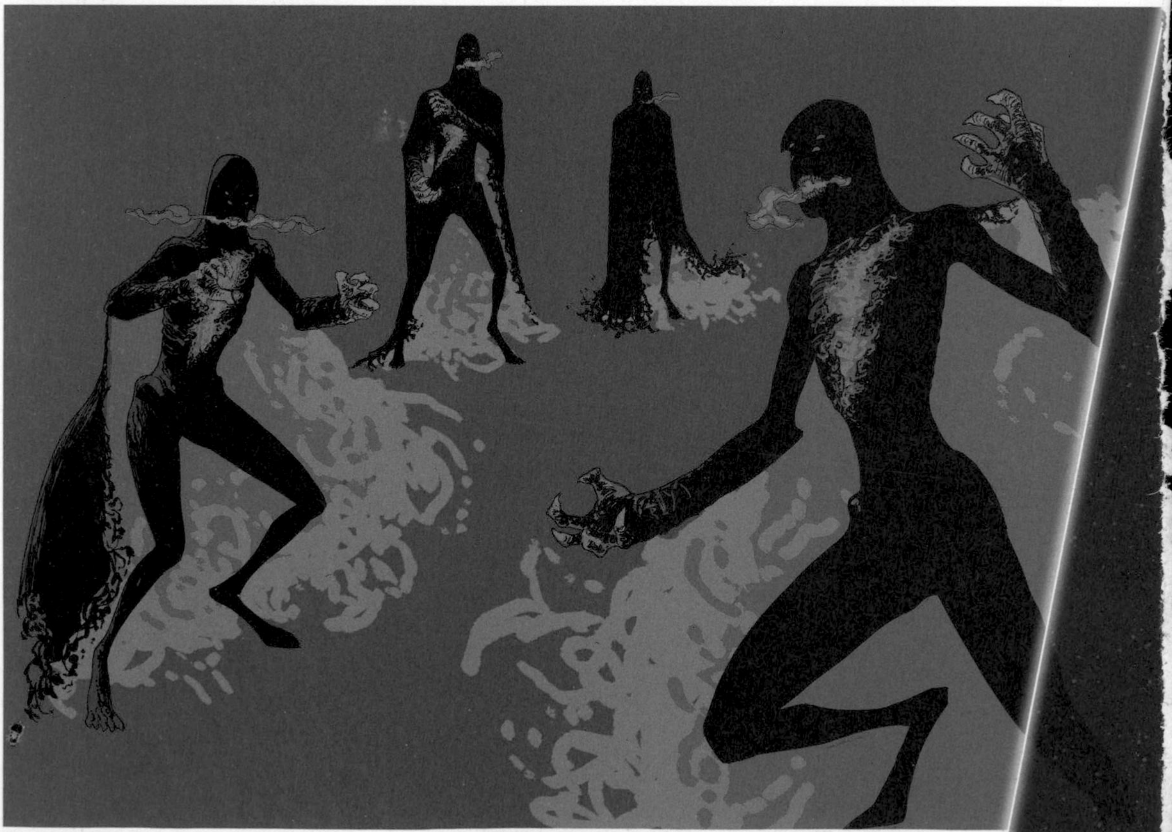